LONDON IN THE EIGHTEENTH CENTURY

Professor Jerry White teaches London history at Birkbeck, University of London. His *London in the Twentieth Century: A City and Its People* won the Wolfson History Prize in 2001 and his bestselling *London in the Nineteenth Century* was published to critical acclaim in 2007. His oral histories, *Rothschild Buildings: Life in an East End Tenement Block 1887–1980* (which won the *Jewish Chronicle* non-fiction book prize in 1980) and *Campbell Bunk: The Worst Street in North London Between the Wars*, were reprinted by Pimlico in 2003. He was awarded the honorary degree of Doctor of Literature by the University of London in 2005 and is a Fellow of the Royal Historical Society.

JERRY WHITE

London in the Eighteenth Century

A Great and Monstrous Thing

VINTAGE BOOKS
London

Published by Vintage 2013

2 4 6 8 10 9 7 5 3 1

First published in Great Britain in 2012 by
The Bodley Head

Vintage
Random House, 20 Vauxhall Bridge Road,
London SW1V 2SA

www.vintage-books.co.uk

Addresses for companies within The Random House
Group Limited can be found at:
www.randomhouse.co.uk/offices.htm

The Random House Group Limited Reg. No. 954009

A CIP catalogue record for this book
is available from the British Library

ISBN 9780712600422

Typeset in Sabon by
Palimpsest Book Production Ltd, Falkirk, Stirlingshire

Printed and bound by
CPI Group (UK) Ltd, Croydon, CR0 4YY

For John Hodgkins and Paul Wilsdon-Tagg,
eighteenth-century men both

'. . . it will, I believe, be allowed to be agreeable and sufficient to touch at those Things principally, which no other Authors have yet mentioned, concerning this great and monstrous Thing, called *London*.'

Daniel Defoe, *A Tour Through the Whole Island of Great Britain*, 2 vols., 1724–26, Vol. I, p. 325

A Description of London

Houses, Churches, mix'd together;
Streets, unpleasant in all Weather;
Prisons, Palaces, contiguous;
Gates; a Bridge; the THAMES irriguous.

Gaudy Things enough to tempt ye;
Showy Outsides; Insides empty;
Bubbles, Trades, mechanic Arts;
Coaches, Wheelbarrows, and Carts.

Warrants, Bailiffs, Bills unpaid;
Lords of Laundresses afraid;
Rogues that nightly rob and shoot Men;
Hangmen, Aldermen, and Footmen.

Lawyers, Poets, Priests, Physicians;
Noble, Simple, all Conditions:
Worth beneath a threadbare Cover;
Villainy – bedaub'd all over.

Women, black, red, fair, and gray;
Prudes, and such as never pray;
Handsome, ugly, noisy, still;
Some that will not, some that will.

Many a Beau without a Shilling;
Many a Widow not unwilling;
Many a Bargain, if you strike it:
This is LONDON! How d'ye like it?

John Bancks, 1738

CONTENTS

ILLUSTRATIONS

LIST OF MAPS

PREFACE

On Tuesday 13 June 1732, after some days of eager anticipation, the pillory had finally been carted from Newgate and assembled by carpenters at Seven Dials. It was to receive John Waller, convicted of perjury, attempting to swear away men's lives for crimes they had never committed so he might profit from the rewards. He was the pretended 'victim' or key witness in no fewer than six prosecutions for highway robbery at the Old Bailey between 1722 and 1732 in which two persons were condemned to death. Not all his victims were virtuous, because one was the notorious James Dalton, leader for a number of years of one of the most active gangs of street robbers in London, who was duly hanged on Waller's evidence in 1730. Waller was sentenced to stand at Seven Dials and then, some days later, outside Hicks's Hall, the magistrates' court at Clerkenwell. He would never keep that second appointment.

No one was more loathsome to the London crowd than an informer. John Waller must have known what fury he would face when he was brought out of Redgate's alehouse in King Street (now Neal Street) for the short walk to the pillory. When he appeared on the platform he was met by a storm of missiles so fierce that the officers were unable to fasten the block. As they struggled to get his head in the pillory several men rushed the platform, among them Edward Dalton, brother of the man hanged by Waller's testimony. Waller was caught by one arm in the pillory but his head was yanked free from the block. He was 'stripped as naked as he was born, except his Feet, for they pulled his Stockings over his Shoes and so left them; then they beat him with Collyflower-stalks', pulled his hand from the pillory and punched, kicked and stamped on him as he lay on the platform. A chimneysweep forced soot into his mouth and it was rammed down his throat with a cauliflower or artichoke stalk. Someone slashed him 'quite down the Back' with a knife.

The excitement was such that the pillory was pulled over, spilling Waller and his assailants onto the stones. 'Waller then lay naked on the Ground. Dalton got upon him, and stamping on his Privy Parts, he gave a dismal Groan, and I believe it was his last; for after that I never heard him groan nor speak, nor saw him stir.'

Waller's body was taken in a hackney coach to the St Giles Roundhouse where a surgeon pronounced him dead, and then back to Newgate. All the way, an exultant cheering crowd followed the coach. Among them were Edward Dalton and Richard Griffith, a meat porter who 'took particular Pleasure in mobbing and pelting Persons appointed to stand upon the Pillory' and who had been prominent in beating Waller to death. At the door of Newgate the prison authorities refused for some time to take the body in until ordered to do so by the Sheriffs. During the delay, Waller's mother, who had been anxiously awaiting her son's return, entered the coach. 'There was a Man in the Coach, and they put me in, and I laid my Son's Head in my Lap . . . My Son had neither Eyes, nor Ears, nor Nose to be seen; they had squeezed his Head flat. *Griffith* pull'd open the Coach-door, and struck me, pull'd my Son's Head out of my Lap, and his Brains fell into my Hand.'[1]

The terrible antagonisms leading to the death of John Waller remind us that London in the eighteenth century was a divided city. Its divisions overlapped one another at many levels. Old separations between London, Westminster and Southwark were still marked physically on the ground, adding to the difficulties of getting round the metropolis. It was a city divided by politics and history, fractures especially deep between the City of London and the court and parliament at Westminster. It was a place of religious discord between churchmen and dissenters and between Protestants and Catholics. The public spheres of men and women were separate in part, their private relations frequently marked by violence and exploitation. Neighbourhoods might be riven by ethnic tensions and family affronts. And everything was complicated by class, for the divide between rich and poor in London was never greater or more destructive in the modern era than in these years. At times these divisions were such that London could seem at war with itself: for a week in June 1780 it really was. There are many narratives that can be constructed from this dramatic, turbulent and disordered century in London's history, but one powerful theme will be how and to what extent the Londoners and their city healed these open wounds.

The fashions of history-writing have swung in recent years towards a celebration of the English eighteenth century as an age of artistic and scientific genius, of reason, civility, elegance and manners. It has often

---

1 OBP T17320906-69; OA17321009; *Daily Journal* 14 June 1732. Dalton and Griffith were both hanged for Waller's murder.

been summarised as the Age of Politeness. And when we think of England in this century it is really London we have in mind, for London led the nation in genius, elegance and manners to an overwhelming degree. There is a great deal of truth in this characterisation, but a proper balance needs to be struck. For this was a city (and an Age) of starving poverty as well as shining polish, a city of civility and a city of truculence, a city of decorum and a city of lewdness, a city of joy and a city of despair, a city of sentiment and a city of cruelty. We might truthfully summarise it as a city of extremes. In Daniel Defoe's epigram of the early 1720s, London really was 'this great and monstrous Thing'.

In transcribing original texts I have followed the originals, with all their eccentricities of spelling, punctuation, italics and capitalisation and without disrupting the flow with innumerable 'sics'. The reader will have to trust me that Joshua Reynolds really did write of the 'Prince of Whales', that a newspaper advert really did refer to a baby's 'Shoos', and so on.

Dates given before the adoption of the Gregorian calendar in 1752 are given in the old style, except that I have made the year begin on 1 January rather than 25 March, as was frequently the case at the time. It is a most disconcerting thing to find a newspaper for 31 December 1705 followed by the issue of 1 January 1705; I have avoided the device of 1 January 1705/06 and given the year as 1706.

Pressures of length have required economy in the endnotes. I have used short titles throughout, with full titles given in the bibliography at the end of the book. And I have confined the notes generally to sources for direct quotations, surprising facts, and some limited suggestions for further reading.

Translating money into modern values is fraught with difficulty. For much of the eighteenth century a regular income – hardly ever attainable, I should add – of 75p a week (say £40 a year) would provide security and reasonable comfort for a family of man, woman and two children; a pound a week would be considered good money for anyone working with their hands, even a junior clerk; and a gentleman could manage to keep up a decent appearance on £200 a year. If we have in mind a multiplier of 250 to translate old values into new we won't go too far wrong.

12d (pence) = 1s (shilling) = 5p
Half a crown = 2s 6d = 12.5p
Crown = 5s = 25p
240d = 20s = £1
½ guinea = 10s 6d = 52.5p
1 guinea = 21s = £1.05p
1 moidore = 27s = £1.35p

INTRODUCTION:
LONDON 1700–1708

LONDON is generally believed, not only to be one of the most Ancient, but the most Spacious, Populous, Rich, Beautiful, Renowned and Noble Citys that we know of at this day in the World: 'Tis the Seat of the *British* Empire, the Exchange of *Great Britain* and *Ireland*; the Compendium of the Kingdom, the Vitals of the Common-wealth, and the Principal Town of Traffic that I can find accounted for by any of our Geographers . . .[1]

BY 1700, after half a century of relentless expansion, London had overtaken Paris to become the largest – if disputably the finest – city in Europe. It stretched in a great arc of continuous building along the north bank of the Thames, some five miles as the crow flies from Tothill Street, Westminster, to Limehouse in the east. It was linked to the south bank and the burgeoning Borough of Southwark – the next largest town in the kingdom if it could ever have been imagined separate from the metropolis – by the 500-year-old London Bridge. The connection seemed more solid somehow when travellers mistook it for just another street until a gap in the houses on either side revealed the swirling river below. North to south, across that single bridge, London was more shallow than broad, just two and a half miles from the 'stones' end' in Shoreditch to the furthest point of Blackman Street, Southwark. This was a walkable city, just three hours across (allowing for obstructions) and less than two hours north to south, and on foot was how most Londoners experienced it. Even so, its size and complexity and dense obscurities already made it unknowable: 'So large is the Extent of *London*, *Westminster* and *Southwark*, with their Suburbs and Liberties, that no Coachman nor Porter knows every Place in them . . .'[2]

That age-old three-part division of 'London', dating back to Saxon times at least, was still real enough at the beginning of the eighteenth century, despite the unbroken continuity of the built-up area. The City of London, the heart of trade, manufacturing and the manipulation of money, had centuries before burst beyond its Roman walls, but confined itself to ancient boundaries east of Temple Bar and west of the Tower. The City of Westminster had two sectors: one around the Abbey, Westminster Hall (the law courts) and the Houses of Parliament, and the other – more aristocratic – around St James's Palace, the royal court. This area around St James's, with its northern suburbs, was just becoming known as 'the west end of the town'. By 1700 the two cities were conjoined by houses and streets almost a mile deep from the river to their outer suburbs and liberties. These outliers in effect formed a township distinct from the cities out of which they had grown, made of once separate villages now fused in a solid ring from St Martin-in-the-Fields in the west to Whitechapel in the east. This ring of suburbs, though highly diverse, was predominantly a workers' district. South of the river, Southwark also had a strong manufacturing complexion, leavened with trade and something of the City's money-getting ways. In the east, on both sides of the river, was an entirely different London, a seafarer's town or towns, places of both poverty and considerable wealth. Seagoing London was most dense along the river's north bank at Wapping, but it had a significant strand along the south bank from Bermondsey, through Rotherhithe, to the quite separate towns of Deptford and Greenwich – neither, in 1700, London at all.

Despite frequent allusions to the cities of London and Westminster and the Borough of Southwark as three distinct places, and despite there being in reality five main divisions, the whole had come to be known and understood as 'London' by 1700. Distinctions, though, remained more than skin deep. Joseph Addison famously summed them up in June 1712:

When I consider this great city in its several quarters and divisions, I look upon it as an aggregate of various nations distinguished from each other by their respective customs, manners, and interests. The courts of two countries do not so much differ from one another, as the court and city, in their peculiar ways of life and conversation. In short, the inhabitants of St James's, notwithstanding they live under the same laws, and speak the same language, are a distinct people from those of Cheapside, who are likewise removed from those of the Temple on one side, and those of Smithfield on the other, by several climates and degrees in their ways of thinking and conversing together.[3]

How many lived in this 'aggregate of various nations'? If only we could answer with confidence. All numbers in eighteenth-century London are to be treated with scepticism, most mistrusted, many dismissed out of hand. Contemporary estimates of London's population around 1700 helpfully ranged from around half a million to 2 million. Historians since have been hardly the wiser. The two most eminent London historians of the first half of the twentieth century adopted astonishingly precise figures of 674,500 for 1700 and 676,750 for 1750. A kind of consensus around 575,000 for 1700 and 750,000 for 1750 has emerged in the last fifty years, but the true figures are unknowable and these will only ever stand as best guesses. If we keep in our minds over half a million for 1700 and under three-quarters of a million for 1750 we won't go too far wrong. Even so, the staggering size for contemporaries of London's population at the beginning of the century is brought home by the estimate for Britain's second city in 1700. That was Bristol, at around 30,000. It is believed that one in ten persons in England and Wales lived in London; and that perhaps one in six had lived in it at some time in their lives.[4]

Just why London's 'nations' proved so populous is an easier question to answer than how many Londoners there were. Its sheer size exercised a gravitational pull on the nation, through wonderment and curiosity and tales retold; and through counties from Cornwall to Cumberland producing and delivering goods for the London market and providing labour-power for every function from serving maid to courtier. London was the kingdom's centre of world trade and shipping, of the emerging banking, brokerage and insurance industries, of finished commodity manufacture not only for the metropolis but for the nation, for European competitors, for the empire and for the world. It was the home of the royal court, with its countless civil-list pensioners; of Parliament, which transacted an immense part of not just public, but local and even private business for the nation; and of uniquely metropolitan institutions like the higher law courts, a monopoly of printing and publishing, and the 'royal' theatres. For all these reasons London was immensely wealthy. And that in itself was a further irresistible allure to rich and poor alike, ever supplementing the 'aggregate of various nations'.

LONDON IN THE EIGHTEENTH CENTURY

A striking feature of this monster city in 1700 was its newness. In September 1666 some three-fifths of the City of London had been destroyed in the Great Fire. The losses were immense – 13,200 houses were burned to the ground and so were most of the great public buildings, including St Paul's Cathedral and eighty-seven parish churches. Rebuilding the housing took well into the 1670s. The public buildings took longer – St Paul's was not considered finished till 1711. And rebuilding was at a much reduced density – some parish churches and livery company halls were never replaced and only around 9,000 houses filled the place of those lost.

Although some lamented a failure to reconstruct the City on rational geometric lines, a different and doubtless improved City nonetheless replaced the old. The new houses were of brick rather than plaster-faced timber as before. They had neat flat fronts, were generally two rooms deep, three or four main floors high, and two or three windows (or 'bays') wide. Attics were set back into the roofline and there were no storeys jutting forward over the pavement, nearly brushing gables with the houses across the way. Old property boundaries had generally been followed. But where opportunity offered, main roads were widened and courts and alleys were opened out, and gradients were flattened when the Thames waterfront was raised three feet. So in 1700, three-fifths of what had been an ancient City, full of Tudor buildings and older, was now a great modern town, just thirty years old or less.[5]

Almost equally important, the Fire had given an added push to suburban development in and around Westminster, as the wealthiest citizens took the chance to seek a convenient home downwind of, but close to, the crowded City. St James's Square's first houses were rated from 1667 and the neighbourhood south of Piccadilly grew apace from then. Great old mansions along the riverside south of the Strand were pulled down and replaced with elegant rows of terraced houses in York Buildings and neighbouring streets from the 1670s. The area around the Haymarket and Leicester Fields (later Square) was also built on from the 1670s, Soho in the 1670s and 80s, Golden Square and around in the 1680s, Seven Dials in the 1690s. In north London, smart suburbs took root around Red Lion Square and at Bloomsbury Square from the 1680s. There was expansion at the same time in some middling and poor parishes at the edge of Westminster and the City, in St Martin-in-the-Fields and St Giles and in Clerkenwell. Further east were new streets in Spitalfields, driven by demand from French Protestant migrants especially from 1685, and in Wapping. Finally, south of the river, the Great Fire of Southwark of 1676 destroyed 600 houses, which were rebuilt in the new brick or in traditional timber and plaster. All this, then, was pretty much spanking new or just coming of age in 1700. Indeed, the up-to-date feel of much of London was a matter of astonishment, its new growth 'really a kind of Prodigy', according to Daniel Defoe.[6]

There was much of charm and beauty in this new London. Contemporary Britons believed it 'the fairest' city 'in all Europe, perhaps in the whole World'. Part of that claim resided in the majesty of old buildings like the Tower and, most of all, Westminster Abbey: rising over the trees of the park, 'with another city arising beyond all', it offered 'a view of such a nature as few places in the world can parallel'. But much was contributed by what was new. The warm pinks and reds of the brick used to build the new City and suburbs were not supplanted by a cooler grey until towards the end of Queen Anne's reign (1714). In paintings of the time and for half a century after, the muted fireside glow of London brick cast the city in a rosy hue. It seems to have proved more resilient to discolouration from London smoke than white Portland stone, used for every grand public building and quickly blackened on the south and west façades by the prevailing winds.[7]

It was not just the welcoming colours of new London that gratified contemporaries, but the regularity of the street frontages in the City and of the streets themselves in many of the newer suburbs. Grandeur too could be found in the new public buildings of the City, in the rebuilt churches wrought or influenced by Sir Christopher Wren, fifty or so gleaming steeples and towers in Portland stone, some soaring 100 feet and more over the buildings around them. Grandest of all was the new cathedral of St Paul's, Wren's masterpiece, massively dominating the City skyline from its elevated position atop Ludgate Hill. Its inspiration – no accident this, given the frequent comparisons between the celestial city and London – was St Peter's at Rome. The cupola of St Paul's stretched some 300 feet into the sky. It would remain London's tallest building for more than 200 years to come, helping strangers find their bearings by a glimpse of the dome over the housetops. Even so, its magnificence was curtailed by London's inherent claustrophobia and the close clustering of buildings around it: 'we can't see it till we are upon it,' wrote one critic, who called for the demolition of the nearby City gate and the opening of a line of view from St Paul's to the river to show its full glory.[8]

This cramped confinement was at its worst in the remnants of old London that had escaped the Fire. These were extensive. Two-fifths of the City represented probably 5,000 houses and other buildings, not all old because of London's ceaseless rebuilding and refashioning but many dating back to the 1400s and many more to the century of Elizabeth and Shakespeare. Not even all these were necessarily bad and not all the old streets were uniformly poor and shabby. But much of this pre-Fire housing in the City was worn and decrepit from generations of multiple occupancy and landlord neglect. The wards of Farringdon Without (or outside the walls) and Cripplegate Without contained much of the worst housing in the old City, with over 300 courts and alleys between them. The former included part of Chick Lane and Fleet Lane near the Fleet Ditch, and Long Lane, Smithfield, all bywords for filth and dangerous disorder. Small enclaves of the worn-out City were dotted here and there, like the Liberty of St Martin's-le-Grand, and the former 'Alsatia' or ancient thieves' and debtors' sanctuary of Whitefriars between Fleet Street and the Thames.

Beyond the City, swathes of the inner suburbs from Charing Cross to Whitechapel pre-dated the Fire. The courts and alleys between St Martin's Lane and Bedfordbury were so interlocking and obscure, so much a law unto themselves, that they were known as the Bermudas or the Carribbee Islands from the early seventeenth century. The narrow streets of St Giles were notoriously poor, filthy and dangerous. Turnmill Street, Clerkenwell, was the archetypal London slum long before the word was invented, its name thrown casually into conversation as symbolising the very lowest of London low life. Names like Rotten Row, Foul Lane, Ragged Row, Dark Entry, Dirty Lane, Pissing Alley ('a very proper name for it') litter the London maps of the time around Long Acre and Drury Lane, Shoreditch and Whitechapel.[9] Perhaps Southwark was as bad as anywhere, the courts and alleys off Bankside 'very meanly built and Inhabited', the Mint (another Alsatia, west of the high street) 'sorry built with old Timber Houses, and as ill Inhabited', and Kent Street, the main road to Dover, very dirty, narrow and mean, with courts of 'old sorry Timber Houses'. But most embarrassing of all was old Westminster. Here, around the Abbey, the law courts and the Houses of Parliament, were densely clustered wooden sheds and hovels, even leaning against the Abbey walls. Some were 'ready to fall'. King Street, the main road from the court and City to Parliament, was a narrow filthy congested way, an affront and obstruction to the Queen and her burgesses. This whole wretched area around the Abbey was known as 'the desert of Westminster'. Its outlook wasn't improved by the extensive blackened remains of the Tudor Whitehall Palace, burned to the ground in January 1698 and still largely undeveloped in the early years of the century.[10]

Throughout this old London, some obscure places had no name at all, outliving any claim to inheritance or title. They were run as fiefdoms by the occupiers until so knocked about they were abandoned altogether, the odd 'backward Place, which now, thro' Time, or other Casualties, is come to Desolation, and has at this Day nothing but Ruins, to shew it was once the Possession of poor Inhabitants'. Houses there and elsewhere frequently collapsed. Indeed, much of old London seemed tottering on the verge. Small wonder that after the Great Storm of November 1703, 'Houses looked like falling scaffolding, like skeletons of buildings, like what in truth they were, heaps of ruins.'[11]

It was this old London that was primarily responsible for the great inconveniences of metropolitan life. Here the streets were generally surfaced with large pebbles and with a central kennel or gutter, at very best uneven and rough. Main streets had footways on either side paved in flat stone, Purbeck stone the preferred material, and were not raised much – if at all – above the roadway. To stop carriages taking advantage of the smooth stones they were protected by stumpy wooden posts at the pavement's edge. But in narrow streets there was no footway and no protection at all for the pedestrian. In any event, the upkeep of pavement and carriageway was the responsibility of the separate occupiers – not even the owners – of houses on each side up to the central kennel or midpoint. It was a duty much neglected. Where undertaken, it was performed as cheaply as possible. No obligation existed to use the same materials, or even repair to the same level, as one's neighbour. The pits and troughs that wheeled traffic had to negotiate were bone-shaking and axle-shattering; the holes and hazards endured by foot passengers were not just prejudicial to bones but to life itself. Stagecoach passengers encountering 'London stones' from the country 'were jumbled about like so many *Pease* in a *Childs-Rattle*, running, at every Kennel-Jolt, a great Hazard of a Dislocation . . . Our Elbows and Shoulders . . . Black and Blew'. The 800 hackney coaches licensed for hire were better sprung apparently than the stages, but even they were teeth-rattlers.[12]

There were other hazards too. The drainage of London in 1700 was

established on a simple system. Common 'shores' or sewers, often
Thames tributaries like the Fleet River or 'Ditch', were intended for
surface water drainage only. On this optimistic assumption, the Fleet
had been canalised in the 1670s below Holborn Bridge to the Thames
and lined with warehouses on either side. Using sewers for foul
drainage, for human waste, say, or blood from the slaughterhouses,
was unlawful. Human waste was stored in cesspools, pits dug often
directly beneath the 'bog-houses' or 'houses of office'. They had to be
emptied in the hours of darkness to mitigate the nuisance, their contents
or 'night soil' brought up by bucket and shovel and carted to the
farmers' country dunghills, or to great pits in Tothill Fields, Westminster,
and elsewhere.

In fact these systems were separate in name only. Night-men took
the risk of a fine and tipped their carts in the common sewers to save
a tedious journey to the fields. Those with properties alongside the
sewers built their bog-houses over them with impunity, or nearly so.
Londoners urinated openly in the streets and defecated more privately
on the stones of courts and alleys. Chamber pots were emptied into
the kennels, which in any event collected the scourings of the streets, the
horse and cattle dung, the dog shit and animal carcasses, and shot them
into the sewers:

> Sweepings from Butchers Stalls, Dung, Guts, and Blood,
> Drown'd Puppies, stinking Sprats, all drench'd in Mud,
> Dead Cats and Turnip-Tops come tumbling down the Flood.[13]

That was Jonathan Swift, whose nose was too tender for many
London lodgings, driven from one to another by the stench of the 'sink'
or drains, even in polite parts of the town like Bury Street, St James's.
Amidst the less polite, things could get very messy indeed. A narrow
lane near Billingsgate 'stunk of *Stale Sprats*, *Piss*, and *Sirreverence*
[human excrement]'. In 'the Hog-keepers yards at *White-Chappel*' the
swine were 'fed with Carrion, and the Offall of Dead Beasts are kept,
whose Smell is so unsufferably Nauceous that People are not able to
go that way'. Worst of all, perhaps, were the places in Southwark and
Bermondsey close to the 'Tide-Ditches' that 'receive all the Sinks,
Necessary-houses, and Drains, from Dye-houses, Wash-houses, Fell
Mongers, Slaughter-houses, and all kinds of Offensive Trades . . .
notorious Fountains of Stench enough to Corrupt the very Air, and to

make People sick and faint as they pass by'. Nor was the atmosphere improved by the habit of storing the scavengers' scourings or street slop in giant mounds or laystalls along the north bank of the Thames and on the edge of the town. Those on the river at Dowgate and Whitefriars and Dung Wharf in the City were thirty or forty feet high, and as wide and long as a city block. The 'mounds' of ashes, street mud and rubbish or 'dunghills' at Whitechapel, Clerkenwell and elsewhere were as big as modern slag heaps, with roadways to the top for carts to tip their loads and to remove the contents for brick makers and market gardeners in the countryside. For Bernard Mandeville, 'the stinking Streets of London' were all a sign of a vigorous trading existence, and so 'a necessary Evil'. Others were less philosophical. Small wonder that the royal family removed from St James's Palace to Hampton Court in hot weather to avoid the stench of London, or that flies were the scourge of every summer in town. In 1708 a plague of flies was so dense that Londoners' feet left impressions 'as visible as in snow' on the dead insects in the streets.[14]

According to Ned Ward, that sparkling though scabrous chronicler of metropolitan low life at the turn of the eighteenth century, who always called a turd a turd, an eclipse of the sun was 'Invisible to us at *London*, by Reason of a Stinking Fog that arose from wreaking *Dung-hills*, *Distillers Fats*, and Pipeing Hot *Close-Stool-Pans*'; and, of course, because of London smoke. Coal smoke, foreign visitors thought, was the 'Bane of *London*' that 'poisons the air one breaths in it'. The London air was said to be notoriously 'thick' and in winter 'Fog and Dirt are the two cheapest things then to be had'. Other irritations included the great swinging signs that, in the general absence of street names on walls and house numbers, alerted the passer-by to shops and inns. By the early eighteenth century a map or directory had become an essential tool for finding a way through London, though choosing which of fourteen King Streets, say, was the one you needed could still tax the ill-prepared. Hence the complex directions given out by shops, as in this case for the supplier of Dr Tilney's Green Drops for 'Ailments and Infirmities of the Seminals and Genitals': 'the furthermost House but one, on the right Hand, in Fountain Court, near Exeter-Change, Strand'.[15]

Getting around this sprawling, opaque and densely interwoven city wasn't easy. Pedestrians had to have their wits about them and sometimes considerable fortitude. 'Taking the wall', keeping as far from the filthy street mud as possible, could lead to arguments, even fights, if one person refused to give way to another. Walkers had to compete too with the trotting chairmen, instantly identifiable by football-sized calves bulging through their stockings. There were 200 sedan chairs licensed for hire – 300 from 1713, to accommodate the growth of the town – and many wealthy residents had private chairs. Supposed to keep to the roadway, many – perhaps all – bullied their way inside the posts: a chairman's 'By your leave!' was less request than ultimatum.[16]

All these dangers were worse by night. By the standards of the second half of the century, the lighting of London streets around 1700 was looked back on, literally, as some dark age. But to contemporaries the convex lamps of the City, introduced in 1695, and the 'globular' lamps of the West End, an innovation of 1709, made London the best lit of all cities. They only shone on 'dark' nights without moonlight, and even then were extinguished long before dawn, but to foreign visitors these lamps were as 'the *little Suns of the Night*'.[17]

Other amenities ranked high among the conveniences of London, especially the four parks that largely defined the boundaries of the city on the western side. They stretched, somewhat larger then than now, from Westminster to Kensington, a village throughout the eighteenth century and connected to London more in the mind than on the ground. Originally they had been deer parks for the use of Henry VIII and his court. In 1700 there was still open country between the town and Hyde Park and Kensington Gardens; building had just about come up to Green Park; and in the south, St James's Park had houses on three sides. High brick walls enclosed the separate spaces to make them less continuous than later became the case.

Smartest was St James's, behind the royal palace in Pall Mall. When Londoners talked of 'the Park' in the eighteenth century, this is generally what they meant. It was 'famed wellnigh throughout the world', a German visitor recorded in 1710. All Londoners of the middling classes and above knew it and all visitors had to experience it. Mrs Percivall, a provincial English lady, breathlessly relayed her impressions to a friend in the country (whose name and whereabouts have not come down to us) around 1713:

[St James's Park] has many Deer in it, 'tis very large and two Canalls and a pond called Rosamonds Pond, here are many Swans, here are abundance of

Lime Trees which makes many fine Walks, some close some open in the Spring this place is very Sweet . . . in this Park all the Fine Ladys and Great Beaus walk at Noon in the Winter and ten a Clock at night in the Summer, there stands a Centinel at every Gate to keep beggars and Masked Ladys from walking here. The finest walk and what is most frequented is the Mall 'tis Gravelled and Rolled.

[Of Hyde Park] 'tis very large many Acres: in some places 'tis quite open and other places are bushes of Trees some in order and others wild this stands very high, and the Coaches come here in the Summer, you shall see some Evenings two hundred Coaches; here is a place called the Ring where they generally go to view one anothers fine Equipage and Cloaths, no Hackneys nor foot men are allowed to come in the Ring, they are always dressed when they come here to the best advantage, the Coaches pass so close that many Assignations are made . . .[18]

Another of London's great assets was the Thames. London's very existence as a great trading city depended on it and the river at work was as much one of the sights of London as the parks at play. Indeed, it was an industry in itself, supporting a host of fishermen who caught roach, barbel, flounder, salmon, even an occasional sturgeon. It was also a great highway and gave work to some 1,400 lighters or one-oar barges, and some 3,000 wherries. Watermen in one- or two-men boats could be hired at eighty-nine 'plying places' either side of London Bridge, mostly to the west of it and on the north bank. On a sunny calm day it was the quickest and most comfortable way between the City and Westminster, or to cross from the Middlesex to the Surrey side. It was not without its dangers, though. Shooting the narrow arches of London Bridge, where the water could suddenly fall a dozen feet or more, was a hazard many avoided by being landed on one side and taking boat again at the other: 'when we had watched our boat passing through the bridge, from the shore we could see neither boat nor boatman, so that one could well imagine that both were being sucked down by the water.' Danger from wind and crowding of vessels led to capsizes and deaths every year – eight people in two separate incidents drowned near Vauxhall in April 1718 alone, for instance.[19]

Around 1700 the Thames was not yet the great public sewer that it would become, but it was polluted enough from the common shores emptying into it: Ned Ward wondered how 'the Lady *Thames*' could 'have so sweet a Breath, considering how many stinking Pills she swallows in a Day'. The evening swarms of rats on the riverbank near the Savoy remained a perpetual nightmare for one Londoner at least. Yet there seemed to be few qualms in taking the bulk of London's domestic water straight from the river, without filtration or even settlement first. Much of it was supplied from the old waterworks at London Bridge, dating from 1582. The sediment of Thames water was said to settle faster in the glass than the New River's, supplying the northern suburbs from a source in Hertfordshire, and from the Thames came apparently the drinking water of choice. Whatever the source, all houses of the middling classes and above had access to a piped supply from one of the several London water companies. The poor were served by common pumps in the courts and alleys and by-streets. The supply to everyone was intermittent, householders storing their water in lead cisterns, usually in the basement. And it was made worse by frequent breakages in the six-inch wooden mains beneath the streets and at the join with the leaden pipes supplying each house. Even so, no city in the world, it was thought, was better supplied with water than London.[20]

There is one further amenity worth dwelling on at this point. No Londoner, even one entombed in the dankest, darkest City alley, was more than a mile or two from something like open countryside. Further afield and the hills of Middlesex and Surrey and the pastures and forests of Essex presented beautiful unspoiled views and smoke-free, stench-free air. But even by 1700 Londoners had begun to take a myriad liberties with this rural innocence. At every point on the London compass the wealthy citizen, his wife or his widow had staked their claim, fattening up the villages here, imposing with a country mansion there. Just a few instances will have to stand for an uncountable many: in the west, Gumley House, Isleworth, for a prominent London mirror- and cabinet-maker (c. 1700), and Gordon House, Isleworth (c. 1718), for Moses Hart, a wealthy London Jewish merchant; in the east, Leyton Great House (1712) for Sir Nathaniel Tench, one of the first directors of the Bank of England, and Wanstead House (begun 1715) for Sir Richard Child, a banker of prodigious wealth. These and many more were

magnificently furnish'd with rich Tapestry, *India* Silks, Damask, gold and silver Plate, *China* Ware and Porcelane, rich Cabinets, &c. and adorn'd with fine carved Work and Paintings as many Palaces: And when it is considered that most of these are only the Summer Retreats of Gentlemen, and that many belong to the Tradesmen of the City of *London*, who perhaps seldom spend but a Day or two in the Week there, surely nothing in the World can imitate it.[21]

Surely nothing could. And it was into this filthy, magnificent, immense and bewildering world of London that James Gibbs stepped, some time in the autumn of 1708.

PART ONE

CITY

James Gibbs

I

JAMES GIBBS'S LONDON, 1708–54

The Architect Most in Vogue: James Gibbs

JAMES Gibbs had more influence than any other architect on the new London that began to emerge in the first half of the eighteenth century. In many ways that is a modest claim, for in those years no single architect stamped his mark on the city as Wren had done on the fifty years before or Robert Adam would do on the fifty years to come. The work of other architects showed greater individuality and genius, and the London churches of Nicholas Hawksmoor in particular have been given the palm by posterity. But Gibbs loved London in a way that Hawksmoor never did. And Gibbs proved a more versatile designer. His influence ranged widely over the city's ecclesiastical, domestic and institutional buildings in a way that no contemporary architect chose to match.

James Gibbs was a Scot and a Roman Catholic, born near Aberdeen in December 1682, the son of a prosperous merchant. By the time he was sixteen his parents were dead. He settled for a time in the Netherlands, probably with relatives. At first destined for the priesthood, he entered a seminary at Rome. It proved uncongenial. But Rome breathed vigorous life into an early genius for drawing and painting, and by 1705 Gibbs had begun to study architecture under a variety of Roman masters. He applied himself with flair and dedication to a subject that clearly delighted him.[1]

It appears to have been the last illness of his sole surviving brother that drew Gibbs back to Protestant Britain in November 1708 rather than any promise of commissions or clear plan of forging an

architectural career there. By the time Gibbs reached London his brother
had died. Instead of proceeding north to Aberdeen, he chose to discover
what the city had to offer him. He was not yet twenty-six, and as far
as we know he had never set foot in London before. Gibbs would make
London his home for the rest of his life.

Perhaps surprisingly, his outsider's background did him no harm.
The Act of Union of 1707 had brought many fellow Scots to London,
and a number were in positions of power. His Catholicism made him
the natural choice of architect for wealthy co-religionists. His strong
Jacobite sympathies with the cause of the Stuarts, exiled in France,
sounded a chord with many. These religious and political affiliations
were closely concealed, but all who needed to know were in on the
secret. More publicly, Gibbs was a Tory and he arrived in London on
the eve of a brief Tory ascendancy under a high-church queen of Stuart
stock. His skills as an architect, schooled in Italian classicism while
retaining a taste for the baroque, won him the admiration of the ageing
Sir Christopher Wren. And an easy charm, always ready to see the best
in people, combined with striking good looks – a full mouth, wide-set
eyes, and not yet marred by the corpulence that would overtake him
in later years – can have done him no harm in polite society.

These were all propitious alignments and they quickly proved fertile.
Aristocratic Scottish clients in London commissioned projects from
Gibbs in both the metropolis and North Britain. They included the
joint Secretaries of State for Scotland, the Earls of Loudoun and Mar,
Gibbs refashioning a house and office for them in Whitehall in 1710.
It was around this time that, for reasons of expediency, Gibbs chose
openly to worship in the established church. He never lost his love for
his old religion, but to practise it openly would have undoubtedly denied
him many of the commissions that would go on to make his fortune.
There were many people at this time active in or around London
political life who were not quite what they seemed and James Gibbs
was one of them.[2]

Whatever his dissimulations in religion and politics, Gibbs needed
to make no compromise in his distinctively individual voice as an
architect. He came to London at a time when architectural fashion was
about to shift from the high baroque of Wren to a new and less decorative classicism inspired by the sixteenth-century Italian architect
Andrea Palladio. Palladianism would become the dominant, though far
from pervasive, building style for prestigious projects in London until

the 1750s. Despite its Italian origins, its clean unfussy ordered lines seemed most completely to express Protestant ideals. Palladianism contrasted strongly with the elaborate decorativeness of baroque, which bore more than a hint of idolatrous Catholicism. The new style could properly become a Whig architecture for a Hanoverian Britain, returning to the plain-speaking veracity of Inigo Jones and the early seventeenth century and rejecting the exuberant and morally dubious baroque of Wren and his pupils Sir John Vanbrugh and Nicholas Hawksmoor. Palladianism was beginning to emerge as a force in 'taste' at around the time Gibbs came to London. In a decade it would be something like an orthodoxy. But not before Gibbs had made his first indelible mark on the face of eighteenth-century London.[3]

In February 1711 the parishioners of Greenwich petitioned the House of Commons for financial help to rebuild their parish church. Its roof had collapsed some four months before. There quickly followed a rash of similar pleas from other places, either for rebuilding a worn-out structure or for replacing a small church with one big enough for the swelling suburban populations of places like Rotherhithe, Putney, Southwark and Shoreditch. In March the House received details of the estimated populations of the London suburbs and the church accommodation available for worship. There was a woeful shortfall, just forty-six churches and chapels for over half a million thought to be living in the most populous parishes. A Commons committee reported in April that the existing accommodation provided for no more than one in three of those who needed spiritual succour from the Church of England. This was an affront to both a pious Queen and a Tory administration that saw the established church as an essential bulwark of the social fabric. The House resolved to legislate to build fifty new churches 'in and about the Suburbs of the Cities of *London* and *Westminster* . . .'[4]

The Fifty New Churches Act of 1711 promised far more than it ever achieved. Just twelve new churches were built under the act and not all those were in the suburbs. Even so, all twelve remain among the most treasured London buildings of the eighteenth century. There were three in the East End: Christ Church, Spitalfields (1714–29), St George in the East in Ratcliff Highway (also 1714–29) and St Anne's, Limehouse (1714–30), all by Nicholas Hawksmoor and all properly suburban. Three were south of the river: St Alfege's, Greenwich (1712–18, Hawksmoor), St Paul's, Deptford (1713–30, Thomas Archer) and St John Horsleydown, Bermondsey (1727–33, John James). Two were in the City: a new church

on the northern edge, St Luke's, Old Street (1727–33, Hawksmoor and James), and the rebuilt St Mary Woolnoth (1716–24, Hawksmoor). One was in north London: St George's, Bloomsbury (1716–31 Hawksmoor). And three were in Westminster: St John's, Smith Square (1713–28, Archer), St George's, Hanover Square (1720–25, James) and St Mary le Strand (1714–23). This last was by James Gibbs.

Nicholas Hawksmoor was one of the two original surveyors to the commissioners tasked with building the fifty new churches. As the list of attributions shows, he was by far the more active. William Dickinson, his fellow surveyor, resigned in August 1713 to pursue other interests. Immediately, the friends of James Gibbs, Wren prominent among them, recommended him as successor. It all came at an important time, for Gibbs was struggling financially. The strongest competition came from John James, who had the support of Sir John Vanbrugh and the Whigs. In November 1713, with the help of his numerous powerful Scottish patrons, now influential in a Tory administration, Gibbs was chosen by secret ballot to succeed Dickinson.[5]

Gibbs's first commission, a most prestigious one, was to build a church

London in 1723

on ground anciently occupied by the maypole in the Strand, just east of Somerset House. There were considerable problems in doing so. The site was tightly constricted but occupied a viewpoint of metropolitan significance in London's most important thoroughfare, linking as it did the two cities of London and Westminster. Gibbs overcame these challenges with great individual flair. St Mary le Strand remains one of London's architectural pearls, among the best loved and most readily recognised of all the London churches. Its three-tier steeple is a particular triumph but was apparently an afterthought, insisted upon by the commissioners when the building was already twenty feet above the ground. St Mary's petite, demure appearance, in virginal Portland stone, was quickly seized upon as exquisitely feminine. The Earl of Mar congratulated Gibbs on his 'fair daughter in the Strand', 'the most complete little damsel in town'.[6]

Gibbs's first commission as surveyor for the fifty new churches would prove his last. Politics once more intervened, this time to his detriment. The lingering last illness of Queen Anne, and her death on 1 August 1714, provoked a constitutional crisis, followed by a rebellion and an invasion. As at numerous prior crises, politics became not just a matter of personal conviction but involved the possibility of arrest, imprisonment and financial ruin. Quite literally, at this point in the century politics could become a matter of life and death. Gibbs, a dissembling Catholic and Jacobite whose real sympathies were well known, found himself on the losing side. With the Whigs in the ascendance, the House of Hanover on the throne and a Stuart 'Pretender' gathering an army in Scotland, Gibbs was sacked in January 1716. He had before then apparently seriously considered joining the rebellion but was dissuaded from doing so by the Earl of Mar, its fomenter in Scotland, and perhaps by Lord Burlington.[7]

Burlington, just twenty-two yet an architect and patron of some renown and owner of a sizeable estate behind his mansion on the north side of Piccadilly (now home to the Royal Academy), was perhaps the most influential advocate for Palladianism as the fitting architecture of Hanoverian Whiggery. In fact, in the closet, he seems to have been a closely secretive supporter of the Jacobite cause. But in the troubled days of 1714–16 he maintained an entirely convincing pose as a loyal subject of George I. In any event, his commitment to Palladianism was unalloyed. He, his protégé William Kent, one of the most brilliant architects and interior designers of the day, and Colen Campbell, a Scot like Gibbs, who became an influential theorist for the Palladian movement, helped popularise a definitive shift in taste from the early years of George I.

Not, though, that architectural practice in London followed their lead with anything like uniform acceptance of the new fashion. Eclecticism was the only consistent characteristic of London building design from the age of Wren onwards. Architects not only pursued a range of styles in their projects; they might happily combine one or more styles in any building coming under their hand. For this reason alone, Gibbs's less than wholehearted espousal of the new fashion deterred few commissions. His talents as an architect were manifest and many. Even some Whigs liked what he designed. Most of all, though, it was Tory clients, the embittered remnants of Queen Anne's last government and their wealthy friends, who ensured Gibbs's setback of 1716 was merely temporary.

Despite dismissal by the commissioners for the fifty new churches, it says much for Gibbs's technical skills and his diplomacy that he was allowed to retain the contract for St Mary le Strand and see the church through to completion. And although the act of 1711 missed its target so widely, the pious urge behind it resonated in a score or more of London parishes where churches were both decrepit and too small for the needs, real or imagined, of a larger congregation. Well into the 1730s, church building or rebuilding continued to be the largest single generator of public architecture in London.

The general satisfaction with which Gibbs's St Mary le Strand was received made him a significant contender for these other projects. In 1719 he was commissioned to add a steeple to Wren's St Clement Danes, just east of St Mary le Strand. And when the parishioners of St Martin-in-the-Fields successfully petitioned Parliament in January 1720 for powers to raise money and replace their outworn church it was to Gibbs they then turned. After a stiff competition, in November he was 'elected by a large majority' of the select vestry who managed parish business. It was a most prestigious project and Gibbs a most surprising choice of architect. For St Martin-in-the-Fields was the parish church of the King and his family, and Gibbs was known by many to be a closet Catholic and Jacobite, as well as a Tory. On the other hand, his talents and achievements as an architect were plain for all to see, and George I had no compunction in laying the foundation stone, 'with full religious and masonic rites', on 19 March 1721. The project did not always run smoothly. Trouble arose from a stream that flowed beneath St Martin's Lane and the portico's foundations had to be built on 'several hundred tombstones' taken from the churchyard and reburied in mortar. But overall the building moved apace for the times and the church was consecrated in 1726. It cost the enormous sum of nearly £34,000, some £14,000 more than St Mary le Strand.[8]

James Gibbs's St Martin-in-the-Fields remains the most famous and distinctive parish church in London. It undoubtedly benefited, ninety years or so after his death, from the opening out of St Martin's Lane and the construction of Trafalgar Square. Until then it was so closely pressed by the surrounding shopfronts that no one could step back and view the church from any satisfying viewpoint. Even so, and despite the sniping of architectural purists, it was recognised at the time as perhaps the finest building of the post-Wren era. St Martin-in-the-Fields was James Gibbs's masterpiece. It is a beautiful building that continues to delight and impress nearly 300 years on. The unlikely combination of a Roman portico, a Gothic steeple and Italian embellishments, all worked through with geometric concepts derived from Wren, was entirely unorthodox yet highly influential. St Martin's 'became the type of the Anglican parish church and was imitated wherever in the world English was spoken and Anglican worship upheld'.[9]

By the 1720s Gibbs was the architect 'most in vogue'.[10] He had made his name with his ecclesiastical architecture in the Strand and St Martin's. But commissions came his way from other directions too. First, in domestic architecture, Gibbs's skills and politics made him the first choice among wealthy Tory clients, like the Earl of Oxford, for whom he designed a new front for his Dover Street house in 1737, and the Duchess of Norfolk, whose house at 16 Arlington Street he built from 1734 to 1740. And his fame spread more widely. He designed a beautiful octagonal addition to Orleans House at Twickenham for James Johnson, a prominent Whig, in the early 1720s; he built a library for the bibliophile Dr Richard Mead, a dissenter, at Great Ormond Street in the early 1730s; he designed a new house at 25 Leicester Fields for Sir Philip Parker Long around the same time; and he was even chosen by that hammer of the Jacobites Sir Robert Walpole to soften the Palladianism of his new Norfolk mansion, Houghton Hall.

Second, Gibbs left other marks on the landscape in an important contribution to the charitable and institutional life of London, especially in his work for St Bartholomew's Hospital, Smithfield, where he was a governor. From 1728 he was architect of the great rebuilding scheme that substantially remains at the heart of the hospital to this day. A charitable man, Gibbs gave his services free to the hospital. His quadrangle of four Palladian four-storey blocks kept separate to prevent the spread of fire included an administrative building with a court room or great hall, the staircase leading to it embellished by William Hogarth's giant canvases depicting scenes of charity. Construction long outlived him, not being finished till 1769. His hospital proved not merely handsome but robustly fit for purpose. Well into the twentieth century it was 'difficult to find . . . any wards fresher, lighter, or more wholesome than those built by Gibbs at St. Bartholomew's'.[11]

Gibbs also played a distinctive part in what we might reasonably consider one of the great metropolitan dramas of the age – the ceaseless outward push of London. Like all his prominent fellow designers, he helped satisfy the ambition of wealthy men for an out-of-town mansion within fairly easy reach of the City and Westminster. He worked on Canons for the Duke of Chandos from 1716, designed Sudbrook at Petersham, near Richmond, for the Duke of Argyll from 1715 to 1719 and remodelled the famous riverside villa at Twickenham for the poet Alexander Pope, a fellow Catholic, in 1719–20. He designed or altered country villas for wealthy Londoners in East Barnet, Stanwell (Surrey) and elsewhere, developing as a speciality the design of garden buildings – orangeries, mausoleums and the like – for landowners improving their estates in the outer suburbs and beyond. More significantly, Gibbs aided the expansion of London's built-up area at its most vigorous point of growth – the north-west.

In Richard Steele's play *The Lying Lover*, the audience at Drury Lane in December 1703 were treated to a knowing chuckle at their dropsical metropolis. Young Bookwit, a true son of London just down from the university, is asked by his father, 'Is not the Town mightily increas'd since you were in it?' 'Ay, indeed, I need not have been so impatient to have left *Oxford*; had I staid a Year longer, they had builded to me.'[12] In fact, as Young Bookwit spoke, the outward march of London had just entered one of its faltering periods, as men and materials and money were sucked into Marlborough's army fighting the War of the Spanish Succession. But even in these years of relative slump Great Marlborough Street and Poland Street extended north-west Soho, for instance, and Queen's Square and Park Street (now Queen Anne's Gate) made an elegant addition to the west, south of St James's Park.

With the Peace of Utrecht in 1713 the restraints on London building were suddenly unshackled. A speculative boom was begun with sufficient energy to push past the financial catastrophe of the South Sea Bubble in the autumn of 1720. The war-stifled demand of wealthy consumers for new and fashionable accommodation was felt particularly in the west end of the town. There was a rapid response from landowners, investors and speculative builders.

All three combined to most effect north of Piccadilly. Lord Burlington was one landowner keen to begin, and his own backyard was the bait. Development in the Ten Acre Close behind his mansion began around 1717 in Savile Row and New Burlington Street. Despite his enthusiasm matters progressed unevenly, with spurts and stops in what would become the eighteenth-century way, not least because of litigious disputes over mortgages, leases and costs. Burlington's holdings in the Ten Acre Close would not be fully developed for another twenty years.

Of even greater significance, just to the north and around the same time, a grand project by the Earl of Scarborough developed a whole new town in the fields west of Swallow Street and south of Oxford Street. Scarborough celebrated the new Protestant succession by naming its centrepiece Hanover Square. It all provided, for a moment in time, the most fashionable addresses in town. Its first occupiers from 1720 were aristocrats and the very wealthiest of City magnates.[13]

Scarborough (certainly) and Burlington (nominally) were Whigs, and most of their friends – prospective tenants and investors – were Whigs too. It would be difficult indeed in these fraught years for a Tory to give his address as Hanover Square or George Street nearby. But the thirst for new building was blind to party lines. And Tory landowners on the London fringe, sorely crossed in politics since 1714, sought solace in speculation.

Edward Harley had inherited through his wife a large tract of the manor of Marylebone (commonly Marybone) north of Oxford Street. Some of it was no doubt profitable grassland, but the unappetising character of much of this sordid edge of town is indicated by names like Dung Field and Night Pitt Field and by a handful of drowned clay pits, the clay lifted and burned for London brick.[14] Plans to transform the Harley fields into new buildings seem to have been in the air from 1715. They grew more tangible when it became clear that Scarborough's Hanover Square development was intended to build up to the south side of Oxford Street, directly across from Harley's land. The prospects for a scheme on the north side seemed by 1717 provocatively ripe.

At Christmas 1717 Harley, 'Finding a great disposition in several persons to build in the Marybone grounds', had instructed surveyors to devise a detailed plan and had signed up half a dozen aristocratic partners among his friends. They 'will in all probability, quickly build the whole ground', he thought. That proved more than over-optimistic but, recognising a sure thing, others would join him in the speculation during the next three or four years. Cavendish Square was to be the centrepiece of what was in effect a new town, self-sufficient with a range of house types from aristocratic to middling-class. It included properties for local tradesmen, with stables for coaches and mews for the coachmen, and was built like any country town, complete with its own church and its own market building, Oxford Market, which was fitted out with shops and provision stalls.[15]

James Gibbs, who had carried out work for Harley's famous Tory father at the Earl of Oxford's country house, Wimpole in Cambridgeshire, was a natural choice as supervising architect. In fact, once the surveyors' plan had been agreed, designs for houses and terraces in this very large development inevitably involved many hands, and there was no dictatorial style plan for Gibbs to enforce. But as part of the development Gibbs provided for himself a financial security that left him never having to worry about money again. He turned speculator on a small scale, leasing land and building four houses in Henrietta Street (now Place) from 1725, including a home for himself.[16] Much of what he designed, including his own development and Oxford Market, has been destroyed. But the Oxford or Marylebone Chapel (1721–4), now St Peter Vere Street, remains a delicately beautiful monument to his art. It was another Protestant church into which Gibbs finessed his secret Roman Catholic soul.

'A Kind of Monster': Growing London, 1720–54

What sort of London was emerging under the influence of James Gibbs, Edward Harley and their peers?

The new suburbs in the west and north-west aimed at order, regularity, and a muted nobility that eschewed the flamboyant decoration of the age of Wren, at least in outward appearance. Not all of this was purely a matter of taste. A certain plainness and sameness were achieved by default as a result of post-Fire building restrictions. These established common treatments like flat fronts to the houses, parapet walls hiding the attics, and party walls projecting through the roof ridge. Windows had to be recessed from the front wall, London fashion from about 1709 dictating that these were sash windows rather than casements. Similarly, high site values traditionally required the London terraced house to be tall and narrow, close to the pavement in front and with little more than a paved yard behind.

These conventions were reinforced from around 1718 by the dictates of Palladianism, with ground floors subservient to a first or drawing-room floor, its grand fenestration contrasting with smaller windows above and below. Sometimes a terrace was grouped into a single palace-like front with a central pediment and occasionally one at each end, as though forming one great town mansion instead of a dozen or so dwelling houses – Palladianism's Protestant virtues, it seems, were not immune from meretriciousness. Finally, regularity was encouraged by the grid-like layout that was most economical when large landholdings in a single ownership could avoid importing field boundaries into street patterns.[17]

Despite these forces tending to uniformity there was considerable variety in the new western suburbs, and for two main reasons. First, the suburb – more properly, the new town – accommodated a diversity of tenants and owners, as at the Harley Estate. That alone led to a mixture of house styles and streetscapes, and an incidental medley of residents.

Second, variety was pretty much assured by the mode of production of the eighteenth-century suburban estate. By 1700 an established method had proved its worth. To spread the risk of a large speculation, a landowner would lease parcels of land to other players, often experienced middlemen who acted as developer or main contractor. Besides the freeholders, it was these men who made most money from the suburbs. Their parcels would be subdivided in turn into sites for one, two or three houses, sometimes a few more. A small contractor would then purchase a building lease of these plots and undertake to put up a house of a certain type and size, detailed in a building agreement. Once finished, the builder retained the property, or disposed of it to a new lessee, for the term specified in the lease, commonly thirty-one, forty-two, sixty-nine or (in the very best class) ninety-nine years. At the end of the term the house reverted to the freeholder. In the most prestigious schemes, building agreements might stipulate a common roof-line, materials, decorative features and so on. But more commonly, the detailed aspects of design and finish were usually left to the builder; hence the subtle fluctuations revealed in most terraces of the time.[18]

The London speculative builder of the eighteenth century would move from one small project to another. He was usually a building tradesman. Carpenters and bricklayers understood more of a house than a plasterer or plumber or tiler and so were usually in the front rank. Some were highly skilled and enterprising and became rich men, like Benjamin Timbrell and Roger Morris, closely associated with James Gibbs's schemes. But in boom years the apparently easy profits to be won from building leases dragged shopkeepers, pettifogging lawyers, even actors and bank clerks into the maelstrom. They would contract with a carpenter or bricklayer to build the shell and then with other trades as necessary to finish them off. Many floundered in the process, especially when demand from tenants faltered. Indebtedness and bankruptcy, with the dreadful prospect of imprisonment at the suit of angry creditors, hung like a thundercloud over the whole class of small London building speculators. Little wonder that corners were cut, bad materials made do for good and jerry-building was one of the curses of the age.

That was especially the case where a short lease made it seem profligate to build something that would stand much longer than the term specified.

Throughout the 1720s and 1730s the western suburbs stumbled on. The Harley Estate was as unsteady as any – Cavendish Square, begun in 1719, would only be considered finished in 1769 and time lags generally affected other streets too. But slow progress was no fatal deterrent to others joining the fray, especially those who had most land to play with. Of these, few were better placed than Sir Richard Grosvenor and his brothers, inheritors of the estate of Mary Davies.

The Grosvenor Estate in the Hundred Acres, Mayfair, became the grandest planned development of London's eighteenth century. Its origins lay in what was going on around it. By 1720 the Hanover Square venture south of Oxford Street had revived development immediately to its west in the Conduit Mead Estate, which had New Bond Street as its central spine. That took house building tight to the eastern edge of the Hundred Acres and it proved the final provocation to begin building there too.

In projecting a scheme for their adjoining land, the Grosvenors planned a new town at what was then the far west of the metropolis. It would make a brick and stone peninsula that struck out into open countryside on three sides. To the north, on the other side of Oxford Street, lay the fields of Marylebone, untouched by the Harley Estate, which lay further east; to the south were the Berkeley Fields, as yet still pasture and brickfield; on the west was Tyburn (later Park) Lane, with Hyde Park beyond. The estate's centrepiece, on what by now was the expected model, was to be a great square. In keeping with the domineering ambition of the scheme, this would be a far more magnificent affair than anything the west end of the town had so far offered. Grosvenor Square would become the largest square in London apart from Lincoln's Inn Fields. Around it were streets on a grid pattern, the grandest leading to each corner of the square.

The first of the sixty-year building leases were granted in the summer of 1720. It was an unpropitious moment. Almost immediately the South Sea Bubble broke both credit and confidence. The first houses in the estate were not ready for occupation before 1725. Building then rushed on until 1733, slowed for a couple of years, before pushing forward once more. Only six new leases were granted between 1741 and 1755, but those were in the least popular sites and so the last to be taken, mainly in the north-west along the Oxford Street (at that western end often called Tyburn Road) frontage and Tyburn Lane. It was a corner stigmatised by the gallows fixed near the junction of these two main roads, along which the hanging crowds rampaged. Building there probably went on into the 1770s, making a half-century or more before the estate was fully developed.

The developers were a host of London builders, some eighty to a hundred, mostly carpenters and joiners and bricklayers, with a spattering of plasterers, plumbers, blacksmiths and others. Their take of the land varied greatly, from half a street and more to just one or two houses. As with the Harley Estate, it is worth stressing just how socially mixed this most aristocratic of London estates was at its beginning. It was built not as a suburb but as a self-contained new town, complete with markets, churches or chapels, and even quartering and stabling for the 2nd Troop of the Life Guards, helpful in keeping the peace. Grosvenor Square, built from 1728, would immediately become home to the richest men and women in England, with a distinctively aristocratic tone, and so would Upper Grosvenor Street, Upper Brook Street and, for a time, North and South Audley Streets. The first tenants of Grosvenor Square included the Duke of Norfolk, the Earl of Coventry, the Bishop of Durham, Viscount Weymouth, the Earl of Albemarle and numerous titled widows. Other smart developments in Mount Street became the homes of fashionable tradesmen, 'upholders' or interior designers and the like, all living and working conveniently close to their clients. But behind these frontages, Palladian and palatial, lay mews and blind-end courts for ostlers and coachmen and laundresses. Dung heaps peppered the stable yards in sniffing distance of drawing-room windows. And to the north of Grosvenor Square was a much more plebeian district, at George Street, Hart Street, Chandlers Street and so on, built at the same time as the square but home to building tradesmen, blacksmiths, butchers, greengrocers and fishmongers with businesses in St George's and Grosvenor Markets in the north-east corner of the estate. Shops and other commercial premises were built into the plans for Oxford Street, but also encroached rapidly into North and South Audley Street and elsewhere. Very quickly, some places in this northern part became poor and miserable: '"takes in vagabonds for Lodgers",' the rate collector noted of one house around 1749.[19]

Other landowners in the west fell similar willing victim to the speculative contagion. The Grosvenor Estate would not remain a peninsula for long. Immediately to the south, building on Lord Berkeley's fields, sometimes known as Brick Close, began from 1738 on ninety-nine-year leases, the last granted around 1750. For the eighteenth century this was a sprightly development. But on the ground, things still moved at a snail's pace. Lady Mary Wortley Montagu leased a house off plan in Hill Street around June 1746. Two years later she could move into just two rooms, with everything in 'great confusion'; decorating wasn't finally finished until the spring of 1751. Even so, yard by yard the ground was filled with brick and stone and slate and tile. By the end of the 1750s the whole block north of Piccadilly was pretty much covered with new buildings.[20]

So in the west during the first half of the century, London pushed out solidly half a mile along Piccadilly and some three-quarters of a mile along the south side of Oxford Street, with a redoubt across the road into the Marylebone Fields around Cavendish Square. Small by later standards, this was nevertheless a dramatic extension of London for contemporaries. When Sir Robert Walpole became able to make London visits again in the 1740s after twenty-one years in office as prime minister, 'he could not guess where he was, finding himself in so many new streets and squares'.[21]

At the northern edge of London things were far quieter than in the west. Great Ormond Street and Queen Square, its north side left open to accommodate views to the Hampstead hills, were developed from around 1708. By 1720 the streets were filled in to Red Lion Square. To the east of that, in Clerkenwell and St Luke's, the edge of London hardly advanced at all in fifty years, though it crept out a little.

But it would be a mistake to think the old City suburbs had stopped growing, as a close examination of the maps reveals. For at the beginning of the century there was still extensive backland – domestic gardens, allotments and wasteland – surrounded by housing. Here London grew by filling in these open spaces. As close to the City as Cow Cross, Smithfield, extensive garden land either side of Eagle Court around 1720 had all been filled with streets and courts by 1746. And east and west of St John Street further north, garden lands were built up with courts and alleys from Clerkenwell Close to Goswell Street (later Road). These are examples merely. Taken together, these infillings amounted to extensive additions to the town, discernible more to locals than to travellers between London and Islington, say, or Hackney, to whom 'the town' looked no bigger. They were replicated at every turn:

from St Giles, where new courts and alleys appeared off Dyot (now Dyott) Street and Bainbridge Street; to Holborn, where Bleeding Heart Yard and other courts appeared behind Saffron Hill to the west, and where new streets filled the area around the Cold Bath; to St Luke's, where new housing pressed north of Old Street, and a riot of interlocking courts and alleys filled the backland between Whitecross Street and the now partly covered Bunhill Fields. So in north London the first half of the century proved more consolidation than expansion, thickening rather than widening. Still, the northern suburbs continued to grow, taking in more houses and more people as a consequence.[22]

There was somewhat more dynamism in the east. Shoreditch continued to develop either side of the high street and a few new smart housing projects in Hoxton, notably Charles Square, pushed out the edge of London from around 1718 into the 1730s. Down the road, Spitalfields and south-west Bethnal Green grew decisively outwards, pretty much filling the fields west of Brick (or Dirty) Lane, and in places just beyond it. This development moved quickest between about 1718 and 1728 but lasted through the 1730s and probably later. Whitechapel filled out and spread in ribbon fashion along the main road to Mile End Old Town, which is said to have grown fourfold in the half-century. South of Whitechapel Road similar ribbon development spread along Cable Street and Ratcliff Highway to Shadwell, and on the riverside the last remaining fields of Wapping had been covered with industrial buildings, including numerous great timber yards, and housing. These East End houses, despite stiff fire regulations forbidding timber construction in the suburbs from 1707, were more likely to be wooden-framed and covered with ship-lap boarding than faced with brick, well into the 1740s if not later. Many were just one room deep, on two, three or four floors, and many were let out by the floor or room to different families.[23]

South of the river, in Southwark, there was a general extension westward from the Borough High Street north of St George's Fields. A filigree of new courts and alleys stretched out to Red Cross Street and some extensive building took place in the Mint. To the east in Bermondsey, the builders had begun to encroach on Snow's Fields from various directions and a maze of courts and alleys stretched its tentacles east of Barnaby Street. Further east still, the long strand of Rotherhithe or Redriff had begun to sprout side streets at its London end, and had become more continuous as it approached Deptford. The number of families living in Rotherhithe was said to have almost doubled from 900 in 1700 to something under 1,700 in 1738.[24]

It is generally stated by historians that London experienced a period of stagnation in the second quarter of the eighteenth century and into the 1760s. There is much speculation that for some time in this first half-century the population may even have declined, a demographic disaster for what was then the greatest city in western Europe, given its enormous growth in the century before. In fact, a relatively high estimate for 1700 of 575,000 and a very modest one for 1750 of 700,000 still suggest population growth of some 22 per cent. That may not be spectacular in the context of what had gone before and what was to come after, but it hardly ranks as stagnation.

On the ground, building moved in step with wider movements in the trade cycle, complicated throughout the century by a constant reiteration of war and peace. In general, as in the case of the Marlborough years, war was bad for building. Even periods of peace were susceptible to shocks like the South Sea Bubble and other financial crises that put money in short supply and made creditors call in their debts. The pattern of London building after the interrupted 'boom' of 1715-25 is said to be stagnant from 1726 to 1738, then 'slump' from 1738 to 1745 (the years, remember, of the Berkeley Fields development) and stagnant again from 1745 to 1761. Actually the evidence is overwhelming that despite all the difficulties and the undoubted ups and downs, there was always some money to be made from new building in London. Never for a moment in this first half-century did London stop growing entirely. And a city that expands while losing population is a contradiction in terms.[25]

Indeed, contemporaries were troubled less by slump or stagnation than by the worrying consequences of a metropolis that continued remorselessly to eat into the countryside around it. A madcap proposal by government to restrict all new London building to the existing foundations of demolished structures was laughed out of the House of Commons in 1710, but the anxieties it reflected were clearly deeply felt. London, as 'a Kind of Monster, with a Head enormously large, and out of all Proportion to its Body' (the nation), had been complained of for many generations. It was looked on as 'no better than a Wen, or Excrescence, in the Body Politic', that by the mid-century had reduced 'the body . . . to skin and bone'.[26]

There was another element to this anxiety, beyond even the ceaseless spread of London. It was the increasingly impertinent tendency of the citizens or 'cits' to usurp the place of their betters in the country villages and hamlets around the metropolis. This had been noticed by Defoe around 1724 and not too unsympathetically. He thought the citizen colonists brought a civilising influence, making the villages 'more sociable than formerly', with 'excellent Conversation'.[27] But by 1750 the cits and their 'little country boxes' had become more matter for satire than respect. These villas were both weekend retreat from City shop and home for the citizen's retirement:

I went last Sunday, in compliance with a most pressing invitation from a friend, to spend the whole day with him at one of these little seats, which he had fitted up for his retirement once a week from business. It is pleasantly situated about three miles from *London*, on the side of a public road, from which it is separated by a dry ditch, over which is a little bridge consisting of two narrow planks, leading to the house. The hedge on the other side the road cuts off all prospect whatsoever, except from the garrets, from whence indeed you have a beautiful vista of two men hanging in chains on *Kennington* common, with a distant view of St *Paul*'s Cupola enveloped in a cloud of smoke.

> 'Tis not the Country, you must own,
> 'Tis only LONDON out of town.[28]

Notwithstanding ridicule in rhyme and prose and on the stage of the cits' aspirations, the villages and hamlets around London proved an irresistible lure in every direction. They grew bloated and cockney-fied in the process: 'Middlesex', it was said in 1730, was 'almost all London'. It was in this century that the metropolitan shadow first fell darkly over countryside that would eventually emerge as Greater London. In Essex, for instance, Stratford ('where there are above two hundred little Country Houses, for the Conveniency of the Citizens in Summer' in 1722), Plaistow, Leyton, Walthamstow, Wanstead and Woodford (where there were said to be 162 'mansions' in 1762) all gained in population and wealth. And though the numbers of new houses totalled probably not many more than a thousand in all these places and more, the proportionate increase must have been staggering to locals. The same was true north of London – in Hampstead, say, and Hackney, which seems to have doubled in size between 1720 and 1761. In the west, Chelsea grew from around 172 houses in 1674 to some 350 in 1717 (including Cheyne Row, 1708–c. 1716) and to 741 in 1777 (including Cheyne Walk in the 1750s). And in the south a pattern of brick-built terraced housing on the London model took root from around 1710 in the main streets of Clapham, Putney, Wandsworth, Richmond and elsewhere.[29]

The popularity of citizens' seats from Acton to Wanstead, and the growth of the metropolitan population in these years, put the age-old problem of traffic and communications to and from London under immense strain. In winter, moving just two or three miles beyond the stones' end was always difficult, sometimes impossible. The condition of the roads in the first two decades or so of the eighteenth century was quite astonishingly bad. Some, through ancient use, were sunk deep into the ground and filled with mud in heavy rains. The 'slough' or 'hole' 'in the way to Hampstead' put men and horses in fear of their lives around 1715. The 'High Road at *Kingsland*' north of Shoreditch 'is full of Quicksands' that needed 'extraordinary Brick-drains, and Bridges over them'. West of Kensington the roads were 'extremely bad' and 'very dangerous to Passengers'; 'many Waggons and Coaches have been stuck, and several overturned . . . and several Passengers on Horseback thrown off their Horses . . .' Even closer to the centre, perhaps the condition of the roads leading to Hyde Park Corner from the west, as late as 1725, might represent the difficulties graphically enough:

Abraham Odell, of *Fulham*, Surgeon, said, That the Road between *Fulham* and *Knightsbridge* is very bad; and has seen Carts set between *Hyde Park Corner*, and the Stones End; and that there are Ruts in the Road 4 Foot deep . . . That several Persons have lately received Damage by passing through the Roads between *Little Chelsea* and *Fulham*; and particularly, a Man that is now under his Care, that broke his Leg by a Fall; and another Person likewise under his Care, being much hurt by a Fall from his Horse in the said Road . . . *John Jones*, of *Fulham*, High Constable, said, That . . . Three empty Drays have been stopped at *Little Chelsea*, and Ten Horses put at Length to draw them out, one by one: That Three Weeks ago he travelled the way with a Chaise, and a Pair of Horses, between *Piccadilly*, and *Hyde Park Corner*; and by the badness of the Way, one of the Horses had like to have been smothered in the Dirt . . .[30]

From 1712 onwards, a substantial slice of parliamentary time was devoted to remedying the roads 'up' to London from Middlesex, Essex,

Surrey and Kent.[31] Beginning with the Stanmore (Middlesex) roads that
January, the solution was to take the roads out of parish control – some
parishes more vigorous than others and none, it was thought, vigorous
enough – and consign them to turnpike trusts. Access to the roads was
through gates and passengers paid a toll. The trustees could borrow
money on the security of the tolls and the contributions from parishes
through which the roads passed. There were hundreds of Turnpike Acts,
many in respect of the same stretch of roads as the original terms of
the trust proved inadequate for local circumstances. And there were
thousands of trustees, though only a small proportion proved active
managers of the roads. By 1750 or so nothing was perfect, if only
because no reliable surface treatment for roads would emerge until the
early nineteenth century – the eighteenth-century way of gravel tamped
on clay became a quagmire after heavy rain. But it was all a great deal
better than previous generations had ever known:

the *Improvement* of the *Roads* near this Metropolis, and the *increasing
Conveniences* of *Conveyance* to all the Villages around it, prevent that
Stagnation of People in *London*, which was formerly; enabling great Numbers,
who have Business to transact in *London*, to come there for this purpose,
during a few Hours only of the Day, and to retire into the *Country* in the
Evening; Which is become a general Practice.[32]

But what would they find when they arrived on the London side of
stones' end?

Obstructions and Inconveniences: Changing London, 1700–54

The growth of London outwards didn't relieve pressure on the centre;
it stoked it. We have seen how the inner suburbs consolidated during
these years through the development of backland as courts and alleys.
It has been confidently stated, and generally accepted, that 'every square
yard of the City was utilised' before 1666.[33] But in fact City backland
continued to be developed in the early eighteenth century in both rebuilt
areas and those untouched by the Fire. Of the latter, for instance,
Bishopsgate Ward Without had extensive back gardens to the west of
the main street, especially north of Bethlem churchyard, even around
1720. Twenty-five years or so later and an extensive network of new

streets, courts and alleys had entirely reconfigured the area in a far more dense and complex pattern. And across the road, on the east side of Bishopsgate Street, an old mansion in a large garden, Devonshire House, was demolished and replaced by an elegant brick-built square by 1708.[34] Inside the walls, much of Coleman Street Ward was destroyed in 1666 and redeveloped with little garden land left by 1720. But in thirty years what there was had sprouted courts to the east of Bassishaw Street and north of Bell Alley; and Brickington Court, just outside the fire-damaged area east of Coleman Street, had also extended into backland.

A similar story might have been told, if not in every ward, then certainly in most. Not all these new developments were for housing – industrial buildings and warehousing were also new-built, especially near the riverside – and some housing would have been swept away for these more profitable uses. Certainly it is hard to disagree with historians who project that the City's population never again reached the numbers before plague and fire struck in the mid-1660s.[35] But there's good reason to think that by 1750 it may well have inched upwards from its first post-Fire reincarnation, at least in the outer wards beyond the walls.

These places of course were of a similar character to those old inner suburbs that we saw thickening in St Giles, Clerkenwell, St Luke's and so on. All these districts were notably poor and it is likely that this fresh accumulation of tiny houses in cramped courts and alleys, entered through arches or tunnels from the side streets, attracted yet more of the labouring class or below and made these inner suburbs poorer still.

Information here is hard to come by but what there is points this way. In 1733 there were 'about 933 Families' in Horsleydown, Bermondsey, 'who pay to the Poor's Rate, and about 4,000 Families who do not pay, there being a very great Increase of Houses lately'. In 1735 it was said that St Margaret Westminster was a poorer parish because of the removal of 'the best and wealthiest Inhabitants' to the new districts on the north-west edge of town. We find the church-wardens of St Botolph Aldgate, on the eastern borders of the City, complaining that over 'these Four Years last past', since about 1738, the poor had doubled in number in the parish. The 'Dissoluteness of Morals, and a Disregard for Religion' among the 'younger and poorer Sort of the Inhabitants' of Bethnal Green was said in 1743 to be driving out 'the better Sort of People', 'to the great Impoverishment' of the hamlet, as it then still was. '[B]y far the greatest Part' of the 1,800 houses there were said to be 'lett out . . . in Two or Three distinct Parts or Tenements' because few could afford to rent a whole house. And lodging houses at 2d a night were rife in St Giles around 1750, with 'miserable Beds from the Cellar to the Garret'. One lodged '58 Persons of both Sexes, the Stench of whom was so intolerable, that it compelled [Saunders Welch, the normally fearless High Constable of St Andrew Holborn] in a very short time to quit the Place'. Henry Fielding came across similar places in Shoreditch around the same time. Whether these common lodging houses had increased in numbers recently is unclear. But many inner suburbs were plainly under pressure from a growing population, and more often than not it was the poor who were moving in.[36]

This congestion of buildings and people in London's outer ring, north and south of the Thames, merely made the filth, traffic and obstructions in the streets worse. And all that was at a time when more and more people – Londoners and others – needed to use them. This increasing press of people on the streets of London had a number of causes.

First, the great new towns of Hanover Square, the Harley Estate, Mayfair and the Berkeley Fields didn't just provide out-of-town modern residences for wealthy citizens to move to. They brought into this expanded metropolis the aristocrats and country gentry who had previously confined any necessary London sojourn to a short stay in stuffy lodgings close to St James's Palace and the Houses of Parliament. Now a town house, even though leased and not bought outright, was fast becoming an indispensable acquisition. Many had their own carriages or used hackney coaches for visiting, adding further to wheeled traffic about the town.

Second, the extraordinary growth of international trade in this first half-century, especially to the West Indies, to North America including Canada, and to the Indian sub-continent, brought more ships and goods to London than ever before. Investors had to meet sea captains and insurers and merchants at a galaxy of City coffee houses. And leisure hours were spent in the chocolate (and gaming) houses of St James's, the brothels of Covent Garden and Charing Cross, the theatres around Covent Garden and public gardens at Vauxhall and Chelsea. All added to the town's whirligig of motion.

Finally, parliamentary sessions became notably longer and busier during this time. Every parish in the nation sent petitioners and counsel to secure the improvement of high roads from Dartford to Glasgow. Every contested election – and there were many – brought aggrieved voters and frustrated candidates from every constituency in the Union. Every land enclosure of commons and heaths, the estate of every defunct landowner dying intestate or leaving property to a minor, every divorce of the impotent and the adulterous – all played out their dramas, with counsel and attorneys and a host of witnesses, at the bar of the House of Commons. The sittings of Parliament, generally November to April with breaks at Christmas and Easter, filled London with visitors. Metropolitan entrepreneurs responded with theatrical performances and shows and extended the town's attractions into early summer with entertainments out of doors. The London season had its origins in the seventeenth century but it was greatly consolidated in the first half of the eighteenth. It was in these years that London began to exert an irresistible tidal pull on the national psyche. The draw was such that every country tradesman, every independent lady and many a foreigner keen to observe the heart of one of Europe's leading military and diplomatic powers would see at least one visit to London as an indispensable credential of civilised life.

As London became more crowded, and more of a national and international showcase, its drawbacks grew less and less tolerable. The frustrations of traffic and communications became the engine of physical change or 'improvement'. Later generations would find different reasons for knocking down old London. But in the eighteenth century it was the sheer inability to get from one place to another that most of all refashioned central London on the ground.

At least, refashioned in some conscious or planned way. There were other forces at work too. It is important to remember that London, even in its oldest parts, never stood still. The needs of fashion required those who could afford it to modernise the appearance of their buildings, refacing in brick or plaster to hide old beams, replacing casements with sash windows, providing lighter and airier shopfronts and so on. But in addition to these scattered market-driven renovations, London's old enemy still had a big part to play.

The old enemy was fire and it was an agent of change that struck haphazardly and cruelly. It was a constant visitor to London, despite many legislative attempts in this period to construct buildings that would deter its spread, and despite the understandable paranoia about fire rife among Londoners. Fire was one of the great anxieties of the age, as the letters of Thomas Gray the poet reveal. He was far from alone. For when fire struck, its ravages could be immense.[37]

Often it was the needy who suffered, because fire was a special threat in London's industrial areas. The biggest conflagrations were thus along the riverside. Some 132 houses were destroyed by fire in Limehouse early in 1717; nearly forty houses burned down when fire broke out at the Queen's Head Punch House, St Katherine by the Tower, in January 1735; next year a fire in Upper Shadwell destroyed forty-two houses, six warehouses and eight sheds; in May 1745 a pot of tar boiled over at a sailmaker's in Horsleydown and caused the loss of twenty-two houses, a 300-ton ship and several lighters; and a fire in a dye-house at Battle Bridge, Southwark, in August 1749 destroyed a brewhouse and cooperage, four wharves and eighty houses, with losses of £80,000. These were merely a few among many London-wide, big and small. But the most notable fire of this first half-century began at a peruke maker's at Exchange Alley, opposite the Royal Exchange, on the night of 25 March 1748. It raged 'with great fury for 10 hours', spread to Cornhill – where the justly nervous Thomas Gray had grown up – and to Birchin Lane and the respectable courts and alleys around. Some eighty to a hundred houses and businesses occupied by prosperous tradesmen and manufacturers were destroyed, among them some of the City's best-known coffee houses. Six lives were thought to have been lost. A Swedish visitor was surprised that he knew nothing of it till next day due to the great size of London and its atmosphere, impenetrably smoky at the best of times.[38]

Half a dozen years later and a historian of London would comment thus on the great fire of Cornhill: 'This, no doubt, was a very great Misfortune to the Individuals who were in it, but the spacious and commodious Buildings raised upon the Ruins prove a great Advantage to the Publick, and an Ornament to the City.'[39]

Now what was destroyed in 1748 had been new-built less than eighty years before and it is striking how quickly succeeding generations of Londoners became jaded with the post-Fire City. Nicholas Hawksmoor, as early as 1715, had privately voiced his disgust at the missed opportunity to build something more rational for the modern age: 'we have noe City, nor Streets, nor Houses, but a Chaos of Dirty Rotten Sheds, always Tumbling or takeing fire, with winding Crooked passages (Scarse practicable) Lakes of Mud and Rills of Stinking Mire Running through them.'[40]

Getting around this 'Scarse practicable' city was already a pressing concern as the century opened. Parliament did all it could to aid attempts to improve things, like giving power to local residents to straighten and widen Jackanapes Alley between Chancery Lane and Lincoln's Inn Fields in 1700, or widening Hemmings Row, opposite the old St Martin-in-the-Fields parish church, in 1702. Though important thoroughfares, both were previously only wide enough for a single carriage. The 'usual orders' of every parliamentary session required the parish constables to keep the way clear of obstruction from Temple Bar to Westminster Hall while members were sitting. But complaints of obstruction and delay, of frayed tempers and the insolence of hackney coachmen and chairmen, even of the constables themselves, became the subject of frequent parliamentary debate and retribution. Proposals to demolish ancient gateways at Westminster and Whitehall were debated from 1706, though they would not be entirely removed for fifty years to come. From 1709 there emerged a parliamentary obsession with the paving of Westminster's streets and dozens of paving acts in this first half-century sought improvements there and in the City and suburbs, with utterly indifferent results. Efforts to protect the 'Common-shoars' from 'Annoyances' date from the same year; and in 1710 there was a bill 'for preventing Abuses and Disorders committed by Cartmen, Carmen or Carroonmen, Draymen, Sedan or Chairmen, or Hackney Coachmen'. [41]

These too were all losing battles that were waged without let-up, not just for years but for generations to come. As late as 1741, Lord Tyrconnel could tell the House of Commons that the Westminster streets continued to oppress the traveller by coach with 'unexpected Chasms' and by foot with 'Mountains of Filth':

The Filth, Sir, of some Parts of the Town, and the Inequality and Ruggedness of others, cannot but in the Eyes of Foreigners disgrace our Nation, and incline them to imagine us a People, not only without Decency, but without Government, a Herd of Barbarians, or a Colony of *Hottentots*. The most disgusting Part of the Character given by Travellers, of the most savage Nations, is their Neglect of Cleanliness, of which, perhaps, no Part of the World affords more Proofs than the Streets of *London*; a City . . . which abounds with such Heaps of Filth, as a Savage would look on with Amazement. [42]

The streets of Westminster would have to wait another twenty years or so for thoroughgoing reform. But the difficulties of getting about, and a growing sense of shame that London was letting itself down in the eyes of travellers from home and abroad, let alone those who had thrown good money at a new house in the western suburbs, eventually produced results. These would necessarily have a disconnected and random feel about them, if only because of London's great size and its chaotic patchwork of local government.

There was, though, one important driver. The growth of wealthy suburbs in the west of the metropolis gave fresh impetus to an old rivalry between the cities of London and Westminster. It found expression from the early 1720s with the plaster still fresh in Hanover Square and the footings of Cavendish Square barely dug:

a great Number of wealthy Traders in and about *London*, at present [1722] reside in the Liberties of *Westminster*, and the Western part of the Town, either thro' a Vanity in themselves, or from the Vanity of their Wives and Families; otherwise we cannot account for the vast number of New Buildings being so well inhabited as Experience shews they are; how many Merchants and Traders more will go to settle in those parts, when they shall find the Stream of Business run there; . . . till at last the City become desolate, and the Houses therein stand empty, or drop down, for want of Tenants to live in them, or Encouragement of Trade to support them.[43]

These anxieties found a voice in the debates over whether London should recognise its new western expansion by building a second bridge over the Thames. The City Corporation had always opposed other bridges over the Thames anywhere in reach of London, as a mortal threat to its trade, to its property in the medieval London Bridge, indeed to its very existence as a city. When a bridge far downriver between the country villages of Fulham and Putney had been unsuccessfully canvassed in 1671 it was said that next to pulling down Southwark nothing could more certainly ruin the City of London. But in December 1721 there would be a threat much closer to home: 'divers Gentlemen, Freeholders, and Inhabitants' of Westminster petitioned Parliament for a bridge across the Thames at either one of the horse ferries to Lambeth or Vauxhall, close to the Houses of Parliament and Westminster Hall. It was made necessary by 'the great Increase of the Inhabitants' of Westminster and around.[44] A bill was brought in but it aroused the opposition of the Borough of Southwark, the City Corporation and numerous other interested parties, from the leaseholders of houses on London Bridge to the watermen and lightermen of the Thames. The anxieties were existential, and there's something resounding here of the affronts and humiliations endured by the citizens under the ceaseless lash of their fashionable foe:

The Birth-right and Privileges of Freemen of *London*, will hereby in a little time become Contemptible: For as *South Sea* has strip'd them of their superfluous Riches, long Wars, continued Taxes, and high Duties, impair'd their Stock, and shock'd their Credit; so a new Bridge will take their Meat out of their Mouths, by drawing off their Supply of Provisions, and pick the Money out of their Pockets, by enabling the Inhabitants of Westminster to Trade at less Expences, Houses being at less Rents, Lodgers more frequent, and no Time or Money spent to qualify them for Shopkeepers.
[. . .]
It will enrich the Inhabitants of *Westminster*, and impoverish the Citizens of *London* . . . in short, it will make *Westminster* a fine City, and *London* a Desart . . .[45]

The bill to construct a bridge at Westminster duly foundered in early 1722. But the City could not remain blind to the competition that Westminster, growing so vigorously in size and wealth, presented. So it was in the City that the age of metropolitan improvement – as distinct from growth – first found expression in the 1720s and especially the 1730s, inevitably with more than half an eye turned to its rival in the west. Great new public and commercial buildings began to refashion the City, with the Custom House in Lower Thames Street (1718–23), East India House in Leadenhall Street (1726–9), South Sea House (1724–5) and the first purpose-built Bank of England (1732–4), both in Threadneedle Street. But the first major public improvement of the age was the City Corporation's project to cover the River Fleet between Holborn Bridge and Fleet Street. Its warehouses on the quay-sides had never taken, profits proved insufficient to maintain the waterway and the Fleet for years had been filled with mud, filth and the leavings of the Field Lane slaughtermen and tripe-dressers further upstream. In 1733 the City obtained permission to culvert the Fleet and turn it into a roadway (the present Farringdon Street) and a market. Fleet Market opened on 30 September 1737 with a central row of shops and a market building complete with clock tower.[46]

The space won by removing this notorious 'common Nuisance' provided an opportunity to fulfil a long-cherished ambition to build a mansion for the Lord Mayor of London during his annual term of office.

The question of just where to put it in the crowded City had long frustrated the scheme. The Stocks Market, selling provisions not shares, occupied a building and sheds in a space where Poultry, Cornhill, Threadneedle Street, Lombard Street and Walbrook all converged. The new Fleet Market now allowed the Stocks Market to close and its tenants to relocate. In its place, on this most prominent City site, the new Mansion House would be a 'palace' for 'the capital city of the world'.[47]

James Gibbs was among those submitting designs to the Corporation in 1735. But the contract was won by George Dance the Elder, Clerk of the City's Works, whose estimate was significantly cheaper. The project was beset by complaints of 'City Corruption and Mal-Administration', and Dance's design in Portland stone, with a giant Corinthian portico and overbearing attic storeys, was much criticised at the time. It also suffered massive cost overruns – the final cost was exactly twice Dance's estimate – and egregious delay. The foundation stone was laid in October 1739 but the Mansion House wouldn't receive its first Lord Mayor, Sir Crisp Gascoyne, till 1753. Two and a half centuries on, though, with the attics thankfully long removed, it is considered the 'greatest surviving building' of the eighteenth-century City.[48]

There was no similar driving force behind civic improvement in and around Westminster. The only landowner capable of playing the part of the Corporation of London was the crown, but the crown was supine and never seized any opportunity to improve London in the eighteenth century. Westminster city government was archaic, impotent and fractured. Parish authorities increasingly occupied that vacuum but were largely impecunious and unadventurous. For the first three decades of the century it was left to small communities of wealthy Londoners, united by a common interest, to improve the patch of London they could see from their front windows. The residents of Lincoln's Inn Fields, Holborn, first combined in this way in 1707, getting parliamentary approval to raise a rate (taxing themselves and their neighbours) to fence, lay out and maintain the open space, long a resort of thieves and beggars; but by 1734 things were once again in 'great Disorder', with the Fields a huge rubbish tip for the neighbourhood, and fresh powers had to be sought.[49] There were similar schemes in St James's Square (Westminster, 1726), Red Lion Square (Holborn, 1737), Charterhouse Square (Finsbury, 1743) and Golden Square (Westminster, 1751).

The state of St James's Square, still easily London's smartest in 1726, instructively reveals both the anarchy of personal liberty, as yet unrestrained by public law, and the general tolerance of the age to mess and filth of every kind. The square's great open space was like 'a common Dunghill'. It contained many 'Loads of Soil and Rubbish' on which 'the Inhabitants have, for many Years past, thrown their Dirt and Ashes, and . . . Cats and Dogs have likewise been cast, on the same'. There were also encroachments, 'particularly by a Coachmaker, who has erected a Shed, about Thirty Feet, in the Square, in which he puts Heaps of Wood, and other Things'. Yet residents at this period included the Duke of Kent, the Earls of Lincoln, Mountrath, Tankerville and Stafford, Viscount Palmerston and many more of that ilk.[50]

Parliament, the most disgruntled observer of Westminster's messy ways, was the enabler of all these local attempts to put things right, and it was Parliament that effectively managed the improvements of Westminster in this first half-century. Its greatest project was that second bridge over the Thames at Westminster.

Fourteen years after the failure of the Westminster Bridge Bill of 1722, a petition was again presented to Parliament by the Burgesses, Freeholders and Inhabitants of Westminster in February 1736, arguing that the great increase in buildings and population made a new bridge essential. Parliament indeed went further, deciding that a new bridge 'would be advantageous not only to the City of *Westminster*, but to many other of his Majesty's Subjects, and to the Publick in general', and duly brought in a bill to empower construction of a second bridge.[51] Again, petitions against were received from many, including the Archbishop of Canterbury, in whose gift the horse ferry from Lambeth to Westminster lay. The City Corporation opposed it as 'destructive of several Rights, Properties, Privileges, and Franchises', and as rendering navigation of the Thames 'dangerous, if not impracticable'. A pamphlet war was waged once more, but this time most voices debated the practicalities rather than the principle. For now the arguments in favour of a new bridge were weighted with fourteen years' more growth in the western suburbs. And this was, after all, the improving decade of the 1730s, with the City's own achievements at Fleet Market already well advanced. Most important of all, Parliament – or at least Walpole's administration after the citizens had bitterly opposed his efforts to extend excise duties in 1733 – had fallen out of love with the City of London. All that was a far cry from the politics of 1721–2. So now the City Corporation was waved away. The Westminster Bridge Act gained royal assent in May 1736.[52]

The project was to be managed by Commissioners appointed by

government. They would return to Parliament on many occasions over the next fourteen years for amending legislation and further financing before Westminster Bridge would finally be completed. That the task was not just to build a bridge had been clear from the outset. The House of Commons was plainly told that a bridge would merely exacerbate Westminster's difficulties by bringing yet more traffic to its impassable streets.[53] There were similar problems on the Lambeth side, though they were more easily overcome. So in 1739 the Commissioners were given powers to acquire land and buildings to widen existing streets and create new ones altogether. Despite many false starts and frustrations, the 'Obstructions and Inconveniences' of old Westminster would indeed be substantially eased.

The new bridge joined Westminster just north of New Palace Yard, the main entrance to the Houses of Parliament. A wide new Bridge Street obliterated an ancient narrow way to the river called Woolstaple and required the removal of the old Westminster Market. North from Bridge Street ran King Street, the main route for citizens approaching Parliament and Westminster Hall from the Strand, Charing Cross and Whitehall. It had long been narrow, filthy and difficult to negotiate. The Bridge Commissioners bypassed it altogether and drove a wide new street parallel to it on the east, connecting New Palace Yard to Whitehall. It swept away Rhenish Wine Yard, Stephens Alley, White Horse Yard and other places, the poorer sort living there being forced to find new homes, probably close at hand. The new road was named Parliament Street, and grand houses began to appear in it from 1750. Finally, Great George Street, a continuation of Bridge Street westwards, provided a straight broad avenue from St James's Park to the bridge. It was built from 1753, with houses appearing four years later, and removed a complex of courts, alleys and yards north of Thieving Lane. Its projector was James Mallors, a prominent Westminster builder, and Parliament gave him powers to purchase land and lay out the street.[54] On the Lambeth side a new street was cut through timber yards and houses to join a new road in open fields. This would in time become Westminster Bridge Road.

Westminster Bridge was designed by Charles Labelye, a naturalised Swiss engineer, no Briton apparently equipped with the necessary skills in bridge design at the time. It was 300 feet longer, at 1,223 feet, than London Bridge, had fifteen semicircular arches and was built of Portland stone. It had two footways, with a 'Horse Road' thirty feet across where horses had a steep climb to the central arch. Inadequate foundations to one pier caused it to sink as it was nearing completion in 1747, delaying

things for a couple of years. Westminster Bridge eventually opened on
18 November 1750. 'All the next Day, being *Sunday*, *Westminster* was
like a Fair, with People going to view the Bridge, and pass over it.
Thirty-two lamps were fixed up, and 12 Watchmen appointed to do
Duty every Night, to prevent Robberies and Irregularities.' Westminster
Bridge was soon 'allowed, by the judges of Architecture, to be one of
the grandest Bridges in the World', 'a monument of glory unequalled in
all Europe'.[55] This was the first modern step forward in overcoming
some of the divisions of London on the ground: Parliament Street eased
the link between the two cities of Westminster and London; and the
bridge connected the Surrey shore at Lambeth – and what would in
time become south London – with the giant metropolis.

James Gibbs lived to witness this greatest metropolitan improvement
of the age. He had been especially disappointed by the loss of the
Mansion House commission and probably felt he could have made a
better job of it than did Dance. Through choice or necessity he undertook no major projects after his sixtieth birthday in late 1742. Most
of his work now lay out of town, apart from a new block for an
apothecary's shop and laboratory at St Bartholomew's Hospital, whose
architect he remained, from about 1745 to 1749. By then he was ill
'with the stone', but not incapacitated, and he seems never to have left
off designing and planning projects even into his last year. Intimations
of mortality were, though, clearly in his mind by May 1754, when he
made his will, and on 5 August he died at his London home in Henrietta
Street, on the corner of Wimpole Street. He was seventy-one years old.

Gibbs died a man rich in money, plate and property. Never having
married and with no family of his own, he bequeathed most to
the Scottish-Catholic interest from which he had sprung, especially
the family of the Earl of Mar, who had done so much to launch
his London career. He remembered his architectural assistants and his
charities, including £100 each to Bart's and the Foundling Hospital.
His collection of architectural books and drawings he left to the
Radcliffe Library in Oxford, which he had designed for the university.[56]
To Londoners ever since, of course, his legacies have been left in brick
and Portland stone at St Peter Vere Street, St Mary le Strand and, most
especially, at St Martin-in-the-Fields.

Within a short time of James Gibbs's death yet another Scottish
architect would arrive, whose legacy to London, though not of such
indelible grandeur, would be more pervasive still.

Robert Adam

II

ROBERT ADAM'S LONDON,
1754–99

'A Kind of Revolution': Robert Adam

THERE are many surprising similarities in the London lives of James Gibbs and Robert Adam, the architect who, more than any other, came to define metropolitan taste in the second half of the eighteenth century. Adam too was a Scot, born 1728 at Kirkcaldy in Fife, his father a prosperous architect of country houses and a prominent government masonry contractor. Robert and his three architect brothers inherited the family business in Edinburgh and in 1754 Robert left there to study on the Continent, Italy his final destination.

Before leaving he had paid a couple of brief visits to London and they made a mark. For it was in Rome as early as 1755 that he determined where he would try to establish a career. As he confided to his sister Nelly, 'what a pity it is that such a genius [as myself] should be thrown away upon Scotland where scarce will ever happen an opportunity of putting one noble thought in execution'. So, after some three years' extensive travel and intense study in Italy, it was to London he came. He was there by January 1758. He brought two foreign draughtsmen along with him, without whom, he confessed, he'd never have had the courage to establish a London office. Like Gibbs fifty years before, Robert Adam would spend the rest of his life in London.[1]

Adam also arrived in the capital at another propitious moment for a brilliant, ambitious and prosperous Scot, one who this time had no Catholicism or Jacobitism to compromise his appeal. A Scottish court in all but name had assembled round George II's grandson, the young

Prince of Wales. Prince George's tutor, John, Earl of Bute, had become almost a surrogate father to him and was a power in the land. The Countess of Bute was told of her talented architect countryman the minute he arrived in London and it was not long before Robert Adam and Lord Bute were introduced. That first meeting with the cold, shy and timid kingmaker didn't go well, but Bute quickly proved a prestigious and generous patron. From the outset of his London career, Adam became a star of the 'Scotch party' that would dominate politics and much of high culture in the early years of George III's reign. It was a solid base from which to conquer metropolitan architectural taste.[2]

Robert Adam's London career flourished early and lasted long. He was hugely energetic and hard-working, blessed by great charm and capacity for friendship. He established an office for the practice at his home in Lower Grosvenor Street, just east of Grosvenor Square, one of the best addresses in 'new' London. The influence of Bute helped him to a government commission, the screen wall fronting the Admiralty building in Whitehall, designed in 1759. The accession of George III in 1760, and the elevation of Bute to prime minister in waiting, brought a rush of private commissions for an architect who quickly came to represent the acme of modernity. In 1761 he became with William Chambers – whose style was inimical to that of the flamboyant Adam – Joint Architect of His Majesty's Works, or architect to the King. But Adam was never an institutional architect. It was in the cultivation of new forms of private taste in building design, and especially the decoration of interior spaces, that his life work resided. The Adam style would become, as he himself put it in 1773, 'a kind of revolution in the whole system of this useful and elegant art'.[3]

The eclecticism of influences bearing on the Adam style was temperamentally well suited to metropolitan taste, ever intolerant of orthodoxy. Palladianism was one strong component, but the architect whom Adam most admired was Vanbrugh, with his eccentric baroque. The European tour had been of fundamental influence and Adam had imbibed ideas from contemporary France, from archaeological remains in Italy, Dalmatia, Syria and Greece (much second-hand from architectural folios), from Renaissance masters and the buildings of Florence, Venice, Ravenna and Rome. It has all been labelled neoclassical, but in fact it was just Adam – light, delicate, feminine, elaborate, flowing, full of movement and colour, sometimes full to bursting.

Adam motifs were astonishingly rich and varied, with the antique and classical strongly emphasised, but where palm leaves might spring from a Corinthian column and a single urn could sprout a lively gavotte of branches, stems and wreaths that seemed to step out for ever.[4]

Robert Adam's reliefs became the pattern of the age, 'found the world over'. They decorated not just walls and ceilings, fireplaces and architraves, but carpets, cabinets, sofas and soft furnishings, lamps and door furniture, vases and pots and wine coolers. On the outside of buildings they erupted in decorative columns and door frames and fanlights, and rusticated stucco and moulded Coade stone. In London they were found everywhere. There the Adam style was pursued single-mindedly from the 1760s to the end of the century by a host of imitators so convincing that it quickly became difficult to detect the real Adam from his multitudinous surrogate sons. And really, especially from the publication of the Adam designs in 1773, there was no difference worth speaking about at all.[5]

Robert Adam's early commissions were most frequently for this fresh art form in the existing homes of the London rich, rather than designing entirely new buildings. The restless desire for domestic makeovers to keep up with changing fashion grew more riotous still in the second half of the eighteenth century. So in the early 1760s Adam adapted the town house of Sir Francis Dashwood, the notorious rake, at Hanover Square, and renovated 19 Arlington Street for Sir Lawrence Dundas, a rich Scot; he refashioned the state rooms at Syon House, Isleworth, for the Duke of Northumberland; nearby he made 'a palace of palaces' for the fabulously wealthy London banker Robert Child at Osterley Park, 'the most superb and elegant thing of its kind in England';[6] in Hampstead, from 1767, he extended and decorated Kenwood for William Murray, Earl of Mansfield, another Scot and the greatest lawyer of the age; and in the 1770s he fitted up a magnificent drawing room in a new wing of the Duke of Northumberland's old London mansion near Charing Cross. Less extensively, Adam was also commissioned to build new houses, the first in 1761 by Lord Bute, which became Lansdowne House, tucked discreetly into the south-west corner of Berkeley Square; this was followed by a superb town house at 20 St James's Square for Sir Watkin Williams-Wynn and another for Lord Stanley, Earl of Derby, in Grosvenor Square.

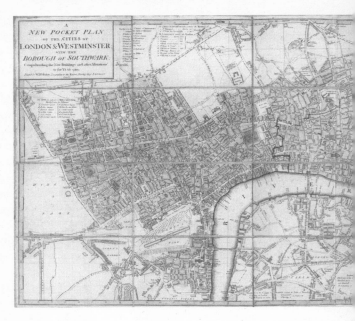

With the arrival of James Adam from Italy in 1763 and the youngest brother, William, around the same time, the firm of Adam became the most active, and one of the most sought-after, architectural practices in the kingdom.[7] In thirty years they undertook over 300 commissions from the greatest in the land and even beyond – Catherine the Great sought a piano design from Robert, for instance. But commissions were not enough for the ambitious Adams. The ever-growing city into which they had thrown themselves offered even richer prizes. They were not content merely to dictate the ways in which the London rich enjoyed their elegant domestic interiors. They wanted to change the face of London itself.

In the 1760s, Durham Yard between the Strand and the river, just east of York Buildings, was one of London's many eyesores. It was the site of a great medieval Thames-side mansion, almost a castle, called Durham House, demolished in the 1660s and replaced by a jumble of industrial buildings (including a waterworks), warehousing and dwellings. Although some smarter houses and shops were built later along the Strand frontage in the 1730s, Durham Yard and its courts and wharves were in a ruinous condition, not helped by local erosion of

London in 1790

the river that had produced a foul-smelling bay at low tide. It was in this unlikely place in 1768 that the Adams designed an extraordinary speculation intended to put their stamp on London for ever.

The Adelphi was the most impressive private improvement of the age. The Adams' intention was to embank the river, build warehouses beneath arches on a quay at the shoreline and put twenty-two great town mansions on top to create a terrace – apparently the first use of the term to represent a continuous row of buildings – of Venetian grandeur. A magnificent promenade in front would overlook the river. More modest houses were to fill several new streets between the terrace and the Strand.

The difficulties were immense. The freehold was not for sale and the Adams had to content themselves with a ninety-nine-year lease from the improvident Duke of St Albans, paying him ground rent of £1,200 a year. The site sloped forty feet vertically from the river to the Strand, so to make ground floors level with the Strand pavement or nearly so required massive foundations and enormous vaulted warehouses, sometimes two storeys deep beneath the terrace. And to make the quay and terrace straight required taking some of the bed of the river, vested in the City Corporation. It required an act of Parliament to secure it to the Adams. The City opposed it with every sinew as 'a violent invasion of their antient rights of conservancy, and an usurpation' of their property, even petitioning the King not to sign the royal assent. But in 1771 the City was out of favour with both Parliament and court and the Adams triumphed. Their influence in the House of Commons had been strengthened by Robert becoming MP for Kinross in 1768. But popular opinion smelt jobbery in 'the Scotch party', the land 'granted by ye Influence of Ld Bute & Mansfield to one Adams a Scotchman & a meer Creature of their own'. Bute and Mansfield were thought to be profiting from the scheme.[8]

In fact, profits proved very hard to make. In June 1772 the banking house of Neale, James, Fordyce and Down stopped payment, a shock to the financial system unparalleled for fifty years past. The Adams were rich but their whole fortune, including that of the Edinburgh firm run by eldest brother John, was tied up in the Adelphi. The credit crisis of 1772 affected many would-be purchasers of the new houses, despite the celebrity draw of David Garrick moving in to number 4, six storeys high with a double basement, on Royal Terrace that April. Takers for the warehouses proved almost impossible to find, and they were the financial (as well as structural) underpinning of the project. Matters weren't helped by the embankment of the river being some two feet too low to keep out the river's highest tides, with quays and warehouses vulnerable to flooding.

Facing ruin, the brothers went back to a friendly Parliament for help. They proposed a Lottery Bill to raise the £218,500 needed to complete the scheme, pay creditors and secure a profit. Again Parliament proved complaisant. The Adam Buildings Act of 1773 permitted the sale of 4,370 tickets costing £50 each. There were 108 prizes but winners had to wait for their houses to be finished; those who couldn't wait auctioned their winning tickets to those who could. Eventually things came right. As the streets behind the Royal Terrace filled with houses, including from 1774 a home for the Society of Arts in John Street, the public clamoured for the smartest addresses in the centre of London. Robert Adam had moved from Lower Grosvenor Street to Royal Terrace in 1772, siting the firm's office round the corner in Robert Street – John, James, William and Adam Streets were all part of the scheme, modesty never one of the brothers' failings. The development contained a chapel, later taken by Mammon into Coutts's Bank on the Strand – a grand house for Edinburgh-born Thomas Coutts was a prominent part of the Adelphi scheme. As a counterbalance, perhaps, the Adelphi New Tavern and Coffee House, later the Adelphi or Osborne's Hotel, opened in 1771. The Adelphi remained a prestigious address for the rest of the century, despite the unhealthy winter fogs said to steal in from the river.[9]

Even while the Adelphi was progressing – and even while floundering – the brothers were engaged in other London speculations. The most important of these were connected with the growth of the town.

When Robert Adam arrived in London the Seven Years War was just two years old and the outward push of the town had flagged almost to a standstill. In general, London's northern boundary in 1758 was Oxford Street, apart from the extension into Marylebone in which James Gibbs had played his part. That had not progressed far beyond Cavendish Square in the Harley – or, as it had become by marriage from 1734, the Harley-Portland – Estate. But demand for new housing at this most fashionable edge of London built up in the war years and developers rushed to satisfy it from the declaration of peace in 1763. One of the most frantic London building booms of the century, lasting a dozen years and more, was the result.[10] The Harley-Portland Estate began to move northwards once more and, on neighbouring land to the west of Marylebone Lane, the Portman Estate joined in to consolidate the invasion of the fields north of Oxford Street. The Adam brothers would be involved in both these important speculations.

They took land first in the streets now emerging north of Cavendish Square. Their first large venture, in 1770, was in Mansfield Street, on what had formerly been a water company's reservoir in open countryside. They built ten houses in two terraces, comfortable three-bay properties on four floors over a basement, stuccoed to the first floor. Each had a tiny courtyard with stables and a laundry room to the rear. The work was contracted out to eight or nine builders working to Robert Adam's designs, and the first tenants or owners were reassuringly aristocratic.[11]

The development in Mansfield Street – all conducted during the anxious years of the Adelphi – proved more easily profitable than the bottomless pit on the Strand. It encouraged the brothers to take more ground as it became available nearby – in Queen Anne Street West, where they built a house for the Duke of Buckingham and Chandos from 1771, and in Duchess Street, where a few years later they constructed a grand mansion for General Robert Clerk, one of the great

Scottish bores of the age but an old friend of Robert Adam. They also took plots in Great Portland Street and Weymouth Street.[12]

The brothers' greatest scheme in this outward surge of the town was Portland Place. As projected, in 1773–4, Portland Place would have been a street of palaces, noble detached mansions individually designed, in keeping with Lord Foley's great house, which formed a boundary to the south. But uncertainties attaching to the American troubles seem to have blunted an appetite for excess in building and ambitions were tempered to the times. The second scheme, though reduced, was grandiose enough, based on long Palladian terraces with a central five-bay pedimented mansion, the whole having the appearance of one great palatial façade. What was finally built, a third scheme, did not quite live up even to this. Yet Portland Place, the widest street in London of its time to accommodate northerly views to the fields from Foley House, protected by act of Parliament, was a staggering speculation. Once more it attracted a flock of aristocratic tenants paying rents of around £350 a year. By 1781 some forty-three houses were completed or on site. But there were gaps in the terraces as some of the twenty or so builders who had leased plots from the Adams struggled to find money in years once more beset by war. By 1792 some sixty-eight houses were finished before yet another war would cut London building to a trickle. Portland Place lay unfinished at the northern end, as did the streets on either side, well into the nineteenth century. It then became absorbed into an even grander town-planning scheme.[13]

When the times proved unpropitious for Robert Adam's street of palaces his involvement in a more modest Portland Place seems to have dwindled and he left most of the design and implementation to James. But Robert's ambitions would be amply fulfilled in his most important contribution on the nearby Portman Estate.

Land in Marylebone to the west of the Harley-Portland holdings had been in the possession of the Portman family since the 1550s. Two hundred years on and the neighbouring developments seemed a provocation to change meadow and pasture to bricks and mortar, but the 1750s, when ambition first surfaced, proved too risky. After 1763, however, the risks seemed reversed – *not* building might miss a new metropolitan neap tide – and so building on the north side of Oxford Street began to spread west towards the Edgware Road. Baker Street formed a north–south spine and off it yet another London square would be the centrepiece of a grand plan – unsurprisingly, it was called Portman

Square, and the earth was first dug there in 1764. It moved – generally these were boom years – at a faster pace than much London development and took just twenty years or so to complete. The Adams seem to have taken by 1775 a good third of the north-west corner and built on part of it a magnificent six-storey five-bay 65-foot frontage town house. It was for the Countess of Home, dowager of an old Scottish family (the Adams never neglected – and were never neglected by – their North British metropolitan compatriots). The Countess took possession of her glorious Robert Adam home in 1778; regrettably, she didn't enjoy it long, dying there in January 1784. Home House happily survives as 20 Portman Square.[14]

The Adam brothers fulfilled scores of London commissions in the 1760s and 1770s, properly their London years – rebuilding houses on old sites from the City to St James's, building new houses from Marylebone to Mayfair, decorating houses everywhere, even designing the new Theatre Royal Drury Lane (1775–6), one of the most popular and prestigious places of public resort in London. And they undertook or assisted some of the great London speculations of the age, the Adelphi an exhilarating but exhausting example. Perhaps there was too much exhilaration, for the 1780s were marked by a shift away from London to private and public commissions out of town, especially in Scotland, where the resources of John Adam's Edinburgh office helped relieve pressure from the London brothers.

After the American War ended in 1783, London building once more began to look hopeful. And it was to the northward march of the town that Robert Adam made the last significant contribution of his long London career. In 1768 Charles FitzRoy, later Lord Southampton, acquired land west of Tottenham Court Road as a long-term building speculation. By 1789 he was ready to build a self-contained suburban new town complete with market, at the centre of which – in that well-established eighteenth-century pattern – was to be a grand square. Robert Adam was commissioned to design Fitzroy Square and the south and east sides were duly built by 1792, magnificent terraces in Portland stone with patent stucco embellishments.[15]

Fitzroy Square would then lie unfinished for over forty years. Building came to a sudden halt, with foundations, at least for the north side, already dug. It seems the war with France from February 1793 killed off every uncertain speculation. Perhaps a local contributing factor was the death of Robert Adam at his home, 13 Albemarle Street, on 3

March 1792, aged sixty-four. He had suffered with his stomach for some years and death appears to have been due to a burst abdominal blood vessel. Like Gibbs, he was unmarried, and left his extensive possessions to his two sisters. James outlived him by just two years.

At the very end of the century Fitzroy Square had become yet another of the terrors of London by night. The Earl of Scarborough's carriage drove into the badly lighted excavations; a footman was hauled out but died of his injuries.[16] But then the terrors of London were legion, despite half a century of 'Improvement'.

'We Have Done Great Things': Improving London, 1754–99

The prickly pride of the City Corporation had taken a body blow from the building of Westminster Bridge, made more painful by the eventual success of the project, plain for all the world to see. Westminster Bridge changed the direction of City thinking. It did not cease to cast a jaundiced eye on any improvement elsewhere in London that might affect its interests, as its hard-fought blocking tactics against embanking the Thames as part of the Adam brothers' Adelphi showed in 1771. But practically there was only one way to respond and that was to fight back.

All this was articulated, as the new streets around Westminster Bridge were still being built, by Joseph Massie, a writer on economic and financial matters about whom we know little. He was probably a West Indian sugar merchant and best known for pamphlets on trade. But though he lived in Covent Garden, his concern for the financial health of the City of London never left him. In February 1754 he published one of the most influential pamphlets of the century on the future of metropolitan improvements. In it he addressed head on the crucial question of city rivalries.

For Massie, the City of London 'has the justest Grounds for being alarmed at the Schemes already laid, and laying, for *new and magnificent Streets, new Inns, Stage Coaches, Livery-Stables*, and *Trades of all Kinds*, in the Neighbourhood of *Westminster-Bridge*'. He asked: 'Shall the City of *London* remain any longer supine and inactive, until it be rivalled, and in some Measure eclipsed, by Cities both Abroad and at Home . . . ?' Assuming the answer would be no, he proposed numerous improvements: removing '*Inconveniencies* and *Inelegancies*' like

'*Nastiness*' at the posterns of the City gates, ruinous houses, the old City wall and streets too narrow for carriages to pass one another; adding '*Ornaments* and *Embellishments*' like public fountains, triumphant arches and equestrian statues, of which the City had none, to numerous places, including London Bridge; and constructing 'fine Openings' at the City boundaries. And he called for a new bridge 'at the Mouth of FLEET-DITCH' across the Thames to Southwark. All this was 'by Way of *Retaliation*, or rather of *Self-Preservation*', in the face of Westminster's aggrandisement.[17]

With Massie's pamphlet acting pretty much as a blueprint, the City Corporation took a momentous step forward. It petitioned for powers to build its own new bridge at Blackfriars, where the River Fleet, still an open sewer south of the new Fleet Market, joined the Thames; at the same time, a petition of London and Southwark citizens and merchants urged the widening of London Bridge by the removal of houses from both sides of its carriageway.[18]

The Committee of the House of Commons established to consider the petitions heard much evidence on the adverse financial position of the City's rents and land tax yield in the years since Westminster Bridge opened. It was said that there were many empty houses in the western wards of the City and that the property around the proposed bridgehead at Fleet Ditch was ruinous. The Committee was assured that all this would be replaced with better housing should the bridge be built and that many merchants who had left the City 'with regret' would move back. In the event the Committee gave leave to bring in two bills: one for the widening of the carriageway on London Bridge – even though that meant demolishing housing built by the City just ten years or so before – and one for building a new bridge at Blackfriars.[19]

Both bills duly passed into law, but the widening of London Bridge proved easier to effect. It began in 1757, the housebreakers wielding hammers and crows from February, a temporary wooden bridge constructed alongside and opened that October. That burned, or was burned, down but quickly rebuilt, yet work on the ancient bridge itself moved slowly – demolition of the houses and laying a new carriageway took till 1762 to complete. Beneath the roadway, two central arches were combined into one to ease the passage for rivercraft shooting the rapids.[20]

Blackfriars Bridge proved a far more difficult project, partly because of its enormous cost. After some three years' debate and parliamentary

niggardliness over funds, a public subscription in interest-bearing bonds
was taken out among the citizens sufficient to raise the £144,000
thought necessary to build it. That alone, perhaps, was some measure
of citizen anxiety for the future of their City. In 1760 Robert Mylne,
a brilliant young Scot fresh from Rome, just twenty-six years old and
with little or no experience of London or of bridges, won in competition the contract to design the City's second bridge. Construction was
arduous and time-consuming. Mylne devised innovative solutions to
the difficulties posed by the swift-flowing river; even so, Blackfriars
Bridge took eight years to build and finally cost some £153,000. It
opened to wheeled traffic in November 1769, a magnificent undertaking
and a most beautiful bridge. But that didn't stop smart carping at the
cits – this time for a blundering Latin inscription on the bridge that a
pamphlet by Busby Birch described as 'wholly ignorant of *Classical
Latinity*'. He suggested that many citizens would have been more
conversant with 'HEBREW'.[21]

While these great works were being projected, the lamentably unfinished business of the streets of London once more claimed attention.
The delay in building Blackfriars Bridge proved more than frustrating
for the City. New dwellings near the bridgehead at Westminster, including
those built for a widened Charing Cross where it joined Whitehall, all
potentially drew rich citizens from their proper domain. In a state of
some anxiety, the City procured an act in 1760 empowering a lengthy
list of some thirty-four street improvements to free traffic and remove
eyesores.[22] In effect, this was an attempt more or less to complete the
programme Massie had laid down six years before. Thirty or so separate
schemes involved the demolition of hundreds of old houses. Blind courts
were broken through to make new streets. Sheds and other encumbrances
built against church walls were cleared away. Important avenues like
Threadneedle Street, Cornhill, Old Bailey, Lombard Street, Houndsditch
and a dozen others less significant had their worst obstructions demolished and 'the ground laid into the street'. Not all the plans were
implemented, and many took a decade or more to complete, but much
was done.

In separate initiatives the Corporation took down the last important
remains of the Roman wall from Moorgate to Cripplegate, leasing the
ground for new houses in its stead. It was an irony of the times that,
just as the 'antique' of Robert Adam was gripping the imagination of
wealthy Londoners, the remains of London's real antique was busily

done away with as a public nuisance. Eight City gates, mostly rebuilt after the Great Fire, were also demolished by the Corporation between 1760 and 1762 to ease traffic congestion. And somewhat later, by the end of the 1760s, access to the new Blackfriars Bridge was provided by culverting over the southernmost run of the Fleet Ditch and conveying it as a sewer some way into the Thames beneath the bridge. The roadway was called Bridge Street, now New Bridge Street.

These were astonishing changes. All around them the citizens saw wooden scaffolding and shuttering, and lived with the inconveniences of streets being closed for a long time before they could be widened. But an even greater transformation affecting most metropolitan streets was also getting under way in this energetic decade. And this was begun in Westminster.

In 1754, the same year as Massie's imaginative proposals for the City, two pamphlets called yet again for the reform of Westminster's streets. The first and more important was by John Spranger. He reiterated a familiar litany, showing how little improvement had been effected in the first half of the century: 'broken or irregular Pavements', 'Foulness and Darkness of our Streets – scarcely passable in Carriages with Safety', 'frequent and melancholy Distresses and Disasters', 'fatal Mischiefs' daily 'to Men and Cattle' (meaning horses), the 'Quantity of Filth . . . so great, that Man and Beast, in some Places, can hardly wade through it . . .' Spranger spelled out the dangers all this held, not just for the hapless Londoner but for the economic well-being of London as a whole, where 'without a free and safe Intercourse between Place and Place by Land as well as by Water, *Trade* cannot subsist, much less flourish'.[23]

An enthusiastic endorsement of Spranger's proposals was soon published by the tireless reformer Jonas Hanway.[24] Central to their plan was the establishment by Parliament of commissioners to oversee the paving, lighting and cleansing of streets in Westminster and nearby parishes. But Parliament had grappled ineffectively with this problem before and these proposals directly countered the interests of Westminster local government. It took eight years for a bill along these lines to be introduced.

At last, from 1762 to 1766, no fewer than five acts of Parliament finally established an entirely new framework for paving, cleansing and lighting the London streets. Instead of responsibility falling on individual householders, paving commissioners were endowed by parliamentary grant to begin a large-scale programme of street improvements. Carriageways were laid in flat stone and kennels moved from the centre to the edges; footways were raised above the level of the roadway and regularly paved; globular lights were erected on poles at regular distances; streets displayed their names and houses were numbered; posts on the pavements, hanging signs and high-level rainwater spouts were all abolished. Once effected, improvements would be paid for by a rate levied on the householders who benefited from them and by an extra Sunday toll at the Middlesex and Westminster turnpike gates. This was a true collectivisation of individual responsibility, and a turning point in the history of municipal enterprise in London.[25]

By 12 July 1765 the transformation of Westminster had come right to the door of the City:

The new pavement from Charing-cross to Temple-bar, which was begun at the first of these places, was this day ended at the latter, and the communication opened for carriages. Those, who have not seen this new pavement, can scarcely imagine the alteration made by it, the taking down of signs, and fixing up of lights in a regular manner. It may be said that no street in London, paved, lighted, and filled with signs in the old way, ever made so agreeable an appearance, or afforded better walking than the Strand does in the new . . . In short, too much cannot be said in praise of those noblemen and gentlemen, who first promoted this improvement, and have so steadily carried it on, in spite of all the obstacles thrown in their way, and all the cavils against their proceedings.[26]

Here, then, was yet further provocation to City rivalry. As late as 1765 a French visitor noted how the City streets were 'eternally covered with dirt' and 'paved in such a manner that it is scarce possible to find a place to set one's foot, and absolutely impossible to ride in a coach'. Comparisons with the new Westminster were both inevitable and invidious. How *could* a resident of Grosvenor Square be expected to shop at a City draper's in St Paul's Churchyard or Cheapside in circumstances such as these? Something had to be done.[27]

It was, and quickly. In November 1765 the City Corporation received a report on the unsavoury condition of the City streets and by May 1766 the City had procured an act that put in place a close copy of the statutory framework established by its neighbour.[28] Southwark won similar powers that same year and so did a clutch of Middlesex parishes by 1770, Shoreditch and St Marylebone among them.

The City Commissioners of Sewers and Pavements proceeded with unwonted vigour for the times. At their first meeting, just a few days after the London Paving and Lighting Act gained royal assent, they established nine professional staff, adopted priorities (the first street to be paved, Fleet Street from Temple Bar, had been named in the act), and agreed the terms of advertisements for tenders. Householders were ordered to remove their 'Signs, Sign posts and Sign Irons' by 24 June, after which the surveyors would be instructed to take them down in default. Carriageways were to be laid in Aberdeen stone (Scotch granite) and the footways in Purbeck stone not less than two inches thick. 'Bulks and Rails' or shop projections were taken away; even flitches of bacon obstructing an alley into Newgate Street attracted the commissioners' attention.[29]

Why so much urgency? There were two main reasons. The first was put to the commissioners by the shopkeepers and others of Holborn and the City streets leading to the north-west: 'since the new Paving of the Strand your Petitioners . . . have sensibly felt a great and general diminution of their Trade' as the carriage-owning classes deserted them for an easier journey within Westminster. Second, because in places things were so very bad. We might instance the pavement outside Miles Nightingale's warehouses in Fore Street, Cripplegate Without, which for thirty-six feet 'lies in an hole eighteen Inches deep from the top of the new paving in the Carriageway, and thereby creates a Slough full of Mud and Water to the great annoyance of the Neighbourhood and all Persons who pass or repass that way'.[30]

Across London, these were momentous changes. They were not comprehensive, because some places like the ancient Liberty of Norton Folgate in Shoreditch, for instance, opted out of parish statutes through the poverty of their residents. And doubtless the commissioners were not always and everywhere as vigilant as they should have been. But the reorganisation of paving and lighting, the naming of streets and numbering of houses, all made London tangibly more manageable. And more modern too. By the early 1770s it could be said with some confidence that 'London is the best paved and best lighted city in Europe.' Its paving remained a wonder to foreigners till the century's end.[31]

Indeed, by then it seemed that London was improving in every direction. In the City the Bank of England was partly rebuilt in 1767–8, a new Corn Exchange was erected in Mark Lane around 1770 and Newgate Prison was demolished and rebuilt from 1776. In the Minories

on the eastern borders of the City, 'wooden hovels and waste ground,
the receptacles of thieves' were replaced by a private speculation of
Sir Richard Hammett's and designed – with unworldly optimism given
the location – in the style of Bath by George Dance the Younger.[32] A
growing government bureaucracy spawned new buildings and fine
architecture from the City (where a new Excise Office was built in
Old Broad Street, 1769–75) to Whitehall. Here, William Kent's fine
Horse Guards barracks was completed in 1759, eleven years after the
architect's death; the Holbein Gate was demolished in 1759, Robert
Adam's Admiralty screen was built soon after and great mansions,
eventually to be used for the public service, arose in the 1770s in an
area transformed by the arrival of Westminster Bridge and its associated street improvements.

Government also accounted for one of the greatest developments of
the last quarter of the century. Somerset House was an extensive Tudor
palace, built on the river next to the Savoy and with a frontage on the
Strand just west of James Gibbs's new church. By 1775, much of it
was in poor condition and for some years it had been let in apartments
to courtiers, pensioners and other tenants – the Royal Academy had
its offices and painting school there from 1771, for instance. By 1775,
too, the Adams' Adelphi scheme was well advanced not far upriver
towards Charing Cross. It inspired government to embank the river
nearby along the ancient Savoy palace and the gardens of Somerset
House and an act was secured that year for doing so. At the same time,
the demolition of Somerset House was proposed, to be replaced by a
palace of public offices designed to solve the accommodation problem,
in particular, of an ever-swelling army of tax gatherers.

The architect chosen for the new Somerset House was Sir William
Chambers, born in Sweden of Scottish parents. Chambers had been the
King's architect jointly with Robert Adam in the 1760s and from 1769
was sole Comptroller of the Office of Works till his death in 1796,
aged seventy-three. His architectural style was more restrained and less
popularly influential than Adam's, but Chambers was one of the most
important London architects of the second half of the century. He
designed Kew Gardens from 1757, fulfilled a number of important private
commissions for town houses in Whitehall and elsewhere, including Lord
Melbourne's Albany speculation behind Piccadilly (1771–5), engaged in
ventures north of Oxford Street, and most of all played a leading role
in London's public architecture. He was a tireless worker and greedy

for power and influence, manoeuvring adroitly to sideline competition in any institution – like the Royal Academy or Office of Works – in which he was involved. On the other hand there was no doubting his talent.[33]

The new Somerset House was a stunning achievement. There was only a small part of the old Somerset House that had a frontage on the Strand. Chambers constructed a great gateway opening into a theatrical drama unfolding within. It was built around a giant courtyard, a paved London square, surrounded by elaborately sculptured palatial buildings on a design heavily influenced by Parisian architecture – a city Chambers knew well. Work on Somerset House was still going on until five years after his death and proved enormously costly. Even so, this new Thames-side palace provided Londoners with a haven from the hubbub on the Strand, and one of the pleasantest riverside walks in the capital.[34]

Of course, in a city built on the restless imperatives of moneymaking, much change was small-scale and wrought by private individuals, alone or in combination. The steady commercialisation of the City, domestic premises replaced by warehousing and workspaces, probably led to the loss of more than one in four houses within the walls between 1737 and 1801.[35] Banks built new premises, as at Asgill's (1757) and Martin's (1793–5), both in Lombard Street, and Drummond's (1760) in Charing Cross (decorated by the Adam Brothers in the 1770s). So did fire and life assurance offices like Amicable Assurance in Serjeant's Inn (1793) and the Westminster Fire Office in Bedford Street, Covent Garden (1795). These and many other corporate initiatives helped drive the constant renewal and replacement of London's older buildings. But all around, the pressures of fashion seeded modernisation in every direction. In the City, by the early 1770s:

The building large magnificent houses for tradesmen is carried now to a pernicious extreme: the rents are exorbitant; the tenants appear to live in proportion; they are often entered upon credit; the professions carried on in them will not always support such increased expences; and how precarious the situation of tradesmen is rendered under the combined effects of all these circumstances, is too well known to be pointed out.[36]

Not all ended up in the bankruptcy courts, though. Thomas Fletcher, a linen draper, demolished and rebuilt a substantial post-Fire mansion at 11 Ironmonger Row, Cheapside, in 1767–8, his firm trading from the same premises for another seventy years.[37]

Just as in the first half of the century, much of this ceaseless renewal was driven by the ever-present menace of fire. Almost every year brought its giant destructive conflagration, the riverside once more especially prone, but the City and old Westminster vulnerable too. Cornhill and the streets around it were badly damaged in November 1759, November 1765 and December 1778. So were the Strand and the courts and alleys off it in December 1762 (destroying part of old Somerset House), June 1765, August 1765 and October 1769. These were merely the largest blazes at two prominent locations. Among scores of disasters close to the river, the greatest fire of these years destroyed half the hamlet of Ratcliff, some 630 houses out of 1,200, in June 1794; 140 tents for the homeless were pitched in a field by Stepney Church.[38] All these fires were followed, some more quickly than others, by rebuilding in modern style. From 1774, new buildings were subject to yet further building regulations designed, among other things, to prevent the spread of fire.[39]

The combination of public improvements, the rearrangement of paving and lighting in the London streets, and the hop, step and jump of private investment had caused something like a transformation in London's built environment by the 1780s. William Hutton, a Birmingham worthy, had first visited London in 1749. He returned in 1784 and marvelled at this 'collection of magnificence', its houses 'on the average, about one storey higher than I have ever seen'. At night, 'Not a corner of this prodigious city is unlighted', though even the new lamps were outshone by the shop windows. He thought, 'The stranger will be astonished at the improvements which have been introduced during the last thirty-five years . . .' Even the insatiable Jonas Hanway, taking stock around the same time, agreed that 'we have done great things of late years . . . insomuch that a *British* subject, who has not seen these ancient cities of *London* and *Westminster* for *forty years*, would scarce know them again.'[40]

Yet the appetite for improvement was unappeased. It was as though success merely sharpened a critical eye on all that remained to be done. James 'Athenian' Stuart, a rare cockney among the architectural alumni of the age, his brilliant talents dulled by drink but still gener-ously admired by Robert Adam, set out proposals in 1771 for further embellishing the Thames waterfront and the London squares, and for further investment in new public buildings, including a modern royal palace. Stuart in turn praised the most remarkable of the metropolitan improvement proposals, that of the architect John Gwynn, a Shropshire man and friend of Samuel Johnson, who had published his richly detailed suggestions for the improvement of the City and Westminster some five years before. Gwynn was less concerned with adornment than with the practical means of getting around this sclerotically congested city, spotting opportunities for new and wider streets at almost every turn. Eminently practical, he proved too far-sighted for his time, though many of his plans would be adopted in the century to come.[41]

For, as Gwynn and Stuart knew, wherever one looked the disabilities of old London, even after fifty years of improvement, were palpably immense. In large measure it was mouldering around Londoners' heads. Every year brought its crop of collapsed houses, some more noteworthy than others. In July 1758 'An old lodging-house in Plumb-tree-court, Broad St. Giles's, fell down' and 'several poor wretches were crushed to death, and many more desperately maimed. There being other houses in the court in the like condition, the mob assembled in a few days afterwards, and pulled them down.'[42] Among many of the notable collapses, we might mention that of two houses in the Mint, Southwark, which fell in August 1774, killing, it was said, fourteen people with nine different surnames, a further two expiring in hospital, while a baby was cut from its dying mother, Mary Middleton – 'we hear it is likely to live';[43] and seven were reported lost after two houses collapsed in Houghton Street, Clare Market, in June 1796.

Just as it had in 1703, bad weather turned a crop of these events into a harvest. A 'most dreadful hurricane' in September 1772 brought numerous 'old houses . . . to the ground' – 'the damage is incredible'; nine empty houses were blown down in Southwark by a 'dreadful tempest' in October 1774; a violent 'hurricane' in November 1795 laid low houses all over London, including one in Fitzroy Square apparently; and so on.

The decrepit state of old London was in many ways hidden from view, especially from those Londoners unfamiliar with City byways and the poor suburbs of St Giles, Clerkenwell, Whitechapel and Southwark, or the back streets of Westminster. That restricted view encompassed all the wealthier residents of London, particularly of new London in the north-west suburbs. They might read of the worst horrors of fire and falling houses in their newspapers, but theirs was an age of incuriosity, when it was 'polite' not to take notice of the poor and their living conditions. Occasionally, though, towards the end of the century, a little more interest in the condition of old London and those who lived there began to emerge. Richard King, a 'Modern London Spy', took his readers through the Desert of Westminster. Between Tothill Street and Petty France around 1781

We . . . involved ourselves in a nest of little streets and lanes, which were so intricate, that Mr Ambler [the Modern Spy's guide] could scarcely extricate himself. Many of these like the Almonry, were inhabited by wretches who were a disgrace to humanity, while in the neighbourhood, as in that of St. Giles's, some hundreds of the industrious poor were scattered up and down. [As they walked through the wind blew down] part of a high stack of chimnies . . . which had absolutely dragged down part of the gable end of the next house with it . . .⁴⁴

In all of this – the dangers of old London at the centre, the filth, the stench, the people – lay yet more reasons why London should continue to grow. And grow it did.

The Mad Spirit of Building: London Growing, 1754–99

The 1750s might have been a relatively quiet period for London house building but it saw the projection of a scheme of great significance for the growth of the metropolis. It had been in the air since at least 1754 but its first parliamentary manifestation was a petition in December 1755 from residents, gentlemen, farmers and tradesmen of Middlesex, London and Westminster, pressing for the construction of 'a new Road from *Paddington* to *Islington*'. Other petitions followed, mainly for but some against, and a House of Commons committee reported in February 1756. The clear purpose of the road was not to 'by-pass' London, as has some-times been said, but to ease east–west communications within it, so that those living in Marylebone having business in the City could reach it more quickly and safely than by picking their way through the unsavoury streets of Holborn, Smithfield and Clerkenwell. Opposition was led by the Duke of Bedford, who held land north of Bloomsbury through which the road would run, to the prejudice of his outlook and of his tenant's valuable corn crop, susceptible to dust from the road. But the committee reported in favour, and the bill enabling it passed into law that session.⁴⁵

The New Road was built in 1756-7 from the Edgware Road at Paddington to Islington at the Angel public house. It connected to the north-western suburbs through Marylebone Lane and Portland Street, the latter junction provided for in the act, and to the City via St John Street to Smithfield and Goswell Street (now Road) to St Paul's. These City connections were soon strengthened by an entirely new private venture. This was City Road, projected by the inventive Charles Dingley, an influential figure behind the New Road. It opened as a toll road from Islington to Moorgate on 29 June 1761, 'has a foot-path on each side, is well lighted, and is indisputably the finest road about London'. Even the Duke of Bedford, implacable critic of the New Road that he was, built his own private road secured by gates and keepers, to connect Bedford House from Southampton Row to the convenient new route. The silver tickets giving leave to travel the Duke's private road were much prized – David Garrick solicited for one in 1760, for instance.[46]

One reason for the Duke's opposition had been the risk of building along the New Road obstructing his views to the Highgate hills. It was not an unlikely prospect, and Parliament had envisaged something similar: it secured that any development along the New Road would be set back fifty feet, giving rise to some abnormally long front gardens there in the years to come. But in 1760 or so, the New Road still lay deep in the fields, nearly half a mile north of Oxford Street and some three-quarters of a mile from London's edge as it approached Islington. Yet with the burst of building that followed the end of the Seven Years War in 1763, it looked as though the greedy metropolis might build right up to the New Road and even beyond. John Gwynn thought so in 1766, and urged that Parliament should make it 'the great boundary or line of restraining or limiting the rage of building'.[47] Parliament didn't listen. But this sense of the New Road as a logical boundary to the town offered mouth-watering opportunities for those with land between it and London.

The juices flowed fastest, as they had done for the half-century past, around the silver spoons in the north-west of the town. For there was a great deal of money to be made from land in Westminster and Marylebone in these hectic years. A 'small piece of ground in Piccadilly', it was reported in 1764, had been bought by a brewer for £30 'some years ago'. He used it to store barrels. But it was lately sold for £2,500, 'so greatly is that part of the town improved even in the memory of man'. And in 1769 land at Hay Hill, Mayfair, just east of Berkeley Square, fetched £20,000, a nabob's ransom. Sixty years or so before,

Queen Anne had given it to the then Speaker of the House of Commons; the gift had been widely decried as a bribe and so he sold it and gave the money to the poor – it fetched just £200. Others beside the land-owners could make profits in turn: the rent of 'a great house' in Grosvenor Square was £500 a year in 1776, over ten years' wages for a plumber.[48]

With inducements like these there was no shortage of building land on the north-west edge of the town where the New Road now marked a sensible place to aim for. Other things could be in short supply, though. The demand for bricks was such that they had no time to cool at the makers': brick wagons caught alight on the road and bricks sometimes reached the bricklayers too hot to handle. And buildings could be so skimped and shoddy, these same bricks made up with more rubbish than clay, that they collapsed before they could be occupied:

> Whene'er a new building I pass in my rout,
> I cautiously take myself somewhat about,
> Preferring a slouch in the mud, over shoes,
> Than under some thousands of bricks to repose.[49]

Despite these hindrances, the progress of building in the north-west of the town astonished all who saw it:

The even.g being very fair and serene tempted me to make an excursion to Marybone Gardens. But as there were no fireworks exhibited I did not go in, chusing rather to strole About & Amuse myself <w^{th}> ye New Buildings both there & Near Oxford Road. Westminster & Middlesex are March.g out of Town as well as London. Such Huge Piles such elegant Improvem^{ts} w^d most undoubtedly Amaze you. They are joyn.g Field to Field & House to House in so unbounded & precipitate a Manner y^t Hamstead will be ere long reckond ye suburbs of this City.[50]

That was 1772. Ten years earlier and Marylebone (more commonly Marybone) Gardens had stood alone in the fields just south of where the New Road would run, but now was joined to London. Another ten years and the Gardens were gone altogether, closed and laid out for buildings on the Harley-Portland Estate, soon to be obliterated by Weymouth Street, Upper Wimpole Street and eventually Devonshire Place. Further west, the Portman Estate moved steadily northwards.

Manchester Square was laid out in 1776, a great mansion for the Duke of Manchester occupying its north side.

As always, building was in fits and starts as war and peace and financial anxieties dictated, but by the early 1790s continuous building from London on the Harley-Portland Estate had indeed reached the New Road at Marylebone High Street and Portland Road. The Portman Estate had filled in three or four blocks to the north of Manchester Square, and ribbon development along the east side of Edgware Road, from its junction with Oxford Street, also ran all the way to the New Road. All of these new streets were marked by their regularity, except where the ancient way of Marylebone Lane imposed itself in the west and some old field boundaries distorted the street pattern further east. Otherwise the Portman and Harley-Portland estates were a model Georgian townscape of parallel streets and three great squares (Cavendish, Portman and Manchester).[51]

All of this was now unquestionably part of London, though still prized for its air and its rural connections: Portman Square, as late as 1782, was thought by Hannah More to be graced by 'the scenery of a country retirement'.[52] But to the south-west of London a whole new town of aristocratic pretension was being built entirely out in the fields – *of* London, perhaps, but certainly not in it.

This was Hans Town at Chelsea's eastern edge. It was a venture along the lines of earlier new towns on the Harley and Grosvenor estates, a self-sustaining country town, and on a very grand scale. It was proposed by the builder Henry Holland, working with his talented architect son of the same name, on land formerly owned by Sir Hans Sloane. The building potential of the villages to the south-west of the built-up area and close to the river had all been enhanced by turnpike roads and new Thames bridges at Kew (1758) and a wooden bridge from Chelsea to Battersea (permitted 1766, built 1771–2). The Hollands took some thirty-four acres and began building in Sloane Street and Sloane Square from around 1776. In twenty years, no doubt with many stumbles, some 550 houses and other buildings were on the ground. They included lodging houses, a school, workshops, a public house, coach houses and stables, a bakehouse, slaughterhouse, shops, warehouse and dairy. There would have been an Anglican chapel but the neighbouring clergymen, jealous of their pew rents, prevented it. It was all very much a mixed development, including 'utilitarian' buildings and 'modest houses for local tradesmen'.[53]

The idea of a new town in the fields resonated elsewhere. Pentonville, a speculation of Henry Penton, the landowning MP for Winchester, began around 1773, with houses north and south of the New Road just west of the Angel public house by the end of the century. Somers Town was begun north of the New Road, still three-quarters of a mile or so clear of London's edge at Bloomsbury, in 1786, the speculator here a builder, Jacob Leroux, on land owned by Lord Somers.[54] Even further afield, building began in Camden Town in 1791. All these were satellites of the great metropolis and rarely appeared on maps of London until the new century.

Year by year, London trudged out to meet them, even though everywhere was more sluggish than at Marylebone. The Duke of Bedford on his Bloomsbury Estate proved far more cautious than the Duke of Portland and Henry Portman, near neighbours to his west. In the thirty-three years from 1732 to 1765 his tenancies increased from 450 to some 550, or around three new houses net a year. The Bedford Estate was not tempted to build in advance of demand from the highly respectable market it aimed at. Even so, over this same period, the rent roll of the estate more than doubled and this, combined with the extensive development of neighbouring land on the west of Tottenham Court Road in the 1760s at Charlotte Street, Percy Street and elsewhere, made building seem attractive once more.[55]

In 1771 the Fourth Duke of Bedford died and in 1774 his dowager took forward plans that had lain on the table for some years. She began a great Bloomsbury speculation, Bedford Square. Building started there in 1776. The Bedford Estate would still be building, on and off, for the next eighty-four years.

Bedford Square was unique in eighteenth-century London in that it was planned and built in one integrated design that ensured all the houses looked alike. Every other square since 1700 had sought to accommodate individual self-aggrandisement at the expense of uniformity. But in Bedford Square a strict and entirely unmetropolitan discipline was imposed on builder and tenant alike. As though in recognition of the long-term nobility of the venture, these were the first ninety-nine-year leases granted on the Bedford Estate. Yet despite its many capital virtues, Bedford Square failed to hit the fashionable market it aimed for. Wealthy tradesmen, and most of all wealthy lawyers – Bloomsbury was always the favourite suburb of the Inns of Court – were the best tenants even the new square could hope for. Not a single member of the House of Lords lived in Bedford Square in 1793, for instance, and just a handful of MPs. Even so there were enough wealthy tradesmen and lawyers to make this western part of Bloomsbury, so near yet so far from the beau-monde, a ready speculation. By 1786 development had filled the ground from Tottenham Court Road to both sides of Gower Street and was creeping north to the New Road.[56]

Further east and from 1790, the Foundling Hospital thought to capitalise on the valuable fields it owned nearby. A talented architect, Samuel Pepys Cockerell, was brought in to assist. His plan inevitably involved squares, one either side of the hospital – Brunswick to the west, Mecklenburgh to the east – with a mix of interconnecting streets aimed like a new town at a broad tenantry from working tradesmen to the wealthy. James Burton, who would become one of the great speculative builders of Regency London, was actively involved in fulfilling Cockerell's plans. The realistic, unpretentious aspirations of the Foundling Hospital Estate were in keeping with the more plebeian development that had characterised east Bloomsbury, between the Bedford Estate beginning at Southampton Row and filthy Gray's Inn Lane (now Road). The new development hit home. Between 1792 and 1802, Burton alone would build 586 houses there.[57]

In the east and south of London, with no aristocratic or fashionable estates to attract the nobility, things moved as much through happenstance as design. So Mile End Old Town, for instance, reacted strongly to the building boom from 1763 and seems hardly to have paused for a moment thereafter: it had around 500 houses in 1768, 727 in 1780 and by 1801 the number had more than doubled to 1,665. Limehouse, on the other hand, seems to have stagnated in the second half of the century. Bethnal Green was estimated to contain 2,000 houses in 1774, 2,400 four years later, around 3,500 in 1795 and had 3,820 (234 of them empty) in 1801. Spitalfields also thickened out slightly, with courts and alleys taking some remaining garden land in these years, and many new streets were built in Mile End New Town, east of Brick Lane and Osborne Street. South of Whitechapel Road growth was modest, filling in some garden and wasteland as demand dictated and opportunity arose.[58]

On the other side of the river, development was more dramatic. Indeed, the road layout and settlement patterns altered out of recognition between 1750 and 1799. On the Lambeth side of Westminster Bridge a new town had begun to emerge between Lambeth Palace and the bridgehead, with extensive building in Lambeth Marsh, Hercules

Buildings (when William and Catherine Blake moved to number 13 in 1790 the houses were about twenty years old) and a cluster of streets near Westminster Bridge. There had been houses in Lambeth Marsh in the 1740s but otherwise virtually everything else was new.[59]

So too was a road network linking Westminster Bridge Road to the new road from Blackfriars Bridge, named Great Surrey Street (now Blackfriars Road), connecting in St George's Fields at a circus and an obelisk. The south bank of the river west of London Bridge had long been built up with wharves and timber yards and workers' dwellings, but until 1765 it had not spread far from the riverside, except along a few country lanes. With the arrival of Blackfriars Bridge, extensive new development spread either side of Great Surrey Street, swallowing up orchards and market gardens and tenter grounds used for drying dyed or bleached cloth, with streets and houses encroaching deep into St George's Fields. The development was irregular and patchy, comprising mixed classes of housing. But Great Surrey Street was good enough for Robert Mylne, who had helped it all happen, to build himself a house there in 1780. And it all represented a considerable expansion of London south of the Thames.[60]

What of the villages around London, still separate from it but falling ever more deeply beneath the metropolitan shade? Two examples might stand for many. Hackney, north of the river, had long been a popular suburban village, indeed almost a town, even by the 1750s: 'tho' long deserted by the Nobility, yet it so greatly abounds with Merchants and other Persons of Distinction, that it excels all other Villages in the Kingdom, and probably upon Earth, in the Riches and Opulency of its Inhabitants . . .' It contained then some 983 houses and in the fifty years to come it grew faster than ever before. There were over 1,500 houses in 1789 and 2,134 (of which eighty-four were empty) in 1801, when nearly 13,000 people lived there. It was still opulent, though popularity would doubtless have dented its appeal to the richest. And despite being a creature of London for centuries past, it remained in part a working rural community of farmers and labourers, industrialists and mechanics in silk mills, colour or paint manufactories, calico printers and so on, all based on the River Lea. So even Hackney was not merely a Londoners' dormitory town but to some extent a self-sustaining economy. Of all Hackney's industries, though, brick making was the most extensive, especially at Dalston, its sights and smells another deterrent to the fashionable by the end of the century. Even so, the parish was prosperous enough to build a smart modern church, St John's, begun in 1791 and opening in 1797.[61]

In south London, Camberwell's church also received attention, being 'much enlarged' in brick in 1786 for a congregation that had outstripped its capacity. It is difficult to get reliable figures for the growth of this parish. In 1725 there were said to be 1,520 living there and by 1787 this had more than doubled to 3,762. That was considered an accurate estimate and around the same time there were around 770 houses. If all this was true, then there was a late-century spurt, for in 1801 there were 1,224 houses (including sixty-two empty), home to over 7,000 people. Though just three miles from Westminster Bridge, Camberwell was a retired place, 'no public road passing through it except to the neighbouring village of Sydenham, which also is no thoroughfare'. It was especially recommended to valetudinarians who, 'from inclination, or for the benefit of the air, are induced to prefer a country residence, tho' business calls them daily to the metropolis'. Indeed, 'So many Merchants and others have capital houses here, that they cannot be enumerated.'[62]

Something like this was happening to every village in the penumbra of what, a century or more later, would become known as Greater London. From Woodford to Wimbledon, Bromley to Barnet, country villages were engorged by prosperous Londoners or by the economic advantages of falling under London's tidal sway.

These great changes were made possible by the turnpike roads, still often under deep mud in winter at the century's end but incomparably better than what had gone before. They not only laid open the villages of Middlesex, Surrey and Essex to the ravages of the coach-owning classes. They brought London closer to the nation. Journey times to London seem generally to have halved during the last thirty years of the century. From Edinburgh to London took James Boswell five days in March 1772. The news of Fordyce's banking crash that same year, which rocked the Adam brothers and had disastrous consequences for Scottish depositors, took a near-miraculous forty-three hours at the gallop to reach Edinburgh. But by the end of the century the coach journey took just two and a half days. Bristol could be reached in nineteen hours, Bath in sixteen, Exeter in thirty-two (it had taken five days in 1750) and so on. And large numbers were making these journeys. By 1775 the average number of stage coach passengers, incredible as it may seem, was ten inside and eighteen out. Roads remained by far the most popular means of transport to and from London, though many also came by sea from Leith, Newcastle and Cornwall. Canals impacted hardly at all on travel to London in the eighteenth century, while the Thames remained as popular as ever. It had its hazards, though, even for a journey from Brentford to the City in 1774, when 'the Wind and Tide was against each tother that the Waves did Roll that it was Very Dangerous'.[63]

All this increase in the ease and speed of travel to London was considered an evil by many. Arthur Young thought 'that giving the power of expeditious travelling, depopulates the kingdom'. How? Because young men and women deserted the countryside for London, that 'region of dirt, stink, and noise'. 'That the over-grown size of *London* is pernicious to the population of the kingdom, there can be no doubt', mainly through wasting and debauching the best of the country's youth and through the high mortality, especially of children, 'in that destructive city'. Young considered it an urgent necessity to 'Finish the enlargement of the capital; and lessen the number of its inhabitants, by such secondary means [he favoured high taxation] as may be judged most proper'. In less cataclysmic terms, most commentators who reflected on London's growth condemned it and called for some restraining hand. Popular novelists satirised metropolitan aggrandisement as 'an over-grown monster' and a curse on the nation. Political economists complained of London's 'Encroachments upon, if not actual Usurpations of, the Rights and Privileges of the rest of the Kingdom'. [64]

Londoners, though, just looked on with awe. Horace Walpole – no more sharp-eyed or witty London-watcher than he – noted how 'Rows of houses shoot out every way like a polypus; and so great is the rage of building everywhere, that if I stay here [Strawberry Hill, Twickenham] a fortnight, without going to town, I look about to see if no new house is built since I went last.' He considered it a barometer of the state of the economy in general, and hardly ever in his long London experience did he find the builders at ease. By 1791 'Indeed the town is so extended, that the breed of chairs is almost lost, for Hercules and Atlas could not carry anybody from one end of this enormous capital to the other.'[65]

'An Epitome of a Great Nation': London, 1799

In June 1782, Carl Philipp Moritz, a literary man from Berlin, climbed to the gallery of St Paul's Cathedral. It was a rare clear day.

Below me, lay steeples, houses, and palaces in countless numbers; the squares with their grass plots in their middle that lay agreeably dispersed and inter-mixed, with all the huge clusters of buildings, forming, meanwhile, a pleasing contrast, and a relief to the jaded eye.

At one end rose the Tower, itself a city, with a wood of masts behind it; and at the other Westminster Abbey with its steeples. There I beheld, clad in smiles, those beautiful green hills, that skirt the environs of Paddington and Islington; here on the opposite bank of the Thames, lay Southwark; the City itself seems to be impossible for any eye to take in entirely, for, with all my pains, I found it impossible to ascertain, either where it ended, or where the circumjacent villages began; far as the eye could reach, it seemed to be all one continued chain of buildings.[66]

Over the course of the eighteenth century London took on extra girth over a mile thick in the north-west, filling a good deal of the ground between Piccadilly and the New Road. In the west it pushed out half a mile from St James's to Hyde Park Corner, and similarly along the northern boundary in west Bloomsbury, Holborn, Clerkenwell and Shoreditch. In the east, Bethnal Green and Spitalfields filled the fields for half to three-quarters of a mile beyond the built-up area of 1700. On both sides of the Thames in the east, from Wapping to Limehouse and Bermondsey to Rotherhithe, the riverside put on more streets. South of the river, Southwark expanded to the west by half a mile and more, and an extensive new district had grown near Westminster Bridge at north Lambeth. Along the main roads from the metropolis, continuous ribbons in brick and mortar reached out to join villages to London in every direction. Within half a mile of London's edge new towns were building in the north and west. Between them and the metropolis, indeed all around, the ground was scorched by London's breath, the fields pocked by brick-workings and clay pits, streets and building plots marked out for the developer, speculations lying half finished, rows of houses standing stark and lonely as hayricks in the open fields.

It was evident that London would not stop where it was. There was much of the coiled spring about it even in the 1790s, when building largely stalled through the demands on men and materials of a global war. Signs of things to come were apparent even in Bloomsbury, where the Fifth Duke of Bedford had inherited all his father's caution and his jealousy of an untarnished view from Bedford House to the northern heights. There was still no building between the Duke's windows and the New Road, three-quarters of a mile or so away. But Somers Town had impudently smudged the skyline on the far side of the road from 1791 and had grown bigger since. In September 1798 it was reported that the Duke had stopped up his private carriageway to the New Road – or 'to Somers Town', as the *Annual Register* infuriatingly put it. He caused some outrage because his road had formerly been used as a footpath through the fields 'from time immemorial'. Eventually, though, he abandoned as a lost cause any future prospect of maintaining aristocratic grandeur at Bedford House. He resolved to demolish his Restoration mansion and lay out the land to the New Road for building. By 1800 he had moved to Arlington Street, Piccadilly.[67]

One reason why the battle to stop London growing was so hopeless was the inexhaustible demand of the cockney for the rural. It infected cockneys of every class. And by 1799 it had made itself felt far and wide. Around the Jew's Harp Tavern and Tea Gardens, north of the New Road at Marylebone,

were several small tenements, with a pretty good portion of ground to each. On the south side of the tea-gardens a number of summerhouses and gardens, fitted up in the truest Cockney taste; for on many of these castellated edifices wooden cannons were placed; and at the entrance of each domain, of about the twentieth part of an acre, the old inscription of 'Steel-traps and spring-guns *all over* these grounds,' with an 'N.B. Dogs trespassing will be shot.'[68]

Similar hutments were noted in Bethnal Green and no doubt elsewhere. And at Paddington a shanty, Tomlin's New Town, had nearly a hundred of these 'small wooden cottages' let from £7 to £12 a year to 'journeymen artificers', a 'little colony of about 600 persons'. Up a rung, formerly smart suburban places by the 1790s had become vulnerable to infiltration by the cocknoi polloi. 'Dined at Turnham Green', Chiswick, the radical playwright Thomas Holcroft confided to his diary in October 1798: 'Complaint of the G— family of the want of rational society. The villas of the place having become the country houses of wealthy but ignorant town tradesmen. Butchers, tailors, tallow-chandlers, &c. who make these their holiday and Sunday seats.' Even London plutocrats could have their cockney moments. 'Old Madam French', with a villa at Hampton, paved over her lawn running down to the river 'with black and white marble in diamonds, exactly like the floor of a church'; and Lord Dudley nearby erected an 'obelisk *below* a hedge, with his canal at right angles with the Thames, and a sham bridge, no broader than that of a violin, and *parallel* to the river'. All this from that true son of London Horace Walpole, owner of a sham-Gothic villa-cum-castle at Twickenham.[69]

So not only London but Londoners too were spreading in every direction at the century's end. London had grown, was growing and (all could see) would grow in years to come. And it was not just bigger than at the beginning of the century. In important ways it was better.

The paving and lighting improvements of the 1760s, and their extensive (though not universal) supervision by commissioners and paid officials, had greatly improved things for all users of London's streets. Foreigners were most impressed by the street lighting: 'nothing can be more superb,' wrote a German military man around 1790, optimistically claiming that there were more lamps in Oxford Street than in the whole of Paris. Frederick Wendeborn, a German resident, noted how London 'exceeds Paris by far in regard to pavement and cleanliness'. These things were not perfect, but no one doubted they had grown very much better during the second half of the century. It was plain, too, that new streets in Westminster near the bridge and Houses of Parliament, at the former Fleet Ditch and in several street widenings in the City had added greatly to the magnificence and grandeur of old London. And the separate centres of the City, Westminster and Southwark had become more closely knit together, more indivisibly 'London', as a result of new bridges and streets. The British capital did indeed look like 'An epitome of a great nation' by the century's end.[70]

But in some ways things were almost certainly worse. The vast majority of old London remained intact. It suffered from the accretion of years on poorly built houses and from landlord disinvestment as capital moved into new building at the outskirts. By the end of the century the classic London slum districts could be easily listed by 'the medical practitioners, whose situation or humanity has led them to be acquainted' with St Giles, Clerkenwell, Holborn, St Luke's, the northern wards of the City, Spitalfields and elsewhere.[71] Old London also suffered from the pressure of population. By 1801 the number of Londoners was at last reliably computed at 866,000 for the built-up area; 959,000 for what would later be London county or Inner London, including places like Kensington, Fulham, Hackney and so on, still detached from the metropolitan edge; and 1.1 million for what would become today's Greater London.[72] So London, constantly growing on the ground, had almost doubled its population over the century.

This pressure of population alone had adverse consequences in old London. One of them began to scandalise Londoners from at least the 1780s. This was the overcrowded state of the London burial grounds, where coffins lay so close to the surface that the rectors' 'hogs root up the bones'. A 'great square pit' at St Giles's churchyard around 1789 revealed 'many rows of coffins piled one upon the other', 'so many putrid corpses, tacked between some slight boards, dispersing their dangerous effluvia over the capital'. And in the early 1790s the retaining wall of a Quaker burial ground in Ewer Street, Southwark, collapsed and the built-up ground, some nine feet high and filled with corpses, toppled into a bricklayer's yard next door, to the 'great horror' of the neighbourhood. Indeed, cheap burials were known to be so temporary that there was a market in second-hand coffins: 'when the Churchyards are full in London, the Sextons take up such bodies as are reduced to Skeletons, throw them back into the earth, and resell the Coffins to make room.'[73]

Similarly, the pressure of numbers at London's centre had made its inadequate sewerage more intolerable still. John Gwynn had called for cesspits to be abolished and replaced with 'publick drains or common-sewers', but he was many years ahead of his time. Cesspools grew in number as the older suburbs of London filled out with backland development in courts and alleys. And the growing numbers of animals killed for food, countless illegal connections to the common sewers intended only for rainwater, and apparently an increasing tendency of the night-men to empty their carts into the sewers discharged even more filth into the Thames. Ned Ward had spoken at the beginning of the century of the river's 'sweet breath'; no one did so at the end, when the water at Blackfriars Bridge was seen to be black with sewage from the Fleet.[74]

Even the great London problem of the age, the difficulty of getting around the metropolis, had failed to ease. Traffic seemed always one step ahead of improved paving, street widening, even new bridges. London just could not accommodate the persons and vehicles that needed to come in, get out or pass through it. Despite the New Road, the centripetal road system and the organisation of transport for hire ensured that most travellers from Harwich, say, to Bristol, or from Dover to York, had to go through London. It was a struggle. John Yeoman made a journey from Berkhamsted, thirty miles north-west of

London, to Brentford, seven miles to the west. With no carriage of his own he had to rely on the coach proprietors' stages and their London inns:

we Set of att Eight o clock with only Two Passengers, but they Still Increaseing till we had twenty one and such fine weather made it a Very Pleasant Journey. we Arived att the Hog in the Pound, Oxford St. about I o Clock . . . and about three o clock we went to the White Horse celler, Piccadily, where was a Couch Just agoing for Brentford, att which Place We Arived about half Past four.[75]

With all these pressures it was small wonder that another wave of City street widenings were under active contemplation by the end of the century. They were urged in press and Parliament by an energetic alderman and Lord Mayor, William Pickett. He had advocated the removal of Temple Bar to ease communications between the City and Westminster, but although that proved a step too far he did secure the purchase and clearance of Back Row and Butcher Row, a shambles of old buildings obstructing the Strand near St Clement Danes Church. And Alderman Skinner agitated successfully to reduce the dangerous gradient of Snow Hill, the entrance to the City from Holborn. The City also, in a larger venture, began to develop land at Moorfields and build Finsbury Square, opening out an avenue to City Road and thence the New Road. These schemes would not be finished till the next century.[76]

In all, London seems to have become even more congested at the century's end than at the beginning. And it was just so full of people:

I believe you will think the town cannot hold all its inhabitants, so prodigiously the population is augmented. I have twice been going to stop my coach in Piccadilly (and the same has happened to Lady Ailesbury) thinking there was a mob, and it was only nymphs and swains sauntering or trudging. T'other morning, i.e. at two o'clock, I went to see Mrs Garrick and Miss H. More at the Adelphi, and was stopped five times before I reached Northumberland House, for the tides of coaches, chariots, curricles, phaetons, etc., are endless.[77]

Just who were these nymphs and swains? And where had they come from?

PART TWO

PEOPLE

Samuel Johnson

III

SAMUEL JOHNSON'S LONDON – BRITONS

'London is Their North-Star': Provincial Londoners

THE greatest Londoner of the eighteenth century – like many great Londoners of any age – was raised in the English provinces. Samuel Johnson was from Lichfield, Staffordshire, born in 1709. His father was a bookseller of fluctuating fortunes who afforded his brilliant son a solid education but couldn't sustain that support through Oxford, which Johnson left in shaming poverty in 1729. Deprived of a gentleman's career in the church or the higher ranks of schoolteaching, he was thrust back on a bookselling life or the petty frustrations of a country schoolmaster. In both his value was undermined less by his stinted formal education than by an affliction of personal oddities and disabilities that only an indomitable will could put in their place. Unusually tall for his times at some six feet, large-framed and big-boned, he would be noticed in any crowd. Worse, his thick-lipped brooding face was scarred by the scrofula (tuberculosis of the skin) that also left him both short-sighted and hard of hearing. Far worse, Johnson suffered from 'the palsy', tics and involuntary movements of arms and legs that could make his shambling gait something close to that of a fairground monster, especially when he felt compelled to perform some wheeling antic ritual that, if tried in the street, would be sure to gather 'a mob round him'. None of this was helped by a lifelong slovenliness in dress or by ravening table manners and a disregard for personal cleanliness: famously, he had no 'passion' for 'clean linen'.[1]

Johnson, then, was a misfit. And his unfittedness for daily intercourse was no aid in overcoming the poverty that dogged him for two-thirds of his life. Even when his wife Elizabeth's dowry enabled him to start a school on his own account – where David Garrick, keen to advance his classical studies, was one of his few pupils – the venture quickly foundered, taking Elizabeth's small nest egg with it.

In March 1737 Johnson decided to leave his 'Tetty' in Staffordshire and seek his fortune in London. Garrick did the same. They walked and rode the 150 miles or so together, sharing one horse between them. No one suspected it at the time, but the arrival of these two young men, Johnson twenty-eight and Garrick just twenty, would prove a momentous conjuncture in the cultural history of London.

Why did Johnson choose London to make his fresh start? Like many provincials of the middling sort, he had some connection with the metropolis. His father had been apprenticed there from Lichfield in 1673 for seven years, his master a stationer called Richard Sympson. Around 1712 the young Samuel made his own London link – and half a memory – when taken to be 'touched' by Queen Anne for the scrofula – the 'king's evil', which many thought could be cured by the royal fingertips. And his uncle Andrew, a pugilist who taught the boy rudiments of self-defence that he would always treasure, had 'kept the ring at Smithfield, appropriated to wrestlers and boxers' and 'was never thrown or conquered'.[2]

Yet Johnson came to London not for the assistance of connection or friends but to pursue an enterprise that would be unimpeded by his physical eccentricities, one more easily pursued in London than anywhere else. He had first offered to write for Edward Cave's *Gentleman's Magazine*, published from St John's Gate, Clerkenwell, in 1734, and Johnson's subsequent failures as a schoolmaster steered him finally in this direction. Literature needed no self-advertisement or silky manners, just a fluent pen. And Johnson's outstanding ability to produce high-quality prose with unerring rapidity encouraged him to try the world's greatest marketplace for print. James Boswell broadened London's appeal for Johnson as 'the great field of genius and exertion, where talents of every kind, have the fullest scope, and the highest encouragement'. In fact, and more helpfully, London uniquely offered Johnson chances that would be unhindered by his disabilities.[3]

As things turned out, London at first was full of bitter disappointment for him. The poverty he suffered, and the disregard he met at every turn, found eloquent expression in *London: A Poem, in Imitation of the Third Satire of Juvenal*, published in 1738. Here London is the site of corruption and false appearance, its vices emasculating the nation's former proud standing in the world, a city of night-time terrors and daytime deceits:

> This mournful Truth is ev'ry where confest,
> SLOW RISES WORTH BY POVERTY DEPREST.

Indeed, Johnson's sojourn in London nearly came to a swift end just a year later. Rapidly, it seems, tiring of London, he vigorously sought a country schoolmaster's position in Shropshire. It came to nothing because he had no MA degree and could not obtain one in the time needed. But we should not forget that Johnson, whose affection for London and London life was second to none in the eighteenth century, had tried to flee from it in desperation within two years of his arrival, and might conceivably have succeeded.

Thrown back on the metropolis, Johnson made his uneasy way there through a succession of temporary lodgings. If we count the rooms he was given by Mr and Mrs Thrale in their four London houses (including Streatham, just beyond the built-up area), Johnson had some twenty-three addresses in forty-seven years.[4] They ranged fleetingly from Greenwich to the new north-western suburbs near Hanover and Cavendish Squares. But Johnson's London was mostly a tightly circumscribed district about three-quarters of a mile long – from Durham Yard, Strand, to Shoe Lane, Fleet Street – and only half a mile wide. When he attended church it was St Clement Danes, just west of Temple Bar, in a crowded mixed parish which included two Pissing Alleys and some very poor property as well as many handsome new streets. Johnson's London, at the meeting point of the two cities of London and Westminster, was the very centre of printing and publishing and a natural home for one who would become the leading literary man of his day.

Once immersed in the London swim, Johnson the misfit at last discovered just how congenial the city was to him. There – perhaps only there – he could be himself: 'The freedom from remark and petty censure, with which life may be passed there, is a circumstance which a man who knows the teazing restraint of a narrow circle must relish highly.' 'No place cured a man's vanity or arrogance so well as London', he thought, because it gathered to it people whose talents and qualities were at least as good as his own. And for a literary man, involved

Strand, Fleet Street, 1761

in the production and dissemination of ideas, and for a curious man, interested in all the vagaries of life, London was 'a heaven upon earth'.[5]

Among those vagaries, London gave Johnson full opportunity to exercise that charity and humanity which even his detractors acknowledged and respected in him. It came not just from religious conviction but from a deep wellspring of egalitarianism. More than any other famous Londoner of his time, Johnson engaged sympathetically with London's lowest depths. He encountered homelessness and probably night-cellars and common lodging houses with his friend Richard Savage, even more penniless than Johnson, in the late 1730s. In later and more prosperous years a friend recalled how 'He frequently gave all the silver in his pocket to the poor who watched him, between the house and the tavern where he dined', and he urged his friends to do the same. When returning home late at night he squeezed pennies into the hands of homeless children sleeping under shop bulks so they might wake up to a breakfast. Finding a hungry prostitute who had fainted in the street one night, he carried her home on his back, fed her and had his household look after her for some time. His friend Mrs Thrale summed up Johnson's humanity: 'He loved the poor as I never yet saw any one else do, with an earnest desire to make them happy.'[6]

His affection found daily domestic expression in the ménage of misfits that he invited into his household whenever he rented a place stable enough to offer them a home. Frank Barber, the freed slave from Jamaica who became Johnson's servant, we'll meet again later. The other three long-standing residents were provincials: Anna Williams, a blind Welsh poet; Robert Levett, a drunken practitioner of physic, born near Hull; and the widowed Mrs Desmoulins, née Swynfen, from Lichfield, whom he took in as housekeeper on a generous allowance with her young daughter. There was also for some time another woman, Poll Carmichael, whose history is obscure. It was not a harmonious arrangement. Mrs Desmoulins hated Williams and Levett with a vengeance. Levett was the oddest of all, attending poor patients for whatever they could give him, often a nip of gin. He had married 'a woman of the town, who had persuaded him (notwithstanding their place of congress was a small-coal shed in Fetter-lane) that she was nearly related to a man of fortune, but was injuriously kept by him out of large possessions'. The marriage failed, with heated recriminations on both sides. Johnson loved

Levett for his charitable physicking of the poor and perhaps because he was even stranger and less of a lover of clean linen than Johnson himself: 'his external appearance and behaviour were such, that he disgusted the rich, and terrified the poor.'[7]

Johnson's 'nests' of provincial Londoners at Gough Square, Johnson's Court and Bolt Court would not have been uncommon in a city of migrants.[8] For migration was one of the great facts of London life in the eighteenth century. Demographers estimate that 8,000 migrants a year were coming to London in the first half of the century, and certain it is that at any point in time a high proportion of Londoners were born outside the metropolis. Just how high is less certain. In 1781 Dr Richard Bland surveyed some 1,600 married couples who were assisted through childbirth by the Westminster General Dispensary. He found that just one in four individuals was born in London, over half were born elsewhere in England and Wales (including rural Middlesex), 8.6 per cent were Irish, 6.5 per cent Scottish and fifty-three or 1.6 per cent were 'foreigners'. Of the migrants, 53 per cent were men. [9]

We should not extrapolate too far from this small sample of the lower-middling classes and the 'poorer sort' who would have made use of the dispensary's services. But there is much circumstantial evidence of large numbers of the provincial-born in eighteenth-century London. Of a sample of 153 beggars arrested in the City between 1738 and 1742, just over half had no 'legal settlement in the metropolitan London area'. A similar survey in 1796–7 of 1,226 English beggars in London, nine out of ten of them women, found 31 per cent had settlements further than ten miles from the metropolis. These need not all have come to London as beggars, of course, for provincials arrived from every rank: in the early years of the century one in four of London apprentices claimed to come from country 'gentry' stock. And although we might reasonably assume that most migrants to London came from those nearby counties most powerfully affected by its draw, and despite the difficulties of long-distance travel, contemporaries noted how 'The numbers of persons, who with their families, find their way to the Metropolis, from the most remote quarters of Great Britain and Ireland, is inconceivable.'[10]

We might instance the truth of that from the poor law records of Samuel Johnson's adopted parish of St Clement Danes. Truly metropolitan, in the heart of ancient London though it was, Londoners down on their luck who sought relief at St Clement's workhouse door had come there from all over England and Wales. A sample of 100 applicants for relief in 1752–3 reveals twenty-seven with clear provincial links or connections to places further afield. We hear of an agricultural labourer from Tiverton, Devon, a stableman from 'Morvan [Malvern] under the hill in Gloucestershire', a deserted wife from Worcester, a widow from Lincoln, a farm labourer from Skeffling, Yorkshire, men and women from Liverpool to Alverstoke in Hampshire – and poor Lucy Holland, just eight years old and alone in London, born at Shrewsbury (Shropshire) 'as she hath been informed both by her Mother and Godfather'. Indeed, this pattern of provincial migration to London is visible everywhere. Even on the gallows, a single execution at Tyburn in August 1746 dispatched highway robbers born in Dorset, Wales, Newry (Armagh), Leicester Fields (London) and two from rural Surrey. In 1841 four out of ten Londoners were born outside the metropolis, the proportion falling somewhat by the end of the nineteenth century. There are no reliable figures for the earlier period but it seems reasonable to assume that around a half of all Londoners and possibly more were born outside the metropolis during much of the eighteenth century.[11]

What brought so many to London? Its magnetic attraction was embedded in those factors we have already noted as influencing metropolitan growth: the increasing fashionableness of a London home for the country gentry, lured there as the seat of sophistication; the ever-expanding luxury that accompanied them, drawing in its wake craftsmen, painters, musicians and actors who otherwise had only constricted provincial opportunities to support themselves; the growth of trade that needed investors, bankers, clerks, accountants, solicitors, warehousemen and shopmen to keep cash and credit in circulation; and the attractions – even the fatal attractions – of London life, made known to every Briton through newspapers and magazines, through novels and plays, and through prints that brought to life the fashions and foibles of the giant metropolis.

London never loomed larger in the life of the nation – and that is saying much – than it did in the eighteenth century. Its appetite for labour of all kinds, but most of all for the ablest in every calling, was unquenchable. Throughout the century it was a truism, engraved into the national consciousness, that London was the true object of talent: 'in most families of *England*, if there be any son or daughter that excels the rest in beauty or wit, or perhaps courage, or industry, or any other rare quality; London is their north-star, and they are never at rest till they point directly thither.' It was said that London to the English was 'as the Mahometans consider the Paradise promised them by their prophet'.[12]

A true galaxy of genius undertook the journey. A respectable proportion of the men and women who made eighteenth-century London its scintillating self – for contemporaries and posterity alike – hailed originally from the English provinces and Wales. In the arts the greatest London painters came largely from country stock. The West Country connection here was prodigious. Francis Hayman, the history painter, and his London tutor Robert Browne were both Devon men. So were Joshua Reynolds and *his* London master Thomas Hudson, and so was Ozias Humphry, the miniaturist. Sir James Thornhill, mentor and father-in-law to William Hogarth, was raised nearby in Dorset. And from the other side of the country, Thomas Gainsborough, a great favourite with fashionable London, was brought up in Suffolk. Only a few of the architects who were most active in shaping the metropolis on the ground were London-born: William Kent was from Yorkshire and so was Thomas Ripley, who reputedly walked to London to seek his fortune; Nicholas Hawksmoor was born in Nottinghamshire and John James at Basingstoke in Hampshire. In literature, even those most associated with London writing came from elsewhere: Ned Ward, the archetypal cockney versifier, was probably brought up in Leicestershire or nearby; Joseph Addison, whose *Spectator* moulded metropolitan taste in the early years of the century, was raised in a country vicarage near Salisbury Plain; Henry Fielding was born not far away in Glastonbury and was brought up in Dorset; John Gay – whose *Beggar's Opera*, set in Newgate, was the theatrical hit of the century – was from north Devon; and William Godwin was from Wisbech, Cambridgeshire. Among prominent literary hostesses, Hester Thrale was Welsh and Elizabeth Montagu a Yorkshirewoman. Even in the substructure of literature, as it were, such distinctively metropolitan trades as printing, bookselling and publishing had many provincial migrants among their most distinguished names: Robert Dodsley the publisher was from Mansfield, Nottinghamshire; John Newbery, famous and rich as a publisher of children's books in particular, was born in Berkshire; John Boydell, print seller, publisher and City alderman, came from Shropshire; the type-founder William Caslon came from Worcestershire; Edward Cave, publisher of the *Gentleman's Magazine* and Samuel Johnson's first London employer, was a fellow Midlander, born in Rugby. The theatre, too, was very largely a metropolitan institution in the eighteenth century, but those who wrote for it and acted in it came from all over. Besides David Garrick of Lichfield – actor, manager, playwright and greatest theatrical celebrity of his age – Elizabeth Inchbald (actress and playwright) was from Bury St Edmunds, Samuel Foote (whose London farces kept audiences chuckling for decades) was a Cornishman, Christopher Rich the impresario came from Somerset; and Richard Cumberland the playwright came from Northamptonshire. Polished most brightly among the London furniture makers were Thomas Chippendale from Otley, Yorkshire, and Thomas Sheraton, from Stockton-on-Tees, County Durham; and among the watchmakers were Thomas Tompion from Bedfordshire and John Harrison, inventor of the famous chronometer that measured longitude, a Yorkshireman. Clerics and philanthropists likewise came from far afield, like 'the unfortunate' Reverend William Dodd from Bourne in Lincolnshire, Jonas Hanway from Portsmouth and Granville Sharp, the anti-slavery campaigner, from Durham. The antiquarians of London had provincials among them, like Daniel Lysons from Gloucestershire, Thomas Pennant, a Welshman, and John Britton from Chippenham, Wiltshire. Even the chief citizens more often than not were from outside the metropolis: of twenty-one of the best-known City aldermen of the century just seven were born in London or the satellite villages around; and of the best-known merchants just one in four was born there.[13]

The draw of London was felt at every social level. Most migrants came for work and most worked with their hands. They included the very humble, like women from north Wales and Shropshire who dominated fruit and pea and bean picking in the market gardens at the edge of west London. Their number, it was said in 1798, 'is astonishing. Their industry is unequalled in Britain, or perhaps in the world. The fruitwomen will labour several hours in the garden, and go to and from the London markets twice a day, though at from four to seven miles distance', all for a daily shilling. Many took their earnings back home with them in the winter, but some stayed and made a home for themselves – the milkmaids of Islington were frequently Welsh girls, for instance.[14]

Certainly a large proportion of migrants to London were young women in domestic service, arriving by 'waggon loads' it was said in 1762. A French lodger in Leicester Fields around this time observed a new servant, 'a fat Welsh girl, who was just come out of the country, scarce understood a word of English, was capable of nothing but washing, scowering, and sweeping the rooms, and had no inclination to learn anything more'. And James Boswell was struck by 'a pretty little Yorkshire maid called Mary' when he lodged in Old Bond Street in 1769.[15]

So the countryside sent servant maids, the ports provided London with sailors, the market towns with building craftsmen and apprentices, the villages with labourers. Welshmen gave London many chairmen, footmen, porters and pettifogging solicitors. 'Vagabonds' came from 'all Parts of the Kingdom', among them 'vagrant Children' who 'cannot, or will not, discover [reveal] the Places of their Settlement', as London's magistrates complained to the House of Commons in 1732. 'LONDON is the grand Reservoir, or Common-Sewer of the World'. Within its 'Scum and Filth' it was said that 'Scotland sends us Pedlars, Beggars, and Quacks'.[16] But as we've already had cause to notice, Scotland sent London a great deal more than that.

'Men Very Fit for Business': North Britons

The Scots had a long history in London. They were even credited with joining the two cities of London and Westminster in the early seventeenth century, when 'the great number of Scotch who came to London on the accession of James I [1603] settled chiefly along the Strand'.[17] But London only truly became the capital of Scotland, and so the place for Scots to seek their fortune as naturally as the English, with the Act of Union of 1707. The Union filled the metropolis, or so it seemed, with Scottish peers, politicians, churchmen, soldiers and professionals of one complexion or another. They were generally resented for their opportunism and cliquishness, and mistrusted for their loyalty to the Jacobite succession. Above all they were envied for their success. At court they were favoured as diplomats and officials and in the middling classes they were just too good at whatever way of life they chose, 'men very fit for business, intriguing, cunning, tricking', without 'much honour or conscience'.[18] This stereotyping of the overweening Scotsman remained pretty constant through the century, perhaps tailing off towards the end, and North Britons were always fair game on the London stage.

This general unpopularity of the Scots in London probably interfered little with the normal intercourse of individuals. Samuel Johnson, for instance, who had great fun goading the North British, had numerous Scottish friends (among them his chosen biographer) and selected five of his six assistants on his famous *Dictionary of the English Language* (1755) from among the London Scots. But there were moments in the century when this simmering prejudice became dangerous. The rebellions of 1715–16 and 1745–6 were largely Scottish affairs, and many were brought to London to suffer for their treason. For decades, Scottish heads on pikes decorated Temple Bar, the gateway between London and Westminster used by thousands each day. They remained a grisly reminder of the old enmity until they finally fell to the ravages of time in the early 1770s.[19] At these moments of high anxiety, Scots in London were at least at risk of a drubbing. In April 1746 Alexander Carlyle, a young Scottish divinity student on his first visit to London,

was in the coffeehouse with Smollett when the news of the battle of Culloden arrived, and when London all over was in a perfect uproar of joy . . . About 9 o'clock I wished to go home to Lyon's, in New Bond Street, as I had promised to sup with him that night . . . I asked Smollett if he was ready to go, as he lived at Mayfair; he said he was and would conduct me. The mob were so riotous, and the squibs so numerous and incessant that we were glad to go into a narrow entry to put our wigs in our pockets, and to take our swords from our belts and walk with them in our hands, as everybody then wore swords; and, after cautioning me against speaking a word, lest the mob should discover my country and become insolent, 'for John Bull', says he, 'is as haughty and valiant to-night as he was abject and cowardly on the Black Wednesday when the Highlanders were at Derby.' After we got to the head of the Haymarket through incessant fire, the Doctor led me by narrow lanes, where we met nobody but a few boys at a pitiful bonfire, who very civilly asked us for sixpence, which I gave them.[20]

The last high point of anti-Scottish prejudice in London was connected with the unpopular rise of Lord Bute as the mentor of Prince George, later the young George III. The Bute camp slotted many Scots into government places and contracts, as we saw in Chapter 2. The London anti-Scottish agitation was fuelled by much aggressive journalism, notably by the radical John Wilkes in the *North Briton*, but it plainly resonated among all ranks of Londoner. James Boswell unwittingly chose this difficult time to make his first extensive stay in London. On the evening of 8 December 1762, at Covent Garden to watch Isaac Bickerstaffe's new comic opera *Love in a Village*, 'two Highland officers came in. The mob in the upper gallery roared out, "No Scots! No Scots! Out with them!", hissed and pelted them with apples.'[21] Even the Scotch granite used to pave the improved streets of Westminster and the City a few years later gave an opportunity for doggerel satire at the expense of the North Britons' insinuating ways:

> The new Scottish pavement is worthy of praise,
> We're indebted to Scotland for mending our way's;
> But, what we can never forgive them, some say,
> Is, that they have taken our *Posts* all away.[22]

Nonetheless, even at the height of their odium, nothing deterred the Scots from coming to London. The top ranks of the London professions were full of them. We have already seen how Scotsmen – Gibbs, the Adam brothers, Chambers, Mylne – dominated the architectural profession in London. Similarly the two greatest lawyers of the century were both Scots. William Murray, the first Lord Mansfield, was born in Perth in 1705. He reputedly rode on horseback from his home to London and Westminster School in 1719 and never returned. 'Much may be made of a Scotchman, if he be *caught* young,' Johnson mused, and it was Mansfield he had in mind. A judge of brilliant acumen and convincing eloquence, he figured large in the major trials and political dramas of his long life, dying at Kenwood, his country house in Hampstead, in 1793. Of a later generation, Thomas Erskine was born in Edinburgh in 1750 and after a few false starts determined to try his fortune at the London bar, entering Lincoln's Inn in 1775. He found he had a genius for advocacy. He had courage too, defending London radicals in the treason trials of the 1790s. Besides these there were Scottish painters (Allan Ramsay, favourite portrait painter of the young George III through Bute's influence), novelists and men of letters (Tobias Smollett and James Boswell prominent among them), poets and playwrights (Joseph Mitchell, David Mallet or Malloch, and James Thomson of *The Seasons* fame, combining in a metropolitan Scottish literary coterie in the 1720s), antiquarians (William Maitland, historian and topographer of London was born in Brechin), even London rakes – William Douglas, the Fourth Duke of Queensberry, was one of the most outrageous gamblers and sybarites of his own or any other age, ending his long-lived days, lustful to the last, at his Piccadilly mansion in 1810.

Of all the professions, the London Scots excelled in two – banking and medicine. In banking, despite numerous smaller fry like Alexander Fordyce, who brought the British banking system to its knees in 1772 through reckless speculations, two names were most gilded. The Drummonds of Charing Cross, who were nearly undone by their suspected Jacobite sympathies in the '45, and Thomas Coutts, in partnership with his brother James from 1761, of the Strand. Thomas Coutts in particular was centrally connected both to plutocratic Scottish life in and out of London and more widely to the metropolitan rich, even financing the gambling debts of its greatest profligates. Once more through Bute's pervasive influence, Coutts became personal banker to George III, the foundation of long-lasting ties between the British royal family and the bank on the Strand.

Finally, the spread of the Scots into London medicine was astonishing. Medical training in Scotland was particularly advanced and once young men had obtained their MD at Edinburgh, Aberdeen, St Andrews or Glasgow, then a London career was open to them, if sometimes with a little difficulty. Anti-Scottish prejudice was rife in London's medical societies, at least in the middle of the century. Smollett, a medical man before a writer, recorded what sounds like a real experience when Roderick Random's examiner at Surgeon's Hall complains that, '"you Scotchmen have overspread us of late as the locusts did Egypt."'[23] Most of the main London hospitals elected Scotsmen to be among their physicians and surgeons. In one branch, obstetrics, the Scots were paramount, following the lead of William Smellie from Lanarkshire, in London for most of the twenty years from 1739, whose textbook and redesigned forceps made him the foremost authority on childbirth in the land. Accordingly, Scottish physicians were appointed to all the London lying-in hospitals and, at the other end of the social spectrum, assisted at births at what seemed like every fashionable address in London. William Hunter, a student of Smellie's, was the leading 'man-midwife' when his tutor left London. At a weekly club for Scottish medical men at the British Coffee House, Hunter's toast was, 'May no English nobleman venture out of the world without a Scottish physician, as I am sure there are none who venture in.'[24]

Besides these brilliant sons of the Scottish enlightenment their plebeian compatriots, both men and women, were no less reluctant to take the high road to London. Thomas Hardy, one of the radicals tried for treason whom Erskine successfully defended at the Old Bailey in 1794, was a Glasgow shoemaker, born in Stirlingshire. Talking to an employer who knew London, Hardy's 'curiosity was excited, and he determined to see it'. Hardy set out on board a smack from Glasgow and arrived eleven days later in April 1774 with 18d in his pocket. He found work before it was spent, helped by a letter of introduction from his former master.[25]

Perhaps we know most of any working man coming from Scotland to London through the unpublished memoirs and diary of Samuel Kevan, born in 1764. His father was forcibly ejected from his farm in 1767 'by the House of Galloway', and the devoutly Protestant family moved to nearby Wigtown. In 1779 Samuel was apprenticed to his brother, a stonemason and slater, for three years. At eighteen or nineteen he determined to 'push my fortune in the Land of comerce & Money' and joined another brother in Liverpool, eventually moving to Stone in Staffordshire.

Passing at the upper part of the Street, the London coach made a stop at the Inn nr the Market it struck me, I should go with it to London . . . and paid the fare, 25 Shillings, and on Wednesday evening Octr 1st 1783 was at the Swan with two necks Lad Lane London –

Four shillings & six pence was my stock of Money when I arrived at the Capital. One shilling I paid for my bed and had no break fast next day –

Here was a young soft lad with out friend or advisor Master of no trade, and without Tools – One spare Shirt & pair of Stockings all the rest at Newcastle [under Lyme]. – Plastering was my pursuit all day on Thursday, but still unsuccesfull, and if I had, I was unable for it. – The evening was drawing on, and I was in Hyde park going from Piccadilly toward Oxford Street, I betook myself to most earnest request for assistance and direction in that trying & forlorn condition in such a manner, as I never had before, nor durst since. The roof of a House appair'd boarded ready for slating I recollected that was the business I was best acquainted with, and shaped my course there; coming near

I met the Master Slater & some men, knowing them by their tools, ask'd for work, was question'd where I lodg'd, if I had tools & and I told a plain tale that I was just arriv'd in Town & Southwood, for that was his name, took me home to his own house [in Store Street, Tottenham Court Road], I slept with one of his Sons – Mrs S. was a little unwilling at first – went to work next day, Friday – This Mr S. had the character of an irregular drinking man, but I rec^d the greatest kindness from him, particularly in being taken to his own house – he gave me near the full wages, 16/ was then the highest.[26]

Kevan made London his home. Others were doubtless more transitory, perhaps like the 'poor young girl', her accent 'broad Scotch', who in 1778 asked the writer Richard Lovell Edgeworth what street she was in. She had just arrived in London and was searching for a friend, Peggy, in service in this street but whose house number and employer's name had been forgotten. Edgeworth accompanied the girl and explained her plight at every door till Peggy was happily discovered.[27]

What of the beggars that Scotland was reputed in the 1740s to send to London? In fact they were scarce, at least in the decades that followed. In the samples of St Clement's poor law applications just one in 100 claimed any Scottish connection in 1752–3 and three in 100 in 1790–91. And out of 2,000 beggars in the streets of London questioned in 1796–7 just sixty-five (or 3.25 per cent) had a settlement in Scotland.[28] Indeed, the largest single group among the beggars, over four out of ten, seems likely to have been women and men (for such were the proportions) born and bred in London or within ten miles of it. And no doubt there were many true cockneys among them.

'Within the Sound of Bow Bell': Cockneys and Citizens

In this city of migrants, where so many Londoners had come originally from elsewhere, it was still the London-born who formed the largest single group. In the absence of firm numbers, it seems reasonable to assume that the London-born clustered most densely at the heart of London, in the ancient City itself and its near suburbs. At least in the early part of the century there still seems to have been some truth in the view that the 'confirmed Cockney' was to be found 'within the sound of Bow bell', St Mary-le-Bow, Cheapside, in the centre of the City.[29]

A number of factors made this likely. First among them were the benefits of 'being free' of the City of London. It was as close to an assurance of being able to make a living as anyone was likely to get in the eighteenth century. A freeman could acquire his advantages through birth, apprenticeship or purchase. Freedom of the City was thus by no means the sole province of the City, or even the London-born, and there were many provincials and others there among the ranks of apprentices and domestic servants. But the son of a freeman would know the utility of taking up his birthright. Freedom offered some protection from kidnap by the pressgang and from some tolls on his goods; it permitted him to trade in the City as shopkeeper, artificer or manufacturer, or waterman, lighterman, carman and porter; only freemen could hold a licence as publican or stockbroker; and if a freeman left orphaned children in their minority the City's Court of Orphans might offer them protection. Even a journeyman who was not a freeman risked dismissal as not entitled to work for a City employer. These benefits probably tended towards residential loyalty to the City from one generation to another.[30]

Secondly, freedom was attainable only through membership of one of the City's guilds or companies, many of ancient establishment and wealthy endowment, which sought to protect the interests of producers in a wide range of London industries, from commerce to manufacturing. All tried to create a monopoly for their freemen members. They had limited success, and their grip on the trades of London loosened as the century wore on. Nonetheless, the companies' influence tended to the location of certain trades in or close to the City: the mercantile businesses involved in importing, shipping, banking and insurance; the wholesale markets in fish, meat and poultry; the great City retailing industries in drapers' goods, haberdashery and dress; and manufactures like brewing and distilling, clock- and coachmaking; and workers in gold and silver, gunsmiths, stationers (including printers, booksellers and publishers) and many more. These traditional London industries were those to which the London-born were most readily apprenticed, because most familiar to them. And their central locations exerted a gravitational residential pull on workers who needed to live close to or over the shop.

For a few instances of this association of the London-born with London trades and continued London residence we might cite William Hogarth, born in 1697 at Bartholomew Close, Smithfield, his father from Westmorland; the young William was apprenticed to a silver plate engraver in Blue Cross Street, Leicester Fields. Or William Shipley, founder of the Society of Arts, baptised at St Stephen Walbrook in 1715, his father from Leeds and mother from Hampshire; William, following in his father's footsteps, was apprenticed to a stationer in Poultry. Or Richard Stevens, organist and composer, born in Bell Alley, Coleman Street, 1757, from Wiltshire wool-spinning stock; his father, a freeman of the Haberdashers' Company but a keen amateur flautist, apprenticed his son to the Master of the Boys of St Paul's to learn singing and the harpsichord. Or William Braund, a rich Portugal merchant, his father from Devon but at William's birth in 1695 a vintner and citizen of London; William was apprenticed to an eminent City merchant, Christopher Emmett. These were all men born to families of the London middling classes, and somewhere in the middle of them. None was sufficiently well off to be schooled for the university and the church or the law, none rich enough to anticipate a life of leisure on rents or dividends. The life chances they inherited grounded them in London.[31]

The London-born poor were subject to different forces, some of which also tended to keep them close to their place of birth. Even in a century of great geographical mobility and adventurousness – those very features that brought men and women from all over Britain to London in their tens of thousands – there were consolations in staying put. A 'settlement' in a parish gave the right to claim some sort of relief in the event of poverty striking in old age or sickness, bereavement or marital desertion. This could be obtained by birth or inheritance: a father's settlement passed to a son or daughter. Settlements could also be secured, among other ways, by renting a house at over £10 a year, by serving an apprenticeship, or by having been a weekly servant for a year or more to an employer in the parish. A wife shared her husband's settlement.[32] In the City and nearby suburbs, the nation's centre of apprenticeships and of inns, coffee houses, manufacturers' workshops, warehouses and shops employing countless 'servants', there were many opportunities to acquire a settlement. The parish of the most recent settlement had to accept the burden of relief. Not moving too far from a place of settlement, even if not the parish of birth, secured relief without the need of 'removal' to a place far away.

The poor law records of St Clement Danes give us some insight into these long-term patterns of residential settlement and mobility within the dense centre of London, tightly circumscribed though it was. These cases are all from 1790–91, of persons temporarily destitute and presenting for relief at the workhouse. And we should note that St Clement's had a reputation as a 'casualty parish', less scrupulous than many about a local connection before offering relief, and so might have drawn more supplicants from other parishes than was normal. We find Margaret Forrest, 'Poor and unable to maintain herself . . . during her lying in', married at St Mary le Strand to a sailor in the Royal Navy, now at sea; he was born at the Artichoke in White Hart Yard, St Martin-in-the-Fields, an illegitimate son. Charlotte Davies, twenty-three, single and pregnant, was born in Union Court, Holborn, her father subsequently renting a whole house in Church Yard, Fetter Lane, St Clement Danes, where he died; her mother would not or could not help her in her present plight. William Fitzgerald, born around 1715, had married at St Mary le Strand, rented a house in Bennetts Court, Drury Lane, and lodged for the past five years in Hemlock Court, both in St Clement Danes. And so on. The pattern for most, from the little indeed that we know about these lives, is a connection with central London in general, rather than with any parish in particular.[33]

Did anything mark out these Londoners from the migrants all around them? There was, of course, the London dialect. It was mostly remarked in the transposition of v and w, betraying even those with genteel pretensions to be of cockney (and thus plebeian) origins, and there were a few other notable peculiarities. Lady Peckham, in Thomas Holcroft's comedy *The School for Arrogance* (1791), gives 'vhat' for what and 'vus' for was, 'wery' for very and 'willin' for villain; she adds a redundant d to 'gownd' or 'ownd' and an n to 'yourn'; and she says 'purtend' and 'purtensious'. Holcroft was born in Orange Court, Leicester Fields, in 1745, his father running a struggling shoe shop, and these linguistic quirks ring true. Something like them had been the stuff of metropolitan stagecraft since the 1760s if not before. We might add the occasional use of 'ax' for ask – by Zachariah Fungus, the commissary in Samuel Foote's farce of that name (1765) – and the ubiquitous 'them there' and 'this here', cockney currency even among City aldermen it was said.[34]

There were other things, too, about the long-term Londoner that struck newcomers to the city. The ceaseless bustle and excitement of the streets – at first so inchoate and perplexing to the stranger – endowed

Londoners with a liveliness of apprehension and quick-wittedness that separated them from country arrivals. It led to a sense of superiority, as Tate Wilkinson, an actor and impresario born in the Savoy in 1739, later recalled: 'till the age of seventeen, I judged every man and woman I saw ignorant and stupid who lived two miles from Richmond and Hampton Court.' Though his father was a clergyman, admittedly loose enough in his conduct to get himself transported, Wilkinson's 'dialect conform[ed] to my brother Cockneys', among whom he was taken as 'a man of knowledge, being a Londoner'.[35]

A tendency to hubris underlay what many saw as the defining characteristic of the Londoner: a truculent egalitarianism. It was markedly true on the Thames, where any waterman plying for hire, a trade passed from father to son in London's waterside districts, claimed the right 'to call out whatever he pleases to other occupants of boats, even were it to be the King himself, and no one has a right to be shocked'. And it was true in the public thoroughfares, where 'A man in court dress cannot walk the streets of London without being pelted with mud by the mob, while the gentlemen look on and laugh', and where a gentleman having a disagreement with one of 'the populace . . . is at once invited to strip and fight'. A London guide of 1768 warned that 'the rabble, or those who compose the mob, tho' much mended in this respect within the last fifty years, are still very insolent and abusive . . . When this happens, it is always prudent to retire and give them their way.' An American merchant complained to a compatriot in 1771 that London 'is the devil of a place, for nobody in the street pays any more attention to him, a well-bred, dressed gentleman than to a porter . . .'[36] Around the same time, however, a German visitor saw another and more positive side to this democratic spirit: 'No minister . . . no titled minion will venture to make the poorest give place to him in the street; and yet they daily pass on foot through the best-peopled and most-frequented streets of London, where they are pressed and elbowed, and bespattered, without once offering to complain.'[37]

The egalitarianism of the streets spilled into the pleasure gardens and public entertainments, where it adopted new forms of Jack's-as-good-as-his-master. Dress and fashion were preoccupations of the age for all ranks and it was not always easy to spot class difference by judging appearances alone: 'To guess at the rank of life of those who appear in the streets, or in public places, is a difficult matter,' thought a German resident in 1791. That was much decried as indicating the spread of luxury and the demise of deference. So apprentices were censured for donning fashionable 'Swords and Tye Wigs, or Toupees' on Sundays, and 'fashionable figures' at the 'gayest places of public entertainment' were 'found to be journeyman tailors, serving men, and abigails, disguised like their betters'. 'In short,' remarked Tobias Smollett in the voice of prickly Matt Bramble excoriating London life around 1770, 'there is no distinction or subordination left – The different departments of life are jumbled together – The hod-carrier, the low mechanic, the tapster, the publican, the shop-keeper, the pettifogger, the citizen, and courtier, *all tread upon the kibes of one another* . . .' [38]

When Smollett combines the citizen and courtier in this way he shows how far, in one degree at least, London had come to eliding the court end of town and the City and making them not two countries, as Addison had put it in 1712, but one. It was perhaps for this very reason, one class usurping what another had long treasured to itself, that the householder and freeman of the City of London was such an object of satire and derision. The citizen – more familiarly, the cit – epitomised trade, a huckster's eye for buying cheap and selling dear, and the unscrupulous accumulation of 'new money' not founded in the eternal verities of land and inheritance. In fact, new money was eagerly sought by out-of-pocket aristocrats with a son or daughter to marry for ready cash. But that awkward truth did not stem for a moment the vitriol directed at the citizen of London in novels and verse, in the journals or on the stage, and in the daily conversation of all in the professions and above who claimed some sort of superiority over the trading sort.

The snobbery was merciless. It lasted throughout the century. Sometimes, indeed, the citizens made themselves easy targets. There was many a chuckle, for instance, at the readiness of City worthies to claim an ancient family line and have it represented in coats of arms, approved by Heralds' College for the appropriate fee. When the herald agrees to invent a coat of arms for the recently deceased Alderman Gathergrease in Steele's *The Funeral*, the undertaker quips, 'let him bear a Pair of Stockings, he's the first of his Family that ever wore one . . .' [39] But in general, satire at the expense of the citizens was wit at its most obvious, relying as always on snobbery's ready stereotypes. They were 'illiterate and under-bred', aspiring to the à la mode but really 'completely old-fashioned', their country boxes with 'a small Chinese gate', an island (with a lamb) on a pond (with a swan, 'a wooden one') and 'a grotto with patterns in shells': grottoes had been smart but once adopted by the cits they were objects of scorn. They worshipped money, and boasted how their West End acquaintances would see how the citizens 'eat gold, and drink gold, and lie in gold'. And they were notoriously greedy, especially at their City feasts on Lord Mayor's Day and other occasions, when they 'Gormandize, like Beasts, not eat like Men'.[40]

This snobbery was at its fiercest when the cits trod on the shoe buckles of those at the polite end of the town by emulating fashionable living:

> yet with all Aids whatsoever, they appear at best but as very mean *Copies* of fine *Originals*; the *Ludgate-Hill Hobble*, the *Cheapside Swing*, and the general City *Jolt* and *Wriggle* in the *Gait*, being easily perceived through all the Artifices the *Smarts* and *Perts* put upon them. A Man may *waddle* into a Church, or Coffee-House, make a Leg to an Alderman, Levee a Common-Council-Man in his Counting-House, he may *D—mn* with a good Air, Dress well, Drink well, and even hum over two or three Opera Tunes, and pass in all the Wards of the City for a well-bred Person; but towards *St. James's* he won't pass muster, he must be . . . return'd back to *Leaden-Hall*, like a counterfeit Guinea that won't go.[41]

In one regard at least, the stereotyping of the citizen as knowing – and wanting to know – only the City and its moneymaking ways had begun to weaken by the century's end. 'Your true Cockney, who never was out of the sound of Bow bell, is uncommon in the present age,' wrote Vicesimus Knox in 1790. 'No persons ramble more than the citizens, to Bath, Tunbridge, Brighthelmstone, Margate, and all other places of fashionable resort.' He thought the old commercial values of the City had been diluted as a consequence. And the withering away of the City's residential function began to dislodge the old ways of 'living over the shop'.[42]

Knox's rambling cockney was undoubtedly a feature of the age. London sent its sons and daughters all over Great Britain, indeed all over the world. Sometimes outward migration was a sign of success – the London merchant taking up his country seat and swiftly satirised for his pains. Sometimes it was to escape a London that had become unbearably harsh for one reason or another. 'I was born in London, in the year 1738,' recalled Mary Saxby. 'My mother dying when I was very young, and my father going into the army, I was exposed to distress even in my infancy.' By the age of twelve or so she had run away from London and gone on the tramp, it seems never to have returned.[43] And sometimes migration was a forcible ejection, tens of thousands of Londoners transported to colonies in the Americas and Australia after conviction at the London, Middlesex or Surrey sessions. So not all found their fortune in London. And for almost everyone, life in London had much of struggle about it.

'A Very Neat First Floor': Living and Dying

There is not perhaps another city of its size in the whole world, the streets of which display a greater contrast in the wealth and misery, the honesty and knavery, of its inhabitants than the city of London. The eyes of the passing stranger (unaccustomed to witness such scenes) is at one moment dazzled by the appearance of pompous wealth, with its splendid equipage – at the next he is solicited by one apparently of the most wretched of human beings, to import a single penny for the relief of his starving family![44]

So wrote Israel Potter, an American prisoner of war who absconded from his British captors and made a life for himself in London for many years from 1781. Those contrasts of flaunting riches and starving poverty were apparent to all with eyes to see, though few were prepared to say so in the forthright manner of the American democrat.

We might start, as contemporaries would have done, in the realms of 'pompous wealth', among the quality, the *ton*, the beau-monde, the fashionable rich who could afford all that London – and so the world – had to offer. And we might take as instances the luxurious lifestyles of two commoners who could rival, though not surpass, the wealth of the richest aristocrats in London.

Among many wealthy Londoners vainglorious to the point of absurdity was George Bubb Dodington, originally from Herefordshire, heir to a tremendous fortune from his uncle. Bubb Dodington was a Whig politician and diplomat, studiedly old-fashioned like something from the Restoration: his 'bulk and corpulency gave full display to a vast expanse and profusion of brocade and embroidery . . . set off with an enormous tye-periwig and deep laced ruffles'. He made do with a country mansion in Dorset, a villa in Hammersmith and a town house in Pall Mall. They were all 'such establishments as few nobles in the nation were possessed of'. His lifestyle in the 1750s was recalled by the playwright Richard Cumberland:

he was not to be approached but through a suite of apartments, and rarely seated but under painted ceilings and gilt entablatures. In his villa you were conducted through two rows of antique marble statues ranged in a gallery floored with the rarest marbles, and enriched with columns of granite and lapis lazuli; his saloon was hung with the finest Gobelin tapestry, and he slept in a bed encanopied with peacocks' feathers in the style of Mrs. Montague. When he passed from Pall-Mall to La Trappe [his villa in Hammersmith, where only men were to be found] it was always in a coach, which I could suspect had been his ambassadorial equipage at Madrid, drawn by six fat unwieldy black horses, short docked and of colossal dignity . . .[45]

Our other exemplar of the London rich is that same Mrs Montagu whose passion for feathers Bubb Dodington shared. Elizabeth Montagu was born in Yorkshire to a landowning family and acquired a fortune through her husband, a coal owner in County Durham. On his death in 1775 she inherited everything. Already famous as one of the great literary 'blue-stocking' hostesses from her house in Hill Street, Mayfair, on her widowhood she bought a giant plot on a ninety-nine-year lease in the north-west corner of Portman Square and instructed James 'Athenian' Stuart to build her a mansion there. Her 'palace' was finished in 1781. Montagu House was of nine bays on three floors, set in a large garden with an extensive courtyard for carriages at the front. The first floor included a 'great room' for assemblies, a gallery for pictures and statues, a vast dining room, a 'room for morning company' and a suite of rooms for Mrs Montagu and her maid. The ceilings were painted by Angelica Kauffman and the finest decorative artists from Italy, the friezes were elaborately delicate plasterwork, and the morning room would eventually be covered in Mrs Montagu's favourite feathers. In this exotic residence, full of rich beauties, Mrs Montagu's guests ranged from George III and Queen Charlotte to David Garrick, Joshua Reynolds and Dr Johnson himself; indeed, ranged wider, for on May Day Mrs Montagu gave an annual feast of beef and plum pudding to the boy chimney sweeps of London, allowing them full reign of her garden, if not the feathered morning room. A few weeks after one of these, in

May 1792, Fanny Burney attended a 'public breakfast' that Mrs
Montagu gave for 'four or five hundred people'. The throng mingled
in 'the Feather Room'. The dining room was decorated 'very splendidly'
with not a seat to be had at the table, but Fanny 'had a very good beau
in Major Rendell, who took charge of any catering and regale'. The
company was at its elegant best, but Mrs Warren Hastings was dressed
like 'an Indian princess, according to our ideas of such ladies, and so
much the most splendid, from its ornaments, and style, and fashion,
though chiefly of muslin, that everybody else looked under-dressed in
her presence'.[46]

This was the London lived by the wealthiest Londoners, probably
fewer than 1,500 households, their influence far in excess of their
number. A few thousand more could count themselves wealthy, with
annual incomes greater than £1,000 and with a town or counting house
to themselves, though still usually rented by the year or on a lease much
shorter than Mrs Montagu's. Relatively few had a freehold. There were
then the many thousands of households of the middling sort, with
annual incomes from, say, £100 to £1,000. As is apparent from the
sums, there was a wide disparity between them. The best off aspired
to their own house, if tradesmen then to their own shop. Almost all
were rented by the year from a landlord who may have been one of
the London rich or may have had just a few houses at his or her
disposal, perhaps only the one; a fortunate inheritance of a single freehold or long lease could provide an income for life sufficient for modest
means. So in 1786 a house in 'the best streets' with a twenty-four-foot
frontage could fetch 100–150 guineas a year unfurnished, and in less
fashionable districts 80–100 guineas. A modest house of eighteen-foot
frontage could be had unfurnished for 30–40 guineas, depending on
area. Location and size were, of course, the main determining factors,
location most important of all.[47]

Middling-sort households renting a whole house would often expect
to defray their expenses by letting out one or more floors as lodgings.
The rent of an unfurnished first floor of two rooms and a closet was
about half the rent of the whole house. A furnished floor would fetch
more but there were advantages in letting unfurnished, because the
tenant's furniture could be seized if the rent was unpaid. Probably the
majority of middling-sort London housing was divided into unfurnished or furnished lodgings in this way, quite often with an element
of board or service into the bargain. Lodgings were what visitors

staying any substantial time in London sought to take as cheaper than hotels. And lodgings were what many long-term residents could merely afford or sometimes preferred over renting a whole house, which brought parochial obligations to serve as constable or other parish officer that the lodger would avoid. The ratepayers of Stepney, for instance, complained in 1727 that 'there are Abundance of Gentlemen who are Lodgers, and Men of Worth' in the parish who 'are not liable to be assessed' for rates.[48]

More fashionable men of worth sought lodgings in 'the best streets', and those most commonly over a tradesman's shop. Rents from lodgings provided a buffer against the vicissitudes of trade and it was generally the case that a shopkeeper occupied the ground floor, renting out the 'best' or first floor to a single household, and perhaps the second floor to another. The garrets, sometimes the cellars, were kept for servants' accommodation, generally the householder's servants but occasionally the lodger's as well. This pattern of the middling sort living in multi-occupied housing was a feature of London throughout the century, though it probably became less dominant towards the end. By 1780 it was noted that in the City crowding had declined and cleanliness improved through 'so many families having quitted lodgings, and living in whole houses.'[49]

As instances of the importance of lodgings for the middling sort in London we might cite Richard Steele, who lodged at 'Mr Keen's An Apothecarye's in Bennett street near S[nt] James's' in 1705. On Thomas Gray's visits to London in the 1750s he lodged in Jermyn Street, St James's, with Roberts the hosier at the sign of The Three Squirrels or at Frisby's the oilman. James Boswell agreed to pay 40 guineas a year for a second floor in Downing Street in 1762–3, his landlord chamber-keeper for the Office for Trade and Plantations, and in 1775 took 'a very neat first floor at 16s' over a tailor's in Gerrard Street, Soho. Laurence Sterne, at the height of his fame as the author of *Tristram Shandy*, lodged over a wig maker's and 'silk bag shop' in Old Bond Street from January 1767, dying there in March 1768. And so on.[50]

The temporary nature of lodgings, while offering flexibility and freedom and no doubt contributing much to the mobility of Londoners in these years, did not suit everyone. Many hankered for a house of their own without having to worry about a lodger's caprice or coming under the supervision of a landlord on the premises. John Thomas

Smith's landlady in Gerrard Street around 1787 would lock up at midnight and open her door to no one, frequently forcing that talented young artist to bribe the constable of the night to let him stay by the fire in the parish watch-house.[51]

We might take Edward Gibbon, the historian, as an example of a lodger who aspired to better things and eventually obtained them. Gibbon was born in Putney in 1737, his father a Tory politician. Living on unearned income, Gibbon was on the edge of the wealthy and the middling classes, though his income was beset by legal difficulties and was never immense. In December 1758, just arrived in London from Switzerland, he took 'a very good first floor, drawing-room bedchamber and light closet with many conveniences for a guinea and half a week' at John Stewart's, a linen draper in New Bond Street. In 1766, after more sojourning abroad, he was at Miss Lake's in St James's Place, 'an indifferent lodging' though costing him 2 guineas a week. In 1769 he was lodging in Pall Mall, 'opposite the Duke of Cumberland's', where he seems to have stayed for over three years. In 1772 he was looking for a London house, and though 'Houses rise to my inquiry every moment' none quite suited him. But soon he leased a 'delightful mansion' in Bentinck Street, at the far western edge of the Harley-Portland Estate. There he had fun planning his bookcases ('painted white, ornamented with a light frize' in 'Adamic') and choosing wallpaper ('a fine shag flock', 'light blue with a gold border'). He called it 'my little Palace': 'all the notions I ever formed of a London life in my own house, and surrounded by my books, with a due mixture of study and society are fully realized.' His happiness lasted a decade or so. Then, oppressed by money troubles, Gibbon left expensive Bentinck Street and England altogether for Switzerland in 1783. When he returned to London for the last time in 1793 it was for medical treatment. He took lodgings once more, this time in St James's Street, and died there after surgery in January 1794.[52]

Before we move to the dwellings of the 'poorer sort of people' it is worth pointing out that some characteristics were shared by the lower ranks of the middling classes and the upper ranks of plebeians, from the journeyman in steady employment to the 'handicraftsman' or artisan working on his own account or employing apprentices and 'hands'. Living in a house let in lodgings was common to all. All could be troubled – as Jonathan Swift was in St James's, we might recall – by the insufficiencies of the London drainage system. And all were subject at one time or another to that London torment, the bedbug. Even magazines aimed at the *ton* gave space to infallible recipes for killing bugs. One, based on the residue of lamp oil and turpentine, 'will rid any bed whatsoever, though it swarms with bugs', it was said in 1771. And a man called Bridges, of Cross Street, Hatton Garden, advertised his services as 'Bug-Doctor to the King'.[53]

So in plebeian London, among the poorer sort, we find very similar patterns to those of the middling classes but with some distinctions. Much of their housing was in cheaper areas with no pretensions to fashion. These too were often older areas where the housing had received generations of hard knocks from crowded lodgers. And a third difference, very important, was the amount of space a working family could afford: most workers could afford only a single room and not a floor.

Francis Place, for instance, a journeyman leather-breeches maker, was born in Vinegar Yard, Brydges Street, Covent Garden, in 1771. His first married home was a furnished room over a coal merchant's 'at the Back of St Clements Church' for which he paid 3s 6d a week. Other furnished rooms followed, sometimes costing 4s a week, by which time (1792) there was a baby. But 'I worked incessantly, and soon saved money enough to buy some good cloaths and a bedstead, a table three or four chairs and some bedding, with these and a few utensils we took an unfurnished back room up two pairs of stairs at a chandlers shop in Wych Street.' In moving from furnished to unfurnished, Place halved his rent to 2s a week. There was further progress in early 1794, when the family moved to another unfurnished room large enough to curtain off a bed space. There was a small yard and a washhouse, both 'great conveniences'. He had other single rooms after that, while recognising the one-room dwelling's pernicious effects on family life – for a time there were four of them in the one room. But by 1796, his circumstances improving, he was renting four rooms in an old house in High Holborn at £16 a year, yet looking out for 'some respectable single man' to lodge in one of them to help pay the rent.[54]

New workers coming to London, with no family home there, often had to start from a lower base. We might recall that Samuel Kevan, the slater from Wigtown, spent his first night lodging at his employer's, sharing a bed with his master's son. Bed-sharing was customary for a single man of the labouring classes who could that way halve the rent of

a furnished room. It was usual, too, for domestic servants to share beds
in this way. Bedfellows were by their nature a transitory phenomenon,
though doubtless some arrangements proved more long-standing. They
could also be uncomfortable when a bedfellow became ill or had 'the
itch' (from the scabies mite) or was more than commonly lousy or
unclean in his habits, no working person having the facilities to keep
his body clean even by contemporary standards. There were other risks:
thefts by bedfellows were an occasional feature of larceny cases at the
Old Bailey, for instance. And Samuel Hurlock was hanged in 1747 for
the murder of John Pitts, an 'old man' who shared his bed in Sugar
Loaf Court, Goodman's Yard, on the eastern edge of the City. He said
he had found Pitts 'lying cross his Stomach' in the night, 'Upon which,
Passion, which is Madness of the Devil, got the Mastery of him', and
Hurlock stabbed him to death with a bayonet.[55]

It is not clear how long Samuel Kevan stayed a bedfellow, but probably only a short time until he was introduced to an employer at Tooley
Street, Southwark. At first he rented a room from a Mrs Sewell, a
married woman originally from Stowmarket, who kept a 'small school'
at her home in Red Lion Court and who 'acted the part of a Mother,
in finding me Shirts, Stockings, &c.' But after some time his master
offered him a room in his own house. It seems to have given Kevan as
much pleasure as Gibbon took from his Bentinck Street 'palace', and
for much the same reason:

This little back parlour M[rs] Tysons 181 Tooley Street was my secret retreat for
about a dozen years, my window look'd into a back yeard, a narrow Tent bed,
a large Table, a chair, & my Chest, with a closet still encreasing in books was
my furniture. This was Taking-up house by myself, finding myself far behind,
I set on with eagerness to obtain knowledge.[56]

There he lodged till 1795, when he heard that Mr Sewell at Red Lion
Court had died of his asthma. Kevan, now thirty-one 'and being unhappy,
& unsettled', thought it time to marry. Mrs Sewell, 'who I always
respected, and had an eye to, if it should please providence to remove
her husband', was his choice: 'no person could be more suitable – She
had all the qualifications of a good wife – had no children, a house
furnished, and a little money beforehand – beside she had a very respectable School that averaged about Sixty pounds per An[m].'

When I call'd upon Mrs Sewell that evening, she was at work in the little back kitchen. I took my Seat at the opposite side of the room. 'I have often said to Mr Sewell, said I, that when he died I would have the widow and I now renew it to yourself.' [']You were always given to a joke replied Mrs S. and *so* you mean to continue it.' [']No, I am now in earnest.'⁵⁷

They married in October 1795, when, after a dozen years or so as a lodger, he became a London householder.

How did the poor fare? Many of course had no home at all, not even the limited comforts of a shared bed in a room they could in part call their own. Homeless children were a feature throughout the century, clinging to the warmth of glasshouses and brick kilns in the coldest nights of winter. In November 1732 the Lord Mayor called for action by the constables to arrest the many 'Poor Vagrant Children who are suffered to skulk in the Night-time, and lie upon Bulks, Stalls, and other Places in the Publick Streets of this City, whereby many of them perish by the Extremity of the weather, and other Inconveniencies ensue'. Each year, though, nameless children died wretchedly on the streets of London, like 'A poor boy' found dead in a dunghill at a stable yard in Holborn where he'd crept from the cold in February 1771. And at the other end of life we hear of old 'Mad Eleanor' or 'The Queen of Hornsey', said to have been of good family but disappointed in love, who slept in fields, doorways and dunghills for twenty years at the end of the century, 'covered with rags, which were hung in bundles about various parts of her body.'⁵⁸ Occasionally, but not often, the public conscience was disturbed by London's homeless, as in November 1763, when two women were found starved to death 'in a ruinous' house in Stonecutter Street, Fleet Market, where they had squatted for warmth. They were found on the floor, quite naked or nearly so, their clothes apparently taken by three other occupants of the house, two of whom were also 'almost starved'. 'Soon after another woman was found starved to death in an empty house in the same neighbourhood.'⁵⁹

Of the poor who had a home, the one-room lodging was all they could hope for. Dreadful cases of poverty infrequently came to light here too, exposed by medical men, magistrates and well-wishers. In the worst places there was almost no furniture at all, 'an old oil cloth' or a rug covered with a ragged blanket substituted for a bed long gone to the pawnshop or the landlord. 'On such a couch,' affirmed

Dr John Coakley Lettsom in 1774, 'I have found a husband, a wife, and two or three children at once chained by disease, without any resources to procure a morsel of bread.' Dr Robert Willan found up to eight family members to a bed later in the century. And in 1797 Patrick Colquhoun, a reforming London magistrate, visited a house in Mile End New Town where five families comprising thirty-three individuals lived – they had four 'miserable corded bedsteads' between them, the fifth family sleeping on straw with no bedclothes. We might close a sad litany in a court near Fleet Market in March 1784. Lodgers 'smelt something offensive up two-pair of stairs', where a family of six lodged. When called upon to open the door the children said they couldn't and so the neighbours broke it in. The mother lay on the bed 'in a state of putrefaction', dead for more than a month. The father had absconded, leaving the children 'naked and almost starved to death'. Three were unable to stand and the eldest 'could just speak to be understood'.[60]

Indeed, death was all around in eighteenth-century London. It was thought at the time – and historical demographers have agreed since – that mortality in the capital was generally higher than elsewhere in the nation. It could take a terrible toll of Londoners of all classes. Among people mentioned in the last few pages, Edward Gibbon, himself a sickly child, lost all six younger siblings, 'snatched away in their infancy'; eight of Mrs Thrale's twelve children died before reaching the age of ten, five of them in infancy; of Francis Place's fourteen children by two marriages, five died in infancy and two more under seventeen years old; all six of Thomas Hardy's children died young, his wife dying in childbirth in 1796; and Samuel Richardson, the cockney printer-novelist whom we'll hear about in later chapters, lost all six children by his first wife and two of six by his second, none of the eight living to see a fourth birthday.[61]

This by no means exhaustive list exemplifies two marked features of London mortality: the extraordinary prevalence of childhood deaths, especially in the first five years of life; and the failure of wealth to give immunity from early death in the metropolis. Ages at burial were first collected by London's parish clerks in 1728. From then till the end of the century, deaths of children under five accounted for nearly half of all burials in the Bills of Mortality in the 1730s and over four out of ten in every succeeding decade. Overall mortality as measured by the number of burials collected in the bills was at its worst in the second quarter of the century, when some 25,000–30,000 were buried each year in London, and seems to have improved from around 1780, when the average number – in a larger population – fell to below 20,000 per annum. Accordingly, fewer children were dying then too, but the proportion of children's deaths to all deaths remained stubbornly high.[62]

Why was mortality in London so prevalent and why did it adopt these particular patterns of chronology and age distribution? Many contemporaries ascribed the very high mortality from around 1725 to 1750 to the popularity of gin, a thesis famously followed by some historians of London subsequently. In fact, no single cause can provide an answer to a question that still baffles modern specialists. High mortality appears not to have been caused by absolute poverty alone, because London was relatively immune from the occasional subsistence crises that beset the nation. The deaths of children played an even greater part in the mortality bulge of 1725–50 than later in the century and so gin, though it may have aggravated parental neglect and may directly have caused a small proportion of infant deaths, is unlikely to contribute much to an explanation. A more fruitful line of enquiry is directed at the special virulence of disease in the first part of the century. Typhus or 'gaol fever', a louse-born disease associated with overcrowding and poverty, bore an epidemic character in London especially in the first half-century and no doubt made a contribution. So did epidemic agues and influenzas and so did smallpox, more common in London than elsewhere and most prevalent in the middle two quarters of the century, when it killed over 2,000 Londoners each year. Almost all London children caught smallpox, it was said, and the disease was a prominent killer in the early years of life. Infantile diarrhoea, a disease peculiarly prevalent in the summer months, was also a major killer and at its worst in the first half-century. It flourished in insanitary conditions and, as we have seen, the state of the streets and open sewers like the Fleet, with so much faecal matter lying above ground, were at their worst in those years too.

Finally we might point to some elements in infant care that made children most vulnerable. Undoubtedly typhus, epidemic fevers and infantile diarrhoea were diseases that impacted most on the poor. They were rife in the northern suburbs of the City, in the East End and in Southwark. But a general ignorance of infant welfare, nutrition and hygiene, an intolerance of ventilation – not helped by the pernicious window tax that blocked up windows in all classes of houses – and a hostility to breast-feeding until late in the century, made children vulnerable irrespective of the rank into which they were born. Once past the dangerous childhood years, life expectancy improved, but was lower than in many other European cities until middle age: it was computed in 1772 that London life expectancy at twelve years old was forty-five and a half and at twenty-five just fifty-one.[63]

If death was all around, then so was the fear of death. Memories of the Great Plague of 1665 were still fresh in the early years of the eighteenth century, and rumour and fear abounded. The plague was said to be in Newcastle upon Tyne, where much of London's sea coal originated, in 1710; its arrival in Marseilles in 1722 caused a panic that found its way into draconian legislative proposals for quarantining London; in 1743 Horace Walpole was 'in great apprehension of our having the plague' which had appeared on the Continent; cases of plague were falsely reported in St Thomas's Hospital in 1760; and rumours of the plague in London were circulating among the poor of Holborn as late as 1799.[64]

Death and disease, then, were two leading features of London life. The fear of fevers and smallpox kept visitors away from London during epidemics and that is no surprise. The poor, as always, were most at risk, but all classes were affected by the great equaliser, to a larger extent than might at first be thought likely. There were, on the other hand, shared aspects to life in London which fortunately were among its many delights.

'Take or Give the Wall': Getting on Together

When I parted with you at the Bell I mounted the ladder of the Coach as slowly as a Criminal does the Ladder at Tyburn with this difference he because his Journey is so short I because my Journey was so long dreading fat A—e's & Sick Stomacks. I found to my inexpressible comfort only a Quaker Woman and her Son – the Woman observed we should be very snug – scarce had she spoke . . . when the door opened and presented to our view a man of enormous bulk he apear'd to be about 60 – he wore a threadbare snuf colord Great Coat his Hat had seen many better days! his Wig had once been curled – had once been Qilld – the flags of his waistcoat peeped from under his great Coat . . . after having seated <himself> safe in the corner next to the Quaker – (who seemed to be very apprehensive for her Linnen) and coverd his Breeches with the flaps of his great Coat he informd us he was happy to see some companions on his Journey that for his part he loved society so well he would not have gone to Town by himself tho he had stayed till that day week – he hoped he said we did not intend to be silent – for himself he had a pretty large collection of stories – which he believed would last us all the way and more over Madam says he (addressing himself to the Female) they are of a very innocent nature.[65]

The young George Cumberland, travelling from Cambridge to London in December 1774, experienced that sociability that was such a striking feature of the stagecoach age. Some intimacy was unavoidable through the collective agonies of a jolting coach; some from the dangers of the road, fear of robbery eliciting anecdote and advice whether welcome or not; and some through the 'common civility' which required a man to pay regard to a woman travelling companion and which rendered a taciturn passenger rather an unsociable oddity.[66]

Stagecoach sociability might end at the coaching inn's courtyard, but just getting around the London streets needed frequent requests for directions, especially before the general introduction of street signage in the mid-1760s, and we've already seen an instance in the case of Scotch Peggy's friend. Street incidents – accidents and rows and eccentric sights – gave opportunity to comment on the shared lotteries of life, and no doubt a pervasive culture of drinking loosened tongues and sloughed off inhibition. A growing tendency to politeness also aided this superficial social intercourse, as a 'Lady' confided to the *Town and Country Magazine* in 1790, struck when 'perambulating the streets' of London by the readiness of people to suggest that the '*lady* at the apple-stall' or the '*gentleman* who is blacking the other gentleman's shoes' would surely help her find her way. If this was merely another dimension to London's egalitarianism, then at least it helped sociability rather than hindered it.[67]

For it was true that all who came new to London needed some help in negotiating the city and in getting on with the Londoner. Hence the ready market for pocket maps, guides and other handy advice on 'the art of living in London'. A number followed Horace's classical town-and-country-mouse conceit where a rural innocent is guided through London's hazards by a more experienced hand, a citizen born and bred or someone who understood the town's pitfalls from long familiarity.

Then there were pamphlets alerting newcomers to 'the tricks of the town', which showed London to be 'a kind of large Forest of *Wild Beasts*'. Others combined advice and amusement in verse, like John Gay's *Trivia; or, The Art of Walking the Streets of London*, 1716, or William Green's *The Art of Living in London*, 1768, much reprinted. And others still, like the Reverend John Trusler's *London Adviser and Guide* of 1786, offered updated rules 'On Walking London Streets'. Among this advice to the newcomer the vexed question of when to 'take or give the wall', the side of the pavement furthest from the street mud, still led to arguments into the 1760s it seems, although Samuel Johnson felt it had long been resolved that those with the wall on their right could claim it.[68]

Besides these printed guides for strangers, many were also in a position to get practical advice from individuals in London. The sheer weight of migrant numbers meant that any new arrival more likely than not had family, friends or acquaintances there who could at least offer a helpful word, sometimes a bed for a night, to soften the blow of landing in town. Networks could widen beyond acquaintances into gatherings based on loyalty and affection, perhaps to supply a gap for those without any friends to hand. Newcomers of the middling classes had county-based associations, though how long each survived must have depended on the energies of a few individuals and doubtless varied from generation to generation. In 1705 we hear of 'a Club or Society of Men born in the City and County of Gloucester' meeting every Wednesday at the City of Bristol Tavern, Friday Street, Cheapside; the Angel Inn near Wych Street, St Clement Danes, was a great resort for Cornish and other West Country lawyers around 1720; a 'club of Nottinghamshire gentlemen' dined at the Star and Garter Tavern, Pall Mall, in 1765 and no doubt there were many more besides.[69]

Some of these associations achieved longevity, especially those sustained by the pride of small nations. The best-known London Welsh association seems to have been formed in 1714 by migrants of the upper-middling ranks as the Society of Ancient Britons, helped by patronage from the Prince of Wales. In 1718 it established a charity school for children born in or near London with a Welsh parent. The children – eventually girls as well as boys – were schooled, clothed and put to apprenticeships at the charity's expense. At first it was held in a room in Hatton Garden, but in 1737 subscriptions were raised to build a new school at Clerkenwell Green; it moved to larger premises in Gray's Inn Lane in 1772. Each year the Society celebrated St David's Day with a church service – in 1798 at St James's Piccadilly, the singing courtesy of 'a society of gentlemen belonging to Portland-chapel' in Marylebone.[70]

The Scottish networks were extensive and operated at many levels, doubtless encouraged by the hostility faced by North Britons in London. Many were informal. Scottish lodgers found Scottish householders to rent from, as Boswell did in Downing Street in 1762. Scottish buyers favoured Scottish sellers: Boswell was shaved by 'old Reid' in the Strand, 'an Athol man in London about thirty years', and Garrick teased him for patronising '"the only Scottish shoeblack in London"'. The Scottish watchman at Spring Gardens alerted Robert Drummond the banker to a fire '"somewhere behind; but I came first to your honour, because you are of my own country"'. Most of all, Scots sought out Scottish companions. Boswell's loquacious diaries are punctuated with social gatherings – in taverns, drawing rooms, even the park – where all around him are North Britons. Sometimes it was congenial, as over breakfast with Captain James Erskine discussing the Clackmannanshire election, where the 'ideas of both countries were well mixed; and London really seemed in my imagination the capital of both, and not a strange capital'. Sometimes it was less so, Boswell's haphazard sensibilities disgusted by his companions' 'forward, coarse, north-of-Scotland manners. We drank a considerable quantity.'[71]

Whatever the outcome, Scottish company in London everywhere found strength in numbers, especially in those 'clubs' of eighteenth-century London which rose and fell like sky-rockets. 'I dined frequently with a club of officers, mostly Scotch, at a coffeehouse at Church Court in the Strand,' recalled Alexander Carlyle of his time in London in 1746. In 1758 he was dining weekly, a club's defining feature, with Robert Adam and other Scots at a coffee house in Sackville Street. Thomas Coutts and a 'little colony of Scotsmen' met weekly at the St Albans Tavern off Pall Mall in the early 1760s. Indeed, a Scotsman of whatever background seemed sure of finding like-minded compatriots in London, as Thomas Somerville, a dissenting churchman with literary aspirations, did from 1769 till the end of the century. They were aided by certain coffee houses that devoted themselves to a Scottish clientele, most famously the British Coffee House – the 'Breetish', Gibbon called it – in Cockspur Street, Charing Cross. It was run by Mrs Anderson, daughter of a Fife merchant, from around 1756 to 1777, and the British seems to have maintained an overwhelmingly tartan complexion for much of the century. In 1770 the place was rebuilt; Robert Adam was the architect.[72]

The Scots in London also combined for convivial and charitable purposes. Their oldest and most prestigious institution was the Scottish Corporation, founded in 1603, chartered by Charles II in 1665 and given further privileges in 1676. From Scotch Hall or the 'Scottish Hospital', Blackfriars, the Corporation administered relief to the London Scottish poor. At first this was in a workhouse, but for much of the eighteenth century it appears to have been given to recipients in their own homes or to help them return to Scotland. Scotch Hall and the Corporation moved to smarter premises in Crane Court, Fleet Street, in 1782. By that time there were several societies of Scots in London organising feasts, balls and Scottish dancing assemblies. The most important event in their calendar was the annual St Andrew's Day celebrations. In November 1787 some 10,000 London Scots were said to have taken part in events organised by the Scottish Hospital, the Highland Society, two Caledonian societies, the Ancient Caledonians and others at London's leading taverns and elsewhere. All was conducted 'with great magnificence' and 'the greatest regularity and decorum', except at a Caledonian Society ball in Ansell's Room, Spring Gardens, where the half-guinea tickets had reached 'improper persons' and the company was regaled with *'musty victuals, and execrable wines'*.[73]

Why were these associations, both informal clubs and gatherings and formal feasts and assemblies, so important in eighteenth-century London? In a city where family ties were necessarily weakened through migration, the dislocations of urban existence and premature death, Londoners sought support from their 'friends', a keyword of the age. The vagaries of life – illness, worklessness, debt, eviction, relationship breakdown, bereavement, accident, fire – came many and fast. Parish relief through the poor law was often niggardly and stigmatising, its funds utterly inadequate for the needs of the time. Without assistance from friends, debtors were imprisoned, the hungry starved, the sick languished and died untended. And to counteract the loneliness and isolation of the greatest city in Europe, a city of strangers, Londoners gained mutual strength – and often much delight – from their associations. Association was built into the structure of communal government in the City's wardmotes and precinct meetings and in the open vestries of many suburban parishes. It operated at work in the City companies or guilds and in journeymen's friendly societies for self-help or combinations against employers. It was the stuff of religious life around the parish church or dissenting meeting house – we might think here of the Society of Friends or Quakers, a strong presence in eighteenth-century London, none more friendly to their sick and poor than they, and none more helpful to their business-minded brethren.

The obsessive desire to associate was most visible in the formation of clubs, small gatherings of friends from every walk of life who met weekly or more frequently in public houses and coffee houses to dine or sup together, drink, gossip, discuss business opportunities, combine in ventures and assist each other where possible. In general, these were gatherings of men. Such was the passion and necessity for association of every sort that Freemasonry was built on nothing more than this cult of fraternity for its own sake and for the mutual advantages it could bring.

Modern Freemasonry was very much an eighteenth-century London invention. With its elaborate mysteries and secret signs of belonging, with local or trade-based lodges ordered by a hierarchy to which, in egalitarian fashion, all ranks could aspire, Freemasonry provided an alternative society where friends could be acquired by the middling classes outside the older established networks of organised religion and parochial loyalty. Wherever it originated, Freemasonry seemed purpose-built for London, an ideal antidote to metropolitan rootless-ness and isolation. It rapidly asserted itself in the capital. The Grand Lodge of England, the oldest in the world, was formed when four London lodges came together at the Goose and Gridiron public house, St Paul's Churchyard, in June 1717. Scores of lodges met in public houses as a regular feature of metropolitan collective life throughout the century. In 1775 a magnificent Freemasons' Hall was built in Great Queen Street, Lincoln's Inn Fields, and next to it three years later a Freemasons' Tavern, large enough for great public meetings and dinners. Among the Londoners we've met so far Sir Robert Walpole, William Hogarth, Sir James Thornhill, James Boswell, William Kent, Sir John Soane, Tobias Smollett, James Thomson and no doubt others were all Freemasons. The Scottish connection here too will not go unnoticed.[74]

Associations of all kinds, then, were a marked feature of London
life in the eighteenth century and we shall meet some of them more
intimately in the pages to come. They were the main bulwark against
that other most salient fact of London life – indifference. The 'freedom
from remark and petty censure' that Johnson rejoiced in turned readily
to a disregard of anyone's business but one's own, with multitudes
single-mindedly pursuing their individual interests. In the 'jumble' of
London the normal safeguards of social life seemed absent. As Henry
Fielding made Joseph Andrews tell his good sister Pamela, '"London is
a bad place, and there is so little good-fellowship, that the next door
neighbours don't know one another."' So it must often have been in a
city where so many were newcomers and where attachments to lodgings were so fragile. But it was not always the case. We might note that
the Old Bailey proceedings during the century contain over 1,200 cases
where 'neighbour' is cited in evidence, most often assisting the victims
of crime in one way or another. And Thomas Legg noted 'Poor people
that lodge in Low Rented Houses, going to each other' at midday on
Sundays, 'and after paying their awkward Compliments, borrowing
Saucepans and Stewpans for the dressing Peas, Beans, Bacon, and
Mackrell for Dinner'; and 'Plates full of Pie, Tarts and Pudding sent
between Neighbour and Neighbour, for big-bellied Women, and sick
Children'.[75]

Londoners' varied interactions generally struck some sort of balance
between the needs of self and its perceived obligations to others.
Nonetheless there is no doubt that indifference bred loneliness in
those on its receiving end. The great paradox of the lonely individual
in the crowded city was a feature of London life much remarked
upon by contemporaries. So London, it was said, made 'the best
hiding-place in the world', 'the only place in the world to be private
in'. Anecdotes were treasured of people secreting themselves from
family and acquaintances just by moving to another London district
not far away: 'there is no being alone but in a metropolis,' thought
Horace Walpole.[76]

Walpole relished it. So did many others, educated women among
them like Eliza Haywood, Elizabeth Carter and Mary Wollstonecraft,
who loved the freedom London lodgings gave them. For the poor and
friendless, of course, loneliness was a nightmare. And there were
moments when the plight of individuals might combine to cast out for
a time whole groups of Londoners from the common weal: Roman

1. London Bridge from the Southwark side, *c*.1751. This was London's only river crossing until Westminster Bridge opened in 1750. In a dozen years all the houses were removed to widen the carriageway and protect the City's position as a place of trade. The cataract of water that made shooting the bridge by boat so dangerous is well illustrated to the left.

2. St Mary le Strand and old Somerset House, *c*.1753 (John Maurer). James Gibbs's 'fair daughter in the Strand' remains one of the most distinctive landmarks in London. The parish watchhouse by the main entrance was considered a disgraceful eyesore by architectural critics.

3. St Martin-in-the-Fields, *c.*1738 (Robert West). James Gibbs's second London church (1721–6) became the pattern for Anglican parish churches throughout the English-speaking world.

4. Cheapside, *c.*1750 (T. Loveday), showing the shop signs and pavement posts before they were all removed by the street improvements of the 1760s. Being born within the sound of the bell of St Mary-le-Bow, on the right-hand side, was said to define a cockney.

5. Mansion House, *c.*1753. Designed by George Dance the Elder, the disfiguring attic stories were removed in the nineteenth century. Even so, this was an early achievement of the City's improving urge that began in the 1730s.

6. Westminster Bridge from the south-west, pictured before it opened fully to traffic in 1750. This second river crossing stimulated the development of Westminster and subsequently Lambeth on the Surrey shore.

7. Somerset House and the Adelphi beyond, 1791 (Joseph Farington), the most prestigious improvement projects in central London. Not all were impressed. Horace Walpole remarked of the Adelphi buildings that they were 'warehouses, laced down the seams, like a soldier's trull in a regimental old coat'.

8. Blackfriars Bridge, 1790 (Joseph Farington). London's third bridge, opened in 1769, was an act of self-defence by the City of London, worried by the growth of commerce and wealth in Westminster.

9. Portland Place, *c.*1796 (Thomas Malton). The widest street in London when laid out by the Adam Brothers in the 1770s, lined with town houses in Palladian terraces, it typified the wealthy suburb of Marylebone, drawing in many aristocratic families among its tenants.

10. St Mary le Strand and Somerset House, *c.*1796 (Thomas Malton). Half a century of improvements are plain to see here, especially on the south side of the Strand with its tall and regular terraces and the palatial frontage of Sir William Chambers's new Somerset House.

11. Butcher Row, St Clement's Lane, drawn by John Thomas Smith shortly before demolition in early 1798. Despite many improvements the condition of much of inner London housing was deplorable, as here in pre-Fire housing divided into single-room tenements for workers' families.

THE HUMOURS OF
ST. GILES'S.

12. *The Humours of St Giles's*, 1788 (Thomas Rowlandson). The parish of St Giles, west of Holborn, epitomised poor London in the popular imagination. Irish migrants had settled there in large numbers since the seventeenth century. Rowlandson captures much fun among the misery.

13. Jewish old-clothes dealers, 1794 (Thomas Rowlandson). The Jewish poor, generally excluded from apprenticeships, often pursued marginal callings in the streets, the trade in old clothes and oranges being particular favourites.

14. A Quack Doctor, 1800 (Thomas Rowlandson), thought to be Dr Bossy, a German quack, who set up his stage weekly in Covent Garden to appreciative crowds, here including a Jewish pedlar. A black boy is one of his troupe of assistants.

15. *Noon*, 1736 (William Hogarth). Another busy street scene demonstrating variety among the Londoners. Smartly dressed French Huguenots emerge from their chapel in Hog Lane, between Soho and St Giles, while a housemaid taking home a pie has her attention distracted by a black footman.

16. *The Enraged Musician*, 1741 (William Hogarth). The 'cries of London' uttered by a variety of street sellers were an astonishing feature of metropolitan life to newcomers and a vexation to anyone seeking peace and quiet. A milkmaid, a sow gelder with his horn, a knife-grinder, street oboist and ballad singer all add to the row.

Catholics during the Jacobite rebellions and the Gordon Riots, or London radicals in the years of repression after 1793, for instance.[77] In these ways even English Londoners could be made minorities. But there were many other minorities in the city who had more or less difficulty in fitting in to London, that 'great moving picture, changed by the different characters and figures not of the country parts of England alone, but of the whole Universe'.[78]

Ignatius Sancho

I V

IGNATIUS SANCHO'S LONDON – CITIZENS OF THE WORLD

'Our Unfortunate Colour': Black Londoners

The gout seized me yesterday morning – the second attack – I looked rather black all day.[1]

THANKS to his witty and wise correspondence we know more of Ignatius Sancho than of any other African Londoner of the eighteenth century. His story had much of romance about it. He was born around 1729 on a slave ship making the Atlantic crossing from Guinea to the Spanish West Indies. There his mother soon died from disease and his father killed himself rather than submit to slavery. The orphaned infant, baptised Ignatius, was brought to England by his master when just two years old. He was given to three maiden sisters living in Greenwich, who raised him for service. They fed him well – too well, for obesity seems to have shortened his life – but starved him of book-learning to frustrate his future independence. It was they who named him Sancho, after Don Quixote's fat attendant. But his untutored aptitude shone through, and Sancho's education was fostered under the aristocratic patronage of the Duke and Duchess of Montagu. Around 1749 he became the Duchess's butler, a responsible position for a man so young. When the Duchess died in 1751 she left Sancho an annuity of £30 – enough for bare necessities as long as he lived; her black 'Groom of the Chambers' was similarly treated.[2] But let loose on London, Sancho rioted in its pleasures, from innumerable bawdy houses to the card tables, where, it was said, he once lost the clothes he was sitting in to a Jewish gamester.

By the time he was thirty, though, he seems to have put dissipation behind him, finding both religion and a wife. He married Ann Osborne – from the West Indies and also of African origin – at St Margaret's, Westminster, in 1758, and eventually rejoined the service of the Montagus, becoming the new Duke's valet in 1766. But gout and corpulence undermined his usefulness and in January 1774 he was helped to take a shop selling groceries and tobacco at 20 Charles Street (now King Charles Street) near Whitehall. There he lived contentedly until, weighed down by a combination of health problems – 'an old man all at once – the failure of eyes – the loss of teeth – the thickness of hearing' – he died in December 1780. He was just fifty-one. [3]

This 'coal-black, jolly African', as he himself described 'Sancho the big', his 'convexity of belly exceeding Falstaff', had a wide London connection. He was well known, up and down stairs, from his years in service with the nobility. His extensive reading in English literature, his true eye for painting and a faithful ear for music – he composed songs and wrote a theoretical treatise, now lost – won the respect of many. He was friendly with Garrick, famously corresponded with Laurence Sterne on the evils of slavery, was painted by Gainsborough, visited by Nollekens the sculptor and loved by many more. He had extensive networks of white friends among the higher classes of domestic servants, with whom he had worked, and among other blacks in London, especially musicians. He was a lively correspondent in private and in public, usually signing his letters to the papers on a range of subjects 'Africanus'. His religion had a touch of Methodist enthusiasm – he could tell a friend of the death of his beloved daughter, Kitty, that 'she drew her prize early – Wish her joy!' But it was marked most of all by a loving charitableness – 'Philanthropy I adore,' he told Sterne – that involved him in practical schemes of assistance and redemption and extended to a passionate espousal of animal welfare untypical of his times.[4]

Sancho, then, was entirely integrated into a London society of the literate middling sort of people. Yet, while London-bred and feeling inferior to no one, his colour marked him out for special gaze. He could never – how could he? – disburden himself from the tragedy of black people during the times in which he lived. 'Look round,' he wrote to Julius Soubise, a black adventurer whom Sancho sought unsuccessfully to counsel, 'upon the miserable fate of almost all of our unfortunate colour – superadded to ignorance, – see slavery, and the contempt of those very wretches who roll in affluence from our labours. Superadded to this woeful catalogue – hear the ill-bred and heart-racking abuse of the foolish vulgar.'[5] Indeed, despite his firm installation in London society, Sancho never secured indemnity from the foolish vulgar, of all classes. After a trip to Vauxhall Gardens in August 1777 with four of his children they 'had a coach home – were gazed at – followed, &c. &c. – but not much abused'.[6] No doubt that night Sancho suffered more for his children's sake than his own. For he could rely on urbanity, wit and learning to give as good as he got. William Stevenson, the artist, 'often witnessed his patient forbearance, when the passing vulgar have given vent to their prejudices against his ebon complexion, his African features, and his corpulent person'. Once, in Spring Gardens Passage near St James's Park, a 'young Fashionable said to his companion, loud enough to be heard, "Smoke Othello!"'

This did not escape my Friend Sancho; who, immediately placing himself across the path, before him, exclaimed with a thundering voice, and a countenance which awed the delinquent, 'Aye, Sir, such Othellos you meet with but once in a century,' clapping his hand upon his goodly round paunch. 'Such Iagos as you, we meet with in every dirty passage. Proceed, Sir!'[7]

There was truly only one Ignatius Sancho. But how many fellow black Londoners shared the city with him? There are no certain figures. Contemporary estimates of 15,000–20,000 appear too high in the light of recent research into marriages and burials of blacks recorded in London's parish registers, and modern historians put numbers in a fluctuating range of 5,000–10,000 at any one time. It seems likely that in the 1780s, when migration of black loyalists from America reached its peak at the end of the Revolutionary War in 1783, the figure would have been 10,000 at least.[8]

But these modest numbers belie the significant visual presence of blacks in London. They were ubiquitous in the domestic service of merchants trading with the West Indies or running plantations there, and widely imported into other rich families as symbols of wealth, status and imperial connections. Their value resided less in their labour than in their public display – answering doors, running errands, walking by a sedan chair or behind a mistress, accompanying a master on horseback, or perched behind the family coach. It was a value recognised uniquely in the public art of the city, at least into the 1760s, in shop, inn and coffee-house signs – in Ludgate Hill alone, for instance, were at one time or another the Black Boy and Comb, the Blackmoor's Head, the Indian Queen and the Little Blackamoor's Head, with the Black Boy Coffee House, known for its book auctions, nearby in Ave Maria Lane. And real blacks had numerous walk-on parts in the London theatre: Richard Cumberland's *The West Indian* of 1771 called for 'several Black Servants, carrying Portmanteaus, Trunks, &c.', for example.[9]

There was much hypocrisy in this high favour apparently accorded to blacks in London, for inhuman oppression was at the heart of their presence there. London was not a slave port, like Bristol or Liverpool, but many of its most prosperous and prominent citizens were slave owners or slave traders, among them rich Quakers like the bankers David Barclay and Sir Francis Baring, and one of the most famous (and certainly wealthiest) Lord Mayors of modern times, William Beckford.[10] So throughout the century, almost all black Londoners of African origin had, like Sancho, been captured or born as slaves. And most of these, when they arrived in London from the West Indies, as so many did, entered as slaves too. They were bought and sold there like any other commodity:

A Negro Man Named Limbrick, lately come from Barbardoes, Aged 16 Years, a handsome Tall Fellow, to be dispos'd of. Enquire at Madam England's near the Sun Tavern in Shadwell.

Daily Courant, 12 March 1709.

A beautiful Negro Boy about eight Years of Age, lately come from Barbadoes, to be dispos'd off, any Person that pleases may see the Boy at Mrs Eades, at the Cabinet on Ludgate Hill near Fleet Bridge; who likewise sells Right Barbadoes Citron Water, and true French Hungary Water.

Daily Post, 26 May 1725.

Advertisements like these appeared most frequently in the first quarter of the century but persist through the 1750s at least. They give no idea of the numbers being brought in by slave masters or merchants for their own use or private sale. Advertisements for runaways, however, were common into the 1770s, the individuals they sought frequently distinguished by old lesions perhaps denoting ill usage:

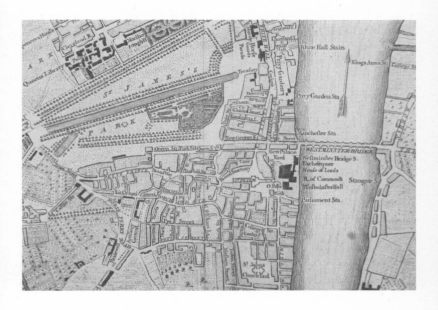

Westminster, 1761

Run away from her Mistress the 15th instant, a Negro Woman, aged about 19 years, full bodied, middle siz'd, very black, with a great bump on her left Hand, and goes by the name of Bambo.

Post-Man, 18–20 January 1705.

Run away from his Master on the 17th Instant at Night, with several Things of Value, a Negro Man named Scipio, about five Foot six Inches high, and pretty thin, had on a light-colour'd Coat, and hath a Scar under his Left Eye, and is lame in his Feet.

Daily Courant, 20 May 1723

If most black servants in London began their employment as slaves, what proportion remained in bondage throughout their service is unclear. Some did, because we know of Jack Beef, servant to John Baker, Solicitor-General of the Leeward Islands, who accompanied his master to London in 1757 and was freed on retirement in 1771; Beef was a keen equestrian, a notable cook of turtle and entirely his master's right hand. And many of the thousand or so wealthy Americans resident in London at any one time until the 1770s brought with them a black slave servant or two, returning with them on departure. There is no doubt that many were given their freedom before retirement, often after baptism, which was popularly though fallaciously thought to bring manumission with it. Once free they could enter the labour market, marry without obstruction, have portable property and cash sufficient to become victims of crime, and so on.

Perhaps most blacks in London, like Sancho and all those he remarked upon, were in this condition. But not all. In 1772 James Somerset, an African slave, then about thirty and baptised, had left service in Baldwin Gardens, Holborn, only to be imprisoned by his former master while he arranged a ship to return him to Virginia. The courts freed him from prison and affirmed his right to remain in the country in a judgement of Lord Mansfield's widely (but wrongly) interpreted as rendering slavery illegal in England. Even after the Somerset judgement, instances of slavery continued to come to public notice in London. In 1774 a case came before Alderman Wilkes, sitting as a magistrate at the Mansion House, of a black slave to a merchant in Lothbury who had been there fourteen years without wages. Wilkes peremptorily freed him and suggested he sue for the back-pay.[11]

By that time the large numbers of free black servants in London had helped them migrate from service with the aristocratic and slave-keeping classes into the households of the London middling ranks. Perhaps the most famous of all was Francis Barber, bequeathed to Samuel Johnson by the son of a friend. Barber was born a slave in Jamaica and came to Johnson when he was about seven, in 1752. Johnson treated him as free and gave him an education. Unable to settle easily, Barber left to work for an apothecary in Cheapside when he was around eleven, and then joined the Royal Navy a couple of years later. But he returned to Johnson, marrying in 1773, and eventually moving his wife and five children into the Johnson ménage at Bolt Court. Johnson left his indispensable Frank most of his small fortune in 1784, including sufficient funds for an income for life of £70, a generous sum.

Barber was one of many. We hear of 'the articulate Joseph Alamaze, who is a black man or negro', a livery servant to Alderman Bull when he was Lord Mayor in 1773–4, and respondent in a salacious divorce suit in 1791. Giacomo Casanova found a black servant called Jarbe for his Pall Mall lodgings in 1763 'who spoke English, French, and Italian with a facility'. Joshua Reynolds had a black footman for many years who featured in numerous portraits: a man was sentenced to death for robbing him in 1769 but was transported at Reynolds's urging. Joseph Nollekens, miserly and filthy in his habits, had Elizabeth Rosina Clements as his long-suffering servant, 'a woman possessing a considerable share of drollery', known to the local tradesmen as Black Bet and to Nollekens's artistic acquaintances as Bronze. When a gentleman was robbed on the highway between Hillingdon and London in December 1780, Tobias Pleasant, who was black, told the court that 'I am servant to Mr. Lane, I have lived with him thirty-two years last November. I was behind his carriage when my master was robbed.' And so on.[12]

Like Ignatius Sancho and Jack Beef, black servants seem to have been fully integrated into that rich, mainly white subculture of male and female domestic servants in eighteenth-century London. But there was also something like a black community based on kinship – Sancho and his family spent much time with Ann's brother, for instance – and fellow feeling. There were informal gatherings, like one in Johnson's house while he was away, Barber entertaining 'a group of his African countrymen' round the fire, 'all turning their sooty faces at once to stare at me'; dancing routs or 'balls' of blacks – probably servants and their acquaintances in the main; black christenings and wakes, like that for Ruth Crook in Red Lion Street, Holborn, in 1763, her coffin 'followed by twenty-eight couple of men and women, all Blacks, and interred in a genteel manner in St George's (Bloomsbury) burying-ground. Plenty of punch and wine was given to those that came to the funeral.' There were demonstrations of mutual support and collective effort – for James Somerset at his court case, when blacks attending the court politely applauded the verdict with many others waiting outside Westminster Hall; for two men imprisoned in the City's Bridewell in 1773, when 200 or more paid them visits; and in the 1780s to agitate for help for the black poor, as we shall see in a moment.[13]

Much of this communal life was founded in the lively fellowship of domestic service, with its bottomless capacity for scandal and mirth, all lubricated by the comforts attaching to the coat-tails of the rich. It was no doubt spiced by the experiences of black Londoners from other walks of life. These too were often employed in London's luxury trades close to the world of higher domestic service. The Duchess of Devonshire had a black hairdresser called Gilbert; Olaudah Equiano was also a hairdresser in London in the 1760s and 1770s, having been apprenticed to a master in Coventry Court, Haymarket; and Julius Soubise, man of fashion and a great favourite among the ladies, taught fencing and horsemanship. There were numerous black sailors in the dockside areas of London, like John Guy, fresh off the *Newcastle* in 1736, who claimed he'd been robbed of his wages at a bawdy house near Rosemary Lane, Whitechapel: 'The oldest of the prisoners pull'd up her Coats, and bid me look at — and told me it was as black as my Face.' And there were black workers like John Commins, a gardener around Stepney, set upon and robbed by four men in March 1782: 'As I passed them, the prisoner said to me, You sulky negro, what do you look at?'[14]

Most prominent among blacks out of livery were musicians. The army was the main employer of musicians in the country and there were frequently blacks among their number. Music teaching and performing offered an independent living outside service, even if not an especially prosperous one. Black musicians, especially horn and trumpet players and drummers, feature in several of Hogarth's and others' London scenes. William Douglas, 'the Black Prince', was one of the King's Trumpeters in 1722; Equiano played the French horn as an amateur, Soubise played the fiddle and Sancho had a great friend,

Charles Lincoln, 'an African', who sailed to India as one of 'the Captain's band of music'.[15]

Some blacks also made a living as performers and exhibits in fairgrounds and public halls. Ned Ward mentions a black woman rope-dancer in a booth at Bartholomew Fair at the opening of the century, a flexible black man demonstrated his double joints in London in December 1751, and unusual instances of skin colouration were exhibited, most famously Amelia Lewsam, a black albino from Jamaica, in the 1760s and later.[16] Black women occasionally entered public notice as prostitutes in riverside brothels and those around Drury Lane. Lord Pembroke told Boswell of 'a black bawdy-house' in 1775, for instance; and in 1782 a black prostitute, Esther Allingham, plying around St James's, was proved innocent of a theft charge at the Old Bailey brought by a welching client: 'I do not chuse to give my carcase up to you for nothing,' she had told him. Black beggars, usually men it seems, were distinctive on London streets, probably more by their colour than by their numbers – they were sometimes called St Giles' Blackbirds. They appear to have been fairly well treated: 'Black people, as well as those destitute of sight, seldom fail to excite compassion,' thought John Thomas Smith, the contemporary chronicler of London's beggars.[17]

Beyond the collective life of black servants in London we have little idea how the black poor lived. Servants out of place through bad behaviour or misfortune, sailors unable to get a berth through injury, runaways hiding from a reward, all ended up in the swarming courts and alleys of central London. Their opportunities to make a living were curtailed in the City by a deliberate act of discrimination, the Corporation preventing freemen from taking on black apprentices from 1731; and 'No negro or mulatto girl' could find a home and training for service at the Asylum for Orphan Girls established in Lambeth by Sir John Fielding in 1758. Besides these penal disabilities, black men were also subject to the press gang – Michael Thomas narrowly escaped impressment at the altar when he married Ann Brandley, his white bride, at St Olave's, Southwark, in November 1770; and they perhaps unduly suffered the inhumanities of the poor law – 'a poor black fellow' too ill to walk was seen dumped from a cart over the City border by parish officers unwilling to pay for his care around 1784, for instance.[18]

In terms, though, of the informal workings of London in street, pub

and lodging house, what evidence we have points to the full integration of blacks into metropolitan plebeian life. It was helped by
intermarriage between black men and white women, common if only
because the proportion of black women in London compared to men
was so small. Perhaps a case that entered the Old Bailey lists in 1781
might reveal something of the day-to-day relationships of blacks and
whites in London's poorest areas.

John Downs, a black man who lived 'at Mrs Williams's in Fleet-
street', was drinking heavily at the Sir John Falstaff in St Giles on a
Monday night. 'Sarah Robinson was there; she asked me to drink,
and said she was very hungry; I gave her three-pence to get something
to eat; she was very ragged; I asked her if she had no better clothes
than those on her back; she said her clothes were in pawn: I gave her
some money to get them out.' Sarah took Downs to Elizabeth James's
bawdy house, also in St Giles. 'This black man came on Saturday
night, between eight and nine, and asked me if I had a lodging; I said,
yes . . . Sarah Robinson was with him; he was very much in liquor
indeed.' During the night, Sarah tried to leave the house and Mrs
James's suspicions were aroused. 'I said she should not go home till
I waked the black man, to see if he was safe or no: I went up stairs
with her, and shoved him about with my hand, but could not wake
him; I persuaded her to go to bed with him till morning', and then
went to bed herself, taking 'the key of the street-door with me'. But
Sarah left through a window, taking Downs's silver watch worth £3,
a pair of pinchbeck shoe buckles, and 3 guineas and 8s he'd had in
his pocket. For good measure she took some of Mrs James's clothes
with her.

Next morning, Downs knocked on Mrs James's room door and
reported his losses. Knowing where to find Robinson, Mrs James went
with Downs and a constable to her lodgings and found her hiding in
a room. 'I told her to pull my gown and apron off, to give me the
Black's things, and I would forgive her as to my things.' The watch and
buckles she'd given to her landlady for disposal and were recovered,
but the guineas had gone. Robinson was imprisoned for theft and her
landlady for receiving. Downs apologised for involving the constable
and gave Sarah sixpence.[19]

Perhaps Mrs James's solicitude for John Downs's welfare was merely
commercially prudent – had he complained to the constable that he'd
been robbed in her house there could have been repercussions, even a

suspicion she had been involved. But there is nothing here to show that Downs was treated less well than any other man with ready money in his pocket. And nor was he excluded from any of the pleasures (and risks) of London life. It's plain, too, that he played his full part in the poor helping the poor.

Not all black Londoners in the 1780s, though, were as fortunate as John Downs. The dog days of the American Revolutionary War and its conclusion in 1783 brought to London probably some hundreds of black loyalists who had served in the land forces or navy. They were ill-connected and ill-equipped to be useful in a metropolitan labour market temporarily dislocated by a post-war slump in demand, made worse by demobilisation. Unable to find work, these newcomers soon became 'alarmingly conspicuous throughout the streets as common beggars'.[20] Others took to crime. Until the 1780s black people appear in the Old Bailey Proceedings as much victims as perpetrators, if not more so. From the summer of 1783 that changes, and blacks accused of property crime become more common, though the number of 'negroes' coming to trial remains very small – just five in 1783–4, for instance.

The condition of 'the black poor' after 1783 drew considerable attention from an anxious London middle class. Anxiety and philanthropy combined in 1786 to project an expedition to settle black Londoners in Africa – hardly resettle, for almost all had been born into slavery in the Caribbean or America. Motives were mixed. For some philanthropists the project was largely a matter of humanity, giving blacks new hope away from a city that seemed unable to grant them either dignity or a livelihood. For others, and for the government that subsidised the venture, humane motives were diluted by the desire to rid London of a potentially disruptive problem. For the blacks in general, though there were some doubters, the proposal was broadly welcomed, Olaudah Equiano for a time playing a part in its practical arrangements. The voyage to establish Freetown, the brainchild of Granville Sharp and the Committee for the Relief of the Black Poor, sailed from London on 8 April 1787, with more than 400 blacks and 'about sixty Europeans, chiefly women'.[21]

The black presence in London, then, was most conspicuous and problematic in the 1780s, but throughout the century it was a striking feature of metropolitan life. It was supplemented in the last forty years or so by growing numbers of 'blacks' from the Indian sub-continent.

There were two main groups – sailors and domestic servants, mainly from India but also the Far East, including Malaysia. The sailors, known as lascars, were in greatest numbers but largely visible only in the north-eastern riverside districts where the East India Company's ships berthed. Indian seamen were employed on the Company's ships throughout the century. By 1767, and for at least the next twenty years, the Company was boarding many of its lascars at the Orchard House, in an inaccessible corner of east Blackwall on the far side of the Isle of Dogs. It was probably a lascar from here, 'lately come from the East Indies', who ventured into London a couple of years later and defaced with a knife the statue of Queen Anne in St Paul's: he was sent to Bedlam as a lunatic.[22]

Most of the London lascars appear to have been Bengalis and 'Mahommedans', though they were called by English names for the convenience of their masters. With a shortage of English seamen caused by the demands of war from the late 1770s and from 1793 in particular, more lascars and Chinese sailors were brought into East Indiamen trading to India, the Malays and China. The last twenty years of the century saw their numbers peak, to around a thousand or so at any point in time. Something like a panic over lascars said to be assaulting and cutting women in the East End of London disturbed the press in February 1780, though the peaceable nature of the foreigners was cited to decry the rumours. Perhaps more concretely, the mix of lascar and Chinese seamen proved explosive. A desperate affray at Stepney in October 1785 involved 'a great riot' with swords and 'long knives' around a lascar lodging house.[23]

There was also a distinctive presence in the west end of the town of Indian servants who, across the century, had been brought to London by the white 'nabobs' of the East India Company and its fellow travellers. They were possessions of status and fascination. Boswell noted in 1772 one director of the Company who 'had an Indian lad and an Indian boy for his servants', and in 1781 a director of the Sun Fire Office with 'extensive properties in the East Indies', with a 'black boy called Tom' who 'attended me well and put on my wig'. William Hickey returned from India in 1780, bringing with him Nabob, 'my little Bengally', who proved more decorous than useful. Not all were treated well. Susannah, just fifteen and with no other name, described as 'a negro' in the Old Bailey proceedings of 1795, in fact came to London with her mistress, Polly Hill Bridges, 'when she was a girl; I brought her with me from the east Indies'. She had been a servant for 'about nine years' but received no wages – 'None at all'. Susannah was transported for seven years for stealing from the Bridges. But it was probably her mistress's testimony that saved her from the gallows: 'I am afraid she has been ill advised, or she never would have committed such a crime'; she had 'A very good opinion of her'.[24]

In sum, among the oppression and abuse of blacks in London we can discern, in the lives of Sancho and others, countervailing moments of kindness, affection and respect. In all, there was a general acceptance and inclusion of blacks in London society, certainly in the ranks of the plebeians and in the middling-rank foothills of domestic service. In an age of considerable hostility to foreigners, not all non-British Londoners would be able to say the same.

'Foreign Varlets': Europeans and Some Others

Europeans in London often had an uneasy time of it. After all, Britain was at war with France and sometimes Spain for much of the century. It was in the nature of things that the French, such close neighbours, would be those most likely to visit or seek their fortune in London. But the only French subjects really welcomed were those refugees who, for reasons of religion or politics, held traitorous notions of their motherland and were keen to aid Britain against its old enemy. That seemed just reward, given that France succoured the Jacobite court that had fled Britain in 1688 and actively fostered the rebellions of 1715 and 1745.

Despite this difficult climate, the place of the French in London life was vibrant throughout the century. By far the most significant French migration to London, for its lasting economic and cultural impact throughout the eighteenth century and beyond, was the Huguenot diaspora. Protestants had been persecuted in France for more than a century before their limited privileges were finally removed by the Revocation of the Edict of Nantes in 1685. For twenty years before that, migration of the Huguenots from their settlements near the extremities of France, most notably around Bordeaux in the south-west, had brought a 'trickle' to England. After 1685 it became a 'torrent' that continued less swiftly into the early years of the eighteenth century.

Most settled in London. By 1700 there were perhaps 25,000 in a city of something over half a million.[25]

The Huguenots made two London districts peculiarly their own. In the west, Soho – an area still in building at the end of the seventeenth century, with much property unlet and available for the newcomers – was substantially a French quarter by the early 1700s. In 1711 probably two out of five inhabitants of the whole parish of St Anne were French, with dense clusters in the south-east around Old Compton Street. Of the 3,000–4,000 French residents, most were lodgers rather than house-holders, yet lodgers with a distinctively middling-class air or above. The charity disbursing relief to the Huguenots in 1705 was assisting 164 'Gentilhommes' and 361 'Bourgeoisie', of no regular profession, who had lived in France 'upon their estates'. Most of the former were in Soho, the latter more widely scattered in Soho, Seven Dials and Spitalfields. This last was the second great area of settlement, on the eastern border of the City of London, a largely plebeian colony of artisans and journeymen silk weavers, but with a significant scattering of bourgeois masters. The Huguenots didn't bring silk weaving to Spitalfields, but their skills in fashionable fine French silks transformed the industry into one of the great forces in London manufacturing. In 1705 many hundreds of these weavers were getting charitable relief of one kind or another, especially in north-west Spitalfields around Wheeler Street, Brick Lane, Petticoat Lane and Brown's Lane (now Hanbury Street).[26]

The Huguenot migration was unique in its size and suddenness and character, for these were newcomers often well educated and mostly armed with marketable skills. Their Protestantism mitigated the fact they were French and in general they found favour in London, though some resentment was initially felt by English weavers in the East End. Huguenots were prominent among London merchants – it was said that a drop of Huguenot blood in the veins was worth £1,000 a year – and among artists and men of science (Louis François Roubiliac, the brilliant sculptor, and John Dollond the occulist, might stand for both Huguenot cultures). And they were inventive and hard-working at everything to which they turned their hands, whether market gardening and flower growing at Chelsea and Battersea, calico printing and felt hat making in Wandsworth, or watch- and clockmaking, gun making, silversmithing and cabinetmaking in the artisan parishes of Westminster.[27]

The Huguenots' enterprise and imagination, steeped in French styles, fitted well into a city where luxury commodities knew no excess of extravagance. Their self-help friendly societies, often based on the regions of France from which they claimed an original allegiance, their hospital in Old Street, their soup kitchen ('The Soup') and almshouses in Spitalfields, all cushioned any burden to the poor law authorities. These were powerful aids to acceptance and assimilation. And apart from a brief but noisy migration in 1707–8 of Camisards, the 'French prophets', whose theatrical convulsions drew large audiences to their services, Huguenot Protestantism was much in the undemonstrative English mould. It espoused both the established church and respectable nonconformity and spawned a shoal of congregations. By 1700 there were nine French churches in Spitalfields and fourteen in Westminster (seven of them Anglican); the great church in Fournier Street, Spitalfields, was built in 1743. Until the mid-century these congregations were generally French-speaking and thriving, but by 1780 the decline of both had become irreversible, and most Huguenots appeared largely indistinguishable from the Londoners around them. The twenty-three French Protestant churches of 1700 had fallen to eleven by 1782 and in 1800 to just eight.[28]

Despite the enduring enmity between Britain and France, London proved an alluring draw to other Frenchmen and women of talent. There was considerable aristocratic patronage of a great cast of Frenchmen working in the luxury trades – hairdressers, wig makers, fencing masters, upholders or upholsterers (interior designers), cooks and confectioners, valets and footmen and ladies' maids, dentists (male and female), clap doctors, dressmakers and tailors, all to the disgust of those who equated a tide of luxurious effeminacy with a corrupting foreign influence. Popular resentment occasionally flared up. There were riots against 'foreign Varlets', or a French acting company, at the Little Theatre, Haymarket, in October 1738, 'a sharp and bloody battle', all in front of the French ambassador; and at the same place in November 1749, when aristocratic supporters of the 'French Strolers' drew swords and wounded some of the opposition. In 1744 a planned meeting of footmen protesting about their Swiss and French fellows turned into a riot against the Bow Street magistrate when he ordered they be locked out of the meeting room. And French servants were frequent butts on the London stage: '"you will find al de doors dat was shut in your face as footman Anglois, will fly open demselve to a French *valet de chambre*"', and so a Yorkshireman turns French to get a job in London in Foote's *The Liar* of 1762.[29]

The association of the French with aristocratic insouciance, their taking the Englishman's roast beef from the very tip of his tongue and their general untrustworthiness as spies in time of war combined to make a Frenchman justly nervous on the streets of London, as Pierre Jean Grosley found in the 1760s:

My French air, notwithstanding the simplicity of my dress, drew upon me, at the corner of every street, a volley of abusive litanies, in the midst of which I slipt on, returning thanks to God, that I did not understand English. The constant burthen of these litanies was, French dog, French b—; to make any answer to them, was accepting a challenge to fight; and my curiosity did not carry me so far.[30]

The connection between French migrants and the luxury trades bound them to the parishes of Westminster, particularly Soho, where Huguenot penetration had eased the way. Many tradesmen and professionals catered for their fellow countrymen, though some French restaurants attracted Londoners of all origins, like the 'ordinaries' in Suffolk Street, behind the Haymarket, and notably Pontack's near the Royal Exchange in the City. And the community seems to have been the only one of the century to sustain a bookshop, Paul Vaillant's in the Strand, or produce foreign-language newspapers in London, the *Gazette de Londres* before 1703, the *Courier Politique et Littéraire, or French Evening Post* in the 1770s, and the *Courier de Londres*, printed in Coventry Street, in the 1790s.

From the earliest years of the century, and in those same Westminster parishes of St Anne's, Soho, St Martin-in-the-Fields, St James's and St Paul's, Covent Garden, the French mingled with artists and artisans from all over Europe, but especially the Dutch, the Germans and the Italians. London drew them as it drew other men and women of genius – because in general it paid better for their talents than anywhere else in the reachable world. Foreigners brought talents that the British lacked until, in the second half of the century, the natives had learned sufficient from the migrants to rival, rarely surpass, continental genius.

Among the painters Sir Godfrey Kneller, a German and 'still Gottfried Kniller when he opened his mouth',[31] was something akin to the father of English portraiture. He founded the first English painting and drawing academy in Great Queen Street, Lincoln's Inn Fields, in 1711, with a Swede, an Italian and a Frenchman alongside three English painters as the co-founders. A Frenchman and a Dutchman established in 1720 another artists' academy in St Martin's Lane – Hogarth was an early member. Among many others we might mention Johann Zoffany, from Bavaria, in London from 1758, who nearly starved in a garret until finding work painting clock faces for 'Rimbault, a celebrated Musical Clock-maker' in Seven Dials, before his genius for portraiture was finally discovered, by David Garrick and others.[32]

Sculpture in London throughout the century was dominated by Dutch masters like Peter Scheemakers (designer of the Shakespeare monument in Westminster Abbey), Michael Rysbrack (in London from 1720, employed – on stingy terms, it is said – by James Gibbs for monuments in St Martin-in-the-Fields, and one of the most commissioned sculptors of the age);[33] and by Italians like Giuseppe Ceracchi (a Roman in London from 1773, with extensive workshops near Cavendish Street) and John Baptist Locatelli from Verona, occasionally commissioned by Robert Adam, who in 1776 took over workshops near the Middlesex Hospital previously used by another Italian called Angelini.

In the first half-century, engraving – so useful for bringing art into the homes of the middling classes – was an entirely continental skill, mainly French. It was fostered by Hubert-François Gravelot, in London from 1732, later keeping a drawing school under the sign of the Pestle and Mortar in James Street, Covent Garden; by Simon François Ravenet, a Parisian commissioned by Hogarth to come to London to engrave *Marriage à la Mode* around 1743 and who never left; by Louis-Philippe Boitard, who illustrated eighty-six *Cries of London* in 1766; and by numerous others. For superfine craftsmanship in the building trades the Italians outstripped all contenders. Gibbs commissioned the *stuccatori* Giuseppe Artori and Giovanni Bagutti for the plasterwork on St Martin-in-the-Fields and other projects, including his own house in Henrietta Street; and Robert Adam used 'an unusual number of foreign artists', among them at least six Italian decorative painters.[34] For much of the century too, as we shall see, Italians and Germans dominated musical life in London.

The luxurious appetites of Londoners magnetised the talents of Europe, most notably in the arts but in other fields also. London's mercantile community made a City cosmopolis almost to match that of the west end of the town. The Germans and Dutch were most prominent, but there were Swedes, Swiss and Frenchmen among them. And, less reputably, London attracted to the cosmopolitan parishes of

Westminster a ragged crew of 'sharpers and adventurers', bankrupts and criminals, seeking there the luck that had run out elsewhere:[35]

> London! The needy Villain's gen'ral Home,
> The Common Shore of *Paris* and of *Rome*[.][36]

Besides the French and the Jews, whom we'll meet in a moment, the only other European migrants to build something like a London community were the Germans. Hamburg merchants in London had settled in sufficient numbers to found a Lutheran church in the City in 1669, and there were enough artisans (clockmakers, tailors, enamellers, glassmakers, shoemakers and bakers) in Westminster to start a breakaway church in the Savoy in 1694, with a second there in 1697. The connections between the court of William of Orange and the House of Hanover were also close enough to establish a German Court Chapel at St James's Palace in 1700. By then or shortly after, a German hotel and guest houses were sharing Suffolk Street with the French, making it the first call for foreign travellers right through the century.[37]

In 1708–9 some 10,000–13,000 mainly Protestant Palatines from south-west Germany arrived in London, migrating for reasons of economic betterment as much as religious persecution. They were mainly herded into temporary shelter in a tented camp at Blackheath and barns at Deptford, Lambeth and Kennington. Many died from 'distemper', cold and hunger, despite a royal bounty and much charitable giving. An entirely rural population by origin, they were shipped to Ireland, the West Indies and America. Few seem to have settled in London, though 200 or so found their way back to Southwark from Ireland in late 1710.[38]

There were, then, many intimate networks of Germans in London even before the Elector of Hanover succeeded to the throne on the death of Anne in 1714. The monarchy would remain as much Hanoverian as British until 1760, and the crown imported from Germany mistresses, courtiers and servants in droves. It all gave further encouragement to German artisans, traders, musicians, theatrical impresarios and dancers – David Garrick's wife, Eva Maria Veigel, arrived from Vienna as a dancer with the Italian Opera Company at the Haymarket Theatre in the 1740s, for instance – to come to London to cling to the gilded curtilage of St James's Palace. There were two main areas of settlement – in Westminster around south Soho and

St Martin-in-the-Fields, and in Whitechapel and Wapping, where German sugar boilers had begun to oust the Dutch from that sweet but sweaty trade by the late 1740s. The long-lived German church at Alie Street, Whitechapel, was founded for these workers in 1762. There was also a small community of Moravians at Chelsea from 1750 till the end of the century, and probably the beginnings of a suburban migration to Hackney, where German market gardeners had established nurseries from 1756.[39]

There would be another dramatic appearance of the German Palatines in late summer 1764, when 600 were abandoned on the Thames by a contractor shipping them to America. Most lay starving in the open air at Goodman's Fields, Whitechapel, until their plight reached the papers and tents and food were provided; they were finally shipped at the crown's expense to South Carolina. And refugees sought succour in London from one or other troubled spot in a troubled century, from Corsican freedom fighters in 1769 and after, to American loyalists from 1775, with larger accessions in 1783.[40]

The most desperate of all came late in the century, and were fleeing for their lives. By the summer of 1790 Horace Walpole noted how Richmond was 'brimful both of French and English', the first wave of an increasingly frantic migration as the terror in France grew yet more merciless. In September 1792 the starving, haggard condition of those arriving was such that it was said poor women seeing them in the London streets spontaneously gave all they had in their pockets as they passed by. Charitable committees were established, one of which by March 1796 was maintaining 6,000–7,000 refugees with government help. But the doles to individuals were so small that 'both Laity and Clergy' had pawned or sold all spare clothing and even 'the beds from under them'. Pregnant women were reported as having to give birth unattended by medical assistance on 'straw, in unfurnished houses, without food or fire, and almost without clothes'. 'Many have died.' The miserable condition of the French refugees continued into the new century, even creating a shabby new émigré suburb at Somers Town. It was unsympathetically nicknamed Botany Bay by Londoners, some of whom could not forget that these were foreigners and French first and refugees second. Walpole recorded in March 1793 that 'Some windows of the poor French émigrés at Richmond have been broken': 'the mob declared it was for having murdered their King.'[41]

We might mention one further group here – the Gypsies. They were a picturesque, sometimes troublesome, feature of life on the edge of London and occasionally at the centre too. Gypsies had been expelled from England under penalty of death by the 1560s. But law was one thing and Gypsies another, and they were well established in London throughout the eighteenth century. They were engaged most of all with horse dealing and fortune-telling at the fairs and markets around the built-up area, but some old connections with the heart of the city lived on, in echoes at least. We hear of Jacob Rewbrey, King of the Gypsies, of St Margaret's, Westminster, in the Old Bailey Proceedings for 1700, convicted of theft. Margaret Finch, Queen of the Gypsies, was buried at Beckenham in 1740 at the age, it was said, of 109: she had settled at Norwood, where she told fortunes, and was so crippled she had to be buried in a square box. Her niece and successor, Old Bridget, Queen of the Gypsies, was buried at Dulwich in 1768. And in 1773, after a funeral attended by 200 'loyal subjects' at Newington churchyard,

The cloaths of the late Diana Boswell, Queen of the Gypsies, value 50l. were burnt in the middle of the Mint, Southwark, by her principal courtiers, according to ancient custom; it being too great an honour for subjects to be clothed in robes of state, and too great a disgrace for her successor to appear in second hand royalty.[42]

Gypsies were found right round London's built-up area – at Harrow on the Hill, Edmonton, Green Lanes in Stoke Newington, famed for its 'gipsy tribe', indeed throughout 'the Bye-Lanes within four Miles of London, making Fires with Sticks pulled out of Hedges, and boiling Turkeys, Fowls, and other Provisions stole in the Night'. But the most famous Gypsy communities were in south-east London, most notably Norwood. George Bubb Dodington took the Prince and Princess of Wales and a large party 'in private coaches to Norwood Forest to see a settlement of gypsies' in June 1750; and in August 1798 a palette of artists, including Zoffany and Joseph Farington, found a Gypsy family and an old woman who named forty things 'the same as the language of the natives of Bengal – 26 of them precisely'.[43]

The penumbra of criminality apparently inseparable from the Gypsy name also surprisingly shadowed the reputation of an even more stigmatised minority of eighteenth-century London – the Jews.

'Offscourings of Humanity': Jewish Londoners

The Jewish community in London around 1700 was probably no larger than a hundred or so families, some 750 people in all. It was officially of very recent date, Oliver Cromwell allowing Jews to settle once more in Britain in the 1650s after a banishment lasting more than three centuries. Spanish and Portuguese or Sephardi Jews, the first to come, had a tradition of international trade, their most prominent men rich merchants dealing with Europe, North Africa and the Ottoman Empire. The Ashkenazim, from Holland and from central Europe, were in general less wealthy but also steeped in trade. At the beginning of the century the two groups were numerous enough each to have founded its own synagogue, the Spanish and Portuguese in Bevis Marks and the Ashkenazi Great Synagogue in Duke's Place. Safety in numbers overcame divisions between one Jew and another, the synagogues a stone's throw apart in Aldgate ward on the eastern edge of the City. And when a new congregation broke away from Duke's Place in 1707, the Hambro' Synagogue was set up a five-minute walk to the south in Magpye Alley, Fenchurch Street.

By the end of the eighteenth century London Jewry had changed in three main ways. First it was very much bigger, with perhaps 15,000 Jews in London by 1800, most of whom had arrived in the past fifty years. Second, the community changed character. Newcomers generally derived from the Ashkenazim of Germany and land to the east – probably just over one in ten of London Jews were Sephardim at the century's end. Many were from poorer, more economically marginal or displaced groups and no longer represented an aristocracy of trade. Third, growth caused the Jewish area of London to spread from Aldgate into Whitechapel, where the City's constraints on freedom of trade – no practising Jew could properly be made free of the City – would no longer frustrate economic enterprise.[44]

Not that the City's restrictive practices, aggravated by a widespread anti-Semitism, could hold back the Jewish merchant class from achieving some astonishing financial successes. Where the City reluctantly tolerated the wealthy Jews in its midst, they made themselves indispensable to crown and government while demanding few political favours in return. When in 1744 several hundred London merchants made public their loyalty to George II as the Pretender gathered his forces in France, more than three dozen Spanish and Portuguese Jews were among them, including six Da Costas, four Francos and five named Mendes. Many Sephardic Jews were well known around the court, then and later, taking pains to stress their Englishness over their religion: 'As they do not wear beards, they cannot be distinguished at all from other people,' a German visitor noted around 1762, his London banker also a Jew.[45]

Among them was Joseph Salvadore, a specialist in gold and silver, sufficiently rich and well connected to broker a government loan issue of £8 million in the 1760s, taking £250,000 of stock himself. Samson Gideon had proved even more vital to earlier administrations of the 1740s, including Sir Robert Walpole's last, subscribing for no less than £600,000 of a £3 million government loan in 1742. Gideon was famed for his liberality, wit and common sense: 'Never grant an annuity for her life to an old woman. They wither, but they *never* die,' was apparently one of his axioms. In the City panic of 1745, when the Jacobite rebels approached Derby, a banker called in a loan of £20,000: 'Gideon sent him a bottle of smelling salts wrapped in twenty £1,000 banknotes.' And Benjamin Mendes da Costa was remembered more for his astonishing generosity than for his wealth, endowing Jewish communities in London and America, sharing 'his bounty' with indigent families (both Christian and Jew) at the cost of £3,000 a year, and ordering that on his death all 'private bonds' or bills in his hands be destroyed to relieve his debtors.[46]

Most Jewish moneylenders, and there were many lending sums small and large, did not share Mendes da Costa's enviable reputation. 'I must get the money from some soft-hearted Christian, for I hope not to have anything to do with the Jews,' wrote the cash-strapped Earl of Carlisle in February 1773, and there is no doubt that the fear of usury, rocketing debt, arrest and imprisonment, driven by a moneylender who *would* have his pound of flesh, was an enduring nightmare of the age. The moneylending 'son of Israel', often a 'shabby old fellow', 'loathsome', 'noxious', was a common anti-Semitic stereotype. Fanny Burney makes Cecilia's heart recoil 'at the very mention of a *Jew*, and *taking up money upon interest*'; 'I dread the whole race,' says another character. On the stage, too, the City Jew was a popular butt, despite the occasional well-known Jewish performer, like the singer Michael Leoni and the comedian J. de Castro. Moses Manasses was a more typical stage Jew, 'Vast finely dressed', keen to take up membership of Boodle's or Almack's but always blackballed – 'perhaps, my religion vas de objection'. Only rarely was there public reflection that the victim could be as much to blame as the stage villain, as in the case of that most reckless and indefatigable gambler of the age, the brilliant wastrel Charles James Fox. At one of his crashes, around 1773, a piece of doggerel entered West End consciousness that was much quoted, in one form or another, for years to come. It seems to take some pleasure in the discomfort of high-dressing men about town, the Macaronis:

> But hark! the shouts of battle sound from far!
> The Jews and Macaronis are at war.
> The Jews prevail, and thund'ring from the stocks,
> They seize, they bind, they circumcise Charles Fox.[47]

Just twelve Jewish brokers were licensed to trade stock on the exchange at any time in the century, and they were likely to have been among the super-rich lending to Fox. But the lending and trading fraternities were widespread and with luck and sharp wits could prosper. Those who did founded an anglicised suburban presence, noted at Hackney Triangle by the late seventeenth century, in Highgate by the 1720s, Stoke Newington from the 1740s and Stamford Hill by the 1760s. Wealthy Jews also provided financial backbone for the institutions of London Jewry. The best-endowed of these were the synagogues and their charitable networks. Duke's Place was rebuilt in 1766, dedicated with prayers to the King and Queen and a performance of Handel's Coronation Anthem, and the New Synagogue opened for an Ashkenazi congregation at Leadenhall Street in 1761. By then there were three Jewish burial grounds along the Mile End Road, others in Hoxton Town and Hackney, a hospital in Leman Street and an almshouse and three charity schools near Bevis Marks. Another hospital, for the Ashkenazim, was projected in the 1790s in Mile End Old Town but not opened till 1806. As the community spread east so did their synagogues, a congregation forming at Rosemary Lane in 1748, and at Gun Yard, Houndsditch, and nearby Cutler Street (for Polish Jews) in the 1790s. And throughout the Jewish districts of Aldgate and Whitechapel the community's dietary and other needs were met by a small host of kosher butchers, ritual slaughtermen, Hebrew booksellers, specialist outfitters and suppliers of sacred objects for the home. There was even a brothel conveniently close to the Aldgate synagogues at 4 Beaker's Gardens, Leadenhall Street, known for its Jewish clients.[48]

This was by no means an entirely separate world from the rest of London. High finance connected the *ton* of Anglo-Jewry with the court, Jewish moneylenders were intimately involved with the lives of debtors among the middling sort of people, and the many Jewish Freemasons in the City shook hands with their Gentile brethren. So too the Jewish poor, encouraged to come to London by the wealth and generosity of its Anglo-Jewish community and the prospects to be had there, had to make a living jostling with the rest of the metropolitan poor. Jewish hawkers, peddlers and old-clothes dealers were familiar figures on the London streets. These were trades they brought with them or fell into because they needed no capital that could not be readily borrowed, not many English words and no tuition. Jewish street traders made certain commodities pretty much their own – oranges and lemons, spectacles, penknives, pencils and more. The City authorities were generally down on hawking as inimical to the freeman in his shop, and Jewish hawkers were at risk of arrest and a whipping in Bridewell. But in the plebeian districts just beyond the City border they were well known, especially in the old-clothes trade.[49]

'The Jews were the only people who went about crying "old clothes" for the purpose of purchasing them,' recalled Francis Place. They were 'ragged' and 'exceedingly dirty in their persons', and 'almost universally wore their beards long'. The old-clothes men sold their wares to shopkeepers in London's thriving second-hand trade. Certain streets specialised in it, like Monmouth Street (Seven Dials), Middle Row (Holborn) and Field Lane (Saffron Hill). But the great old-clothes market of London was Rag Fair, in Rosemary Lane, Whitechapel, where 'it is amazing to see the great number of Jews who resort to it every afternoon with such things as they have purchased during their morning walk through the streets of London'. Some of the traders there were famously wealthy, dealing with country shopkeepers and exporting 'to foreign parts'.[50]

We know very little of those poor Jews who made a living in the London streets, but on the rare occasions they appear in the records their lives and deaths seem hardly different from those of the poor all around them. In January 1794 a City inquest heard of the death of Joseph Moses, of 10 Bartholomew Court, Arrow Alley, Houndsditch. He lodged in a garret and 'used to go about the Streets calling Sticks and Slippers'. He was a heavy drinker and would 'hardly come home sober one night in a week'. His sister found him at the bottom of the stairs after he had apparently missed his footing when drunk. She called a surgeon but Moses was dead when he reached him.[51]

Buying cheap and selling dear could hardly avoid the taint of cheating and taking advantage, whoever was involved in the trade. Sometimes cheating was intrinsic to the enterprise. The most profitable, though risky, end of the 'second-hand' trade was dealing in stolen property. Every thief needed a 'fence' and every plebeian district of London had its publican or pawnbroker or other dealer who would buy what was stolen and sell at a profit. The vast majority of fences were not, of course, Jewish. But a Jewish fence with connections on the Continent was well placed to give a good price for stolen gold and silver. The Jewish receiver of stolen property became a stock figure of the age and there was indeed some foundation to the stereotype. In 1770 the community itself was sufficiently alarmed by the phenomenon, real and imagined, for a synagogue to advertise a reward for anyone securing the conviction of a Jewish receiver.[52]

This was one more connection between Jewry and other Londoners. Relations between Jewish fence and Gentile thief had to be intimate and based on a great deal of trust. 'When Nokes brought the Jew to us; he said he was a good honest fellow; he had known him a great many years, and was what they call an Old Fence', a Smithfield thief turned King's evidence swore at the Old Bailey in January 1764. The fence in question was Hyman Levi, in Houndsditch seven or eight years: 'I am an old cloathsman, and dress old hats. I was crying old cloaths in Bread-street in the city; Nokes called me behind, and said, will you buy a parcel of cloaths?' A few years later and a watchful citizen reported, 'I saw the two prisoners,' one a boy of eleven, 'near Houndsditch; they were enquiring for a Jew, whose character, I have heard, is that of a notorious receiver of stolen goods'. 'Old Mrs Moses' offered £100 for banknotes stolen from the Norwich mail outside a pub in Mile End Road in 1780; when she didn't come to collect them the thieves panicked and fled to Ireland. Henry Lee, aka Levy, aka Hetsey, 'a noted receiver of stolen goods', was found red-handed with both the thieves and a large quantity of 'thread lace' at a house in Smithfield in 1781: he absconded from his bail and didn't stand trial. Whether he was the 'Mr Levy' of Frying Pan Alley, Petticoat Lane, suspected of handling stolen aniseed liquor in 1787 is unclear. There were numerous similar references in the Old Bailey Proceedings till the century's end.[53]

All of these cases involved 'Christian' thieves, but there was a notable fringe of criminality among the Ashkenazi migrants of the second half of the century. Jews, like other City men, were not immune from the crime of forgery of bills and Bank of England notes, and Jewish swindlers and fraudsters from Germany and Amsterdam were said to have set up in London from around 1762. But the character of crime in the Jewish community shifted decisively from about 1770. A visitor from Germany, where there were many penal restrictions on Jewish life, tarred all with one brush when describing the position in London of 'the German Jews, a class of men, detested as the offscourings of humanity', living by 'cheating and nocturnal rapine'. But it is clear that there was a small minority among the new migrants who followed crime as their profession.[54]

A few were desperate men. In June 1771 a gang of eight or nine Jewish thieves broke into the farmhouse of young Mrs Hutchins, a widow, in the King's Road, Chelsea, terrorising the household, shooting dead a manservant and making off with plate, linen and money. Four of them were hanged at Tyburn. Duke's Place synagogue pronounced an anathema on all those yet to be discovered. In February 1775 about forty 'Low Jews and Christians' armed with cutlasses and pistols combined to rescue Patrick Madan, a troublesome and notorious London thief, from Moorfields watch-house, almost demolishing it in the process. When thirteen came to trial in Clerkenwell that April 'the mob of low Jews and Christians round Hickes's-Hall was greater than ever remembered'. Jewish housebreakers around Houndsditch were said in the 1780s to be equipped with crucibles and furnaces for melting plate; they were connected to dealers in Holland, who disposed of their spoils on the Continent. And a dozen Jews and Christians combined again in a desperate attempt to rescue a suspected Jewish forger from the New Prison, Clerkenwell, in 1795.[55]

When the City Recorder sentenced the burglars of the Chelsea farm in December 1771 he 'called attention to the laudable conduct of the principal Jews, and hoped no one would stigmatize a whole nation for the villainies of a few . . .' Well he might. For among the common people of London – just as in the corridors of the Guildhall and the salons of the great – Jews were deeply disliked. They may have received official toleration to trade and practise their religion and traditions, but economic obstacles were put in their way, they were grossly libelled in the press as child-killers, and in 1753 a bill to permit the naturalisation of certain rich Jews in very limited circumstances drew a campaign of vilification against London Jewry distinguished by unreason and prejudice in equal measure. The City Corporation was predictably among the bill's, and the Jews', noisiest detractors. They were joined by pious Christians in flocks. The 'Jew Bill' duly foundered.[56]

Only one outbreak of collective violence against the Jews has come down to us. In June 1763, when crowds were celebrating the young king's birthday, a crush at Tower Hill killed six and wounded many others. In the melee a Jewish pickpocket was caught stealing from a sailor. After being ducked as usual in the nearest standing water,

he pretended to have his leg broke, and was carried off by some of his brethren. But the sailors discovering the trick, and considering it as a cheat, pursued him to Duke's Place, where, at first, they were beaten off by the inhabitants; but presently returning with a fresh reinforcement, they attacked the place, entered three houses, threw every thing they met with out at the window, broke the glasses, tore the beds, and ript up the wainscot, leaving the houses in the most ruinous condition; with the furniture three children sick of the small-pox were thrown out, but happily received no damage.[57]

This was a year of demobilisation and violent industrial dispute, and sailors could be truculent at the best of times. But if the daily interaction between Jews and other Londoners only very rarely partook of collective hostility, it remained frequently nervy and uncomfortable for the Jews throughout the century. Carl Philipp Moritz, a German literary scholar friendly to the Jews who visited London in 1782, thought the 'antipathy and prejudice against the Jews' was 'far more common here, than it is even with us'. It readily expressed itself in scornful looks and physical Jew-baiting. One instance came to public notice in 1776 when a woman in charge of a Westminster pub was prosecuted 'for assaulting and greasing the chin of a Jew with pork' and had to pay him £10 damages. According to Francis Place, such outrages were commonplace:

It was thought good sport to maltreat a Jew, and they were often most bar-barously used, even in the principal streets . . . "Go to Chelsea" was a common exclamation when a jew was seen in the streets, and was often the signal of assault. I have seen many jews hooted, hunted, kicked, cuffed, pulled by the beard, spit up, and so barbarously assaulted in the streets, without any protection, from the passers by, or the police . . . Dogs could not now be used in the streets, in the manner many jews were treated.[58]

Place thought the treatment of Jews improved once they felt confident enough to retaliate. And retaliation was encouraged, according to Place, by the remarkable Daniel Mendoza, born into poor circumstances in Aldgate in 1764. Apprenticed to a glass-cutter, he was discharged for fighting his master's son. Working for a Jewish fruiterer, he found himself battling the local youths, who insulted his employers on account of their religion, and soon 'I became the terror of these gentry'. By the age of sixteen he was fighting for a purse and soon 'Mendoza the Jew' was one of the most celebrated prizefighters in an age which valued highly such profitable prowess. In 1786 he opened a boxing school at Capel Court behind the Royal Exchange, and had numerous Jews among his scholars.[59]

There will have been many reasons why the treatment of Jews in the London streets slowly became less barbarous, not least an increasing refinement of manners and politeness among most ranks during the timespan Place had in mind. But at the margins it may have been that the rise of Mendoza and what we might christen 'muscular Judaism' was one factor influencing events towards the century's end. Certainly, readiness to use one's fists was always a useful attribute in eighteenth-century London. It was frequently resorted to by a London minority of great importance in the history of the metropolis: the Irish.

'Get Up, You Irish Papist Bitch': Irish Londoners

The Irish, of course, were well known in London, but that did not necessarily make them welcome to the general run of Londoners. The Irish poor have received most attention from historians – and provoked most hostility at the time – but in fact London proved an irresistible lure to all classes of Irish throughout the century. '*London* has very attractive Charms for most People, as our *Irish* Nobility and Gentry sufficiently evidence, by spending the greatest Part of their Time and Fortune there,' wrote Laetitia Pilkington in 1748, and she was living proof that the metropolitan dragnet swept more widely still. For it was the men and women 'of energy, ambition, talent, and character' who were tempted most by London, to the detriment of Ireland but to the glory of the metropolis.[60]

Irish soldiers, lawyers, Protestant clergymen, politicians, scientists and doctors all made names for themselves in London, among them stars enlightening any galaxy, like Edmund Burke, the political philosopher, and the philanthropic physician and scholarly collector Sir Hans Sloane. Most of all, the Irish shone in the visual arts, the theatre and in print, where domestic opportunities for the display of genius were absent or constrained. The rich metropolitan market for pictures brought to London Robert Barker from County Meath, inventor of the panorama, coining the name and making a stir with it in the capital in 1792. Displayed at the rotunda he had specially built in Leicester Square, his huge 360-degree canvases won the admiration of the greatest artists of the age. Barker's 1799 panorama of the Battle of the Nile was called 'the most correct picture of any event I have ever seen' by Horatio Nelson. A more troubled close contemporary, James Barry the history painter, born near Cork in 1741, was brought to London by Irish patrons to work under James 'Athenian' Stuart. Barry won some notoriety for his rather blatant treatment of female nudity, and his intractable nature created discord in the Royal Academy. He declined into paranoia and self-neglect, dying at his house in Castle Street East (now Eastcastle Street) on the Harley-Portland Estate in 1806.[61]

Actors and actresses dissatisfied with the rewards of the Dublin stage tried their luck in London, often moving between the two, and with great success if the brogue could be suppressed sufficient to appease metropolitan humours. Charles Macklin, probably from County Donegal, left Dublin for England in 1708, eventually making a name for himself in London in 1733; famously short-tempered, he killed another actor during a row by pushing a walking stick into his eye – he was acquitted of murder at the Old Bailey but branded on the hand for manslaughter. Macklin died at his Covent Garden home in 1797, aged nearly 100. Thomas Sheridan, from Dublin, spent much of his theatre career from 1758 in London, subsequently overshadowed by his brilliant son. Margaret 'Peg' Woffington was already famed in Dublin before moving to London in 1740. A celebrated beauty, she was Garrick's lover, living with him for a time before his marriage. One of the most popular actresses of the day, she died at her home in Queen's Square (now Queen Anne's Gate) in 1760 and was buried a Protestant, though born a Catholic. Woffington had drawn some fire for her free and scandalous relations with men, and another Irish actress from Dublin, Gertrude Mahon, became one of the most successful London courtesans of the 1770s. Another, Mrs Rudd, the courtesan mistress of Joseph Salvadore, was born in County Armagh.

But it was in the world of letters that the Irish truly showed their genius. The contributions of Jonathan Swift, Laurence Sterne and Oliver Goldsmith in fiction, verse, political pamphleteering and history writing helped mould the culture of the times; the London stage had among its brightest playwrights Isaac Bickerstaff, Arthur Murphy, Richard Brinsley Sheridan and Richard Steele, even better known as an essayist in the *Tatler* and the *Spectator*; Edmond Malone was a leading literary scholar and Laetitia Pilkington a fascinating memoirist and poet. All these mingled indistinguishably among the clubs (where Murphy and Goldsmith were great friends of Johnson) and the soirées of literary London; the Irish painters were equally welcome (Barry aside) in the schools and academies as their British peers; the Irish politicians played as full a part in the House of Commons as any Englishman. These we might think of as the City and West End Irish, and their contribution to London life in the eighteenth century cannot be overestimated, or allowed to be overshadowed by the more fraught presence in the capital of their poorer countrymen.

Even the most brilliant, though, shared something of a common inheritance – impecuniousness. It was not universal. Edmund Burke, in London from 1750 aged twenty-one, lived in Charles Street (now Charles II Street), St James's Square, from 1767; a year later he could write to a friend in Ireland, 'We have purchased an house, rather superb for us, and about 600 acres of Land just by Beconsfield' – he kept up both establishments for many years.[62] And the Irish middling sort in funds could keep up a high style of living. An Irish clergyman, whose name has not come down to us, called at the Irish Walk in the Royal Exchange in August 1761 to raise 'English money' on his letters of credit. An Irish merchant invited him home to dine with 'some of my Countrymen':

And I must confess for yᵉ Honour of old Ireland yᵗ he generously gave us a very elegant Entertainment. The table was coverd wᵗʰ 5 or 6 substantial Dishes after wᶜʰ was servd up A Desert of the finest Fruit out of his own Garden Accompanied wᵗʰ Forreign and Domestic wines of a rich Flavor proper to such a service. W^ch partak'g of plentifully we Nobly Closd y^t Convention wth 2 or 3 Bottles of most Excellent French Claret by way of Bonn Bouche.[63]

In general, though, the limited circumstances that drove the Irish to London travelled with them, an incubus often impossible to shake off. The bailiff and the debtors' prison stared gauntly out at many. And there was much of desperation characterising those who sought to make their mark as adventurers, bluffing their way within London society and grasping at whatever fell within their reach. The tribe was frequently satirised in the first half of the century as 'The Society of Irish Fortune-Hunters', silver-tongued footmen prominent among them, some assuming military rank or aristocratic titles and all seeking to woo and marry a dowry. One came undone when marrying 'the pretended Widow of a Shopkeeper in the *City*', she 'of the County of *Kerry*', for there were Irish fortune-hunters of both sexes. When satirised on the London stage, it was the Irish adventurer and soldier of fortune who most often stepped boldly forward, always with a furious temper, though markedly generous when his ends were won.[64]

In real life some prospered, like Lord Nugent, plain mister when he arrived in London, 'a jovial and voluptuous Irishman, who had left Popery for the Protestant religion, money, and widows'. He married three times and augmented his fortune and estate with every stride to the altar. He never lost his 'coarse and often licentious, but natural, strong, and ready wit', nor his Irish accent. And one Concannen, originally from Dublin, in the 1790s keeper of 'the fashionable gaming house in Grafton Street', Mayfair, was said to have deceived and been deceived by a 'young Lady' – both flaunting a fortune that neither possessed. They made the best of it, moved to Paris and lived by gaming until the revolution incommoded them. In 1796 Concannen was said to be worth £25,000. But most fared less well. In 1730 Stephen Dowdale was hanged as a highwayman at Tyburn Tree. Born in Ireland, he had been sergeant in an Irish regiment in Flanders but couldn't prosper back home after demobilisation. He came to London, 'apply'd himself to the Gaming Tables' and 'resolved to raise Contributions on the Highway'. He 'acted the Beau for some Years . . .'[65]

Perhaps the vicissitudes of the 'Irish literati' in London most spanned the full range from flagrant wealth to plunging poverty. Their sufferings were legendary. Laetitia Pilkington, around 1742, contemplated suicide after 'three Days, and three Nights without Food of any Kind'. She lived hand to mouth on charity, often screwed from the better-off London Irish, under the roof of a grasping landlady in Duke Street, St James's. There she found a 'young Woman, who lodged in the Garret, whom I . . . to the uttermost of my Power supported, as she was my Countrywoman, and in great Distress'. Eventually her landlady had Pilkington arrested by bailiffs for rent arrears – '"Get up, you *Irish Papist Bitch*, and come along with us"' – and she landed for a time in the dreaded Marshalsea.[66]

Oliver Goldsmith was the son of a Protestant clergyman in County Longford. When his father died while Goldsmith was at university the family was left in poverty. Graduating without distinction at Dublin, he took a medical degree in Edinburgh and came to London in his late twenties in 1756, setting up at Bankside, 'a poor physician to the poor'. His Irish background probably telling against him when competing for places as a doctor, he preferred to live by literature. His character was irregular and prodigal – when he had money he spent more than he had, always optimistically anticipating an uncertain income – yet open-hearted and generous to his own detriment. In 1759 a friend visited him in his 'wretched dirty room' in Green Arbour Court near the Old Bailey. Goldsmith relinquished the only chair in the room and seated himself in the window. While they were talking 'a poor ragged girl of very decent behaviour, entered, who, dropping a curtsey, said, "My mama sends her compliments, and begs the favour of you to lend her a chamber-pot full of coals."' The coals were duly scraped together. In and out of debt for most of his busy literary life, he frequently sought refuge from the bailiffs – and the taverns' temptations – in a country retreat at Canonbury House, Islington, yet was still arrested and in sponging houses from time to time. Some of his many difficulties lay in the charity he gave when in funds, especially to his fellow Irish in London. He died owing large sums in 1774, aged about forty-six, 'indebted to the forbearance of creditors for a peaceful burial'.[67]

There are no reliable numbers for the Irish-born in London until 1841. Then they made up 3.9 per cent of the population, after some decades of increasing emigration from Ireland. Demographers have estimated there were some 23,000 Irish in the capital in 1780, less than 3 per cent of the population. The only contemporary figures gave higher proportions but for very specific groups. In the early 1780s, some 8.7 per cent of 3,236 married persons seeking help from the Westminster Dispensary were born in Ireland, with men in the majority (58 per cent). Somewhat later, a census of 2,000 London beggars in 1796–7 claimed that 679 or just over a third were from Ireland. In all it seems that we won't go too far wrong if we think of the Irish-born as making up some 3 per cent of London's population across the century, or something fewer than 30,000 people by its close.[68]

Most, just like the large majority of all Londoners, were working people who laboured with their hands. Among skilled men from Ireland's towns and cities we hear of plasterers, plumbers, engravers, tailors, silk weavers and calico printers in London. Among the labouring poor were female domestic servants, men who were general labourers 'doing any sort of servile work',[69] and porters; most famously there were Irish chairmen and coalheavers, both depending on great bodily strength. And then there were Irish old-clothes dealers, street sellers and beggars of both sexes. Some trades determined where the plebeian Irish lived in London: old-clothes dealers near Rag Fair and Monmouth Street, coal-heavers in Wapping, silk weavers and tailors in Spitalfields and Whitechapel. For the nondescript labouring poor, St Giles-in-the-Fields was home to several thousand of the poorest, who had settled there in the seventeenth century. In all these districts there were many Irish at the lower fringe of the middling sorts – publicans, shopkeepers, lodging-house keepers – more often than not catering for their own countrymen.

Why did Irish workers come to London? The metropolitan draw exerted its usual magnetic influence, but the push factors from Ireland were notorious. There was periodic agrarian distress and industrial dislocation throughout the century, all acting on a population as poor as any in Europe and with no poor law to assist their plight. Indeed, chronic want in the Irish countryside had long made some traditionally dependent in part on the London economy. Each year many hundreds of men and women came from Ireland to the fields about London to help bring in the hay, arriving often in May and returning home at the summer's end. They were, according to Saunders Welch, a London magistrate, 'useful, faithful, good servants to the farmer' and 'of real use to the kingdom'. Nor were they likely to have been among the poorest of the Irish to come to London: 'Every hay-maker is expected to come provided with a fork and a rake of his own', though the farmer had to provide rakes when labour was hard to come by. Irish women were common among the milkmaids of Islington, known (like the Welsh) for their strength. And Irish potato pickers seem to have been employed in the Essex fields close to London by the 1790s.[70]

But when Irish workers settled in London they had much against them. They had no significant Anglo-Irish aristocracy wealthy or selfless enough to stop them becoming a drain on the London poor law, or a nuisance from begging in the streets. Their church, for most of the poor were Roman Catholic while their middling-sort peers were generally Protestant, was outlawed and had no capacity to establish charitable institutions. Back-street mass-houses were persecuted when they came to light, like one in the garret of a little alehouse in Shoreditch in 1735, where near a hundred were gathered, most 'miserably poor and ragged, and upon Examination appear'd to be *Irish*', the priest escaping from a back door. Indeed, 'Popery' was one reason for their unpopularity, and when Jacobitism was resurgent in 1715 and 1745 the Irish were mistrusted as rebels: in 1714 Irish officers were recruiting for the Pretender in London and in the '45 government sent an Irish adventurer to spy out disaffection among the Middlesex haymakers, though he 'found none who had any Regard for the Pretender's Cause'. There were rumours in 1754 that the Pretender planned to kidnap the King with the help of '"1500 Irish chairmen, or that class of people"'. And the religion of many Irish continued to be a source of antagonism late on in the century, with Irish Catholics singled out for ill-treatment in the Gordon Riots of 1780.[71]

Most collective hostility against the Irish, though, was for economic reasons. The worst outbreak of the century took place in the summer of 1736, beginning in Shoreditch and spreading quickly south to Spitalfields and Whitechapel. That year the seasonal haymakers were, or were thought to be, accompanied by Irish workers making inroads into other East End industries. Nearly a week of rioting began on Monday 26 July when workers in Shoreditch took to the streets complaining 'of being underworked, and starved by the Irish, *down with the Irish*, &c.' The immediate cause was an allegation that the contractor building the new church of St Leonard's, Shoreditch, had 'discharged at once a great number of all sorts of labourers, and took in at once Irishmen, who served for above one-third less a day'. True or not, the charge was widely believed, especially among the silk weavers in Spitalfields, who blamed Irish migrant weavers for driving down wages in their own competitive trade.[72]

The rioters' aim was nothing less than to drive the Irish out of east London by destroying the pubs and houses where they lodged. There was serious disorder. For several nights houses had their windows broken and attempts were made to pull them down. A public house in Brick Lane was defended with firearms and a young rioter was killed and seven or eight injured. From Tuesday the crowds were reported to be 4,000 strong and the Tower Hamlets militia was mobilised, strengthened with guards from the Tower. Once the troops appeared 'the mob retired, shifting from one street and alley to another, and gave no resistance', but still sought new targets.[73]

By Friday the disturbances had moved south into Whitechapel, where it was said 'the Mob were come out of Spittle Fields'. Clearly there was some plan in mind. A witness later told the Old Bailey:

On Friday Night, July 30, between 9 and 10, I was at the End of *Red Lion Street*, and I saw the Mob coming down *Bell Yard*, with Sticks and lighted Links. One of them made a sort of a speech directing the rest to go down *Church Lane*, to the *Gentleman and Porter* . . . There was about 50 or 60 of them, and they had 2 or 3 Links with them. One read from a Paper the Signs of the *Gentleman and Porter*, the *Bull and Butcher*, and the Tavern in *Well Street* . . . they had great Sticks, like Stakes out of Bakers Bavins.

That night an Irish lodging house or pub in Leman Street was attacked by 'several hundreds' when Justice Phillips arrived with a party of Guards from the Tower, marching 'quietly, without beat of Drum, and in the dark'. Phillips drew his sword and arrested a man breaking a window with a club: 'I told him, if you don't surrender, I'll run you thro'.' The house escaped with all but its windows intact, and an armed guard had to protect the watch-house where the arrested men were taken. In Rose and Crown Alley, Church Lane, an Irishman fearing for his life jumped from a 'Window into the Hog Yard, and heard the Mob crying *d—n it, which are the Irish Houses?*' and '*d—n them, have their Heart's Blood*'.[74]

Among the rioters, in both Leman Street and Cable Street, were one or two soldiers; and one convicted rioter was a plasterer, confirming that this was not solely a riot of weavers. That weekend the trouble spread outwards. The Horse Guards had to disperse rioters 'gathering in *Ratcliff-highway*, to demolish the Houses of the *Irish*', and 'Mobs arose in *Southwark*, *Lambeth*, and *Tyborn-Road*, and took upon 'em to interrogate People whether they were for the *English* or *Irish*?'[75]

Even in a century and a city prone to riotousness, these were unusually violent and protracted events. They may have achieved something of their ends, too, for it was thought that some master weavers were now too frightened to contract with Irish workers. And there were a number of other sharp exchanges involving the Irish in years to come. On St Patrick's Day 1740 there was a 'fierce Battle' between the Irish and the butchers of Clare Market, parading the streets with a grotesque effigy of an Irishman, that had to be put down by 'a File of Musqueteers' from St James's barracks. This we might term a cultural conflict, but often the cause of anti-Irish aggression was more plainly economic. A West Ham calico printer employing Irish hands in 1750 received death threats ordering him to discharge them, '"as the English are starving for want of work"'. Five years later there was a riot of Irish 'haymakers, chairmen, &c.' against the English in St Giles, once more requiring troops to put it down. At the Westminster election of 1763, rioting sailors battled with Irish chairmen and destroyed their chairs, the only one left intact 'having on it these words "This belongs to English chairmen."' In July 1774 'A dreadful affray' lasting three days between Irish and English haymakers broke out at Hyde, Mill Hill (Hendon), spreading to the districts around, in which three people were said to have been killed, among them a child. The Irish were there by custom and with the support of the farmers, but this year the English had resolved to keep them out. And in the Gordon Riots of 1780 it was difficult to disentangle anti-Catholic prejudice from anti-Irish.[76]

In and around these flashpoints, the simmering antagonism between Irish and English didn't take much to boil up in pub or street or lodging house. This was true even in areas where the Irish had made their homes for generations, like St Giles. It is now difficult to distinguish assailant and victim in a welter of conflicting evidence, but there is no doubting the vehemence of anti-Irish hatred among some sections of the London poor.

'*You Blood of a Whore, there's* Dublin *for you*,' Stephen Jones shouted while beating William Swinney in Bowl Yard, St Giles, in July 1740. Jones had 'asked him what Countryman he was', and when Swinney said he was Irish Jones 'gave him a Blow, and said, if he would not fight he would make him fight'. Swinney died later from the punches and kicks he received. A row in the Ship, Bainbridge Street, St Giles, in August 1765 led, an inquest jury thought, to the death in the Middlesex Hospital of Philip Barry. His wife had been drinking with him when a woman began 'd—ning the Irish; I said, *Mistress, what occasion have you to d—n the whole country for one or two bad?* she

said, *D—n your blood, are you Irish, you b—h?* I said, *I am indeed.*'
The woman then called her husband, Tom Bradley, 'a fighting man'
who 'fights for money'. Despite a warning from the blind publican,
Barry went out into the street to fight and suffered a broken rib and
head injuries. There are numerous other cases in the Old Bailey
Proceedings that point to what must have been daily anxieties for the
Irish poor in London.[77]

On the receiving end of abuse, refused lodgings (as many were) and
employment on the basis of their nationality, with poor relief given at
the reluctant whim of overseers who saw them as an importunate and
alien burden on parish funds, the Irish poor were often forced to become
among the most desperate and marginal of Londoners in some of the
capital's most filthy and decrepit districts. Unsurprisingly, the connection of the Irish with crime was a strong one; most often they acted
alone or with their countrymen as accomplices. Irish women were as
likely to come before the courts as men, and both were most commonly
noted as sneak thieves, pickpockets, street robbers and coiners.

Those were offences common enough among the indigenous poor
of London. But there were two particular problems of disorder which
the Irish made their own. One was a disregard for authority that the
police of the metropolis found especially difficult to deal with. And the
other was a spirit of internecine contention that imported Irish troubles
into London's courts and alleys. These tendencies could combine, and
they seemed to do so most commonly towards the century's end.

A wake over a dead child at Oxford Buildings, Oxford Street, in
June 1793 led to a row in which a number of watchmen were severely
beaten, the captain of the patrole dying of his wounds; a party of Foot
Guards were pelted with brickbats and no fewer than fifty-six arrests
were made. A row in a pub at Broad Street, St Giles, in November
1796, 'for many years . . . the resort of the lower and most abandoned
class of Irishmen', left many 'desperately wounded'. Another fearsome
affray over a corpse took place in March 1798 when three or four died
in a row between Irish families over who should have responsibility
for burying the woman concerned. And on Boxing Day night that same
year, St Stephen's Day a particular time of celebration for the Irish, the
crowded King's Arms, Maynard Street, St Giles, was scene of a battle
between fifty constables and Bow Street officers searching for rogues
and vagabonds who might be pressed into the army. The police entered
with cutlasses drawn, and one was killed in the melee.[78]

No migrant group then in eighteenth-century London proved more problematic than the Irish poor – or less popular among other poor Londoners. Religion was one source of contention, but so it was with the Jews, many of the French and others, without, however, producing the flare-ups that beset relations between plebeian Londoners and their Irish neighbours. In the end, class and culture told most strongly here. Irish pugnacity was a particular provocation in an age when fists and feet and sticks were quickly wielded to supplement an argument. But most of all it was the fear that the Irishman's low standard of living enabled him to take short wages, and with them the bread from the Londoners' tables. For how to make a living in London was the greatest challenge of all.

PART THREE

WORK

William Beckford

V

WILLIAM BECKFORD'S LONDON – COMMERCE

'That Which Makes London to be London': Trade

His figure was pleasing, and majestick; but when he was angry, one of his eyes became so terrible, that no person could bear to behold it; and the wretch upon whom it was fixed, instantly fell backward; and, sometimes, expired.[1]

THERE was a great deal of the Caliph Vathek about Alderman Beckford as reimagined by his novelist son: 'much addicted to women', surpassing 'in magnificence all his predecessors', not as Caliph but as Lord Mayor of London, and possessor of that 'terrible eye', William Beckford was a dominating figure in metropolitan business and political life in the middle decades of the eighteenth century. Apparently with obscure forebears in seventeenth-century Clerkenwell, Beckford was a Jamaican, born in 1709 into the wealthiest sugar-growing family on the island. At fourteen he was shipped to London and Westminster School. There he acquired a facility in the classics and some lifelong friendships, among them with the future Lord Mansfield, while never shaking off his Jamaican accent or an overbearing manner that presumably had much to do with his upbringing. From Westminster he went to Balliol, Oxford, and then studied medicine in Leyden and Paris. But in 1735 his father died and Beckford was summoned home to help his elder brother, Peter, run the family estates. Two years later Peter died too and Beckford became sole owner of eleven sugar plantations with 1,737 slaves and part owner of nearly a third as much again. Prominent in Jamaican politics, he also kept that 'terrible eye' trained on the London end of his sugar trade through an agent, James Knight, usually addressing letters to him at the Jamaica Coffee House, Cornhill. Through Knight, Beckford encouraged the migration to Jamaica of 'white Inhabitants of any Sort'. He bore none of the resentment of the Londoners towards North Britons, 'who are men of strong Vigorous, and goodly Constitutions & (if I am not misinform'd) Luxury has no Great share in their Educations'. On the plantations he did not flinch from that cold-blooded tyranny on which a sugar fortune was based, equipping loyal slaves with arms to hunt down Maroons: 'they keep our Woods clear of Runaways, & if a Negroe Starts they are sure to bring him or his Head back.'[2]

Before the end of 1744, Beckford left Jamaica for good, overseeing and enlarging his estates from London and serving the sugar interest in the House of Commons and in the City Corporation. He sat from 1747 for the pocket borough of Shaftesbury in Dorset and from 1754 as one of the four representatives of the City of London. Like most West India merchants, he supported too the interests of America – William Hogarth, a friend, featured him as the colonists' defender in *The Times* (Plate 1, 1762) – and he fought against taxes on sugar and any other impediment to Atlantic trade and his own profits.[3]

Of all the West India merchants Beckford was the richest and on his death in 1770, during his second term as Lord Mayor, he left his one legitimate heir 'England's wealthiest son'. By then he had become the owner of 3,000 slaves and thirteen plantations of more than 22,000 acres, a fortune augmented by large dealings in the public finances in London. He took £100,000 of government war bonds in 1759, for instance, paying just £10,000 up front and selling the stock at a profit. His wealth rendered him profligate in all directions. At least eight illegitimate sons and daughters by a harem of mistresses were treated generously in his lifetime and remembered in his will; perhaps there were others, for he once claimed that the air of Richmond was so unhealthy that '"I lost twelve natural children there last year!"' His public ostentation at City feasts was said to have been greater than anything seen since the time of Henry VIII. On one occasion during his second mayoralty 600 dishes were served on gold plate, allegedly costing him £10,000. When his mansion at Fonthill in Wiltshire burned down in 1754 his response to his steward on being told the news was, 'Let it be rebuilt.' It was, on such a scale that it became known as 'Splendens'. And on the floor of the House of Commons his unrestrained disordered loquacity – he once boasted 'that on a single idea he had poured forth a *diarrhoea* of words' – made him something of a laughing stock among his opponents and even some of his allies. Despite that, he was a figure of genuine moment. Rendered independent by his great wealth and never losing sight of its basis in trade, he was an opponent of West End aristocracy and kingly pretensions, and a pugnacious defender of City democracy. He was reputedly the first commoner in England to die a millionaire.[4]

Beckford's virile extravagance, unpolished by charm or circumspection, embodied the commercial character of the City of London and, indeed, much of the metropolis as a whole. This was above all a city based on commerce, on buying and selling in markets far and wide – in a word, on trade, 'Which is that which makes *London* to be *London*'.[5]

The lifeblood of London trade, and so of eighteenth-century London itself, flowed through the River Thames. The port of London had been rebuilt after the Great Fire and then remained pretty much unchanged until the end of the eighteenth century. At its heart were the twenty-one 'legal quays', including Billingsgate Dock, along a continuous embankment on the north side of the river from London Bridge to the Tower. They were just 1,419 feet long and forty feet deep. Small coasting vessels pulled alongside the quays but most ships, from Tyne colliers to great West Indiamen carrying sugar and rum, had to moor in the river and unload into lighters and barges which then took cargoes to the quays. The legal quays had never been big enough to handle all the business of the port, so 'sufferance wharves' on the south bank were permitted by the customs officers to unload specified cargoes when the need arose. They provided a further 3,700 feet of quay frontage, but even when added to the north bank London had barely more quay capacity than the port of Bristol. From the sufferance wharves all goods intended for the City and Westminster had to be carried over London Bridge until 1750. From the legal quays goods were taken through ten narrow turnings into Thames Street, the noisiest, busiest, most dangerous street in London, and then stored in warehouses or carted on to purchasers in the metropolis.

Downstream of the port proper there grew some facilities to ease congestion in the upper pool. There was a small wet dock at the

Hermitage in the middle pool, and others at Shadwell and Lime-Kiln Dock in the lower, all on the north side of the river. On the south bank, St Saviour's (or Savory) Dock, 'the port of Southwark',[6] took coals from Newcastle and timber from the Baltic; and just downriver, from 1703, the Howland Great Wet Dock at Rotherhithe provided the largest dock in the port, where 120 merchant ships could unload away from the risks of the river. It was dedicated at first to timber and then from 1763 to the whaling trade, its name changing to Greenland Dock around that time. All of these havens were on the London side of the noose-like loop of the Isle of Dogs, one of the river's greatest hazards to shipping, where vessels were frequently lost in adverse winds while yet so close to their journey's end. To avoid its dangers the East India Company, whose ships were the largest on the river by far, established a port at Blackwall, on the east side of the Isle of Dogs and before the huge bend began. East Indiamen were received in a wet dock built there during the first years of the early seventeenth century. There was a shipbuilding yard for East Indiamen alongside and another (till around 1782) at Deptford on the south side of the river. From 1789, the port at Blackwall was modernised by John Perry. Perry's Brunswick Dock could refit and provision thirty East Indiamen at a time and thirty smaller ships as well. Cargoes were brought by lighter from the ships anchored in the river, either to the legal quays or to Blackwall, from where they were removed by road, under armed guard, to the Company's warehouses on the eastern side of the City. These great depositories increased in number during the century.[7]

They had good reason to multiply. The port of London had largely stood still from the seventeenth century. Yet trade in the eighteenth century expanded beyond all precedent. The population of London, we might recall, probably grew by something less than a factor of two across the century. But the number of ships entering the port more than doubled, from around 6,900 in 1700 to 14,800 in 1795; their tonnage quadrupled; and the value of goods shipped grew from £10.3 million to £31.4 million. The pace of growth accelerated from around 1770, so that the increases of the first seventy years of the century doubled again in the last thirty. The expansion of other British ports, notably Bristol and Liverpool, meant that London was taking a smaller share of the nation's trade at the end of the century than at the beginning. Even so, London handled over 70 per cent of Britain's imports in 1790 and 56 per cent of its exports.[8]

The international reach of London was extraordinary, its national penetration comprehensive. From the East Indies came tea, porcelain, drugs, muslins, cottons, silks, pepper and spices; from the West Indies sugar, rum, coffee, cocoa, pimento, ginger and hardwoods; from Africa fruit, wax, gum, elephants' teeth, palm oil and wine; from the Southern Ocean fishery and from Greenland whale oil, spermaceti, blubber, whalebone and seal skins; from America tobacco, rice, indigo, cotton and corn; from the Mediterranean and Turkey wine, oil, fruit, wool, cork and drugs; and from Russia and the Baltic timber, iron, pitch, tar, hemp, linens and tallow. The coasting trade brought linen, corn, hides, tallow and butter from Ireland; coals from Newcastle; and herrings, salmon and linens from Scotland. In return, London exported linens, woollens and haberdashery to India, Jamaica, the Cape and America, and British manufactures throughout the world. And it shipped the products of the world to every tiny port along the coasts of the British Isles, and often deep inland through the canal system. Beale's Wharf in Southwark, just one of twenty-nine operating coastwise in 1793 and by no means the biggest, loaded and discharged vessels weekly from Faversham, Milton and Maidstone; Falmouth, Penzance, Truro 'and all places adjacent in Cornwall'; Portsmouth, Gosport, Southampton, the Isle of Wight, Christchurch, Havant, Petersfield, Salisbury and Winchester; Plymouth, Fowey, Looe, Mevagissey 'and all places adjacent'; Stockton, Darlington, Durham, Yarm 'and all places adjacent' once more.[9]

This frantic business all went on in the face of formidable difficulties. The crowded state of the port had long given London's merchants – 'merchant' in the eighteenth century meant someone trading with abroad – ripe cause for complaint. The West India merchants petitioned the City for an enlargement of the port as early as 1674 and petitioned Parliament in 1705. They became more clamorous still from the end of the Seven Years War, seeking power to extend the quays and build docks in 1762–3, 1765 and again in 1795–6. This last campaign was begun by William Vaughan, the far-sighted son of a London merchant with interests in marine insurance. In 1793 he had proposed four sites where docks could extend the port downriver from the Tower, at St Katherine's, Wapping, the Isle of Dogs and Rotherhithe. All would be built during the first thirty years of the new century.[10]

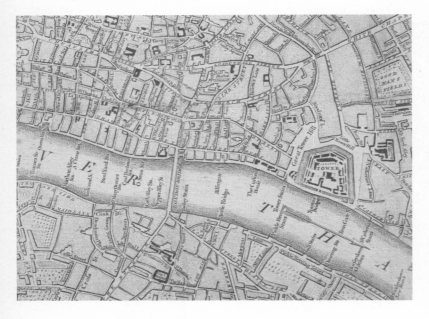

City and the Upper Port, 1761

The proposals of Vaughan and others were examined by a Committee of the House of Commons, whose first great report of 1796 showed how the Thames had become the sclerotic victim of its own success. Congestion at the undersized quays and sufferance wharves left craft waiting interminably to discharge their cargoes and to load them. In the upper pool, moorings for 545 ships were 'frequently' occupied by 775, some in water so shallow that they 'sat down upon their Anchors' at ebb tide, causing damage and sometimes total loss. Timber ships unloaded their cargoes on to the river in rafts eleven or twelve times the size of the ship, often till the timber was sold to a merchant. The 350 or so West India ships all ended their annual voyage to London between May and October, the same summer months when colliers were also most crowded on the river. Besides the ships were lighters, barges (it needed sixteen to discharge a single collier) and small boats, so that on any day some 3,500 craft were 'in active Service and Navigation on the River' between London Bridge and Limehouse Reach on the west side of the Isle of Dogs. In the daily melee fatal accidents were common. Seven men and a boy on their way to unload a corn ship drowned when their boat was struck by a lighter in January 1780, for instance. Trinity House pilots, who supervised use of the river, reported it sometimes 'so filled up with Shipping, that a Boat cannot pass', that vessels 'often run foul of each other' and that ships and pilots could wait seven days at Deptford for the river to clear sufficient for them to come up, and five days at Shadwell before a passage opened seawards. We should remember too that throughout the eighteenth century there was a lively fishing industry on the Thames. Even in the 1790s Thames salmon, appearing mid-February, was 'in great estimation, and sells at a vast price', with shad as big as eight pounds, lamprey in amazing quantities, and roach, dace, bleak, eels and flounders taken even among the shipping in the upper pool. Further down-river, amidst the East Indiamen at Blackwall Reach in July, whitebait 'in multitudes innumerable' made for famous suppers in the taverns of Greenwich. All this activity aggravated the busyness of the river. [11]

The crowded Thames was an insufferable nuisance to the merchants of London, yet the volume and value of merchandise continued to rise decade by decade. The framework of mercantile activity in London shifted from the early years of the century. Before then, companies founded by royal charter in the time of Elizabeth and the Stuarts sought to impose trading monopolies that linked particular merchants to certain parts of the globe and no other. So the Muscovy merchants (Russia Company), the Turkey merchants (Levant Company), the Royal Africa Company or Guinea merchants, the South Sea Company (trading to South America and the Spanish West Indies), the Hudson Bay Company and others were awarded crown authority as sole traders in their various regions of the world. Europe, the West Indies and America were open trading areas for any merchant, though there were natural advantages from familiarity in specialising in one rather than dealing with many. In fact, these chartered companies' monopolies were never entire and under pressure of competition from independent traders the system had largely broken down by 1750.[12]

The claims to monopoly of the greatest of all, the East India Company, formed in 1600, proved more robust, largely because it backed up its trading activity with considerable force of arms in the Indian sub-continent. It monopolised British trade with India and China, and though it too was vulnerable to foreign competition and private traders it energetically protected its interests. The Company generated wealth from two main sources. Trading activities took second place to the spoils its servants made for themselves. The London nabobs were less likely to be those directors meeting at East India House in Leadenhall Street than the administrators and military officers who rendered Company services to one competing maharaja against another.

The number of Company ships making their annual return voyage to the east was just a dozen or so around 1710, about twenty in 1740 and fifty-three in 1797. The value of their exports was modest, and though that of their imports was less so, it still accounted for around just 19 per cent of British imports by value over the last quarter of the century. On the other hand, those of the Company's servants who survived the ardours of climate and combat returned to become among the richest of Londoners. William Hickey, an adventurer in both Bengal and Bond Street, travelled home from Calcutta with a Captain Bentley, reputed 'little removed from an idiot', who carried with him 200,000 silver rupees in 'eight strong wooden boxes', a sum to set him up for life. And the wealth of those with greater talent – or rapacity – was legendary.[13]

In general, and in the long run over the eighteenth century, the merchant community of London increased and prospered wherever it traded. It was a community that defied simple classification. There was no single way into merchant life, for instance. Entry might be by inheritance (like William Beckford), apprenticeship, quick wits or good luck, or because it offered an attractive place to invest family money. Once a merchant, the shifting fortunes of trade drove men to diversify their interests where opportunity arose, even if it took them from the trade in which they began. But in all they did, the world of the Thames was never far from their daily concerns.

All this speaks loudly enough through some of those London merchants' careers that have come down to us. In 1763 the nineteen-year-old Samuel Hanson inherited his father's grocery business – the concept was more grand then than it later became – in Botolph Lane, the centre of the orange trade, between the river and East India House. With the business came over £3,000 in cash and stock in the South Sea and East India Companies and the Bank of England, together with a freehold house in Cornhill let on lease and a country mansion in Sutton, Surrey. The firm imported oranges and lemons from Cyprus and Spain, raisins, muscatels, figs and sultanas from Spain and Greece, and almonds from the Balearics. Most were then sold wholesale to grocers all over Britain, shipped out from the river or carted by road. Hanson was not content to rest on his father's fortune and actively diversified, trading in rum and sugar, cochineal, even silks, broadcloth and Guinea redwood. At some point, probably in the 1770s, he bought a three-sixteenths share in the *Neptune*, ready-fitted for a voyage to Jamaica, later selling two of his sixteenths in separate transactions that nearly recouped his initial outlay. His annual profits seem to have averaged around £1,800, a considerable sum, though whether he became worth 'a plum', or £100,000, the contemporary equivalent of a millionaire, is uncertain.[14]

For one who definitely did we might take another wholesale grocer, Abram Newman of Fenchurch Street, who bought a partnership in a re-export firm dealing in coffee, tea, chocolate and sugar in 1764. He died worth £600,000 in 1799, 'one of the richest citizens of London', who even after retirement 'came every day to the shop, and ate his mutton chop at 2 o'clock (the good old City hour) with his successors'.[15]

These men were City insiders, born into the merchant class. But we have already glimpsed the numbers of provincial or Scottish merchants active in London trade. Many sons of country gentry and upper tradesmen were apprenticed to City counting houses and won a fortune in the greatest trading city on earth. So too did others who leapfrogged the apprenticeship route and cold-shouldered the livery companies and the expensive benefits, what were left of them, of City freedom. These more marginal men, devising loose associations from family connections and from friendships, found London a congenial place to operate as long as they had ready money to command. The initial stake of £3,000–4,000 or so necessary to fund a new merchant in London was raised from family and friends, who of course would share in the profits by receiving interest on their loans. Once reputation was established, credit would follow.[16]

Capital was just one necessity for mercantile success. For trade to flourish, information was an indispensable requirement. In eighteenth-century London there were several channels, other than the river itself, through which it flowed.

The Royal Exchange, between Threadneedle Street and Cornhill, was the general meeting place of London's merchants and their clients, and indeed anyone wishing to send goods or book a passage to any port in the world. Rebuilt after the Great Fire on the site of the Elizabethan original, the Exchange was on two floors around an open courtyard. On the first floor in the early decades of the century were some 200 shops which had been turned over to offices or left empty by the 1750s. In the cellar were warehouses for pepper, wine and other goods. The ground floor was the merchants' haunt, a covered piazza divided by tradition into 'walks' where merchants trading with certain parts of the world were to be found – the Norway, East India, Jamaica, Virginia, Scotch, East Country Walks and so on; the Jews had their own walk between the French and the Spanish. It was a cosmopolitan place even at the beginning of the century. Mr Spectator witnessed 'disputes adjusted between an inhabitant of Japan and an alderman of London', 'a subject of the Great Mogul entering into a league with one of the Czar of Muscovy', all among 'a body of Armenians', 'a crowd of Jews' or a 'group of Dutchmen'.[17] Throughout the century it never lost this Tower of Babel character:

I ought never y^{e}less to tell you wth w^t Astonishm^t I was struck when I first enterd ye Change. I heard such a confusd Hum & Buzzing like as bees pointing different ways to collect those Precious Sweets to supply their respective Calls. They speak here as many Languages Modestly Assort'g as Mithridates King of Pontus . . .[18]

The Royal Exchange opened six days a week at noon, the main business done from twelve till two; and on a Sunday the piazza on the south side of the Exchange fronting Cornhill would swarm with merchants and their clerks at midday. But although the Exchange kept restricted hours, business never slept. It found its insomniac haunts in the City's coffee houses.

It is difficult to exaggerate the significance of the coffee houses in City business life. They were used for business meetings; for entertaining; for auctions of everything from ships and silks to wine and books, all sold 'by the candle', bids having to stop when a candle-end burned out; as company offices; as *postes restantes* where letters could be addressed and left till called for; as reading rooms stocked with newspapers and journals; as refreshment houses providing meals and coffee and everything stronger; as a lost or stolen property office; as a listening post for hackney writers; as a home-from-home for gatherings of friends or 'clubs'. At any one time there were scores in the City – some 124 within the walls in 1737, for instance, and perhaps another sixty or so without. A number lasted for generations under the same name but different management, while others were fly-by-night affairs drowning quickly in a hogshead of debt. Some could nurture a very special character, like one entered in the summer of 1790 by a Russian visitor who was astonished to find that 'all the people there began to address me in Russian!' It 'was the meeting place of merchants who trade with Russia. All of them had, at one time or other, lived in Petersburg and know our language.' Some, indeed, were the stuff of legend. And they were clustered so tightly about the Royal Exchange that the great fire in Cornhill in 1748 destroyed the New Union, Tom's, the Rainbow, the Pennsylvania, Jonathan's, the Jerusalem, the Marine, Elford's, the Jamaica, Garraway's, Baker's, Cole's and Sam's coffee houses. Many, in that resilient City way, were quickly rebuilt.[19]

The business of the City coffee house was less coffee than information. The eighteenth century was its heyday, at least until the last quarter of the century, when the development of offices and purpose-built exchanges began to replace an older, less formal way of doing business. It was from the coffee houses too that information on stocks and shipping and business news – as well as City gossip – found its way into an ever-rising tide of newsprint.

Another channel of information was of such sophistication even by the early years of the century as to be one of the wonders of London, indeed of the world. This was the postal service, especially the London Penny Post.

The General Post Office in Lombard Street connected London with the rest of the British Isles and the Continent, with mail packets sailing twice weekly to Calais, Lisbon, Corunna, Hellevoetsluis, Holyhead and other places. Mail coaches were sent all over England and Scotland on three days each week and to Wales twice. The Penny Post delivered only in London and certain places ten to fifteen miles around. At the beginning of the century some 400–500 coffee houses and shops acted as 'receiving houses' where letters could be left with the penny fee. Messengers took them to be stamped in one of six offices – four in the City – and from there they were delivered to the addressee. Out of London proper, the recipient also paid a penny. By the 1790s, after some rationalisation in the name of efficiency, there were just two offices, in Abchurch Lane in the City and Gerrard Street, Soho, some 110 suburban receiving houses and around 180 in the metropolis. There were six deliveries each day in London and three in the towns and villages in London's shadow, all made by what foreigners thought of as a huge army of letter carriers. No other city in the world had such a system: 'I am of opinion,' wrote the German Londoner Frederick Wendeborn around this time, 'that no nation is more given to letter-writing than the English.'[20]

There was one final element quickening the flow of business information in London. Right through the century the City merchant, like the City tradesman, often lived all week over or next to the shop, in a house close to 'Change or the Bank or to his shipping interests near the quays. Merchants' country houses were fashionable and ubiquitous among the wealthy. But their town houses generally combined rooms for partners, clerks and visitors on the ground floor, a dining room and kitchen on the first, bedrooms on the second and servants' chambers in the garrets. When an American merchant, Joshua Johnson, moved from rooms in Westminster and rented such a counting house in Tower Street in 1771 he found the decision to live over his City shop had 'not been without its good effects with the staid citizens'. And in these years, perhaps surprisingly, the same was true for those men who dealt less in goods than in another City essential: money.[21]

'Most Infamous Sett of Gamblers': Money Matters

The business of holding cash deposits safe from theft and fire, of lending money out on interest and paying money to third parties on an order to pay (a cheque) had begun with the London goldsmiths. It was a trade that centred on Lombard Street, where, at the sign of the Grasshopper, Sir Thomas Gresham is generally accounted 'the father of English banking'.[22] Gresham operated there from the 1540s, but it was a century later, in the turbulence of civil war, that the richest goldsmiths' 'running cashes' became an indispensable component of the financial system. 'Bank' entered the English language in the 1640s. The foundation of the Bank of England in 1694, based first in part of Grocers' Hall behind Poultry and not relocating to its own building in Threadneedle Street till 1734, was a dramatic boost to both public and private financing. The Bank sold stock to private investors and then loaned the money at interest to government on the security of future tax income. It also acted as a bank for private individuals, issuing notes for cash deposited and giving interest.[23]

At first the goldsmiths opposed the Bank and did all they could to subvert it. But as trade flourished and wealth grew there was a bigger pool for bankers to fish in, and the banking side of the goldsmiths' business enlarged sufficiently to be separated from their traditional craft of working gold. This was a process that took some time. Even in 1722 there was a confusion of identities and something of novelty about the business:

The *BANQUIERS* commonly called *Gold-Smiths*, are in *Lombard-street*, about the *Royal-Exchange*, and on each side of *Temple bar*. They may very properly be called *Banquiers*, rather than *Goldsmiths*, for they keep all the private Cash of the Nation; and in every Shop you will see daily Receipts and Payments made as in a Bank.[24]

The twenty-four private banks in London in 1725 had emerged from this goldsmith tradition. They included some great names: Child's (c. 1665) at the Marygold, Fleet Street, adjoining Temple Bar; Hoare's (1672) at the Golden Bottle, Fleet Street; Campbell's, later Coutts's, at the Three Crowns towards the west end of the Strand; Martin's (c. 1711) at the Grasshopper, Lombard Street; Drummond's (1717) at the Golden Eagle, Charing Cross. From the beginning, then, there was a geographical duality in the London banking system. The City node around Lombard Street catered very largely to the mercantile interest and the needs of international trade; the banks of Fleet Street and the Strand, while inevitably involved in mercantile affairs at the beginning, by around 1720 had begun to look westward for their business, to the West End gentry and aristocracy, who could offer land as security. This separation was never exclusive, but it was distinctive nonetheless and became more so as the century grew older, with most moneyed Westminster residents banking west of Temple Bar or just inside.[25]

As the wealth of London increased through expanding trade and the growth of the town, especially the western suburbs, so London's banking system enlarged accordingly. There were twenty-nine private banks in London in 1754, forty-two in 1770, sixty-two in 1792. The City and West End duality remained a marked feature at the century's end. In 1792 there were thirty-nine banks in the Lombard Street area, fifteen of them in Lombard Street itself, and another three nearby; there were four in Fleet Street or near it and five in Charing Cross and the Strand; and elsewhere in the West End of the town were a further ten, including three each in Pall Mall (the first appearing in 1756) and Bond Street. There was just one south of the Thames, in St Margaret's Hill, Borough.[26]

With the proliferation of banking houses came some modernisation and adaptation of old premises. Yet even purpose-built banks copied the counting-house tradition of a ground-floor banking hall with living accommodation for a partner overhead. Thomas Coutts refashioned 59 Strand in 1769 in sumptuous Adam style, with a drawing room later decorated in 'China' paper. When premises were acquired at the rear in the Adelphi, a 'Bridge of Sighs', said to be reminiscent of that in Venice, tied the Strand bank at first-floor level with buildings in William and John Streets from 1799: the personal connection between home and bank could not be severed, even by a street's width.[27]

The numbers show that the spread of banks in London was very much concentrated in the second half of the century and that was true for the country as a whole. Edmund Burke thought in 1750 'there were not twelve "bankers' shops"' outside London, whereas in 1790 there were at least 230. But provincial banking did not grow at London's expense. For the country bankers needed City banks and brokers to handle their business with metropolitan merchants.

Obtaining and giving credit were necessary parts of a merchant's business. The 'bill on London' – a note promising to pay at a future date that could be cashed as readily as a banknote or sold on at a discount if the possessor couldn't wait till the due date – was in universal circulation at the century's end between merchants and their customers at home and abroad. For some merchants it was a short step to use their capital not, say, for ship-owning or stock purchases but for lending out to others. Among the founders of what would become Williams Deacon's in Birchin Lane, Lombard Street, were men who had begun their careers as sea captains in the East India trade, then bought shares in ships chartered to the East India Company by syndicates of owners, then became managing partners or 'ships' husbands'. They were joined by merchants who had traded to India. Each of them was able to invest a stake of £5,000 in the new venture. Founded on a capital of just £20,000 in 1771, three years later the bank had deposits of some £340,000, of which £250,000 were loaned out to merchants and their clients on the security of discounted bills, and £20,000 invested in stocks and ships. Sir Charles Raymond, one of the original sea captains, died in 1788 worth £200,000. Other merchants founded banks that came to rival their goldsmith antecedents in reputation: Sir Richard Glyn, a merchant in salt and chemicals, began his banking career in 1754; David Barclay, a linen merchant, inherited part of the bank that took his name in Lombard Street in 1776; Sir Francis Baring, a grocer, established a banking arm separate from his merchant's business in 1777.[28]

Another financial industry with roots in trade and shipping, and another product of the commercial revolution of the second half of the seventeenth century, grew even faster than banking. The disaster of 1666 had focused the citizens' minds on the question of risk, especially of course from fire but not exclusively so. The first response emerged from the collective life of the City coffee houses: mutual protection. The idea was simple enough. A number of friends and acquaintances came together to share the costs should any one of them suffer damage from fire. Each contributed a sum of money proportionate to the losses they wished to insure against. They then advertised for people to join them in the venture on the same basis. When sufficient capital had been raised they established a company or 'society' and offered the same protection to all others who wished to join. The capital was invested and a dividend paid annually to the society's members, less the cost of any claims during the year. This was the basis of the Hand-in-Hand or Amiable Contributors for Insuring from Loss by Fire, formed in 1696 at Tom's Coffee House, St Martin's Lane, with about a hundred initial investors. The business quickly grew, so that in 1704, for instance, the Hand-in-Hand issued 7,300 policies insuring premises (not contents or merchandise) within five miles of London.

The friendly society basis of the Hand-in-Hand was not the only way in which the insurance industry of eighteenth-century London established itself as one of the capital's great financial services. An eccentric projector, Charles Povey, set up a company insuring goods as well as premises that in 1710 became the Sun Fire Office. It conducted its first business from Causey's Coffee House near St Paul's, then took two rooms in a house in Sweeting's Alley by the Exchange, then the old South Sea House in Threadneedle Street in 1727, and finally moved to the new Bank Buildings there in the 1760s.

The Sun opened an office for West End business in Craig's Court, Charing Cross, in 1726, and the polarisation of City and Westminster business we saw in banking affected the London insurers too. The Hand-in-Hand had originated in a Westminster coffee house and put its first office there. But a great deal of its business was City-based and early on tensions arose between citizen directors and those at the West End of the town. In 1701 a City office opened for two days a week at the Crown Coffee House near the Royal Exchange, but grumbling discontent persisted. In 1711 there was a series of City coups. A majority of the society resolved that all its general meetings should be held in the City and that half the directors should live there. By the end of the year a new office was opened at Angel Court, Snow Hill, and the securities were removed there from Tom's Coffee House. The office at Tom's was closed in 1714 and all business conducted east of Temple Bar. Aggrieved by the 'hardships and indignities' suffered at the hands of the dictatorial citizens, the West End directors formed their own Westminster Fire Office in 1717. The 150 original subscribers 'were mainly craftsmen and tradespeople of Westminster', paying subscriptions of £5–50. After some years at Tom's, where it eventually took over the whole building, in 1766 it moved to new premises in Bedford Street, Covent Garden.[29]

In 1720, a product of the fashionable joint-stock enterprises bringing investors together for a range of ventures, two chartered companies were established providing fire and other insurance: the London

Assurance Company at Birchin Lane and the Royal Exchange Assurance upstairs in the Exchange itself. For insuring against fire, that perennial nightmare of the Londoner in the eighteenth century, these companies and the older societies were joined by the Union Fire Office at Maiden Lane in the City (a spin-off formed in 1714 from the Hand-in-Hand to insure goods and merchandise only), the Phoenix (Lombard Street and Charing Cross) formed in 1782 and the British Fire Office in 1799 at Cornhill and the Strand. Each venture had its own distinctively uniformed fire brigade of eighteen to thirty or so watermen, paid by attendance at fires. Insured houses were identified by the lead or iron company mark fixed high on one of the walls, though in fact the company brigades would fight any fire, whether of insured property or not. They had the use of a handful of company engines and the single engine that each London parish had by law to maintain, and were accompanied by uniformed porters to remove goods and protect them from plunder. From 1791 the Sun, Phoenix and Royal Exchange Assurance combined their brigades in 'The Fire Watch', under a single superintendent.[30]

The London Assurance and Royal Exchange Assurance extended their cover to shipping, but once more marine insurance had its origins in the seventeenth-century City coffee houses, and again there was an important element of mutuality. Merchants wishing to hedge the risks of a trading venture might come together to ensure that losses were not borne by just one of their number. This was a common feature of the important London coal trade, for instance. By the early years of the eighteenth century a group of specialists in underwriting risks of this nature had emerged, meeting for business at Edward Lloyd's Coffee House, at first in Tower Street and from 1691 in Lombard Street. Merchants wishing to insure the risks of a voyage employed brokers to visit the underwriters in their boxes at Lloyd's who gave a price for the proportion of the risk to be covered. Once full cover had been secured, the broker returned to his client with a policy that listed the underwriters and their prices. The broker could shop for the best price at Lloyd's and elsewhere, for other underwriters at other coffee houses were involved in the business. The assurance companies' premiums tended to be higher, though there was less risk of default, and marine insurance remained largely in the hands of underwriters at the century's end. It was a system that worked well. 'It is notorious to all the Mercantile World,' it was said in 1735, 'that as the English

Insurers pay more readily and generously than any others, most Insurances are done in England.' Confidence, trust, reliability, all depended on the underwriters' sure-footedness, and that was aided by sophisticated information mechanisms that again emerged from the coffee houses: *Lloyd's News* published shipping information from 1696, and *Lloyd's List* from 1738, some twenty-five years after the death of the man who had given his name to an important London industry.[31]

The final, less scrupulous form of insurance established in these years was on lives. Life insurance had awkward beginnings in eighteenth-century London. Of all insurances it smacked most of gambling, that reigning vice of the age, and occasionally must have had a more sordid and deadly side:

> The Office of Assurance of Money upon Lives is at the Rainbow Coffee-house in Cornhill, where Men or Women may Subscribe on their own Lives for the benefit of their Children, or other Persons Lives for the benefit of themselves, and have them approv'd without their Knowledge or Consent, paying 10s. Entrance, and 10s. towards the first Claim for each Life, and shall have a Policy for 1000 l. for each Life subscribed upon in the said Society.[32]

That was an advertisement from 1709, but sixty years later the speculators at Lloyd's were at similar tricks, in effect opening a book on lives, especially of persons noted in the newspapers to be ill. The potential for fraud was infinite, because newspapers hungry for copy would often print what they were given. Yet in an insecure world the desire for some financial assistance on the death of a breadwinner was understandably acute. Again the most stable and reliable life insurance emerged on a mutual or friendly society basis. The Amicable Society for a Perpetual Assurance Office was established in 1706 as a friendly society in Serjeant's Inn, Fleet Street. Numbers were limited to 2,000 members between the ages of twelve and forty-five, paying an entrance fee and an annual premium of £5. The London and Royal Exchange Assurances also offered some life cover, preferring to insure the lives of the middling sort and above, the London Assurance favouring clergymen and army officers, for instance.[33]

Life assurance was put on a more scientific basis when the Equitable Life Assurance Company, founded in Nicholas Lane, Lombard Street, in 1761, began to use mortality tables to calculate risks and premiums. The Equitable was a mutual that required its members to have an 'insurable interest' in the life assured, so from the outset forestalling gambling on lives. Even so, 'interest' was generously interpreted. Creditors were considered to have an insurable interest in their debtors' lives, for instance, and moneylenders and tradespeople insured their clients for the period and value of a loan or until a bill was paid.[34]

The insurance industry, then, in all its branches, was one of the most significant developments in London's economy in the eighteenth century, marine insurance raising the credit of the City as a financial centre worldwide. Speculation, and the love of gambling with well-informed odds, had something to do with marine insurance and much to do with the insurance of lives, at least in the early years. But speculation came into its own in the taverns and coffee houses in and around Exchange Alley at the heart of the City. For in the Ship and Castle Tavern, at Garraway's Coffee House, Sam's, the Marine and most of all Jonathan's, and even out of doors in the crowded Alley itself, were to be found the brokers and jobbers in stocks, 'yᵉ most infamous sett of Gamblers yᵗ ever existed', who had 'converted Trade entirely into gaming'.[35]

A market in stocks and shares had developed by the end of the seventeenth century. It depended on a number of factors: sufficient wealth in the hands of numerous men and women, a significant volume of securities or shares in company ventures and the public finances, and simple procedures for buying and selling them. All these elements strengthened from the early years of the eighteenth century, when Bank stock, government stock and East India stock were most favoured by the rich. They were added to from 1711 when the South Sea Company was formed with a charter giving it exclusive access to the Spanish market of South America, with its silver mines, logwood and dyes like cochineal. In exchange for this monopoly the Company accepted the burden of £9 million of the national debt, issuing shares to raise the money. The excitement caused by these new opportunities in the stock market was one important reason, Daniel Defoe thought, for 'the prodigious Conflux of the Nobility and Gentry from all parts of *England* to *London*' and the 'constant Daily Intercourse between the Court Part of the Town, and the City'.[36]

Trading in stocks was nominally in the hands of a hundred brokers licensed by the City Corporation. They acted for private clients to secure the best price when selling stock and the cheapest when buying. The price was given by jobbers, or dealers in stock, who were ready to buy from the brokers and sell to them. All of this eased access to the market for investors and those needing to exchange securities for ready money. But the market attracted to it a less scrupulous fringe of men fully alive to its moneymaking opportunities. For in reality the City was ineffective in regulating just who marketed securities, and legislation designed to restrict gambling on periodic fluctuations in the price of stock, or 'time bargains', was very largely a dead letter.

Stock dealing was generally a coffee-house industry, and the sharpers had as much right to be in the public coffee room as anyone else. In 1762, 150 of the more substantial brokers negotiated the exclusive use of Jonathan's to keep out the more feckless traders. But one disgruntled broker excluded from a haunt used by stock dealers 'from time imme-morial' won a case in the courts that re-established public access. In 1773 a group of brokers acquired a building in Threadneedle Street as a 'Stock Exchange', but it allowed anyone access for sixpence a day. More exclusive entry to stock dealing was not established till the early years of the nineteenth century. Until then it was all much of a free-for-all.[37]

Speculation in company stock was the immediate cause of the greatest financial scandal of the age, the South Sea Bubble of 1720. The South Sea Company had never engaged much in trade to its exclusive Eldorado in the Spanish Americas. It put most energy into competing with the Bank of England for a share of the national debt in return for interest payments guaranteed by tax revenues. Its plan to take a further £7.5 million of public debt and issue shares to raise the money was approved by Parliament in April 1720, a process assisted by bribery on a kingly scale to lords and commoners alike. When South Sea stock was offered to the public that May its price rose astronomically. The promise of easy money attracted all with cash to spare in a city and nation where it seemed there had never been so much to spend. When cash couldn't be had, then property was mortgaged and sold to buy South Sea stock:

Surely such another Time of general Confusion never happened; for prodigious Numbers of People resorted daily from all Parts to *Exchange-Alley*, the Theatre of Destruction, where, by their wild Deportment and excessive Noise and Hurry, they acted like so many Persons just escaped from their Cells and

Chains; for all Thought of Commerce being laid aside, nothing was thought of but this iniquitous Traffick, and buying and selling Estates; for many Persons from nothing having got immense Sums of Money, were willing to lay them out in Purchases; and, as they lightly came by their Wealth, stood not for Price, but would give double, or treble the Value . . .[38]

At the height of the bubble that September the price of South Sea stock, which had first sold at £86, stood at around £1,100. Other stock had seen a doubling or trebling in price and some more meteoric still – Royal Exchange Assurance shares jumped from 5 guineas to £250, for instance. And a rash of over 150 City projections by 'bubblers', some of which were entirely fraudulent – among them schemes 'for inoffensively emptying Bog-houses', 'for curing the Grand Pox', 'for a Flying-Engine' and 'for assuring of Maidenheads' – tickled the pockets of those outpriced elsewhere. The crash later that month and early the next brought South Sea stock back to its starting point. The ruin was general across the moneyed and trading classes and even beyond, 'of merchants of great credit, and of clergymen, lawyers, physicians, and tradesmen: some of whom after living in splendor, proved unable to stand the shocks of poverty and contempt, but died broken hearted, while others withdrew to remote parts of the world to hide themselves and never returned'.[39]

The fraud at the heart of the South Sea scheme of 1720, and 'bubbling' more generally, continued to plague City and Parliament through the century. In October 1731 came the failure of the Charitable Corporation, formed in 1708 to provide small loans to the industrious poor on better terms than pawnbrokers would provide, when the capital of £488,000 disappeared along with the warehouse keeper and the cashier, George Robinson, MP for Marlow. Two more MPs involved in robbing the charity were also expelled from the House of Commons. A lottery was established to repay investors in the Corporation, among whom were many pious widows, eventually recouping 10 shillings in the pound.[40]

The biggest banking failure of the century, that of Neal, James, Fordyce and Downs, of Clement's Lane, Strand, which stopped payment in June 1772, was also caused by defalcations. Alexander Fordyce, a fashionably high-living and flash-dressing Scotsman sometimes called 'The Macaroni Banker', had disastrously speculated with his clients' money and lost, fleeing to France to avoid arrest. The biggest repercussions were in Scotland, where investors had unwisely trusted in the

fabled prudence and frugality of their countrymen, but for a time the
commerce of London was thrown into chaos. Joshua Johnson,
the Maryland tobacco merchant, reported the general consternation to
his partners back home:

every man seems afraid of each other; there has already a number stopped
and a continuance of them daily. Where it will end, the Lord only knows . . .
Distress seems pictured in each countenance on Change and no credit given
to any house who is capital in business, so that I may say with justice such
small people as we, seems now the greatest.

Among the 'stoppages' were 'two of whom has shot themselves'. [41]
   The Fordyce affair produced the worst financial crisis since the South
Sea Bubble. There would not be such alarm again until the very end
of the century, when a run on gold at the Bank of England in 1797
stopped payment in cash rather than notes. That was a panic induced
by the anxieties of war, something not seen since 1745. But between
these moments of general commercial distress, the daily travails of
business inevitably brought many to their knees. The vicissitudes of
trade, aggravated by war and the rumour of war for so much of the
century, affected all involved in international commerce and the world
of ships; the weather affected shipping, harvests, rents, the price of
provisions and wage demands; the London season, the Lord Mayor's
Show and the uncertain court calendar of births, weddings and deaths
affected artisans and others serving luxury consumption; fluctuations
in the cost of money and access to credit affected everyone in trade.
There were, then, so many uncertainties. They combined most painfully
in London, where the risks of indebtedness, inability to pay, arrest,
failure and bankruptcy were more commonly experienced than elsewhere, in part a function of the greater competition to be found there
in most areas of economic life. Nowhere was competition more rapacious than in an industry of vital significance to London life: retail
trade. [42]

'They Swim into the Shops by Shoals': Retail

The shopping streets of London were one of the city's marvels. Foreigners
in particular were stunned by what they saw. Even in 1703, 'The Number

of Shops both in the City and Suburbs [is] so great, and indeed so far beyond any foreign City, that it is to Strangers a just Matter of Amazement.' So it remained throughout the century. Its shops were 'the most striking objects that London can offer to the eye of a stranger', thought Pierre Jean Grosley in the 1760s, 'all brilliant and gay', 'a most splendid show, greatly superior to any thing of the kind at Paris'. And thirty years later Archenholtz found the 'magnificence of the shops, and warehouses . . . particularly striking in London': 'Nothing can be more splendid than the shops of silversmiths . . . The greatest shops of this sort at Paris, in the Street St Honoré, are mean in comparison with these. I know some of them in Cheapside, which contain goods to the amount of an hundred thousand pounds.'[43]

'The four streets – the Strand, Fleet Street, Cheapside, and Cornhill – are, I imagine, the finest in Europe,' wrote César de Saussure in 1725, and this long unbroken avenue of shops remained one of London's great arteries throughout the century. Even then its glories might have been extended a little at both ends to encompass Charing Cross in the west and Leadenhall Street in the east. It was a route some two and a half miles long, the bulk of it – about two-thirds – lying in the City. End to end it was pretty much lined with shops with living accommodation above. This main metropolitan shopping street ran along the south side of St Paul's Churchyard, then Ludgate Street and down Ludgate Hill to Fleet Street. By mid-century a northerly but less continuous cross-town shopping route had emerged, still emptying into Cheapside at its eastern end but turning north of St Paul's along Newgate Street, up the steep, twisting and narrow Snow Hill to Holborn, and then through Broad Street, St Giles, to Oxford Street. And with the growth of the town in the west, and its taste for luxury and distaste for the citizens, shopping districts had planted themselves in Covent Garden and St James's before 1700. In the early years of the eighteenth century these grew significantly north of Piccadilly along Bond Street. Yet even at the end of the century, despite a growing tendency to disconnect home from shop among the trading classes, the deep pockets of the citizens and the traditional reluctance of tradespeople to desert the place they knew best retained for the City more than an equal share in London's shopping attractions.[44]

If the City of international trade, shipping, banking, insurance and stock dealing was very much a man's world – though by no means exclusively, because there were many wealthy women investors in all these sectors – the world of retail was in the larger part a feminine sphere:

St. *MARTIN at LUDGATE* is indeed but a small Parish, but has the greatest Resort of Ladies of any other in the City, because 'tis here the fair Sex are furnish'd with Materials to make their Conquests. There are many young Ladies, and what is worse, old Ladies . . . that every *Saturday*, while their Houses are cleaning, they take a Tour to this Parish [where] they swim into the Shops by Shoals . . .[45]

Ludgate was indeed the place for haberdashers, mercers and drapers, but so too were Gracechurch Street and Lombard Street, Cheapside and Cornhill. There were so many of them. They clustered together in these streets, gaining strength in numbers from the passing trade they attracted and the great pleasure to be had there. It was a pleasure that faced two ways – looking and being looked at. 'The shops are really very entertaining,' thought Fanny Burney's Evelina, 'especially the mercers', after she had 'been *a shopping*', as her companion called it. 'At the milliners, the ladies we met were much dressed, that I should rather have imagined they were making visits than purchases.' The delights of shopping could be enjoyed even without stepping inside. Sophie von la Roche noted how the 'fine high windows' displayed material in 'a cunning device' that showed how it might fall when made into a dress, either at the shop or by a dressmaker who called at home. 'Behind great glass windows absolutely everything one can think of is neatly, attractively displayed, and in such abundance of choice as almost to make one greedy.' Choice was indeed bewildering. 'I thought I should never have chosen a silk,' complained Evelina, 'for they produced so many, I knew not which to fix upon.' Small wonder, when Edward Nourse at the Turk's Head, Cheapside, could offer:

All Sorts of Genoa, Dutch, & English Velvets, Paduasoys of all Colours, Tabbys water'd or unwater'd, Rich Brocades, Damasks, & all Sorts of flower'd Silks, Rich Florence & English Sattins, Figur'd & Stript [Striped] Lutestrings, Ducapes, Mantuas, Sarsnets, & Persians, Likewise all Sorts of half Silks, as English, & Turkey Burdets, Cherry-derrys figur'd and stript Donjars. Also all Sorts of Black Silks for Hoods, & Scarves, Worsted Damasks, Plodds, Superfine broad Camblets, Calimancoes, Camblitees, Black Russells, fine Callimancoes [sic] for

Pettycoats and Yard wide Tammys or Stuffs. Likewise Short Cloaks, Manteels, Mantelets, & Velvet Hoods, ready made, with all other Sorts of Mercery Goods, Wholesale & Retail at yᵉ lowest Prices[.][46]

And the West End had early on developed clusters of retail shops to rival, or at least compete with, the City: shoes in Cranborne Alley, near Leicester Fields, as well as St Martin's-le-Grand in the City; linens and mercery in Bond Street and Bedford Street, Covent Garden, and 'Petticoat Shops' nearby in Henrietta Street, as well as Ludgate Hill and Cheapside, for instance.

We should not let these specialist retail clusters disguise the primary character of the main shopping streets – their diversity. Dotted among the mercers of Cheapside, for instance, were cutlers, map sellers, braziers and ironmongers, goldsmiths, vintners, portmanteau sellers, booksellers, perfumers, cane and stick makers, musical instrument shops, druggists, stationers and so on. And in 'lovely Oxford Street', where a new retailing force had established itself by the 1780s, it did so along similarly diverse lines. Sophie von la Roche noted watchmakers, silk shops, fan stores, china shops, glass shops, 'spirit booths' or gin shops, which she found 'particularly tempting' because of the lights behind shelves of crystal flasks, confectioners, fruiterers, lamp shops providing 'a dazzling spectacle' and all 'so beautifully lit'; in the end, though, she thought 'the linen-shops are the loveliest'. 'Up to 11 o'clock at night there are as many people along this street as at Frankfurt during the fair, not to mention the eternal stream of coaches.'[47]

Indeed, everything was to be had in London. When a West Country agriculturist wanted a 'bushel of Surinam potatoes, for planting', he asked his friend Hannah More to obtain them, not from Bristol, but from 'the warehouse in George's Yard, Oxford Street'. And when the young architect Robert Mylne required 'a common case of mathematical instruments' while in Rome, he asked his father in Edinburgh to order them from 'John Bennett near Golden Square in London', 'with two dozen of his threepenny black pencils, a stick of his best Indian ink and a few ounces of French soft black chalk'.[48]

Perhaps the greatest shopping street of all throughout the eighteenth century was the Strand.[49] Its fortunes were far from stable. It had benefited from the push westwards after the Great Fire, even incorporating two 'exchanges' in imitation of the shopping bazaar built over the City's Royal Exchange. But the thirty-six shops in Exeter Exchange, on the north side of the Strand opposite the Savoy and dating from the 1670s, were foundering by 1720, though the building struggled on till 1829 in other guises. New Exchange, on the south side of the street, by the early 1700s housed 128 shops famous for their millinery – and for their assistants. It seems to have done well at least till 1730, but then lost caste and was demolished in 1737 to be replaced by a terrace of purpose-built shops, one of which, number 59, became Coutts's Bank.[50]

We might use the Strand and the New Exchange to remind ourselves that shopping didn't delight just 'the Ladies'. It was, though to a lesser extent, a man's world too. Many men worked in them, of course, Evelina remarking on the 'six or seven men belonging to each' mercer's shop she visited; 'and such men! so finical, so affected', ever 'bowing and smirking', figures of amusement to the customers but of scorn to all who deprecated the spread of luxury and effeminacy.[51]

But gentlemen were keen shoppers too. They all loved their 'taylors', till the bills came in, and many shops specialised in masculine requirements, from guns to walking canes and pocket watches to shoe buckles. James Boswell, for instance, in the Strand in November 1762, felt the need for a new 'silver-hilted sword', but felt too few guineas in his pocket. At 'Mr Jefferys, sword-cutter to his Majesty,' he found what he wanted and asked Mr Jefferys to trust him. '"Upon my word, Sir," said he, "you must excuse me. It is a thing we never do to a stranger." . . . However, I stood and looked at him, and he looked at me. "Come, Sir," cried he, "I will trust you."' So Boswell chose a belt, put the sword on, and made his serene way into the Strand, duly paying next day: '"We know our men,"' he was gratified to hear Mr Jefferys say.[52]

At the New Exchange, 'The Chiefest Customers . . . were Beaus'. The reason was well known: 'Oh! but, Son, you must not go to Places to stare at Women. Did you buy any Thing?'

[M]y Choice was so distracted among the pretty Merchants and their Dealers, I knew not where to run first – One little lisping Rogue, Ribbandths, Gloveths, Tippeths – Sir, cries another, will you buy a fine Sword-knot; then a thirds pretty Voice and Court'sie – Does not your Lady want Hoods, Scarfs, fine green Silk Stockings – I went by as if I had been in a Seraglio, a living Gallery of Beauties – staring from Side to Side; I bowing, they laughing – so made my Escape . . .[53]

And when young Dudley Ryder visited 'the glass warehouse' there in November 1715 it encouraged that devout though lustful nonconformist law student from Hackney to explore his foppish side: 'There is indeed a noble collection of looking-glass, the finest I believe in Europe. I could not as I passed by there help observing myself, particularly my manner of walking, and that pleased me very well, for I thought I did it with a very genteel and becoming air.'[54]

There was commerce in old as well as new. There was a large market in second-hand furniture, the rich in their carriages picking up bargains at house sales forced by creditors and every poor shopping street and alley having its dealers. Some streets – Lower Moorfields, Wych Street and Holywell Street in the Strand, Thieving Alley by Westminster Abbey, Turnstile Alley off Drury Lane, Harp Alley off Fleet Market and no doubt many others – specialised in the trade. Some 200 or so licensed pawnbrokers sold unredeemed pledges like bedding, watches, snuff boxes and other personal possessions. And Moorfields was the place for second-hand books across the century.[55]

The trade in old clothes was the largest of all. It was frequently combined in the same streets with a large ready-made clothing trade for plebeian customers, especially in and near Houndsditch, on the eastern borders of the City. Sometimes the two trades combined in the same shop. Kenelm Dawson, for instance, at the sign of the Jolly Sailor, Monmouth Street, made and sold 'all sorts of Mens & Boys Cloaths', bought and sold 'all sorts of Second hand Cloaths, both Rich & Plain' and offered 'Gentlemen' a bespoke service for 'Suits and Liveries . . . at Reasonable rates'. This Monmouth Street, Seven Dials, was the great second-hand clothing mart at the west end of the town. 'Monmouth-street finery' might have stood for tawdry showiness but it was certainly the fashionable end of the second-hand market. When William Hickey returned from Bengal in all his finery, a friend pretended to mistake him for the Lord Mayor's trumpeter. He promptly sold his Indian suits to a Monmouth Street salesman for 47 guineas – a year's income for a carpenter – 'for what had, I suppose, cost me seven times that sum, and most of them were nearly new'. It was just as useful for those who wanted to buy. Smollett's Roderick Random, a cash-strapped medical man and Scotsman to boot, who wished to keep up appearances but was conscious he had been seen too much in the same clothes, sold them in Monmouth Street 'for half the value, and bought two new suits with the money'. It was also a great place for countrymen to fit themselves out. John Yeoman from Somerset visited it in 1774: 'Master don't you w[ant] Some Cloathes [I'll] Sute you. It is Imposable to go thro' the Street without buying Something.' He bought some breeches.[56]

Rag Fair, at the eastern end of the town, was a very different place. Its origins are obscure but it seems to have emerged at the end of the seventeenth century. By 1700 it was thriving. Every afternoon except Sunday, from around two o'clock and into the night, the carriageway of Rosemary Lane, east of the Tower of London, was choked with street sellers offering old clothes, hats and shoes from sacks, barrows or just a blanket on the ground. The sheds, shops and houses on either side, and in the courts and alleys off, were also generally turned over to the old clothes trade. And just as in Monmouth Street, some shops dealt in new ready-made clothing: James Lackington, a Somerset shoe-maker who eventually made a fortune in London's second-hand book trade, bought a new greatcoat in Rag Fair for 10s 6d around 1773 – he'd first been asked 25s for it.[57]

It was the street-selling aspect of Rag Fair that called down the wrath of the authorities, the City magistrates attempting to suppress it at the western end near Little Tower Hill around 1700, again in 1737 and 1741, and perhaps more frequently still. But the marshals and constables proved helpless against the rag pickers and old-clothes men and women, 'for their Number bids defiance to all Molestation, and their *Impudence* and *Poverty* are such, that they fear neither *Gaol* nor *Punishment*'. This was a commerce that dealt in farthings, sometimes in barter, in stocks 'so very small, that I found Two-pence, or Three-pence, was accounted, amongst some of them, considerable Takings'. Yet, Ned Ward recounted, 'I saw not one Melancholy or Dejected Countenance amongst 'em . . .' There was good reason for both buyers and sellers to be pleased: around 1790 the London chronicler Thomas Pennant was so fascinated by one transaction that at the end of it the salesman called on him to observe his customer 'going off with his bargain . . . *For*, says he, *I have actu-ally clothed him for fourteen pence.*'[58]

Many other markets in London catered for the poor. A London guide of 1785 lists thirty London markets, eighteen of them selling meat, often with other provisions. These were only the most prom-inent. We do not know how many places there were like 'the long Market near *Swan-Alley*, *Goswell-Street*', selling 'Lumping Bargains of Meat, (such as it is) . . . to poor People', for generally they were too humble to notice. Much marketing by the poor took place late at night just before the stallholders closed and while they were anxious to get stale stock off their hands. Between midnight and one on a Sunday morning, for instance, 'The Markets begin to swarm with the Wives of poor Journeymen Shoemakers, Smiths, Tinkers, Taylors, &c. who come to buy great Bargains with little Money.' And uncountable little shops, often in the cellars of side streets and back alleys of poor neighbourhoods — 'I keep a Fruit-Cellar under the King's-Arms tavern', in or near Wild Street, Drury Lane, a woman told the Old Bailey in 1734 — offered provisions as pinched and wan as their customers. 'The stock-in-trade of a green-cellar, for instance, might be "no more than a gallon of sand, two or three birch-brooms and a bunch of turnips".'[59]

On the other hand, the 'wholesale' markets of London were at the heart of the capital's domestic commerce, selling mainly to retailers but also by retail to private customers. Leadenhall was the City's great market. It had about a hundred 'standing Stalls for Butchers' selling beef alone, 140 for those selling 'Veal, Mutton, Lamb, &c.' and accommodated fishmongers, poulterers and sellers of fruit and vegetables (or 'herbs'). Billingsgate marketed fish and coals; Newgate mainly butchers' meat but with herbs and fish too; and Smithfield of course was the City's market for meat on the hoof and for horses. The West End of the town had Covent Garden for fruit and herbs — 'the best garden in the world' to James Boswell — and there were general markets at Bloomsbury, Soho (Carnaby Market), Holborn (Brook's Market for meat), Clare Market in St Clement Danes for general provisions, particularly for meat, fish and poultry, and Fleet Market on the western edge of the City; at the court end of the town were St James's Market, the Haymarket (living up to its name throughout the century), Shepherd's Market north of Piccadilly, and Westminster Market for meat, with James Gibbs's Oxford Market in the western suburbs and Spitalfields Market (for meat and herbs, chiefly roots and greens) in the eastern. South of the river, Southwark Market was said to be 'the most plentiful and reasonable Market about the City of *London*, for the supply of the Poor'. It was held three days a week in the Borough along the way to London Bridge, and was such a nuisance to traffic by 1755 that it was abolished and moved a short distance away to a new site called the Triangle.[60]

All these markets brought in 'country-killed meat' and garden produce from Middlesex, Surrey and Essex, especially from the market gardeners along the Thames in the west. Fulham was famous for flowers, Battersea for cabbages and asparagus, Hackney and Stratford for exotics, Chelsea for '"fruit trees, and ornamental shrubs and flowers from every quarter of the globe"'. Indeed, 'every species of garden luxury' was sent to town by market gardeners within twelve miles of London. Choice made Londoners fussy. The fledgling farmer Edmund Burke at Beaconsfield, with 'a very great quantity of Carrots' on his hands, complained that 'the London Market will take off only those which have an handsome appearance'.[61]

The wholesalers and shopkeepers that constituted that 'London Market' in the first instance made up a large part of the city's middling sort, but they were no homogeneous group. It cost £1,000–5,000 to establish a woollen draper in business and up to £10,000 for a mercer, huge sums that often required a partnership to put together. Butchers and fruiterers might need much less to start up – £50 or even less – but a good shop in a prominent location could call for £100–500.[62] These were big differences and it need not surprise us that, in a hier-archical age so conscious of status, they brought with them conflicting identities. To those for whom all trade was tainted, the 'ridiculous distinctions which tradesmen make among one another' were merely risible. From the inside, though, the daily battle with debtors for cash and with suppliers for credit, the hard-fought scrimping to invest capital in stock and buildings, the jockeying and half-truths needed to attract and keep customers, all made distinctions like these part of the armour of self-respect. Key to it all was reputation – for integrity and fair dealing, for 'punctuality, and exactness', for 'honour' and honesty most of all.[63]

Maintaining reputation had perhaps never been more difficult, certainly never more costly. In a luxurious age shopkeepers competed in premises that had to be up to the moment and in the fashion. Daniel Defoe in 1726 noted the 'modern custom', 'wholly unknown to our ancestors', for tradesmen to 'lay out two-thirds of their fortune in fitting up their shops' with 'painting and gilding, fine shelves, shutters, boxes, glass doors, sashes, and the like'. He cited a pastrycook's that had cost £300 to fit out in 1710 with new sash windows with 'looking-glass plates' and great mirrors, candlesticks, lanterns and the like.[64]

Not all, of course, won or maintained the necessary reputation on which they could base a modest fortune. Failures within every rank of the shopkeeping classes were common enough, often dictated by the vagaries of fashion. Sometimes reputation was sacrificed to Mammon – or to Venus. John Perrott, from Newport Pagnell, Buckinghamshire, inherited £1,500 when he was orphaned as a child. His guardians apprenticed him to a relative in trade and in 1752 he opened a linen draper's shop on Ludgate Hill. From then till 1759 'he returned annually about two thousand pounds; and was remarkably punctual in his payments. Having established his reputation', he traded on it, taking goods on credit to the value of £25,000 and then employed someone to sell them at a loss to raise cash. He then summoned his creditors to tell them he couldn't pay what was owed and to reach an accommodation. This was a risky fraud and Perrott was hanged in Smithfield, close to the scene of his crime, as an object lesson to the City's trading classes. The cause of his downfall became clear from the account he gave to the commissioners in bankruptcy: 'Expences attending the connexion I had with the fair sex' amounted to £5,500 in a single year, all spent on his mistress, Mrs Ferne.[65]

But it was not John Perrott who characterised the London tradesman for contemporaries. It was the stories of their trading success that resonated most strongly. They took on an almost mythic quality, the living embodiment of London's opportunities, proof that gold really could be scraped from its paving stones. 'How ordinary it is to see a tradesman go off the stage, even but from mere shopkeeping, with from ten to forty thousand pounds' estate to divide among his family!' while country gentlemen struggled to keep their estates together. 'I remember John [Walker] when he was a shopman with a grocer and chandler in Wells-street, Rag Fair, for a stipend of £16 per annum, which he thought himself very happy to get. He died worth £200,000', his money made as a sugar baker. Richard Crossley was employed by a spoon maker in Paternoster Row to carry fuel for the furnaces, winning the name of Charcoal Dick. But being smart, sober and frugal, he saved £100, set up as a spoon maker himself in Giltspur Street, and when he left off was worth £80,000. Sir William Plomer, Alderman of London and Lord Mayor in 1781–2, 'began life in a dark oil-shop in the neighbourhood of Aldgate' and married the niece of a washerwoman known as '*check-apron Sall*' – or so the story went. A fortune, it seemed, could be made from anything. When Aaron Gibbs died at his house in Clerkenwell in 1725 worth £40,000, he was described as 'an eminent rag merchant'. 'Who can say,' asked Joseph Brasbridge, silversmith and cutler of 98 Fleet Street, whose own business was undermined by his cheerfully confessed 'dissipation', 'that a man has not as good a chance of making a fortune in London, as in the East Indies, or any other part of the globe?' And certain it was that there were many enterprising ways to turn a penny in eighteenth-century London.[66]

'Clean Your Honour's Shoes': Streets

The Thames, the Royal Exchange, the coffee houses, Leadenhall Market, Cheapside and the Strand – somewhere among these great marketplaces we can rank the streets of London. They were open for business all day every day, and almost all night every night. The calls of the street sellers were a defining feature of metropolitan life. 'There is nothing which more astonishes a foreigner, and frights a country-squire, than the Cries of London,' thought Mr Spectator in 1711, and so it proved through the century. Seventy years later and Israel Potter, an American taking his first sight of London, 'was almost stunned, while my curiosity was not a little excited by what is termed the "cries of London" – the streets were thronged by persons of both sexes and of every age, crying each the various articles which they were exposing for sale, or for jobs of work at their various occupations . . .' [67]

The cries of London were in everybody's heads: Handel used one as the idea for an aria in *Serse* in 1738, actors rang them out in the theatre, artisans mimicked them at the bench. They proved irresistible to artists – and they were irresistible because they sold well. The 'Cryes' of Marcellus Lauron (1688) were republished throughout the century, and sentimentally redesigned by Louis Philippe Boitard in the 1750s. Paul Sandby, the great figure-drawer of the mid-century, issued *Twelve London Cries done from the Life* in 1760, harsh energetic portraits with nothing of sentiment about them, their subjects grabbing attention through seduction or aggression. In the 1790s came a return to prettiness in Francis Wheatley's cries of 1792–5, thirteen of them turned into popular engravings, each selling at the high price of 7s 6d plain or 16s coloured.

Hardly a portrayal of London's streets could leave out their street folk. They abound in Hogarth, often also 'drawn from the life' with well-known characters in mind, reaching an apotheosis in *The Enraged*

Musician (1741), who is plagued by a street oboe player, a ballad singer, a knife grinder, a dustman with his bell, a sow-gelder with his horn, a fellow crying fish and a maid calling milk. They teem in the street scenes and caricatures of Thomas Rowlandson and James Gillray, and in the topographical drawings of John Thomas Smith – a true Londoner he, born in a hackney coach somewhere between Seven Dials and Great Portland Street; Smith's ancient London buildings vie for attention, not always successfully, with his beggars and street sellers, often characters well known in their day.[68]

We have no idea of the numbers who turned to the streets of London to earn a living or part of a living. There must have been many thousands, even though the streets were a hotly contested space to conduct commerce. Shopkeepers resented the street sellers as a blight on their trade, and so did the City markets. Numerous regulations were in place to stop hawkers and peddlers trading, especially in the City. In a clampdown near Christmas 1738, for instance, many hawkers were arrested and imprisoned, their goods forfeited.[69] An expensive bureaucracy was established to license those who were tolerated, and it is likely that throughout the eighteenth century – much as we saw with Jews in the orange and other trades – street sellers of all denominations were more common in the suburbs and in Southwark and Westminster than in the City itself.

What sort of people were they? Most seem to have been women. After domestic service and laundering, and working with the needle or loom in the weaving and clothing trades, street selling was the next great industry for women. A few trades like chair mending and knife grinding seem to have been largely male preserves and men entered numerous others, but in general buying in the markets and selling in the streets was largely a woman's trade. Women or men, this was a poor labour force but one by no means entirely without resources. Money had to be raised for stock, for a basket or a barrow, and the knife grinder's bench or a street musician's instruments represented fixed capital for many. Barrows, handcarts and organs could be rented. Even so, rental and stock had to be paid for somehow, as often as not on credit. So on the security of clothes or possessions a pawnbroker would lend stock money for the week. One who loaned heavily to the street-trading community told the House of Commons in 1746 that he had taken 24,328 pledges in the previous twelve months, lending on average 3s for each pledge. Doubtless too, as in the nineteenth century, there were entrepreneurs emerging from street selling who found it more profitable to rent out barrows and provide sellers with stock, taking 'half profits' at the end of the day or week. Some saved enough from their arduous tramping to win public notice. We hear of a Stepney man who in 1785 left £10,000 to his local church, money made from hawking quills about the streets; and of 'Poor Jo, all alone', famous for his long beard and great age, who sold matches and ballads, and turned a penny from conjuring tricks, leaving over £3,000 to widows and orphaned children in 1767.[70]

Perhaps the most useful street sellers, both to London and the London economy, sold food. The well-informed agriculturist John Middleton thought 'consumers are much indebted' to 'the jack-ass drivers, barrow-women, and other itinerant dealers . . . who buy of the gardeners in the market, and hawk through the streets of London, and its environs, vegetables and fruit at a very moderate price'. Food vendors of one kind or another were legion. Milk was carried in tubs and pails by women from the cow keepers at Islington and around. Usually they called 'Mew!' to announce their presence; 'one wench', who walked about Soho Square, was unkindly remembered for her 'inarticulate scream . . . as if her posteriors were then actually piercing by a cobbler's awl'. We hear of a rice-milk seller still at work in St Giles between four and five on a summer morning, the 'Geneva' or gin sellers without whom 'No modern mob can long subsist', the 'sassafras' or 'saloop' sellers in the fields early on Sundays. The pie sellers, often with a bell, were so common that John Thomas Smith marked a milestone in his early years as 'the age when most children place things on their heads and cry "Hot Pies!"' And '"Muffins! muffins! Ladies come buy *me*! pretty, handsome, blooming, smiling maids,"' was cried by a crippled muffin man about Soho Square in the 1780s. Fish was sold from a basket by men and women – Sandby portrayed a female fury of a mackerel seller – among them the occasional distressed fishmonger, like John Bryson, once rich, who at the end had only nuts in his basket while crying 'every sort of fish from the turbot to the periwinkle'. 'Holloway cheesecakes' was a famous cry of the 1740s; the offal sellers called tripe, neats' feet, calves' feet, trotters, hearts, liver and lights; 'A pudding-a-pudding a hot pudding'; 'Rare Meltin Oysters, rare stewing Oysters'; 'Will you buy my Crabs come buy my Crabs'; 'Sweet China Oranges'; 'Fresh Gathered Peas Young Hastings'; 'Round & Sound Five Pence a Pound Duke Cherries';

'Strawberries Scarlet Strawberries'; 'Hot Spice Gingerbread Smoking Hot!'; 'Turnips and Carrots ho!' There were sausage fryers, apple roasters, walnut sellers: just about everything that could be carried and eaten was sold on the streets of London.[71]

So too for domestic goods and not a few domestic services. Brushes and brooms, iron candlesticks and sticks 'to beat your Wives or Dust your Clothes', mouse traps and rat traps were all hawked about the streets. So were nosegays and flowers, stationery, crockery, cutlery, matches, stockings; 'baubles and trinkets' were sold at the gates of Ranelagh Gardens; Anne Henley, said to be 104 when she died, had lived by making pincushions, sitting 'at various doors in Holborn' to sell them; the dramatist Thomas Holcroft's mother 'hung a basket with pins, needles, tape, garters, and other small haberdashery, on her arm, and hawked them through the outskirts and neighbourhood of London'. Some animal doctoring seems to have been a street profession, like sow gelders and horse quacks who 'trudge through the streets with a melting ladle and gally-pot, filled with horse-turpentine'. Link boys waited at theatre and tavern doors at night to light passengers home with their torches or rushes. Shoe-blacks, boys and men, were found on many street corners and were 'very numerous on Sunday mornings'. They charged a halfpenny for much of the century but a penny by the end, and were equipped not just with blacking but with a purpose-made 'buckle brush' as well:

> His treble voice resounds along the *Meuse*,
> And *White-hall* echoes – *Clean your Honour's Shoes*.[72]

Knife and scissor grinders were common in the streets and so were chair menders who restored the cane bottoms of cheap kitchen chairs. Israel Potter's 'constant cry through the streets of London, from morning to night' was '"Old Chairs to Mend"', and it 'yielded a tolerable support for my family' until doctors' bills for his children ran them into debt and Potter into prison.[73]

Potter combined his street trade, as no doubt many did, with 'finding': 'I collected all the old rags, bits of paper, nails and broken glass which I could find in the streets, and which I deposited in a bag, which I carried with me for that purpose', selling them to the rag merchants for 'a trifle' which helped feed 'my poor wife and children'. Finding was the foul end of commerce in the streets. 'Bunters, with Bits of

Candle between their Fingers, and Baskets on their Heads, rummaging the dirty Dunghills at the Entrance of Lanes, Courts, Yards, Alleys, &c. for Rags and Bones, to purchase the ensuing Day's Dinner', were a feature of the streets in early morning, according to Thomas Legg in 1764. A 'whole Company of Finders' scoured the markets at night as soon as they closed for discarded scraps of meat, fruit and herbs, and those bones so valuable for making 'mock ivory' knife handles, or burning and crushing to make into crucibles: 'A paste made of burnt bones will stand a stronger heat than anything else,' Samuel Johnson, a repository of practical esoteric knowledge, explained to Boswell. Even orange peel found in the streets, he said, was taken to a place in Newgate Street for scraping and drying before sale to the distillers.[74]

An equally arduous but more prosperous living could be made by those who sought to attract and amuse the public in the streets. The ballad sellers who sang their wares were the most prominent and numerous, and generally they too were women. Francis Place recalled how common they were in the 1780s, and how obscene the material they sometimes sang and sold. Some had fixed pitches and 'There was always a considerable crowd of fools idlers, and pickpockets to hear them.' Applause was proportionate to 'the vileness of the songs and the flash manner of singing them':

Two women used to sing a song opposite a public house the sign of the Crooked Billet, at the back of St Clements Church in the Strand . . . I can only remember the last two lines.

'And for which I'am sure she'd go to Hell
For she makes me fuck her in church time.'

I remember these words in consequence of the shout which was always set up as the song closed with them.[75]

Fiddlers and harpers played hornpipes and jigs in the streets and public houses, often attracting a happy little group of dancers – or 'nimble-footed, noisy, drunken Fools' as they appeared to some. Certainly, not everyone appreciated their efforts: 'a fellow is at this moment winding a cursed Clarionet under my Office Window', complained George Cumberland, a clerk at the Royal Exchange Assurance, in the freezing January of 1776, 'which is a proff a man may move his fingers, tho possibly he plays in Gloves for the Musick is so miserable as to produce no Ideas, that Frost and Snow will not'. On the other hand, Mary Wollstonecraft in George Street, Southwark, told her sister in November 1787 that 'an organ under my window had been playing *for tenderness framed* – and *welladay my poor heart* – my spectacles are *dim . . .*'

'Humstrum' or hurdy-gurdy players, puppeteers with their theatres carried on their backs, dancing dogs, mountebanks or quack doctors whom we'll meet again in a later chapter, acrobats, jugglers, clowns, and a snake charmer who cheated risk by extracting his vipers' teeth were perpetual or occasional features of the streets of London.[76] Certainly there was talent to be had, like this trio 'parading the streets of London' in the summer of 1799. One carried an organ on his back, another blew 'a reed-pipe' and the third was a tambourine player who 'frequently during the performance of a tune cast up the instrument into the air three or four feet higher than his head, and caught it, as it returned, upon a single finger; he then whirled it round with an air of triumph, and proceeded in the accompaniment without losing time, or occasioning the least interruption'.[77] And there was always some event that prompted street entrepreneurs to try their luck. 'I have been this morning at the Tower,' wrote Horace Walpole to a friend in August 1746, 'and passed under the new heads at Temple Bar, where people make a trade of letting spying-glasses at a halfpenny a look.'[78]

Some of this street earning, of course, came close to begging, or was combined with it. A link boy, for instance, would often have to ask charity to buy a torch, and no doubt some costermongers did for their stock or just to keep themselves alive: 'She sold gingerbread and oranges, in a very poor way, little better than a beggar,' the Old Bailey heard of Mary Cox in 1765, and the same must have been true of countless more.[79] For begging was a considerable feature of the streets of London throughout the century.

The numbers of beggars on the streets caused the authorities to take periodic alarm throughout the century. There were crises in 1703, 1729, 1737, 1740 and 1741; in 1751 there were complaints of another 'prodigious and scandalous Encrease of publick Beggars', and constables neglecting to arrest beggars were threatened by the City with prosecution in 1760; and so on. There may well have been times when the numbers of beggars rose through economic distress or post-war demobilisation, but the fact is that begging was perceived to be a problem right through the century. '[Y]ou will no where find such multitudes of unemployed persons, loiterers, vagabonds and beggars' as London, thought Sir John Fielding, chief magistrate at Bow Street, around 1776. He shared a common view that beggars had been largely removed by vigorous police action from the City, much like its suppression of street sellers. Even so, the City had to repeat its warning to prosecute constables for negligence in dealing with beggars as late as 1798.[80]

Despite facing a whipping and imprisonment in Bridewell for their importunities, beggars were highly visible on the London streets. Indeed, it was their business to be so. They were especially prominent on Sundays, at street corners and around the doors of churches, to 'teize the Parishioners', and in the countryside north of the City where 'vast quantities of field mendicants' with 'their dismal stories' charmed pennies from holidaymakers. And the pennies do seem to have come. 'The city abounds with beggars,' thought William Hutton, visiting from Birmingham in 1784. 'It is hardly possible to travel the streets of London, and keep money in one's pocket; not because it is picked out, but drawn by our own consent. Distress and compassion are inseparable companions.' Indeed, it seems likely that one reason for the large numbers of beggars in London was the freedom with which Londoners gave alms when they had them to give.[81]

It was a generosity much criticised by magistrates and reformers, many Christians among them. One justified reason for some suspicion concerned the means by which pity might be evoked. There seems little doubt that many professional beggars resorted to shams of one sort or another to wring pennies from Londoners. Beggars pretended to be dumb or lame; some 'tie their arms in their breeches, and wear a wooden stump in their sleeve'; some faked epileptic fits; some women pretended to hang themselves, cut down by an accomplice who then raised a clamour for alms – a trick with a history, for we hear of it in 1731 and again in 1752; one old soldier plastered his leg with a mixture of sheep's blood and flour to simulate 'mortification'. Some were said to

raise artificial sores on their bodies . . . by burning crow's foot, spearwort, and salt, together, and, clapping them at once on the face it fretted the skin; then, with a linen rag, which sticks close, they tear off the skin and strew on a little powder of arsenic which gives it an ugly and ill-favoured look: these sores are, in the canting phrase, called *clegms.*

Such 'Faquir-like . . . austerities' were also said to account for mutilated limbs.[82]

Not all of course were impostors. 'If any person is born with any defect or deformity, or maimed by fire or any other casualty, or any inveterate distemper which renders them miserable objects, their way is open to London; where they have free liberty of shewing their nauseous sights, to terrify people, and force them to give money to get rid of them,' it was said around 1730, and doubtless it was true that compassion was most quickly raised by blindness and missing or deformed limbs. It was raised too by children. Children could be hired out from Petticoat Lane for 8d a day in 1772 to beggars who presumably made a profit from their bargain. By the 1790s the price had apparently risen to 2s, for Archenholtz claimed to have overheard one 'beggar woman' scold another for paying so much '"for so fine a child as that! I would not give more for a monster."' It's hard to believe, but there is some evidence that children were mutilated to increase their earning power. Anne Martin or Chapney was sentenced at Clerkenwell to two years' imprisonment in 1761 for 'putting out the eyes of children, with whom she went a begging about the country'. And poor Elizabeth Parker, who died at Moorfields in 1767 at the age, it was said, of 103, had been stolen from her parents when young and 'her eyes put out, and carried about by two beggars to move charity'.[83]

Like other professions, those who made a livelihood from begging chose to cluster together. Places in St Giles, like the 'old shattered building' called Rat's Castle in Dyot Street, or in the Borough, like Pike Yard in the Clink Liberty, Three Tun Alley off White Street, or Kent Street, 'chiefly inhabited by *Broom Men* and *Mumpers*', were notorious beggars' haunts. Like stockbrokers in their coffee houses, beggars shared information and a convivial time in taverns such as the Case is Altered, Kent Street, or Welsh's Head (also the Old Blind Beak's Head), Dyot Street. And privacy was assured by 'the cant language, sometimes called Pedlar's French, or St. Giles's Greek, slang, slum, &c.'[84]

This begging fraternity proved endlessly fascinating to the middling sort, despite its 'low' character in the Age of Politeness. Some found

fame through the artist's pencil, like Hogarth's Philip-in-the-Tub in
Industry and Idleness (1747) among others, or Old Simon Edy, who
begged at the gate of St Giles churchyard and was pictured by Thomas
Rowlandson and John Thomas Smith – 'he was one of my pensioners,'
the kindly Smith recalled. Any connection between begging and riches
was always newsworthy, both as a wonder of nature and a deterrent
to credulous giving. We hear of John Cornwall, 'the Cripple of Kent',
who died at Kent Street aged ninety-one in 1765, leaving 'a woman,
whom he called his wife, upwards of 400 guineas in gold, and a considerable sum in silver'. Mary Simes, 'a beggar woman aged 109', was
said to have been worth £1,500 when she died in the Mint, Southwark,
in 1772. Mary Jones, a beggar for over forty years, who died in Hedge
Lane (now Whitcomb Street), Charing Cross, in 1780, had ninety half-
crowns in a mug in her lodgings and, like any other woman of capital,
had over £600 'vested in the funds'.[85]

Such exceptional cases tell us little of the realities of the begging life,
except that beggars, real or sham, had some among them of an avar-
icious and hoarding turn, just like merchants and tradespeople. The
generality was more mundane. We know, for instance, that most beggars,
like the majority of the street folk, were women. Of 2,000 London
beggars interviewed by Matthew Martin for the Mendicity Enquiry
Office around 1796–7, no fewer than 1,808 were women: perhaps male
beggars were less ready to be questioned. Of the women, 127 were
single, 1,100 married and 581 widowed. Of a smaller sample of 120
from the same source, there were twenty-one men, mostly maimed,
aged or sick; of the ninety-nine women, forty-eight were widows, about
a third were aged, some crippled, some without work; many did not
know how to get parochial relief or were afraid of applying for it,
perhaps because they would be 'passed' to their home parish or forced
into the workhouse. For these women the greatest problem was 'want
of work', sometimes because of a baby – over half had two or more
children not yet old enough to be sent to work. 'To all of them, the
gift of a little food, and the hearing of their melancholy story, afforded
some comfort.'[86]

No doubt there were numerous impostors among the men too shy
to be interviewed. But there were many hard cases also. Prison reformers
noted how discharged prisoners of any background had no recourse
but 'begging in the streets for subsistence'. And foreigners remarked on
the extraordinary number of wooden legs in London, far more than in

any other city in Europe, testimony no doubt to the victims of Britain's almost ceaseless wars. We may reasonably assume that, despite the large numbers of shams, the majority of London beggars were casualties of this kind, 'cripples, blind men, old men, women, and children'; and potentially all that large number of Londoners who had just a finger-grip on the economic life of the metropolis.[87] And that was an economic life of unlimited diversity.

Francis Place

VI

FRANCIS PLACE'S LONDON – INDUSTRY AND LABOUR

'Minute Movement and Miraculous Weight': Made in London

FRANCIS Place would never give up. His courage he inherited from his father, his stoicism and a kind heart from his mother, but his far-sighted intelligence and determination to improve both himself and the lives of the London workers from whom he'd sprung were products of his own indomitable personality.

He was a cockney and illegitimate, born on 3 November 1771 in Vinegar Yard, Brydges Street (now Catherine Street), between the Theatre Royal Drury Lane and the tiny burial ground of St Mary le Strand. Simon Place, his father, kept a Marshalsea debtors' lock-up or spunging house there, and later one in Ship and Anchor Court, Strand, till such places were abolished at the end of 1780. He then took the King's Arms public house in Arundel Street, close to St Clement Danes Church – all very much in Johnson's London. Simon Place was from Bury St Edmunds, Suffolk, where he was apprenticed to a baker but ran away to London when very young. He was a drinker, a womaniser, a gambler, a fighter and a terrible bully to his two sons, beating Francis with a rope's end and once breaking a stick over his head. If one of his boys met him in a narrow passage or doorway 'he always made a blow at us with his fist, for coming in his way, if we attempted to retreat he would make us come forward and as certainly as we came forward he would knock us down'. But he was staunch and loyal to all who sought his aid, much respected for his advice and common sense, and never went back on his word. These more admirable qualities Francis took from his father, as well as the strong physique and good looks that stayed with him almost till his death, aged eighty-three, in 1854.[1]

Place got no love of learning from Simon, who 'could sign his name, but could not write a letter of business, and never I conclude, had read a book of any kind in his life'. But Place derived a passion for books and learning from a schoolmaster, Mr Bowis, who ran a day school near St Mary le Strand. Bowis encouraged not just learning but reasoning, 'the talent of distinguishing, of separating matters and drawing conclusions', that Place would endeavour to practise all his life. In this way he reasoned his way out of religion while still a boy. There was, though, much of Simon in the way Francis gratified his passion for books. His penny a week from his father didn't allow him to buy any, but he found ways of getting money nonetheless. Once he 'raked the kennel' of filthy Water Street, running down to the Thames, for old iron. He sold it and bought materials for a paper kite taller than himself, decorating it with paper stars and flowers. He chopped wood after school for a chandler's shop for 3½d an hour, bought twine, flew the kite in the fields and promptly 'sold it on the spot twine and all for half a guinea. From this time I never wanted money. I made models of boats and rigged them', and 'Moulds for Cocks and Dumps', lead shies that were hard to knock down. He gathered the lead from the burnt carcass of a house near Holywell Street, Strand.[2]

When Francis approached fourteen in 1785 his father was keen to apprentice him to a lawyer, 'but I had an antipathy to Law and Lawyers' – the spunging house perhaps darkening his mind in that direction – and he risked his father's ire by refusing to countenance it. He expected to be sent to sea as a punishment, but his father reacted mildly. That evening, in the bar of the King's Arms, he offered his son to anyone there who would take him as an apprentice. 'A little man named France said he would, and I was sent the very next morning on liking for a month to learn the art and mystery of Leather Breeches making.'[3]

Old Joe France lived and worked in Bell Yard, Fleet Street, just on the City side of Temple Bar. He and his wife were heavy drinkers, his three daughters prostitutes, his two sons thieves. Place became apprenticed for a term of seven years. It was not a propitious base to learn a trade for life, and the trade itself seemed unlikely to sustain Place for long. France 'had nearly outlived his customers' in the gentleman's bespoke trade, young men abandoning leather breeches in the face of competition from corduroy and other materials. To pay his way France made 'Rag Fair breeches' for the cheap ready-made trade, using substandard leather damaged by water or worm. Through application and a lively curiosity Place took to the craft and quickly earned 6s a week on journeyman's piecework. With his keep all found, 'I became a great man for my age and associated with from fifteen to twenty youths who were also apprentices mostly living in Fleet Street all turbulent unruly fellows, scarcely under any sort of control.' Their money was spent in taverns on drink and prostitutes and on their 'sweethearts', respectable daughters of citizen tradesmen and artisans.[4]

Like many others, Place never served out his apprenticeship. Around 1788 Old Joe France and his household fled his creditors in the middle of the night – 'shooting the moon' or doing a moonlight flit – and hid over the river in Lambeth. Shortly after, France was imprisoned in the King's Bench for debt. In July 1789 Place relinquished his indentures. The exigencies of fortune and the changing tide of fashion now threw him on to the London labour market as a journeyman at the age of eighteen. There was still a living to be made in leather breeches and at first he prospered. His prospects were good enough for him to marry Elizabeth Chadd at Lambeth Church in March 1791 – he nineteen, Elizabeth just sixteen. They set up home in a furnished room 'at the Back of St Clements Church', close to where he'd been brought up.[5]

Place now faced the greatest crisis of his working life. The leather-breeches trade suffered another downturn in 1791–2. He sought to protect his position by experimenting with other materials, but he couldn't keep up with more experienced men and the leather work fell away. He and Elizabeth lived hand to mouth in the single room where they worked, ate and slept. One week they had no money at all, 'in the depth of winter and we had neither food nor fire', until a single pair of breeches on which Place worked for two days without rest rescued them.[6] Worse came when the journeymen struck for better wages in the spring of 1793. It was a disastrous miscalculation by the Breeches Makers' Benefit Society, at a time of low demand and when the Society's funds were inadequate for the numbers depending on them. The masters enforced a general lockout – to Place's surprise, because he hadn't heard a strike had been called. But his good sense and energy pushed him to the front of the agitation and he found himself the Society's treasurer, with a major hand in strike tactics: for the rest of his days he would be in demand as a drafter of articles, rules and petitions for innumerable workers' associations in London. At the end, though, the men were forced back to work with no gains in wages or conditions, and in May 1793 Place was perpetually blacklisted by the masters. A month before, in the middle of the strike, his baby Ann had died of smallpox in their one room above a chandler's in Wych Street, Strand.

For eight months Place could find no work, 'either in my own trade or in any other way'. He and his wife pawned everything 'but what we stood upright in' and slowly starved. 'My wife was a fine, handsome young woman, and I was most affectionately and sincerely attached to her . . . and when I sometimes looked at her in her comfortless, forlorn, and all but ragged condition, I could hardly endure our wretched state . . .' Then, in an unforeseen turn, a master breeches maker relented on seeing Elizabeth's piteous plight, defied the ban and gave Place as much work as he could handle. With his wife's help, he made up for lost time. There would be later setbacks but this was a turning point. Place narrowly avoided what he saw all around him: that 'poverty kills apace. Those who having been once well off in the world fall into poverty seldom long survive their change of circumstances.'[7]

Rejecting the vulnerabilities of a journeyman's life, he began making on his own account, running up leather and stuff breeches with material bought from City drapers on short credit and selling his goods to retailers. After four years, in April 1799, he took a partner and opened a tailor's shop at 29 Charing Cross. In 1801 he took a grander shop at 16 Charing Cross, with 'the largest plate-glass windows in London, if indeed they were not the first', and had thirty-six men working for him. By that time he had involved himself for some eight years in the movement to improve the wages, conditions and political influence of London's working people. Then, and ever after, Francis Place would be 'the Radical Tailor of Charing Cross'.[8]

There was much in Place's life that was unique to his own unquench-able spirit. But there was also much that he shared in common with his times: his unruly and disordered apprenticeship, ending through his master's failings; the fluid labour market affected by the shifting tide of fashion; the insecurity of a working life stalked by penury; the diversity of opportunity – as a journeyman for numerous masters, as a worker on his own account, and eventually as a master himself, making and selling direct to the customer; and the turbulent and bitter industrial relations of eighteenth-century London. And we might note among these common features the pot luck assigning him to 'the mystery

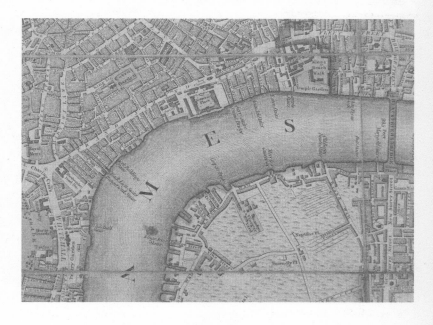

St Clement Danes to Charing Cross, *c.*1799

of Leather Breeches making' that might so easily have taken him in a different direction. For Place grew up among mathematical-instrument makers, chair carvers (he almost took up the trade), sculptors' modellers, silk mercers, law stationers and lightermen (to whom his brother was apprenticed).

There had always been a good chance, though, that Place would be bound to a manufacturing trade, for London was the greatest manufacturing centre of the nation, probably of the world. After wholesale and retail distribution, manufacturing was London's largest business sector, most likely accounting for between a quarter and a third of all London enterprises. It was marked by extraordinary variety and by detailed specialisation. The division of labour that Adam Smith proclaimed the driver of productive power and efficiency was found pre-eminently in the workshop districts of London, with infinitely divided industrial processes run as separate businesses but often clustered close to one another. In many trades, though not all, this was a flexible, innovative and competitive industrial environment.[9]

Much of what Londoners used in their homes or wore about their persons was made by other Londoners. The manufacture of finished commodities had to accommodate the pockets of all from the humblest to the richest, from necessities to luxuries. Soap, candles, floorcloths, wallpaper, cutlery, tableware, dishes in metal or porcelain or earthenware, chairs and tables, beds and cabinets, all were made in London. So was nearly every item of clothing to be found in the drapers' warehouses, in cotton, woollens and silks, and the 'toys' and watches that graced the pockets and dressing tables of the quality. As often as not these goods were not made wholly in one master's workshop but passed through the hands of numerous workers and finishers in their own one- or two-room homes nearby. And they were made all over London: in the inner suburbs of Whitechapel, Spitalfields, Shoreditch, Clerkenwell, Holborn and St Giles; in the parishes of Westminster from St Clement's to St James's; in Southwark, a great manufacturing town in its own right; and, most of all, in every street and turning in the City of London itself. Some districts had a special association with a particular trade. But the general truth is that the production of almost any commodity was widespread in London, and every London district was marked more by diversity than by any single industry.[10]

Southwark, for instance, was known best for its leather trades, established in Bermondsey well before 1700, and sure enough in a

London directory for 1781 we find skinners, tanners, wool staplers, hatters, glue makers and all the by-trades this great industry spawned. But we also find brewers, distillers, maltsters, snuff makers, shipwrights and shipbuilders and barge builders, copper and brass and iron founders, coopers and iron-hoop makers, sailmakers and mast makers and rope makers, white-lead makers, dyers, confectioners and biscuit bakers and gingerbread bakers, engine and pump makers, glassmakers, anchor smiths, block makers, sugar refiners, pin makers and needle and fish-hook makers, potters, card makers, soap makers, watchmakers and clockmakers, upholsterers, copperas makers, starch makers, shot makers and gun makers, colour makers, coachmakers, turners, oilcloth makers, pewterers, silversmiths and goldsmiths.[11]

The workshops of the City were equally diverse, though with much more in the garment, printing and stationery industries and the luxury trades. The great fire of Cornhill in 1748 destroyed the premises of milliners, cabinetmakers, shoemakers, a pewterer, a stocking-frame knitter, tailor, saddler, hatter, watchmaker and button maker. Just about everything was made in the City. When four men were tried in May 1790 for a conspiracy to murder the King, the court was told of their efforts to commission a metal or wooden tube for the airgun they were supposedly about to use, approaching a brass founder in New Street Square, another nearby in Shoe Lane and a turner in Bartholomew Close, Smithfield. Some manufacturers were more neighbourly than others: six died when Mrs Clitherow's fireworks factory in Halfmoon Alley, Bishopsgate Street, blew up a few days before Bonfire Night in 1791. And many places had their specialties. There was a whalebone boiler in Whalebone Court, horners made 'Lanthorns, Inkhorns, Giggs [whipping tops], Spoons, small Dishes, and other things of Horn', in and around Inkhorne Court, off Petticoat Lane; flax and hemp dressers were found in Moorgate, leather dressers and curriers at London Wall, candlestick and bell founders in Lothbury, tinware and fishing-tackle makers in Crooked Lane, off Fish Street Hill; turners clustered in Spinning-Wheel Alley, Moorfields, famous for its go-carts; barbers and wig makers gathered around St Andrew Holborn – they employed women homeworkers to pick grey hairs from the tresses used in their wigs; Addle Street near Aldermanbury was noted for its cabinetmakers, Great Wood Street for its cake bakers, Jewen Street for its button-mould makers, Gutter Lane, Cheapside, for the makers of wooden chimney surrounds, and St Martin's-le-Grand for its shoemakers.[12]

Some of these City manufacturing industries employed large numbers. The gold and silver wire trade centred on St Giles Cripplegate in the north-west of the City was said in both 1712 and 1743 to give work to over 6,000 people, probably half of them children. In 1712 eighty-five 'Sheds' with 255 'pair of Wheels' for spinning the fine wire in gold lace were employing some 1,700 alone. It was an industry not confined to a single parish but a feature of many others in the City and beyond, with workers even in Westminster at Covent Garden and St Martin-in-the-Fields.[13]

This was the case too with one other great City industry, the working goldsmiths and silversmiths making the 'toys' – jewellery and trinkets and decorative cases for watches – so popular at the time. They were to be found especially near Goldsmith's Hall, Foster Lane, in the City's north-west corner. It was a trade that might have been expected to follow the drift of wealth and luxury consumption westward from the City, and to some extent it did. That was a movement already well established by 1720, when perhaps one in three London goldsmiths were located west of Temple Bar, the Huguenot influence specially marked in Soho, St Martin-in-the-Fields and Covent Garden. But despite the growth of the town – and of gilded wealth – in the west, that proportion seems hardly to have changed by the end of the century. From 1780 to 1799 the largest concentration of goldsmiths was still to be found in narrow and crowded Noble Street, Gutter Lane, Foster Lane, Aldersgate Street and around. By then, in the West End of the town, the makers and sellers of Huguenot influence had died away in favour of Oxford Street and Bond Street in particular.[14]

Even so, the parishes of Westminster, especially those like Francis Place's closest to the City, could boast a manufacturing economy almost as diverse as anything east of Temple Bar. About 30 per cent of Westminster's householders who voted in the general election of 1784 were manufacturers of one complexion or another, among them 565 tailors and 548 shoemakers. There was a great medley among the rest, who combined in that typical London pattern of clustering and inter-mingling mixed. Every shopping street was a manufacturing street too: Joseph Bramah made and sold his patent water closets at 14 Piccadilly in the 1790s, Richard Poole of Jermyn Street made and sold pewter ware, and Thomas Dobson of 427 Oxford Street 'Makes and Sells all Sorts of Leather Pipes, for Brewers and Engines, Buckets, Jacks, Canns, Portmanteaus, Fire Caps, Shoes, Boots', for home and export. Some of these places had hands enough to call themselves factories, like Mr Aimable Michelle's or Mitchell's Artificial Flower Factory at 14 Dover Street, Piccadilly, where Rhynwick Williams, the so-called London Monster who slashed women's clothing from behind, worked with a dozen or so others in 1790.[15]

Occasionally the clustering of an industry in particular neighbourhoods reached that perfection of subdivision of labour that turned a single district into a factory in all but name. The most celebrated coachmakers of London were to be found in and around Long Acre, between St Martin's Lane and Drury Lane. John Hatchett of 121 Long Acre, the royal coachmaker, employed several hundred workmen on three floors, from smiths to gilders, around 1786. But hardly any coachmaker made a complete coach. Bits of the enterprise were farmed out to specialist trades like draughtsmen, 'coach livery lace-makers' and wheelwrights, some seventeen different trades in all, if not more, and each a few minutes' walk from one another. Similar patterns were strongly marked in cabinetmaking, tailoring and shoemaking, with considerable outwork done at home, and much of the work in tailoring involving women at the needle.[16]

London's great watchmaking industry took subdivision furthest of all. No man was expected to make a complete watch, although those describing themselves as watchmakers were legion. The watchmaker commissioned the watch and engraved 'his Name upon the Plate, and is esteemed the Maker, though he has not made in his Shop the smallest Wheel belonging to it'. Those serving an apprenticeship as a watchmaker were expected to be able to make most of the movements, but in practice they were given to hands of varying skill to make. At least twenty-one makers, most working at home, were involved in the separate processes of building a watch; chains to drive the wheels, for instance, 'are frequently made by Women in the Country about *London*, and sold to the Watch-Maker by the Dozen for a very small Price'.[17]

The ingenuity of the London makers and the great beauty of the watches they made were famous all over Europe throughout the century. Names like Daniel Quare of Exchange Alley, Thomas Earnshaw of High Holborn and John Arnold of Devereux Court, Strand, were of world renown. Arnold famously 'made' a watch set in a ring for George III in 1764, incorporating 120 moving parts 'of minute movement and miraculous weight'. Fine London watches didn't come cheap. When Horace Walpole commissioned a watch for a friend in Florence he could find nothing respectable under '100 guineas, with two seals for 16 more', from John Deard of Dover Street, Piccadilly.[18]

Watchmakers, then, were found all over London. The City, with large numbers of makers in the gold- and silversmithing areas around Goldsmith's Hall, had still the greatest cluster even in the 1790s. By then the workmen had spilled over from the City into Clerkenwell, where makers like Christopher Pinchbeck had settled around 1720: his famous alloy of copper and zinc gave 'toys' to the masses. By 1797 about a third of all Clerkenwell residents depended on watchmaking for subsistence, with around 1,600 workers making 120,000 watches a year between them. The trade leapfrogged into Somers Town, where French refugee watchmakers settled in the 1790s, and spilled over into Shoreditch. When a shark nine feet three inches long was caught in the Thames at Poplar in 1787 a silver watch and chain bearing the maker's name, Henry Watson of Shoreditch, was found in its belly; a man had bought it for his son bound on a voyage to the Cape but the youth had been lost overboard in a squall off Falmouth two years before.[19]

Cabinetmaking was another London manufacturing industry of great fame and value, with even more scope for flamboyant self-expression within the shifting tastes of the times. The cabinetmaking industry at the west end of the town furnished the houses of the rich not just in the metropolis but nationwide. Thomas Chippendale's *The Gentleman and Cabinet-maker's Director* of 1754 brought his designs to the attention of every great householder – and every provincial furniture maker – in the land. From his house and workshop in St Martin's Lane, where he moved in 1755, he supplied furniture for noblemen and celebrities probably without laying much more than a finger on the pieces going out under his name. Even employing some forty or fifty workers, there was still the need to put out gilding, cloth dyeing and paper staining – for Chippendale was an 'upholder' or upholsterer who designed and decorated the rooms which his furniture graced. He worked closely with Robert Adam on a number of grand projects in the 1760s, for instance.[20] Wealthy tradesmen like Chippendale, or the Linnell brothers, cheek by jowl with aristocratic customers at 28 Berkeley Square from 1754, and Thomas Sheraton, in Bloomsbury, Mayfair and Soho in the 1790s, were less furniture makers than arbiters of taste, both in the metropolis and far beyond.[21]

Furniture of course was needed by Londoners of every rank and degree and there were large differences between these great men at the

West End of the town and the general run of the metropolitan cabinetmaking trade. Like many other London industries, there was a
polarity along the axis of fashion. Right through the century, City
makers from the Mansion House to Houndsditch in the east, and around
St Paul's Churchyard in the west, held their own making furniture for
the citizens. George Seddon, at Aldersgate Street from around 1750,
was employing some 400 hands in the 1780s, supplying both 'the needs
of the needy and the luxurious'. Cabinetmaking was an industry that
undoubtedly grew in London, especially in the second half of the century,
but it seems to have grown pretty much equally across Westminster
and the City. At the century's end there was very little penetration into
Shoreditch, St Luke's and Bethnal Green, the great furniture-making
districts of the nineteenth century, although the famous chair maker
George Hepplewhite had his workshops mainly in Clerkenwell.[22]

Not all London's industries flourished as heartily as watchmaking
and furniture. Shipbuilding on the Thames suffered fierce competition
from builders on the Tyne and fell away during the century for all but
the largest East and West Indiamen and the smallest fishing and coasting
vessels. The Thames accounted for just one in ten of the 1,156 ships
built in 1790–91. The high costs of London labour, rents and taxes
were no doubt factors in the decline, as they were in the move of
stocking-frame knitters to Nottingham from the early years of the
century, many shoemakers to Northampton from mid-century, and some
hat factories to northern towns in the 1760s. Similarly, the rise of
provincial centres of production in metals at Birmingham and the West
Midlands no doubt adversely affected London's needle- and pin-making
trades, though without extinguishing them entirely. Provincial towns,
drawing labour from the countryside to work in industry, proved less
resistant to fresh ways of working than the old-established manufacturing trades of London, especially in the use of machinery. That was
the case in the silk industry, for instance, where London faced competition from Manchester in handkerchiefs and Coventry in ribbons.[23]

Silk weaving was one of London's great manufacturing industries
but, partly for reasons of provincial and foreign competition, one under
great pressure for nearly all the century. It was concentrated, though
not exclusively, in the East End parishes of Spitalfields, Bethnal Green
and Shoreditch and, as we have seen, was energetically advanced by
Huguenot migrants at the end of the seventeenth century. Silk was
imported 'raw' from Turkey and the East Indies or already 'thrown' or

spun into thread from Italy. It was then worked in London by 'a vast Number of Families, Men, Women, and Children' employed in 'Throwing, Dying, Winding, Warping, Weaving, and Dressing' to make 'Lustrings, Plain and Figur'd Silks, Rich Brocades, Ribbons, Stockings, *Norwich* Crapes, and other sorts of Wrought Silks'.[24]

Work was commissioned and sold wholesale by master weavers living mainly in the finest streets of Spitalfields and the eastern part of the City. In the early years of the century most of them had French names. Designs were drawn mainly by English artists, prominent among them talented women like Anna Maria Garthwaite. Silk was worked and woven in the master's own workshops above or behind his dwelling house, its characteristically wide windows or 'weavers' lights' providing as much daylight as possible for the fine work involved. More commonly the work was put out to an army of artisan weavers who had looms and reels in their one- or two-room homes, and lived three or four families to a house. There were many women working on their own account as ribbon weavers, for instance, and many more who assisted men weavers, most often their husbands. These were family enterprises and children helped their parents from an early age. The numbers involved were very large. There were said to be some 10,000 looms in London in the early eighteenth century, each probably keeping three persons at work, including children, with some 40,000–50,000 in all dependent on the trade.[25]

Silk spun a skein that connected the ragged poor of Spitalfields and Bethnal Green at the east end of the town with the richest in the land at the west. Silk dresses remained at the pinnacle of London fashion throughout the century, and the beauty and mystery of its production evinced a sense of wonder among even the fashionable themselves. 'Lady Middlesex, Lord Bathurst, Mr. Breton, and I waited on their Royal Highnesses [the Prince and Princess of Wales] to Spitalfields, to see the manufactory of silk,' George Bubb Dodington noted in his diary in June 1750. They went on to Robert Carr's silk mercery at the sign of the Queen's Head, Ludgate Hill, to sample the finished article in full splendour. Carr dealt with a dozen or so of the top Spitalfields masters and was an enthusiastic purchaser of Anna Maria Garthwaite's designs. He also imported much of the silk his contractors wove for him.[26]

Silk, then, was a great London industry that depended, as so many did, on the Thames for its raw materials. But it remained, in general, an industry of small-scale production, much of it relying on self-employed

artisans, a flexibility readily exploited by masters who could stop production at a moment's notice. Nor was it a forward-looking industry, at
least in London, where resistance to machinery was a frequent source
of trouble, as we'll see shortly. In this, silk manufacture was typical of
much London industry, but by no means all of it. For there were also giant
industrial undertakings in London that had more of what we might consider
the industrial revolution about them, dependent on steam power – London
had 109 steam engines at work in 1800, 7 per cent of the national total
– and employing many hands.[27] These businesses, too, frequently relied
on the Thames for their livelihood.

The brewing of ale and porter, and of vinegar, the distilling of a
number of liquors and mineral water production were all heavily
capitalised industries that especially followed both sides of the Thames.
The river provided water, power and transport for raw materials and
finished commodities. It was the axis of a metropolitan industrial
periphery. Along its banks and its tributaries a host of industrial villages
and townships had settled by the century's end. Wapping, in the east,
was a port-side township making everything for ships and sailors –
rope, sails, blocks, pumps, cabin hooks, clay pipes, scientific instruments, guns – with several sugar refiners and, of course, breweries.
Bow was famed from about 1750 to 1776 for its fine porcelain made
at 'New Canton' on the Essex bank of the River Lea; at its peak it
employed some 300 hands, ninety of them painters, most living at the
works. At Hackney's Temple Mills on the other side of the Lea were
brassworks, sheet lead manufacturers, needle makers, wooden water-
pipe borers, papermakers and calico printers; and a renowned 'colour'
or paint factory was established in Homerton in 1780 by Louis Berger,
originally from Frankfurt. Nearby, Stratford and West Ham were
known for their calico printers and dyers. Navigation of the Lea was
improved for bringing raw materials by barge to the industries of
Hackney, Bow and Stratford by Thomas Yeoman's canal, the Limehouse
Cut, in 1767–70.[28]

Across the river at Woolwich, close to the great royal dockyard where
ships of the line were built, was the huge ordnance factory and depot at
Woolwich Warren, where about 1,500 artificers and labourers, including
some 300 boys, made artillery and ammunition; an army of 'poor women'
homeworkers in Woolwich town sewed canvas bags for use at the works.
The associated manufacture of gunpowder was so dangerous that it had
to be exiled to common land far out of London, at Hounslow Heath,

Waltham Abbey and elsewhere: the gunpowder mills frequently exploded, four at Hounslow in 1758 alone, for instance.[29]

Back along the river, at Deptford, close to another royal dockyard, was the earthenware manufactory of 'Deptford-ware'. And further west, from 1769 Lambeth was home to Eleanor Coade's artificial stone factory in Narrow Wall, turning out weather-resistant decorative features and statues for the façades of London's finest town houses; and there were several manufactories of plate glass, lead shot, stoneware, vinegar and printed linens. At Battersea from about 1750 was the famous enamels factory established by Sir Stephen Theodore Janssen, employing French artists and engravers; Janssen failed in 1756 but the works were continued under other hands till about 1780. Over the river, the famous Chelsea porcelain factory was founded by Nicholas Sprimont, from Liège, with Huguenot partners about 1744, reaching a pinnacle in the early 1750s and closing around 1768; it employed a hundred or so workers, many fine artists among them, and a hundred charity apprentices. The works were subsequently used for the manufacture of Derby ware and then for wallpaper, London the centre of that fashionable trade. At the end of the century there were Chelsea factories making artificial stone, earthenware, painted silk, floorcloths, and an iron foundry making bells and cannon. Fulham was famous for its glazed earthenware potteries, there even before 1700, and for its carpet factory begun by French makers around 1753.[30] And in the far south-west was a chain of industrial villages along the River Wandle, at Wandsworth, Wimbledon, Carshalton and Merton, where the remains of the abbey were turned over to a variety of works in calico printing and a copper mill – a thousand people were employed within its walls at the end of the century.[31]

Indeed, all round London, from Walthamstow to Knightsbridge, industrial enterprises of one sort or another were making things for Londoners or for consumption elsewhere in the nation or the world. And all these things had to be moved in and around the giant city.

Fellowship Porters, Lumpers and
Snuffle-Hunters: Moving Things Around

We should start, once more, on the river, for much movement of commodities began and ended there. The port was a major employer of labour. At any time a few thousand seamen were active on its waters and around 7,500 others found employment of some sort in loading and delivering cargo from ships. Patrick Colquhoun, a London magistrate with a special interest in the port at the end of the century, thought there were 1,400 'lumpers' who loaded and discharged ships, 400 of them 'generally complete Seamen', 600 less qualified but pretty fully employed and 400 occasional or casual workers who resorted to the river 'when great Fleets arrive'. Four hundred journeymen coopers worked in the port who went on board vessels in pairs to unload commodities shipped in barrels, like sugar and rum from the West Indies. Around 1,500 lightermen were involved in transferring cargoes from ship to shore by barge, and a thousand watchmen employed to protect goods left overnight on ships and barges, or while waiting to be moved from wharves or quays. At the margins of port labour, 'Snuffle-Hunters' or casual porters were hired by the hour or day to move goods round the quays and help get them ashore. These, Colquhoun thought, were 'literally composed of that lowest class of the community, who are vulgarly denominated the *Tag-Rag* and *Bobtail*', or 'the Scum of Society'. He thought there were about 500 of them, though the shifting tide of men seeking this sort of employment no doubt defied enumeration. They were 'generally found at the *Water Side*, to which they resort, in crowds, in the throng Seasons, and obtain occasional employment through a want of a better Class of Labourers'. All had to scratch around for work elsewhere: two footpads executed in 1774 were described as porters at the wharves in the winter and haymakers in the summer, for instance. Snuffle-hunters were also found as an addition to the thousand or so warehouse labourers storing and dispatching goods from the port to their destination.[32]

Of all these men only the coopers and lightermen served an apprenticeship and were bound by the rules and prices of a City livery company protected by statute. Similar protection had been sought for many years by another important branch of port labour, the coalheavers. At the end of the century there were said to be a thousand of them, though this may understate the number because higher figures had been given in earlier years and since then the growth of London's coal trade had continued unabated. It was arduous labour digging coal out of the holds of innumerable colliers and stowing it in barges and lighters. The coalheavers were generally 'remarkably stout well-made men'. Among them were serving 'Soldiers in the Guards' and many more were migrants: 'it will be difficult to find men so adapted, from strength, &c. to execute this laborious task of coal-heaving, as the Irish are,' it was said in 1768.[33]

Among the workers in the port were some 900 watermen employed in conveying people, letters and packages, goods and provisions. Many more were busy elsewhere on the river. There were 3,000 registered watermen's wherries on the Thames and over 12,000 members of the Watermen's Company, including lightermen, in 1796. About 8,000 in all were active on the river. For most Londoners, watermen meant the fellows who plied for hire in their wherries at the various Thames stairs. They took goods across and along the river, and carried men and women on business or pleasure. Their fees were fixed by statute, a pair of rowers (called 'oars') getting twice the rate of a single oarsman ('sculls'). Watermen had to have served a seven-year apprenticeship; anyone else working as a waterman was subject to a fine. And an elaborate statutory code determined just where and how the watermen should work, enforced mainly by their own Company. This was a craft proud of its traditions, and the watermen's wherries were among the sights of London, 'very attractive and cleanly kept', a French visitor thought, 'painted generally in red or in green' with awnings to match in summer and a strong canvas tent on rainy days. But the watermen were a truculent bunch, notorious for their 'immodest, obscene and lewd Expressions, towards Passengers, and to each other', despite a Company order of 1701 threatening to fine miscreants.[34]

Safe on dry land, goods and passengers were moved by a small army of carriers and carters. The proportion of workers employed in moving things around was almost certainly higher in London than anywhere else in the country – hardly surprising, given the size of the port, the extent of the town and the wealth of its people.[35] As with the watermen, the importance accorded the movement of goods in London life was frequently reflected in statutory codes of behaviour setting the numbers of workers and the fees they could charge, enforced by societies that also governed access to the trade and prevented too much competition doing any man out of a living.

The City porters, for instance, retained their privileges and protection throughout the century. A country porter might carry goods *into* the City but none out of it and none from one part to another 'unless he be a freeman; otherwise he is liable to be arrested'. These freemen were organised into four 'brotherhoods' or 'fellowships' whose tasks and names are variously described. The focus of their business was the port of London and the river on both sides from Queenhithe to the Tower. Some 700 fellowship porters, answerable to the alderman of Billingsgate Ward, landed and handled coals at Billingsgate Quay, as well as salt, corn and other commodities 'measurable by dry measure'. Around 2,000 or more ticket porters, their names stamped on a metal ticket hung from their belts, were authorised to ply for hire at one of ninety-two stands about the quays and in the streets. They humped goods around the town and were of great strength, expected to bear up to three hundredweights on their shoulders; stout wooden posts or 'pitching-places' were dotted about the streets so they could rest their burdens. When the German traveller Carl Philipp Moritz arrived on the quays in 1782, a porter 'took my huge heavy trunk on his shoulders with astonishing ease; and carried it till I met a hackney-coach'. Some of these fellowship and ticket porters were in effect porterage contractors, respectable men of the middling classes hiring others to carry, as it were, under a ticket of convenience. But all City porters, it was thought, 'generally make a good Livelihood of it'. So good that casual or unofficial porters seem to have been tolerated from a silence in the statutes or from long usage or to serve the necessities of trade. The women fish porters of Billingsgate, famous for their thumb-rings, foul language, stout build and robust temper, unsurprisingly held their own throughout the century. Outside the port and away from the riverside, in the outer City parishes and suburbs and in Westminster, porterage was unrestricted, unknown numbers seeking a living in the trade.[36]

As we have already seen, people as well as goods were carried by men around the streets of London. At the end of the century there were 400 licensed hackney chairs and probably 1,500 or so chairmen. They wore distinctive coats and specially fortified shoes for both offence and defence, and were otherwise distinguishable by their giant calves and no-nonsense manners: Jonathan Swift, a frequent chair passenger, was in an accident in February 1711 when 'the chairmen that carried me squeezed a great fellow against a wall, who wisely turned his back, and broke one of the side glasses in a thousand pieces'. These hackney chairs plied for hire at the stands in Covent Garden and elsewhere and charged 1s for the first half-mile and 6d for every half-mile after. Many noble or rich families kept a private chair, with or without a coat of arms on the sides, carried by liveried retainers or by chairmen hired for the hour or day.[37]

Despite the great volume of transportation of goods and people on foot throughout the century, it was horsepower that drove the wheels of commerce on London's streets and roads. There were said to be over 20,000 horses in London in 1722, over 5,000 of them stabled in the crowded City and half of these saddle horses for the citizens to ride about town and into the country. The numbers must have grown as London and its trade grew, but by how many is unknown. The rise in licensed hackney coaches, from 700 at the beginning of the century to 1,000 at the end, seems but a modest indication of the increase of population in the period. Probably a rise in the numbers of stables hiring private carriages by the day and the growing private ownership of carriages, chariots, chaises and horses, even among the tradesmen's ranks, filled something of the gap: the cit 'wheeled down to his snug Box', his wife driving her own 'one-horse chair', were common causes of satire from mid-century on.[38]

The drivers of hackney coaches, though themselves duly licensed by the Commissioners of Hackney Coaches and Chairs in Somerset House, bore but a blotchy reputation. They were liable to be fined for 'Damage, Abuse or Imposition'. Charges by the hour and by distance were carefully regulated, and passengers' rights fully spelled out in the London guides. Tables of fares, even more elaborate than for the watermen, were another feature of the guides, one of 1783 running to more than fifty pages of fares from prominent stands to all parts of the town: Aldersgate Street to Lincoln's Inn Fields 6d, to the King's Bench Prison 1s 6d, to Marybone Church 2s, and so on. Nevertheless, the hackney coachmen were notorious for overcharging and demanding a penny or two extra to drink their fare's health. Drink was indeed a problem, a drunken coachman drowning his team and himself when he drove into the Thames down Iron Gate Stairs, just east of the Tower, in February 1774. Francis Place recalled hackney coachmen 'lashing the peoples umbrellas with their whips as they drove along' to register their disgust for that newly popularised invention taking the bread from their mouths in wet weather. And there was worse, for 'flash coachmen' working at night were said to be in league with burglars, watching out for them and carrying the spoils to receivers. Richard Scurrier, just eighteen when he was hanged for stealing a firkin of butter in 1725, measured all his misfortunes from the time he drove a hackney coach: 'for (said he) many of the Hackney-Coachmen are the worst Men upon Earth . . .'[39]

City carters were also regulated by statute and governed by their own Company. Christ's Hospital licensed the drivers of 420 cars or carts to ply for hire at assigned stands and wharves and the City Corporation imposed on them a variety of obligations, including a one-way system for entering and leaving cluttered Thames Street. Their charges were also fixed, depending on distance and weight carried; they had to help the hirer load and unload and refrain from abuse or insult. The coal and wood mongers about the wharves had a further 120 'great Carts' and there were sixty-seven for hire in 'the Out-Parts' around 1737.[40]

There was then a very substantial industry built on carrying people and goods into London and out of it to every country town or village of note across the land. This network was the nation's nervous system, based on London, for it carried not just goods but information in newspapers and journals and by word of mouth. Its nodes were at least seventy-five coaching and carrying inns at every point of the London compass. So that, for instance, wagons taking parcels, goods and unfussy passengers to Wareham in Dorset left the Angel Inn, Fleet Market, on Monday, Wednesday and Friday mornings at 11; the Saracen's Head in Friday Street, off Cheapside, on Monday mornings at 10, Thursday mornings at 3, and Saturday nights at 9; from the Bell, also Friday Street, on Monday, Wednesday and Saturday mornings at 10; and coasting vessels left Chamberlain's Wharf, Southwark, when wind and tide and trade permitted. Narrow Friday Street had yet another inn, the White Horse, 'large, of good resort', but the Saracen's Head was the busiest, 'very large, and of a great Resort and Trade', with an unusual double courtyard. It was the starting place for the Somerset stage coaches to Taunton and Yeovil, besides the Dorset wagons. Many City tradesmen dealing with the country towns would hire warehousing space at inns like these for the easier transport of their goods.[41]

Most of these places were very old, or at least of very old origins, and built to a pattern. There was usually an unpretentious frontage on a main street with a covered way driven through it leading to a great courtyard. On one side was stabling and on the other were two or three extensive floors for guests, often entered from a gallery or open corridor. Visitors were never far away from the stench and bustle of London: the well-known White Hart Inn, Borough High Street, was said to accommodate 200 guests who had to share its courtyard with what tradition had declared should also be a common laystall, or dung heap. The George Inn, close by and still surviving as the last of the galleried inns that had their heyday in the eighteenth century, was of similar fame.[42]

Most celebrated of all was the Golden Cross on the north side of Charing Cross, facing Francis Place's tailor's shop. Its enormous court-yard occupied the space now just about taken by Nelson's Column. Once more it had a small frontage but made the most of it with a giant iron stanchion reaching beyond the pavement for its painted sign of the Golden Cross, at least until the signs had to come down. It was home to 'The Portsmouth Flying Machine', offering a daily service at a guinea a ride in 1756; in later years the Comet and the Regent to Brighton and the Tally-Ho to Birmingham began and ended their jour-neys at the Golden Cross. Trunk makers' shops clustered nearby to remind travellers of their needs. The Golden Cross, like all these coaching and carrying inns, was one of London's greatest hotels throughout the century, for visitors from home and abroad. They were, then, among the large employers of another of the capital's main employment sectors: domestic service.[43]

High Life Below Stairs: Domestic Service

No industry made a greater impact on the daily lives of Londoners in the eighteenth century than domestic service. Servant keeping among households of the middling sort and above was pretty much universal. The numbers of those households rose in London during the century, through inward migration, the growth of business and the country-box-keeping habit of the citizens. As a consequence the numbers of servants increased too. There would have been even more, but the demand for them, contemporaries thought, always outstripped supply, at least the supply of those deemed fit to serve. Certainly, servants were to be met everywhere in London, scrubbing doorsteps and sweeping pavements, washing down mud-splashed walls and windows, running errands, carrying packages and letters, walking behind their employers in the streets, whether on foot or in a chair, driving a coach or riding behind it. And hidden from view in basement kitchens and out-house sculleries were others who not only polished the comforts of the well-to-do but made possible that keystone of London's domestic economy, the house let in lodgings.[44]

Just how many servants there were in London isn't known but has been guessed at. Contemporary estimates ranged from one in nearly every five Londoners working in service to one in eight and as few as one in eleven. Whatever the case, the numbers were very large, if only because the servant-keeping habit ranged up and down the social scale. It stretched well beyond the tradesman class into the ranks of the artisan and corner shopkeeper in plebeian streets. Working on his own account around 1794, Francis Place, who had almost certainly grown up with one or more servants in the home, found himself and his wife with enough work on their hands to occupy them all day in their single room in Wych Street: 'We employed the wife of a hackney coachman who lodged in the Garret to Cook and wash and clean for us.'[45]

As here, women made up the majority of domestic servants right across the century. They dominated service in the very large number of small households keeping servants, but there were also many women who never 'lived in' but cleaned others' homes as charwomen or took in washing. Overall, domestic service remained a very important source of employment for women: probably some 80,000, or half of all employed women in London, were working in the sector at the century's end. If we add to that a further 20 per cent who were menservants, then we get close to 100,000, or one in ten Londoners, working in domestic service. The numbers having daily contact with servants, of course, were many times larger.[46]

There was an enormous variety among the servant-keeping households of London and consequently in the types of servants they employed. The Duke of Bedford might represent the wealthiest end in his great mansion at Bedford House, which filled the north side of Bloomsbury Square. His was a large household of forty servants in 1753 and forty-two in 1771, under the day-to-day supervision of a male house steward. There was a clerk of the kitchen, a French cook, a confectioner, a butler and under-butler, a groom of the chambers and two ushers – all men – and up to eight footmen. In charge of the female staff was a housekeeper, with three or four housemaids and two or three laundry maids; there was then a personal maid for the Duchess and later one for her daughters; there were four or five kitchen maids and a confectioner's maid. Outside the house were a first and second coachman and two post-chaise drivers, postillions, grooms, stable men and boys, a head gardener and a number of liveried watchmen, often troublesome through drink.[47]

There could have been only a few score London retinues of this size, maybe a hundred or so. Henry and Hester Thrale's Streatham mansion, which had eighteen to twenty servants, might stand for the very rich commercial classes, an extensive group in London. And most wealthy households were more modest even than that. John Baker, the West Indian attorney, had eleven servants in Red Lion Square from 1757, Jack Beef among them; and when Mr B brought the newly married Pamela to Hanover Square in Richardson's novel of 1740–41 their 'family' comprised two male stewards 'and six men-servants, including the coachman. The four maids are also with us.' In all these larger households, by no means rare in London at any time in the century, men predominated in the servant household: in 1780, for instance, nearly a third of male servants on whom employers paid tax in Westminster lived in households where there were ten or more menservants.[48]

From the much more numerous moderately well-to-do London ranks and below, women servants were in the majority. Mary Berry, a friend of Horace Walpole, thought that comfort in London without '"pinching economy and pitiful savings"' demanded three menservants and four women. London houses for tradesmen and clerks and minor officials presumed that accommodation for three or four servants – two maids and one or two footmen – would suffice: the maids more often than not shared both bedroom and bed. In the small tradesman and artisan class the manservant tended to be an unaffordable luxury: in a sample from one City ward around 1700, where 80 per cent of households surveyed kept just one or two servants, 81 per cent of all servants were women.[49]

If overall demand outstripped supply, competition within the servant world meant that there were always far more applicants for the top posts with elite families than would ever be needed. These were filled by promotion within the household, by word of mouth among employers and servants both – as significant a recruiting ground as any at this end of the market – or by newspaper advertisements. Word of mouth helped lower down the scale too, and so did 'register' or 'intelligence' offices, bringing employers and servants together in an employment exchange, some of which had better reputations than others. For general maidservants, who took on much of the work in the homes of the middling ranks and lodging houses, London girls were apparently discriminated against as being too knowing, too work-shy and perhaps too sexually promiscuous – these were the common anxieties in any event. And the Irish bore a stigma – as much from their Roman Catholicism striking a dissident voice in Protestant households as from any other prejudice, it seems. So the country girl from the British mainland found most favour, though not if promoted above her station: '"don't mention the *tramontaine*"', Sir William Stanley tells Lady Julia, who has brought her lady's maid from home, in a novel by the Duchess of Devonshire. '"She might do tolerably well for the Welsh mountains, but she will cut a most *outré* figure in the *beau monde*."'[50]

Her name was Win, and even a Win could do well. For service in general had many compensations and offered many opportunities. They were greater for men than for women and they were more readily encountered in wealthy households than the lower ranks of the middling sort of people. But compared to the working lives of many in eighteenth-century London, the privileges and comforts of a servant's existence were highly valued: a servant in place did not, in the great majority of cases, go hungry or ragged. And there were many ladders for advancement.[51]

The most public expression of the comforts of servant life was in matters of dress. Whether in livery or out, a servant's appearance epitomised the standing and spending power of the employer who sent her into the world. The result was a cause of some wonder to foreign observers: 'The servant-maids of citizens wives, the waiting women of ladies of the first quality, and of the midling gentry, attend their ladies in the streets and in the public walks, in such a dress, that, if the mistress be not known, it is no easy matter to distinguish her from her maid.'[52] Even a City bookseller's porter, a Welshman like his master, 'sported a powdered head and pig tail, black satin breeches, stone set knee buckles, silver shoe buckles, blue silk stockings, and frilled shirts'. A superior footman's gold-laced waistcoat and matching jacket was one of the sights of the London streets and such perquisites were much sought after: a servant comfortably situated in all other circumstances might leave one place for another just because of the livery he wore about the town.[53] In private, too, servants generally lived well. Most important, they fed well, even in lower-middling ranks where they ate similar fare to their employers.

There were other ways they were looked after also. Employers often sought to improve their servants' skills, like Elizabeth Montagu, who offered to train a cook for her service by paying for a temporary posting to 'the King's kitchen, or to any famous Tavern to learn cookery' in 1742.

When servants were sick, many employers were duly solicitous – inevitably with something of self-interest in their concern – providing doctors, using their influence to get staff admitted to hospital and so on. In 1778, for instance, Hester Thrale found that 'Some of our Servants had got the Itch this Summer, so I set 'em apart, and had them well anointed.' She showed her maid 'the Animal magnified; & told her how it burrowed under the Cuticle, how that it was catching as Lice were catching &c.'[54]

The intermingling of ranks that domestic service involved gave much encouragement to emulation and many opportunities for getting on in the world. Just five men and four women in the Duke of Bedford's household in 1753 were not literate enough to sign their names and towards the end of the 1760s the proportion having some capacity to write seems to have risen further.[55] Sometimes a rise could be spectacular, and not just in fiction. Hester Thrale, whose intelligence and noble good nature in the face of dreadful setbacks never ceases to astonish, materially assisted one such case. She was approached by a Southwark riding master called Carter, whose large family was overwhelmed by debt, to find a place for Laura, his eldest daughter, some time in the early 1770s:

I promised to get her a place, but finding She could neither read, nor write, nor work, nor wash, I found no body would be plagued with her but myself and taught her prayrs, her Catechisme &c. I then put her to School to learn washing – ironing Lace-mending, clearstarching and such like, paid a Master to instruct her in writing & then took her into my Nursery – to compleat her Education[.] She was encouraged by her Mother however to be saucy, She insisted on the Servants calling her *Miss* forsooth, would not dine at their Table, & in short made them all abhor her, besides that She soon appeared to be a Lyar in Grain.[56]

Hester helped Laura to a place elsewhere and 'clothed her elegantly that She might not be despised', but Laura fell out with her new mistress, was turned out of doors and 'I would see her no more'. A dozen or so years later, however, in 1787, Laura Carter entered Hester's life once more at a fashionable London assembly, this time as Laura Rush, now 'become a fine Lady & very rich', 'the finest of the fine at every Publick Show'. Her husband, W. Beaumaris Rush, would at the end of the century be knighted as Sheriff of Suffolk, when Laura became Lady

Rush. Some of Hester's early disappointment in the girl clearly lingered: 'I could not guess who the Wench was when She addressed me.'[57]

Not all prospered through service. Broken-down former domestics, incapacitated by age or accident or otherwise unworthy of hire, made up a significant portion of those seeking help from the parish. And young unmarried maidservants were notable among women asking for relief while out of work through pregnancy or for help to support a baby. Servants hired for a year on an annual contract gained a settlement in the parish where they were employed and so had ease of access to relief that was denied to others: a lodger's servant gained a settlement that was denied to the lodger himself, for instance. So at St Clement Danes, with its many middling-sort households and inns and lodging houses all reliant on domestic service, we find among several other former servants Ann Stevens, a yearly servant some twenty years earlier with Mrs Giles, a dealer in old clothes in Houghton Street; and Sarah Knight, twenty-four, single, a servant at a lodging house in Arundel Street, Strand, pregnant by Richard Wright, 'Gentleman', 'having had carnal Knowledge' of her several times in the house; and many others.[58]

Despite the tangible benefits of service – perhaps in part because of them – the relationship between servant and employer was not an easy one. In households of the middling sort and above, servants held most of the cards. In general there were more places available than servants to fill them and it was relatively easy for an experienced servant to give up one position and find another. John Macdonald, a Scottish footman who worked in and out of London, had twenty-seven masters in thirty-four years from 1746 to 1779. Passed over unjustly, as he saw it, for promotion to a valet's post, 'I was angry, and told my master so', duly giving notice. Another master, Colonel Dow of Lisle Street, Leicester Fields, 'spent so much money on women that I was tired of waiting on them; though, if many an hungry fellow had had in my place, they would have taken care of it, if there had been a thousand ladies. I gave warning merely on that account.'[59]

It was this marked independence among London servants that lay behind the litany of employers' complaints and grievances expressed everywhere in newspapers, magazines, letters, diaries, fiction and, of course, on the stage. James Townley's *High Life Below Stairs*, a hit at Drury Lane in 1759, excoriated the servants of a rich young man's household. They cheat him, run riot on his cellar and pantry, copy the ways of their betters in fine dress, snuff taking, tea drinking, gaming at cards and looking down their noses at honest citizens and tradesmen. In all, they are a gaggle of 'idle unnecessary servants, who are the plague and reproach of this kingdom'. The finely dressed servant maids who so impressed foreign visitors were universally condemned by London pamphleteers for being 'puffed up with Pride' and ever clamouring for higher wages.[60] And complaints of laziness and inattention to employers' interests were legion. We might savour just one, from Domenico Angelo of Leghorn, the most famous riding and fencing master in London mid-century. He had returned to London unexpectedly from the country on 5 August 1763. In writing that evening to his wife to tell her what he had found, his indignation understandably muddled his powers of expression, in English at least:

I am arrive'd at home this two hours, I find only the Cook wasching the back stars, and not a soul mor in the house, Jhon, Peghi and Catherin I belivd they are all gone to the Devil; I find my pooure Little Sophi in Mr Vernon's Room setting upon a chaire, Paris and Mr Vernon firs a slip upon the bed. My dear Girl as soon as shee sa me shee scrime loud my dear Papa weken'd the two Pig's and the sweet soul was pleas'd to come in my arm's. the bed chamber all in confusion and y'am in doubt if this two beecches will com' for make my bed. you must preperd at your return to send them away I can not have patience no Longuer. Your Mother shee is just come to see the Dear Sophi, which the Pooure Soul shee is so darti as shee newer was wasch'd, with a shift without one slive and her arms and faces so darti that shee stink. Now is eight a clook if thei are not at home in one hour thei schall not come in to the house. I have set out from Salisburry last night at 11 & I am ded of slip, and no appierence to have what I want. I beg my dear to come home as soon as is possible, I aspect you thusday next. I hope my dear sweet Kitty well Kiss her great dill for me. My Comp^s to our dear friend Mrs Wood and all the family. I intend to go to see harry tomorrow morning. belive me my dear Betyi that I love you with all my hart and soul. your aff^n husband

Angelo[61]

The misdeeds of domestics who considered themselves above their station were thought to infect other 'servants' like apprentices and clerks, about whom similar complaints were made. But there was one category of servant who drew most ire: liveried footmen, or 'the most *useless, insolent* and *corrupted* Set of People in *Great Britain*'. Their unruly conduct in street, park and playhouse – where they took for themselves the upper gallery and reserved seats in the boxes till their employers arrived – attracted general condemnation. They were known for hard drinking and for fighting while drunk or sober – Lord Barrymore kept a footman, one Hooper, just for his bare-knuckle skills. The footmen of MPs and peers were immune from arrest for debt while Parliament was sitting, a privilege not calculated to restrain insolence and one only removed by a change in the law in 1770. But most of all it was the connection between footmen and 'vails' that caused most annoyance and which came to a head in London in the 1760s.[62]

There was a long tradition of giving vails or tips to domestic servants that was apparently unique to Britain. Guests at dinner in a London mansion would, on departure, find the servants lining the passage to the front door, all expecting recognition of their service during the evening. The imposition could mount up: 'to a gold-laced coat you cannot offer a solitary shilling; you must slip two shillings and sixpence into his hand.' A visitor enquiring of porter or footman for their master would be denied entry or information without a gratuity, the size of which depended on the status of the employer. Mrs Pilkington, who for part of the 1750s depended for her livelihood on the kindness of a few among the London rich, calculated it cost her £1 17s 7½d to write to a great man, 1½d for pen, ink and paper and the rest in vails to his servants to deliver the letter and obtain a reply. From profits like these it was said that Sir Robert Walpole's porter could get more in vails than many country gentlemen from their estates.[63]

Over the years there had been several unsuccessful attempts to stamp out vails-giving, but in 1757 a campaign began in Scotland – 'Sir, you abolished vails, because you were too poor to be able to give them,' Johnson told Boswell – which was taken up in London from the early 1760s. A large meeting of nobility and gentry at Almack's assembly rooms in 1764 '"unanimously determined neither to give nor allow any vails to servants"', and in the next few years metropolitan vails-giving fell into general (but not universal) disuse.[64] Servants' wages had to rise as a result, but even so this was not a struggle that the truculent footmen of London were disposed to give up peacefully. On 11 May 1764

A great disturbance was created at Ranelagh-house, by the coachmen, footmen, &c. belonging to such of the nobility and gentry as will not suffer their servants to take vails. They began by hissing their masters, they then broke all the lamps and outside windows with stones; and afterwards putting out their flambeaux, pelted the company, in a most audacious manner, with brick-bats, &c. whereby several were greatly hurt, so as to render the use of swords necessary. In the scuffle one of the servants was run through his thigh, another through his arm, and several more otherwise wounded.[65]

As that evening at Ranelagh shows us, London's workers were hardly behindhand in standing up for their rights. And in that especially turbulent decade of the 1760s, they were never shy of using violence when doing so.

'At the Eve of a Civil War': Masters and Men

Wage rates in London did not greatly alter across much of the eighteenth century. An unskilled labourer earned 8s to 12s a week, and a journeyman in most of the manufacturing and building trades 12s to 18s: 'every poor man's labour may be estimated, at an average to be worth two shillings and sixpence per day' (or 15s a week), it was said in 1783, and that's not a bad rule to keep in mind. Skilled workers could do better: building craftsmen earned about 21s a week, compositors around 25s, the finest cabinetmakers 30–40s, a respectable income for the lower end of the middling sort. In general, though, it was a fortunate working man whose wage could in theory bring him £50 a year. Women's wage rates were – in general once more – about half those of men. In domestic service the gap was usually even wider: a housemaid was paid around 4–6 guineas a year between 1700 and 1760, 6–8 from 1760; a footman 14–16 guineas in the earlier period and 15–20 in the later. Very low wages could be paid to women even for very hard labour. As late as 1797, 'A woman is only paid 6d. for carrying a very heavy basket of fruit from Ealing or Brentford to Covent Garden, near 9 miles', at a time when many other wages had risen significantly.[66]

That rise from the late 1780s but especially from the 1790s was to accommodate a sharp increase in the cost of living. Living costs had remained pretty stable for the first sixty years or so of the century, with just occasional periods of high prices in the wartime period of 1708–10, in the very cold winter of 1739–40 and in 1756–8, the opening of the Seven Years War. This was a long period of relative prosperity. 'Real wages', wage rates set against fluctuations in the cost of living, showed significant gains, especially from 1730 to 1755. The last forty years of the century, by contrast, were marked by general inflation in the cost of living, with which wages failed to keep pace. For most years, from 1766 till the end of the century, real wages were some 20 to 30 and even 40 per cent lower than those enjoyed in the 1740s.[67]

There was another factor influencing the living standards of London's workers across the century, of even greater importance than the cost of provisions. This was irregularity of employment. For almost no one could expect his half-crown a day week on week throughout the year.

Nearly every manufacturing trade was subject to fluctuations in demand from changing fashion and the dislocations of the London season, when the nobility and country gentry were most commonly in town. In the first few decades of the century London was fullest from about November to June; from the 1740s the season shrank from January to July, and again from March to July by the end of the century. These were the frantic months in the London luxury trades like tailoring, silk weaving, cabinetmaking and so on, with diminished demand during much of the rest of the year and a local depression in most years from November to January. Trades depending on the port, including transport, were affected by the seasonality of shipping and the vagaries of the weather, which also took its toll on most commodity prices, especially coal. The interaction between the weather and economic distress was plain for all to see and it was markedly worse in the second half of the century compared to the first: there were twenty-two very cold winters after 1750 but there had been just seven before. In these bad winters insufficient work combined with high prices to double the misery for many Londoners. Indeed, everything was worse in bad weather. London was at its most terrible in the biting cold: a drunken man who'd stumbled into the frost-stiffened mire of Fleet Ditch was found 'standing upright and frozen to death' in January 1763, for example; and several poor fishermen, caught in pack ice in the river during the long frost of 1767–8, also froze, 'the youngest of them, a youth about seventeen, was found sitting as erect almost as if alive'. All the working people of London, apart from domestic servants living in comfortably off households, were vulnerable to the shifting fortunes each year might bring.[68]

Not all, of course, succumbed. Many working people in London could live well on their wages and could afford to put a little by during the busy times of the year. A man's wages could also be supplemented by the casual earnings of wives and children – taking in washing, char-ring, running errands, street finding – and by the perquisites of many jobs, like 'cabbage' in the tailoring trades and 'spare' materials in building or woodworking. The little put by was usually in portable property, possessions about the home that could be sold or pawned in the bad times. The care with which many working people dressed themselves, and which so impressed foreigners while exasperating those who bemoaned the luxury of the times, was one such resource, so was investment in furniture, and so were the surprisingly valuable posses-sions that could be found in many humble dwellings. 'I live in Brick-lane, in the parish of St. Matthews, Bethnal-green', Thomas Leachman told the Old Bailey in 1786; 'I am in the turnery way, and making utensils for weavers', it seems as an artisan. Three men broke open his house and were sentenced to death for stealing an eight-day clock worth £5, a quart silver tankard valued at £3 and a table spoon at 10s. And there are many similar cases in the records.[69]

There were other resources available to many working people that did not merely rely on the individual or family to marshal. We have already seen how mutuality or collective self-help was an important feature of London life, from social gatherings in club or lodge to the foundations of a great industry like insurance. Mutuality extended across London's industrial sphere. The livery companies (or guilds) of London were institutions of mutual protection still active in the City. Some of the ninety-one London companies were of great antiquity and over the centuries their power in the working life of the metropolis had begun to wither away in favour of charitable enterprise. Fees from admitting apprentices and selling City freedoms were spent partly on junketing at the fifty-two company halls and partly on charitable disbursement in pensions for derelict members and their families, in running schools and maintaining almshouses. But in the first half of the century a few were also engaged in industrial protection, attempting to maintain a monopoly of trade or manufactures by keeping out 'foreigners' – non-freemen and journeymen who had not served a seven-year apprenticeship. Some had the power to search premises in the City and its environs to ensure that proper standards of manufacture were being upheld.

Besides protecting their interests against outsiders, the companies' industrial activities also reflected the division of classes within the livery. The interests of large manufacturers were put above those of the small 'garret-master', assisted by wife and family and perhaps an apprentice or two; and both were put above the interests of the journeyman, whether time-served or not. An attempt to revive the flagging industrial power of the companies was made by an act of the City's Common Council in 1712 designed to suppress non-free journeymen and tradesmen. Searches were renewed by the coopers and others, and sometimes met with much resistance. In general it was an act most observed in the breach, although from time to time till mid-century companies prosecuted non-free employers – the Glovers and the Bakers in 1732, the Gunmakers in 1733, and so on. But by 1749, during a tight labour shortage in London, the masters found the tables turned when time-served journeymen in some trades combined to prosecute employers of non-free workers in an attempt to drive up wages. By the end of 1750 the exigencies of trade overcame the weight of tradition. The City granted licences to masters to employ foreigners in the absence of free journeymen, essentially ending one of the great planks of protectionism in the City trades and further undermining the companies' relevance to the needs of modern London.[70]

As the stonemasons, painters and others who reported their masters to the magistrates showed in 1749–50, there was a great deal of mutual self-defence among the journeymen of London. Men of the same trade shared information at the 'houses of call', public houses where masters paid out wages at the 'pay-tables' late on Saturday nights and which acted much like employment exchanges for the trade in question. They were also home to friendly societies based on trades, a weekly penny or two saved for Christmas boxes and for funerals and other emergencies. Some, like the Taylors' Friendly Society of 1708 at the Cross Keys, Wych Street, were ambitious ventures similar to insurance societies, and could generate large funds useful in an industrial dispute. Others were small-scale and local and vulnerable to fraud or theft: in 1736, when some Spitalfields weavers sued the pub landlord 'where their Club was kept, for a Sum of 30l. lent him out of the Box', the court threw out the action because 'they were not a legal Society'. Pubs hosting 'burial clubs' used to display a miniature coffin lid and some trades had special funeral traditions: John Wilkes took James Boswell one night in 1776 into Parliament Street 'to see a curious procession pass: the funeral of a lamplighter attended by some hundreds of his fraternity with torches'.[71]

These were collective shields against the shifting fortunes of daily life, including the whims and petty oppressions of victimising employers.

But attack, according to a saying current at the time, was the best form
of defence and there were many ways to wage the class struggle in
eighteenth-century London. Some were in the hands of the individual
worker. The depredations of journeymen in the workplace, whether in
the workshop or their own homes, were – according to their masters
at least – shameless and profligate. The thefts, frauds and abuses of
journeymen shoemakers were brought before the House of Commons
by employers in 1723, by journeymen armourers and braziers and dyers
in 1727, by journeymen goldsmiths and watchmakers in 1744 and
doubtless others. Parliament acted to stamp out some common abuses
in a number of trades in 1749.[72]

Collective offensive action was occasionally taken against labour-
saving machinery, understandable when the insecurity of employment
was among the greatest evils of plebeian life. The most spectacular
instance was Charles Dingley's wind-driven sawmill at Limehouse, built
in 1767 and capable of doing the work of many hand-sawyers. On 10
May 1768 it was attacked by some 500 men, who overwhelmed the
two armed watchmen, destroyed the machinery with axes and nearly
pulled down the counting house; but a year later, helped by compensation from Parliament, the mill was once more in operation. And there
was suspicion of arson in the destruction by fire of the giant steam-
driven Albion flour mills near the south side of Blackfriars Bridge in
April 1791. Certainly its fate was applauded by workers who saw the
Albion as a citadel of monopoly at a time of high bread prices.[73]

But the main means of collective attack were the combination and
the strike for higher wages or better conditions. It was all a dangerous
business, because combinations were questionably lawful and ringleaders
could be prosecuted for conspiracy.[74] On the other hand, the masters
could hardly take to court hundreds of workers who refused to work
and in general they were forced to treat or try to starve them back to
work by a lockout.

Despite the difficulties, labour disputes were common in London
throughout the century. There was trouble among the shoemakers in
1714, with 'tumultuous' meetings and some arrests. Proceedings against
combinations of clubs and societies in the woollen trades were taken
in 1718. There were similar moves against clubs of journeymen tailors
in 1721, some 7,000 said to be organised at fifteen to twenty houses
of call. The journeymen wheelwrights struck three times between 1718
and 1734. There was a strike of shipbuilders at the royal dockyard in

Woolwich on the eve of war in 1739; it had to be put down by a battalion of guards and a troop of horse. In 1744 perhaps up to 15,000 journeymen tailors and stay makers struck for higher wages in a violent dispute that threatened arson against employers' houses and involved attacks on blacklegs. The dispute rumbled on into 1745, the men complaining of prosecutions leading to imprisonment, and masters contriving to have strike leaders impressed into the services or transported to the plantations. It flared up again in 1751–2, with complaints of abuses on all sides and rewards offered for those tailors who had sent threatening letters to the masters, and there was another month-long strike in 1756.

But the most truculent workers by far were the silk weavers of Spitalfields, Bethnal Green and parts of Shoreditch, known generally as the Spitalfields weavers. With so many depending on the weaving lofts for their subsistence, and with so many labourers in a conservative trade that bred generations to the loom, any interruption in production quickly brought misery in its train. This, on and off, was the great fact of life for the Spitalfields weavers all century long: in January 1700 we find complaints to the House of Commons of 'the great Decay of the Silk Manufactory', with distress among the weavers and throwers; and in January 1798 we hear of a soup and potato charity at 53 Brick Lane keeping over 3,000 poor weavers' families from starvation.[75]

The Spitalfields weavers wouldn't lie down under their intolerable burdens. Their very numbers, the credit their industry gave them, with many wealthy consumers at the court end of the town, and a readiness to exercise their collective might with violence if necessary made them a power in the land for the first three-quarters of the eighteenth century, most certainly a power on the streets of London. In 1721 competition from printed Indian calicoes led the master weavers to seek protection from Parliament against foreign imports. When the bill outlawing importation and threatening to fine anyone who wore the offending prints was temporarily stalled, the weavers interpreted it as political faint-heartedness. Thousands of men, women and children converged on Parliament and had to be dispersed by the Horse Guards. Offending gowns were torn from ladies' backs or splashed with 'pernicious liquids'. Threats were made 'to demolish the House of a *French* Weaver, and rifle that of the *East India* Company', but peace was kept by military force until the bill passed. Some years later, on 5 November 1739, a large number of journeymen weavers attempted to pull down the house of a master in Spital Square. He was accused of trying to get silk winding done free as part of the price of a weaving job. Guards were brought from the Tower, the Riot Act read, and 'Several Soldiers . . . were dangerously wounded, by Bricks and Tiles thrown on them from the Tops of Houses.' And unemployment in the summer of 1745 renewed the weavers' agitation against Indian silks and calicoes, though this time protests seem to have been confined to petitioning the Weavers' Company for more vigorous enforcement of the law of 1721.[76]

The long half-century of relative prosperity in London and the nation ended in the early 1760s. There was terrible distress in a severe frost lasting from Christmas Day 1762 to the end of January 1763 which 'put a stop to several handicraft trades' and pushed all prices up except butchers' meat, as the farmers about London drove their cattle to town for slaughter rather than see them starve in field or barn. In October 1763 the first signs of desperation among the Spitalfields weavers brought several thousands on to the streets to attack a master's house. They 'destroyed his looms, and cut a great quantity of rich silk to pieces'; his effigy was driven about in a cart, hanged on a gibbet and burned. Troops were called out to quell the disturbances. The master's offence has not come down to us.[77]

With the cost of living continuing to rise and with a labour market overstocked by demobilised servicemen at the end of the Seven Years War, worker militancy spread to other trades. There was renewed trouble among the tailors in the spring of 1764. Some forty journeymen at a meeting in 'the Bull-head in Bread-street', City, were arrested at the instigation of some master tailors and imprisoned in the Wood Street Compter, unlawfully as it turned out. They were suspected of being 'Flints', refusing to work for the masters' prices as ratified by the magistrates, 'in contradistinction to those who submit, and are in derision stiled . . . *Dungs*'. That same April several thousand silk weavers marched from Spitalfields to present a petition to the King, protesting against the importation of French silks that were once more undermining their livelihood. They petitioned Parliament in similar terms in the following January of 1765, and peruke makers and hatters protested against foreign workers in London around the same time.[78]

The first great crisis erupted in spring 1765. In April a combination of journeymen tailors was broken up and the ringleaders imprisoned in Newgate, and there were fights between Flints and Dungs in a public house at Cloth Fair, and perhaps elsewhere. But the Spitalfields weavers

put all that in the shade. The end of the war with France two years
before had opened up a clandestine trade in silks to which the authorities seem to have turned a blind eye. Master weavers in Spitalfields
and mercers in the City commissioned fine but cheap silks from the
Continent rather than have goods made in London. A bill to strengthen
the penalties for importers passed the House of Commons but was lost
in the Lords, apparently on the instigation of the Duke of Bedford, the
only peer opposing the measure. On 14 and 16 May the weavers and
their families 'assembled by beat of drum' many thousands strong and
marched in protest against the defeat of the bill. On 17 May some
50,000 advanced in separate columns from Spitalfields and Moorfields
through the great townships of the poor in Holborn, St Giles and
Southwark, and converged on Parliament. They marched under black
flags to mark their misery, which 'their pallid looks and emaciated
carcases', in the words of the *Annual Register*, 'made sufficiently evident'.
On their way back east tempers frayed and at Bloomsbury Square there
was a concerted attack on Bedford House. Part of the courtyard wall
was pulled down in front and so were fences in the gardens behind.
The house was saved by Horse and Foot Guards, who were pelted with
paving stones; one crashed through the Duke's carriage window, cutting
his hand and bruising his head. 'Bedford House is like a fortress besieged,'
Thomas Gray reported to a friend; 'soldiers looking over the walls, &
patrolling round all the avenues. he immured within, & the Dutchess
ill with fright. the mob curseing him without . . .' A mercer's shop in
Ludgate Hill thought to be importing French silks had its windows
broken and so did several master weavers' houses in Spitalfields. For
some days rumours of riots and of country weavers marching on London
to aid the poor of Spitalfields shook nerves at the polite end of the
town: 'we have been at the eve of a civil war,' Horace Walpole told a
correspondent at the end of May. Peace was eventually secured by a
combination of force of arms, a promise by the masters to recall French
orders and 'a seasonable subscription' among the rich for the weavers'
relief. A year later almost to the day came a political victory, too, when
Parliament tightened controls on foreign silks and other goods. Several
thousand weavers accompanied the King from St James's Palace to the
House of Lords to assent to the bill, 'streamers flying, music playing,
and drums beating'.[79]

The weavers' peace proved short-lived. The third terrible winter in
five years in 1766–7 caused great disruption to trade and huge rises

in the price of bread and coal. Misery was made worse by flooding on both banks of the river. In the aftermath of these dreadful hardships, the master weavers chose to lower the prices given for woven silk. They were able to do so through the introduction into the London trade of improved looms. 'Two classes of weaver were mutually combined to distress each other, namely the engine and narrow weavers.' It was said that an engine worked by one man could weave as much silk in a single day as a narrow weaver could in six. From October 1767 the two factions fought it out on the streets of Spitalfields and around. Silk was cut in the loom and engines were destroyed. Both sides armed themselves with 'rusty swords, pistols . . . cutlasses, hatchets, &c.' From time to time, for five months to February 1768, weavers assembled thousands strong in the night-time. Magistrates and police were overwhelmed, guards were called from the Tower, and numerous arrests were made. That winter, once again, saw a severe frost, storms, floods, unaffordable prices, great distress and extensive fires in the City and Westminster that 'rendered the season truly deplorable'.[80]

The misery of the London poor provoked both anxiety and, partly as a consequence, charity among the London rich; among the disbursements was £200 in January 1768, collected among 'the nobility and gentry' frequenting 'Almack's tavern', Pall Mall.[81] But no amount of charity could have pacified the trouble to come. For it was at this moment that two new elements complicated further a period of economic distress and industrial strife that London had not seen for generations. In February 1768, as a result of events to be discussed in a later chapter, John Wilkes returned to London after more than four years' exile in France. He promptly stood as parliamentary candidate for the City, sparking a lengthy period of fevered politics in both capital and nation. His effect on the mood of the times was to render compromise not just unfashionable but unthinkable. And in April a bloody industrial conflict extended London's bitter struggles between worker and master, worker and worker, to the River Thames.

The London coalheavers were more powerful than numerous. On a thousand or so men depended the coal that Londoners needed for survival and, in the swift dispatch of their trade, the efficient operation of the upper port. But despite this, and despite their famously robust physique salted with Irish temper, the coalheavers had traditionally been oppressed and exploited by the undertakers or gangmasters who organised their work, and held them in financial thrall. These were a few publicans along the river who dealt with the coal factors and put together gangs to unload the coal ships. They required men to take part of their wages in truck, charging over the odds for drink, provisions, shovels and lodgings. The coalheavers had petitioned Parliament to improve their lot as early as 1700, but from around 1750 their grievances seem to have sharpened. In 1768, under the lash of high prices, with family resources diminished by the dreadful winter just passed, their patience broke. Unsurprisingly, given all we know about the men and the trade and the masters, it was a struggle marked by great violence: 'Of all the tumults,' thought Horace Walpole, reflecting later on the times he had lived through, this was 'the fiercest and most memorable'.[82]

Responding to the coalheavers' grievances, an attempt to organise them under the auspices of the City Corporation was made by act of Parliament in 1767. William Beckford, as alderman of Billingsgate Ward, had the task of establishing a scheme to register coalheavers and determine standard prices for their labour. The practical work fell on a deputy agent, John Green, licensee of the Round About tavern, New Gravel Lane, near the river at Shadwell. But a rival scheme proposed by a local magistrate, Justice Ralph Hodgson, found favour with the coalheavers; they had been pressing for higher wages, which Hodgson was prepared to accept. When Green advertised for coalheavers to be registered to work under the new arrangements none came. So Green advertised for any able-bodied men willing to work at his prices and duly filled his gangs.

In the middle of April 1768 there was 'a desperate affray' at Wapping between the newly registered coalheavers and those who had formerly done the job but were now out of work: 'many persons were wounded, and three or four houses almost destroyed'. It was all probably aggravated by tensions between English and Irish, the latter prominent among the dispossessed coalheavers. On 20–21 April, after many threats and a serious attack on the premises just a few days before, a crowd of 400–500 coalheavers, some crying 'Wilkes and Liberty', besieged the Round About tavern with the intent of pulling it down and having Green's life. With the help of a sailor drinking in the bar and a lodger or two, Green barricaded the house against the crowd: 'stones came up very fast' and broke his windows. Armed with a brace of pistols, a musket and a blunderbuss, Green fired down on the crowd from his upstairs windows. Around midnight his assailants armed themselves with muskets and returned his fire – Green later counted more than 260 'bullet marks' in the ceilings and walls at the front of the house. The siege continued all night and into the morning. No magistrate or police came to Green's assistance. Eventually, in the daylight, Green escaped from the house. He had killed two men, so he surrendered to Justice Hodgson, who committed him to Newgate with the words, 'Mr. Green you are one of the bravest fellows that ever was.'[83]

A few days later, with disruption causing delay and congestion on the river, the coal ships' sailors attempted to discharge their own cargoes, but the coalheavers stormed the ships, with fierce fighting on both sides. In May sailors on other ships took advantage of the chaos to strike for a wage increase, bringing outward-bound vessels to a standstill. They marched on the Royal Exchange and then petitioned the King, 'colours flying, drums beating, and fifes playing'. That same month the watermen petitioned the Lord Mayor, journeymen hatters struck, the sawyers destroyed Mr Dingley's mill, the tailors were in dispute once more and so were the London glass grinders.[84]

The coalheavers seemed to have negotiated peace with a wage rise in the early part of May but it didn't hold and the colliers' crews once again tried to move their cargoes. On 25 May more fierce fighting broke out between sailors and coalheavers in which James Beattie, a young sailor, was stabbed to death. The river remained a turbulent place, with fierce battles and many injuries right through June. Peace was finally forced on the coalheavers not by industrial means but by a ferocious display of judicial retribution. On 6 July two Irish coalheavers were sentenced to hang for the murder of Beattie; and another seven coalheavers, six of them probably Irish Catholics, were condemned for the attack on the Round About tavern. On 11 July James Murphy and James Dogan were hanged at Tyburn and 'delivered to the surgeons to be anatomized'. More dramatically, on 20 July, in a provocative flaunting of state power in the heart of the coalheavers' community, the seven convicted of the Shadwell attack were taken in carts from Newgate to makeshift gallows at Sun Tavern Fields, a few minutes' walk north-east of Green's tavern. Before the carts rode the two City sheriffs, accompanied by 'a prodigious number of peace officers'. The executions were watched by 'an incredible number of people'. Some 300 soldiers were deployed nearby in case of trouble but there was none: 'our mobs are subsided,' a relieved Horace Walpole wrote to a friend a week or so later.[85]

The coalheavers had indeed had enough. But the much larger body of Spitalfields weavers were about to enter the most violent period of their struggle to protect their livelihoods. Less than a month after the executions in Sun Tavern Fields, weavers attacked two houses in an obscure place called Pratt's Alley and cut silk from the looms: Edward Fitchett, just seventeen, was shot in the head with a pistol by one of the attackers and died. There was further trouble in March 1769 with threats, extortion and violence against masters, and in July there was more cutting of silk. In August, the silk-handkerchief weavers rose against the low prices paid for their work and extorted a levy of sixpence a loom for their cause. Some masters armed themselves rather than pay and sharp fighting followed. On one night the silk was cut from fifty looms and on another night a hundred. 'Pistols were continually kept firing during the whole night, but only to deter, it is thought, any person from opposing' the 'cutters'. The violence grew through September, when masked cutters armed with blunderbusses, pistols and axes sealed the entrances to Hoxton Square and broke open a house in search of a master weaver who had offended them, but they failed to find him. On 30 September a party of soldiers raided the Dolphin alehouse in Cock Lane, Spitalfields, where some cutters were meeting. Firing began on both sides and two weavers and a soldier were shot dead. With Spitalfields under something like martial law from a special barracks built there for the troops, numerous clashes with armed weavers and soldiers led to further deaths on the weavers' side.[86]

These turbulent events reached a climax with the execution of two weavers convicted of the affray at the Dolphin, John Doyle and John Valline. At the Old Bailey on 21 October, the Recorder had ordered their deaths at 'the usual place of execution', meaning Tyburn. But on the personal orders of the King the hanging was moved to Bethnal Green, in the heart of the weavers' quarter. Apprehensive of trouble, the City sheriffs protested in a lengthy correspondence with the law officers until judges ruled the King's order lawful. On 8 December Doyle and Valline were hanged at a gallows in the crossroads at Bethnal Green, near the Salmon and Ball public house. There was 'an inconceivable number of people', who threw 'many bricks, tiles, stones, &c' at the sheriffs and peace officers. The sheriffs had declined military assistance as a further provocation to the weavers. Three other cutters, despite petitions for clemency, were hanged at Tyburn a few days before Christmas.[87]

There was a grisly sequel, emphasising the repugnance of the crowd for anyone caught informing against a popular cause, when vengeance was both pitiless and unrelenting. In a field at Bethnal Green on 16 April 1771, a pattern drawer for master silk weavers named Daniel Clarke, 'the principal evidence' or informer against Doyle and Valline some eighteen months before, was cornered by a crowd over 2,000 strong and stoned to death. He had been hunted in and out of one house after another and dragged about the streets for over an hour, beaten, kicked and whipped at intervals, until thrown into a pond and stoned. Many brickbats seem to have been thrown by boys in the crowd. It was said that 'Never did any poor mortal suffer more than he did; he begged of them several times to shoot him; but they kept stoning him till he died in the greatest agonies.' Two of the crowd, one of them a weaver, were hanged for Clarke's murder on the same spot that July.[88]

By then, indeed from after the hangings in Bethnal Green at Christmas 1769, a grudging peace had been stamped on the weavers of Spitalfields. It was made permanent, shortly after further disturbances, when Parliament passed the first of the Spitalfields Acts in July 1773. This established that wage rates should be determined and enforced by the magistrates, protection that the tailors had secured for many years past. But legislation unwittingly condemned the silk-weaving industry in London to a lingering demise. It stifled mechanical innovation – always the dread of most in the community – by requiring masters to give the same price for any measure of woven silk at the handicraft rate, even if produced by an 'engine'. More favourable conditions out of London encouraged much production to drift away at the expense of Spitalfields, where the work shrank faster than the workforce for the rest of the century and beyond.[89]

This insurrectionary industrial violence that lasted without much remission from October 1763 to December 1769, with its centre east of Aldgate and quelled only by brutal force of arms, would prove of unequalled ferocity in the history of modern London. It was a merciless struggle on both sides. The masters' interests were finally buttressed by a draconian rule of law and the armed forces of the state. And it was sharpened though not determined by the peculiar political conjuncture brought about by 'that Devil Wilkes'. Taken all together, these few years truly did look – and look still – like the eve of a civil war in the metropolis.

Something like normality returned from early 1770. Amid grumbling discontent, through years marked by high prices that always outstripped London's low-wage economy, some trades erupted from time to time. There were agitations and strikes by cabinetmakers, royal-dockyard workers, carpenters, seamen, bookbinders and others. By the 1790s, the strength of workers' organisations in London was such that many employers were prepared to negotiate higher wages to match the rise in prices – and so avoid the sort of conflagration seen across the Channel.

Nor were these merely struggles waged in streets or public-house taprooms or on the river. In 1765 a satirical pamphlet attacked an unnamed nobleman, probably the Duke of Bedford, for saying that if he were a Spitalfields weaver he could live on 10d a day. With Swiftean irony the author proposed an act to allow weavers to keep within this budget by selling their children at the Royal Exchange to 'people of fashion and fortune' to 'provide themselves with as many infants as they think proper'. We do not know the author, who purported to be a weaver and possibly was. But it was more likely to have been one of that great army of writers for hire who came into their own in London in the eighteenth century.

ELIZA HAYWOOD.

Parmentier pinx.   Vertue sculp.

Eliza Haywood

VII

ELIZA HAYWOOD'S LONDON – PRINT, PICTURES AND THE PROFESSIONS

'Purse-Proud Title-Page Mongers': The Business of Words

'Well,' said Mrs. Eccles, 'how do you like my books? are they not prettily chosen?'

'I assure you,' replied [Henrietta], taking down one, 'you chose very well when you chose this; for it is one of the most exquisite pieces of humour in our language.'

'I knew you would approve of my taste,' said Mrs. Eccles, 'but what have you got? – O! The Adventures of Joseph Andrews – Yes; that is a very pretty book to be sure! – but there is Mrs Haywood's Novels, did you ever read them? – Oh! they are the finest love-sick, passionate stories; I assure you, you'll like them vastly; pray take a volume of Haywood upon my recommendation.'

'Excuse me,' said Henrietta, 'I am very well satisfied with what I have . . .'[1]

Now, Mrs Eccles, a Westminster milliner, is also a bawd who lets out rooms for illicit liaisons and has an interest in softening Henrietta's virtue with a little well-directed bedtime reading. Eliza Haywood was two years dead when this dubious memorial found its way into print, but at least it recognised her place in the reading public's affections in the 1750s, even alongside the greatest novelist of the age. Henry Fielding would prove more durable. Even so, Eliza Haywood's successes with a popular readership, especially among women, were sustained over a long and varied writing career.

The details of Haywood's personal life are obscure. She was born Eliza Fowler, probably in London to a father 'in the mercantile way', some time around 1693. By her late teens she had married and she appeared, as Mrs Haywood, as an actress on the Dublin stage from 1714. By 1717 she was back in London to act at the theatre at Lincoln's Inn Fields and two years later she published her first novel, *Love in Excess*. By then, 1719, she was single once more, whether widowed or separated is unclear, though she retained her married name till the end of her life.

As Mrs Eccles points out, passion and Eliza Haywood the novelist were no strangers, and so it proved in real life. In the early 1720s she was the lover of that wayward and unreliable genius Richard Savage – ungrateful too, for he later satirised 'the divine *Eliza*' as Cytherea, a prostitute in the Temple of Venus. By 1729 it seems she had grown large but yet with something of her old attractions about her: 'yon Juno of majestic size,/ with cow-like udders, and with ox-like eyes'. And she had 'Two babes of love' out of wedlock, possibly with William Hatchett, a little-known playwright who stayed loyal to her till her death at her home in New Peter Street, on the edge of insalubrious Tothill Fields, Westminster, in February 1756.[2]

While many of Haywood's personal circumstances remain hidden from us, her well-documented writing life proves strikingly representative of her times. Women writers flourished in every literary field during both halves of the eighteenth century, especially prolific as novelists and playwrights. Women readers were among the most fervent devotees of print, especially of fiction, and they were of many ranks, from ladies of quality through all the middling station to the higher ranks of domestic servants. Indeed, many thought women read too much. As early as 1705 a banker's niece 'has made a World of her own' by spending 'all her Solitude in reading Romances', in Richard Steele's *The Tender Husband*, and this complaint – for such it generally is – was reiterated, even by those men and women writers who benefited from it, throughout the century.[3]

Haywood directed much of her output to women readers, but not exclusively so, for few writers attempted as many genres as she. In a thirty-seven-year career she published some eighty works and a number of collected editions of her writings. At beginning and end she was a novelist, or writer of fictional 'histories' as they were most often described. Some of these were modest affairs of thirty or forty pages, a few ran to three or four volumes, and most explored the difficulties of love and the perils of seduction, or 'the undoing Artifices of deluding

Men', that great literary theme of the age. But in between she tried her pen at just about every form that London's business of words had so far invented. Using 'an education more liberal than is ordinarily allowed to persons of my sex', she made extensive translations of French memoirs and fiction. She wrote poems – some of fawning awfulness in praise of her wealthy and powerful mentor, Aaron Hill. She used her stage experience to write several plays, she collaborated in an opera libretto with Hatchett and she wrote dramatic criticism for the newspapers. She produced a moral tract for servant maids that praised timidity and obedience. She dabbled in politics and was arrested for writing a Jacobite pamphlet in 1749, which probably put an end to her 'modest career' as a publisher. And she edited periodicals for women, most famously the *Female Spectator*, a monthly which ran from 1744 to 1746.[4]

This was a modernisation of Addison and Steele's *Spectator* of more than thirty years before but directed at women. It used the same tone of moral rectitude and politeness of manners, and the same device of a number of imaginary contributors with their own individual experiences and points of view, but addressed to the female condition and its anxieties. Almost certainly Haywood wrote it all. Her name was absent from the title page but many readers would have been familiar with her identity and her notoriety. She introduced what would be a very popular magazine – the first successful magazine edited by a woman for women – with a personal confession. It is easy to see what appeal wisdom won through experience might have had for women readers of all ages:

I never was a beauty, and am now very far from being young . . . I have run through as many scenes of vanity and folly as the greatest coquet of them all. – Dress, equipage, and flattery were the idols of my heart. – I should have thought that day lost, which did not present me with some new opportunity of shewing myself. – My life, for some years, was a continued round of what I then called pleasure, and my whole time engrossed by a hurry of promiscuous diversions. – But whatever inconveniencies such a manner of conduct has brought upon myself, I have this consolation, to think that the public may reap some benefit from it . . .[5]

Eliza Haywood, then, was adept in many fields. That alone could earn her the equivocal honour of a 'writer for hire', a 'hackney writer', or 'prostitute scribbler' as Samuel Johnson – the greatest writer for hire of them all – would term it. In this she was one among many in London's business of words, when the field of those seeking to earn a living by writing had never been larger. She was typical too in her readiness to engage in the war of words that so infected popular writing in the eighteenth century. Her targets were political, satirising Walpole and all his works, as so many did; and they were personal, directed against the authors with whom she competed for public attention, a small world where almost everyone was known to each other. She attacked, apparently without provocation, a woman friend of Alexander Pope – unwisely, because Haywood achieved some sort of immortality as that Juno in Pope's *Dunciad* of 1729, the prize in a pissing competition between two rascally booksellers.[6] She wrote *Anti-Pamela*, a lewd satire on Samuel Richardson's celebrated though improbable *Pamela* of 1740–41. And she attacked Henry Fielding, who had employed her as an actress in his plays, in wounding terms in perhaps her best novel, *The History of Miss Betsy Thoughtless* (1751), accusing him of hypocrisy after his appointment as a Westminster magistrate: 'the town is perfectly acquainted both with his abilities and success; and has since seen him, with astonishment, wriggle himself into favour, by pretending to cajole those he had not the power to intimidate'.[7] Fielding, who had mildly satirised Haywood as Mrs Novel in *The Author's Farce* of 1729, took it rather well and seems, as often, to have borne no personal ill-will. But for Pope and Savage, Haywood was one of those 'dunces' who flattered and multiplied the follies and vices of the age through a common prostitution of the writer's 'art'.

There was one further way in which Haywood was representative of her times. London life dominated almost everything she wrote. City manners, both vicious and virtuous, occupy a number of her early novels, and London locations, and the moral hazards encountered there, give some buttress of reality to *Betsy Thoughtless* and *Jemmy and Jenny Jessamy* (1753). White's Chocolate House in St James's Street, a brothel in Chick Lane, another in 'a handsome house' near Hatton Garden, a house of assignation in Tavistock Street, a bagnio in Orange Street and another in Silver Street, a duel behind Montagu House, Great Russell Street, a fashionable wedding in Golden Square, Langford's auction house in Covent Garden Piazza, all ground the reader in the bustling life of the town:

'Happening to have some business the other day to cross the park,' continued she, 'I met Willmore in the narrow passage leading from thence to Spring-Garden, – he had two persons with him, who I suppose, by their habits, were officers in the army; – they were all three arm in arm, and took up so much of the way that it was impossible for me to pass them without brushing.'[8]

During Eliza Haywood's lifetime, and even more quickly in the fifty years after, the opportunities in London to make money from words flourished as never before. Figures for adult literacy in England in the eighteenth century can only be guesses, and the guesses – even the meaning of literacy – are contested areas. But probably six out of ten men could read and write by 1750 and 40–50 per cent of women were readers to some extent. All agree that Londoners were more literate than country folk. And it seems reasonable to think, though this is disputed too, that literacy expanded with the enlarging world of print in the second half of the century: a sample of 100 men applying for relief to St Clement Danes in 1752–4 reveals that sixty-seven could sign their names, and of 100 women thirty-one; similar samples in 1785–92 show seventy-eight men signing and thirty-eight women.[9]

It was the newspaper that revolutionised the importance of words and reading, in London in particular. It was almost entirely an eighteenth-century innovation and of metropolitan growth. The first London daily newspaper was the *Daily Courant*, begun on 11 March 1702, published alongside a number of others that came out three times a week or less. By 1709 it was still the only daily but was accompanied by sixteen others published two or three times a week. Many were ephemeral. But despite the imposition of a newspaper stamp, or tax, which pushed prices up from 1d to at least 1¼d a number from 1712, the demand for newsprint proved inexhaustible. The steep growth in political journalism in the 1720s and especially the 1730s, with papers subsidised by opposition and by government, made them 'so multiply'd, as to render it impossible, unless a man makes it a business, to consult them all'. By mid-century there were six London dailies, six tri-weeklies and six weeklies; by 1785 there were nine London morning newspapers (all dailies), ten evening newspapers (all bi- or tri-weeklies) and three Sundays, a total of twenty-eight titles; and by 1793 there were thirteen London morning dailies, eleven evening titles (mainly three times a week) and eleven weeklies, thirty-five in all. At that time there were sixty-seven English country papers, nearly all weeklies. The nation's daily news originated almost

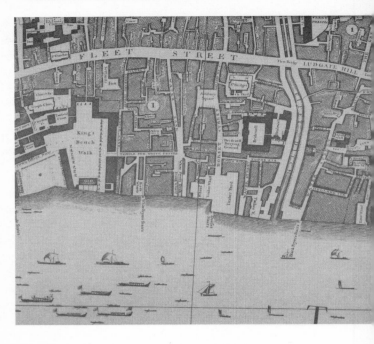

entirely from London. And a small stable of monthlies, beginning most prestigiously with the *Gentleman's Magazine* in 1731, sought to distil for leisured readers the important gleanings of Grub Street with a leaving of more learned contributions.[10]

Circulation numbers varied but probably averaged 1,500–3,000 for most titles in the final quarter of the century, though some like the *Gazetteer* and *Morning Post* claimed 5,000 and others like the *Public Advertiser* and *Daily Advertiser* perhaps more. On any day in London in the 1790s it seems there were at least 40,000–50,000 papers in circulation for a population of 900,000 or so. Newspaper *buyers* were thus a pretty small proportion of Londoners. They bought them in the street from the hawkers or 'mercuries', or they had them delivered for a small additional charge by a 'newswalk'. These were run as a monopoly claiming the right to deliver any paper in set districts of the town, and could be bought and sold as real property: William Henry (WH) Smith's parents had one around Berkeley Square from 1790, his widowed mother carrying it on till her death in 1816.[11]

Newspaper *readers* were far more common. Reading the paper was

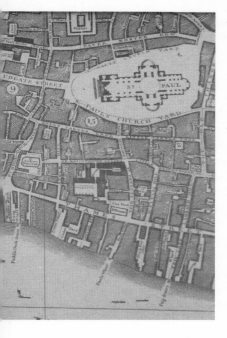

Fleet Street to St Paul's
Churchyard, *c.*1740

'a real passion for the English', noted Archenholtz at the end of the
century. And they were read mainly in the coffee houses:

People go to them chiefly for the purpose of reading the papers, an occupation
which in England is one of the necessaries of life. The best frequented coffee
houses take in ten or twelve copies of the same paper not to make persons wait,
together with the best periodical publications. The papers are bound up in large
folios at the end of the year, and carefully kept, as they always find readers.[12]

It was politics that underpinned this passion for the papers, and
party polemics that undermined the value of the news they printed.
Writers who had given or sold their abilities to a party wrote 'without
a Wish for Truth, or Thought of Decency', complained Samuel Johnson
in 1757, launching the *London Chronicle*, a daily that he claimed would
mark a new departure for journalistic reliability. Politics aside, more
general criticisms of inaccuracy stuck to those many newspapers that
relied overwhelmingly on word of mouth for the news they printed.
Johnson himself was not above inserting false paragraphs into a paper

to torment Hester Thrale's mother, an inveterate retailer of the news to all about her, who would then astonish the company by reading them out. The *Flying-Post*, an early London paper of Queen Anne's reign, became popularly known as the *Lying-Post*. And this propensity to false reporting and manufactured paragraphs – '*Grub-street News . . . 'tis Grubstreet*, all *Grubstreet*' – plagued the London newspaper industry throughout the century.[13] 'It is all in the papers,' the elderly skinflint Whittle is told, of news of his impending marriage to young and energetic Widow Brady, which now he wants to disavow:

Whittle. So much the better; then nobody will believe it.[14]

Nor did truthfulness prosper under the shift to scandalmongering, that most successful means of selling papers in the last quarter of the century. The *Morning Post* under the Rev. Henry Bate Dudley, from 1775, was 'that *Hydra* of scandal' for Georgiana, Duchess of Devonshire, who was well placed to know. It was matched or even exceeded by the potted biographies of flawed worthies published in the *Town and Country Magazine* from around the same time.[15]

The burgeoning business of news during the eighteenth century was matched by the business of books, at least from the 1740s. Before then some 2,000 or so titles (books, plays, pamphlets) were published in London each year, accounting for over 90 per cent of all English publishing, with the busiest decade the 1710s, and stagnating or declining slightly in the twenty years after. But in the 1740s a publishing surge brought the annual total to around 2,800 a year, rising to 3,300 in 1780 and 4,600 in 1790, and growing still through the last years of the century. By then London was publishing just over three-quarters of the books published in England.[16]

Books were part of London popular culture from the earliest years of the century. When Dudley Ryder and 'Cousin John' walked out with two young ladies in the fields near Hackney in March 1716, 'Our conversation turned very much upon a book that they had lately read called *Lindamira*, a kind of a romance which they very much commended and admired. This led us naturally into a discourse about love', an irresistible subject to the eager young law student; three days later, perhaps seeking tips, he was reading *Lindamira* himself. Those who didn't read were satirised on the stage, which as ever reflected London manners. Henry Fielding's egregious Lord Formal was driven against his inclination to the booksellers because to be agreeable to 'the ladies . . . a man must understand something of books'. He found it uncongenial, for reading just a dozen pages 'vastly impaired the lustre of my eyes. I had, Sir, in that short time, perfectly lost the direct ogle . . .' Lord Formal apart, the interest in books was sufficient to have bred three literary monthlies by the 1750s, with more by the century's end, and a shoal of reviewers prominent 'amongst other Disturbers of Human Quiet', in Samuel Johnson's heartfelt phrase. Indeed, the appetite for books was attested daily in the newspapers, the *London Chronicle* of 2–4 March 1780, for instance, carrying advertisements for fifteen new titles and four magazines.[17]

By then readers didn't have to buy a book to stay in the know. Circulating libraries operating on a private subscription basis opened in London from the 1740s on. By 1760 there were around twenty and probably a few more by the century's end. They were very popular, not least among those seeking a living through words. Mrs Pilkington, 'not having a Library of my own', was 'a constant Customer' at Mr and Mrs Ryves's in Brook Street, who 'hired out Books by the Quarter' around 1743. Laurence Sterne confessed to finding some ideas for *Tristram Shandy* from a book he borrowed, probably from Hookham's Library in Old Bond Street, close to his London lodgings, around 1758. The prolific Bishop William Warburton used to 'send out for a whole basketful of books, from the circulating libraries' to fuel his store of anecdotes when overwintering in London during the 1770s. Charges varied, the principal six – five of them in Westminster and just one in the City – demanding around 3d a volume for new publications, with a membership fee of 4s a quarter. John Bell's British Library in the Strand claimed to have 10,000 volumes in 1771, 50,000 in 1778 and 150,000 in 1793. And the London Library at Ludgate Hill, membership a guinea entrance and a guinea a year, offered readers 'clean books, which is seldom the case at circulating libraries'.[18]

Clearly, these great places were aimed at the reading middling sort and above, rather than the labouring classes. Even so, it would not be surprising to discover small businesses in obscure streets catering for artisans and journeymen, by the 1790s at least. And none of this deterred book buying. James Lackington, prominent mainly in the second-hand trade and selling 100,000 books a year from his shop at Chiswell Street, Finsbury, thought book sales had increased more than 'fourfold' in the twenty years after 1775, despite the borrowing habit in London.[19]

Who were the writers that supplied this giant industry? They were enlisted, in general, from all those varied ranks of the middling sort who were forced to earn a living rather than relying on inheritance. That was a swelling number throughout the century, especially in London. The basic requirements were not great – probably most readers at some time contemplated the possibility of writing for money in an age when letter writing and journal keeping helped polish a style. The temptations and opportunities to do so were greater after an education at a grammar school, at home with tutors or even at the university. The rewards of a professional life in the church, the law or medicine might often prove disappointing. The business of words, on the other hand, theoretically offered a potentially easy road to fame and fortune amid the excitement of being around others in the public eye. And the attractions of a literary life could be tasted every morning at the coffee houses, every evening on the stage and every quiet hour in the closet. Never before had so many men and women tried to earn a living by writing: it was, as Johnson said, 'The Age of Authors'.[20]

The pitfalls, though, were legion, and for one simple reason. Just like the riverside with its snuffle-hunters, or Spitalfields and its weavers, this polite refuge of the literate middling sort was hopelessly overstocked. It could never give work to all who flocked there pen in hand. This, rather than the reluctance of rich patrons to support genius, as many writers lamented at the time, was the primary cause of discontent in the writing trade. The travails of the hackney writer (low earnings, exhausting hours, irritating working conditions) never ceased to rouse the pity of . . . the hackney writer. And there was much of bitterness in every writer's complaints that was characteristic of the times. By birth, by education, by understanding, it seemed that those who made their livelihood the business of words were due more regard from a society that had bred them to better things:

The poet's poverty is a standing topic of contempt; his writing for bread is an unpardonable offence. Perhaps, of all mankind, an author in these times is used most hardly; we keep him poor and yet revile his poverty. Like angry parents who correct their children till they cry, and then correct them for crying, we reproach him for living by his wit, and yet allow him no other means to live.[21]

Perhaps of all mankind? No other means to live? Oliver Goldsmith spoke from his own bruised heart, but his words would have had a cracked ring among the coalheavers of Wapping or the sempstresses of St Giles.

Indeed, this reserve army of labour of the middling classes had more in common than poverty with the 'poorer sort of people'. It was, for instance, a workforce divided within itself. The great divisions were based on background and upbringing, on party-political allegiance formed as much from convenience as conviction, and on conflicting values that characterised literature as an aid to politeness and reformation on the one hand and to Grub Street pandering to the low taste of the times on the other. At the bottom, in a frequently described hierarchy, were the scavenging writers for the newspapers who haunted the coffee houses and taverns for gossip or news that might provide a paragraph at sixpence a throw. These made up, in the popular mind, the denizens of Grub Street (now Milton Street), although few (if any) writers of any complexion seem to have lived in this miserably poor place on the northern edge of the City, close to Barbican, at least in the eighteenth century. It was so obscure that Samuel Johnson confessed towards the end of his life that he had 'never paid his respects to it himself'. Yet 'Grub-street writer' or 'Grub-street writing' was a phrase so frequently heard that foreign visitors asked directions to it, expecting to find 'a great part of the London literati and some eminent booksellers'; they found ragged shoemakers instead.[22]

A hackney writer, however, could cover a multitude of styles and might well be a more respectable character, often educated, sometimes learned, each turning his or her hand to what would pay in the business of words and generally ignoring any other way of making a living. Almost all, like Eliza Haywood, were forced into wide versatility to make words pay. Samuel Johnson (poet, essayist, critic, translator, political pamphleteer, playwright, novelist and most famously projector and author of the *Dictionary of the English Language*, 1755), Oliver Goldsmith (critic, poet, playwright, essayist, novelist, historian, scientific writer), Henry Fielding (playwright, newspaper editor, novelist, essayist, social scientist, memoirist), all wrote mainly for the magazines or booksellers – publishers we would call them now – on commission, or struck out on their own account, hoping to tempt the public. The lesser fry who made their living in the business of words ranged widely in background, education and talents. Robert Sanders, a Scotsman who taught himself Latin, Greek and Hebrew in spare moments at his trade as a comb maker, called himself Doctor of Divinity, wrote biographies for the booksellers and produced an annotated Bible that he paid a real clergyman to put his name to, sharing the profits. Charlotte Lennox was an American who came to London in 1735 when she was fifteen, publishing her first novel in 1750; she won extravagant praise from Johnson, was a friend of Henry Fielding and satirised Eliza Haywood's fiction in *Henrietta*, made translations from the French, wrote poems and plays, edited the *Lady's Museum*, a women's monthly, in 1760–61 and published her last novel in 1797. There was, then, little similarity of background among the hundreds of other hackney writers who might serve as examples, except an origin somewhere among the middling sort. One group of writers, though, of great importance in the century, often did come from one stable, or at least had experience of it: many playwrights, like Haywood, had been actors and knew stagecraft from the inside – like Susannah Centlivre, Samuel Foote, David Garrick, Thomas Holcroft, Elizabeth Inchbald, Charles Macklin, Arthur Murphy and numerous others.[23]

Relatively few of this large field of professional writers had attended the university sufficient to obtain a degree. Even so, there were many university graduates who made part of their living by the pen. There were many writing clerics and writing lawyers and medical men. And there were many others, with private incomes inherited from rich relatives or aristocratic patrons, who earned money from their pen but happily without having to rely on it for a livelihood. It was from this quarter in the first half of the century, most effectively from Alexander Pope, Jonathan Swift and their circle, that Grub Street came under most sustained attack. Hackney writers were censured for their immorality, their pandering to fashionable vices and mindless enjoyments, their lack of learning and the absence of intellectual stimulation to be had from their writings. Less forgivably, they were vilified for their poverty – 'their debt, their habitations in the Mint, and their want of a dinner'.[24]

This great division in London's republic of letters, apparent well into the mid-nineteenth century if not beyond, gained much bitterness in these early years from politics, sometimes intensely and personally felt. Alexander Pope was a Catholic and a Tory, and had a father who made great wealth in City trade, though how much of it benefited his son is unclear. Pope's rich Jacobite patrons encouraged the greatest poet of the age for the potent political gall that fell from his pen. It was a gall that didn't flinch at mocking his opponents' poverty or physical or family shortcomings – and his enemies gave as good as they got, Pope's deformed spine and weak frame ready sources of ribaldry. It was thought sufficient to reveal a man's brother as a shoeblack or his father as a saddler or himself as a 'Son of Love' whose mother was an oyster seller to justify calling his writing 'the Refuse of Wit' and the writer 'the very Excrement of Nature'. Small wonder that this virulent ill-will spilled over into innumerable threats of summary violence, into dirty tricks, even bloody duels.[25]

Yet this bitter animosity among writers was one sharp spur to the conviviality and mutuality that so marked the world of words in London in the eighteenth century. Factions flocked together and found many places to roost. When William Beloe, a clerical schoolmaster in Norfolk, decided to try his hand at 'LITERATURE' in London around December 1783 he found it easy 'to form literary connections':

Generally speaking, in London at least, there is great liberality among literary men, a ready disposition to interchange communications, which may be mutually useful, to accommodate one another with the loan of books, to point out sources of information, indeed to carry on, by a sort of common treaty among one another, a pleasant, friendly, and profitable commerce.[26]

Beloe found the booksellers' shops and book auctions ready places to meet like-minded literary men. The Chapter Coffee House in Paternoster Row also had a literary flavour from around 1715, and so did Tom's in Russell Street, Covent Garden, from at least the 1720s, when it was a distinctively Tory haunt. Numerous taverns around the Strand, Covent Garden, Soho, Fleet Street and the City were much frequented by hacks and other men of words, Samuel Johnson forming his first 'literary club' at the King's Head, famous for its beefsteaks, in Ivy Lane, near St Paul's, around 1749, for instance.[27]

More privately, numerous printers and booksellers had great reputations for generosity to writers – the brothers Dilly, in Poultry, often gave dinners to Boswell, William Strahan the famous printer in New Street, Shoe Lane, was always good to any fellow Scot pursuing the literary road to London, and Mary Wollstonecraft was helped to a writing career by Joseph Johnson of St Paul's Churchyard, who even found suitable London lodgings for her. And once connections were made writers did indeed stand together, supporting one another with alms (as Pope did Savage), putting pieces of literary work their way (as Boswell did for 'a poor man, Cochran'), urging friends to buy subscription copies in advance of publication (as Samuel Johnson did for blind Anna Williams), even writing copy to enliven a friend's prose (as Johnson, again, did for Charlotte Lennox).[28]

It is clear from the largesse of publishers and printers that the republic of letters in eighteenth-century London was not a community of equals. Some had more power than others and most powerful of all were the booksellers and printers. They were a diverse group in every way except geographically, for in general they were found tightly shelved in the old-established printing and publishing terrain of London: in and around St Paul's Cathedral, including Paternoster Row and Ave Maria Lane in the east; and in and around Fleet Street and the Temple, spreading through Temple Bar and along the Strand in the west. These were the two ancient districts of London learning based on church and law, and where the printing press had long set up headquarters. Printers and booksellers were often combined in one and the same person in the early years of the century, but were largely divided into separate trades by the 1750s.[29]

Print was a large and important London industry, heavily capitalised in plant, building and stock, though not employing large numbers of men. There were said to be seventy-five master printers in London in 1724, 124 in 1785 and 216 in 1808. On average, they ran something less than three presses each, a press giving work to five or six men. Very few firms, a handful at most, employed more than fifty, so there were probably fewer than 3,500 workers in all at the century's end. In and around the master printers lay a small constellation of printers' joiners and smiths, typefounders, bookbinders, ink makers and printing stationers making account books and so on. Printing and these by-trades were concentrated in the City: of the 124 London letterpress printers of 1785, seventy-four or 60 per cent were located in the City's square mile.[30]

The printing workforce may not have been large but it was nonetheless important. There was some seasonality to book production, which was quiet in the summer, but in general printing was that rare London employment, offering steady work at a reasonable wage. Compositors, who set the type and laid out the page, could earn at least a guinea a week 'with little mental power and corporeal labour', as Johnson put it. Compositors fluent in Latin might earn more, and those few with Greek more still. Pressmen, who inked the type and screwed the hand-press, used even in newspaper printing, could earn some 3s a day or 18s a week, more if there was a rush. It was an industry proud of its skills and its traditions in the 'chapel', the old name for workers combined in a single shop, and the infinitely detailed schedule of piece rates and shop rules were pored over as devoutly as any prayer book. Apprentices were sworn to uphold the chapel secrets in initiation ceremonies that doubtless varied from shop to shop, and similar loyalty was expected from new journeymen. Benjamin Franklin, in London for eighteen months or so from Christmas Eve 1724, worked at a printing house near Lincoln's Inn Fields, where he found his fellow workers demanding 5s beer money not just on his admission to the shop, which he paid, but on his removal from the press to the composing room, which he wouldn't. But he found his work upset by 'the chappel ghost', 'mixing my sorts, transposing my pages, breaking my matter, etc.', and he was forced to pay up.[31]

As in many other London trades there were great opportunities for advancement and some extraordinary triumphs. John Barber, a barber's son born in Gray's Inn Lane around 1675, had 'but [a] narrow' education and was apprenticed to Mrs Clark, 'a Printer and a Widdow' in Thames Street. From a journeyman, with application and drive, he became Mrs Clark's manager and then set up business for himself, settling in Lambeth Hill, Old Fish Street, near the Monument. His Grub Street acumen can only have been helped when he became the lover of Mrs Delarivière Manley, a novelist with much of scandal about her, and his wealth was swollen by timely investments in the South Sea Bubble. He bought a country estate at East Sheen, became a City alderman in 1722, a sheriff in 1729–30, Lord Mayor in 1732–3 and a Tory thorn in the side of Sir Robert Walpole from the excise excitements of 1733. He died in 1741 and was said to have left legacies to a number of Jacobites, including Pope and Swift. In the more respectable years after Barber's death several other printers won fame and fortune. Luke Hansard came as a very young journeyman from Norwich to London around 1770, and found work with John Hughs of Turnstile, Holborn. Hughs had been at Eton with Lord North and became Printer to the House of Commons under North's premiership in 1763. On Hughs's death, in 1774, the meticulous and indispensable Hansard, just twenty-two, was taken into partnership; from 1799 the firm continued in his sole name, which soon after entered the English language. Most astonishing of all was Samuel Richardson, whose roots were in London and who frequently proclaimed himself a cockney though born and raised in Derbyshire. He was apprenticed to a printer in Golden Lyon

Court off Aldersgate Street, from 1706 to 1713, and became a journeyman compositor and hawk-eyed corrector of the press. When his
master died in 1720 he set up on his own account and prospered. But
it was his ventures as a published novelist from 1740 – an art that
seems to have sprung from nowhere – that made him one of the most
famous men of the age.[32]

There would be no other voice in English literature quite like Samuel
Richardson's. More typical of his brother master-printers, though, was
his charitable support for the many less fortunate workers in the business of words:

SIR, I am obliged to entreat your assistance. I am now under an arrest for
eighteen shillings. Mr. Strahan, from whom I should have received the necessary help in this case, is not at home; and I am afraid of not finding Mr. Millar.
If you will be so good as to send me this sum, I will very gratefully repay you,
and add it to all former obligations. I am, Sir, Your most obedient and most
humble servant,
    SAMUEL JOHNSON.
    Gough-square, 16 March [1756].

The good Richardson sent 6 guineas.[33]

Printers were often the bankers of the hackney writer and so were
booksellers like the Scot, Andrew Millar, to whom Johnson would also
readily have turned. But if the great printers were the plutocrats of the
business of words, booksellers who were publishers were the adventurers
and the speculators, taking much of the risk in ventures where 'almost
as much Paper is wasted, as is sold'.[34]

It was not an easy business. The competition was fierce, with some
seventy booksellers publishing books in London in 1760 and perhaps
150 in 1785. The text itself was usually not a financial risk. Payments
to authors were generally low. Many copyrights were very cheap, just
£5 to £27 for most novels, sometimes with further payments depending
on sales. But other costs (printing, binding, advertising) were high and,
much as in other risky ventures of the time, booksellers might hedge
their bets by combining in a partnership or 'conger' to purchase an
expensive copyright between them. Auctions of copyrights in halves,
quarters and sixteenths – just like any sailing ship – took place at
Stationers' Hall for some large ventures. Other combinations were
constructed in advance. Five booksellers, individuals and partnerships,

commissioned Johnson's *Dictionary* in 1746 at a price of £1,575, for instance.[35]

But at some time all booksellers were prepared to shoulder a high risk on their own account. Robert Dodsley, a former footman, was aided by Alexander Pope and others to set up as a bookseller in Pall Mall in 1735. Dodsley's investments were various and extensive and generally successful. He paid 10 guineas for Johnson's poem *London* in 1738, bought one-fifteenth of the *London Evening Post* for £150 in 1746, a quarter of the *London Magazine* for £350 in 1748, brought out the *London Chronicle* as his own speculation in 1757 and began the *Annual Register* in 1758, paying Edmund Burke £100 a year as its editor and main writer. Perhaps of all the London booksellers it was Andrew Millar, apprenticed in Edinburgh, who proved most venturesome. He was in London by around 1729, settling at 141 Strand, near St Clement Danes Church, in 1742. He was one of the partners in the *Dictionary*, compiled nearby in Gough Square, and famously the publisher of Henry Fielding, to whom he paid £600 for the copyright of *Tom Jones* (1749) and £800 for *Amelia* in 1751. Between 1754 and 1762 he paid David Hume some £4,000 for his multi-volume *History of England*. 'I respect Millar, Sir,' said Johnson: 'he has raised the price of literature.' On his death in 1768 he was worth £60,000.[36]

Millar died before a judgement in the House of Lords in 1774 ruled that booksellers had no perpetual copyright in the works they bought, copyright reverting to authors after fourteen years. It seemed to spell ruin and the booksellers proposed a parliamentary bill to restore what they had lost, without success. In reality little changed, most profit deriving from the first years of publication in any event, and perpetual copyright was already vulnerable to piracy by unscrupulous printers and booksellers, especially in Ireland. Popular books were pirated in Dublin and shipped to London almost as soon as they appeared in their proper livery, a trade that seems to have relied on extensive bribery within the London printers' shops. To his chagrin Samuel Richardson saw the sheets of his last novel, printed in his own shop and jealously watched over, in the hands of Dublin pirates even before London publication: he dismissed two of his workers as a consequence.[37] And besides piracy, booksellers were frequently liable to have a copyright suppressed as a libel against an individual or the crown, especially in those politically fraught periods that so frequently punctuated the century, as we shall see in a later chapter.

The frequent success of the booksellers, even against all these odds, rankled with authors. Some published their own works themselves. A popular device till around mid-century was the subscription, where purchasers paid part of the price of a book on a proposal and the rest on publication. In this way Pope made at least £4,000 from his free translation of the *Iliad* in 1715–20, in addition to selling the copyright to the London bookseller Bernard Lintot for 1,200 guineas. It was a scheme that lost caste when authors began canvassing subscriptions for books they had no intention to write. Others had their works 'printed for the Author' and undertook their own distribution. Charles Churchill, a much-feared satirical poet, was offered a handful of guineas for *The Rosciad* but quickly made £700 when he published it himself in 1761. Others followed suit, with varied success. Most, though, needing money upfront and unable to contemplate the sometimes heavy costs of printing and binding, had to fall back on that 'purse-proud Title-page Monger', the bookseller.[38]

That it was, in fact, possible to make a living from hackney writing in the eighteenth century we can see in numerous careers, from Samuel Johnson (aided by genius) to Eliza Haywood (sustained by ceaseless hard labour). Even for these it was a vulnerable living, as Johnson's letter to Richardson makes plain; and Johnson, we should remember, often abstained from drink and always avoided extravagance. Many, not so talented or well disciplined, foundered. 'Poet', 'garretteer', 'hack' and 'hackney writer' were bywords for poverty throughout the century. There are many instances in the records, but we might pick out just two.

Samuel Boyse was a talented poet in Latin and English, the son of an English dissenting minister and privately educated in Dublin. He was a difficult man, said to be 'voluptuous, luxurious, and boundlessly expensive', and 'intoxicated whenever he had the means to avoid starving', which was not always. Stories were told of him having pawned his clothes, confined to 'a bed which had no sheets: here, to procure food, he wrote; his posture sitting up in bed, his only covering a blanket, in which a hole was made to admit of the employment of his arm'. A letter of July 1742 from Boyse at the Crown Coffee House, a spunging house in Grocer's Alley, Poultry, begs help from Edward Cave, bookseller and editor of the *Gentleman's Magazine*, 'having not tasted any thing since Tuesday evening'. It was now Thursday. He 'sometimes raised subscriptions for non-existent poems, and sometimes employed his wife to give out that he was dying'. When commissioned to translate a book he pawned it after producing a sheet or two, the publisher having to redeem it. Johnson once raised a subscription to get his clothes out of pawn; they were straight away pawned once more. When his wife died, 'to signify his sorrow . . . he tied a black ribbon round the neck of a lapdog, which, to acquire the character of a man of taste, he used to carry in his arms'. He died in 1749 'in an obscure lodging near Shoe-lane, and was buried at the charge of the parish'.[39]

Boyse was a professional hack. For writing as the last refuge of the middling sort we might cite Charlotte Charke, the wayward actress daughter of Colly Cibber, actor, playwright and much-derided Poet Laureate, who was disowned by her father after a family row. As an actress she specialised in breeches parts and for part of her life wore men's clothes off-stage, going under the name of Mr Brown. Deserted by her husband and with a daughter to keep, Charke found her acting career badly damaged by stage licensing in 1737; she had acted in Henry Fielding's company, at whom the new controls were chiefly directed. She was in and out of various employments – making and hawking sausages for a time, running a tavern in Drury Lane, acting occasionally and marrying again in 1746, though soon left a widow for the second time. Eventually she took to writing. Around 1754 she was visited by a writer and poet, Samuel Whyte, who recorded his impressions in an article published six years later. He found Charke in 'a wretched thatched hovel' near the New River Head, Clerkenwell. She was

sitting on a maimed chair under the mantle piece, by a fire, merely sufficient to put us in mind of starving. On one hob sat a monkey, which by way of welcome chattered at our going in; on the other a tabby cat, of melancholy aspect! and at our author's feet on the flounce of her dingy petticoat reclined a dog, almost a skeleton! he raised his shaggy head and eagerly staring with his bleared eyes, saluted us with a snarl. 'Have done, Fidele! these are friends.' The tone of her voice was not harsh; it had something in it humbled and disconsolate . . . A magpie perched on the top rung of her chair, not an uncomely ornament! and on her lap was placed a mutilated pair of bellows, the pipe was gone . . . they served as a succedaneum for a writing desk, on which lay displayed her hopes and treasure, the manuscript of her novel. Her ink-stand was a broken tea-cup, the pen worn to a stump; she had but one![40]

After two novels and a celebrated memoir, Charke took once more to the stage and died at her lodgings in the Haymarket in 1760, aged forty-seven.

Charke's *Narrative* of her extraordinary life brought fleeting fame but little fortune. Yet fame and fortune could be won by the author's pen. Perhaps, if fortune was sufficient, fame was more important. Certainly, authors produced some of the greatest celebrities of an age when birth and fame were coming to be valued in equal measure. Samuel Johnson, son of a struggling bookseller at Lichfield, too poor to sustain an education at Oxford, too ill-qualified to pursue a profession in the law or church, to which he'd have been gloriously suited, was eventually welcome in every drawing room in England, despite his shortcomings in dress and manners. He dined more than once at the invitation of the Duke and Duchess of Devonshire. A contemporary recalled the Duchess, 'then in the first bloom of youth' and one of the most celebrated women in the land, 'hanging on the sentences that fell from Johnson's lips, and contending for the nearest place to his chair'.[41]

And a generation earlier, around 1742, the young Joshua Reynolds was sent to a London auction room to buy a picture for his master, Thomas Hudson. The sale was 'uncommonly crowded'.

Reynolds was at the upper end of the room, near the auctioneer, when he perceived a considerable bustle at the farther part of the room, near the door, which he could not account for, and at first thought somebody had fainted, as the crowd and heat were so great. However he soon heard the name of 'Mr. Pope, Mr. Pope,' whispered from every mouth, for it was Mr. Pope himself who then entered the room. Immediately every person drew back to make a free passage for the distinguished poet, and all those on each side held out their hands for him to touch as he passed; Reynolds, although not in the front row, put out his hand also, under the arm of the person who stood before him, and Pope took hold of his hand, as he likewise did to all as he passed.[42]

Pope was misshapen, a son of City trade, a Catholic, a Jacobite, and it was his writings alone that had won him this secular beatification among the public, including (one imagines) those who had never read him. Small wonder that, for all the risk of meagre rewards, the world of words remained a beacon for the middling sort, many members of the genteel professions among them. And the world of the professions was penetrated by print to an uncommon degree throughout the century.

'Overburdened with Practitioners': Print and the Professions

I am sometimes very much troubled, when I reflect upon the three great professions of divinity, law and physic; how they are each of them overburdened with practitioners, and filled with multitudes of ingenious gentlemen that starve one another.[43]

That was in 1711 and the professions listed by Mr Spectator would remain overstocked for the rest of the century. To avoid starvation many sought refuge in print.

We shall meet the professors of divinity in a later chapter and they were indeed major contributors to the published word – if not literature – of the age. But it was the lawyers who provided the readiest supply of hackney writers of one kind or another in the eighteenth century. 'The Lawyers! Why those are our People,' says Henry Fielding's Scriblerus Secundus in 1731: 'there hath long been the strictest Union between *Grubstreet* and the Law . . .' Some hackney writing was commonly regarded as lawyers' perquisites, like theatre criticism, where they 'exerted their judicial capacity, and have given judgment, *i.e.* condemned without mercy'. But there was a close affinity between almost any aspect of print and the law, so intimately shackled in the close confines of Fleet Street and the Inns of Court. William Cowper, the poet, was called to the Bar but never practised; William Combe, a hackney writer too proud to put his name to a title page as demeaning to a gentleman, was a student at the Inner Temple but never became a lawyer; Boswell, himself counsel at both the Scottish and the English Bar, had his great biography of Johnson proofread by a corrector of the press who had also been a barrister but 'was now getting his livelihood by *certain* diligence'; John Britton, the London antiquary, spent years as an attorney's clerk in the 1790s; and so on. Nor was it all one-way traffic. Some professional writers sought financial security in the legal profession, if only as a part-time lawyer, to bolster their income. Henry Fielding turned to the law after stage licensing, becoming a member of the Middle Temple in 1737 and later combining advocacy and magistracy with novel writing. And Arthur Murphy was a playwright before being admitted to Lincoln's Inn in 1757; called to the Bar in 1762, he successfully prosecuted the case against perpetual copyright in 1774, while continuing to write for the stage and the booksellers.[44]

It is unclear how many lawyers of all sorts lived in London at any time in the century but the total seems likely to have been large. There were said to be 4,000 'attornies sworn in the two courts of *King's-bench* and *Common-pleas*' in 1731. To that can be added solicitors in Chancery, conveyancers and scriveners, or contract lawyers. Somewhere at the margins, but a numerous crew by all accounts, were the pettifoggers 'pretending' to the profession of an attorney, who 'will undertake any dirty work for reward'. All in all we might put the attorneys and their kin at some 5,000, a figure that seems unlikely to have shifted greatly across the century. Only some 1,700 attorneys, including a number of partnerships, are listed in the law directory for 1791, but that was the respectable end of a profession that struggled throughout the century to rescue its reputation from public opprobrium.[45]

An Act for the Better Regulation of Attorneys and Solicitors in 1729 required all formally practising in either branch to take an oath of honesty and to have served an apprenticeship as an articled clerk for five years. In order to keep the profession select, no attorney could have more than two clerks in articles. A decent grammar-school education was thought necessary for an apprenticeship in the law – Luke Hansard, for instance, had some Latin but not enough to be put to an apothecary or attorney, having to make do as a printer as third choice. The division between solicitors and attorneys was removed in 1749, when each was allowed to deal in the business of all courts, though demarcation disputes between scriveners and attorneys over who should draw up deeds and contracts rumbled on until 1760, when a special jury of City merchants ruled in the attorneys' favour. And shortly after the 1729 act took effect a Society of Gentlemen Practisers in the Courts of Law and Equity was formed in London, the forerunner of the Law Society; but its membership in the eighteenth century never exceeded 200 and it had no premises to itself, generally meeting in taverns about Fleet Street.[46]

Despite these efforts to regulate the attorneys they were not popular men: 'an Attorney and a Knave are very near become Terms synonimous', it was said in 1747. Inefficiency, encouraging expensive lawsuits, suborning evidence and defalcation of clients' funds were all common complaints. Many dabbled in moneylending and loved to pursue their debtors for the costs sticking to the debt. And it didn't help that the courts and legal processes of the time were so complex that no single lawyer could hope to master them all – a London guide of 1708 lists some fifty-six courts and administrations, some with many offshoots, from the Bails and Postea Office to the Philazers and Exigenters of the Common Pleas and Queen's Bench, each with their own dominions and eccentricities. Richard Campbell, the indispensable chronicler of work in London at mid-century, attributed the lawyers' dishonesty first to a culture of 'Cheating, Lewdness, and all manner of Debauchery' while serving an articleship and then to their great number: 'They are so numerous that there is not Bread for half of them', their very poverty 'an Enemy to Virtue'.[47]

The highest branch of the law, and one generally free from the taint of knavery, was the Bar. The number of barristers was much smaller, just 4,366 called in the century as a whole, and by no means all of these in practice. Around 400 were listed as counsel or special pleader in the law directory for 1791. Entry was through the universities or through the Inns of Court, where, in all reality, law studies were meagre, sometimes non-existent. Law students could be as uproarious as any apprentice: it was said that the Temple was for beaux, Lincoln's Inn for lawyers and Gray's Inn for whorers. Even so, it was considered a gentlemanly profession for those needing to earn a living and attracted the brightest sons of trade. Dudley Ryder of the Middle Temple was the son of a wealthy Cheapside linen draper. His nonconformity barred him from Oxford and Cambridge and after schooling at a dissenters' academy in his home village of Hackney he pursued his studies at Edinburgh and Leyden. He was Walpole's solicitor-general from 1733 and attorney-general from 1737, a consummate politician though a mazy lawyer in argument, and not always on the side of right. He ended his days as Chief Justice of the Court of King's Bench, dying in 1756 aged sixty-four, leaving a 'great estate' of £110,000 in cash and securities and £3,000 a year in land. And William Blackstone, the greatest academic lawyer of the age, was born in 1723, his father a Cheapside silk draper who died five months before his son's birth. Although much of his life was spent at Oxford, he returned to London and died less than a mile from his birthplace in 1780. Blackstone, of course, was no stranger to the world of print, publishing extensively from 1750, his *Commentaries on the Laws of England* (4 vols., 1765–9) one of the most successful books of the century. The ninth edition was ready for publication when he died, and the *Commentaries* and the lectures on which they were based were said to have made him some £15,000.[48]

The printed word, in one form or another, was no less indispensable to that other great secular profession of the time – medicine. As with law, the very education of a physician or surgeon, often at a university, always requiring limited facility in Latin and Greek, tempted some medical men to change tack and use their skills to write rather than practise. Oliver Goldsmith, born into an impecunious family of the middling sort in County Longford, north-west of Dublin, obtained after many travails a degree at Trinity and then pursued desultory medical studies at Edinburgh and on the Continent. With what seems to have been little knowledge and less application, he set up as a physician in Bankside, Southwark, around 1756, but quickly determined that print offered more profit than patients. Occasionally it did, but for the rest of his life he shifted uneasily between comfort and destitution, or something close to it. Tobias Smollett, from Dumbarton, studied surgery and medicine at Glasgow University, leaving without a degree and coming to London at eighteen when the family finances were too low to keep him in education. He brought with him a play on which he pinned great hope, but had to turn back to medicine. He passed the examination of the Company of Barbers and Surgeons in 1740 and became a naval surgeon, serving in the War of Jenkins' Ear. In 1743 he set up in Downing Street as a surgeon, but didn't thrive. Smollett never lost the urge to write and in a few years he abandoned the saw for the pen, helped by a marriage in 1747 to a Jamaican heiress whom he'd met while in uniform. There were numerous other medical men who turned authors. Benjamin Hoadly, the playwright, graduated MD from Cambridge in 1728. George Crabbe, the poet, was a struggling surgeon in Aldeburgh when he abandoned medicine for London and the literary life in 1780. And the *Grub-Street Journal* of 1730–37, espousing the *Dunciad* view of what was proper to literary men, was begun by two young doctors, John Martyn and Richard Russel.[49]

To this extent and more, the worlds of medicine and letters were very close. But there were other aspects. '"A young physician must publish himself into practice,"' William Combe, active in London hack work from about 1775, later told an acquaintance: '"I have helped more than one in this way,"' claiming to have written John Hunter's first book, *A Treatise on the Natural History of the Human Teeth* (1778). Certainly, the many celebrity physicians and anatomists of the age published widely, to spread their name among medical men and no doubt incidentally to draw rich clients on to their professional lists.[50]

It is no surprise that doctors should have attracted great public attention in the eighteenth century. We have already glimpsed the vulnerability of all ranks in London to sickness and premature death, in both childhood and the prime of life. Ineffective pain relief made many conditions hard to bear and the prospect of surgery a nightmare. The agents of infection were unknown and there was no effective control on their spread. No rules of basic hygiene, even in the sickroom, won general acceptance within the profession or among the public. In the face of so much ignorance, so much fear and pain, a well-educated and sophisticated man skilled, so far as the times would allow, in anatomy, pharmacology or surgical procedure, arriving with the recommendation of genteel clients and a reputation in the profession, seemed blessed with something close to divine authority.[51]

Of course, there were doctors and doctors. Physicians were top of the tree, though numerous sceptical voices questioned their right to perch there. The Royal College of Physicians was in Warwick Lane, a short step from Newgate Prison, which often provided corpses for anatomy lessons. At any one time there were only some fifty Fellows, all graduates of Oxford or Cambridge who had passed the College's examinations. Licentiates, just three or four admitted each year, also had to pass the exam but entered the profession by apprenticeship or hospital pupillage. A physician's art didn't extend to surgery, relying mainly on knowledge of anatomy and diagnosis, and treatment with bloodletting and medicines run up on prescription by apothecaries, oversight of whose drug supplies was formally in the hands of the Royal College. Even the physicians were a mixture, from 'the pert Coxcomb' with 'a Licence to kill as many as trust him with their Health' to those who acted with tact, kindness and skill. 'A large wig and a red coat, an air of great importance and sufficiency, with an absolute and authoritative tone of voice, are the ingredients which compound a physician here', a London guide claimed in 1768; a short sword and a gold-headed cane – one famously passed between five celebrated physicians as a talismanic heirloom – were also part of the garb in one or other of the coffee houses physicians used for consultations.[52]

Some became as rich as merchants and bankers. Dr Richard Mead, born in Stepney in 1673, was physician to Pope, had a rich practice of £5,000–6,000 a year in his prime and spent prodigally on book, coin and picture collections at his house in Great Ormond Street: Johnson said of him that he 'lived more in the broad sunshine of life than almost any man'. Hans Sloane, a near contemporary of Mead's, was another collector whose museum in Bloomsbury Place became one of the sights of London; it was bought for the nation on his death in 1753 and became a founding collection for the British Museum. Many physicians had reputations of being 'greedy after fees', as Samuel Richardson put it, but numerous others had a deep sense of charity, among whom John Coakley Lettsom, a Licentiate of the College, has already found mention here; he died worth less than £7,000 though, apart from his benevolence, he lived very well indeed. And in the hospitals – Mead was physician at St Thomas's for a time – the post of physician was no sinecure. At the London Hospital, for instance, John Lewis Petit died in office in 1780 after six years' service, aged about forty-four; John Gideon Caulet died after two years in 1784 'of a fever', aged about thirty-five; and William Austin 'died in office of a rapid febrile disease' in 1793, aged thirty-nine.[53]

Surgeons were a somewhat different breed. In general they were not university men but apprenticed to a practitioner and examined in anatomy and surgery at the College of Surgeons, which separated from the Barber-Surgeons in 1745. The surgeons were generally reputed practical and expert men, though in fashionable life a French surgeon was valued over an Englishman because of tuition in the busy Paris hospitals. 'The only honest and certain part of the art of healing is surgery,' wrote Richardson in 1749. Surgeons in general missed the great rewards of the fashionable physicians – in the hospitals the fee for even a major operation was just 6s 4d – but it could give a comfortable living if a man was able to bear the strain of it all. John Abernethy, brilliant surgeon of the London Hospital for many years, 'rarely undertook an operation without vomiting'. Patients were given brandy but not drugged and were generally tied or held down to the table. Experience could mean that the agony didn't last long: William Cheselden at St Thomas's could remove a bladder stone in less than thirty seconds, for instance. Advances in anatomical knowledge and surgical procedure made the surgeon more effective as the century advanced, with real progress in midwifery in particular. Their reputations even remained undamaged despite the treatment of venereal disease being entirely in their hands. In London it was said that 'three Parts in four of all the Surgeons in Town' depended on the clap for a living, though perhaps Richard Campbell exaggerated to make a moral point. He certainly drew one reasonable conclusion: 'if all knew as much as they pretend, they would not have half so many Patients'.[54]

The apothecaries, who had their own Company and College, were the third and most numerous branch of the healing profession. They were often at bitter odds with the physicians for trespassing on their terrain, giving advice and selling drugs direct to patients, taking over much cheap doctoring to the poor and the struggling middling sort. An attempt to heal these divisions was initiated in 1773 by John Coakley Lettsom. The Medical Society of London was formed of thirty each of physicians, apothecaries and surgeons, and proved of lasting usefulness by sharing knowledge of medical advances in the capital.[55]

The limited effectiveness of doctoring in eighteenth-century London gave much scope for quackery – indeed, there was unavoidably something of the quack in the greatest physician in the land. Fear and pain made people turn to those who made extravagant claims for their medicines. Sometimes those who made the medicines believed the claims they made, many having spent time in an apothecary's shop and knowing something of drugs. Sometimes, too, those who took the remedies felt better for them and recommended them to their friends.

For all these reasons the London quack was ubiquitous throughout the century. Quacks imitated the confidence of the physicians and advertised their coffee-house consulting hours in handbills 'distributed in the papers, and at the corner of almost every street in London'. They proclaimed themselves the poor man's doctor, avoiding the horrors of the hospitals, in witty monologues from a stage at the London fairs, weekly at Covent Garden and almost daily at Tower Hill and Moorfields. Some of these public aspects of quackery had diminished by the end of the century: the rise of the charitable dispensary brought the apothecaries' knowledge within the reach of the poor, and the redevelopment of Moorfields around 1790 removed the classic ground for the quacks' daily shows. But Dr James's Fever Powders, sold by John Newbery the bookseller and his heirs (even Horace Walpole swore by them), Evans's

Worming Powder (which Hester Thrale discovered were just James's Powders dyed red with 'Cinnabar'), Daffy's Elixir, Godbold's Vegetable Balsam for asthmas and Velno's Vegetable Syrup all had great followings and made their inventors fortunes.[56] There were quacks in all departments of healing: famous oculists who combined preposterous blindness cures with skill in operating (without anaesthetic) on cataracts; Dr Graham, with his notorious Temple of Health and Earth Bath, which offered a cure for sexual impotence and barrenness; and fashionable dentists like March, a Frenchman, who attended 'the very, *very* fine set' in the 1770s:

My poor sister Caroline, who had the finest set of teeth I ever beheld let herself be teized into going to him. He told her she would lose them soon because they touched each other, therefore must be separated by filing; after which operation they never recovered their former strength and firmness. I believe he was a complete Charlatan.[57]

It was the newspapers, of course, that daily brought the attention of the middling sort and above to the quacks' promises. Every disorder was apparently remedied, but the disorders claiming most attention were venereal. There were famous quacks in this area, like Dr John Misaubin, who featured in Hogarth's *Marriage-à-la-Mode* (1743) and whose pill was sold after his death by his widow, Martha.[58] And there were many less famous, some of whom held little back from the public gaze:

Richard Rock, M.L., In King's-Arms-Court, Ludgate-Hill, Cures all Degrees of the Venereal Distemper, whether of longstanding or recently acquired, by a regular and approved Method, in short Time, without the Knowledge of the most intimate Relation, and without the least Constraint or Obstruction in Business; whether the Symptoms be Internal or external; as for Instance Pains in the several Members, Pustules all over the Body, and in the Mouth, Nose and private Parts; spots like Measles on the Glands, tumefied Scrotum, Spreading Ulcers, Pains in the Joints, scaly Pustules of divers Sorts; Blood slimy and corrupt, nocturnal Pains, broad scaly Scabs, Heat of Urine, occasioned by a Gonorrhea, the Urinal Passage being ulcerated, phygenous Ulcers of the Jaws, Nose and Palate, and many other bad Symptoms, too tedious to enumerate in this Advertisement.[59]

Print, then, played a large part in all aspects of medical life in London. And physicians, lawyers, writers were frequently brought together by this shared medium, valuable nourishment as it proved to them all. Samuel Johnson's literary clubs, which he helped form at various points in his life, included lawyers and physicians as well as literary men, who were often outnumbered. Yet *the* 'Literary Club', founded in 1764 and meeting weekly at the Turk's Head Tavern, Gerrard Street, till 1783, was suggested by none of these but by the greatest portrait painter of the century – Sir Joshua Reynolds.[60]

'Painting from Beggars': The Business of Pictures

Art was one of the great industries of eighteenth-century London. The art took many forms and the artists came in many guises, but there is no doubt that the production and popular consumption of art increased greatly in the century following 1700. It was valued very highly. An appreciation of painting and sculpture was one of the most important benefits to be derived from the young Englishman's grand tour of continental Europe, that final polish to a university education – sometimes an alternative to it – that became a badge of leisured wealth in these years. To discern animation in a sculpture and the truthful expression of 'the passions', nature and character in a painting were proper 'amusements . . . of a man of parts'. And a cultured, appreciative and enlarged public for painting and sculpture was seen as one of the achievements of an age which in print had too often celebrated the vulgar.[61]

The connection between art and the Continent influenced greatly the character of art production in London in the first half of the century. In the early years especially it was largely a migrant trade. London was the Mecca of foreign artists, the only sculptors, painters and engravers credited among metropolitan art buyers with talent, certainly with genius; and the best education for an artist was to be had not in London but in Rome and Venice. History painting – generally scenes from the Bible or antiquity – was most valued among connoisseurs, but of the history painters just one of any note was English, Sir James Thornhill. English portrait painters were better regarded, but even then the leading artist was Sir Godfrey Kneller, German by birth and schooled by Rembrandt, who had come to London when he was twenty-nine in 1675. It has been said that at the opening of the eighteenth century 'the arts in this country had sunk almost to their lowest ebb'.[62] On the other hand the appetite for art in London, among those who had cultivated taste abroad and among the growing numbers of the middling sort keen to decorate their houses and commemorate their wealth and progeny, was sharper than ever before. Much of the first half of the century was spent in finding ways to nurture British talent to satisfy this rising popular clamour for pictures.

The need for an academy to school artists in London was recognised early on as an essential first step. The normal training in art for a talented youth was through apprenticeship to an acknowledged master, for which the apprentice paid by way of premium, just as in any other trade. It was a practice that held good through the century. Thomas Hudson, a renowned portrait painter of the 1730s to the 1750s, had been apprenticed to Jonathan Richardson at Holborn Row, Lincoln's Inn Fields, some time around 1718. Hudson was from Devon and in 1740 he took a fellow Devonian, Joshua Reynolds, to be an apprentice and lodger in his home at Great Queen Street, Lincoln's Inn Fields; Reynolds in turn had John Northcote, yet another Devon boy, as a pupil and assistant but with no premium – Northcote's family had no money to spare – in his Leicester Fields home in 1771. The apprenticeship system had much in its favour but in reality no practising artist had time or resources to acquaint a pupil with all the various skills of drawing and painting.[63]

John Evelyn, the diarist, had suggested a London academy in 1662. But the first attempt to establish one came nearly fifty years later, in 1711. It was an initiative led by foreigners, four of the six founders a German (Kneller), a Swede, an Italian and a Frenchman, with Richardson and Thornhill representing the natives. The academy was set up in rooms in a run-down mansion in Great Queen Street. A guinea subscription paid for a season's membership and allowed models to be hired for figure drawing. At this time the streets around Lincoln's Inn Fields were very much an artists' district, but they were even then beginning to lose their appeal as artists followed the westward drift of fashion. So when this first academy dissolved in factions and splits, its new incarnation appeared in St Martin's Lane, just west of Covent Garden. Its full title was sometimes given as the Academy for the Improvement of Painters and Sculptors by Drawing from the Naked and its founders were French and Dutch. But among the first students in October 1720 who paid their fee of 2 guineas was the greatest English artist of the first half of the century, the single-handed moving force behind the creation of a new English school in art. He was William Hogarth.[64]

Hogarth was a Londoner, born in Bartholomew Close, Smithfield, in 1697, his father a struggling schoolmaster originally from the Lake District who tried unsuccessfully to make a living by writing Latin and Greek textbooks. His father's failures – for a time he was confined in the Fleet Prison for debt – frustrated any ambition of a university education, and Hogarth was apprenticed to a silver engraver in Cranbourne Street, Leicester Fields. A genius for drawing took him to St Martin's Lane while pursuing a livelihood as a designer and engraver of trade cards, tickets and invitations, just beginning to speculate in prints satirising the follies of London life. Only five feet tall – all bristle – the disappointments and anxieties of his early years left him with an intolerance of authority and a fierce determination to make an unaided way in the world. Hogarth resented the influence of foreigners in London art and the fawning and sometimes ignorant praise lavished on them by 'men of taste'. But most important of all he had an astonishing facility that showed in portraiture, history painting and engraving. There was no more versatile artist than Hogarth in eighteenth-century London. And no artist relied more on London and the Londoner for his inspiration. Posterity has come to see much of eighteenth-century London through Hogarth's eyes, and we have the compliments of contemporaries to certify the accuracy of his extraordinary vision.[65]

Besides attending the Academy at St Martin's Lane, Hogarth studied at the free drawing school that Sir James Thornhill opened behind his house on the north side of Covent Garden Piazza in 1724. Five years later, and not entirely it seems in line with Thornhill's wishes, Hogarth married his daughter, possibly after an elopement. Thornhill died in 1734, leaving his drawing school fitments to Hogarth. A year later, Hogarth used them to establish a new St Martin's Lane Academy after the old foundered in a financial scandal, the treasurer absconding with the subscriptions.[66]

By then, 1735, Hogarth was already a celebrity. The first of his great morality series, *A Harlot's Progress*, a complex and allusive London narrative in six pictures, was completed in 1732 and immediately engraved and published. The prints proved hugely popular. They were followed by *A Rake's Progress*, publication of the eight engravings delayed till 1735 so that copyright could be secured to the artist under a new law which Hogarth himself had initiated through friends in Parliament.[67]

From the 1730s Hogarth's popularity added a new dimension to the business of pictures in London that further fuelled the thirst for art and opportunities for artists. It was a thirst that spawned new schools – George Michael Moser, a brilliant gold-chaser originally from Germany, opened a drawing school in Salisbury Court, Fleet Street, for instance, and Hubert-François Gravelot, the French engraver, one in James Street, Covent Garden. It continued to attract to London foreign artists and others from all over Britain to take advantage of the great popular demand there for portraits and decorative work. It began to address the lack of spaces in London for artists to show their work, the auction rooms supplemented by permanent exhibitions of art at the Foundling Hospital from the 1740s. And it encouraged the artists to establish their own institutions to value and expand the place of art and the role of the artist in the nation: the Society of Arts was established by William Shipley, a drawing master and painter, in 1754, eventually having premises built in the Adelphi in 1774; a Society of Artists of Great Britain was founded at the Turk's Head Tavern in 1762 and incorporated by royal charter three years later; a rival Free Society of Artists was formed about 1765; and the Royal Academy was founded in 1768, Sir William Chambers, the architect, its main mover and Sir Joshua Reynolds its first president. One or more exhibitions of artists' work were held annually in London from 1760. William Hogarth, the man who in so many ways had breathed new life into English art and who revolutionised the London art world, died in his house in Leicester Fields in October 1764.[68]

By then there were many ways indeed to make a living from pictures in London. Artists responded to the needs of a marketplace in which tastes were always shifting; and some of those tastes were created by the artists themselves.

Portrait painting made up by far the largest part of the art market in London. Demand for it grew as the numbers and disposable income of the middling sort grew. It was a demand that outstripped easy supply and in the early years the most fashionable painters turned to division of labour on the workshop model to fulfil their commissions. Sir Godfrey Kneller spent little time with his sitters, taking the face back to his studio and assigning hat, wig, coat, ruffles and so on to one or more assistants.[69] 'Drapery-painting' became a sub-genre of the portraitist's art and there were many specialists, the painting travelling from the limner's or face painter's studio to the drapery painter's and back again.

The most celebrated drapery painter of the century was Joseph van Aken, from Antwerp, who had his studio at King Street, Seven Dials, and who seems to have painted for most of the celebrated portraitists of his day. Even country painters would send van Aken cloths on which a whole family's faces had been painted for him to supply costumes and background as he saw fit. Allan Ramsay, the famous Scottish painter who settled in London in 1738, used van Aken and so did Hudson, Reynolds's master, then considered 'the greatest painter in England'. Northcote later related what Reynolds must have told him, perhaps with some exaggeration in the telling:

after having painted the head, Hudson's genius failed him, and he was obliged to apply to one Vanhaaken to put it on the shoulders and to finish the drapery, of both which he was himself totally incapable. Unluckily Vanhaaken died, and for a time Hudson was driven almost to despair, and feared he must have quitted his lucrative employment: he was, however, fortunate enough to meet with another drapery-painter, named Roth, who, though not so expert as the former, was yet sufficiently qualified to carry on the manufactory.[70]

Not all portrait painters used drapery men. Joseph Highmore of Holborn Row, Lincoln's Inn Fields, a contemporary of Hudson, didn't and nor did Hogarth. Perhaps his business in portraits was insufficiently extensive to call for it or perhaps his pride and independence couldn't tolerate it. And on van Aken's death in 1749 he captured the portraitists at the Dutchman's funeral, lamenting both his passing and their own future dissolution.[71]

There were numerous other collaborations. Equestrian portraits often involved a figure painter and a horse painter; a specialist dog painter might be employed for a family 'conversation-piece' or a huntsman's portrait; pictures of London pleasure grounds might employ an architectural painter skilled in perspective and another whose ability was in figures; when Philip James de Loutherbourg was commissioned to paint the siege of Valenciennes around 1794 he took with him James Gillray to capture the faces of officers to be commemorated; and so on.[72]

Collaboration was one reason for artists to cluster their studios in certain districts of the town. In general these were close to fashionable clients and as fashion moved west the artists moved with it. There were notable clusters in and around Covent Garden Piazza throughout the century – at least ten artists in the Piazza in the

1760s, for instance; another round Leicester Fields, where both Hogarth and Reynolds overlapped from 1760 to 1764; and in between lay St Martin's Lane with its Academy, and numerous artists and elegant cabinetmakers. Some houses passed from artist to artist, 104 St Martin's Lane home to Sir James Thornhill, John van Nost (a sculptor), Francis Hayman and Joshua Reynolds. And all these districts were graced by convenient artists' haunts for dining, drinking and gossip: Old Slaughter's Coffee House in St Martin's Lane, near Hogarth's Academy, and the Turk's Head Tavern, first in Greek Street but more famously when it moved to Gerrard Street, just north of Leicester Fields. From around 1770 another strong cluster arose north of Oxford Street and west of Tottenham Court Road, especially in Newman Street, Marylebone.[73]

The old-fashioned collaborative work in portrait painting had led to a great deal of sameness and formality in drapery and posture, and the new generation of artists that followed Hudson rejected the drapery painter as an enemy of truthfulness and nature. It was Joshua Reynolds who most famously developed this new informal feeling in English portraiture. His genius found increasing respect among a fashionable and aristocratic market. By June 1753 his sitters included the Duke and Duchess of Devonshire, Henry Fox, Admiral Keppel and the Duke of Grafton among others, and 'I am told that the Prince of Whales intends to come and see my Pictures.' Soon the volume of work required even Reynolds to seek some assistance with drapery work, sometimes putting pictures out but often using assistants within his own studio.

Giuseppe Marchi, a Roman whom Reynolds first took as a pupil, was later paid about £100 a year, with board and lodging, for this important work. By the 1750s Reynolds was charging the same as Hudson, 12 guineas for a head and 48 for a full length, the sitter paying half on commission. As his fame enlarged so did his prices: a head in the 1760s was 35 guineas and 50 in 1779; a full length rose from 150 to 200 guineas around the same time. Thomas Gainsborough, another portraitist of genius, in London at Schomberg House, Pall Mall, from 1774, began charging 160 guineas for a full length from 1787, just a year before his death.[74]

Reynolds and Gainsborough were exceptional in every way. But other artists could thrive in London, too, and in a variety of forms. History painters were commissioned to decorate important public buildings – Sir James Thornhill painted the great hall of the Royal Naval Hospital at Greenwich (1708–17) and the dome of St Paul's (1715–20); Hogarth's *The Pool of Bethesda* (1734–6) was painted for the staircase at St Bartholomew's Hospital; and at Hogarth's instigation the rotunda and boxes at Vauxhall Gardens were decorated in history scenes, many by Francis Hayman. Private commissions for histories and landscapes decorated the walls of many London mansions. But landscapes were popular too among the middling sort as decorations for walls, chimney pieces and door panels. Around 1714 Joseph Highmore came across a Dutch painter who had hired a long attic near Drury Lane to paint landscapes on canvas the length of the room. From large pans of paint he made first the skies in blues and 'what he called "cloud colour"', 'then the middle portions, and finally the foregrounds'. The lengths were then cut and '"sold by parcels"'. He and his assistants could make each day some thirty landscapes selling at 40 or 50s apiece, and they were not, thought Highmore, '"altogether devoid of merit, for he had something like genius and taste . . ."'[75]

Some painters specialised in copying old masters, for which there was a popular market at all prices. Some, like de Loutherbourg, specialised in scenery painting at the theatres and for private theatricals. Some specialised in still life, one Thomas Keyse making a name as a 'beef and mutton painter'. Some painted coaches and signs, and we met the numerous painters of Bow and Chelsea china in an earlier chapter. The work of miniature painters was very popular, among whom the celebrated Jeremiah Meyer was Jewish, his religion not appearing to hold him back. Some artists used other materials than pencil and paint. Beautiful Mrs Worlidge made landscapes with her needle in silk and wool. Mary Knowles, another beauty, made portraits in needlework for which Queen Charlotte once made her a present of £800. The miniature painter Anne Louisa Lane and her sister Mary made many hair pictures, including seascapes and a 'Portrait of a Nobleman worked with a needle in his own hair', in the 1770s. The American Mrs Patience Wright made models in wax and the famous Mrs Salmon made caricature wax figures about six inches high. Isaac Gosset's wax composition hardened like ivory and sold for 4 guineas a portrait, with copies of royal sitters for the public at a guinea each – but they were pirated in fakes made of plaster of Paris and sold everywhere for pennies. Silhouettists took portraits with a candle lantern that threw an outline on paper and used a device to reduce it so that it could be traced and cut out in black card – one Joliffe reputedly had the whole of White's

Club sitting for him in 1758. James 'Athenian' Stuart made a living painting fans at a factory in the Strand when he was a boy in the 1720s. And so on.[76]

Sculptors also made a living in London and not just from chiselling stone, an art still often in the hands of foreign genius through the century. Making figure and other models from plaster casts was an extensive London industry. John Flaxman the Elder had studios at the Golden Head, New Street, Covent Garden, and later at 420 Strand. He employed numerous workmen who frequented Simon Place's King's Arms. They 'dined in a large box which had a small fire in it' and brought 'prepared clay with them and with bits of stick model one anothers heads, generally caricaturing some feature, they also modelled my father and mother and some other persons'. Journeymen like this could earn 20–25s a week.[77]

John Flaxman the Younger made figures in relief for Wedgwood's pottery factory and later carved wonderful monumental sculpture. John Bacon modelled in terracotta and had a large workshop in Newman Street, employing some twenty assistants. He was chief designer at Eleanor Coade's artificial stone manufactory in Lambeth and created the statue of Samuel Johnson in St Paul's Cathedral. William Wilton made papier-mâché and plaster ornaments at workshops in Hedge Lane, Charing Cross, and Edward Street, Cavendish Square. He kept 'hundreds of people, including children . . . for several years constantly employed'. His son Joseph became a well-known London sculptor who made money while in Italy casting copies of antique statues for English collectors. Indeed, London's 'virtuosi' employed a small army of artists to copy or find originals for their collections: that of Charles Townley in Park Street (now Queen Anne's Gate), Westminster, became one of the sights of London, for the quality at least.

Many artists who couldn't readily sell their wares made a living by teaching. Some taught pupils privately in their own homes – a royal patron provided gold-plated cachet – or opened schools. Teachers made much of the varied career opportunities in art open to their pupils. William Shipley had a drawing school at Craig's Court, Charing Cross, and later at Castle Court, Strand. In 1757 he advertised his

endeavour to introduce Boys and Girls of Genius to Masters and Mistresses in such Manufactures as require Fancy and Ornament, and for which the Knowledge of Drawing is absolutely Necessary; Masters or Mistresses who want Boys or Girls well qualified for such manufactures may frequently meet with them at this School . . . A genteel Apartment is provided for the reception of Young Ladies of Fashion, who are attended every day from Eleven to one.[78]

The careful attention to gender in Shipley's advertisement is one further reminder of the importance of women in London's business of pictures, especially in the second half of the century. The celebrated Swiss 'paintress' Angelica Kauffman was said to have made some £14,000 from portraits and historical paintings over her sixteen years in London from 1766 to 1782; the City portraitist Mary Grace, of Shorter's Court, Throgmorton Street, apparently earned £20,000 from her work; Mary Black was a skilled copyist of old masters and teacher of pastel painting to the royal family and the quality; and Caroline Watson, engraver to Queen Charlotte, engraved Sir Joshua Reynolds's last great self-portrait for the printsellers. Kauffman was a member of the Royal Academy and so was Mary Moser, 'the famous Painter of flowers', recognition of something approaching equality of the sexes that marked both print and pictures during these years; and the Society of Artists gave honorary membership to a number of other women painters.[79]

The business of pictures in London encompassed more than artists. The painters' neighbourhoods of St Martin's Lane, Covent Garden, Leicester Fields and Newman Street attracted the colourmen, suppliers of all types of paint, painting 'cloths', pencils (as brushes were also commonly known) and drawing materials. Oil paints were sold 'tied up like little puddings, in pieces of bladder', to be pricked and squeezed as the artist required and sealed again with a tack. Among the best-known colourmen were James Newman in Gerrard Street, near the Turk's Head; Thomas and William Reeves of Holborn Bridge who invented 'soluble cakes' for watercolourists; and Dorothy Mercier at the Golden Ball, Windmill Street, Golden Square, who around 1760

Sells Flower Pieces in Water Colours, Painted by her self, from the Life. And Fanns for Ladies, in a New & Elegant Manner. Also all sorts of Shop Books, Finest Writing Paper Both Gilt & plain, in all sizes. English, Dutch, & French Drawing Paper, Abortive Vellum for Drawing, Writing Vellum, the Silk Paper for Drawing with Different Sizes of Mesage Paper, & Mesage Cards. Fine Black, Brown, and Blue India Ink.[80]

Others, too, had reason to be grateful to the thriving artists' communities in these years. An unknown number of anonymous Londoners appeared in artists' work, sometimes in the most famous paintings and sculptures of the age. We have already seen how Londoners populated Hogarth's street scenes, the antiquarian prints of John Thomas Smith and the 'London Cries' of Sandby and others. And sometimes they could make a little money from the business. James Dyer, a trooper in the Horse Guards, was one of the four male nude models at the Royal Academy, paid a 5s weekly retainer and 1s a night's sitting – nude female models earned half a guinea for a sitting of two or three hours. Dyer was later exclusively employed as a model by Benjamin West, the great American history painter, at his studio in Newman Street. George White, a well-built London paviour originally from Yorkshire, was a favourite model of Reynolds, who was also '"for ever painting from beggars"'; and in his *Nativity* of 1779 he modelled boys and girls from the London streets. His sister Frances, also a painter, took her infants from the life, '"some beggar woman's child which is laid naked on a pillow in the mother's arms"'. Joseph Nollekens, the sculptor, hired 'abandoned women' to sit for his Venuses and the flowing locks of an Irish beggar for his bust of Johnson. And a monument by Louis François Roubiliac to Sir Peter Warren in Westminster Abbey incorporated a Hercules whose legs 'were copied from a chairman's and the arms from those of a waterman'.[81]

There were other ways in which the world of art reached the notice of ordinary Londoners, even the poorer sort, in these years. Some 20,000 people paid 1s each to view John Singleton Copley's *Death of Chatham* in 1781, and free annual academy exhibitions were so mobbed by large and disorderly crowds that a charge for admission was eventually made to keep the poorest out. But no one could stop crowds gathering at printshop windows and it was the extensive industry of printmaking in London that properly brought art to a mass audience.[82]

It took some time to develop. Before the 1740s many prints were imported, the best considered to be French. When Hogarth, proud Englishman though he was, wanted engravers for *Marriage-à-la-Mode* in 1744 he gave the job to two Frenchmen living in London and brought over Simon François Ravenet from Paris. There were noted printsellers like Thomas Bowles and his successors in St Paul's Churchyard and John Overton near Newgate, but their best wares were foreign and their English prints often cheap and bad copies of masters like Hogarth – it was these citizen pirates that 'Hogarth's Act' was aimed at. The great City printsellers supplied a ready market for glazed prints to be hung in houses of the middling sort – Hogarth's own pictures showing how cluttered were contemporary walls at the time; fine art prints for collectors tended to be the province of sellers at the west end of the town, again mostly imported wares.[83]

It was the printseller John Boydell of Cheapside who at last provided encouragement to English engravers by commissioning prints of the portraits, landscapes and histories that were becoming such a feature of London life in the second half of the century in particular. Originally from Shropshire, he was led by a love of drawing at the late age of twenty to seek an apprenticeship with an engraver at Holborn in 1741. From selling prints of his own landscapes he amassed £150, with which in 1751 he took his first shop. By importing prints – he taught himself French to ease the trade – by buying up others' engraved plates, by commissioning artists to paint pictures and having the best engravers make prints of them, he became the largest printseller in England, probably in Europe. The public taste in prints was frequently refreshed by the use of various technologies, mezzotint from the 1760s, aquatint from the 1770s and stipple in the 1780s, and Boydell's wealth became such that he was elected alderman for the Ward of Cheap from 1782 and Lord Mayor in 1790–91. The alderman's showroom at 90 Cheapside, some seventy feet long, was one of the sights of the capital; and so was his Shakespeare Gallery in Pall Mall, built in 1789 to house paintings of scenes from the plays, commissioned by Boydell. Sophie von la Roche described the large shop windows at Cheapside and the wide pavements that 'enable crowds of people to stop and inspect the new exhibits'. Boydell continued to prosper until the dislocations of the French Revolutionary War in the 1790s destroyed his lucrative European export trade.[84]

By then a distinctive new market had grown up side by side with the fine art trade. The great age of caricature had origins in the 1720s and was stimulated further by the moral satires of Hogarth, who denied that he was a caricaturist while exploiting the art of exaggeration in his more comic studies. But from the 1760s on, four decades of political turbulence would create an extraordinary flourishing of the satirical caricature. It reached its golden age with James Gillray, Thomas Rowlandson and others, from around 1780 till beyond the end of the century. Gillray was a political satirist of genius and Rowlandson the comic observer of all about him in the London streets. Posterity has come to view late-eighteenth-century London through their joyously anarchic vision.

It was a vision that could be had for 6d plain and 1s coloured, and caricatures were found pinned or stuck to the walls of cheap lodgings and workshops and backstreet taverns throughout London. In the 1790s folios of caricatures could be hired out by the evening and printshops like William Holland's at 50 Oxford Street advertised '"the Largest Collection of Humorous Prints in Europe. Admittance 1 Shill^g"'. The huge popularity of caricature was closely associated with a rise in printshop numbers, and the printsellers were closely associated with the artists who provided their profits. Rowlandson lived for a short time in the 1790s over Mrs Lay's printshop in Pall Mall, near Carlton House. Gillray lived over Hannah Humphrey's shop at 18 Old Bond Street from 1793, moving with her to 27 St James's Street in 1798 and dying there in 1815. In 1785 there were some twenty-five major printsellers in London, of whom eleven were in the City, thirteen in Westminster and one in Holborn. And the appetite for prints was further fostered by growing numbers of illustrated books and magazines, with glorious coloured prints in the *Botanical Magazine* from 1787 and coloured fashion plates in the *Lady's Monthly Museum* from 1790.[85]

It all made work for artists and for a growing army of engravers. As early as 1772 Horace Walpole had complained of the 'exorbitant imposition' of London engravers' charges that deterred him from commissioning further plates for his private press. For a youth talented in drawing engraving offered many rewards, journeymen of the highest skill earning 3 guineas a week in a trade that demanded patience and great accuracy using a variety of techniques. A master engraver could profit greatly. Sometimes the profits were not always licit. William Ryland, engraver to George III and master of 'a very capital printshop in Cornhill', forged bills of exchange when he overreached himself in trade. The young William Blake was nearly apprenticed to him but presciently begged his father to take him away: 'Father, I do not like the man's face: *it looks as though he will live to be hanged.*' He would be, twelve years later in 1783. His widow, though, lived on and prospered as a printseller in Oxford Street and later New Bond Street, her late husband's productions 'meeting with an extensive sale'.[86]

This passion for pictures was an extraordinary feature of London life in the eighteenth century. It gave employment to some thousands of artists and printmakers and associated tradesmen. It showed itself in every domestic interior of the middling sort and above. It was plain for all to see in the crowds at 90 Cheapside and to hear in the gusts of laughter outside Mrs Humphrey's window. Pictures also provided some of the great public spectacles of London life in the annual exhibitions of the Royal Academy and the Incorporated Society of Artists. Among the throngs of spectators of the quality and many ranks below were those, never few in number, who had come more to be seen than to see. And that was true for London's varied public pleasures in general.

PART FOUR

CULTURE

Teresa Cornelys

VIII

TERESA CORNELYS'S LONDON – PUBLIC PLEASURES

'High Lords, Deep Statesmen, Dutchesses and Whores': Carlisle House

TERESA Cornelys was a cultural entrepreneur of whimsical genius and tireless energy. She held the leading strings of London's public pleasures in the 1760s and 1770s, when luxury and show heeded no bounds. She was 'the Queen of Extravagance', the 'reigning Empress of the "vast regions of state and magnificence" in Soho', the 'celebrated Mrs Cornelys' whose entertainments were lauded by contemporaries and recalled with wonder a generation or more after her heyday. But public gratitude for the pleasures she provided proved shallow and Mrs Cornelys would die in penury and obscurity before the century was out.[1]

She was born Teresa Imer in Venice, probably in 1723, her father an actor and theatre manager. She took to the stage as an opera singer but she was a beautiful girl and her looks and charm suggested easier means of making her way in the world. From 1740 to 1759 she combined a stage career, singing at opera houses in many Italian cities, in Denmark, Germany and Holland, while moving as mistress from one rich keeper to another. She married an Italian dancer in the mid-1740s and bore a son by him, and she had a daughter with the Margrave of Bayreuth, but she took the name of Cornelys from a Dutch merchant who was her lover in the late 1750s. A near contemporary of Giacomo Casanova's, their cosmopolitan rambles often intertwined, a first liaison apparently dating from Teresa's early singing years in Venice. Casanova accepted paternity of one of her children, a daughter Sophie, who accompanied her mother to England.[2]

In October 1759 Teresa Cornelys arrived in London. An English musician playing in Rotterdam, an adventurer calling himself John Freeman or Fermor, suggested to her the many opportunities to make a living by music there. He helped her produce a series of concerts at the Little Theatre in the Haymarket. And it was Fermor apparently who suggested they might develop a programme of fashionable concerts and assemblies. Cornelys was encouraged in the venture by Elizabeth Chudleigh, notorious for appearing naked beneath a diaphanous night-gown at a Ranelagh Gardens masquerade in 1749, and by other ladies of fashion a little more respectable. In April 1760 Mrs Cornelys took the lease of a Restoration mansion on the east side of Soho Square. She was not yet fluent in English and Fermor acted as her agent in the purchase.[3]

Carlisle House faced Soho Square, with a long garden and outbuild-ings stretching down Sutton Street (now Row). The first season's successes encouraged Cornelys in an extravagantly bold scheme of expansion, with a new extension along Sutton Street for a concert hall, ballroom and supper rooms of great magnificence. Further additions were made in future years for which Thomas Chippendale was one of the contractors, an indication of the quality of the work. This new Carlisle House offered a bewildering variety of spaces, giving great scope to Mrs Cornelys's fervid imagination. There were 'Tea-rooms', a 'Great Gallery' for '*Contre Dances*', the Bridge Room 'for dancing Cotillons', the Pavilion 'ceiled with looking glasses' and 'laid out [in February 1776] in a delightful Garden' with 'the choicest Flowers . . . and bordered with a Thicket of the most curious Shrubs'; the Supper Rooms included one great room with 'an elegant Walk, bordered with two regular green Hedges' and on either side a 'curious Plat-form' with round supper tables, 'each of which is enriched with Trees'; and there were the Star Room, the Stage Room and the Chinese Room 'decorated, as to afford the most enchanting *Coup d'oeil*'. When Casanova caught up with Mrs Cornelys in June 1763 she was both celebrated and rich, reputed to keep thirty-three servants, two secretaries, six horses and a country house. She employed 'a *writing puffer*' at 'a considerable salary' to keep her name constantly aglow in the newspapers. And there must have been a host of hirelings to attend and cater for the grand entertainments that made her famous and set fashionable London in a blaze.[4]

Staple fare at Carlisle House was the masked ball, or masquerade.

There had been masquerades in London for some fifty years before 1760. The first great age of masquerades was brought to the capital around 1711 and pursued with vigour by Count Johann Heidegger four or five years later. Heidegger was Swiss, primarily an opera impresario, but masquerades proved a fashionable and profitable venture, taking full advantage of the splendour of the Opera House, or King's Theatre, in the Haymarket. They were held right through the 1720s and 1730s. But by the late 1740s masquerades had fallen out of fashion, more through vitiation of taste it seems than from the almost constant attack in press and pulpit (let alone Hogarth's vigorous pencil) on their luxuriousness, their licentiousness and their foreign origins.[5]

Certainly the masquerade was a controversial entertainment. But then so were most, perhaps all, of London's public pleasures. Metropolitan society was deeply hierarchical – in theory. The nobility and the gentry, 'the quality' so called, lived private lives modelled on an exclusivity deriving first from birth and second from wealth. Yet even privately this was a lie, as the frequent intermarriages between impoverished titles and heavily capitalised citizens eloquently testified. When nobility and gentry moved outside private bounds to enjoy themselves in the public realm, then hierarchy was compromised from the very first step. They found their pleasures shared with the great commingling of ranks who bought their entertainment just as they did any other commodity in any other market. The public pleasures of London, then, were sites of turbulence, as rank jostled rank and deference wrestled mischief, all with many unintended consequences.

The masquerade was often designed as a truly exclusive public entertainment – restricted nominally to 'subscribers' who bought tickets in advance – but even then it too proved subversive of hierarchy and order. The mask self-consciously satirised a society based so very much on appearances. It could turn a rake into a bishop, a kept woman into a nun, a man into a woman. It was a place of great sexual danger for virtuous wife and maid alike, the scene of downfall in novels throughout the century: '"May I be damned, madam,"' cries Henry Fielding's Booth, '"if my wife shall go thither"', when Amelia's landlady provides two tickets for a masquerade.[6] It encouraged licence for tongues to seduce and hands to roam. The promiscuous mingling of people who, moralists thought, should keep their distance from one another never ceased to generate anxiety, often disguised (another mask) as contempt:

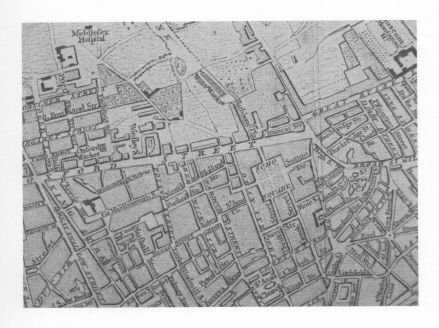

Soho, 1761

> And now, in crowds, press'd through the yielding doors,
> High Lords, deep Statesmen, Dutchesses, and Whores;
> All ranks and stations, Publicans and Peers,
> Grooms, Lawyers, Fiddlers, Bawds, and Auctioneers;
> Prudes and Coquettes, the Ugly and the Fair,
> The Pert, the Prim, the Dull, the Debonair;
> The Weak, the Strong, the Humble and the Proud,
> All help'd to form the motley, mingled Crowd.[7]

The metropolitan hierarchy, then, proved permeable at every level, and permeability was lubricated by foreign influence. We have already seen the high regard for continental taste that encouraged European servants, craftsmen and artists to settle in London, foreign painters and sculptors prominent among them. The cachet of the masquerade in the 1720s and 1730s owed much to its encouragement by a foreign royal family and continental entrepreneurs. Mrs Cornelys found her exotic background in the opera house and the bedroom more help than hindrance when, from the early 1760s, she took the *ton* by storm.

Her first successes were marked by that exclusivity so valued by her subscribers but so difficult for the businesswoman to sustain at a profit. She sold 450 tickets through a committee of ladies for a ball in January 1764 in honour of the Princess Augusta and her new husband, the Duke of Brunswick. 'All the beauties in town were there, that is, of rank, for there was no bad company.' But if profit were to be made there had to be some leavening of rank along the lines of 'Publicans and Peers', 'Dutchesses and Whores'. For later events non-subscribers would be admitted on the night for 2 guineas, reduced to 26s or less when that price proved too high; occasionally she gave balls for '"the upper servants of persons of fashion"', and others were marked by 'great numbers of *filles de joye* and Votaries to Venus'.[8]

Even so, Mrs Cornelys's masquerades could be sensational events, as here, late in her heyday, on Monday 26 February 1770, when 'near 800 of the Nobility and Gentry' attended a masked ball at Carlisle House:

Soho Square and the adjacent streets were lined with thousands of people, whose curiosity led them to get a sight of the persons going to the masquerade, nor was any coach or chair suffered to pass unreviewed, the windows being obliged to be let down, and lights held up to display the figures to more

advantage. At nine o'clock the doors of the house were opened, and from that
time, for about three or four hours, the company continued to pour into the
assembly . . . The richness and brilliancy of the dresses was almost beyond
imagination; nor did any assembly ever exhibit a collection of more elegant
and beautiful female figures . . . Some of the most remarkable figures were, a
Highlander (Mr R. Conway.) A double man, half Miller, half Chimney-Sweeper
(Sir R. Phillips.) A political Bedlamite, ran mad for Wilkes and Liberty, and
No. 45. A figure of Adam in flesh-coloured silk, with an apron of fig-leaves.
A Druid (Sir W. W. Wynne.) A figure of Somebody. A figure of Nobody. A
Running-Footman, very richly dressed with a cap set with diamonds, and the
words, 'Tuesday night's club', in the front (the Earl of Carlisle.) His Royal
Highness the D. of Gloucester in the old English habit, with a star on the
cloak. Midas (Mr James the Painter.) Miss Moncton, daughter to Ld. Galway,
appeared in the character of an Indian Sultana, in a robe of cloth of gold, and
a rich veil. The seams of her habit were embroidered with precious stones, and
she had a magnificent cluster of diamonds on her head; the jewels she wore
were valued at 30,000l. . . .

About two o'clock the company began to depart, in effecting which there
was much difficulty, and at six in the morning, three or four hundred remained
in the rooms . . . Most of the carriages that came to the masquerade were
chalked by the populace with 'Wilkes and Liberty'.[9]

There is other evidence that this extravagant flaunting of wealth and
hubris at masquerades provoked resentment in the poorer sort of people.
'An Independent Whig' expressed in 1774 his disgust at 'the Exactors'
of high taxes 'revelling at Mrs. Cornelys's Masquerade, at the Expence
of more Money for one Evening's Amusement, than the wretched hard-
working Man . . . can earn by half a Year's severe Labour'. And two
years later the innovation of a summer masquerade at Carlisle House
provoked 'the mob' to think 'they had a right to take extraordinary
liberties with the Masks as they went to their coaches in the morning;
to this we ascribe the insolent licence of their tongues; such things were
said by the "greasy rogues in rags", as would have shocked the most
profligate.'[10]

There were other offerings too at Carlisle House. Mrs Cornelys never
forgot the reason she first came to London and she tried hard to make
Soho Square a more serious place for London's public pleasures in the
way of musical concerts. Orchestral music was a passion among
Londoners but it was a minority passion encouraged most vociferously

by the nobility and gentry. Throughout the century music was an art sustained by foreign performers, who made up many of the composers and the bulk of soloists, orchestral principals and music teachers in London. Unlike painting, which saw the birth of an English school in this century, the best musicians in London were most frequently foreigners, as dominating in the 1790s as they had been in the days of Queen Anne.[11]

Opera was the most fashionable (and generally most foreign) of musical entertainments, as we'll see in a moment. For concert performances London was less well served, at least in the early years. Hickford's Rooms in James Street, Haymarket, from 1697 and moving to Brewer Street in 1738, was the most distinguished venue: the nine-year-old Wolfgang Mozart and his sister Nannerl famously gave a recital there in May 1765. There was also a concert room in York Buildings, off the Strand, from about 1680, taken on as a commercial speculation by Richard Steele from 1713, but it seated only 200. A number of other private ventures rose and fell, like 'Mr Coignand's Great Room, Cross Street, near the Globe Tavern, Hatton Garden', offering 'A Compleat Consort of Musick, Vocal and Instrumental' in 1719; and most remarkably the attic room over a coal shed in Clerkenwell, where Thomas Britton, the 'Musical Small-Coal Man', organised concerts for those brave enough to negotiate the ladder-like external staircase and the discomforts of a ceiling so low a tall man couldn't stand upright – even Handel played the primitive organ there before Britton's death in 1714.[12]

Teresa Cornelys needed first-rate orchestral music for the dancing at her masquerades and her cosmopolitan connections must have assisted the flow of foreign musicians to London – she had a long association with Felice de' Giardini, a violinist and composer, who directed much of her music. But during 1764 she enlisted the help of two master musicians not long in London to devise concert seasons at Carlisle House in a development that greatly enlarged access to music in the capital. Karl Friedrich Abel and Johann Christian Bach – who took his new home so closely to his heart he was known as 'the London Bach' – ran concerts there for three years, beginning in January 1765. Subscribers paid 5 guineas for a season of fortnightly concerts, the two composers directing the orchestra and writing new music for the occasion. The concerts proved so popular that Mrs Cornelys had to install an extra door in the Soho Square frontage to alleviate the crush of subscribers disgorging from carriages and chairs.[13]

The astonishing success of Teresa Cornelys as London's greatest impresario of the 1760s contained the seeds of her eventual downfall. To attract fresh audiences every season she spent lavishly in an annual round of costly magnificence and innovation. Returns on her investment grew harder to yield when other entrepreneurs, senses quickened by the palpable success of Carlisle House, set up to compete for the quality in one or other of the pleasures pioneered so successfully by Mrs Cornelys.

The first blow fell in 1768. William Almack had kept a coffee house in Curzon Street, Mayfair, in the 1750s and then an alehouse in Pall Mall, which he later ran as a fashionable gaming house. He prospered sufficiently to build new assembly rooms in King Street, St James's Square, opening in February 1765. There he provided weekly balls and gaming tables and extended his premises with a 'great room' fit for concerts in 1767. Like Mrs Cornelys's early ventures, *ton* was assured by a 'Ladies' Coterie' who vetted subscribers to exclude the unfashionable. And it was under their protection that Bach and Abel were seduced from Carlisle House to open a new concert season at Almack's from 1768. Eventually the Hanover Square Rooms, built in 1775 with Bach and Abel in mind, at last provided a new and more permanent concert hall for Londoners. It was here that Joseph Haydn's concerts organised by the impresario Johann Salomon took place in the 1790s.

The second blow, aimed directly at the masquerades at Carlisle House, was the Pantheon in Oxford Street, an elegant rotunda in the Italian style designed by James Wyatt, thought to be the best modern building in London. It opened with a masquerade in January 1772 and the Pantheon quickly stole the place in London's public pleasures that Mrs Cornelys had won a decade before.[14]

In fact, Mrs Cornelys's difficulties had begun even earlier, and they began over money. Her 'singular . . . taste and invention', as Horace Walpole put it, brooked no compromise as regards the luxuriousness of her fittings and furnishings and decorations. Costs outstripped profits and by 1768 she had to reach an accommodation with her creditors that made her relinquish control over the spending at Carlisle House and most of its income. Her ambitions, though, were as expansive as ever. In early 1771 she took advantage of a fracas within the management of the King's Theatre, Haymarket, and decided to stage operas in Soho Square. She succeeded too well. Prosecutions for holding unlicensed stage performances were pursued by the King's Theatre and she was twice fined £50. The opening of the Pantheon a few months later proved a near-fatal shock. Three or four months later, by April 1772, Mrs Cornelys had locked herself in Carlisle House to avoid her creditors, emerging only at night and on Sundays; but by October she had been arrested and was in the King's Bench Prison for debt; a month later she was bankrupt; and in December the lease of Carlisle House was bought at auction by two creditors in what may well have been a rigged sale. From this time on, her daughter Sophie would have nothing more to do with her.[15]

Nonetheless Teresa's flair and tireless energy remained her creditors' best means of getting their money back and for much of the 1770s she wove an eccentric track between Carlisle House and a variety of venues, often as contractor in others' schemes, always teetering on the verge of ruin. She was involved in a plan to hold assemblies at 'The Hotel' in Southwark in 1773 and organised summer balls and masquerades at fashionable Southampton in 1774; in 1775 she arranged entertainments at Ranelagh, where she provided the catering for the great Thames regatta, and was planning new 'Casino Rooms' in Great Marlborough Street; she was back at Carlisle House again at Christmas 1775, through 1776 and into 1777, when she imported some French singers to bring the joys of the *Opéra Comique* to London. Later that year she successfully fought her eviction from Carlisle House, Lord Mansfield and a sympathetic jury won over by 'several instances of cruelty and oppression' at the hands of her creditors; her masquerades there continued through 1777 into early 1778, when her connection with Soho Square seems at last to have ended. Her final masquerade was probably held at Great Marlborough Street in May 1779. The unrespectable 'Promenades' at Carlisle House in the winter of 1780, often associated with her name, had no connection with Mrs Cornelys.[16]

Indeed, by then things had gone precipitately downhill for her. In October 1779 reports in the London press of her death in the Marshalsea Prison were swiftly corrected to say she lay 'extremely ill' there. By the spring of 1780 she had been moved to the more salubrious Fleet Prison. In the Gordon Riots that June she and the rest of the prisoners were freed by the rioters as the prison burned and she went into hiding from her creditors, as numerous others must have done.[17] It's said she took the name of Mrs Smith – if so, then for once her imagination failed her. How or where she lived remains a mystery. Her son, whom she had given a good education and who became a tutor to the nobility, apparently made her a small allowance, and she had a benefactress in Lady Cowper and perhaps others who recalled the days she had so richly gladdened.

Yet the decade after 1780 proved even bleaker for Carlisle House than for Teresa Cornelys. It hosted a debating society and scientific lectures and attempted to revive something of past glories in occasional concerts and masquerades. But by 1784 it lay empty, in 1785 its fate was in the hands of the Court of Chancery and in 1791 the old Carlisle House on Soho Square was demolished and replaced by two new houses. A year later and Mrs Cornelys's assembly rooms on Sutton Street were converted to a Roman Catholic chapel. Both houses and chapel were finally removed in 1891 and replaced by St Patrick's Roman Catholic Church, Soho Square.[18]

Mrs Cornelys outlived the house she had made one of the most famous in London. In 1795 or 1796, after sixteen years' obscurity, she embarked on an unlikely new venture, selling asses' milk and breakfasts from a large wooden building at Knightsbridge, then still a rural place. It's unclear whether new debts floored her or old creditors battened on her once more, but she was arrested and confined again in the Fleet. On 12 August 1797, 'at a very advanced age', Teresa Cornelys died 'in the hospital room of the Fleet, which the humanity of the Warden bestowed on her'. An acquaintance reported that she died '"in the most shocking agonies"', possibly of breast cancer. We might hope that fate was kinder to her. Some kindness she did receive and as a result we know that till the end she remained indefatigable. For she was made

a liberal allowance from a lady related to the family of the earl of Cowper, who would have increased that allowance, and have fastened it on her for life, if she would have renounced her *projecting turn*, which flattered her with the hope of reviving all her influence in the fashionable world. These visionary prospects, however, she would not resign, and, while she was dreaming of a palace, she died in a gaol![19]

'Down on Your Knees': The Stage

Teresa Cornelys, we might remember, had been an opera singer and that was a vocation that alone would have endeared her to the *ton*, or much of it at least. For opera was a hugely fashionable entertainment in London. It had grown with the century, very much an imported art form when London's first opera house was built in the Haymarket by Sir John Vanbrugh and others in 1705, and then adorned for nearly fifty years by the greatest stage composer of the age, George Frideric Handel. The sensational success of Handel's *Rinaldo* at the Haymarket in 1711, a year or so before he made London his permanent home, provoked Mr Spectator into almost weekly denunciations of this foreign invasion. The golden lures drawing continental singers to London and the huge salaries paid them when they arrived – £2,000 a season for the great sopranos and castrati in the 1720s, 2,000 guineas still in the 1790s – cast the whole enterprise as exorbitantly luxurious at the expense of British purses and native talent.[20]

Once established there grew other grounds for controversy. Opera became quickly infected with that presiding genius of the London stage in the first half of the eighteenth century – faction, much of it political. A great deal of the *Spectator*'s anger was Whiggery directed at a Tory court, and those battles would never quite go away. The great singers and the great (and not so great) composers attracted zealots whose only object was to drive their enemies from the opera house, even from London itself. In 1726–7 the quality divided over the merits of two rival sopranos, Cuzzoni and Faustina, their supporters wearing opposing favours in the streets and hissing and cat-calling their rivals on the stage. The King's Theatre became a gladiatorial spectacle, with crowds round the doors throwing insults and punches at prominent supporters on either side. On 6 June 1727 the disturbance in the house reached such a pitch that the singers themselves tussled on the stage.[21]

Next year, London's foreign opera cult and its two leading ladies were satirised in the most successful theatrical production of the century, John Gay's *The Beggar's Opera*. This was less an opera than a play with music and was produced at the New Play-House in Lincoln's Inn Fields. It was a satire much in the *Spectator* mould, a celebration of sturdy English patriotism decked out in traditional ballads. But it imported a sharper political edge with a thinly screened attack on the 'Great Man' – Macheath the highwayman in the play, Sir Robert Walpole the prime minister in real life – and on the web of institutional corruption within which the Great Man moved in both dimensions. If the Faustina–Cuzzoni rivalry had subverted order in and about the playhouse, Gay seemed to subvert confidence in both administration and the institutions of law and order. *The Beggar's Opera* brought the public in droves to Lincoln's Inn Fields, ran for an extraordinary ninety nights from 29 January 1728 and was frequently revived – to the horror of moralists and the magistracy – for the rest of the century. *Polly*, Gay's projected sequel of 1729, potentially more outspoken on Walpole's character, was suppressed by the Lord Chamberlain.[22]

Political faction and anxieties over disorder continued to dog the world of opera in London for the next twenty years. Handel had been attacked by the Bishop of London for wishing to stage operas in English with librettos based on biblical stories and had been condemned from pulpits up and down the land. The birth of oratorio, a largely new pleasure for Londoners, with dramatic scripts and scores produced without stage action, emerged from the controversy, with *Esther* its first fruit at the King's Theatre, Haymarket, in May 1732.

Handel was to suffer worse humiliations. He had always relied on the enthusiastic support of the royal family, but became the unwitting victim of factionalism in court soon after the accession of George II in 1727. The King and his son, Frederick Prince of Wales, were embroiled in a bitter quarrel that spilled over into politics. The violent opposition in Parliament and the country to Walpole, who soon became indispensable to the new monarch and his court, attached itself to Frederick. An alternative court buzzed like wasps about the prince's mansion, Leicester House, occupying the north-east side of Leicester Fields or Square. It anathematised Walpole, the King, the rest of the royal family and all their works. In 1733 the Prince and his faction made opera their battleground and established a rival house to Heidegger and Handel at the Haymarket with a new company at the theatre in Lincoln's Inn Fields, the champion of 'English opera' even before Gay's triumph. 'An anti-Handelist was looked upon as an anti-courtier, and voting against the Court in Parliament was hardly a less remissible or more venial sin than speaking against Handel or going to the Lincoln's Inn Fields Opera.'[23] Despite the backing of the King, Handel was driven from the Haymarket in January 1734, though his music would win a place in the heart of music-loving Londoners that long outlived his death in 1759. *Messiah*, composed to a libretto by Charles Jennens and first performed at Dublin in April 1742, became a perpetual favourite. From 1784 frequent Handel celebrations or festivals, assembling vast musical forces, were held at Westminster Abbey and elsewhere.

What, in general, was the audience for opera in London? It was thought to attract a greater proportion of the quality than the theatre, and seat prices were higher accordingly. 'The inhabitants of the Boxes at the Play-House, make up Pit and Box at the Opera,' wrote James Ralph in 1728. 'The Pit at the Play-House is the first Gallery in the Opera. The first Gallery and middle Part of the upper Gallery in the Play-House, have no Representatives in the Opera; there are but few of that Country who care to part with a Crown for a Song.' The opera's second gallery was filled with noisy footmen but the first was 'supported either by some of our most substantial, plain, sober Tradesmen, their Wives and Children . . . or by Officers of the Army, Members of Parliament, Gentlemen of good Characters and plentiful Fortunes . . .' The dress code for an opera audience was also more elaborate than for the play, full dress for men, 'or at least French frocks with swords', it was said in 1779, with a 'genteel deshabille' in the lower gallery.[24]

Even so, and even at the end of a century when politeness is said to have penetrated every rank, it was the 'tittering and loquacity', the rowdiness and disorder of an opera audience, that most struck the music-lover in London. Joseph Haydn went to hear William Shield's opera The Woodman at Covent Garden Theatre in December 1791:

The common people in the galleries of all the theatres are very impertinent; they set the fashion with all their unrestrained impetuosity, and whether something is repeated or not is determined by their yells. The parterre and all the boxes sometimes have to applaud a great deal to have something good repeated. That was just what happened this evening, with the Duet in the 3rd Act, which was very beautiful; and the pro's and contra's went on for nearly a quarter of an hour, till finally the parterre and the boxes won, and they repeated the Duet. Both the performers stood on the stage quite terrified, first retiring, then again coming forward.[25]

At that time Covent Garden was more theatre than opera house, indeed one of the great theatres of the metropolis, and it is difficult to exaggerate the place of the stage in London's public pleasures. At any one time there were several to choose from. The oldest continuous

London playhouse was the Theatre Royal, Drury Lane, first built in 1663, replaced after a fire with a new house by Wren in 1674, and demolished and rebuilt on a larger plan by Henry Holland in 1794. The theatre on the south side of Lincoln's Inn Fields was slightly older, dating from around 1660, but its use was discontinuous. A second theatre on the same site was built by the playwright William Congreve and others and opened in 1695, coming under the canny management of Christopher Rich, a lawyer, who had it rebuilt again in 1714, when the management passed to his son John. It was under John Rich's tenure at Lincoln's Inn Fields that *The Beggar's Opera* became such a runaway success: it made, the wits quipped, Rich Gay and Gay Rich. With the money, Rich built an entirely new playhouse in a more fashionable part of the town, moving his company to Covent Garden Theatre, entered through a long passage from Bow Street, in December 1732. The house at Lincoln's Inn Fields continued under various companies – Handel produced operas there for some years after 1734 – but it closed as a theatre in 1756. The Theatre Royal, Covent Garden, as it quickly became, prospered and was rebuilt and enlarged in 1792.

On the west side of the Haymarket, Vanbrugh's Opera House of 1705 burned down in 1789 and was promptly rebuilt the year after. And more or less opposite, the Little Theatre in the Haymarket was built by a carpenter, John Potter, as a speculation in 1721. It had many famous days. Henry Fielding's company was based there in the 1730s, Eliza Haywood among the actresses; Samuel Foote, the author of brilliant satirical farces, had it from 1747 to 1777, during which time it became a Royal Theatre, able to play legitimate or spoken drama; and George Colman, another talented comic dramatist, took it over, passing it to his son in 1790. A few other small theatres rose and fell in both the east and west ends of the town and in the suburbs, where Sadler's Wells in the fields of Clerkenwell secured a permanent place in the pleasures of Londoners. But one more is worth noting here. Goodman's Fields Theatre in south Whitechapel originally dated from 1729 but was quickly rebuilt by a new manager, Henry Gifford, in 1732. Its place in history is assured because it was here that David Garrick first appeared on the London stage, as Richard III, on 19 October 1741. Gifford's theatre was rebuilt again in 1746 and seems to have continued playing until 1802.[26]

So until 1721 the Opera House was accompanied by two main theatres; from then till 1732 three; and after that for the rest of the century four or five, with a period of extensive modernisation in the last decade or so. All of them were in constant rivalry to secure the leading actors, the best plays and the biggest audience, engaging in constant makeovers to enhance their luxuriousness and convenience. Sometimes they combined against a common enemy. As often as not that was the London public, with whom theatre managers were frequently in a state of civil war.

Almost all ranks patronised the London theatres to some degree. Their prices were designed to accommodate different classes, with boxes at 5s, the pit 3s, the first gallery 2s and the upper gallery 1s, prices that hardly fluctuated across the century. When the new Covent Garden Theatre opened in September 1792, after expensive rebuilding, the managers apologised to the public for having to dispense with the 1s gallery in the new house, leaving a single gallery at 2s. The news was greeted with a riot on the first night that threatened to undo all the work of the gilders and upholsterers; the managers reopened the upper gallery at 1s on 1 October. Higher prices in the pit (3s 6d) and boxes (6s) were permitted to stand.[27]

A shilling was a manageable sum for an artisan and an occasional treat for a journeyman or apprentice. All but the poorest, then, could share in London's greatest pleasure. And on several nights throughout the season they might find themselves sharing it with the King. From journeyman to monarch, all sorts and conditions of Londoners were to be found in the theatre and all had their place:

In our Playhouses at *London*, besides an Upper-Gallery for Footmen, Coachmen, Mendicants, &c. we have three other different and distinct Classes; the first is called the *Boxes*, where there is one peculiar to the King and Royal Family, and the rest for the Persons of Quality, and for the Ladies and Gentlemen of the highest Rank, unless some Fools that have more Wit than Money, or perhaps more Impudence than both, crowd in among them. The second is call'd the *Pit*, where sit the *Judges*, *Wits* and *Censurers*, or rather the *Censurers without either Wit or Judgment*. These are the *Bully-Judges*, that *damn and sink the Play at a venture* . . . in common with these sit the *Squires*, *Sharpers*, *Beaus Bullies* and *Whores*, and here and there an extravagant *Male* and *Female Cit*. The third is distinguished by the Title of the *Middle Gallery*, where the Citizens Wives and Daughters, together with the *Abigails*, Serving men, Journey-men and Apprentices commonly take their Places; and now and then some desponding Mistresses and superannuated Poets . . .[28]

The audience, all agreed, was a spectacle as fascinating as much of the action on stage, the theatres 'glittering and gaudy, because our spectators love to be an exhibition themselves'. The house lights were undimmed throughout the performance for ease of observation. Fashionable people in the boxes were most regarded and had most regard for each other: 'Gentlemen and ladies ogled each other through spectacles; for my companion observed, that blindness was of late become fashionable.' It must all have been great fun, though uncomfortable for some. Sophie von la Roche, at the Little Theatre in the Haymarket in 1786, saw four ladies enter a box 'with such wonderfully fantastic caps and hats perched on their heads, that they were received by the entire audience with loud derision' and laughed from the house.[29]

Business was conducted, flirtations indulged and disputes prosecuted as readily in the theatre as in park or street or coffee house. A 'terrible alarm' of fire at Drury Lane that caused a near-fatal panic in 1751 began with a row behind the boxes when two gentlemen drew swords. And Horace Walpole witnessed in 1789 a 'boxing match' between two ladies in the boxes; the pit 'hinted to the combatants to retire, which they did into the lobby, where a circle was made, and there the champions pulled one another's hair, and a great deluge of — powder ensued; but being well greased like Grecian pugilists, not many curls were shed'.[30]

Moments like these proved more memorable than the play. They were no doubt exceptional, though not very rare, and individual bad behaviour posing a danger to players or the audience was stamped on by parish constables, who seem to have attended every performance for just such an eventuality. But low-level misbehaviour was a notorious feature of the London playhouses. Carl Philipp Moritz joined the audience in the pit at the Little Theatre around 1782. 'Often and often whilst I sat there, did a rotten orange, or pieces of the peel of an orange, fly past me . . . Besides this perpetual pelting from the gallery . . . there is no end to their calling out and knocking with their sticks, till the curtain is drawn up.' And he found himself frequently annoyed by quarrels in the galleries and by a young fop behind him who rested his feet on Moritz's bench and even on the German's coat 'to display his costly stone-buckles with the utmost brilliancy'.[31]

Yet despite these discomforts the theatre proved irresistible to the Londoner. On some evenings everyone wanted to go. Popular actors and plays could produce a great crush at the doors that sometimes proved dangerous and worse. The greatest crushes of all were caused by the attractions of the audience and not the stage. In 1768 'all the avenues' to Drury Lane were filled with 'an immense crowd' for some hours before the King of Denmark was due to take his seat in the house; the pit grew so crowded near the doors that people were 'riding on the shoulders of others below' and ladders were brought to the stage to help those climb out who had 'fainted or were compelled to give up the struggle'. The worst crush of the century was at the Little Theatre in February 1794. Fifteen died when someone tripped descending a staircase to the pit, among them a mother and daughter who had come with a party of tradesmen and their families from Tooley Street, south of the river, dying alongside two gentlemen heralds from the College of Arms. The show went on, the King only learning of the tragedy once the performance was over.[32]

When the audience stopped regarding one another and duly paid attention to the action on stage they saw – as often as not – themselves. London life proved an inexhaustible subject for playwrights and play-goers alike. *The Beggar's Opera* and *The London Merchant, or the History of George Barnwell* (George Lillo, 1731) were two of the great theatrical sensations of the century; almost as popular were the London farces of Arthur Murphy, George Colman, Elizabeth Inchbald and Samuel Foote, who satirised living personalities to devastating effect – he resisted the considerable temptation to put Samuel Johnson in a play because 'he knew I would have broken his bones'; the moral comedies of Richard Cumberland selected a run of London types as main characters and the satires of Richard Brinsley Sheridan chose London drawing rooms and playhouses for their scenes. Frequently, too, the prologues and epilogues spoken by a leading player directly addressed the audience with fond banter or flagrant flattery, sometimes downright sycophancy:

We are your servants – it is agreed,
SERVANTS should *follow* – MASTERS should *precede*.[33]

Yet that was really no exaggeration. The London playhouse was a tyrannous democracy. Its will was fickle. Its power could be abused by the corruption of a cabal who might hiss a play from the stage solely for reasons of politics or personality or private interest. It showed none of the deference that genius might have received in another public place.

It was – as many commentators remarked who saw the quality in the boxes and pit at the mercy of the gallery's contemptuous fusillade from above – the world turned upside down.[34]

These turbulent spaces at the heart of London's public pleasures were subversive of politeness, deference and order. The object of subversion was not anarchy or revolution but the assertion of those traditional values we have already seen associated with the Londoner. The playhouses were temples of egalitarianism and fairness in a city divided by caste and inequality. As we saw with Covent Garden, audiences brooked no interference with the rights of the poor playgoer to a shilling seat. And when footmen were banned from the upper gallery of Drury Lane in March 1737 they broke down the stage doors with 'staves and *truncheons*', beating anyone who stood in their way; they were at length seen off by the Foot Guards but their privileges were quickly reinstated.[35]

The audience frequently asserted control over how the stage should entertain, rioting when a favourite player didn't appear, calling on players to 'speak louder!', hissing an actor who sipped a glass of wine on stage while the gallery was stifling, demanding the action be stopped, even in the presence of the King, so that a sickly playgoer could be carried out, and so on. And they enforced cockney prejudices against the foreigner and all things foreign, with riots against French players and satires of French manners roundly applauded, as we saw in an earlier chapter. When David Garrick lavished time and a great deal of money on a Chinese Festival at Drury Lane in October 1754 its very foreignness, aggravated by rumours that there were French players in the cast, caused a riot against both the stage and the people of fashion in the boxes who were ready to applaud it. 'Swords were mutually drawn, and blood shed', the rioters 'demolished the scenes, tore up the benches, broke the lustres and girandoles' and they carried their fury beyond the theatre doors, smashing windows in Garrick's town house and threatening to pull it down. 'He found himself reduced to the necessity of seeking protection from the soldiery.'[36]

Cockney patriotism was more frequently and less riotously expressed in a fierce love of country, most fervently in the presence of the King. A sceptical American visitor squeezed with difficulty into Covent Garden Theatre in April 1795 – a year of war, as so many were throughout the century – and 'was surprised to see *his Majesty* pleas'd with the flattery so grossly offered, as the whole gang of Actors &

Actresses *several* times came out and roard out God Save the King & Rule Britannia and then the choruses was so charmingly echo'd from the Boxes, Pit and Gallery'. Indeed, these two songs, both products of the century, came to epitomise the patriotism of the London theatres. 'God Save the King' was first opportunely published in 1744, and 'Rule Britannia' was an aria by the London operatic composer Thomas Arne from about the same time, though only popularised later at Covent Garden in 1753 in his *Alfred the Great*. In the rebellion of 1745 it was said that 'the loyal acclamations of "God Save the King" might have been heard from *Drury-Lane* to *Charing-Cross*'. In this and other ways 'the audience has been known to enter into the immediate business of the Drama' and in fact became the drama itself.[37]

In matters of taste, London's playgoers demanded laughter, tears, bawdiness and variety, and the greatest of these was variety. The combination changed little across the century. In any evening at the theatre comedies predominated, a tragedy went rarely unsweetened by a farce, and every opportunity was taken to insert music, dance and sometimes singing into the action, whether appropriately or not. At the Theatre Royal, Drury Lane, in March 1740, *Timon of Athens* ('Alter'd from Shakespeare') had 'proper Decorations of Singing and Dancing'. These included 'M'selle de Chateauneuf's kicking the tambourine, till she shows herself naked to the waist'. 'I have not seen it,' Mrs Anne Donnellan wrote to Elizabeth Robinson, later Montagu, 'but I have heard it very lively described; she kicks twice for the King and once for the audience to the great edification of the spectators.' Under Garrick, in February 1760 at the same theatre, *Romeo and Juliet* was played 'With the Additional Scene, representing The Funeral Procession. The Vocal Parts' by a number of singers, with a 'Masquerade Dance proper to the Play' and a Minuet, all followed by Charles Macklin's farce *Love-à-la-Mode*. And at the close of the century Drury Lane offered *Romeo and Juliet* with a 'new Musical Entertainment' called *A Friend in Need*; and Covent Garden *The Merry Wives of Windsor* with a 'Comic Opera', *Netley Abbey*, alternating with pantomime (February 1797).[38]

David Garrick, whose naturalistic acting and convincing exploration of character did so much to enrich the pleasures of the London stage from 1741 till his retirement in 1776, played a large part in the movement that installed Shakespeare at the head of English drama. But it was a Shakespeare, as the above instances show, that had to accommodate the tastes of the time.[39] A manager might gently steer the public taste but he could never afford to ignore or rebut it. Garrick was a much-loved celebrity of the age and a highly fashionable man at a time when actors were prized guests at the richest drawing rooms in London and actresses arbiters of taste for ladies of the quality. When he died in 1779, his burial at Westminster Abbey was of almost unparalleled magnificence for a commoner and attended by vast crowds. But when presenting entertainment on the stage as manager of Drury Lane he was of no more account than any apprentice or pettifogging lawyer.

His Chinese Festival had been one dangerous moment among many. In 1750 the audience was disgusted with 'an old play not acted these fifty years call'd friendship in fashion'. When, at the end of a performance accompanied throughout by catcalls and groans, it was given out that the same play would be performed the next night too, the audience demanded that Garrick should come to the stage. But he wasn't in town so 'they began ripping up yᵉ benches of pit & Gallery and throwing these on yᵉ stage, broke down yᵉ King's Arms & did a great deal of damage'.[40]

That kind of event might punctuate any season. But nothing quite matched what happened in January 1763. Drury Lane was to be opened after an expensive refurbishment. To help recoup his costs Garrick took the risky step of announcing that the old practice of charging half-price admission for people arriving after the third act of a play would be stopped. At the best of times, any change to the traditional privileges of the London playgoers was tantamount to a declaration of war on the audience. And these were not good times, because Garrick seems to have made enemies among some of the 'Bully-Judges' of the pit. A disturbance was got up by a cabal motivated more by personal spite than an outraged sense of public justice. Handbills protesting against the change were given out in the streets. On the opening night the audience 'began the cry for *Garrick, Garrick!* which was immediately universal all over the house'. He duly appeared 'with a deportment of propriety and respect'. 'At last the hissings and yellings from a thousand throats began to subside' and a man in the centre of the pit rose to his feet: '"*I call on you in the name of the public to answer for your RASCALLY impositions.*" On which, the word RASCAL was echoed throughout the pit . . .' The spokesman continued, '"*Answer it, Sir; answer me, Sir.*"' Garrick clearly knew his opponent and tried to reply man to man. '"*Speak to the audience, Sir; speak to the house*"', which Garrick tried to do, but the hubbub was too much for him and he retired. The actors came out several times but couldn't be heard. Around 8 o'clock the protesters called on the ladies to retire as 'the house might be burnt and destroyed' and when they had done so the new glass lustres were smashed, spilling lighted candles into the boxes. Worse was only stopped by soldiers kept at the ready by the magistrates.

In consultation with Garrick, Covent Garden had applied the same policy on half-price admission but when the managers met next morning they found their position hopeless. That night Garrick was once more summoned to the stage and the same 'orator' 'demanded a Yes or No: "*Will you, or will you not, admit the public after the third act at half price, to all entertainments, except the first winter of a new Pantomime?*"' Confronted by the prospect of his theatre being torn to pieces before his eyes he answered that he would. It was not enough. Two actors were summoned to the stage by the audience who demanded an apology for their actions in obstructing the rioters the night before. One of them, a fiery Irishman, John Moody, made a sarcastic reply that 'gave great offence and the audience ordered "*knees, knees, down on your knees*"'. '"I will not, by God",' said Moody, and left the stage. But Garrick was summoned once more and, humiliated and ready now to agree to anything, shamefacedly conceded to the audience that Moody should not act again at Drury Lane while 'he was under their displeasure'. What playwright could compete with drama like this? In September, Garrick left for a European trip and didn't return to the London stage for eighteen months.[41]

'Sights and Monsters': The Lions of London

There was only one Lyoness. The Keeper threw a Dog for her to devour she fawn'd on it, and of all the Meat that was brought her would give him part and got him between her Paws, and lick him: For all this tenderness the Dog was very uneasy:[42]

Mrs Percivall's memorable visit to the menagerie at the Tower of London in the winter of 1713–14 was part of an itinerary that was shared by almost all visitors to London across the century. The Tower, St Paul's, the Royal Exchange, St James's Palace, Westminster Abbey, Westminster Hall, the theatres, pleasure gardens and exhibitions – these were the 'Lions of London', described in every guidebook and meticulously recounted for friends and family in letters home or travel diaries for sharing on return. Some of these places were the quintessence not merely of London but of the nation past and present. Like the Tower, still a gaol for state prisoners and the Mint for the national coinage, with its lions, 'Indian cats', wolves, eagles and a tiger, the country's only peren- nial collection of 'wild animals' until a menagerie opened at Exeter Exchange in the Strand in 1770; and yet so resonant of past glories with its horse armoury and crown jewels that 'dazzled . . . by dim candle-light, shewn by a woman behind some rails, who recites her lesson faster than a nun recites her psalms'.[43]

These were all attractions for visitors to London rather than for Londoners themselves. Even the Tower, one imagines, may well have been taken for granted by the cockneys. But one of the Lions seems to have had a universal fascination. Bedlam or Bethlehem Hospital for lunatics and the insane moved to new premises on the south side of Moorfields in 1676, where Finsbury Circus now stands. It was built by the City of London, designed by its surveyor Robert Hooke and was 'more like a Royal Palace than a Place of retirement for poor senseless Creatures'. Over the piers of the entrance gate reclined two large figures carved from Portland stone by Caius Gabriel Cibber, father of the actor-playwright, representing melancholy and furious mania. This great institution symbolised for many the national genius for philanthropy. It exerted a fascination on visitor and Londoner alike for, in order to pay witness to the order, cleanliness and care the patients received, the public were given access on visiting days. For Samuel Johnson, who took advantage with Boswell of a visiting day in May 1775, and who was himself burdened throughout his life with fears for his reason, 'the general contemplation of insanity was very affecting', and no doubt many shared that view. Visitors were thought to be beneficial to the prisoners by importing '"jollity and merriment"', and the penny or two reportedly paid by most encouraged a few to give more generously to Bedlam's coffers.[44]

On public holidays the hospital wore something of the apparel of a fair with nut, fruit and beer sellers plying in the galleries and freely mixing with patients and those who'd come to see. But a visitor in

1753 complained of '"a hundred people, at least [who] were suffered unattended to run rioting up and down the wards making sport of the miserable inhabitants. I saw them in a loud laugh of triumph at the ravings they had occasioned."' Bedlam's fascination extended to all classes, as Hogarth's Plate 8 of *The Rake's Progress* (1735), said to be an accurate representation of a new incurables' ward at the hospital, plainly describes. Eventually doubts about the propriety of Bedlam as a public show led to male visitors being excluded from the women's side in 1769, and admittance wholly restricted by ticket a year later, when visitors were accompanied by 'keepers or nurses'. On this basis visiting seems to have continued for the rest of the century, a Russian traveller noting in July 1790 that 'Many of the men made us laugh. One imagines that he is a cannon and keeps firing charges through his mouth. Another grunts like a bear and walks on all fours.'[45]

'From the highest to the lowest, this people seem fond of sights and monsters,' Oliver Goldsmith makes his 'Chinese Philosopher' say on a fictional visit to London around 1760, and it's true enough that London's entertainments had much of the monstrous about them. Giants were great favourites: an Englishman seven feet four and a half inches tall was shown at the Sun, Queen Street, Cheapside, in 1701; 'The Tall Black' or 'Indian King' was to be seen about the same time at the Golden Lyon, Smithfield; a few years later an Essex giantess 'near seven feet high . . . though not nineteen' was shown at the Rummer, Three King Court, Fleet Street. Dwarfs proved equally popular. In 1723 a German dwarf called Matthew Buchinger was shown at the Two Blackamoors' Heads, Holborn; though without legs or hands, he used 'a curious piece of machinery to play upon the violin and german flute'. Women dwarfs were often called 'fairies' or 'fairy women': in 1700 a German woman just two feet eight inches tall, danced and sang at 'the Brandy Shop, over against the Eagle and Child', in the old Stocks Market. And around 1742 a married couple, Judith and Robert Skinner, Judith the taller at two feet two inches, were exhibited in Westminster with much success; after a year or so they were said to have saved enough to retire and keep their tiny carriage, specially made for drives in the park.[46]

Exotic animals could also draw a crowd, like the 'noble Female Rhinoceros, or real Unicorn', its 'Hyde . . . Pistol Proof' and a 'surprising Crocodile' from the Nile, the first ever 'shewn alive in the King's

Dominions', both at the Red Lion, Charing Cross, in January 1752; or the 'learned pig' who knew his letters, exhibited for 5s in a room in Pall Mall in 1789, though the price eventually came down to 1s. So could monsters that must have teased both nostril and credulity, like a 'sea-monster or white bear with wool and webbed feet' that John Baker saw exhibited in Castle Street, Leicester Fields, in June 1758; or the 'Syren or Mermaid' with breasts 'fair and full, but without nipples' and 'in all respects like the cod-fish' from the waist down, shown in London in May 1775.[47]

Exotic people were also a sensation, like the exhibitions of former slaves with special talents or unusual skins we've already encountered. The periodic arrival of American Indians drew great crowds. Some Iroquois visited in 1710 and Cherokees in 1729, 1762 and 1782: the three Cherokee chiefs and their wives who came at the expense of the government in 1762 were allowed to become a profitable exhibit at Marybone Gardens, where they ate their supper and smoked their pipes each evening in front of admiring crowds. All three wives were said 'to be with Child before they left Marybone by little Bob the waiter to whom they took a fancy & whom on their account became almost as much beloved by their Husbands . . .'[48]

Mechanical shows were legion throughout the century. Ingenious, sophisticated, illusory, they depended on individual flair, even genius, and they astonished those who came to see. James Cox's Museum in the Great Room at Spring Gardens, Charing Cross, from 1772, with its jewel- and gold-encrusted mechanical animals and curios – a screeching peacock, crowing cock and more – delighted Samuel Johnson among many others; part of the collection was acquired by Catherine the Great's Hermitage. Speaking 'Automatons' were all ventriloquism, Hester Thrale thought in 1784. There were competing waxworks in Fleet Street and the Strand – 'The Figures were the worst I ever Saw – one Shilling admittance', groaned John Aspinwall in 1795. Puppet shows like the Italian Fantoccini of Carlo Perico at the Great Room in Panton Street were a sensation from 1770. Shadow shows with clever lighting, cut-out figures and translucent screens, like the *Ombres Chinoises*, were a hit under Philip Astley's management at 22 Piccadilly in 1779. And Loutherbourg's Eidophusikon, exhibited first in 1781 at his home in Lisle Street, Leicester Square, showing magical views of London or Italy or the Niagara Falls on a stage six feet wide and eight feet deep, delighted polite audiences in the 1780s; it would continue past the end of the century under others' hands.[49]

Giants, dwarfs, wild animals, monsters, puppet shows, mechanical exhibits, waxworks, theatrical performances with farces or 'drolls' based on London life, food stalls and drinking booths, music and dancing, swingboats and roundabouts, jugglers and rope dancers, boxers and wrestlers, quack doctors and tooth drawers, card sharpers and dice rollers all came together in a grand climacteric at the various fairs held annually in and around London. The greatest was Bartholomew Fair, Bartlemy, established even before a royal charter of 1133 formally permitted it to run for three days from St Bartholomew's Eve, 23 August. By 1700 the fair had extended to a fortnight, to the discomfort of the tradesmen of Smithfield but to the joy of the thousands who flocked there for profit or amusement. From the beginning of the eighteenth century there was a continual battle between the showmen and the City authorities to rein back the fair to three days and to ban the theatre booths, the drolls considered inimical to morality and the dignity of the City of London. From about 1735 the fair was indeed restricted to three or four days but theatre remained a permanent feature past the century's end.[50]

Southwark Fair, famously the subject of a brilliant satire of the times by Hogarth in 1734, had also probably been in existence long before its charter of 1462. It opened in September on the close of Bartlemy and was likewise running for some two weeks by the beginning of the eighteenth century. It was suppressed by the City Corporation in 1763 as productive of disorder, immorality and an obstruction to trade. May Fair, held from May Day in that part of the suburbs which eventually took its name, was put down by the Westminster authorities in 1708 but subsequently revived until brought finally to an end by a combination of private interests and judicial force of arms around 1764. There were smaller fairs at Tottenham Court and other inner suburbs, and a number of more rural fairs at Greenwich, Charlton (the Horns Fair) and others, some surviving into the nineteenth century.[51]

As the suppression of fairs sealed off some of the seams of joy in London, especially for the poorer sort, the quantity and quality of polite public pleasures continued to increase in the second half of the century. The British Museum opened at Montagu House in Great Russell Street in 1753. Access to its collections was free, but strictly confined to those applying in writing for a ticket, with a further seventy-five persons let in on each of the three opening days every week, 'if none of the persons are exceptionable'; the Museum's officers could also invite 'persons of distinction for rank or learning' as their guests. 'Free' access thus proved far more exclusive than places that made a charge. Sir Ashton Lever's collections of natural history and ethnographic items – the Holophusikon, he called it – could be seen at Leicester House, the Prince of Wales's former mansion. The entrance fee varied from 2s 6d to over 5s. But the charge never reimbursed Lever's costs and in 1786 the collection was sold by lottery, moving to a purpose-built rotunda, the Leverian Museum, on the south bank by Blackfriars Bridge in 1787, entrance 1s.[52]

Along the river in Lambeth, on the Surrey side of Westminster Bridge, was Philip Astley's Amphitheatre. For many years from about 1769, this was the home of extravagant horsemanship and acrobatic skills, Astley a cavalryman of almost superhuman powers. Entrance charges were precisely segregated but plebeian, as befitted the south side of the river, ranging from 6d in the side gallery to 2s 6d in the boxes. By the end of the century Astley had a rival in the New Royal Circus at St George's Fields, Southwark, offering in 1799 'an entire Grand oriental Spectacle', complete with music, 'Elephants, Camels, Dromedaries, Chargers in Equestrian Armour' – and the pantomime of the Harlequin Highlander.[53]

By the 1790s Leicester Square and the streets around had become the centre of London's public pleasures. The new circular building for Robert Barker's Panorama at Leicester Square opened in 1794 and displayed in the spring of 1799 a view of Windsor and later 'Lord Nelson's Victory at the Mouth of the Nile'. Nearby Miss Linwood's exhibition of embroidery was showing at Leicester House and so was Mr Martin's 'grand Mechanical Display of the Universe', 'The Newtonian System of Astronomy Refuted', for 1s. In the assembly room at Lisle Street were readings of Molière in French given by Anthony Le Texier, actor and impresario; a new Eidophusikon was showing at Panton Street, first seats at 3s, second at 2s; and a show of Italian pictures was available at the Exhibition Room, Whitcomb Street. Elsewhere in the west end of the town that spring of 1799, besides theatre and opera, and concerts at Willis's Rooms (late Almack's), King Street, and the Hanover Square Rooms, were public debates, lectures, picture exhibitions and mechanical wonders. By this time monsters, giants and dwarfs had faded from fashion but were still to be had at Bartholomew Fair: 'the Windsor Fairy', a six-legged ram, Miss Biffin who painted miniatures without arms, and 'A Surprising large Fish, THE NONDESCRIPT', were all favourites of the 1790s or just beyond.[54]

Not all of London's public pleasures had to be paid for. The streets were a rich source of mirth and spectacle. The Lord Mayor supplied an annual pageant from St James's Palace to the Mansion House every October or November. The arrival of George I into London in September 1714, magnificent funerals like that for the Duke of Marlborough in August 1722, the astonishing display of wealth and power at the coronation of George III on 22 September 1761, victory processions and peace celebrations all provided sensations for Londoners and memories for a lifetime. And every royal birthday and christening offered the excuse for a splendid turnout of carriages, costumes and livery around St James's Palace: 'it must be confessed that a court is a fine thing', thought Boswell.[55]

Private pleasures also spilled into the public sphere. The party for the King's birthday in June 1764 at Northumberland House, Charing Cross, saw 1,500 guests arrive in coaches and chairs; there were two bands of music and 10,000 lamps in the gardens. Private illuminations for events like the King's recovery from illness in March 1789 were publicly enjoyed: 'The Transparency, & manner of lighting up *our* House was particularly admired,' Hester Thrale noted in her diary at Hanover Square. Even small house parties could have a public dimension. A former officer in the Irish army, 'Count' O'Rourke, ended a hospitable evening around 1778 'at his lodgings, a second floor in Wardour-street, Soho', with 'fireworks in the street (catherine wheels and flower pots)'. And fireworks, coloured lamps, 'mutual cordiality and cheerfulness' were very much the stuff of those ornaments of London that this age most especially perfected: the pleasure gardens.[56]

No Equal in Europe: Pleasure Gardens

Permanent among them, pleasure gardens in all but name, were the parks. They were the daily recreation grounds and trysting places of Londoners, available throughout the year and the venue of any set-piece splendour too large for London's streets to accommodate. They were jealously prized by all classes, used by King and commoner alike:

'rose early to see the King take his usual ride in the Park', one visitor
confided to his diary in September 1761. Foreigners were shocked that
in St James's Park 'the first quality blended with the lowest populace.
Such is the taste of the English, who pride themselves on this, as a
proof of their liberty.' It shocked the foreign royal family in St James's
Palace too. George II's queen, Caroline, once asked Sir Robert Walpole
what it would cost to enclose the park for the sole use of the court.
He replied, '"Only a *crown* Madam."' To her credit, Queen Caroline
lavished improvements on Kensington Gardens and Hyde Park, the
Serpentine one of her changes, wrought in the 1730s.[57]

Throughout the century the parks brought something of the country
into London, with fallow deer so tame they would eat from the hand
and milk had straight from the herd of cows at Spring Gardens:
syllabub – fresh milk and Spanish wine with a herbal cordial – was
all the rage there in 1741. Between 7 to 10 o'clock on a summer
evening it was said that St James's Park was so filled with 'Society'
'that you cannot help touching your neighbour', the Mall 'one thousand Paces long, the finest and most frequented Walk in *London*';
both figured in plays and novels across the century. And apart from
these great open spaces at the western edge of the town the citizens
had much-frequented walks at Moorfields, Goodman's Fields, Lincoln's
Inn Fields and elsewhere. Taking the air at Gray's Inn Walks was a
popular Sunday excursion, especially when a new gown was to be
shown off in public. Later in the century the popular spectacle of
ballooning tended to favour these smaller parks, the first voyage in
England undertaken by Vincenzo Lunardi from the Artillery Ground,
Finsbury, on 15 September 1784.[58]

The greatest celebration of the whole century in London was for the
Peace of Aix-la-Chapelle, held in Green Park on 27 April 1749. A huge
wooden palace 144 feet long and adorned with statues and paintings
was built to hold a firework display – it was four months in the making.
For a week before the celebration, Horace Walpole thought 'the town
was like a country fair, the streets filled from morning to night . . . and
coaches arriving from every corner of the kingdom'. Handel had
composed spectacular *Music for the Royal Fireworks* – the rehearsal
at Vauxhall Gardens six nights before attracted a crowd of 12,000
paying 2s 6d for admission; the traffic lock of carriages trying to cross
the river at London Bridge lasted three hours. On the night itself he
had at his command forty trumpets, twenty French horns, and winds

and kettledrums to match. When the music stopped a single rocket shot up, 101 cannon roared from Constitution Hill and the display began of more than 160,000 fireworks under the control of an Italian maestro. Within an hour the wooden palace had caught fire and a complete fiasco was averted only by the bravery of carpenters who dismantled part of the blazing structure and of firemen stationed nearby with their engines. The fireworks continued and only three deaths were reported as the result of accidents among the tens of thousands in the park. 'Our mob was extremely tranquil,' thought Walpole.[59]

The river, too, though generally neglected for its scenic possibilities by developer and architect, was occasionally a place of spectacle. The Lord Mayor's procession each year undertook half its route by water, the City companies' ceremonial barges making a wonderfully colourful pageant. The annual watermen's sculling race for Thomas Doggett's Coat and Badge drew crowds to the river every August from about 1716. Royal flotillas had been popular in the reign of George I, Handel's *Water Music* of 1717 composed for one concert on the royal barge that was accompanied by 'numberless' boats for spectators. River pageants continued to play a part in state events, like the arrival of two Venetian ambassadors in April 1763 and a visit to the City by the King of Denmark in September 1768, with 'water music playing in the stern' of the City's 'state barge'. And there was much private music on the river for the rest of the century: Granville Sharp, the anti-slavery campaigner, had a barge on which he hosted musical entertainments, for instance.[60]

But the greatest event of the century on the Thames was the regatta of Friday 23 June 1775, a procession and boat race that filled the river 'with vessels of pleasure' from London Bridge to the Ship Tavern at Millbank, all to watch the '*Regatta furor*'. There was a 'perfect fair on both sides the water, and bad liquor, with short measure, was plentifully retailed'. There were 'regatta cheesecakes, and regatta cherries, and on the Thames regatta coffee-houses; nay, the ladies of easy virtue had decorated themselves with regatta ribbons'. With all the craft on the river, 'The Thames was now a floating town.' It ended with some 2,000 of the quality descending on Ranelagh Gardens for a supper, organised by Mrs Cornelys, and music led by Giardini with an orchestra and chorus 240 strong.[61]

It was thus no accident that the two most prestigious pleasure gardens of London chose the riverside for their location, in part for the view and in part for the charm of arriving by water. Ranelagh was unquestionably the smarter. Ranelagh Gardens, with its famous Rotunda for music and display, opened in April 1742. They were built in the grounds of a former mansion and were the speculation of James Lacy, then patentee of the Theatre Royal, Drury Lane. Ranelagh attracted the quality and the respectable middling sort – Samuel Johnson, who went a number of times, thought the Rotunda's '"*coup d'oeil* was the finest thing he had ever seen"'. It was certainly enormous, 150 feet across, made mainly of wood, with fifty-two dining boxes at ground level and a gallery of boxes above for observing the perpetual circular promenade of the visitors, 'the best market we have in England' for marriages, thought Edward Gibbon, though he never took advantage of it himself. There were a few refreshment tables near a great central fireplace for cold nights, and a large stage and organ to one side. Giardini was in charge of music here for many years – perhaps too many: 'He played like a pig,' thought Haydn when he visited Ranelagh in May 1792.[62]

If Ranelagh proved the most fashionable of the London pleasure gardens then Vauxhall was by far the most famous. It was 'an entertainment, which has no equal, that I have ever heard, in Europe,' Baron Bielfeld wrote in the 1760s, though a German compatriot noted 'many feeble imitations' on the Continent by the end of the century. Vauxhall Gardens had the advantage of longevity, originating under the Restoration as New Spring Garden, famed for 'fashionable gallantry and intrigue', a reputation it carried into the 1730s. The Gardens were then entirely reinvented by Jonathan Tyers, whose wealth seems to have come from the Bermondsey leather trade, as a place of polite resort with a decidedly musical flavour. He opened the new Vauxhall Gardens with a *Ridotto al fresco* or open-air masked ball in June 1732 for a fashionable company of 400 or so. Frederick Prince of Wales 'staid two Hours' and for years proved a loyal supporter. Even under Tyers's reign the company at Vauxhall quickly became more mixed. The entrance fee was fixed at 1s by 1737, the cheapest price of gallery admission at the theatres – Ranelagh was 2s 6d. Music was free, the musicians in an 'orchestra' with organ built in the middle of the Gardens' main open space, the players brought into a Great Room or rotunda in bad weather. And also free were dancing and strolling in the grounds with their 'Dark Walks' and lamplit avenues, and so was nestling in the arbours. Food, though, was notoriously both mean and expensive, the ham transparent though a shilling an ounce, the 'chicks' 'half-a-crown a-piece, and no bigger than a sparrow'. But Tyers spared no expense on polite taste, with history paintings in the eating booths, mainly by the much-admired Francis Hayman but also by Hogarth, and a famous statue of Handel by Roubiliac, in place from 1738. And the Gardens' musicians and singers were of the best, English composers especially favoured with Vauxhall commissions. On any evening some 2,000 people could be expected in the Gardens, but 11,000 or 12,000 on gala nights.[63]

The plebeian entrance fee, the artistic quality of the grounds and the music and art to be found there ensured that Vauxhall attracted a wide mix of ranks. That very fact aroused snobbery of course, but even Horace Walpole and a most aristocratic though high-living assemblage of the quality were joyously at home there in June 1750, though more interested in flirtation than the music.[64]

Forty years after his own magical visit, Walpole thought the polite patronage of Vauxhall had done much to moderate the outrageous language and behaviour of the Thames watermen, the river the favoured means of travel there until Westminster Bridge opened in 1750. And the easy mixing of ranks at Vauxhall was, he felt, a tribute to the nation: 'Admirable it was in a country of so much freedom & so little police, to see Princes & Peeresses mixed with tradesmen & their Wives, wth apprentices & women of pleasure, & so very seldom any indecorum or want of order, nor scarcely ever any disturbance happening even from young men flushed by wine.'[65]

Yet despite Walpole's retrospective encomium it was inevitable that Vauxhall Gardens were to some extent associated with disorder. In eighteenth-century London politeness was always compromised to some degree. In 1744 Mrs Haywood warned 'the young and beautiful of our sex' to beware of beaux bent on seduction or worse at Vauxhall, and insulting behaviour of one kind or another seems to have been a constant risk run by women in the dark walks and other places, even under Tyers.[66]

A row was, if not too serious, part of the fun. In June 1763 Boswell saw 'a quarrel between a gentleman and a waiter. A great crowd gathered round and roared out, "A ring – a ring," which is the signal for marking room for the parties to box it out. My spirits rose' – 'flushed by wine', perhaps – 'and I was exerting myself with much vehemence', but a constable appeared with his staff of office and calmed things down.

Henry Angelo, comparing the 1770s with more respectable times fifty years later, remembered Vauxhall as 'more like a bear garden than a rational place of resort, and most particularly on the Sunday mornings. It was then crowded from four to six with gentry, girls of the town, apprentices, shop-boys, &c. &c.' At any time, 'Rings were made in every part of the gardens to decide quarrels; it now no sooner took place in one quarter, than, by a contrivance of the light-fingered gentry, another row was created in another quarter to attract the crowd away.' But for contemporaries of Walpole, Vauxhall Gardens were far less exceptionable than many other places. Except perhaps on the last night of the season. From the 1770s, if not before, the closure of the Gardens in early September was traditionally greeted with a riot in which every lamp was broken and so, no doubt, were a few heads.[67]

Apart from Ranelagh and Vauxhall, there were numerous other pleasure gardens around London that attracted the middling sort and above through every spring and summer for at least part of the century. Best known and smartest were Marylebone Gardens, in the fields on the east side of Marylebone High Street (either side of present-day Devonshire Street to Harley Street). The Gardens were entered through the Rose Tavern and had once been bowling greens and walks even before the Restoration. They were turned into something resembling Vauxhall by Daniel Gough and opened in 1738 with orchestral concerts. A year or two later they had a Great Room for balls and suppers. In the 1750s Marybone was famous for its cakes, baked under the supervision of Miss Trusler, the proprietor's daughter. Admission was 1s, or 2s with breakfast or supper, sometimes 3s on special nights. There were occasional masquerades and fireworks. From 1763 to 1768, their heyday, they were run by the former star tenor at Vauxhall, Thomas Lowe, though like Mrs Cornelys he ended in financial difficulties. Under his creditors the Gardens survived after a fashion, but music was expensive and seems to have been in short supply from 1774. By then it was 'a wretched place'. The entrance fee was dropped to 6d, 'which could be exchanged for liquor to that value'. Marybone Gardens closed in 1778 and the site was let to builders. By 1790 London had virtually swallowed it up and by 1799 completely so. Similar stories could be told for other less grand suburban attractions for the middling sorts, like Bermondsey Spa (famed for its paintings), Cuper's Gardens downriver from Vauxhall (notorious for its whores), Pancras Wells, the Assembly House at Kentish Town, Hampstead Wells, Belsize House and more, many based on the health-giving qualities of a local spring, so sought after in that age of quackery.[68]

There were then a host of similar places – with waters both natural and fortified – that set out successfully to attract the poorer sort of people. They were dotted in the fields all round London, north and south of the river. But there was a famously joyful cluster around Clerkenwell and Islington, from Hoxton in the east to Battle Bridge (later King's Cross) in the west, that were the favoured resort of the city's labourers, apprentices, 'milliners, mantua-makers, and servant-maids', artisans and small tradesmen and their families. At any one time there were a dozen or more on offer: from east to west there was the Shepherd and Shepherdess in City Road; the Barley Mow and the Castle Inn near Lower (Essex) Road, Islington; the Mulberry Garden, the New Wells, the English Grotto, Merlin's Cave, the Islington Spa ('Spaw' the word was spoken, and often written) or New Tunbridge Wells, and Sadler's Wells, all to the west of St John Street and the Islington Road; the Spa Fields (or 'Sixpenny') Pantheon, the London Spa, Bagnigge Wells, the Sir John Oldcastle and Lord Cobham's Head, all alongside the River Fleet on the road to Battle Bridge. Moving west again along the New Road and Pentonville Road were St Chad's Well, Belvedere Tea Gardens (formerly Busby's Folly) and Dobney's Bowling Green. Further north was White Conduit House, and further north still but within walking distance of the City were Copenhagen House and Canonbury House Tea Gardens. Others might be added to the list. The great day for all of them, the only day of the week when London's enormous working population had a formal holiday and the only day when, for most wage earners, pockets were full or at least had cash in them, was Sunday.[69]

All these places had their histories, affected by the changing fashions of the times and the financial frailties of their promoters. They rose and fell and sometimes rose again, till finally falling under the inexorable tide of brick and slate moving over them from London. Of all, just Sadler's Wells proved indestructible because infinitely adaptable to the changing tastes of Londoners. It had begun as a wooden Music House built by one Sadler around 1680 and was soon a spa selling water from an ancient well found on the site. By the end of the seventeenth century the place was laid out in gardens, evening concerts were given, monsters shown and the occasional prizefight held. In the first decades of the eighteenth century it had a low reputation, its loneliness deep in the fields requiring link boys to light parties to London. Its 'usual diversions' by 1740 were rope-dancing, tumbling, singing and pantomimes with elaborate stage sets and machinery. Sadler's Wells flourished most under the management of Thomas Rosoman, a local speculative builder, who introduced free admission to pit and gallery on purchase of a pint of wine, though boxes remained at 2s 6d. Rosoman rebuilt the theatre in 1765 and had to amend his charging (though not his drinking) policy. The new seats had ledges at the back for those behind to rest their bottles and glasses, and admission to the gallery was 1s, with a pint of wine for 6d more. Giuseppe 'Iron Legs' Grimaldi was ballet master and chief dancer in the 1760s, his famous son, the clown Joseph, first treading the boards there in 1781 at the age of two, as a monkey. At the end of the century there were 'numerous avenues with delightful tables and benches for visitors, under trees hung with lamps', an 'open temple' in which 'lower-class lasses, sailors and other young people were dancing', and of course the theatre with its 'Great Variety of Performances' including comic dances, operettas, posturers and rope dancers, balancers and jugglers, battle spectacles, Chinese processions and more.[70]

Sadler's Wells was decidedly plebeian in its taste and its audience, with some leavening of fashionable sightseers, but we might spare a thought for Bagnigge Wells, entrance 3d and very much the resort of the poorer and lower-middling sort, sited on the west of the present day King's Cross Road (Cubitt Street and Wells Square). The water drawn from the well at old Bagnigge House was discovered to be chalybeate or rich in iron and so the house and gardens were opened to the public in 1759. It soon became a popular resort. The purgative effects of the water were quick-acting and wags made much of the proximity of Bagnigge Wells to the River Fleet, where a 'holey Temple' was built for water-drinkers to 'offer up their Morning Sacrifice', and where 'Reverberates the Thunder of the Bum'.[71]

The popularity of the 'spaw' waters brought all sorts and conditions, from 'genteel females' to John Rann, or Sixteen-String Jack, the highwayman, a brief favourite here before his execution at Tyburn in 1774. By then there were music and dancing in a Long Room, and seats and tables near the Fleet for smoking and ale and cider drinking. The gardens were laid out in walks with statues, and rustic bridges criss-crossed the river; a grotto and cockney cottage were decorated with shells, fossils and fragments of coloured glass, and there were a bunhouse, bowling green and skittle alley, a 'small round fishpond' with goldfish and 'a curious fountain, representing a cupid bestriding a swan which spouts three streams of water through its beak to a great height'. The many delights of Bagnigge Wells survived into the nineteenth century.[72]

For moralists, however, the waters and other pleasures of the Wells and its neighbours in and about 'the Spaw-field' were less invigorating than corrosive. Sunday luxuries for the labouring poor always aroused anxiety and hostility in equal measure. One of the delights at Bagnigge Wells was its famed negus – port or sherry, hot water, sugar and spices. And no luxury provoked more hostility than drink.

'Too Busy with Madam Geneva': Drinking and Socialising

Drink played a large part in the culture of every rank in eighteenth-century London. James Boswell's drinking bouts, for instance, faithfully but shamefacedly recorded in his diaries, might make a slim volume on their own. At the chaplain's table at St James's Palace in December 1793, 'that exquisite wine' champagne confined to France by the wartime blockade, the company had to make do with 'madeira, sherry, hock, port, and claret, and good malt liquor; and I took enough to warm me rather too much'. 'Madeira, sherry, port, old hock circulated' at a private dinner given by a vintner two or three months later, 'and we had a glass both of burgundy and champagne. And lastly came an elegant dessert and *Scotch pints* of very capital claret' – a Scotch pint some three times larger than the English variety: 'The generous bottle circulated so as to produce in me a total oblivion till I found myself safe in my own bed next morning.' Even his twelve-year-old son Jamie, at Westminster School, was 'forced' by the scholars 'to drink burgundy till he was intoxicated'. When John Yeoman, a Somerset dairy farmer and potter, spent a night in London on a visit in 1774, 'we made to free with the Duce of the Vine. Mr. Forrester Was quite full, went home to his house Where he was so Sick that it flew out att both ends like a Bedlamite.' Business was punctuated with drink, whether among the merchants at the Royal Exchange or servant maids sending out for their pot of porter to ease the pains of washday. Ben Franklin, an American and a water drinker, found his fellow workers at Watts's printing house 'great guzzlers of beer' around 1725. 'We had an alehouse boy who attended always in the house to supply the workmen. My companion at the press drank every day a pint before breakfast, a pint at breakfast with his bread and cheese, a pint between breakfast and dinner, a pint at dinner, a pint in the afternoon about six o'clock, and another when he had done his day's work.' 'They were much more often drunk then than now,' recalled Francis Place, looking back on the journeymen of his youth when an elderly man in 1834: 'there are no such abominable places' as Bagnigge Wells and others 'now'.[73]

It was the drunkenness of London's journeymen and labourers that gave cause for anxiety among reformers and not the insobriety of a Boswell or Mr Forrester. Drink damaged the capacity for labour and was a common cause of violence and riot. Many of London's public pleasures were regulated, as Mrs Cornelys found to her cost, but drinking was the most regulated by far. Any place selling alcohol – alehouse, public house, inn, tavern, coffee house, pleasure garden – had to have an annual licence from the magistrates, who could hear both applicants and objectors in public. These were old arrangements, in place for at least 150 years before 1700. But in eighteenth-century London regulation had no great deterrent effect on the numbers of places of one kind or another selling alcohol. In 1737 William Maitland recorded 207 inns, 447 taverns (generally selling only wines and spirits), 531 coffee houses (most licensed to sell wines and sometimes beers) and 5,975 alehouses, 7,160 in all. According to his estimate of the numbers of houses in London, one house in every 13.4 was licensed to sell drink. In 1784, in a larger metropolis, there were 330 inns, 550 taverns, 656 coffee houses and 6,786 alehouses, 8,322 in total; it is possible that numbers may have fallen by the century's end, when there were apparently just 5,620 alehouses in 1794.[74]

Both the regulatory framework and the drinking culture of London's labouring poor were thrown into turmoil in the first half of the century by gin. Distillation of 'English brandies' from the dregs of beer making or spoiled grain had developed in the second half of the seventeenth century, encouraged by a taste for 'Hollands', a spirit that accompanied the accession of a Dutch king in 1689. 'Geneva' ('English gin') is first mentioned as a drink in the Old Bailey Proceedings in 1715 and 'gin' four years later. From about 1720 the drink was made more palatable, mainly through the addition of cordials and flavourings. Because its production was at first encouraged by Parliament, as a British product that took trade away from France and the rest of the Continent, it went untaxed. This and the continuing use of substandard materials in its production, made it very cheap. Gin became the quickest way to oblivion for the poor: 'We have observed,' recorded the *Gentleman's Magazine* some years later, 'some Signs, where such Liquors are retailed, with the following Inscriptions, *Drunk* for *a Penny*, *dead drunk* for *Two-pence*, *clean Straw* for *nothing*.'[75]

It is very difficult to disentangle myth from reality when considering the place of gin in London life in these years, especially in the first half of the century. There were notable moral panics around 1725–9, 1735–6 and 1750–51, when the effects of gin on bishops, magistrates, moralists and reformers seem to have been more maddening than on any sot in Pissing Alley. The cause of reason hasn't been helped by some generations of historians swallowing, neat as it were, the tendentious rhetoric of the hanging classes.[76]

Nevertheless, the penetration of gin or dram drinking into the culture of London's labouring poor was undoubtedly extensive. Gin was cheap and quick-acting. It offered speedy if temporary relief from the anxieties of poverty, hunger, homelessness and abuse. In excess it no doubt took lives and some backstreet distilleries occasionally produced something close to poison: 'Four persons drinking Geneva together in an Alley near *Holbourn* Bridge, dy'd next day, and about ten more were mentioned in the *News Papers* of this Month, to have kill'd themselves in the same manner', though this was in the great panic of 1736, this was Grub Street, and all was limited by the primitive forensic understanding of the time. In excess it no doubt led people into mischief, as sometimes they had cause (or felt it advisable) to plead in mitigation: Elizabeth Plat of St Giles Cripplegate, found in a house with some goods bundled up for removal, claimed in her defence that 'she had been that Afternoon a little too busy with Madam Geneva'. And there is no doubt either that it contributed to the anger and loss of control that made London such a violent place in home and street in these years. In all these ways, and in the disruption of the capacity to earn a living for those who took too much, gin added to the miseries of the poor. On the other hand, for what must have been the majority who enjoyed it in moderation, gin was a welcome stimulant to beat off many ailments, from lassitude to the cold; and in more relaxed circumstances, a moment's enjoyment after work or on Sundays, gin seems very often to have accompanied a pint of ale in what later generations called a 'chaser'.[77]

For those not feeling the excruciating pinch of poverty gin held terrors of quite another kind. The 'whole town of London swarmed with drunken people of both sexes from morning to night', 'more like a scene of a Bacchanal than the residence of a civil society'. 'Half the Work is not done now as formerly' because of gin; it was 'so diuretick, it over-strains the Parts of Generation, and makes our common People incapable of getting such lusty Children as they us'd to do'; it spoiled women's nurse-milk; it was destroying the health of 'the Soldiery'; it caused fewer children to be born at all; it was 'the Source of most Evils, and principal Cause of the Robberies, Murthers, Blasphemies and other acts of Violence and Impiety'; it provoked 'the greatest Villanies, such as were formerly scarce known to our Nation'.[78]

Some of this was fantasy, much else was dubious. But the evidence for the widespread consumption of gin in London, especially from 1721 till around 1758, is overwhelming and extraordinary. William Maitland in 1737 claimed to have counted the astonishing number of 8,659 'Brandyshops' in London, compared to 4,531 bakers, butchers, cheesemongers, fishmongers, 'herb stalls' and poulterers put together. If brandy (that is, gin) shops are added to inns, alehouses and so on, then something like one in every six houses in London was selling alcohol. And in 1751 there were still said to be 'upwards of 17,000' 'private gin-shops' in the metropolis, not too far from Maitland's total figure of nearly 16,000 places selling alcohol in 1737.[79]

Allowing for imprecision and some exaggeration, these numbers seem to be somewhere around the truth. Contemporaries noted the tendency of even the smallest chandler's and backstreet provision shop to keep a gallon or two of gin for sale by the quartern (quarter pint) or half-quartern. 'Chimists' and apothecaries customarily sold gin as a pick-me-up. Investing in small quantities of gin, hawking it door to door or selling it from a cellar or front room had become a way for many women to supplement earnings from the needle or taking in washing. It seems true enough: gin was everywhere.[80]

Most of this trade, and all of it in the hands of the petty vendors, was unlicensed, partly because of uncertainty in the law and partly because it had grown so fast. It was this unlicensed trade in gin that Parliament sought belatedly to control with a series of acts, the first in 1729 and the eighth in 1751, this hectic parliamentary activity some testimony to the urgency and difficulty of the problem. The most dramatic was the act of 1736 for suppressing gin entirely, by a combination of a punitive tax on sales and a £50 annual licence to sell it that no one could afford to buy. As no one did, then all gin sellers were breaking the law. The law was enforced by 'the common informer', any person laying information before the magistrates on which a summons was issued and proceedings begun. The informer received a £5 reward for each conviction. With thousands of gin sellers in London, a small industry grew up around the suppression of the gin trade. But the informer's business proved more dangerous than lucrative.

Rioting against the 1736 Act – 'No *Gin*, No *King*' – was succeeded by even fiercer rioting against the informers. Many were severely beaten and 'two killed by the Populace', it was reported in November 1737; in 1738 a new Gin Act had to be passed to give special protection to informers. By July 1738, though, the numbers of gin sellers prosecuted were formidable. Some 12,000 were said to have been convicted in London, with 4,000 sent to the Bridewells or houses of correction, unable to pay the mandatory £10 fine. But it all had little effect on the sale of gin. Some of the trade went underground, with elaborate ruses to keep the identity of the seller secret. Of those convicted, many must have resumed from the point at which they were interrupted. For the production of gin in England and Wales, and presumably its consumption, continued to rise: some 3.4 million gallons of spirits had been produced around the start of the gin craze in 1723, almost doubling to 6.4 million in 1735. That fell to 4.3 million in 1737 but then rose sharply, peaking at 8.2 million in 1743 – an extraordinary figure not matched again for a hundred years, and then in very different circumstances (with a far larger home population and a big imperial export trade). In 1743, admitting defeat, another Gin Act reversed the policy of prohibition in favour of regulation by means of an affordable tax and a cheap annual licence.[81]

From that point gin selling more readily gravitated to the public house and the production of spirits declined to 6.6–7.1 million gallons in 1750–51. Those were years of the final gin panic, stimulated by a perceived increase in crime in London, and accompanied by much fevered prose and a masterstroke of propaganda. Hogarth's magic pencil in *Gin Lane* and *Beer Street* (1751) probably did more for the anti-gin cause than all the ink spilled in the previous twenty-five years. It certainly fixed in the mind of posterity an awful vision of the age of gin that more than any other has come to define the first half of the eighteenth century in London. The final Gin Act of 1751 raised the spirit excise duty, and so the price of gin, and tried to come down hard once more

on unlicensed sellers. Rather than revolutionising policy in this area
the act of 1751 encouraged the shift towards corralling the trade in
the public house that had begun in 1743. The fall in spirit production
gathered pace, with 5.1 million gallons distilled in 1755, and 3.7 million
in 1758, after which levels returned to those before 1723.

By 1759 the gin craze was over. A combination of enforcement,
anti-gin publicity and a rise in real wages from the early 1740s all did
something to weaken the reliance on gin that had transformed the
drinking habits of the London poor. Even so, gin remained a favourite
stimulant among the labouring classes. In the Old Bailey Proceedings
from 1720 to 1751, Geneva or gin is mentioned in 399 trials or ordinary's accounts, with some double-counting; the number in the admittedly longer period from 1752 to 1799 is 820. And spirit production
rose again in the 1790s, years of financial hardship and falling living
standards once more, with a peak of 4.7 million gallons produced
in 1796.

Alongside these great temporary changes in the drinking habits of
the poorer sort of Londoner, beer never lost its favoured position nor
the public house its popularity. Like all the pleasures of the poor, the
pub was seen by moralists as the root of much evil. In the 1790s the
reforming magistrate Patrick Colquhoun noted a tendency 'for whole
families (men, women, and children) of the labouring poor' to frequent
the public house, 'where all their little earnings are spent in eating
expensively, and drinking ale and spirits'. He especially deplored the
use of the pub among women, formerly confined to public holidays or
the haunt of 'infamous prostitutes'.[82] On the other hand it was possible
to see this socialising of drinking in a positive light, breaking down a
culture of hard drinking by labouring men that can only have been detri-
mental to family life. And it was one further example of the infinite capacity
of the public house to adapt to the changing needs of Londoners – all
classes of Londoners at that.

We have already seen some of the guises in which the London pub
draped itself in the eighteenth century. For many journeymen the
taproom's pay table was where they received wages late on a Saturday
night, and where the landlord was often banker for their friendly societies, box and burial clubs; some were 'houses of call' or employment
exchanges for trades from shoemakers to actors, where worker and
master could be put in touch with one another. These encounters took
place within relatively comfortable and convivial surroundings, shared

by neighbours, in a city where domestic comforts of the most basic kind were often hard to come by.

Even for the labouring poor, and notwithstanding Colquhoun's observations late in the century, the pub's taproom was a largely male environment in the working week. And for the wide ranks of the middling sort the public house – and to a similar extent the coffee house, with many characteristics common to both – was the very fundament of male sociability in the eighteenth century.

Freemasonry and other quasi-secret societies, for instance, proved greatly popular among higher artisans, tradesmen, professionals and above. Between about 1720 and 1780 there were several thousand Freemasons and others in London, and all their lodge meetings seem to have been held in public houses, from the famous Crown and Anchor Tavern behind the Strand in Arundel Street to the lowly Anchor and Crown in Short's Gardens, Seven Dials. Clubs of every sort met in pubs and coffee houses across London, involving every rank of the middling sort and the quality: from the No Pay No Liquor Club at the Queen and Artichoke in the Hampstead Road, where new members had to wear a hat in the shape of a quart pot and drink the health of their brethren in a gilt goblet of ale, to the Je Ne Scai Quoi Club at the Star and Garter, Pall Mall, where the Prince of Wales and his brothers were members in the 1790s.

Learned societies frequently began their existence in a public or coffee house, like the Society of Arts at Rawthmell's Coffee House, Henrietta Street, Covent Garden in March 1754; and some found no other home, like the Mathematical Society of Spitalfields, founded at the Monmouth's Head in 1717, moving to the White Horse, then to the Ben Jonson's Head, then in 1772 to the Black Swan in Brown's Lane (now Hanbury Street), where in 1783 it merged with a local historical society, formerly held at the George in Carter's Rents. Meeting weekly on Saturday nights, its members limited to 'the square of eight', it had a library of over 400 volumes, a loan collection of some fifty mathematical instruments and subscribed to the *Annual Register* – all for just sixpence a quarter.[83] The pub was also often the birthplace of London's charities: the famous Thatched House Tavern in St James's Street, for instance, housed the weekly meetings of the Society for the Discharge and Relief of Persons Imprisoned for Small Debts from 1772, before it was strong enough to set up an office in Craven Street, Strand; and the Thatched House was frequent home to the most prestigious and select of London's many musical fraternities, the Noblemen and Gentlemen's Catch Club, founded by the Earl of Sandwich and others in 1761.[84]

Besides this important role as host to London's associational and institutional fertility the pub supplemented the city's performance venues. The White Swan in Exchange Alley, Lombard Street, held concerts in the 1720s and 1730s, the Queen's Arms Tavern in Newgate Street was well known for its chamber music recitals in the 1780s and there were many others. Exhibitions of monsters and so on were frequently held in pubs and coffee houses, as we have seen, and so were debating societies, most famous of all the Robin Hood, Essex Street, Strand, but with numerous others nearby. As debating attracted larger audiences it tended to move into the great rooms of Carlisle House, and the Casino in Great Marlborough Street, home to the Female Parliament, solely for women debaters, from around 1780, or Mr Greenwood's Room in the Haymarket, home to La Belle Assemblée, another women-only society, around the same time.

The pub was also the traditional home of the 'spouting club', 'so frequent in this town' its chief magistrate complained in 1769, where amateur actors tried their nerve and others' patience at soliloquies or small group performances in front of what must often have been a testing audience. Spouting clubs emerged around the beginning of the century and were flourishing by the end. They were particular favourites in the labouring quarters of London. We hear of a spouting club at Jacob's Well, Barbican, for instance, and in an upstairs room at a pub near Tyburn Turnpike, 'Where young people generally resort, some for amusement, and some with a view to qualifying themselves for the stage', around 1780; and in the second-floor back room of a 'shabby public-house in Whitechapel', where 'we found a group of plebeians of both sexes most ridiculously mispending their time by neglecting their respective vocations'.[85]

A moment's pleasure away from bench or counter was enough to raise the ire of the scribblers of Grub Street, paragons of sober duty as no doubt they were. But, of course, the public house was an irresistible lure for all ranks of the middling sort too. Joseph Brasbridge, admirably frank about the weak will that undermined his City silversmith's business from around 1785, was a member of the Highflyer Club at the Turf Coffee House, founded by one of the Tattersalls, where singing and hard drinking and horsey talk combined. He was often at the Globe, among company favoured by Boswell and others, at the

Cider Cellar in Maiden Lane and the Spread Eagle in the Strand, very lively once the theatres closed; he belonged to the Free and Easy under the Rose, a club of long-standing at the Horn Tavern, Fleet Street; and he often played a hand in card clubs at the Crown and Rolls, Chancery Lane, and the Queen's Arms, St Paul's Churchyard.[86] For inevitably the public house had a part in that other great craze of the age, longer-lived than gin and attracting all ranks: gambling.

'This Extravagant Itch of Gaming'

There was 'no Nation in Europe so much addicted to Play as we are', it was said in 1751, 'nor any City where there are greater Sums lost' than London. Gaming in London had many faces both public and private. It was an integral part of many public pleasures because most sport, if not all, drew a significant part of its spectators from those who were betting on the outcome, and many sporting men and women competed for prizes of one kind or another. Gaming was a frequent accompaniment to other pleasures: rooms were set aside for cards at Carlisle House on masquerade nights and at other balls, masked or otherwise. And it was a large London industry in its own right. The various lotteries sanctioned by Parliament – for buying collections to endow the British Museum, to preserve the Adelphi from ruin and many other public purposes – spawned a host of 'Lottery Offices' attracting ticket buyers with the sort of array of coloured lamps that Mrs Cornelys had first popularised at Carlisle House: 'if the passion for play cannot be suppressed,' wrote the satirist Samuel Foote, 'all that human wisdom can do, is to turn private vices to the use of the public.' Certainly, gambling made work for many hands: a 'List of Officers' in 'the most notorious Gaming-houses' ran to more than eighteen job titles, including 'Two *Crowpees*, who watch the Cards', 'Two *Puffs*, who have Money given them to decoy others to play', a *Porter*, who is generally a Soldier of the Foot-Guards' and '*Common-bail, Affidavit-men, Ruffians, Bravoes, Assassins*' to enforce debts with the aid of 'a *Newgate* Solicitor'.[87]

Gaming often had much of both high and low life about it. Many sporting – that is, gambling – occasions brought together all ranks of Londoners, mostly men but not invariably so, to enjoy the action, the excitement of winning and losing, and the fun to be had from an incongruous assembly.

Cockfighting, for instance, whose sole object was betting and which according to foreigners was a uniquely English pastime, was popular among all ranks of gamblers throughout the century. It was a bloody business. The cocks were bred for aggression and armed with sharpened silver spurs. Bets were paid out only on a death or near mortality, two cocks too exhausted to continue rendering the bets void. Contests were divided into individual 'battles', for a purse of a few pounds, or 'mains', where a champion cock would emerge from thirty-two contestants and win some hundreds of pounds for his owner. Interest was further stimulated by cock owners being advertised as 'the Gentlemen of Essex' against 'the Gentlemen of London' and so on. The most fashionable venues were the Royal Cockpit on the south side of St James's Park (entrance 2s 6d, the same as Ranelagh) and the Gray's Inn Cockpit, north of Jockey's Fields, but there were numerous hole-and-corner places in districts high and low: a cockpit in James Street, Haymarket, was suppressed as a nuisance in 1761, and we hear of others like the New Red-Lion Cockpit in Horseshoe Alley, Middle Moorfields, in the 1750s and one in Pickled Egg Walk, Ray Street, Clerkenwell, in the 1770s, for instance. But the Royal Cockpit was full of the quality. Richard Rigby told George Selwyn in 1745, 'I am just got home from a cock-match, where I have won forty pounds in ready money', and the Duke of Ancaster and others were making bets of 100 guineas or more on a match at the Royal Cockpit in 1762. It was said at various times in the century that cockfighting had lost favour with the quality, but as late as 1799 the papers continued to advertise battles at 10 guineas and mains at 300 at the Royal Cockpit in the prime cocking season of early spring.[88]

By all accounts cockfighting was a spectacle confined to men and so probably were the many other betting sports where beast was pitted against beast. Bear- and bull-baiting, where a chained animal was set upon by dogs usually brought by the spectators, flourished in the early years of the century at William Wells's Bear Garden in Tothill Fields, Westminster, at the New Bear Garden, Marylebone, and most famously until 1744 at 'The King's Bear Garden' at Hockley-in-the-Hole, now Ray Street, Clerkenwell. Baiting appears to have been a spectacle of the labouring poor especially, though there were always visitors enough from the middling sort to record their impressions. It required hard hearts to feel nothing for the animals' torture. Zacharias von Uffenbach visited a show in June 1710 where a bull was baited by some thirty butchers' dogs, two or three at a time, some having to be prised from their grip on the bull's throat with poles; a young bear was similarly treated, and a bull was dressed with lighted fire-crackers with several dogs 'let loose on him on a sudden', resulting in a 'monstrous hurly-burly'; and a jack-ass, not tied down but 'saddled with an ape on his back', fought dogs a couple at a time. Prizes were given to dogs judged the bravest. Bear-baiting, and the rare shows of tiger- and leopard-baiting, seem to have grown out of fashion in the second half of the century, while bull-baiting continued at Tothill Fields past the century's end. Even so, a bear was baited on the ice when the Thames froze opposite Rotherhithe as late as January 1789, and bear- and badger-baiting continued at notorious Black Boy Alley, Chick Lane, past the century's end. Other forms of animal torment with betting as a side-show were cock-throwing, where sticks were shied at a captive cock, especially on Shrove Tuesday, largely but not entirely suppressed at the century's end; duck-hunting with dogs, sometimes enlivened by tying an owl to the duck's back, also out of favour by the 1790s; and dog-fighting in the fields around London, popular throughout the century and beyond.[89]

If much organised fighting between animals was a largely plebeian affair, with the notable exception of cocking, prizefighting attracted all ranks of Londoner. Hockley-in-the-Hole and James Figgs's Amphitheatre at the Boarded House, Marylebone, were favoured venues: 'These are the schools that have made so many brave men,' Mrs Peachum tells Filch the pickpocket in *The Beggar's Opera*. Even Mr Spectator reported from Hockley-in-the-Hole, that resort 'of the lower order of Britons', in July 1712. He witnessed a bloody contest slugged out with swords and staves and there were women in the audience. Fights like these were made more exciting by public challenges printed on handbills and in the papers. Men fought men, women fought women, and occasion-ally women fought men. César de Saussure saw a match in February 1728 between a 'stout Irishwoman' and a 'small Englishwoman' who fought in 'little bodices and very short petticoats of white linen', with two-handed hacking swords. Action had to be halted while cuts were sewn and bandaged in the ring. A bad cut would conclude a contest: the Englishwoman won after the other was cut three times, once across the throat. No doubt many of these gladiatorial combats were fixed to secure the most profitable outcome. Nonetheless they were very popular in the first half of the century and took place at many venues.[90]

Fighting with swords and staves seems to have been rare from the late 1730s, but women's prizefighting with bare knuckles and nails continued to the century's end. A contest between two women and two tailors in the Spaw Fields for a 4-guinea prize ended in victory for '"the ladies"' in 1768; and a match between two 'female pugilists' at Camberwell, the *'fair* ones' ending 'nearly in *buff* ', was savoured in the *Bon Ton* as late as March 1791.[91]

The big money, though, went on the male bare-knuckle champions. They were one of the most fashionable objects of gaming in the last two or three decades of the century at country venues like Moulsey Hurst, Barnet, Finchley, Kentish Town and many other places. They drew the quality, of course, but the rag, tag and bobtail followed uproariously in their wake. In early 1788 at the village of Odiham in north Hampshire, several hundred of the *ton* arrived in their carriages and paid a half-guinea each to enter the paddock where a ring had been erected for Daniel Mendoza, the Jewish champion, to fight Richard Humphries. A guard of prizefighters armed with clubs protected the paddock from the thousands more who'd turned out to have their fun and their fling: 'but what can resist the shock of an English mob? The paddock was broken down, and the torrent rushed in.' Humphries won. The *Annual Register* wryly noted that, against the grain of London life, 'upwards of 20,000l. sterling of bets will be transferred from the Jews to the Christians – *rather to the* Gentiles.'[92]

Very great sums were also at stake on the annual festivals of horse racing at Newmarket and Epsom Downs, markedly popular from the 1730s on, with less profligate meetings at Banstead Downs, Hackney Marshes, Hampstead, Belsize, Kentish Town, Tothill Fields and elsewhere. It was indeed an age of horsemanship and men could win big bets by galloping upright in the stirrups for two miles at Barnet Common in the 1780s, or by racing from Colchester to Whitechapel for a purse of £50 in 1761, or from Shoreditch to Ware in Hertfordshire in less than an hour for 100 guineas in 1738 – the bet was won but the horse died. And horses weren't the only sporting animals: 'My Lord Rockingham and my nephew Lord Orford have made a match of five hundred pounds, between five turkeys and five geese, to run from Norwich to London,' Horace Walpole reported in 1756.[93]

Any human endeavour was also worth a wager. There was much

betting on tennis matches, on cricket – a match between women's teams of six wives and six spinsters at Moulsey Hurst in 1775 had 'great betts depending on it' – on carriage racing, on Thames rowing and swimming matches, on target shooting, on skittles and bowls, and especially on foot racing. They were all '*Sham Matches*,' the cynics said, 'to draw in strangers, and to impose upon them, by a few rascally Cheats and Tricks'; no doubt there was much truth in that, but it didn't diminish their popularity. 'Running footmen' were employed not just to make a show on the streets but to be champion racers and money earners for their employers. Four Welsh women walked from Westminster Bridge to the Boot and Crown at Deptford in less than two and a half hours for a wager of £20 in 1761; a Chelsea fish hawker ran seven miles from Hyde Park to Brentford with fifty-six pounds of fish on his head and a coachmaker's journeyman ran a wheel eight miles in one hour on St George's Fields, both in 1763.[94] And in 1733 Baron Pollnitz watched a man wager to run round St James's Park within a certain time. To aid his progress, or perhaps as part of the bet, 'he stripped himself stark-naked, so that his Hand served him for a Fig-leaf':

In this State of Nature he travers'd along the Mall, thro' an infinite Concourse of People. The Ladies, astonished at such a Sight, knew not how to keep their Countenances: Some turned their Heads aside, others hid their Faces with their Fans, but they all made a Row as well as the Men to let him pass by. After he had finish'd his race, he gravely put on his Cloaths near *Whitehall*, where he left 'em; and as he had won the Wager, abundance of people, instead of checking him for his Insolence, threw him Money. Judge by this, if any People are so good-natur'd and happy as the *English*.[95]

This obsession of the age played itself out most ferociously not in the prize ring at Odiham or Moulsey Hurst but in the drawing rooms and private clubs of St James's. Gambling in fashionable life had gone on in the early years of the century but had tended to be a male passion and somewhat disreputable, with 'sharpers' or professional gamesters having a significant part of the play. But it seems that the gambling climate, and the lure of easy money, in which the South Sea Bubble blew and burst, openly encouraged all sorts of play. Richard Seymour's *Court Gamester* of 1719, an instruction manual, puffed his wares by advising that 'Gameing is become so much the Fashion among the *Beau Monde*, that He, who in Company should appear ignorant of the *Games* in Vogue, would be reckon'd low bred, and hardly fit for Conversation'. The games in vogue then, he claimed, were ombre, picquet and chess.[96]

Seymour's guide reached an eighth edition by 1754, when the games in fashion had greatly expanded, with twenty-two card games alone. By then play had become very much a passion for women of the quality as well as men. The winnings of the King, Queen and princesses at play on Twelfth Night were reported in the papers, giving royal sanction to 'this extravagant itch of gaming'. Lord Hervey, a great favourite of the ladies in and around the court of George II, was said to have lived on his winnings at quadrille, his victims entirely female. Eliza Haywood lamented in the *Female Spectator* that '*now* [1744], not to *love play* is unpolite'. Card tables were the main attraction of fashionable 'routs' or 'drums' in the 1740s and after. Given by lady hostesses for mixed company, these evening assemblies also combined dancing, food and conversation. They were an important part of women's domestic amusements at the west end of the town, and cards were an irresistibly fascinating part of them. In June 1759 Walpole noted how 'Loo is mounted to its zenith; the parties last till one or two in the morning: We played at Lady Hertford's last week . . . It is now adjourned to Mrs Fitzroy's . . .' As always, a few were more concerned with the dark side of play. The Bluestockings' intellectual gatherings in these middle decades of the century self-consciously eschewed gaming, and for the novelists who made up some of their number card play was a common and destructive fictional theme. Inevitably, and brilliantly, William Hogarth warned of its dangers to virtue in *The Lady's Last Stake* (1759).[97]

From the 1760s and 1770s this domestic play became deeper, so deep indeed that some were swallowed whole. Even in the City, assemblies were infected with the West End habit, one 'very near the *Tower*' in April 1773 had 'two very genteel rooms crammed with card-tables, great caps, and maccaroni heads' of fashion-conscious women and men, with 'a large proportion of wine and punch constantly offering itself at your elbow . . .' At routs of the quality at the west end of the town, faro tables passed from one assembly to another, their proprietors paying the noble hostess up to 50 guineas for the favour. Huge losses could accumulate. A 'lady, at the west end of the town' was reported to have lost 3,000 guineas at loo at a single sitting in 1766. And Lord and Lady Spencer, the parents of Georgiana Duchess of Devonshire, had lost most of their fortune at the gaming tables by 1784; by 1786

Georgiana herself owed at least £100,000 in gambling debts and in 1789 was effectively bankrupt, her creditors including Thomas Coutts's bank in the Strand.[98]

Men's play could be even deeper, the consequences even more disastrous. The most serious play tended to take place at private gaming houses or clubs, some more exclusive and private than others, all apparently needing an introduction rather than accepting casual callers off the street. Gaming houses were a feature of London life from the 1720s. Raids by the magistrates on these 'disorderly houses' were spasmodic from at least 1731 but did nothing to deter their numbers or their flagrant defiance of authority. In 1744 Eliza Haywood 'could name a certain spot of ground within the liberties of *Westminster*, which contains no less than fourteen public gaming-houses in the compass of two hundred yards', probably Covent Garden, where houses run by Lady Mordington and Lady Castle were publicly shamed by the Middlesex Grand Jury that same year. By 1791 the *Bon Ton* reported that 'The gambling-houses in St James's-street and Pall Mall are multiplying faster than ever', not including 'the Pharo Tables of about a dozen women of quality, Lords, Baronets, &c. which are to go from house to house during the winter . . .' And the gambling houses did much to make themselves immune from the London police. A raid on 19 Great Suffolk Street, Haymarket, in April 1798 took an hour to break through two 'very stout doors, strongly bolted and barred'. The house was empty when entered, gamblers and the people of the house escaping 'by a subterraneous passage, through a long range of cellars . . . terminating at a house in Hedge-lane [now Whitcomb Street]'.[99]

Most famous of all were the private members' clubs for the richest and smartest men in the land. Though their primary purpose was gambling they were invulnerable to official assault as a private undertaking, new members added by election and not by purchase, and reckoned too smart to be disorderly. The best-known were Boodle's (founded 1762, Pall Mall, moving to the east side of St James's Street, 1782); Brooks's (1764 at Almack's, Pall Mall, moving to the west side of St James's Street in 1778); and White's, oldest of all, beginning as White's Chocolate House in St James's Street in 1693. At first White's was run as any other coffee house, though an exclusive club was formed in part of it some time in the 1720s and by the 1740s it seems to have become entirely private. In 1755 it moved to new and larger premises opposite Brooks's on the east side of St James's Street. These two clubs attracted not only the richest men in London but the most brilliant. By the 1780s they had taken on opposing political complexions, 'so that from opposite sides of the same street, White's & Brooks's were the head=quarters of the Court & Opposition Camps . . .'[100]

But it was the extraordinary recklessness of the gaming at these places that most firmly seized the imagination of fashionable Londoners from the 1770s on. Losses in a single night at hazard, a game with dice with up to twenty men playing, frequently reached £4,000–5,000. In 1772, in one continuous session lasting twenty-two hours, Charles James Fox lost £11,000; over the next two nights he and his brother Stephen lost a further £21,000 between them. At the end of 1773 Horace Walpole reported to a friend that Lord Holland, the two boys' father, was dying and 'is paying Charles Fox's debts, or most of them, for they amount to ONE HUNDRED AND THIRTY THOUSAND POUNDS – aye, aye . . . but while there is a broker or gamester upon the face of the earth, Charles will not be out of debt'. It was true. In 1781 the bailiffs were in possession of Fox's house in St James's Street, 'two carts at Charles's door filling, by the Jews, with his goods, clothes, books, and pictures', 'Charles's dirty furniture in the street . . .' All the while Fox was at play at Brooks's, trying to restore his fortune. And for a time he did.[101]

Samuel Johnson was famously sceptical of the stories of disasters at play: '"Depend upon it, Sir, this is mere talk. *Who* is ruined by gaming? You will not find six instances in an age."' But gaming played its part in the miseries of eighteenth-century London nonetheless. It was thought to have been at least a contributing factor in some fashionable suicides: Lord Milton's son, Mr Damer, hired a room with four prostitutes and a blind fiddler at the Bedford Arms in Covent Garden before dismissing the company and shooting himself in the head in 1776; he was a married man of a depressive cast but owed part of £70,000 gambling debts with his two brothers. And Mr Skrine, an MP, shot himself at a tavern in Newgate Street in 1783 having lost heavily at Brooks's shortly before.[102]

Brooks's and other clubs also kept a Betting Book where wagers could be noted, memories proving fallible in such matters. Hundreds of bets were listed. There were bets on lives – that X would die before a certain date or before Y – on politics, on others' bets, on every vagary of public and private life. So, at White's, we read that 'Mr O'Brien bets Mr. Rigby ten guineas to five, that Coll. John Waldegrave is not married to Miss Peggy Banks in a twelvemonth' (1747); and at Brooks's, 'Ld.

Cholmondeley has given two guineas to Lord Derby, to receive 500 Gs. whenever his lordship fucks a woman in a Balloon one thousand yards from the Earth.'[103] Their lordships remind us that sex and London's public pleasures were never far apart.

The Young Wanton

IX

MARTHA STRACEY'S LONDON –
PROSTITUTION

'How Do You Do Brother Waterman?': Prostitutes

Stracey was a poor, ignorant Woman, not 19 Years of Age. She own'd she had been a common Strumpet and Thief for five Years. – She confessed robbing Humphreys, the Chairman; but declared there was nobody with her at the Time of the Robbery.[1]

WE know little more about Martha Stracey or Tracey than this terse newspaper account of her hanging at Tyburn on 15 March 1745. She had been reluctant to tell the Ordinary of Newgate any details of her short life in the days before her execution. He found her 'of a mean Capacity and slow of Understanding', but perhaps it was just that her plight weighed too heavily with her: 'When I spake to her, she always wept bitterly . . .'

At the end he gleaned something. Martha was born in the parish of St James Westminster; she didn't know when but thought she was eighteen or twenty years old. Her father had been a chairman – ironic, because she was hanged for robbing a chairman of a guinea – but he died when she was about two and her mother died also just six years later. Martha was taken into the workhouse as an orphan and when about eleven was bound to a 'Market Woman, whom she serv'd for three Years, and was very well treated by her. She bought her Cloaths and sent her to School.' But her mistress left London and put Martha to another woman, a drinker who neglected the girl and pawned her clothes. Martha left when about fourteen, tried to set up for herself but fell into bad company and went on the town as a prostitute, boosting her earnings through petty theft.[2]

On 23 December 1744, at around 12.30 in the morning, Martha approached William Humphreys in the Strand, near Charing Cross. Their accounts of the encounter differed. Martha told the Ordinary that Humphreys negotiated to have her in an alleyway for a shilling. Humphreys's evidence at the Old Bailey had a harsher ring: 'the prisoner met me, and said, *where are you going, my dear*; I said, *what is that to you, you bitch.*' He swore that two men then attacked him and pulled him backwards on to a step while Stracey rifled his pockets. But Humphreys grabbed Martha's coat and wouldn't let go. He told the court she then shouted, '*d—n him, kill him, he squeaks.*' It was almost certainly these words that would hang Martha Stracey three months later.[3]

The row attracted two watchmen and a crowd and the men thought to be Stracey's accomplices disappeared in the confusion. At St Martin's watch-house Martha's pockets were turned out but no guinea was found. The constable of the night ordered one of the watchmen who 'has got a pretty good hand at searching' to 'search her behind and before (I ask pardon, my Lord)':

I pulled off her stockings, searched all her clothes, and found 2s 4d and a bag of tobacco; then I searched her arm pits, and every where that I could, but could not find the guinea; then I said, *D—n you open your mouth*; she opened it, and turned out her tongue double; I put my finger in her mouth, and brought the guinea out: she said something afterwards in a vulgar manner, but I could not tell what it was.

The constable pressed Martha to identify the men but she refused. Then as he was leaving the watch-house she appeared to change her mind, pulled him back and 'whispered me in the ear . . . Mr. Constable, *I know it is in your power to leave the watch-house door open, and let me go out, if you will, you shall have a — whenever you please.*' Had Martha herself 'squeaked' and named the men who wrestled Humphreys to the ground she would probably have saved her life.

Prostitution, with all its attendant violence and humiliations, was one of the great facts of London life in the eighteenth century. It seemed that prostitutes were everywhere. Travellers in particular were struck by this peculiarity of London. Von Uffenbach in 1710 noted the 'vast number' of 'harlots . . . here especially by nights in the streets', and by the 1720s it was a commonplace that 'no City in Europe' – some said

17. The Custom House, Lower Thames Street, *c.*1750 (Benjamin Cole). Once discharged onto the busy quays, goods were stored in the large warehouses attached to the House until customs duties were paid. This was the third Custom House on the site, the previous two having been destroyed by fire.

18. Wapping, *c.*1800 (Thomas Rowlandson), passengers and crew taking boat for the ships anchored in the river. The upper pool was so congested around this time that ships could wait a week at Deptford for sufficient passage to manoeuvre upriver.

19. The Royal Exchange piazza, 1788 (Philip de Loutherbourg). The merchants' main City meeting place was divided into 'walks' assigned by place of trade or category of merchant (the Jews' Walk, the Jamaica Walk, Irish Walk and so on), though Loutherbourg captures as many dogs as merchants.

20. Smithfield Market, c.1800 (Thomas Rowlandson). One of the sights of London, Smithfield was the greatest market for cattle, sheep and horses in Europe. It was also the main meeting place for town and country, the market and nearby inns swarming with farmers and their men from all over England.

21. *The Walking Stationer* – 'God bless you, pity the Blind', *c.*1760 (Paul Sandby). The Londoners were said to be especially generous to blind beggars, and to black people begging in the streets.

22. *Rare Mackerel*, 1760 (Paul Sandby). Most street sellers and beggars – the line between them was often blurred – were women, this mackerel seller a particularly fierce amazon of the tribe.

23. Thomas Coe, *c.*1745. Trade cards were a popular form of advertising, giving work for the artists, engravers and printers of London as well as their clients. Many, as here, were exuberantly elaborate.

24. *Industry and Idleness*, Plate I, 1747 (William Hogarth). This great morality tale opens in what is considered a truthful representation of a master silk-weaver's workshop in Spitalfields, one of the great manufacturing trades of London – and one of its most turbulent.

25. *The Distrest Poet*, 1737 (William Hogarth). The poverty of the hackney writer was legendary and lamented interminably by the writers themselves. A bare garret, debt (the milk-maid showing her unpaid tally), a slaving and loyal wife, a hungry bawling child – all were often the lot of those educated men and women condemned to write for a living.

Fun upon Fun, or the first and second part of Miss Kitty Fisher's Merry thought. No Joke like a True Joke. Come, who'l Fish in my Fishpond?

26. *Street Seller of Literature*, c.1760 (Paul Sandby), hawking the first and second parts of the memoirs of Kitty Fisher, the courtesan, competing with the ballad seller over the way. The Londoners were more literate than any other part of the nation and had an insatiable appetite for print.

27. *Twelve London Cries, done from the Life*, 1768 (Paul Sandby). London life was an inexhaustible subject for the artist, and artists had never prospered as they did in the eighteenth century.

28. *Old Joseph Nollekens and His Venus*, 1800 (Thomas Rowlandson). Artists frequently used London prostitutes as models. Here the notoriously lecherous sculptor takes an appreciative look at his subject.

29. Green Park, 27 April 1749 (published by Bowles and Carver). To celebrate the Peace of Aix-la-Chapelle of the previous year a gigantic wooden palace was erected for a fireworks display. Handel's *Music for the Royal Fireworks* was written for the occasion.

30. Ranelagh Gardens, Chelsea, 1752 (Canaletto). These were the smartest of the London pleasure gardens, the Rotunda – where visitors walked round and round for all to see – was 'the best market we have in England' for marriages, according to Edward Gibbon.

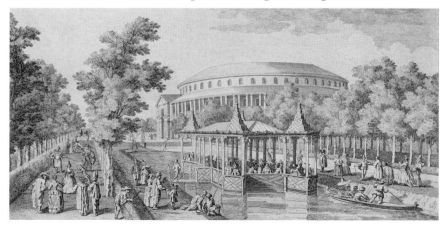

31. Vauxhall Gardens, 1785 (Thomas Rowlandson). Vauxhall offered musical and open-air entertainment for most classes of Londoner except the very poor. Foreign visitors thought there was nothing to match it in Europe, and Rowlandson has populated his print with a bevy of celebrities of the time.

32. Bartholomew Fair, c.1808 (Thomas Rowlandson). London's annual bacchanalia ran for a fortnight or so from St Bartholomew's Day, 24 August, filling West Smithfield with theatrical and dancing booths, menageries, exhibitions of monstrosities, swing-boats, and street sellers of food and liquor.

'the World' — 'can shew an Example of this, but our own'. Even in Paris, 'Men meet no Temptations in the Streets', and it was true that Frenchmen were among those most shocked by 'the extraordinary licentiousness that reigns openly in London'.[4]

None of this seems to have abated at any time in the century. Saunders Welch, a prominent Westminster magistrate, complained in 1758 that 'Prostitutes swarm in the streets of this metropolis to such a degree' that it seemed 'the whole town was one general stew', or brothel. Another Frenchman in the 1760s noted how London's prostitutes were 'more numerous than at Paris, and have more liberty and effrontery than at Rome itself . . . Whole rows of them accost passengers in the broad day-light, and above all, foreigners.' And at the end of the 1780s, far from declining in the age of politeness, the London debating societies of the middling sort were pondering the causes of 'the encrease' and 'the Prevalence' of 'Female prostitution' in the capital.[5]

It was in these years that magistrates and others began to bandy around stupendous estimates of the numbers of London prostitutes — 40,000 in the 1780s, 50,000 in the 1790s, even 65,000 or one in seven or so of every female in London aged nought to a hundred. They were all guesses of the flimsiest kind. Patrick Colquhoun's influential number of 50,000 in the mid-1790s contained 25,000 'in different ranks in Society' living 'partly by Prostitution, including the multitudes of low females, who cohabit with labourers and others without matrimony', so turning every common-law wife into a whore.[6]

It probably didn't take more than a few score flaunting women in the flickering lamps of the Strand at night to appear a 'herd' or a 'swarm'. But it is probably safe to assume that prostitution was a large source of employment for young women in London, at least as great as the street-selling trades, with which prostitution was sometimes combined. At any one time we might safely reckon there were some few thousands of active prostitutes in London's streets and bawdy houses, somewhere say from 3,000 to 7,000.[7] And for contemporaries from the provinces prostitution in London was entirely exceptional. No doubt there were prostitutes in every town, but nothing like the numbers involved and nothing like the free and anonymous market within which they operated in the metropolis. Indeed, prostitution was one of the attractions of London, actively drawing young men to the capital. In January 1758 that morally upright publisher of Pall Mall, Robert

Dodsley, tried to woo the poet Richard Berenger back to London from the country in these terms:

Come to Town, therefore, if not for our sakes at least for your own. The Piazzas of Covent Garden afford in January a better shelter than any Grove in Christendom; and what are your mossy banks and purling streams in the Country, to a sparkling bowl & and a downy bed at the Hummums? Your Naiads, your dryads & and your Hamadryads are enough to starve a man to death; but with ye Nymphs of Drury you may be as warm as your heart can wish – and warmer too: And will not these comfortable considerations invite you to Town?[8]

Who were these nymphs? Reliable statistical material is hard to come by but what there is shows, unsurprisingly, that most were young. When twenty-five prostitutes were taken out of bawdy houses in Hedge Lane in one night-time sweep in 1758 their ages ranged from fifteen to twenty-two, with eleven of them eighteen or nineteen years old. Eighteen was also the age they most frequently went on the town, though two claimed to have begun when they were twelve, one at thirteen and four at fourteen. Prostitutes prosecuted at the Old Bailey whose ages were recorded in the 1790s showed an older profile, with many in their twenties and peaking at thirty, but these were women charged mainly with picking pockets and other property crimes against their customers and older hands were probably over-represented.[9]

The majority of these women were almost certainly migrants to London, if only in reflection of the make-up of the metropolitan population as a whole. A sample of seventy-eight prostitutes committed for trial and held at the Southwark Compter in 1814–29, the closest we can get to our period, showed forty-seven to be migrants and thirty-one London-born, and provides probably a representative glimpse of the likely proportion in the century before. William Hutton, the historian of Birmingham, who wrote up his London journey of 1784, talked to 'many' of the smarter class of prostitute he observed around him, 'Some of the finest women I saw in London'. 'Most of the ladies I conversed with were not natives of London, but were a sacrifice to the metropolis offered by the thirty-nine counties.'[10]

The social backgrounds of these women, whether newcomers or cockneys, seem to have been very mixed. Many came from poor homes like Martha Stracey's and, as in her case, poverty was sharpened and

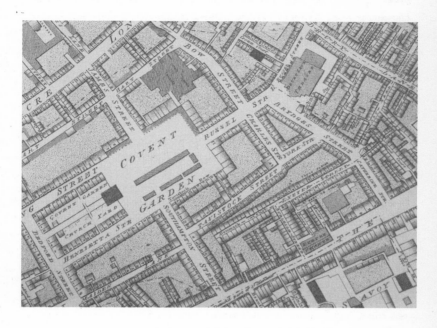

Covent Garden and Drury Lane, *c.*1795

home life disordered by the death or desertion of one parent or both. 'What is it that People in the continual Want of Food, hungry, starving, and perishing, will not be induced to do?' wrote Jacob Ilive in 1757, contemplating the lives of the numerous 'Molls' or 'loose Women', 'debauched because they are poor', among his fellow prisoners at the Clerkenwell House of Correction.[11]

What indeed? The temptations around a pretty girl born into poverty must have required an unnatural obstinacy to resist. We might cite here Mary Brown, born on board ship from Ireland, orphaned and brought up by her godmother, a washerwoman at Rotherhithe, but who ran away when about eleven years old 'and since that time she has been upon the Town'; or Ann Catley, born 'in an obscure Alley off Tower Hill' in 1745, her father a hackney coachman and mother a laundress for soldiers at the Tower. She had a sweet voice and sang in public houses for coppers from the age of ten, losing her virginity at fourteen and then 'taking any fee that was offered'.

Poverty even led parents to recognise the value residing in their daughters' maidenheads: the case of a mother writing to a 'gentleman' offering 'her daughter as a prostitute, being about fourteen years of age' was highlighted in the *Annual Register* of 1759 as one instance of a crime 'oftener practised than detected'; and Hannah More in 1792 came across the case of a well-educated girl of sixteen sold by her father to a fellow prisoner in the King's Bench. Indeed, maidenheads could be sold or forcibly taken in the common belief 'among the lower people, both males and females,' that venereal infections could be cured by passing them to someone not infected – over fifty 'children' were received into the Lock Hospital for this reason between 1746 and 1752.[12]

Country girls might also come from poor backgrounds like these. A man and woman were arrested in the City in 1766 trying to sell for 30 guineas 'a fine girl of eleven years of age'; she was an orphan, taken from Bodmin workhouse in Cornwall by her uncle and brought to London to secure the best price. And in the spring of 1763 Boswell picked up a girl in St James's Park 'who submitted to my lusty embraces'. She was 'a young Shropshire girl, only seventeen, very well-looked, her name Elizabeth Parker. Poor being, she has a sad time of it!'[13]

From these poorer ranks it was probably domestic service that proved the most fruitful source of recruitment for women of the town. In the lower class of servant-keeping households the work could be unremitting ill-rewarded drudgery. Hutton, as a result of his conversations,

thought there were many reasons why women chose or fell into prostitution as a career, 'But the principal cause is idleness. To the generality
of the world, ease is preferable to labour', and no doubt in general he
was right. Yet servants were peculiarly vulnerable, not just to the lure
of idleness but also to the sexual exploitation of men, often within the
household among the employer's family, fellow servants or visitors. It
is young women of the servant class who are largely over-represented
in reports of infanticide, like a poor servant maid at a place near
Execution Dock who gave birth by herself in 1758: 'the infant was
found torn in two, wrapt up in a flannel petticoat, and hid under her
bed. She is secured.' Very many turned to the parish when pregnant
and dismissed from their place: like Lucy Slaughter, twenty-four, yearly
servant with Mrs Poole at Thanet Place on the Westminster side of
Temple Bar, made pregnant by her mistress's son; or Jane Murray, a
yearly servant in Cecil Court, Strand, pregnant by one 'Sinclair of the
Kingdom of Ireland', a law student and 'a Tall thin Genteel Man [who]
generally uses Cecil's Coffee House in Term when he is usually in
England'. Many young women caught like this had little option but to
end up on the town, and so did others who could not stand the dull
and unremunerative vexations of servant life: like Mary Parker, about
twenty-four, formerly a yearly servant at the Lyon and Cat, a bawdy
house in Carey Street, now in 1789 'upon the Town as a Street Walker
and [cannot tell] who is the Father' of her baby daughter; or Betsy
Smith of Dean's Court, Old Bailey, whom Boswell tried to persuade to
take a place rather than be '"At the mercy of every brutal ruffian." She
said masters and mistresses had bad tempers' too and that she would
rather 'be her own mistress'.[14]

Above the servant class, milliners' hands and shop girls were often
connected with prostitutes, and milliners' premises were one of the
common resources of prostitution. 'Take a Survey of all the common
Women of the Town, who take their Walks between *Charing-Cross* and
Fleet Ditch,' thought Richard Campbell in 1747, 'and, I am persuaded,
more than one Half of them have been bred Milliners, have been
debauched in their Houses, and are obliged to throw themselves upon
the Town for Want of Bread, after they have left them.'[15] And higher
still, many ranks of the middling sort encountered that nightmarish
prospect, a lively theme of many eighteenth-century novels, of their
wayward daughters fleeing or seduced to London and living on the
town.

The case of poor Ann Bell, sometimes Sharpe, might stand as one instance. It became a cause célèbre in late 1760. 'She was of a reputable and opulent family in the county of Norfolk,' wrote a friend of her parents, 'deceived, ruined, and debauched' by an army officer quartered near her village. Her reputation lost, she was set to a trade and for a large fee of 72 guineas was apprenticed to 'a very reputable chamber-milliner in Leicester-square'. It was an unfortunate choice. Contact with the fashionable world merely inflamed her 'strong inclination for intriguing'. She abandoned her indentures for lodgings 'in several places, and by several names', including at Madam Modena's in King Street, Soho, and Sarah Parker's at Spring Gardens, Charing Cross, bawdy houses we can assume of one type or another.

While at Sarah Parker's, around September 1760, Ann Bell and another 'young lady, Miss Young', shared in a hard-drinking debauch, lasting three days and nights, at Haddock's Bagnio on the north side of Covent Garden Piazza. Their male companions were Sir William Fowler, an army officer, a wealthy London merchant's son called Willy Sutton and John Moody, that Drury Lane comedian whose bravado we've had cause to admire in another context. The evidence is inconclusive but it appears that Sutton grew violent in drink; he beat Ann Bell on occasions, threatening to cut her with a penknife, and finally stabbing her in the anus and perineum. Despite medical care paid for by a remorseful Fowler, Bell died of a fever, possibly brought on by her infected wounds, in October 1760. Sutton was prosecuted for murder at the instigation of Bell's father and his friends but acquitted at the Old Bailey in February 1761, amid much medical uncertainty over the cause of death. Sutton was doubtless also assisted by his family connections: his younger brother James was a prominent politician, soon to become MP for Devizes. Fowler, on active service in Germany at the time of the trial, shot himself rather than return to testify against his friend.[16]

There were, as the contrasting lives of Martha Stracey and Ann Bell reveal to us, many ranks of prostitute. Even beggars and street finders collected enough coppers to enjoy the lowest class of 'punk' or 'bunter' or 'Hackneyed Whore'. 'I never saw them in the Streets, that I know of,' a watchman of St Bride's Fleet Street testified in 1743 at the Old Bailey about a raid on James Newbold's disorderly house in the appropriately named Love's Court: 'they are not fit for the Streets, they are such poor ragged dismal Toads, and drunk; I believe they ply about

George-Alley, and by the Ditch Side.' Poor and ragged they might have been, but dismal? Another watchman 'was called in there one Night; and they asked me if I would see *a burning Shame*, and one of the Women stuck a lighted Candle – [Counsel.] Let us have no obscene Descriptions.'[17]

Innumerable other women of this same class or just above let us hear their chirpy voices in the Old Bailey Proceedings. One night, also in 1743, Francis Palmer, a garrulous constable of Chick Lane, was checking his own front door in that lively neighbourhood. He had previously given sixpence for some women to have a dram and one of them, Mary ('Moll' or 'Poll') Rosum, had the cheek to follow him. On his doorstep she said, 'Well, I thank you, my Dear, God bless your Cock, or something to that Purpose: She clapp'd her Hand to my Breeches, and went away directly. I did not miss my Watch at that Time . . .' At the Old Bailey, charged with theft, Rosum claimed that Palmer was one of her customers but he told her 'you are too old to be a Whore now . . . I submit to the Court, whether they think I would have to do with such a Creature as that, when there are fine Girls enough to be had . . .' But Polly stuck to her story: 'I have been guilty of no Misdemeanour, but what I did in private to pleasure my Master. Mr Palmer knows I am trusted by the Heads of the Parish, and never wronged any Body.'[18]

When Francis Palmer spoke of fine girls he might have had in mind someone like Hannah Rossiter. She approached Thomas Bigee late one October night in 1741 near Hungerford Stairs with 'How do you do Brother Waterman?' and asked him for a drink. He went along with her to a room in the Haymarket and called for a pint of wine. The tired Bigee lay down on the bed and felt her 'take the Handkerchief off my Neck' but when she began to rummage in his pockets enough was enough: 'said I, you fancy impudent W—e, can't you be content to take my Handkerchief, and not my Money? D— your Eyes, said she, did I take your Handkerchief?' Things got livelier and Bigee called a watchman, who told him 'he knew her to be a Whore and a Thief from her Cradle'. Committed by the justices to prison to await trial, she left the court with Bigee and the police officers: 'she shew'd her white Stockings, and said, do you think these white Stockings can walk to the Gatehouse? No, D—n you, I will have a Coach; and so because she should not plague us, I gave them a Shilling to get Madam a Coach.'[19]

We are given a fleeting but privileged glimpse into the collective life of streetwalkers like this by Jacob Ilive, fascinated by the Molls in Clerkenwell House of Correction:

They take great Delight in sitting in a Ring, and telling Stories of their own Adventures; – how many Men they had bilked, what Sums they had robbed 'em of, and how many Watches they had masoned. Tell who had their M—ds; – how they were first debauched; – how long they had been in Keeping; – how many Children they had had, and what was become of them; – promise how good they would be, when they got out of their present Trouble, – relate their Dreams, tell Stories of Spirits, they could take the Sacrament on it, they had seen; and how often they had heard, they were sure of it, as sure, they would affirm, as God is in Heaven, the Blocks and Beetles beat Hemp of themselves in the Dead of Night, &c. &c. How often, and where they had been in Confinement; whether for Debt or Hard Labour; – how often they had bunted it down to *Portsmouth*, and other Sea-Port Towns; – how they had been at *Bath*, *Sunning*, *Scarborough*, &c. Who had taken them to the Play, gallanted them there, with so many Etcaetera's, that it would fill this, and many of the following Pages, to relate.[20]

Young women like these lodged one or two to a room in the cheap accommodation to be found even in the wealthy parts of London. But if they brought men home, then their lodgings tended to be part of a specialised housing market that grew up around women of the town. Rents were higher, the householder taking a share of his or her lodgers' earnings, some compensation for the risk of prosecution for running a disorderly house. John Cleland's Fanny Hill took lodgings in Covent Garden 'that, by having been for several successions tenanted by ladies of pleasure, the landlord was familiarized to their ways; and provided the rent was duly paid, everything else was as easy and commodious as one could desire', and Cleland was accurate here as in much else. Private lodgings like these ranged across the full spectrum. Miss Oliver at 40 Frith Street, Soho, in 1779 'has elegant lodgings and is company for a nobleman'. A Covent Garden woman, 'not of the common sort', had her own maid and 'a first floor tolerably well, but rather fantastically furnished. The chimney was loaded with silly Chinese ornaments, and festoons of flowers, disposed in a very aukward manner.' Miss Atkins in Henry Mackenzie's novel of 1771, *The Man of Feeling*, lives near Somerset House 'up three pair of stairs' in 'a small room lighted by one narrow lattice, and patched round with shreds of different-coloured paper. In the darkest corner stood something like a bed, before which a tattered coverlet hung by way of curtain.' And, at an even lower end of prostitutes' lodgings, Boswell, the worse for drink, was taken home by a 'red-haired hussy', somewhere in Westminster: 'Horrid room; no fire, no curtains, dirty sheets, &c . . . About six in the morning I decamped. I was despicable in my own opinion for having been in the very sink of vice.'[21]

The dividing line was a fine one between houses turned over to prostitutes' lodgings where men could visit and the bawdy house. The term covered a multitude of places to sin but in general its function was somewhere prostitutes might take their customers for the night or a shorter time. Prostitutes could thus use bawdy houses (night houses or accommodation houses as they were also known) and remain discreet in their lodgings and in their private lives. But bawdy houses might also provide lodgings for prostitutes for whom discretion was unnecessary. They were of many types, from the ragged squalor of Love's Court to houses where the bawds, often women, sometimes married couples, charged their lodgers high rents and loaned them fine clothes to make a bigger splash on the streets. It was from houses like these that women showed themselves at upstairs windows to passers-by to advertise their presence. At worst, bawdy-house exploitation could look much like slavery. Mary Caton testified at the Old Bailey in July 1766 that she was a prostitute in Margaret and Michael Cassady's bawdy house at Eagle Court, Strand:

It was agreed between us, for me to give her all that I got, and she was to give me victuals and drink, lodging, and cloaths; she used to ask me, when any gentleman had been with me, for what they gave me, and I used to give it her all; she never allowed me any thing; there were other young women in the house, they used to do the same.[22]

Some of these places had a coffee room where company assembled and an unlicensed dram might be had, and these slid imperceptibly into that host of taverns and coffee houses that combined licensed sociability with a trade in prostitution. The Denmark Coffee House, Brydges Street, the Hummum Tavern at Charing Cross, Hayward's public house in the Haymarket, Moll King's Coffee House and the Bedford Arms Tavern in the Piazza, the list of these places notorious as houses of call for prostitutes and their customers, where a bed was to be had at any time of night or day, is endless. Most infamous of all perhaps was the Shakespeare's Head Tavern at the north-east corner of Covent Garden Piazza, where Jack Harris was head waiter and 'Pimp-General to the People of England' at mid-century: 'when I entered into the profession', he wrote in 1769, 'I found it on a very mean footing. By Pimp nothing more was signified than to run about the neighbourhood, and bring the first bunter, then come-atable, to the gentleman at the tavern I belonged to . . . The poor wretches used to come in such a tatter-demalion condition, that I saw great room for an amendment to the profession of pimping.' So he made contact with prostitutes at the other end of the town as fresh faces for the Shakespeare's customers, some-times getting them to dress as citizens' wives as an aid to excitement. From 1757 he put pimping on a more scientific basis still, exploiting the power of the printing press to issue *Harris's List of Covent Garden Ladies*, giving 150 or so names, addresses, descriptions and specialities of the women coming under his notice. Put together on Harris's behalf by Grub Street hacks, it ran as an annual publication under numerous different hands till 1795.[23]

Similar to the bawdy taverns and coffee houses were the bagnios, where warm baths could be had as a convenient (no doubt often neces-sary) precursor to an assignation in a room elsewhere on the premises. By no means all bagnios were of this character: the Royal Bagnio in Newgate Street lasted throughout the century and operated separate days for men and women bathers while offering furnished lodgings for 'Gentlemen', and there were others too of this entirely respectable nature. But bathhouses like the Charing Cross Bagnio under Mrs Harington, where Boswell once took a 'wholesome-looking, bouncing wench', the Cross Keys in Little Russell Street, Drury Lane, Lovejoy's on the east side of the Piazza and notoriously Haddock's on the north side were all established for the trade in women of the town. Here, 'as to the neighbouring taverns, girls are sent for to wait on gentlemen; and, out of their receipts, pay so much in the pound to the waiters for pimping for them . . .'[24]

And then there were brothels. These were almost always, it seems, run by women who specialised in providing a varied stock of young prostitutes, novelty the attraction for rich clients. In reality the boundary between brothel and bawdy house was blurred, but the brothel relied most on the stable of 'nuns' maintained by the 'Abbess' or 'Mother'.

These were select places and so not legion, but they were famed in the Grub Street prints and in general conversation. Mother Needham, whose most celebrated brothel was at Park Place off St James's Street in the 1720s, was immortalised as the procuress who snared Moll Hackabout as she alighted from the York coach in Hogarth's *Harlot's Progress* (1731, the year of Needham's death).

Whether any of these women trepanned many girls who did not want to adopt the life on offer is very much open to doubt. But it is clear they had a ready eye for servant girls new to London and pretty newcomers at the milliners'. And they were doubtless well stocked with seductive tales of the easily won comforts that a life on the town could offer above all other employments for girls seeking a living in London. By the last quarter of the century King's Place, a narrow alley between King Street, St James's, and Pall Mall, close to Almack's, had become synonymous with the smarter London brothel; and for coarser tastes Wetherby's in Little Russell Street, Drury Lane, where a surly porter scrutinised callers through a small wicket in an iron-clad door, offered a drinking den as well as young women on the town.[25]

At any one time at the west end of the town there were scores, maybe a hundred or two, of bawdy houses and brothels of one kind or another. But most encounters with prostitutes began elsewhere even if they eventually ended up in a bawdy house or lodging. By no means all did so. For at night prostitutes were to be found almost anywhere that Londoners took their public pleasures. In St James's Park, for instance, where in the 1760s James Boswell frequently foraged for relief: 'She was ugly and lean and her breath smelt of spirits. I never asked her name. When it was done, she slunk off.' Even the Mall was said to be out of bounds to the quality in the evening, when it was turned over to 'the more publically-complying females'. All open spaces were probably used by prostitutes in this way, for display in the daytime and business at night, the Abbé Prévost noting how 'courtezans swarm' in Lincoln's Inn Fields and Gray's Inn Walks in the 1740s, for instance.[26]

The London pleasure gardens were similarly endowed. 'Wanton Venus keeps her Court' in Vauxhall Gardens, Mrs Percivall wrote in 1713: 'I could not help thinking it a kind of Mahometan Paradice for the delights that abound here are all sensial . . . 'tis pitty it should be made the Sconce of Ludeness and debauchery.' Even under Jonathan Tyers it proved impossible to keep the dressier kind of prostitute out and there is some evidence that her business was consummated in the grounds: Lord Pembroke told Casanova how he was bilked by a girl to whom he'd given 20 guineas 'to take a little walk with me in a dark alley' but ran off. And around 1782, when a party of German diplomats and visitors set up camp in one of the boxes they were 'astonished' by 'the boldness of the women of the town; who, along with their pimps, often rushed in upon us by half dozens; and in the most shameless manner importuned us for wine, for themselves and their followers'. The spas, gardens and great rooms at Hampstead, in the fields near Islington, places small (Cromwell's Tea Gardens at Brompton were 'much frequented . . . by the numerous ladies of pleasure who reside in that neighbourhood') and great (like Marybone Gardens, where Fanny Burney has Evelina, insulted by some men, seeking protection from two 'ladies' who turn out to be prostitutes), were important resources for women of the town throughout the century. Even Ranelagh had its 'pretty ladies of the town', like Miss Ledger, a star of *Harris's List* for 1779, who was a 'constant frequenter' there.[27]

Miss Ledger no doubt took her conquests home to her 'little black foot-boy' and lapdog at her lodgings 'next the Bookseller, May-fair', but much street prostitution, as in parks and even in pleasure gardens, was consummated in the open air. That was at least the case at the cheapest end of streetwalking occupied by women like Martha Stracey and the 'civil nymph with white-thread stockings who tramps along the Strand and will resign her engaging person to your honour for a pint of wine and a shilling'.[28] So said Boswell, who took his chances in alleys, doorways and even, famously, in one of the niches on Westminster Bridge.

The Strand was indeed the great highway of London street prostitution in the eighteenth century. Streetwalking pushed beyond Temple Bar into the City along Fleet Street up to Blackfriars. Its epicentre was the half-mile or so from Bedford Street and Half Moon Street at the southwest corner of Covent Garden to the courts and alleys near the lawyers' haunts of the Temple and Clifford's Inn. Of all the many places notorious for street prostitution along this main avenue of the metropolis, contemporaries most frequently singled out Catherine Street, almost opposite Somerset House and leading north to both Covent Garden and Drury Lane. John Gay named it among the terrors of the London night in 1716:

> O! may thy virtue guard thee through the roads
> Of *Drury*'s mazy courts, and dark abodes,
> The harlots guileful paths, who nightly stand,
> Where *Katherine-street* descends into the Strand.[29]

William Green accorded it the same honour as 'that street where Venus holds her reign' some fifty years later. And Francis Place recalled 'these girls' of 'St. Catherine's Lane' as he remembered them around 1788 with their 'long quartered shoes and large buckles' and their generally 'clean stockings', for 'it was to them the fashion to be flashy about the heels'; but 'many of that time wore no stays, their gowns were low round the neck and open in the front', their hair worn 'straight and "hung in rat tails" over their eyes, and was filled with lice, at least . . . considerable colonies . . .'[30]

Catherine Street was two minutes' walk from the Theatre Royal Drury Lane and, from 1732, just three or four minutes from the Theatre Royal at Covent Garden. The metropolitan theatres were great lures for women of the town and for the houses that provided for and lived off them. It was said that with the construction of the Opera House in the Haymarket over 300 '"Nymphs and Goddesses in Drury Lane and all the little Courts and Alleys adjacent"' decamped '"to the further part of Pick-a-dilly and the Haymarket, that they may be conveniently seated against the opening of the new Theatre"' in 1705. The arrival of a theatre in Goodman's Fields in 1728 quickly drew a profusion of taverns and other bawdy houses to batten on the male playgoer. 'Went to playhouse,' wrote Dudley Ryder of an evening at Drury Lane in 1715. 'The whores are always in the passage to it and continually lay hold of me.' Inside the theatres, well-dressed prostitutes, sometimes masked in the first half of the century, were found in the lobbies and pit – on the lookout for country visitors it was often said – with the poorer sort in the 'Flesh Market' of the upper boxes. Even in the 1790s the Little Theatre in the Haymarket was said to be 'half filled with prostitutes and their paramours' who 'disturb the rest of the audience', although one American visitor to Drury Lane was more appreciative: 'In the lobbies and the Rooms are a great number of Girls of the Town who appeard very Genteel and are many, very handsome. They generally come in at Half price when the Play is over & the entertainment begins.'[31]

Prostitution flourished around the theatres as well as in them. There was a great deal of streetwalking in the theatre districts, but they were primarily great concentrations of the bawdy-house trade in lodging houses, taverns, coffee houses, bagnios and brothels. Drury Lane, because of its venerable Theatre Royal, was the oldest, 'the hundreds of old Drury' a synonym for prostitution throughout the eighteenth century and before. The Rose Tavern, a favourite drinking haunt of the nymphs of Drury at the Brydges Street corner of the passage leading to the theatre's west side, was famed by 1700 and is supposed to feature as the tavern in Plate 3 of Hogarth's *Rake's Progress* (1735).[32]

But the whole neighbourhood was a cornucopia of pleasures and dangers in something like equal proportions. 'I being a Country-man, and a Stranger in this Town, was going to my Quarters between eight and nine at Night, and meaning no harm,' Henry Lee testified at the Old Bailey in December 1735. In Long Acre he 'happened upon' Ann Allen and Ann Evans, who persuaded him to go to their lodgings in what they called 'a very civil House' in Earl's Court, 'in Drury Lane'.[33] They had a bowl of punch and drams of 'brandy'. 'I had no disorderly Dealings with them, though they did what they could to bring me to it, for they took up their Coverings, and shewed me what Ware they had, and then they would needs examine mine.' When he had paid the reckoning the landlady left the house with him, 'pretending to shew me the way to my Quarters', but he soon 'mist five Guineas; and a Moidore out of my Fob'. Lee complained of the loss to the landlady, who immediately proposed returning to the house, 'But instead of going back, she took me down a contrary way to lose me, when a Man hearing me complain of losing my Money, said, why do not you lay hold of her Countryman? And with that she run away, but tumbled down, near her own House, and so we took her' and called the watch. Back at the house in Earl's Court they asked 'another disorderly Creature' for Allen and Evans. Making a distinction not generally apparent in the Old Bailey Proceedings, the girl told them 'she was a Whore but no Thief, and she would go with us to find them. We found Ann Evans asleep on the Stairs at the Hamburgh Coffee house in Drury-lane' and Ann Allen back at Earl's Court 'with a Gentleman'. Perhaps because of the punch and drams there were contradictions in the evidence and the jury acquitted both women.[34]

It was the area round Covent Garden that, despite Drury Lane's historic precedence, held the palm as the leading London bawdy-house district of the eighteenth century. There were bawdy houses all over the West End of the town, from Charing Cross to Soho Square, with significant clusters of 'Brothels and irregular Taverns' in the parish of St Mary-le-Strand (about thirty), St Martin-in-the-Fields (about twelve) and Hedge Lane near Leicester Fields (about twenty), but 'The principal of these Houses', according to Sir John Fielding in 1770, 'are situate in *Covent Garden*.' Its notoriety pre-dated the arrival of the theatre, its chocolate and coffee houses even in 1726 furnished with barmaids and waitresses who were 'beautiful, neat, well-dressed, and amiable, but very dangerous nymphs'. It was, according to Fielding again, 'the great square of Venus'. 'One would imagine that all the prostitutes in the kingdom had pitched upon this blessed neighbourhood for a place of general rendezvous. For here are lewd women in sufficient numbers to people a mighty colony.' A critic of Fielding's magistracy claimed that as a consequence 'it is dangerous for a modest woman to appear even at noon-day', and even in Bow Street where the police office was situated.[35]

As London's pleasures began to consolidate in the district around Leicester Fields by the last decade or two of the century it is likely that there was some westward drift of street prostitution and bawdy houses to the Haymarket, Coventry Street, Piccadilly, Pall Mall and other places. But Covent Garden seems never to have lost its special place in metropolitan venery in the eighteenth century. And the fact is that prostitution was found all over London, certainly everywhere that men with money in their pockets came together for enjoyment, from Hockley-in-the-Hole to Mrs Cornelys's masquerades in Carlisle House, Soho Square: 'the *filles de joye* . . . are generally deemed the life, and soul, of a Masquerade', it was said in 1777, when it was a matter for public lament that 'Not an *Abbess*, or a *Nun* was to be seen from King's-Place!'

Even in the City, where policing was more vigilant and where business-minded neighbours might be expected to take affront at disorderly houses, prostitution was not confined to the purlieus of Fleet Street. By the end of the century there were significant clusters of bawdy houses in Aldgate Ward and over the boundary into Whitechapel; and throughout the century relatively large numbers along the banks of Fleet Ditch (and from 1737 Fleet Market), around Smithfield (street prostitution especially rife at the time of Bartlemy, when the cloisters of St Bartholomew's Hospital provided a conveniently sheltered promenade), and immediately to the west in the courts and alleys around Chick Lane, one of the most dangerous districts in the whole of London.

Indeed, prostitutes were available everywhere, from the obscure alleys of Southwark to the new streets of Marylebone, and from the soldiers' women of the Almonry near Westminster Abbey to the ragged beggars' women of Rag Fair, Rosemary Lane.[36]

The sale of sexual services and the profits of casual thieving were not the only ways of turning a penny for these young women. The hectic London art market meant that some pin money could always be earned as artists' models at the Royal Academy and in many private studios. They were often in demand for just part of their bodies to complete a portrait where the sitter's face had been taken but not much else – Joshua Reynolds would send to a number of brothels for, as he put it, 'a nek'. Not much was earned, though, from the notoriously mean Joseph Nollekens, who had women of the town sit 'for his Venuses' at his studio near Cavendish Square. Some were provided by Mrs Lobb, 'an elderly lady, in a green calash, from the sign of the "Fan", in Dyot-street, St Giles's', who sent models 'just arrived from the country' around 1780. She once complained that Nollekens kept Bet Belmanno eight hours '"without a thread upon her, or a morsel of any thing to eat or a drop to drink, and then give her only two shillings to bring home! . . . How do you think I can live and pay the income-tax?"'[37]

Prostitution, then, was a young woman's business in an overstocked labour market where alternative employment usually paid worse, was always far more arduous and had generally very limited prospects. There was only a remote possibility of earning sufficient from the needle, in service or at the washtub to raise a woman above poverty and, if single, to avoid an old age in the workhouse. Prostitution offered economic independence, at least for a time, if a woman could escape the clutches of a grasping bawd; and numbers of course, knowing the business so well, turned bawds themselves. There were huge risks from beatings and abuse, from the ill-effects of drink, to which prostitutes were understandably prone, and from venereal disease, sores sometimes mortifying to cause an early death. And for those who turned thief as the quickest, easiest and most profitable way to win more than a half-crown or shilling a customer there were the risks of savage punishment from the criminal law. The cases of Martha Stracey and Ann Bell are eloquent restraints on an over-optimistic assessment here.

When prostitutes' earnings were exhausted by age or a disliking for the life, then the low-paid London unskilled labour market still remained open to them. In the first six years of the Magdalen Hospital, a reformatory for prostitutes established at Goodman's Fields in 1758, 583 women were admitted. Of these 196 were placed in service and sixty-three were returned reconciled to 'friends', of whom fifteen were 'since well married'.[38] So for poor women a life on the streets closed down few opportunities to change their prospects. And during a prostitute's career, opportunities of advancement for those combining beauty first and quick wits second were genuinely on offer; no doubt more than a dash of ruthlessness was of great assistance in the process, but that was a lesson learned early.

Of course, the contemporary expectation of the wages of sin was far from cheerful. When in 1762 Boswell tried to find Sally Forrester, who had taken his virginity two years before, he returned to the address where he'd met her. But Sally had disappeared, and so had another girl he sought. He feared the worse. 'Good heaven, thought I, what an amazing change in two years! I saw in the year 1760 these young ladies in all the glow of beauty and admiration; and now they are utterly erased or worse.' Yet at fashionable Ranelagh some seven months later he found Sally once more. 'She said she was married to Captain Peter Grant, a Scotch officer, and she would not allow me to renew my joy', and her companion told him she was also married. 'They surely joked about their marriages', and probably they did, but at worst they were in faithful and profitable keeping, at least for a time. In 1796 Hannah More, the evangelical writer, found the girl whose father had sold her in the King's Bench some years before, in keeping with 'a great lawyer', who had 'put infidel books into her hands'. That seemed to have been the worst of it for 'she is very accomplished, understands music, drawing, fine works, and has a mind much cultivated'. And in 1770 William Hickey discovered that 'my favourite Fanny Hartford . . . had married a gentleman of fortune who resided entirely in the country', and he heard no more of her.[39]

These women may have begun with advantages, but occasionally we hear of real rags to riches stories. Ann Catley, the washerwoman's daughter from an alley near the Tower and a prostitute from fourteen, was lucky enough to come across the actor Charles Macklin, who paid for her singing voice to be coached and introduced her to a stage career. She became 'the celebrated Miss Catley' whose 'Catlified hair', cut in a fringe 'like a fan', became in great vogue 'among the lower classes' of London streetwalker in the 1780s. Not everyone appreciated the transformation: she had 'all the appearance of an impudent battered woman of the Town', Sylas Neville, in the pit at Covent Garden and watching her in *The Beggar's Opera* in October 1776, confided to his diary, though perhaps the part called for something like the Catlified style. She died at the age of forty-four, married to General Lascelles or living as his wife, having borne him eight children, 'much respected by the better sort of people in their neighbourhood' at Ealing 'and beloved by the poor'.[40]

Then there was Ann Elliot, daughter of a shoemaker in Tunbridge Wells, debauched at fifteen, pregnant not much later, who was thrown out by her parents soon after the baby was born, though they undertook to care for the child. She came to London and became a woman of the town at a bawd's in Covent Garden. Beautiful but 'vain and idle', she was schooled by Mrs James to become an 'artful reserved courtezan'. Many men fell for her and showered her with gifts; some took her into expensive keeping. Arthur Murphy, her infatuated lover, trained her for the stage, where she combined acting with a hectic life as a courtesan. She died in 1769, just twenty-seven, of some intestinal disorder. 'The bulk of her fortune, amounting to near ten thousand pounds, she bequeathed to her indigent relations.'[41]

Ann Catley and the frail but fascinating Nanny Elliot were by no means unique in straddling bedroom and green room. It was an irresistible combination for those men of all classes who already found prostitution among the great joys of London life.

'The Whoring Rage Came Upon Me': Men and Prostitution

Hawkins has given Me up to yᵉ fucking world again, & my poor miserable Prick is come out of his Hands quite sound with only the loss of a fraenum; I have not yet ventur'd to make use of it . . .[42]

Thus Richard Rigby – 'Bloomsbury Dick' – writing to his friend Sir Charles Hanbury Williams, some time in the early 1740s. Rigby came of rich London merchant stock and he would go on to become MP for Sudbury and later for Tavistock. He was a government minister from 1755 and paymaster-general of the armed forces from 1765 to 1782, loaning liberally to his friends the money under his command and spending lavishly on his extensive personal needs. When he died in 1788 he still owed the public purse an uncollectable £150,000.

Rigby was one of a select set of politically well-connected and wealthy young men attached to Sir Charles, who was born in London in 1708, with a substantial fortune anchored in the Welsh iron industry. Many years after his death the editor of his witty verse would pay tribute to the 'lively acuteness' of Williams's talents; 'the elegancy of his manners, and an incessant gaiety of heart' drew to his side 'eminent men, who delighted in retreating from political labour and party agitation to a social privacy into which only wit and good-humour were admitted'.[43] But not only wit and good humour. Their 'social privacy' had one more component in common. The fascinating world of London prostitution was at the very heart of it. Williams's correspondence in the early 1740s is filled with details of the shifting allegiance of his friends from one woman of the town to another; his memorandum books leave notes for posterity on the Covent Garden characters of the day; his private odes and ballads provide obscene commentary on the sex lives of friends and enemies alike; and letters from his wife reveal all the horror and despair that his own dealings with prostitutes brought disastrously into their marriage.

Prostitution penetrated deeply into the lives of some of the most brilliant and favoured men of the day. It was a part of their lives that had to be kept secret from their wives, if possible, but not from their mistresses, and was a matter of easy social intercourse among friends. Dick (Richard, Second Baron) Edgcumbe 'did lately call at Olivers but finding no pensionaires he was obliged to bugger an externe & has told all particulars of the action in very publick company'; Charles Wyndham, Second Earl of Egremont, writes from Somerset to say he has 'been blessed with the conversation of a Sylvan Nymph of the Frome Wood lands, whom her own Mother brought me as a pure Virgin. Pure she might be, but to my great discomfort & disappointment, most capaciously wide';[44] Richard Rigby laments that:

however lucky I was with my numberless Bunters all the Winter, Fortune gets Home upon me now with Cordees & Heat of Urine. In short at Lord Waldegrave's where I was gone to stay some time, three days ago I had a most humming Clap come down, which is at present so violent as to wake me every morning with a Cordee . . . I am obliged to a very famous Lady for it & one who has been much in Fashion these three weeks or Month I mean Polly Henly. Numbers will have ye like obligation to Her I believe in a few Days for she has been liberal of her Favours. Amongst ye rest our great friend her

Neighbour will have good luck if He escapes, having fuck'd Her the day after I lay with Her, she lives in Conduit street.[45]

Next summer, recovered from 'the Drury-Lane Ague' or 'Garden Gout', he is active once more. 'I have lain two nights at Douglass's since I came to Town with diff'rent bitches you may be sure, one of 'em *a maid* but a week before, at least He & yᵉ Girl agreed in the same Lye & I believ'd 'em & that's as well as if it was true –.'[46]

The overweening power of class and gender that enabled Rigby to write so coolly of his 'bitches' was a common theme. Nor was the lively, acute, elegant and gay Williams above a witticism at the expense of a prostitute's poverty:

Bunter. A Female who not caring to be seen by day . . . generally makes her appearance by Night . . . Her usual Walks are in St James's Park or about Temple Barr. She is excessively civil & courteous to ev'ry Gentleman she meets and will go with Him any where, but especially to Supper having usually not din'd at Midnight and having naturally a very keen and large Stomach.[47]

In Williams's set the world of the brothel provided both titillation and tittle-tattle. 'Olivers' has not been much noticed by posterity but 'Douglas's most certainly has, though it is interesting to note that there must have been a Mister for at least some time alongside Mother (Jenny or Jane) Douglas, the most famous London bawd of the 1740s. Inevitably she features in a Hogarth engraving, *The March to Finchley* (1749), where a houseful of women of the town watch the soldiers making to depart for Derby against the rebels of '45. Tradition has it that it is Mother Douglas who clasps her hands in prayer for the safe return of her customers; she wears a mob cap, which some say she invented.[48]

Sir Charles Hanbury Williams knew the brothel world well. The 'Hôtel Douglas' was in the north-east corner of Covent Garden Piazza, conveniently just next door to the Shakespeare's Head. Mother Douglas herself, according to Williams, was 'A great, flabby, fat, stinking, swearing, hallowing, ranting Billingsgate Bawd, very well known to most Men of Quality & Distinction in these Kingdoms'. Despite, perhaps because of, these attractions she is said to have borne a child to 'Earl Fitzwilliam for the Beauty & Delicacy of whose Face I appeal to both Sexes; particularly to Mrs Douglas of the one & Lord Hervey of the other'. Mother Douglas was the centre of a little industry, not just of sex but of its accoutrements: 'J. Jacobs. Hominum Salvator & Cundum Maker, lives in Oliver's Alley in the Strand and furnishes Mrs Douglas's House with Cundums by wholesale which she retails to her Customers.' She was a purveyor of-false promises, 'an untasted Lass . . . the greatest Rarity that House can afford, if ever it afforded it'. And among her 'best Customers', besides those 'Men of Quality & Distinction', were 'East India Captains':

Upon this head I remember a very expressive and grateful saying of Mrs Haywards (a Sister of Mrs Douglas's) who declared that if a Dog was to come into her House from India she would give him a Dinner as an Acknowledgement of the many handsom Presents She had receiv'd from & the many long Bills She had been paid by Christians who came from those parts.

The presents were 'Chintz, Damask, Rack, Tea & China'.[49]

Prostitution did not penetrate the lives of only the young well-born Whig intelligentsia of the 1740s but every class of men in every decade of the century. Most prostitution was by poor women for poor men in unfashionable neighbourhoods and we've seen numerous instances already. Many men of all ranks no doubt eschewed the trade and remained faithful or celibate. But no man in London could be unaware of the leers and lures all around him, and even for those who remained untempted the sexual exploits and comeuppances of friends and work-mates must have provided lively conversation at the bench or round the kitchen fire. Horace Walpole, an active correspondent of the Williams set at this time, appears to have been largely or entirely celibate, but he was keen to receive and pass on gossip about his friends' antics with women of the town and could turn his hand to a ballad as obscene as any by Williams himself. Samuel Richardson once claimed to a biographer that '"I never, to my Knowlege, was in a vile House, or in Company with a lewd Woman, in my Life."' Richardson was a truthful man and we can believe what he said. But his literary imagination must have been thoroughly schooled by what others had told him and by what he had read, because the many bawds and harlots and bawdy houses in his novels ring strictly true. And if the 'barbarous Mrs. Jewkes', the 'wicked procuress' turned housekeeper in *Pamela* (1740–41), isn't Mother Douglas I'll eat my quill pen.[50]

Indeed, the large part that prostitution played in the minds and behaviours of many men, as revealed in their diaries and elsewhere, was extraordinary. The women of the town were so available, many were so fine and so tempting, and there were so very many of them, that lust and fear of the consequences of satiation battled nightly in men of all ranks, young and old alike.

We might take Dudley Ryder as one such instance. He was a law student of twenty-four and his struggles were complicated by religious avowals, by his awkwardness near young women of any caste and by fear of discovery. Even so, 'whores' were pretty much always on his mind. On his way home to Hackney from the Middle Temple in August 1715, 'had a great mind to have met with a whore and talked with her, to give me an assurance and confidence, for it has put me sometimes into a strange kind of condition when a whore has taken hold of me and asked me to go with her'. A few days later, 'came from the tavern at near 12. As I came along Fleet Street had a mind to attack a whore and did so', in fact two, talking to both: 'It makes me a little uneasy for fear somebody that knows me should have seen me' – things had a habit of getting back to his father. A couple of weeks on, coming home from a gathering of friends or 'club' at John's Coffee House, Bow Lane, near the Exchange, 'I was so raised with our discourse about women that I was extremely inclined that way and I looked for a whore with a resolution not to lie with her but to feel her if I could. However, I am very glad I did not find one', which puts those 'swarms' and 'herds' a little into perspective. In November, after the club:

Met with a whore. Went with her into a corner. After she had asked me several times to go with her she asked me if she could do me any other service. She told me her name was Barker. She is a little black woman . . . The action stings me with remorse after having done it. It was not pleasure to me and my inclinations were not raised at all. I don't know but it may give me a disgust for women a good while.

In April 1716, after the club, 'I was very warm with drinking wine and had a mighty inclination to fill a whore's commodity' – a City term presumably – but merely had 'some little discourse'. In July 'I had a mind to walk about the streets and have some talk with the whores and go the furthest I can without lying with them' to 'learn something of a boldness and confidence'. In August, after the club once more, 'Had a mind to fill a whore's commodity and went about the streets in order to do it, but could not conveniently do it without hazarding my reputation'. Next month he seems to have achieved his objective, but with a disappointing outcome: 'I had a great mind to a whore and wandered about the streets till I found one to my mind, and gave her 6s., but she picked my pocket of a handkerchief.' Made more cautious, in November 'I had a mind to feel a whore and went about the streets on purpose to find one which I did, but she would not let me before I gave her money, which I would not do and so came away.'[51]

As we can see, Ryder's relationship with women of the town was extensive but anxious and fraught. Nothing here, then, of the apparently freewheeling exploits of the drunken Boswell when 'the whoring rage came upon me'.[52] His diaries record scores of encounters with prostitutes, mostly pursued to completion but often followed, as we've already glimpsed, by self-loathing at loss of caste and terror of the consequences, all to be forgotten with the next pint or two of wine. John Wilkes had a large connection among women of the town, his address lists containing dozens of names like 'Fanny Johnson at Mrs Clarke's, Mercer's Street, Long Acre'; 'Peggy Bailey at Mrs Butler's, No 14 Devereux Court, Temple'; 'Kitty Fowler at Mrs Ballard's, No 16 in Gouge Street, Rathbone Place'; the famous brothel of 'Mrs Godby [Goadby] at the green lamp in Great Marlborough Street, five doors from the Shakespear Public House', and many more.[53] And when Henry Thrale married Hester in 1763 he just went on being single. James Worsdale, the painter, used to pimp for him, perhaps from among his models, and Henry's various women-in-keeping found their way into the newspapers, much to Hester's chagrin. In 1776 'Mr Thrale told me he had an Ailment, & shewed me a Testicle swelled to an immense Size', caused by the pox. 'I am preparing Pultices . . . and fomenting the elegant Ailment every Night & Morning for an Hour together on my Knees . . .'[54]

We have seen this openness about kept women as a feature of the life of William Beckford with his innumerable 'bastards', and it was indeed open enough for women to advertise in the papers for keepers:

To the Gentlemen. A young LADY, of an active disposition, and other perfections, that would be improper for the advertiser to mention, is in immediate want of an Hundred Pounds. And as some Gentleman's situation may require a strict attention to be paid to the preservation of health, in conjunction with secresy, the advertiser flatters herself, no opportunity can possibly offer . . . an equal certainty of every punctilio being strictly observed.[55]

There were other anxieties than secrecy and 'the preservation of health', for some men plainly fell in love with, or were for a time infatuated by, their chosen 'frail'. Boswell was much struck in 1785 with Betsy Smith of Dean's Court, Old Bailey, for instance, and Charles Hanbury Williams wrote wistful verse to Kitty Walker, expressing his love for her and jealousy of her other amours.

Even so, when all was said and done, the main anxiety really was the fear of disease. Venereal disease was more common in London than elsewhere in the country and some thought it partly accounted for the excess of deaths over births there.

> Down each Street the Bunters flow,
> Picking Pockets as they go
> Gently they each Corner call,
> Sultry Urine scorching all.
> . . .
> All alone, yet in Her Lap,
> The Temple Beau may get a Clap,
> Where, Pox'd, & Poxing, they shall own,
> The Pains of Love, are Pains alone.[56]

Williams spoke from experience. The symptoms of venereal disease were so painful and so potentially dangerous, treatment with surgery and other mechanical intervention so agonising, 'salivation' with mercury so tiring and debilitating to mind and body, it is a wonder that the power of the prostitute was sufficient to obliterate these risks from the minds of those tempted to engage with her. But she proved indeed ever more powerful. In the autumn of 1742 Sir Charles and those close to him were to learn the terrible costs of succumbing to the prostitute's lures.[57]

Williams had married Lady Frances Coningsby, youngest daughter of the Earl of Coningsby, at St James's Piccadilly in July 1732. He was twenty-three and she twenty-two. They had two daughters, Frances born in 1735 and Charlotte in 1738. It appears that from the outset Sir Charles was unable to relinquish his taste for the women of the town, for Lady Frances later had cause to remind him that 'you *begun*, your *Life*, with me, by an *Injury*, wch might possibly have endured to the *End* of it . . . But tho' I was *blind* to my *own unhappiness*, I was ever too fond of *your ease*, to bear the thoughts of interrupting it, by the least *appearance*, of *discontent*, or *displeasure* towards you . . .'[58] It seems likely, from everything we know about his life in these years, that he was poxed several times – Boswell, it is said, had seventeen infections over a long period – and the '*Injury*' Lady Frances complained of may have been one such.

In any event, in the summer of 1742 Sir Charles was forced to retire to Bath with what his physician there declared to be the worst case of syphilis he had ever seen, although it's no doubt true – as Henry Fox told Williams in an anxious letter – that Bath was a 'Place nobody was ever sent for Y^r Complaint, & of which therefore the Faculty there have no Experience . . .' Sir Charles told Lady Frances he had gone to Bath to cure his 'Cholick' but she herself soon began to manifest venereal symptoms. Now aware of the possible truth, she consulted a Dr J. Oldfield in the City and received the diagnosis of advanced syphilis. Lady Frances moved from the family home at Albemarle Street to lodgings in the City to be near her doctor for treatment. By early September the secret was out. Sir Charles seems to have accused Dr Oldfield of indiscretion but probably the truth became known through Lady Kildare, Lady Frances's aunt and her closest relative, whose dignified fury at 'the Imparable Iniury you have done my Neice' remains unimpaired by her eccentric spelling: 'I am ye onely parent she has, & I will stand by her to the last moment of my life, and she shall never be trusted into ye hands that has bin so Cruell to her'. With London gossip finding its way to Bath, Williams committed the final error that would end his marriage. He accused Lady Frances of giving him the infection:

To add the charge of the most *shameless* & *infamous Crime*, I could commit, to the *Cruelest injury*, I could suffer. This you have done, without the least Colour of *Suspicion*, to support you in your aspersion, & in the most glaring light, of your own *Guilt*. [She demanded] the *most Express* & *direct acknowledgment*, & *satisfaction*, for so *outragious* & *horrid* an *Imputation* . . .[59]

Williams fought the idea of a separation but eventually agreed, relinquishing the care of both daughters to Lady Frances and paying back her contribution to the marriage settlement. He maintained contact with his daughters and made them appropriate allowances, and seems to have kept all his male friendships intact. In late 1746 he began a distinguished diplomatic career with postings to various European courts. But it ended around ten years later when he began to show signs of insanity, possibly connected to his syphilitic infection. Returning to London, Williams was declared officially a lunatic and died in Lord Bolingbroke's house at Chelsea in November 1759.[60]

The flaunting profligacy of female prostitution in London, and the open enjoyment with which it was shared between men friends, were of a very different order from the collective life of gay men, a term that did not then have the connotation it has gained in recent years. Homosexuality was inevitably a secret affair, though by no means invisible. Even so, there were similarities between this hidden world and the extravagance surrounding women of the town. There were some male prostitutes, for instance; and promiscuous 'sodomites', 'sodomists', 'Mollies' or 'Madge Culls' ran the same risks of disease, with some other complications the 'whorers' avoided. But the primary difference that made secrecy literally a matter of life and death was the general loathing with which sodomy was regarded among the majority and the appalling severity with which it was treated as a crime. The severity itself made for a sordid penumbra of blackmailers who might batten on men considered effeminate or in some way vulnerable to the charge and who threatened to swear evidence, false or true it mattered little, against them. Men could be hanged for sodomy and were throughout the century. The pillory for a Molly – the term men seem most to have used about each other at the time – could itself become a most hideous death sentence, as we shall see in a later chapter. Yet despite these swingeing risks, men who loved men had many opportunities to take their pleasure in the anonymous sociabilities of eighteenth-century London.

Historians tell us that a collective life among homosexual men in England only becomes written about some time around 1700, though no doubt the fact pre-dated the notice taken of it. Certainly it was sufficiently in place to be satirised by Ned Ward in an article on 'Mollies Clubs' in 1709 and in a mock advertisement for a *Brief History of Modern Sodomy*, 'Sold by *Ezekiel Manlove*, at the Sign of the *Rump*, on the Back-side of the *Royal-Exchange*', in 1708. And a decade or two later the public prints and courts of law were swept up in a moral panic; at the end of the 1720s it was said there were 'ample Proofs, that this Town abounds too plentifully with a Sect of brutal Creatures called *Sodomites* . . .'[61]

By that time all the features of Molly society were in place. Some taverns and coffee houses hosted clubs of men interested in men, in the same way that the musically or literary-minded gathered together in other places, with this definitive difference, that their activities had to be kept secret from all those who might make mischief, and in particular from the parish police. 'About twenty' of these 'Houses of Resort' were known to the authorities it was said in 1729 and probably a modest two dozen or so might reasonably stand for the number of 'Molly Houses' active at any time in London throughout the century. Most were run by men, sometimes married couples, and occasionally by women, the unfortunately named Mother Clap's in Field Lane, raided in February 1726, being one of this nature. They were spread widely over the town. Many favoured hole-and-corner plebeian districts, and besides Mother Clap's we hear of a 'Cellar in *Marygold Court*, over against the Fountain tavern in the *Strand*', of 'an Ale-house by the Seven-Dials' where 'several Persons' were arrested 'on Suspicion of Sodomy' in 1730, of Jonathan Muff's at Black Lion Yard, Whitechapel, in 1728, the Magdalen Coffee House in Southwark in 1780, and others at Billingsgate, the Mint, Clare Market and so on. But there were also some in the fashionable quarters of the town, like the Royal Oak public house near St James's Square, a house in Windmill Street north of the Haymarket, another in King Street, Westminster, and more.[62]

The first point of Molly contact, however, tended not to be in places like these but – as for prostitution – in streets and parks. In the streets there seems to have been some connection between link boys, shoeblacks and male prostitutes. But it was in the parks that Molly culture found freest expression. A path in Upper Moorfields was known as 'The Sodomites' Walk' and there were numerous other 'Molly Markets' like 'the *Royal Exchange*, *Lincoln's-Inn Bog-Houses*, the South-side of St. *James*'s-*Park*, the Piazzas of *Covent-Garden*, St. *Clement*'s *Church-Yard*, &c.'[63] Moorfields retained this reputation until it was built over late in the century, but it was often said that one place in particular was the most popular contact point – at least in the fashionable part of the town – and that men used secret signs to become acquainted there:

the chief place of meeting is the Bird-cage Walk, in St. James's Park, whither they resort about twilight. They are easily discovered by their signals, which are pretty nearly as follows: If one of them sits on a bench, he pats the backs of his hands; if you follow them, they put a white handkerchief thro' the skirts of their coat, and wave it to and fro; but if they are met by you, their thumbs are stuck in the arm-pits of their waistcoats, and they play their fingers upon their breasts.[64]

One reason for the popularity of the south side of St James's Park as a meeting point was its proximity to barracks at Birdcage Walk and Horse Guards. For soldiers played a large part in Molly life in London, sodomy one way that the hard-pinched private could turn a penny – and blackmail another. In 1785 Richard Cope, a soldier in the Guards, was convicted of 'assaulting and imprisoning a gentleman, of great eminence, fortune, and honour, in Lincoln's-inn, detaining him in a place, called the Black-hole, without fire or candle, all night . . . and charging him with an unnatural crime, in order to extort money from him . . .' He was sent to prison for five years, with an annual pillorying at Charing Cross, 'to the great satisfaction of a crowded court . . .'[65]

The popular prejudice against homosexual men – even the tolerant Hester Thrale couldn't stand 'the unnatural Vice among the Men', to which she thought the 'Scotch . . . strangely addicted' (she blamed the kilt) – and the harsh penalties that could attend a conviction drove many to extreme solutions. Isaac Bickerstaff, a popular Irish playwright who had been commissioned in the marines and other regiments, fled the country after the papers noted an allegation by a blackmailing soldier in 1772; he died obscurely on the Continent many years later. William Beckford Junior, the alderman's only legitimate son, also fled for a time from 1785, leaving his pregnant wife at home when rumours circulated of a fling with a seventeen-year-old nobleman in a country house.[66]

One of the most celebrated of these cases involved Captain Robert Jones, a fashionable young former army officer who had been an enthusiastic and applauded masquerader at Mrs Cornelys's Carlisle House. In July 1772 Jones was tried for sodomy on the convincing evidence of a twelve-year-old boy, Francis Henry Hay, an apprentice jeweller at his uncle's shop in Parliament Street. Jones used to buy his shoe buckles there and got to know the boy to speak to. One afternoon in St Martin's Lane they met by accident and Jones asked the boy to go with him to his lodgings over a china shop in St Martin's Court to collect a buckle that needed mending. In the dining room, it seems Hay was overawed by this young man of quality and Jones buggered him over an armchair. He gave the boy 'some halfpence, about a groat [fourpence], and told me not to tell any body'. There was one further encounter, also in Jones's lodgings, and then Hay fell ill. Frightened by his illness and fearing it might have a connection with Jones, the boy told another jeweller what had happened to him. Jones was arrested, charged, found guilty at the Old Bailey and sentenced to death. Soon, though, it became known to the press that many fashionable people were exerting interest to get Jones a royal pardon. After much public speculation and debate, the King pardoned Captain Jones on the condition he left the country. His subsequent movements in Europe and the Middle East remain obscure.[67]

This leniency shown Jones need not surprise us. For vice and fashion were intimately connected in London throughout the eighteenth century, with many surprising consequences.

'Damn Your Twenty Pound Note': Fashion and Vice

From the monarchy downwards every rank of men in London mingled in some way with women of the town and others who were prepared to trade their charms for money. The lascivious courts of George I and II, which to some extent licensed the sexual manners of the aristocracy from 1714 to 1760, though highly amusing and doubtless deplorable in any family, need not concern us here. The court of George III, puritan by contrast and restrained in fact as it was, provided merely a brief interregnum until 1780, when the sexual japes of the Prince of Wales resurrected the upstanding traditions of his forebears for the rest of the century and beyond.

Perhaps insufficient attention has been paid by historians to the role of the women of the town in the rise of democracy and the dilution of deference in the eighteenth century, with London and Londoners once more the democratic crucible. There was, indeed, a great deal of mixing, high and low. 'William Duke of Cumberland, used to amuse himself in the dark walks', recalled John Trusler of Marybone Gardens in the late 1750s, 'and gave way to a number of unbecoming frolics with the women, which would have disgraced one of the lowest class in society, and which to relate would disgust the reader. He was supported in these unprincely acts, by two *honorable aid-de-camps*, too often pandars to a prince's vices.' And the antics of another royal prince thirty years later similarly disgusted Hester Thrale: 'The Duke of York second Son to our King & Queen gave a Ball to the Blackguards and Women of the Town the Night Pitt gave his to Our first Nobility, &c. in honr of the King's Recovery – for Spite, and Malicious Fun; What Children some people have!'[68]

It was said that the Duke of Norfolk '"had almost as many mistresses . . . as King Solomon"' and at the end of his life maintained a long list of pensioners, 'women of various grades', to whom his bankers paid a quarterly allowance. Lord Baltimore 'openly maintained a harem of "five white and one black women"' and paraded them in the park; he had to flee the country to avoid a trial for rape after kidnapping a sixteen-year-old girl from her father's shop at Tower Hill. Lord George Gordon was well known among women of the town and reportedly asked one who lodged in Tottenham Court Road, whose company he much favoured, to marry him – she sensibly declined. And among many other acts of aristocratic condescension we might mention the insatiable Duke of Queensberry, who built a house for 'the notorious Kitty Frederick' or 'Kate Fred' at 133 Piccadilly.[69]

The condescension wasn't all one way. Many low-born women throughout the century became courtesans of such celebrity that aristocrats, even princes, manoeuvred and outbid one another for their favours. They became trophies, testifying to a man's wealth, caste, charm and power; and they were trophies unburnished by birth or upbringing.

Fanny Murray, probably a musician's daughter from Bath, though some said she was London-born, was seduced by the grandson of the First Duke of Marlborough when she was twelve, in 1741. She became a dress-lodger in a bawdy house in the Old Bailey, where it is said she was given just sixpence a week pocket money for all her pains. From the late 1740s she prospered with the help of Jack Harris and became lover of the Earl of Sandwich. She went on to marry an actor and settled into respectable prosperity, dying when she was almost fifty. She is best remembered for a famous moment of insouciance around 1748. One night she complained to her then keeper, Sir Richard Atkins, 'of want of money'. Sir Richard 'immediately gave her a twenty pound note; she said, "Damn your twenty pound note, what does that signify!" – clapped it between two pieces of bread and butter and eat it'.[70]

Kitty Fisher, born probably Catherine Fischer around 1741 into the family of a struggling German artisan in Soho, became one of the most famous women of the late 1750s, painted several times by Joshua Reynolds, the subject of satirical verse and Grub Street 'memoirs'. She was apprenticed to a milliner, that dangerous trade, where it seems she fell victim to a dashing army officer. She then moved from one wealthy keeper to another. Her name was connected to the Duke of York, Lord Montfort, the Earls of Sandwich, Harrington, Poulett and Pembroke and doubtless others, before she married the MP for Rye. She died very young, apparently of tuberculosis. Her eyes, recalled Hester Thrale, were 'a Species apart . . . their Colour was of a Sky Blue, like a Ribbon, I never saw so beautiful a Brilliant Blue . . .'[71]

This list of low-born women emotionally and commercially entangled with high-born men in London could be considerably extended, and we'll have cause to dwell on one special feature of the connection in a moment, but we might close it with a celebrated but tragic case. John Montagu, Fourth Earl of Sandwich, has found a place already in this narrative in different contexts and will recur once more. He was one of the great rakes of the age, in a great age of rakes. Some time around 1761 he seems to have been struck by a young mantua maker, born near Covent Garden, called Martha Ray. It is said that Sandwich paid her father, a stay maker, £400 and a pension to purchase her honour. Sandwich was married but separated from his mentally unstable wife and Ray became his mistress, the manager of his country household and his constant companion in town. There seems to have been real affection on both sides, on Sandwich's even love. Ray had a beautiful singing voice – Sandwich a musical man, we may recall – and she was given the best training London could afford, often performing for the large private concerts that her keeper arranged in the country. Ray bore Sandwich eight or nine children in their seventeen years together, five of them surviving their mother and all provided for by their father. Martha Ray was shot dead by an obsessed follower, the Reverend James Hackman, on 7 April 1779. She was stepping into Sandwich's coach on leaving Covent Garden Theatre, where she had spent the evening watching *Love in a Village*.[72]

And it was the London stage, theatrical and operatic, that provided the most spectacular marketplace where talent and beauty displayed itself for sale to aristocratic bidders. This turbulent arena of metropolitan democracy was a fit setting for some extraordinary instances of social mobility, dramatic in all senses of the word. And the stage held this power undimmed throughout the century.

A most celebrated case was connected to London's favourite play, John Gay's *The Beggar's Opera*. Lavinia Fenton was the first Polly Peachum, the female lead. She was born illegitimate in 1710, probably in St Margaret's Westminster, her mother later running a coffee house in Charing Cross. Lavinia was a beautiful girl and it is said her mother tried to negotiate the sale of her virginity for £200 and £200 a year

while continuing to please, but Lavinia ruined things by freely giving
all to a Portuguese nobleman: no doubt some details have been embellished in the telling. In 1726 she went on the stage and was sufficiently
accomplished to play Polly from its first night. She was the star of the
show and played the part for sixty-one nights. At some point during
this legendary run she captured the heart of Charles Powlett, Third
Duke of Bolton, twenty-five years her senior and separated from the
wife his father had forced him to marry. Unsurprisingly, Hogarth put
it all on canvas in 1729, the Duke staring fixedly at Polly from the
seats in the wings then reserved for important spectators. On the sixty-
second night Polly was played by a newcomer, for Lavinia had been
installed as the Duke's mistress on a settlement of a £400 annuity
'"during pleasure, and upon disagreement"' £200. There would be no
disagreement. They lived happily together for many years, Lavinia
bearing the Duke three sons, who entered the church, army and navy.
In 1751 the estranged Duchess died and the Duke took immediate steps
to marry Lavinia and make her the new Duchess of Bolton. She outlived
him, dying a rich widow in 1760.[73]

By then others had made their way along the same path. The aristocratic passion for everything operatic and everything continental had
revived, especially among the set attached to the Earl of March, later
Duke of Queensberry, who vied with one another over the mistresses
they bought from the stage. Lord Halifax broke off a profitable marriage
engagement to settle down with a Drury Lane actress as his mistress
in 1760. Nancy Parsons, a ballet dancer in the opera and a scintillating
beauty, as her portrait by Gainsborough testifies, combined the stage
with well-paid prostitution, charging a guinea a time and capable, she
said, of earning 100 guineas a week.

Society was outraged – cynical political point-scoring rather than
moral repugnance, it seems – when the Duke of Grafton, who was
prime minister and a married man, appeared with Nancy on his arm
at the opera in April 1768. She went on to marry Viscount Maynard
at St Marylebone in 1776 but they later drifted apart, Nancy Lady
Maynard dying many years later on the Continent.[74]

In all this time the celebrity of the courtesan, actress or no, was embla-
zoned across the town by the rising genius of English portraiture. Besides
Kitty Fisher, Joshua Reynolds painted Nelly O'Brien, Grace Dalrymple,
Emily Warren as *Thaïs*, a courtesan of ancient Greece, and others like
Elizabeth Armistead and Frances Abington, who both began womanhood

in brothels but went on to grace the stage. Not all these paintings were the commissions of temporary lovers. Some were made as a speculation by Reynolds, for the engravings of Fisher and others proved hugely popular in the print shops; others, it seems, were a provocation to see how far erotic art might be acceptable to the fashionable public.[75]

The highpoint of the celebrity actress-cum-courtesan, constant fare in the public prints and the artist's studio, arrived in 1780 with the affair between Mrs Mary Robinson and the Prince of Wales. Robinson, known generally as 'Perdita' for the part she made famous at Drury Lane, was twenty-two and living in an unhappy marriage with a faithless and feckless husband who seems to have been her pimp to keep the household finances barely afloat – he was in the Fleet Prison for debt, Mary living with him, some time before she took to the stage in 1776. When the affair began the Prince was just seventeen and a lovely and impressionable youth. Wit, intelligence and experience were all on Mrs Robinson's side. Despite that, the glamour of a royal connection was so seductive that finally she was persuaded to relinquish a profitable stage career. The Prince's passion proved as unreliable as his purse, with compensation that was eventually settled at £500 a year for life irregularly paid. For that he bedded, and was frequently seen in the company of, one of the most beautiful women of the age, as portraits by Reynolds, Gainsborough, George Romney and especially John Hoppner attest.[76]

The affair with the Prince was over in months. He transferred his attention to 'The Armistead', equipped for the role by brothel and stage, her list of lovers glittering. Through much of the 1780s the lives and loves of a succession of actresses – Perdita, Armistead, Mrs Jordan, Mrs Billington, Mrs Abington – with the greatest princes and noblemen in the land titillated the majority and scandalised the few. The world of London fashion, always neurotically alert to the shifting tastes of the great, now found itself in thrall to talented women of easy virtue whose celebrity came not from birth but from beauty and a realistic sense of its worth in the market. Some men and women with birth to fall back on withheld respect from these objects of fascination. But that was not the case among the generality of people in the streets and parks of London. And Laetitia-Matilda Hawkins, daughter of Samuel Johnson's first biographer and a sharp-eyed, sometimes shrewish, chronicler of these years, recalled with admiration the extraordinary impact that Mary Robinson in her prime had on London in the 1780s:

She was unquestionably very beautiful, but more so in face than figure; and
as she proceeded in her course, she acquired a remarkable facility in adapting
her deportment to her dress. When she was to be seen daily in St. James's
Street and Pall Mall, even in her chariot this variation was striking. To-day
she was a *paysanne*, with her straw hat tied at the back of her head, looking
as if too new to what she passed, to know what she looked at. Yesterday she,
perhaps, had been the dressed *belle* of Hyde Park, trimmed, powdered, patched,
painted to the utmost power of rouge and white lead; to morrow, she would
be the cravatted Amazon of the riding house; but be she what she might, the
hats of the fashionable promenaders swept the ground as she passed.[77]

The reign of the courtesan had a political and not just a cultural
dimension. The power of a mistress whose influence as well as her
person seemed potentially for sale provided much ammunition for the
political opposition – Martha Ray, almost certainly blameless in this
regard, was reputedly in a position to secure naval promotions through
Lord Sandwich's control of the Admiralty, for instance.[78] And the all
too visible adulation of the courtesan and the trail of wreckage she left
in the royal family and the greatest houses in the land can only have
dented the deference due to rank, as the countless satirical cartoons on
the subject reveal. Nor was deference bolstered by the frequent public
exposure of the promiscuity of many female aristocrats, almost as free-
ranging as any rake.

There were many instances but few more public or risible than the
trial and conviction of the Duchess of Kingston – that Elizabeth Chudleigh
whom we have met as an early supporter of Mrs Cornelys – in April
1776 on a charge of bigamy. The case involved the cynical manipulation of rank and reputation with the unwitting assistance of the arcane
jurisdictions of the law courts. As the Attorney General, prosecuting
the charge, succinctly put it, 'dry Lucre was the whole Inducement, cold
Fraud the only Means to perpetrate that Crime'.[79]

The eighteen-year-old Elizabeth had been married in 1744 to Augustus
Hervey, brother to the Earl of Bristol, but both resolved to keep the
marriage, and the subsequent birth and death of a son, a secret to avoid
adverse consequences in the Hervey household and to Elizabeth's position as Maid of Honour to the Princess of Wales. They continued to
live apart for many years. But in 1759 the Earl of Bristol seemed at
death's door and, facing the prospect of becoming Countess of Bristol

on her husband's succession, Chudleigh took steps to assert the marriage long kept secret by carefully compiling documentary and affidavit evidence. The Earl, however, inconveniently recovered. Saddled with a marriage that neither she nor Hervey wanted, and with her own marriage prospects dramatically improved through the infatuation of the Duke of Kingston, in 1768 Chudleigh took steps in the Ecclesiastical Courts to declare that the original marriage ceremony had in fact been a sham, despite the evidence accumulated a decade before, and that no proper marriage had ever taken place. In all of this she had the help of clever but unscrupulous lawyers and the vital assistance of Hervey, who did nothing to resist her claim. The 'evidence' to disclaim the marriage depended on false affidavits, chiefly that from Chudleigh herself, and suborned witnesses. None of the evidence was challenged and the court duly declared that there had been no marriage and that Elizabeth Chudleigh was a single woman. Not for long. Some days after the verdict in 1769 she became the Duchess of Kingston.

In 1773 the Duke died, leaving all the income from his estate to the Duchess for life. Enquiries by his nephew and heir led to the prosecution for bigamy, tried at Westminster Hall in front of the House of Lords in April 1776. All 119 peers found her guilty. She fled to the Continent to escape punishment, as so many did, dying in France just before the revolution broke.

Part of her lawyers' arguments at her trial had apparently attacked the act under which the charge against her was brought as 'made for *Beggars*, not for *People of Fashion*'. But the Attorney General rejected the argument as an affront to 'the impartial Temper' of justice. He must also have provoked some shivers among the gentlemen of the long robe when, addressing the learned proctors of Doctors Commons, he asserted that any among them who knew the truth and yet assisted her in putting her case to the Ecclesiastical Courts 'are Accessories to her Felony; and ought to answer for it accordingly'.[80] The fraudulent and bigamous marriage of the Duchess of Kingston reminds us that crime and criminals knew no bounds of rank in eighteenth-century London.

Brothel Thieves

X

MARY YOUNG'S LONDON – CRIME AND VIOLENCE

The Republic of Thieves: Plebeian Crime

Judith Gardner. Last Saturday Night, between 6 and 7 o'Clock, I was coming out of *Sherbourne-Lane*, and had 13*s*. and an Half-penny in my Pocket; the last House I came from was the *Black-Bull* Alehouse. There were some Boards laid over a wet Place at the corner of the *Mansion House*, and a Man laid hold of my Arm, and said he would help me over the Boards; I said if I wanted any Assistance, I could give the Man a Half-penny; notwithstanding that, he held my Arm up a great Height, so that he numm'd my Fingers that I had no use of them. While he was doing this the Prisoner *Young* came before me, and immediately I felt her Hand in my Pocket; upon that I put my Hand into my Pocket and seized her by the Wrist; – her Hand was clench'd in the Bottom of my Pocket; upon my doing this, she with her other Hand struck me a great Blow on the side of my Face, so that I was obliged to quit her Hand which was in my Pocket, else I should not have lost my Money. I then took fast hold of her Cloak and never left her 'till I got Assistance to take her from me. The Man immediately quitted me, and ran away; I cry'd out, *For God's Sake stop that Man, for he has held me, while the Woman has robbed me*: A Coal-heaver happening to come by, laid hold of him by the Collar, and that other woman *Davis* went up to the Man and help'd to get him away, she said she knew him for he was a *very good House-keeper* and lived the other Side of *Moorfields*.[1]

MARY Young's fatal last move among the 'gang' of thieves whose leader she was said to be would lead remorselessly to her execution at Tyburn on Wednesday 18 March 1741. By the time she drew up at the gallows, not in any common cart but as a lady in a mourning coach, she had become the most famous London female thief of the century. For some years past she had been known as Jenny Diver after the pretty prostitute and pickpocket, companion of Macheath the highwayman in *The Beggar's Opera*. And she won immortality of a kind when her exploits were sensationally detailed in the Ordinary of Newgate's account published soon after her death.

Despite her celebrity in print few of the facts of her life can be verified. Her date of birth is estimated at around 1704, which would have made her thirty-seven at death, but she might well have been younger. According to the Ordinary, she was born probably in the north of Ireland, where she was given some education and bred to the needle, but she had 'an itching desire to see London' and reached it, apparently with a male companion, when she was about fifteen years old. Although she did not mention to the Ordinary any involvement in prostitution, it is likely that she combined thieving with a career on the town, as so many women did: certainly a Grub Street pamphlet published after she was sentenced to transportation in 1738 had much, perhaps fanciful, detail of her whoring life. She was possibly the Mary Young imprisoned in the City's Bridewell in November 1737 for 'raising great disturbances' in Hanging Sword Alley, Fleet Street, with other 'loose idle and disorderly persons & comon Street Walkers'; and again for a similar offence in January 1738 with one Anne Webb, both 'Night Walkers'.[2]

The linked names in that last account are suggestive, for it was as Jane Webb that Young was tried and convicted of picking a lady's pocket as she left St Paul's Cathedral after attending a rehearsal for the Feast of the Sons of the Clergy in April 1738. A witness of the 'Crowd at the Rehearsal' said that in an hour or two he saw Young pick 'a great many Pockets' before she moved close to his window for her final sally, when he called out to her victim. Another claimed, 'I have known her for a Pick-pocket these 5 Years, and saw her pick 20 Pockets that day. She is so well known, that I could have brought a Dozen People to have prov'd this, if I had imagin'd it would been necessary.'[3]

Young was duly transported to Virginia in June 1738, probably for seven years, but quickly returned to England, facing a near-certain death sentence were she discovered. By 1740 she had resumed her old career as a thief in London.

There were distinctive features about Young that place her at the very top of her profession. She had around her a number of loyal and skilled thieves, both men and women, who could take part in a theft, interrupt anyone interfering at the scene, or give evidence of character or alibi at a trial, though the numerous witnesses appearing for her in 1738 were treated with great scepticism by the jury; sadly for Young, the events of 1741 moved so fast she couldn't make similar arrangements. By all accounts, Young was the leader of this crew. In addition, she was fearless, imaginative and a convincing actress. A favourite deceit was to wear a fake belly to fabricate pregnancy, with a pair of false arms and hands clasped across it: sitting next to prosperous dissenters at a chapel meeting, for instance, she was able to use her needlewoman's fingers at will, the hollow belly having storage capacity for the loot. A pregnant woman stumbling or fainting in the street could quickly gather a sympathetic crowd, rich pickings for her associates. And a pregnant lady in distress would always find succour in a prosperous dwelling, where she and her 'footman' could speedily plunder anything within reach. As a pickpocket she favoured the City over the west end of the town, working in the crush of London Bridge or among the crowds round the Royal Exchange. Her victims were women and not always the wealthiest. But with her gang she ranged widely, to provincial towns like Bristol and any country place where a fair or race meeting drew a crowd, in a time-honoured tradition of smart London thieves taking a working holiday from the dangers of the metropolis.

With all this she prospered, as her rich clothes and funeral coach proclaimed, moving from the City to lodgings in Covent Garden with her lover – they had a child who was about three when Mary died – and keeping a personal maid. It was a good life, and how she clung to it. When sentenced she sought to avoid hanging by declaring herself with child – ironically, given her favourite deception – but a 'jury of Matrons' found her not quick. When the halter in which she travelled to Tyburn was put round her neck at Newgate 'she was very much shocked'. And when the cart was pulled from under her feet she was said to be crying for favourable treatment in the afterlife.[4]

There were nineteen others hanged that day with Mary Young – there would have been a total of twenty-two but two died in the cells at Newgate. Sixteen of the twenty were men: three for burglary, eight for robberies of one kind or another, two for stealing horses, one (a soldier) 'for sheep-stealing at Paddington', one for forgery and a returned transport. The four women comprised two condemned for 'robbing a Countryman' at 'an House of ill Fame', one for house-breaking and

'Mary Young, alias Jenny Diver, for a Street-Robbery', the dividing line
between that and picking pockets a narrow one depending on whether
violence was employed.[5]

It will be remarked that all twenty on that notable hanging day were
executed for crimes against property, and it was theft of various kinds,
rather than murder or criminal assault, that largely occupied the London
courts of sessions and the London hangman. At the Old Bailey in the
eighteenth century there were trials or hearings involving some 49,000
offences where the evidence or judgement has come down to us. Almost
95 per cent were property-related, the remainder concerning killings
and lesser criminal assaults. If this disguises the amount of day-to-day
violence in Londoners' interactions, as we shall see shortly, it doubtless
recognises the overwhelming preponderance of property crime in those
offences thought worthy of a trial by jury.[6]

An analysis of charges brought against some 750 individuals at the
Old Bailey sessions beginning 4 December 1782 through to 29 October
1783 brings us closer to the sort of crime that came before the courts
in a very busy year.

The most common category of crime by far, 178 of the 751 charges,
involved stealing from dwelling houses where the house had not
been broken open. It was a crime especially favoured by women –
35 per cent of all the 220 women in this sample, against 19 per cent
of the 531 men, were charged with this offence – and involved a
variety of techniques: slipping through an open door, reaching
through a window, taking washing or possessions from a yard,
absconding with a landlord's property and stealing from the rooms
of fellow lodgers.[7] In general, this most frequent of property crimes
involved the poor preying on each other, though a further nineteen
servants or apprentices, sixteen of them men, were charged with
stealing from their employers about the home or workshop. Stealing
from shops, including the more subtle forms of shoplifting as well
as the opportunist snatch, was the next largest category, comprising
109 offences; once more, women were over-represented, with fifty
charges.

Stealing from the person was a more complicated affair, favouring
men rather than women as perpetrators. Where women *were* concerned,
the close connection between prostitution and theft is very clear. Some
twenty-nine women were charged with picking pockets or taking possessions during the act of prostitution; just one was charged with picking

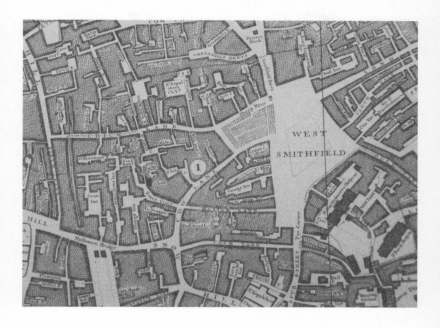

Chick Lane, *c.*1740

pockets in the streets where prostitution was plainly not a factor, and seven more with otherwise stealing from the person, often fellow lodgers. A further six were charged with violent street robbery, the offence for which Mary Young was hanged, and two of these used prostitution as a lure.

On the other hand fifteen men were charged with picking pockets in the street or elsewhere – two in the great hall of the Bank of England among the noonday crowds – and twenty-six with stealing from the person in pubs, lodging houses and elsewhere. Then there was a very large category of seventy-two charged with robbery with violence in the streets as footpads, a crime we'll return to in a moment. A very large part of stealing from the person, even by prostitutes and street robbers, had poor men and women as their victims.

There was then a large volume of crime where houses or other buildings were broken into. This was generally though not exclusively the work of men – fifty-three were charged with burglary, for instance, against eight women, many of whom were accompanying male companions – and thirty men were charged with other thefts from warehouses, thirteen with stealing lead, usually from houses that were empty or under construction, and six with taking goods from 'the keys', generally sugar. The public house was also a place notoriously prone to petty theft, pewter pots proving a popular way of raising a few pennies for women even more than men (twenty-nine charges of thefts from public houses, fifteen by women).

It was men, though, who were almost exclusively involved in stealing goods when they were at their most vulnerable, during transit. 'Freshwater pirates' preyed on barges, wherries, even ships moored in the river (fifteen charges); and there were numerous thefts of bundles from porters, and thefts of boxes, parcels and trunks from carts, coaches and inn yards (thirty). Animals were similarly at risk, with nine men charged with stealing sheep from the fields, thirteen with taking horses, and a few others for thefts of poultry and pigs. Fancy dogs were stolen, too, usually hanged for their skins. And graves were robbed of their corpses, which were then sold to the surgeons for training apprentices in anatomy. Victims here were of the middling sort rather than the poor.[8]

Among a long list of miscellaneous offences one stands out. Counterfeiting coin was a minor London industry in an age when the quality and even the sufficiency of the coinage were greatly impaired. The manufacture of false coin was a 'Royal Offence', investigated by officials of the Mint at the Tower, and conviction almost always carried the death penalty. Ten women and twenty-one men faced trial for coining in this sample. Most often they fabricated low-denomination coins avoiding close scrutiny like halfpennies, even farthings. Again it was the poor who suffered most from crimes like this. They were unlikely to lose from the gilded sixpences and shillings that could pass for half-guineas and guineas in a dim light, but a bad halfpenny or two could mean the difference between a meal and going hungry. The amount of false coinage in circulation in London was very large: the toll at Blackfriars Bridge between 1775 and 1779 produced gross takings of £26,367 13s 6½d, but £2,058 12s 3d was in bad money.[9]

The Old Bailey trials made up only the most visible peak in a mountain range of crime whose extent is incalculable but prodigious. Much of the property crime coming before the Old Bailey must have been opportunistic rather than the work of professional thieves but even so the numbers of those thought by contemporaries to be making a living by crime were very large. Patrick Colquhoun, that energetic speculator in social statistics, thought at the end of the century that some 63,000 'support themselves in and near the Metropolis by pursuits either criminal – illegal – or immoral', and that excluded prostitutes, bawdy-house keepers and the like. Within that total he considered there were some 2,000 'Professed Thieves', 3,000 coiners and utterers of fake coin, and 10,500 pilferers who lived partly by crime, 2,500 of these stealing entirely from river trade.[10]

No doubt these were exaggerations to some degree while, on the other hand, ignoring the large numbers of working Londoners of the lower or middling condition who were ready to take advantage of easy pickings should they safely come their way. Whatever the numbers, crime was thought to be among the greatest problems of the age. The volume of crime in London in the eighteenth century is unknown and cannot be measured by the shifting numbers of offenders processed through the law courts. Even so, it seems clear that throughout the century crime was perceived to be generally and worryingly high, and that at times it appeared out of control.

Several historians have found periods of intense criminal activity, 'crime waves' a later age would call them, especially post-war years when returning soldiers and discharged sailors were thrown on labour markets already depressed by diminished demand for many manufactures. Contemporaries too thought this was the case and it certainly seems to have been a factor on some occasions when the numbers of offences appeared to reach a crisis; indeed, even without demobilisation, serving soldiers were frequently apprehended as footpads and thieves in London.[11]

But moments of high anxiety punctuated the century even more frequently than these temporary dislocations. In 1702 robberies and burglaries grew to such a pitch that the arrangements for the City's watch had to be urgently augmented. In March 1712 a great scare involved the 'Mohocks', rakes reckless and ruthless who were said to be beating and stabbing respectable citizens of the middling sort, though the whole phenomenon seems to have been largely imaginary. In 1718 it was said there were so many thieves in the City that people were afraid to shop or visit the coffee houses after dark 'for fear that . . . they may be blinded, knock'd down, cut or stabbed . . .' A rise in highway robberies led the Middlesex justices to petition Parliament for improvements to the watch in 1720. Rewards for apprehending highwaymen robbing the mails were doubled to £200 in 1722. There was a justifiable panic about crime in 1728–9 when the audacity of street robbers was such that coaches were held up during daylight in the main streets and there was apparently a conspiracy to rob the Queen in her coach, all compounded by the gin scare and doubts over the moral impact of *The Beggar's Opera*. Another fright over highwaymen on the main roads to London in 1735–7 seems to have been based largely on the exploits of Richard Turpin, an Essex man with strong links to the East End of London. The City Corporation petitioned the King in 1744 for assistance in suppressing '"divers confederacies of great numbers of evil-disposed persons, arm'd with bludgeons, pistols, cutlasses, and other dangerous weapons . . ."' There then followed another great crisis of 1749–52, at the end of the Spanish War, when robberies and atrocities of one kind or other seemed daily occurrences in the streets of London and when the prisons, it was said, were packed with footpads and highwaymen: 'think what shambles this country is grown!' wrote Horace Walpole in March 1752; 'One is obliged to travel even at noon as if one was going to battle.' The panic of those years would not be repeated. Even so, in the second half of the century there were great alarms about 'Murders, robberies, many of them attended with acts of cruelty . . .

never perhaps more frequent about this city than' in late 1761; 'Villainy . . . now arrived to such a height at London, that no man is safe in his own house' in 1772; 'the town abound[ing] with desperadoes' through 1781–2 and again in 1786; and in every year that followed criminals and their depredations filled columns in the daily newspapers.[12]

All Londoners were affected in some way by crime in the eighteenth century and a large proportion must have been victims. They included many of those we have already met in these pages or will meet shortly, and doubtless more might be added to the roll call. So, for instance, Jonathan Swift had his pocket picked in the Mall in August 1711, the house where he lodged at Little Panton Street, Haymarket, was broken into in January 1712, and he feared to stir out for the Mohocks a couple of months later. Dudley Ryder's family home in Hackney was burgled in September 1715. Cecile de Saussure had his pocket picked of a valuable snuff box in February 1726. John Baptist Grano, trumpeter and prisoner at the Marshalsea, allowed out to beg from his friends, was knocked unconscious and robbed 'under Somerset House Wall' in May 1729 by several men 'who left me for Dead'. Charlotte Charke's small oil and grocery business in Long Acre was upset by a link boy making off with her brass weights in 1737. Louis François Roubiliac, the sculptor, was robbed by three men not far from his door in Dean Street, Soho, in 1750 – they presented a pistol to his head and took his money and watch. Tobias Smollett lost his watch and money when his stage coach was held up between Chelsea and London in December 1754. The Rev. Dr William Dodd and his wife were robbed and shot at by a highwayman near Tottenham Court turnpike in 1772 – William Griffith was executed at Tyburn for the crime a year later. Thomas Hardy the shoemaker had his room broken into soon after his arrival in London in 1774 by thieves who 'left him almost naked'; and his first married home, a shop and dwelling, was 'stripped' of boots and shoes and all the couple's clothes at Christmas 1781. James Lackington the bookseller was robbed by nurses brought in to care for his sick wife in 1775. Around 1781 Israel Potter the American was robbed by six men in Hyde Park who put a pistol to his breast and took 5 guineas and some copper. That same year the Thrales' 'favourite Abroad-Clerk' absconded from their Southwark brewery with £2,000 – 'I have been running after him I think into all the hiding Places of this filthy Town,' Hester noted in her diary, but she 'lost him at last'. Henry Angelo was robbed by footpads of his hat near Spa Fields and lost a handkerchief to a pickpocket near the Botanical Gardens at Kew some time in the 1780s. In September 1784 Edmund Burke lost much valuable plate when his country house at Beaconsfield was robbed by burglars who travelled by phaeton from London for the job. Around the same time, the sculptor Joseph Nollekens had his collection of gold and silver foreign coins stolen in a burglary at his home in Mortimer Street, Cavendish Square, and Joseph Brasbridge the silversmith had gold and silver trinkets lifted from his shop at 98 Fleet Street. Around 1790 Thomas Rowlandson was robbed near Poland Street, Soho, by a man who knelt on his chest while taking his money and watch, and John Coakley Lettsom, the philanthropic medical man, was held up by a highwayman on his way home to Camberwell. In February 1793 the Barnet house of James Adam the architect was attacked by thirteen armed burglars from London – a gun battle with household staff on the leads ended in the deaths of two intruders.[13]

Even at the end of the century, as that shows, the effrontery of thieves knew no bounds. A single highwayman held up and robbed the Lord Mayor 'in his chaise and four, in sight of all his retinue' near Turnham Green in September 1776. The Neapolitan ambassador was robbed in his coach by four footpads in Grosvenor Square – three held pistols to the servants and one robbed him of a gold watch and money. The Lord Chancellor was burgled at home in Great Ormond Street in March 1784, losing 'the Great Seal of England' in the process. The official home of the Speaker of the House of Commons in Whitehall was robbed in January 1785 by 'fresh water pirates' who took many valuables including his 'gold robe of state'. The Archbishop of Canterbury lost plate worth £2,000 when Lambeth Palace was burgled in October 1788. Fanny Burney's footman stole silver from Buckingham House in 1791, Fanny a lady-in-waiting to the Queen. And there was an attempt in January 1792 to rob the Prince of Wales at a levee in St James's Palace, 'a gang of fellows' importing the tactics of a street robbery even into the royal family's drawing room.[14]

Horace Walpole, it seems, led a veritable life of crime – as victim at least. In November 1749 he was held up in his coach in Hyde Park by James Maclean, a famous highwayman, whose pistol accidentally fired, the ball grazing Walpole's cheek and stunning him. His home at

Arlington Street was broken into in June 1752 and again in March 1771. Two footpads tried to stop his coach and rob him near Twickenham in June 1776 and he was robbed there by a highwayman in June 1782. And in October 1791 a servant absconded with some silver, hanging himself apparently in remorse for the crime.

Walpole seems rarely to have gone abroad without his coach but we might take our final instances of victimhood from James Boswell, whose fondness for walking and dislike of coach fares rendered him specially susceptible to the nightly hazards of London's streets. He was most vulnerable when drunk, which he often was, and so were all foot passengers likely victims when abroad in that lamentable condition. So he lost to pickpockets a handkerchief in April 1775, silver coins and a key in August 1785, another handkerchief in February 1786 and even proof sheets and the relevant manuscript of *The Life of Samuel Johnson* in July 1790. In June 1793, at the age of fifty-three and drunk once more, he was on his way home from the City to Great Portland Street when he was knocked down and robbed not far from his door by a single footpad. This would, he thought, 'be a *crisis* in my life. I trust I shall henceforth be a sober, regular man.' But he was back to his old ways again just a few weeks later.[15]

As we saw from the Old Bailey trials in 1782–3, robbery with violence in the streets of London was a common charge, and a week's run of any daily newspaper through the century shows it to have been an even more common crime. It was the great peril of the London night and although street robbery was more frequent at some times than others it was an endemic threat and constant fear. Fear resided most in the degree of violence that might be used. Being taken in the act was the street robber's greatest risk and the consequences of being taken were generally fatal. To guard against it, footpads had to ensure that they had the advantage not just of darkness and surprise but of strength too. A single footpad armed with a cudgel might tackle a woman or a drunken or infirm man. But to rob wealthy men, often armed with a sword and bristling with all the pride of rank, or men and women travelling in a coach or chair, thieves sought strength in numbers and in arms. These larger gangs of street robbers frequently went armed with cudgels, knives, cutlasses, pistols. And the dreadful consequences of capture made them ever ready to use them.

James Dalton, who eventually 'turned evidence' against his

companions, led one of the notorious gangs of the crisis years around 1728, four or five men all armed with pistols, who stopped and robbed coaches in Holborn, St Paul's Churchyard, Lombard Street and elsewhere, sometimes in broad daylight. Passers-by were too terrified to intervene, and who can blame them? When four footpads of another gang held up a coach one early morning in July 1730 in the Strand, 'three Soldiers came along, but we went up to them, and, presenting our Pistols, threatened to shoot them through the Head, if they offered to molest us, and so they went down a Turning by the *Savoy*, and left us to do what we pleased'.[16] Shootings were indeed a common feature of footpad robberies: in the neighbourhood of Berkeley Square, for instance, a chairman was shot dead protecting his fare in 1755, and a watchman was shot dead and a robber died of a pistol shot and sword stab during an attempted street robbery in October 1756. And in May 1770 two tradesmen returning home from the pub were shot dead by three footpads in Redman's Grove, Stepney. Crimes like these remained, if not common, then frequent enough throughout the century.[17]

The fields on the outskirts of London were particularly dangerous. With so many possible escape routes, thieves could gather with relative impunity even in the daytime, like the eight or ten pickpockets who jostled worshippers outside Pentonville Chapel one noonday in July 1789: when a gentleman cried out the common warning, 'Take care of your pockets!' he was knocked to the ground with a blow to the head. And at night, even at the very end of the century, the fields could be terrible. In May 1797, around eight or nine in the evening, Sydney Fryer, an attorney's clerk, was walking with his fiancée near White Conduit House, Islington, when they were set upon by three footpads. Fryer was armed with a swordstick and put up some resistance but was shot in the head and then robbed of his watch and money: two men were hanged for his murder. And a year later on Hounslow Heath, a small party of City men returning from a stag hunt were held up in their carriage by three footpads. Although no resistance seems to have been offered one of the party was shot above the right eye. He was taken to an inn nearby, where he died two days later: the surgeon on his way to attend him 'was stopped and robbed by the same gang'.[18]

If the footpad was the perennial terror of the London streets and the fields around, then the highwayman rendered the heaths, commons, forests and high roads of London's outskirts equally threatening. Well mounted, armed with a brace of pistols at least, often committing two or more robberies in a night, able to move quickly from one profitable robbing place to another, and with his cry of 'Stand and deliver!' — no myth that — the highwayman was a figure of great notoriety in eighteenth-century London. He — a very occasional woman was reported on the highway, but almost all were men — haunted the imagination of everyone travelling to and from London by carriage, stage coach or on horseback. Any horseman met on the road might become an object of fear. The anxieties of four companions riding to town after dining at a country house in Willesden in September 1761 were vividly recorded by an Irish clergyman in his journal:

When we came as far as Paddington wch leads directly to ye Moveable Gallows at Tyburn we thought we smelld Powder as this at Night is a very Dangerous pass. The two Doct^rs y^t were behind were in a sad pannic about two Horsemen y^t passd & were talking Gibberish. Their money & watches began to tremble in their places. Whilst they were thus engag'd two Fellows wth Carabines on their shoulders passd y^m whom I heard say y^t one man might Robb y^m Both. I believe he might, provided Gentlemen twas not so near ye Gallows — When they espied me they stood & s^d God, Master, we never thought of y^t — & so pass^d on.

Despite these anxieties much romance attached to highwaymen. They often operated single-handedly, seem not generally to have used the gratuitous violence meted out by footpads, and ran great risks of injury from the habit of travellers and servants going armed with guns. Stories of gallantry to lady passengers or the poor were propagated and received with relish by the reading public. And so was any indication — and there seem to have been several instances — of young men of the middling sort taking to the road to counter ill-fortune and rebuild their finances. James Maclean, 'the Gentleman Highwayman' who gave Horace Walpole such a fright in 1749, was one such, a Scottish Presbyterian minister's son who had sought, found and squandered a small fortune in London before taking his chances on the highway; he prospered sufficient to have lodgings in St James's Street at 2 guineas a week.[19]

Even so, the almost certain death penalty on capture rendered the highwayman ruthless when cornered. Richard Turpin shot dead a servant belonging to one of the keepers of Epping Forest who tried to track him down for the bounty on his head in May 1737, and there were many cases of highwaymen shooting once passengers opened fire. This kind of highway robbery remained a feature of London life throughout the century. Despite the small number of charges coming to trial at the Old Bailey in 1782–3, we read in the *London Chronicle* for the first six months of 1780 of robberies by highwaymen in Lewisham, Clapham Common, Hounslow Heath, Gunnersbury, Vauxhall (two), Hammersmith, somewhere on the road from Staines to London, Holloway (three), Kingston, Merrow Downs near Guildford, Islington, Kent Street, Wandsworth and Blackheath; and a resident of that last busy interchange recorded that highway robberies there and nearby in 1789–91 'were exceedingly frequent; they were sometimes perpetrated in broad daylight, and even in the midst of a large concourse of people'.[20]

The other great terror of London was the burglar, especially burglars who operated in gangs and went armed. Samuel Johnson seems not to have been a significant victim of crime during his many years in London. But his big-boned physique and thick walking stick would have been a caution to footpads; and the robustness of his door at 17 Gough Square, Fleet Street, with its chains and bolts and spiked iron bars across the fanlight, still testifies eloquently to the precautions felt necessary by the London householder to guard against thieves forcing entry in the night. Other common deterrents included house-dogs and a blunderbuss prominently displayed behind a barred window. Unsurprisingly, London was a centre of the lock- and safe-making trade at a time when most families still kept their valuables and cash about the home.

Aggravated burglaries of a mob-handed type were most common in the countryside around London where the alarm could be raised only with difficulty. Before taking to the highway, Richard Turpin had been a member of Samuel Gregory's gang, some eight or ten strong, who specialised in forcing their way into isolated farmhouses and country villas on the outskirts of London, terrifying – even torturing – the householders into revealing the whereabouts of plate or money. That was 1734–5, but in every decade of the century there were gangs who adopted similar brutality: we might remember Mrs Hutchins's farm near the King's Road, Chelsea, attacked by burglars in June 1771 in a crime that caused such difficulties for London Jewry; and four years later an elderly couple in Portugal Court, Deptford, were found with their throats cut and their house robbed.[21]

Tactics for gaining entry varied. The connivance of a servant was always helpful but not necessary where brute force could be used. In town, trickery was more often resorted to where forcing doors with crows and hammers would have attracted too much attention. But everywhere, force of arms and fear of capture made men reckless and brazen in equal measure. In February 1785 the maid of Mrs Abercrombie in Charlotte Street, in a crowded and reasonably prosperous new district north of Oxford Street, opened the door to a man who pretended to be a postman. Seven men 'armed with swords and pistols, rushed into the house' and robbed her mistress, wife of an East India Company ship's captain, of her jewellery and some 50 or 60 guineas in cash. They were packing up the plate for removal when they realised the maid had escaped and raised the alarm. 'A great crowd immediately assembled about the house, and the ruffians sallied forth, with dreadful menaces, waving their swords, and directing their pistols at the mob, who tamely suffered them to escape without making the least resistance.' And burglaries where householders of the middling sort were threatened with death and tied up by armed men while their houses were ransacked were common enough through to the century's end.[22]

Who were the men and women who committed offences like these? In general, it seems, most had backgrounds like any other Londoner making their way in the giant city. Mary Young had been a seamstress from the north of Ireland, John Maclean had come to London from Scotland as a butler with an urge to join the army, Richard Turpin was an Essex butcher who had bought stolen venison from Samuel Gregory and had stumbled into more lucrative criminal ways. And in the various accounts of those criminal lives soon to be ended at Tyburn it is their very ordinariness that strikes the reader: James Dupree, thirty, a Spitalfields silk weaver hanged for burglary in 1726, 'of mean Parents, no Education for Letters'; Richard Lynn, about twenty-four, of St Sepulchre's in the City, hanged for burglary in 1727, a time-served ivory-turner who could read and write and earn a good wage; Mary Allen or Smith, twenty-six, a shoplifter hanged in 1747, 'born of honest and respectable Parents' in Goswell Street, Finsbury; on the gallows with her were Henry 'Gentleman Harry' Simms, thirty, of St

Martin-in-the-Fields, at first in service and then a driver of a hackney coach before turning highwayman; and, among yet others, John Ryley, about seventeen, of very poor parents in Old Street, a thief from about nine years old, who trained by picking his own father's pockets when the man 'was in Liquor'.[23]

Just Ryley among this typical sample was likely to have been born into great poverty. Starving poverty was most certainly a factor when evaluating the reasons why individuals took to crime, opportunistically or as a main way of life. It was generally the case among the many hundreds of children, orphaned or abandoned by their parents, who at any time grew up scavenging and homeless on the streets of London. These were the so-called 'blackguards', huddled under shop bulks or round the warmth of the Whitechapel glasshouses, from whom the ranks of link boys, shoeblacks and resourceful sneak thieves were recruited: children like William Winter, 'a lad', caught stealing clothes from a bundle in the passage of a porter's house in Phoenix Street, St Giles, in late 1783 – he tried to hide 'a pair of nankeen breeches under his breeches' but 'he was so bare of clothes he could not conceal them'. Boys like Winter could also be preyed on by those few real-life Fagins, men and women who lived by schooling sneak thieves and 'divers' and who lived off their pickings – a 'club of boys' trained like this by a man 'who kept a public house in Fleet-market' was discovered by the City authorities in March 1765, for instance; and Ann Hickey of Crown Court, St Giles, kept lodging houses for destitute and homeless boys and girls in 1787 and seems to have trained them to steal and go on the town.[24]

Juries of householders at the Old Bailey and elsewhere frequently recognised the great temptations in the way of those going hungry or near-naked. They often wrote down the value of goods stolen so that thieves could avoid the harshest penalties of the law. Occasionally they went further, an Old Bailey jury establishing a 'liberal collection' for the family of a man caught stealing sugar 'off the keys', his wife and five children ill of the smallpox and 'in great distress' in January 1763, and no doubt there were similar occasions.[25]

In general, though, it was not absolute necessity that drove most thieves to steal. The rest in our sample had reasonable starts in life and several were educated and bred to a trade. For the majority by far of those committing crime in London stole not to live but to enter more fully into the age of plenty that was all around them and which, as the century grew older, became ever more abundant – not just in the possessions and commodities of domestic life but in the delightful entertainments and conspicuous daily consumption of the metropolitan collective. The gap between what London could offer and what the many could afford was everywhere apparent. Those excluded from London's delights might endure torments of desire and frustration that only gaining money at almost any cost could assuage. It was no accident that the volume of cases coming before the Old Bailey in the second half of the century rose steeply in that age of multiplying public pleasures, luxurious shopping and flamboyant fashion. Of 49,000 offences recorded in the century at the Old Bailey nearly 30,000 or 61 per cent were heard between 1750 and 1799; the proportion of property crime also grew in these years – it was 93.4 per cent between 1700 and 1749 but 95.7 per cent in the second half of the century.[26]

Many people of any social background were capable of committing crime and falling foul of the criminal justice system. But it seems reasonably clear that a significant minority, whether we believe Colquhoun's figures or not, adopted theft as a full-time career choice. Having done so, a professional thief entered a world – a subculture we might call it – that was at once set apart from, yet intimately connected to, the rest of eighteenth-century London. It was a subculture that operated on a number of levels. One was morality, where the highest values worthy of respect were dauntless courage, loyalty and fair dealing with companions. They were values that proved as fragile as truthfulness, honesty and chivalry in the wider society. Much of eighteenth-century policing relied on one gang member 'turning evidence' against the others, as the Old Bailey Proceedings readily testify. Even so, many stood by their code, and we might recall staunch Martha Stracey and those who bore false witness for Mary Young at some considerable peril to themselves.

The economy of criminality also had close ties to the generality of moneymaking in London. Thieves had their public houses of call much like shoemakers or tailors or coalheavers. Locksmiths turned out skeleton keys and blacksmiths made crows to order. Skilled engravers sculpted dies and stamps to make halfpennies and shillings. Goldsmiths turned over their crucibles to melt and recast stolen plate. Armourers readily provided second-hand cutlasses, knives and the ubiquitous pistol – when Lambert Reading, a country-house burglar, was arrested in his room in Brick Lane in 1775 he was found 'in bed with his girl, ten loaded pistols lying by him', to give one extreme example. And receivers of stolen property or 'fences' were always to be found among backstreet publicans in the thieves' houses of call, with a few pawnbrokers, numerous jewellers (including Jewish buyers and sellers in the eastern part of the City trading to Amsterdam and elsewhere) and especially second-hand-clothes dealers, who seem generally to have taken whatever thieves brought them – a 'gang' of boy pickpockets from the same charity school could sell sixty handkerchiefs in a night to a single dealer in Whitecross Street in 1774; he gave them 4d for each piece, 'good and bad together'.[27]

These shadowy economic margins of the metropolis combined the proceeds of crime with more legitimate trade in ways that were designedly hard to disentangle. Keeping the unlawful components obscure from public gaze required secrecy, and secrecy was aided by the peculiarities of language adopted by thieves and those who dealt with them. There were varieties of thieves' cant. Backslang was the most secret of all. It could be spoken as quickly as any other language and was utterly impenetrable to the non-speaker: this was presumably the 'Gibberish' overheard by the Irish clergyman on his way home from Willesden. Other elements of thieves' vocabulary naming the various techniques of crime leaked into print throughout the century. Mary Young's doings gained added spice in the Ordinary's account from her use of cant terms for cutting off women's pockets ('Cheving the Froe'), or standing at a distance to receive a pickpocket's loot ('stand Miss Slang all upon the Safe') or relieving a beau ('Rum Muns') of his ring ('Glim Star'), and so on. And numerous other thieves' lives or prison literature were littered with slang lexicons to titillate or alarm the reading public.[28]

Much as the London economy adapted itself to the very considerable trade in stolen goods and the manufacture of thieves' materiel, the London housing market was also distinctively affected by the traditions of crime and criminality in the capital. There were obvious reasons for thieves to cluster in certain areas – for information, for proximity to economic outlets, most of all for mutual protection from the forces of order. It would be misleading to call these 'criminal areas', because there were many living there who pursued trades and callings in the mainstream London economy and who were no more (and no less) criminal than the residents of Hanover Square or Pall Mall. But there were numerous districts where the concentration of thieves and prostitutes rendered a place dangerous for the unwary foot passenger and doubly so for the parish police, for bailiffs and for others bent on enforcing the laws. They could be dangerous too for landlords, who might find rents uncollectable and their tenants impossible to evict, and where properties became derelict and were abandoned to those who could make some use of them. Over time the reputations of areas like this rendered them terrible to the respectable. And over time the very worst of them became largely (though not exclusively) the resort of the very poor who could afford nowhere else and the lawless who moved there by choice.

All parts of old London had districts like this, some no larger than a court or two, some much more extensive. In Southwark, west of Borough High Street, lay the Mint, a peculiarly lawless district with numerous seventeenth- and even sixteenth-century houses and a tradition of lawlessness all its own. To the west of Westminster Abbey were networks of old streets around Thieving Lane and the Almonry, where beggars and outlaws had once claimed sanctuary from the Cathedral Church of St Peter and were still traditional 'Alsatias' for thieves. In the City similar ancient sanctuaries had left a residue of lawlessness in Whitefriars, on the riverside east of the Temple, and in St Martin's-le-Grand, with its numerous courts on either side, running north from Newgate Street. Indeed, any poor district from Whitechapel in the east to St Giles in the west would have its streets, courts and alleys notoriously more troublesome than those around: like Dyot Street St Giles, which produced some eighty-seven case references in the Old Bailey Proceedings as a hiding place for thieves and as somewhere crime was committed.

Perhaps the most notoriously criminal district in London throughout the eighteenth century was that centred on Chick Lane, straddling the boundary between Farringdon Ward Without in the City and the parish of St Andrew Holborn. Chick Lane was long and narrow, linking Smithfield Market in the east with Saffron Hill and crossing the open Fleet Ditch at its western end. From it opened a maze of some thirty or forty courts and alleys on either side of the way. Of these, Black Boy Alley was the most notorious, on the north side towards the Fleet Ditch end. Chick Lane alone was referred to in over 300 cases in the Old Bailey Proceedings across the century.

Here were to be found at one time or another some of the most desperate gangs of street robbers and burglars in London. We might instance Edward Burnworth, William Blewit and their gang, six of them hanged for the murder of Thomas Ball in the Mint, Southwark. They had planned this killing of a false friend at an alehouse in White Horse Alley, Chick Lane, in January 1726. Eight men were involved with four or five pistols between them, the bullets cast by Burnworth 'in a Mold. He was very expert at it': perhaps his trade as a buckle maker, apprenticed in Grub Street, was of help to him. To make sure the pistols fired true they tested them in the fields by Copenhagen House. On their way back towards Chick Lane they happened upon Captain Walker, keeper of the New Prison at Clerkenwell, from which Burnworth had recently escaped. There were high words between them in Turnmill Street and a 'Mob' gathered and followed the gang as they turned towards Chick Lane. At the entrance to narrow White Horse Alley the gang swore 'we would shoot the first Man that follow'd us' and Walker and the crowd stood back. Crossing the river by wherry, they found Ball and shot him dead in his home. A crowd once more assembled but 'the prisoners came to the Street Door, discharged another Pistol, and said, *Now follow us, who dare?* And so they went their ways.' There then followed an energetic spate of robberies up and down London in which Burnworth and his gang members combined with other thieves, robbing the Earl of Harborough in his chair in Piccadilly, burgling a distiller's house in Clare Market and carrying out 'a great Number of Robberies'. Hanged at Kingston Gallows, the bodies of Burnworth and Blewit were gibbeted in St George's Fields, 'over against the *Two Fighting Cocks* in the *Mint*', close to the scene of Ball's murder.[29]

Two years later, in 1728, James Dalton's evidence led to the arrest of some members of his gang in Chick Lane, armed with pistol and sword. In 1730 another gang of enterprising young footpads, their leader Hugh Morris, just seventeen, were arrested for numerous street robberies of foot passengers and coaches at night. Morris had been to school and apprenticed to an upholsterer, but apparently told the Ordinary 'that his total Ruin was owing to some Places about *Chick-Lane*, where Numbers of the vilest Miscreants, Street Robbers, Thieves, Pick-pockets, House-breakers, Shop-lifters, and other Monsters of Wickedness, meet in great Companies, and there they drink and carouse' in 'Hell-fire Clubs' – these the Ordinary's words, one imagines, not Morris's.[30] And in 1744 a gang of footpads based in Black Boy Alley grew so persistently obnoxious that the City Corporation petitioned the King to make it clear that none would receive royal clemency when they were apprehended. At last one man was arrested and turned evidence, naming ten others in the gang, and admitting to a campaign of armed robberies that sometimes amounted to six or more attacks in an evening. Five were hanged on Christmas Eve 1744; and through 1744–5 a further five men and seven women, all with Chick Lane connections and mostly street robbers, were hanged at Tyburn. From this time, Black Boy Alley was said to have been known as Jack Ketch's Common.[31]

The criminal resources of an area like this were no doubt manifold but we might pick out two. The first was a collective solidarity against the outside world. Matthew Brown was on his way home through Chick Lane on a snowy night at the end of December 1739 when Thomas Hawkins (alias Dumplin) leaped out of Thatched Alley, knocked him to the ground, snatched his watch and ran back into the alley.

As I ran down the Alley after him, I cry'd *Thieves! Murder! I am robb'd of my Watch!* But 2 Women held out their Arms and stopp'd me; I gave one of them a Blow on the Breast and knock'd her down; then I ran past them and followed the prisoner into the House. As soon as I got in, the Prisoner turn'd himself round, look'd me in the Face, and then laid himself down on a Bed, in the Ground Room. I charged him with taking my Watch, and would have taken him off the Bed, but some Men and Women (who were in the Room) would not suffer me to take him. The Landlady of the House said, d—mn you, you son of a Bitch, bring a Guinea or 20 Shillings and you shall have your Watch again To-morrow Morning. Says the Prisoner, (who lay all this while on the Bed) if the poor Man will bring 10 Shillings he shall have it again. I insisted upon having my Watch, or the Prisoner off the Bed, upon which they all fell a thumping me, and knock'd me out of Doors . . . Then I call'd out for Assistance, and a Soldier coming by, I told him a Thief was gone in there, who had robb'd me of my Watch, and I would give him Half a Crown, if he would call a Constable. Another Soldier came up at the same Time, and bid me give 'em the Money first. I said, I would give them a Crown, as soon as they brought me an Officer, but I did not care to give 'em the Money before-hand. Upon this, they likewise began to thump me about: I told them I believ'd they were all alike, and ran Home to my Wife . . .

When Brown returned to the house that night with a constable and a justice's search warrant a woman – possibly Hawkins's wife – threatened to cut the officer's nose, 'but he gave her a Thump on the Breast and said, – d—mn you, you B—ch, whose Nose will you cut? Upon which she sat down and was quiet.' At his trial Hawkins produced eight witnesses among his neighbours who swore to a different story but to no avail: Hawkins was sentenced to death, but was transported at His Majesty's pleasure.[32]

Another local resource lay in the houses themselves. During or soon after the Gordon Riots of June 1780 an officer of the London Military Association told the philanthropist Jonas Hanway what he'd seen:

We were twice on duty, attended by peace-officers, particularly two, who have been long employed in the art and mystery of thief-taking. One of our detachments visited *Chick Lane, Field Lane, Black-boy Alley*, and some other such places. From the first-named, we escorted several persons to prison. These places constitute a kind of separate town or district, calculated for the reception of the darkest and most dangerous enemies to society; and in which, when pursued for the commission of crimes, they easily conceal themselves. The houses are divided, from top to bottom, into many apartments, with doors of communication to each; and also with the adjacent houses, some having two, others three, others four doors opening into different alleys. To such a height is our neglect of police arrived, the owners of these houses make no secret of their being let for the entertainment of *thieves*. One woman, a rosy veteran, being questioned on this head, answered, *Where are they to go, if we do not admit them?* Thus they support, on principle, the propriety of maintaining the republic of thieves. In many of the rooms I saw six, seven, eight, nine, and ten men in bed; in others, as many women; all pictures of *misery*, as you may easily imagine. In one loft, I saw eight men in bed, without shirts. Into this apartment we crept through a trap-door, our bayonets and pistols in our hands.[33]

Some time in the 1790s Chick Lane was rechristened West Street. But anonymity failed to purge its traditions or erase its reputation. Even when its western end was demolished fifty years later as part of the Farringdon Street improvements, the days of the Gordon Riots and before were sensationally recalled by the demolition of 'The Old House' on the corner of Brewhouse Yard, west of Black Boy Alley and backing on to Fleet Ditch. It had once been an alehouse, the Red Lion, was thought to be some 300 years old, and was sometimes called Jonathan Wild's House, reputedly one of that crafty thief-taker's storehouses for stolen goods. It contained 'dark closets, trap-doors, sliding panels, and secret recesses . . . A skull, and numerous human bones, were found in the cellars'. There was a tunnel to Fleet Ditch and in the garrets 'a secret door, which led to the roof of the next house, from which any offender could be in Saffron-hill in a few minutes'.[34]

This, then, was the archetypal district of the criminal poor in London. But not all London's criminals would have been at home in Chick Lane – or anywhere like it.

Virtue Overborn by Temptation: Genteel Crime

With the growth of trade and the unstoppable rise of the middling sort who depended on it came new opportunities for crime and new devices to make crime pay. We might remember that the frenzied speculation promoted by the South Sea Bubble of 1720 was accompanied by a feast of fraud as bubblers dreamt up proposals to tease guineas from the pockets of the credulous: one was said to have advertised that, for a 2-guinea fee, subscribers would receive a £100 share in a project to be disclosed in a month – his impudence apparently won him over £2,000.[35] That may have been the moment of greatest collective idiocy among the middling sort and the quality, but no year throughout the century was free from some metropolitan chicanery or other. Indeed, as trade, banking and insurance grew, then so did deception, forgery and fraud. Unsurprisingly, and in common with property crime generally, at least as reported in the Old Bailey Proceedings, charges of deception (mainly forgery and fraud) were disproportionately common in the second half of the century. Overall there were 1,075 such charges brought between 1700 and 1799, but 769 (or 71.5 per cent) were heard from 1750 onwards.[36]

Fraud took many forms and new tricks blossomed as old ones grew stale. All depended on appearance, that most unreliable feature of the times. Anyone with the confidence, dress, speech, air of the quality or the moneyed citizen seemed able to winkle the most extraordinary array of goods from tradesmen on credit. Thomas Pitkin, 'late of

London, Linen-Draper', was sought in 1704 for obtaining by deception 'great Quantities of Woollen-Cloth, Linen-Cloth, and divers other
sorts of Goods, Wares and Merchandizes, to the Value of Seventy
thousand Pounds, and upwards'. Smaller hauls were commonplace
and women were as active in the trickery as men. One 'who went by
several different names' at Dean Street, Soho, was committed to the
Westminster Gatehouse in August 1758 charged with embezzling
goods: 'She was carried to gaol in a chair, attended by one of her
footmen.'[37]

Another favourite trick in this age of influence was to pretend to
'an interest' with the powerful through whom a public appointment
might be obtained. William Fuller – 'Cheat-Master-General of Great-
Britain' he was called in 1718 – obtained £150 from a woman in
Ratcliff Highway 'to help her to be *Chief Laundress* to the late
Queen'. He later pretended to be Lieutenant-Governor of the Tower
of London and Warden of the Mint, 'selling' places at the Tower and
in the customs to a lighterman, an oar maker, a victualler in Grub
Street and others. Extraordinary sums were sometimes extorted in
this way, a public place a lifetime sinecure worthy of investing an
inheritance to obtain: in 1777 David Brown Dignam Esq defrauded
£1,200 from a man wishing to become clerk to HM Customs at
Dublin and £1,000 from another for an imaginary place as 'Gazette-
writer to the ministry'. The shamelessness of some of these tricks
knew no bounds: fraudsters even visited those condemned to death
in Newgate pretending influence to obtain a pardon if a large sum
could only be made available.[38]

The ever-increasing volume of merchant and banking transactions
relied largely on vast numbers of bills of exchange, promises to pay
endorsed by merchants, tradesmen and others who had accepted
responsibility for the sum named in the bill when due. These bills
could be readily altered or forged. They could then be used to raise
cash or credit by the person presenting them. It could be a difficult
offence to prove in court. Samuel Fisher was said to have been acquitted
nine times at the Old Bailey for offences of this kind, claiming that
he was the innocent victim of someone who had passed the false bill
to him. When eventually he was transported in 1769 he was said to
be 'worth several thousand pounds'. By the time John Dyer, a former
scholar at Westminster School, counterfeited an accepted bill for 10
guineas in 1790 the courts had come to take a less lenient view of

his crime: just twenty-two, he was convicted and hanged despite having the services of the famous William Garrow as counsel for the defence. And in June 1798 it was reported that three gentlemen were executed that month 'for the same modern but now unhappily common crime of forgery'.[39]

There were some truly sensational cases of fraud involving this kind of forgery. That of 'the unfortunate Doctor Dodd' we'll glimpse in a later chapter. But none, perhaps, was more multilayered in its contemporary resonance than that of the Perreau brothers and the fascinating Mrs Margaret Rudd. It concerned an attempted fraud on Drummond's Bank at Charing Cross when Robert Perreau, a prosperous and by all accounts honest apothecary of Golden Square, presented a forged bond for £7,500 for payment from the account of a rich client of the bank. Daniel, Robert's brother, was a more shadowy and less successful West India merchant who yet seemed to have money enough to run a household in Harley Street and to keep the expensive Mrs Rudd as mistress. In all likelihood the plot and the forgery were all Mrs Rudd's doing, but it was the brothers who were hanged at Tyburn in January 1776 and Mrs Rudd who remained a London celebrity, combining notoriety with considerable sexual allure: James Boswell was much struck by her and became her rather shamefaced lover for a time.[40]

The rise of paper money – cheques, banknotes, headed bills of exchange – gave opportunities to skilled engravers to copy and reproduce the increasingly complex designs on watermarked paper that finance houses used to combat counterfeiting. William Ryland, that skilled and famous engraver to the King to whom the young William Blake took such marked exception, was hanged in 1783 for forging an East India Company bill, copied from one that had lawfully come into his hands. Forging or altering Bank of England notes had been a capital offence since 1697; in 1725 uttering them became capital too; and in 1773 the death penalty was extended to papermakers who used the Bank's name in a watermark. Even so, these severe penalties and the difficulties of engraving the intricate plates and manufacturing the moulds did not deter those who saw forging banknotes as an easy way to big money, false notes for £10, £20, £50 and £100 in circulation by the century's end.[41]

There were numerous other opportunities for fraud in the expanding financial sector of eighteenth-century London. Insurance companies were cheated by arsonists, stockbrokers defrauded clients of shares and attorneys plundered them of savings or rents. Many of these were principals stealing to fund a luxurious way of life or to stave off a crisis of credit. But even more involved that weakest link in the business chain: the humble clerk.

A Little, Thin, Prim Man, about 20 Years of Age, an Attorney's Clerk, slow of Speech, and goes very Upright, has a bald Place on one side of his Head toward the hinder-part; did wear a full bob Wigg, a Light-colour'd Coat and Waste-coat, and Leather Breeches, his right Name is William Croose; he is suppos'd to be flush of Money, having run away from his Master (on Monday the 24th of this instant January, 1709) with a considerable Sum; Whoever Apprehends him, and gives notice thereof to Mr. Samuel Robinson an Attorney in Aldersgate-street London, shall have 5l. Reward, and reasonable Charges. And if he will surrender himself, within a short time, shall be Genteelly receiv'd: Otherwise, all possible Means shall be us'd to bring him to Punishment.[42]

There were many aggravating financial pressures on clerks in eighteenth-century London. They were paid no more than £50 or £60 a year, about the same as an artisan, yet 'all are obliged to wear clean linen, and decent apparel', with all the laundresses' and tailors' bills that entailed. Maintaining a respectable address denied access to the very cheapest areas of London and for a family man necessitated at least a housemaid to help his wife and some sort of schooling for the children. Clerks thought of themselves as, and in common parlance were so called, gentlemen. Yet living within one's means meant penny-pinching and self-denial. And it meant renouncing those pleasures in which London abounded, particularly in the second half of the century, and which were designed to attract the custom of men and families in these lower-middling ranks. The only way for most to partake fully of what London offered was to run into debt. 'In these circumstances,' as a correspondent to the *Gentleman's Magazine* put it in January 1751, calling for higher salaries for clerks to guard against forgery and theft, 'the virtue must be great indeed that is not overborn by temptation . . .'[43]

We have seen earlier how prostitution – not in itself a crime of course – could offer some talented women a way out of poverty and into comfort, even celebrity and riches and a landed estate. The talented clerk, on the other hand, was set on a respectable route to solid comfort, an assured key to social advancement of a kind, but never to riches. Could crime offer the same means of upward mobility through many ranks that prostitution provided for women, and could it offer the clerk not just solid comfort but true wealth?

Possibly it could. It is in the nature of the evidence available to us that we hear most often of the failures, those who were caught and prosecuted and appeared in the dock at the Old Bailey, receiving their final comeuppance at Tyburn. Even of these, most seem to have aimed modestly low in their depredations. We hear of William Guest, clerk at the Bank of England, caught filing guineas to sell the gold dust in 1767; when discovered he tried to cut his throat but the gallows got him in the end. And of Francis Fonton, a clerk in the 3 per cent annuity office at the Bank for more than twenty years, executed in 1790 for forging a name on a bill to gain a few hundred pounds.[44]

Those who aimed higher at least might have the resources to flee to the Continent. Even so, they remained at great risk of pursuit and capture. John Waite, a cashier at the Bank of England, absconded with East India Company bonds worth some £10,000 in May 1741. A reward of £200 was put on his head, increasing to £500 when the trail went cold. At the end of 1742 he was spotted in Dublin by a City merchant's clerk, arrested and brought to London. He stood trial at the Old Bailey for his life in February 1743 but was acquitted on a technicality: he had been tried for a felony but the precise nature of the crime he had committed had only become a capital offence as a result of his actions and the law was not retrospective. But the relentless Bank had him arrested as a debtor in a civil suit for over £14,000 and he was duly found liable in July 1743. He is likely to have lived out his days in a debtors' prison, most probably the Fleet.[45]

But it is worth noting that both Thomas Pitkin and that 'Little, Thin, Prim Man' seem to have evaded capture and no doubt others also fared successfully. We might cite Thomas Shuttleworth, who at least had the capacity to have become a rich man as the result of his crimes. He absconded in May 1745 with 'a large sum of money', said to be over £20,000, taken from the South Sea Company, where he had been a clerk. At that time the Company's clerks could also act as brokers engaged in buying and selling its stock, an arrangement ended as a result of Shuttleworth's misfeasance. A reward of £200 for his arrest was promptly published but he was soon reported to be in The Hague. The newspapers claimed that he sought a passport from the French authorities to travel to Montpelier 'to undergo a certain genteel Operation', but was refused. By June he had become plain Thomas Smith and at the end of the month he was in Rome. There he suffered a setback, reported with some relish in Grub Street:

The famous Mr. Shuttleworth, alias Smith, who is gone to make the Tour of Italy; and that he might do it with greater Eclat, had taken Letters of Credit from a Merchant in Holland on a Banker at Rome for 10,000l. has had the Misfortune to have his whole Correspondence discover'd, by which Means the Money is very like to come back to its right Owners again; and Mr. Smith is in danger of making a much *lamer* Figure at Rome than he intended.[46]

Even so, Shuttleworth seems finally to have evaded the tentacles of the South Sea Company with at least £10,000 remaining to his name, enough to make a comfortable way in the world for the rest of his life.[47]

Deception involving confidence tricks and forgery was the archetypal crime of the middling sort in eighteenth-century London. But the middling ranks were not immune from other forms of theft and occasionally were involved in ventures more commonly associated with Chick Lane and Dyot Street. In September 1793 a banker's clerk delivered a bill for £120 to a client's premises in Hatton Garden. Once inside he had a cloth thrown over his head and was bundled to the floor. A voice threatened to cut his throat if he made a noise, his hands were tied and his feet chained to a copper in the scullery. Food and drink were put within reach – handily, for it took him some six hours to escape. The main assailant, there were four in all, was Lawrence Jones, a former army officer who had sold his commission and seems to have lived buying and selling jewellery. Jones was sentenced to death but managed to hang himself in his cell with his 'knee-strings' a few days before his execution.[48] His case reminds us, if we need reminding, that violence was an unavoidable daily reality of eighteenth-century London life, and that it was no respecter of rank.

'Save Me Woody': Violence

The fact that London was a violent place in these years hardly needs stressing. We have already glimpsed violent reactions against foreigners in London's streets and against Jews and the Irish, even in areas they had long settled. We have witnessed the murderous struggles of workers against employers and against other workers in industries like silk weaving and coalheaving. We have seen the readiness to pull up benches and smash the furnishings of the London theatres at the smallest provocation. And we will see in later chapters collective violence in the name of religion and politics, and the state-sanctioned brutality enshrined in the administration of the criminal law.

Historians tell us there was a marked diminution in this culture of violence, in the metropolis and the nation as a whole, as the century grew older. They cite trends in the Old Bailey Proceedings in support, with 536 charges of murder brought in the first half of the century against 409 in the second half, with similar downward trends in other charges of killing. On the other hand, charges of violent property crime at the Old Bailey and serious charges of breaking the peace moved in the opposite direction (2,101 of violent theft in the second half of the century against 1,330 in the first, and 175 compared to seventy-six for breaking the peace); and, as we shall see in a later chapter, the worst collective violence of the century by far took place in 1780 during the Gordon Riots, when London seemed truly on the brink of civil war. In the absence of reliable statistics we can say generally that the frequency and severity of violence in personal (though not collective) interactions did decline in the second half of the century compared to the first, but that London remained a strikingly violent place even at the century's end.[49]

Violence infected all classes. The uncertainties of economic life troubled almost every rank, and the turmoils of business and the risks of play took a heavy toll on the middling sort and above in particular. Desperation drove many to suicide, considered very much an English disease by foreign visitors.[50] It was indeed a common malaise and reports of suicides were gloomily relayed in the newspapers and in private conversation:

On Saturday last [in September 1713] one Batch, an attorney, shot himself through the head, the same day two women and a boy hanged themselves in other places in this city, and one Jubb, a highwayman, having been convicted at the Old Bailey . . . cut his throat in the bail dock, he is not yet dead, so that it is thought the work may be still finished at Tyburn.[51]

Yet suicide, as some measure of desperation in London, also showed a decline in the Bills of Mortality as the century grew older, averaging 44.4 burials a year in 1740–44 and falling to 28.8 in 1789–93, despite the rise in London's population in the intervening years.

Suicide, like other forms of violence, was readily assisted by the general availability of lethal weapons. The right to bear arms was enshrined in the Bill of Rights of 1689 and for the whole of the eighteenth century there was an uncontested ability for Protestant persons of the middling sort and above to go armed in self-defence. The right of the poorer sort of people and Roman Catholics to carry weapons was far more dubious. In the earlier years of the century it was customary for gentlemen to wear swords as part of daily dress. They added a dangerous element to London life, the insouciance of rank gaining bravado from going armed. In November 1721 Robert Bembridge, annoyed by a drunken prostitute in Princes Street, Leicester Fields, gave her a wound from which she developed complications and died: '*I have stuck an old Whore in the Arse and have sent her about her Business*,' he told the watchman. Edward Strafford, 'a Gentleman of Quality', drew his sword against a porter who had insisted on a larger fee for running an errand and ran him through, killing him instantly: he was 'brought in *Lunatick*' at his trial in July 1731. And a waiter at the Shakespeare's Head in the Piazza 'was run thro' the body' trying to separate two quarrelling gentlemen in April 1756. That may have been an accident, and certainly accidents often happened with the pistols and blunderbusses and 'watch-guns' set to guard against burglars in houses of the middling rank, or carried about on any journey during the hours of darkness, guns being universally accepted as a lawful means of self-defence in these circumstances, as we have seen.[52]

Throughout the century swordplay was considered a necessary skill for gentlemen. Even around 1788 there were over thirty fencing masters in London.[53] And sharpened by the sword, gentlemanly insolence seems to have been bred in the bone and polished in the public schools. A case that came to trial at the Westminster Quarter Sessions in May 1779 aroused much public indignation. Six scholars at Westminster School were tried for an assault on a man who had somehow offended them. They 'beat and wounded him in a most shocking way' in Dean's Yard, just outside the school. After the beating one, 'with a drawn knife in his hand, said, "If you don't kneel down and ask pardon, I will rip you up," which the man was compelled to do'. One boy was acquitted, another fined a shilling for a minor role and four fined £25 each and sentenced to Bridewell for a month. The prison sentences were revoked by a majority vote among the magistrates when the father of one of the boys complained his son might lose his place at Oxford by beginning term late. The press duly savaged 'the atrocious barbarity of the petty classical bravoes'. And many must have pondered the difference in fate between a Westminster scholar and a lad of Chick Lane in similar circumstances.[54]

The most common form of gentlemanly violence, however, was the duel to settle a matter of 'honour'. It was common throughout the century and there were numerous celebrated cases. Juries were reluctant to convict a gentleman of murder even where a charge was brought, most verdicts coming in as manslaughter, with a frequent penalty to be burned in the hand and a fine. Not all approved of duelling – Richard Steele was a wise and outspoken critic – but it was deeply engrained in gentlemanly conduct for much of the century, despite judicial condemnation. The Journals of every parliamentary session, at least until the 1750s, recorded that members had to intervene to prevent a 'quarrel', the business of the House fomenting personal slights and affronts demanding satisfaction: in March 1743 Horatio Walpole and William Chetwynd fought with swords outside the lobby of the House of Commons, Walpole saved by a button from a fierce lunge and Chetwynd wounded in breast and hip before a clerk intervened and they put up their swords. And a particularly notorious duel took place at the Star and Garter Tavern in Pall Mall in January 1765. The quarrel, over dinner and wine, had a trivial point at issue, whether William Lord Byron had more game on his Nottinghamshire estate than his neighbour William Chaworth.

The company, however, had apprehended no consequences, and parted at eight o'clock; but Lord Byron stepping into an empty chamber, and sending the drawer for Mr Chaworth, or calling him thither himself, took the candle from the waiter, and bidding Mr Chaworth defend himself, drew his sword. Mr Chaworth, who was an excellent fencer, ran Lord Byron through the sleeve of his coat, and then received a wound fourteen inches deep into his body. He was carried to his house in Berkeley Street, – made his will with the greatest composure, and dictated a paper, which they say, allows it was a fair duel, and died at nine this morning.

Byron, a fierce man by all accounts, was acquitted of murder by his fellow peers but found guilty of manslaughter. His rank spared him the indignity of branding and he walked free on payment of court fees.[55]

Duels were very common, and not just among the quality. Before 1750 or so the field behind Montagu House (from 1753 the British Museum) in Great Russell Street, Bloomsbury, had been a noted duelling place, but thirty years on there remained many others to choose from. In the first six months of 1780 the *London Chronicle* carried reports of duels between army officers in Hyde Park, using pistols; between an earl and an MP, also in Hyde Park with pistols, where the MP was shot in the groin; between an army officer and a man shot dead in a field near the Dog and Duck tavern in St George's Fields; another in Hyde Park between two Irish gentlemen – the pistols misfired; and another near Kensington Gravel Pits between 'two young gentlemen of fortune with pistols'; no doubt there were others involving protagonists too insignificant to notice.[56]

Among the lower ranks of eighteenth-century Londoners violence was just as readily resorted to when pursuing or settling a quarrel, though it was more rarely attended by such fatal consequences. Just how commonly we can glimpse from the notebook kept by Justice Henry Norris of Hackney between February 1730 and July 1741. Over three-quarters of the alleged offences brought before him claimed an assault of one kind or another, from uttering threats to homicide. Of some 210 allegations of assault, eighty-five were by men on other men, a large number taking place while drinking in and about public houses. There were then eighty-three complaints of men assaulting women. At least twenty of these were husbands beating or threatening wives, and domestic violence was undoubtedly more common than that, because any number of the remainder may have involved assaults on cohabiting partners. Once more, the pub was a common setting for these flare-ups. Then there were eleven cases of men complaining they'd been assaulted by women, and twenty-seven of assaults by women on women.[57]

Most victims of violence and threats here, then, were women and there is no reason to think that the justice's notebook misrepresented the picture London-wide or century-long. That is, violence for its own sake rather than in furtherance of a crime, though as we have seen women were frequently the victims in street robbery and burglary too. And there is cause to believe that rape and other sexual assaults, including some dreadful sexual mutilations, were fairly common but not much recorded or prosecuted.

The hatred of some men for women knew no bounds. Among the worst cases of violence against women were murders in and about the home. One night in August 1733 a desperate Christian Lamb clamoured at the door of her neighbour Mary Wood in Nicholas Alley, Chick Lane: *'Save me Woody, or I shall be kill'd to Night.'* Though she knew the answer, Mrs Wood asked, *'Who'll kill you?'* *'My Husband will, says she.'* Mrs Wood asked her in and fetched 'a Pint of Drink' for her, but her furious husband discovered she was there and burst in, punched Christian to the floor, 'kick'd her in the Belly' and dragged her home. A man tried to intervene as she was being beaten in the alleyway but Richard Lamb would not be placated. Next day Mrs Lamb was found terribly bruised about the body and with her skull fractured by a blow from a stick or a boot. She died two or three days later. 'I live not far from the prisoner,' Mr Lee, a surgeon, told the Old Bailey, 'and have many times had her as a Patient, with violent Bruises and Cuts, when she has been beaten by her Husband, and I have often told her, he would certainly kill her some time or other.'[58]

Violence was used to enforce power relations in the home in other ways – we might recall Francis Place's brutal father, for instance, and there were numerous dreadful cases of child cruelty, even murder, by mothers and fathers throughout the century. Indeed, the home was the environment in which sadism most commonly had space to flourish. This chronic maltreatment of women by men, and of children by women and men, was an enduring undercurrent of life in London. But the home was also very often a workplace and it was those cases concerning the brutal treatment of servants that seem to have most shocked contemporary Londoners.

Even at the end of the century there were numerous horrifying examples of cruelty against servants and apprentices, often orphans or abandoned children put out to work with a small gratuity by the

parish authorities. A chimney sweep called Gay was imprisoned in
1791 for beating and torturing a climbing boy under the care of the
parish of St Martin-in-the-Fields; the boy was released from his
apprenticeship by the court. Theophilus Bridges, a Southwark button
maker, was charged in July 1796 with the murder of Elizabeth Monk,
one of seven girls apprenticed to him by the nearby Asylum for
Female Orphans. The girls were worked from four in the morning
till eight or ten at night and beaten and starved for misdemeanours.
The medical evidence at the trial was vague and Bridges was acquitted
but kept in custody to be tried for a rape. And a few months later
Elizabeth Hale, a Bermondsey 'pin-header', was given six months for
overworking two parish apprentices, beating them with her fists and
'the kettle ladle', and with a pickled rod on their bare skin.[59]

The worst cases of the century came to light in the 1760s. Sarah
Metyard made silk nets, purses and mittens at her haberdasher's shop
and manufactory at Bruton Street, Hanover Square. She employed
five parish children as apprentices, living in, aged from eight to thirteen. They were kept at work long hours in a tiny room, were beaten,
never given enough to eat, and were allowed out once a fortnight
but not alone. One, the eldest, Anne Naylor, was especially badly
treated. She contrived to run away but was brought back. Starved
and beaten, she managed once again to slip out of the house door.
Mrs Metyard's daughter saw her go and shouted out for her to be
stopped. Anne was grabbed by a passing milkman. She begged him
not to take her back to the house: 'I have had no victuals a long
time, and if I stay here, I shall be starved to death.' Feeling that he
had to stop a runaway apprentice, the man returned Anne Naylor
to Bruton Street for the last time. There she was beaten, tortured,
starved of food and water, and eventually died. The Metyards kept
the body in the house for two months, until it grew so offensive it
had to be got away. To make the job easier they decided to cut off
the limbs. A hand from which the girl had lost a finger – a whitlow
had become poisonous through neglect, the finger removed by a
surgeon – was burned to prevent identification. The rest they took
'to the great gully hole in Chick-lane, where the kennel water runs
into the common shore' of the Fleet. The gully was guarded by a
grating set in a high wall. They tried to throw the head and body
over the wall but couldn't and left it wrapped in cloth 'in the mud
and water before the grate', where it was discovered by the watch.

That was in the bitterly cold December of 1758 and no, or no sustained, endeavours were made to identify the victim or her killers. It seems the authorities thought the body had been removed from a grave for the use of the surgeons and discarded when it decomposed. So matters lay for more than three years. But things were not easy between the Metyards. There was much loathing between mother and daughter and in their frequent rows the younger Sarah – who had contributed much to Anne Naylor's ill-treatment – would taunt her mother as 'the Chick-lane ghost' and 'the perfumer'. Eventually she was persuaded by a tradesman, Mr Rooker, who had become their lodger in Bruton Street and who had taken a shine to her, to reveal the story of poor Naylor's death. He reported it to the parish authorities of Tottenham High Cross, in whose care she had been, and in July 1762 both mother and daughter were convicted of murder and sentenced to death. Despite Rooker's efforts to gain a pardon for the younger Sarah, both the Metyards were hanged at Tyburn that September in front of a crowd said to be 50,000 strong. Their bodies were given to the surgeons for dissection. Rooker, clearly besotted with the young Metyard, never forgave himself for being the cause of her death and cut his throat in February 1763.[60]

Five years after the execution of the Metyards another vile case of mistreatment of parish apprentices came to light in Flower-de-Luce Court, linking Fleet Street with Fetter Lane. James Brownrigg, a house painter, had taken two girls to assist in his trade by grinding white lead and undertaking other duties in home and workshop. Mary Clifford, one of the girls, 'had the misfortune of wetting the bed', as her fellow apprentice Mary Mitchell put it, and was singled out for special savagery by Brownrigg's wife, Elizabeth. Both girls were often kept naked, or nearly so. Mary Clifford was seen by a male apprentice wearing just shoes and stockings – she begged him for something to cover herself with. She was frequently tied naked to a hook screwed into a ceiling beam and whipped about her head and body by Elizabeth; she was starved and chained by her neck to a door, the chain just loose enough not to choke her. A neighbouring baker, alarmed by the cries so often heard from the Brownriggs', told a worker to climb on to their roof and look through the skylight, where the girl was seen bloody and nearly unconscious. The authorities were alerted and forcibly removed the girls. But it was too late for Mary Clifford, who died of her injuries some days later at St Bartholomew's

Hospital. The apothecary who sent her there told the Old Bailey that 'she was in a most shocking condition, I never saw such an object in my life . . .' James Brownrigg was acquitted of murder but he and his son were subsequently fined a shilling each and sent to Newgate for six months for assaulting Mary Mitchell. Elizabeth Brownrigg was hanged at Tyburn on Monday 14 September 1767 before a crowd 'so great, that several persons were much hurt' in the crush.[61]

The crowd was notable for other reasons. 'It is the opinion of most people,' the newspapers reported, 'that if the Clergyman and Lay Preacher had not attended Mrs. Brownrigg in the Cart to Tyburn, she would not have reached to that place alive. – A great many things were thrown at her, and the repeated hissing and shouting going to, and at the place of execution, sufficiently demonstrated how much the populace were incensed against her.' Such fury was by no means uncommon when the cruelty of a malefactor's crime had outraged Londoners. Nor was something else uncommon that was noted that day. The size and excitement of the crowd from Newgate to Tyburn offered rich plunder for pickpockets, a Lincolnshire grazier losing a purse of 50 guineas to a thief in St Sepulchre's churchyard, for instance. And by the gallows itself 'a lad was detected in picking the pocket of a young man, and was taken into Hyde-park and severely ducked'.[62]

These expressions of collective outrage were a feature of London life in the eighteenth century, and we have met them before. They had many causes. But one made plain in these two instances on that tempestuous day in September 1767 was the desire to avenge injustice.

There was good reason for the crowd to wish to take the law into its own hands. Official justice was often haphazard, ineffective and inappropriately harsh. A ducking or a 'pumping', even though a man might be half-drowned in the process, was preferable to transportation or a death sentence – though sometimes, it's true, a ducking was followed by a trip to the constable or the round-house, where the nightly watch kept their prisoners. And there were other cases, as we shall see, where the violence of the crowd redoubled the savagery of the penal law and became in turn murderous. Very often, however, a crowd could be readily provoked to remedy wrongdoing that seemed likely to be beyond the reach of official justice.

A particular flashpoint for collective retribution in the 1740s and 1750s, for instance, was the bawdy house. Its suppression could only be achieved by the parish authorities at considerable expense and there were many ways for keepers to frustrate any efforts that might be made against them.[63] Many Londoners saw this not as a question of legislative inaptitude but one of parochial and magisterial corruption. Where a bawdy house became for some reason obnoxious it seemed that judicial process was unlikely to remedy any grievance caused and in these years, at least, the crowd stood ready to take the victim's part.

There were riots against seven bawdy houses by sailors in Farthing Fields, Wapping, in September 1753 when it was thought the mate of a collier had been so ill-used in one of them by prostitutes' bullies that he had died of his wounds. And in August 1757 a bawdy house in Covent Garden was attacked when a drunken man died after falling into its basement area.[64] But the worst rioting took place some eight years before that, and it turned into something like a concerted attack on bawdy houses mainly in and around the Strand.

In late June 1749 three Royal Navy sailors were reputedly robbed of 30 guineas, four moidores, a banknote for £20, two watches and more in a bawdy house, the sign of the Crown, near St Mary le Strand. They failed to get satisfaction from the house and left, vowing vengeance. On the night of 1 July 'a great number of armed sailors' descended on the house, destroying furniture and clothes, turning the women into the street and breaking the windows. Next night the sailors returned and two other houses were attacked in the Strand 'in presence of multitudes of spectators, who huzza'd them'. Similar places in the Old Bailey and Goodman's Fields had the same treatment. It is clear that the 'spectators' in fact did more than watch and cheer, for a constable told the magistrate that in Old Bailey 'he saw a great Mob assembled' but that only 'several of the said Mob were in Sailors Habits'.[65]

One of the houses attacked that night in the Strand was a bawdy house run by Peter Wood at the sign of the Star. His furniture was dragged into the street and burned, his windows were broken, and Wood and his wife were knocked about by men armed with sticks: 'I was beaten almost to a jelly,' Jane Wood claimed at the Old Bailey. Ropes and iron bars or wooden staves were attached to the windows and attempts made to 'pull the house down' by dislodging frames and brickwork. There were cries of 'Down with the Bawdy Houses', and some involvement in the riot by the middling sort. When Wood tried to bribe the rioters not to pull his windows out a man called Wrench, 'of credit and reputation' and who later successfully resisted a charge of riot in the magistrates' court, 'said, my boys haul away', and they did.[66]

The soldiers summoned to help the constables made three arrests at Wood's, including a journeyman shoemaker, John Wilson or Willson, and Bosavern Penlez, a journeyman peruke maker, originally from Devon and by all accounts a clergyman's son. It appeared as though Penlez had been helping himself to some clothes and linen, saving for himself stuff not consigned to the flames. Wood claimed all three had been active in the riotous attack on his house. Despite the Riot Act not having been read by a justice ordering the crowd to disperse, Wilson and Penlez were found guilty of a felony and condemned to death. The jury recommended mercy in both cases, in part because of their previous good records but largely, it seems, because the bawdy houses and their keepers had become objects of public opprobrium, the riots against them taking on something of a popular movement.

In the event, Wilson was reprieved the night before his execution in October 1749, but Penlez duly hanged. There were apprehensions of a rescue by sailors during the procession from Newgate to Tyburn and at Holborn Bars a party of Foot Guards waited to escort it beyond the City. But Penlez was the prisoner of the Sheriff of London, Alderman Stephen Theodore Janssen, who, 'holding his white wand', dismissed the soldiers 'very civilly' and duly led the procession to Tyburn, a triumph, it was thought at the time, for the civil power.[67]

The hanging of Penlez drew much execration from the press, and much adverse reflection on the harshness of the criminal law as it applied to a poor rioter and its leniency when faced with a prosperous bawdy-house keeper. The animadversions of Grub Street drew a spirited response from Henry Fielding, the magistrate who had committed Penlez for trial. Fielding plied his vigorous pen in defence of the King and his laws and those appointed to uphold them. In his pamphlet on the Penlez case he reprinted much of the evidence that had come before him. When the jury's recommendations for mercy were considered by the Privy Council the King was minded to reprieve both men but the trial judge was adamant that at least one should suffer as a deterrent to all crowds minded to take the law into their own hands. But which one? Penlez, caught with a bundle of linen in his arms, had also been charged with burglary by the grand jury, but the charge had never come to trial. It was this allegation, never tested in front of a jury, which Fielding chose to represent to the Privy Council as a means of discriminating between the two men. His representations effectively sealed Penlez's death warrant, and according to Fielding Penlez 'deserved his Fate'. Now, Fielding was a lawyer and proud of it. But it was an unseemly slip of the long robe that justified hanging a man for a crime he had never had to answer and for which he'd never been convicted. Such shallow justifications, though, were not untypical. For much of what passed for justice in eighteenth-century London had a great deal of this rough-and-ready callousness about it.[68]

PART FIVE

POWER

Henry Fielding

Sir John Fielding

XI

THE FIELDINGS' LONDON – POLICE, PRISON AND PUNISHMENT

Mr Fielding's Men: Thief-Takers

THE brothers Henry and John Fielding have had a very good press as the most far-sighted and energetic reforming magistrates of eighteenth-century London. In part that's not surprising, because they were ever ready to praise themselves in print and they were able, through part ownership of the *Covent Garden Journal* and later the *Public Advertiser*, to conduct a Grub Street chorus that daily thrust their justicing into the public gaze. They worked hard to establish a contemporary reputation for infallible wisdom and unsullied probity. In general they were successful, though not all were convinced.

That good name has survived, especially among historians of the English police. Much credit is indeed due, especially to John Fielding, whose tenure as chief metropolitan magistrate at Bow Street was much longer than that of his elder brother, and especially for their achievements in crime detection and thief-taking. But these were men who inevitably shared the flaws and limitations of the public life of the times in which they lived. Both were arrogant, proud and wilful in office. Both clamoured privately and publicly for an untrammelled enlargement of their power. Both despised and feared any collective expression of the London poor and waged war on their pleasures. And in the case of Henry Fielding, surely one of the greatest hypocrites of the age, a reputation for magisterial wisdom and probity seems now overdue for reappraisal.[1]

We have of course met Henry Fielding before, as a satirical playwright and unquestionably one of the greatest novelists of the century. He was born in 1707 in Somerset, raised in Dorset and educated at Eton, his father a high-ranking and high-spending army officer with aristocratic connections. Edmund Fielding's loose way with money was matched by prodigality in the bedroom – he had thirteen children by his first two wives and married twice more. Though Henry was the eldest child of a distinguished line, he found himself disinherited and forced to earn a living. By the age of twenty he was trying to live by his pen in London, mainly writing for the stage, where he propelled himself into the pleasures of the metropolis. Strikingly tall and strong, though with a long nose and chin not considered classically handsome, Fielding charmed by his vivacious conversation and sociable wit. He drank heavily, ate well, spent lavishly at the expense of landlord and tradesman, and was well known in the brothels and bawdy houses at the west end of the town, some of them featuring as stage sets in his plays. Charles Hanbury Williams, a contemporary at Eton, was favoured among his friends.

Fielding's uncertain income on the one hand and proud birthright with a fittingly luxurious lifestyle on the other fostered an overriding ambition – not to write great works of fiction, which he did, but to find a sinecure from the public purse where he would not have to write at all. He tirelessly solicited places of one kind or another from Sir Robert Walpole, but when rebuffed turned one of the minister's sharpest critics, so sharp that stage censorship was introduced in 1737 largely to keep him quiet. With theatrical writing denied him, he took to the law to equip himself better in the battle of life. He was called to the Bar at the Middle Temple in June 1740. It was not a haphazard change of direction: the law and the doings of bailiffs, pettifoggers and justices had of necessity long held his interest.

In the event, Fielding's pen proved of greater financial worth than the barrister's art, interspersing pro-government polemic – Walpole out of power from 1742 – with some very profitable novels, as we have already seen. But his lawyer's calling helped him to his first public office as High Steward of the New Forest in April 1746 and after much solicitation he was appointed a Westminster magistrate in July 1748. With the help of his patron the Duke of Bedford, ground landlord of Covent Garden, Fielding was able to take the tenancy of the famous justice house at 4 Bow Street that December. That was a property qualification enabling him also to become a Middlesex magistrate in January 1749.[2] The City of London, we should note here, was entirely outside his jurisdiction, its magistrates, the aldermen and Lord Mayor sitting at the Guildhall and the Mansion House.

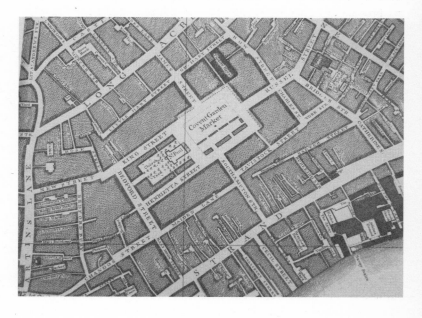

Covent Garden, *c.*1740

Armed with both Westminster and Middlesex jurisdictions, his will-
ingness to serve the ministry helped him become the 'court justice',
responsible for advising and assisting the judicial interests of government, and principal magistrate for the metropolis, excluding the City.
We have glimpsed in the case of Bosavern Penlez the court justice as
pamphleteer-apologist for an unpopular prosecution and even less
popular execution. And as principal magistrate none was more down
on bawdy houses as tending to 'the overthrow of Men's Bodies, to the
wasting of their Livelihoods, and to the indangering of their Souls';
none more critical of the infection of luxury – he meant pleasure
gardens – among 'the very Dregs of the People', keeping them from
their employments with 'Show', 'Music', 'Gluttony and Drunkenness',
'every Kind of Dainty' and 'the finest Women . . . exposed to View';
and none more ready to clamber on the bandwagon of gin as poisoning
'the Health, the Strength, and the very Being' of those 'most useful
Subjects', the wage-labouring poor.[3]

The extraordinary case of Elizabeth Canning lets us look more closely
into the judicial practice of this 'disinterested and public-spirited . . .
social reformer'.[4] Elizabeth Canning was an eighteen-year-old domestic
servant in Aldermanbury, in the City. On 1 January 1753 she disappeared on her way home from relatives who lived in a notorious place
near Rag Fair called Saltpetre Bank. Some four weeks later she arrived
home in a ragged, famished and filthy state. She claimed she had been
kidnapped near Moorfields by street robbers. They had taken her to a
house out of London run by women who had taken her clothes and
tried to starve her into a life of prostitution. Imprisoned in an attic,
she was able to glimpse the Hertford stage, the coachman of which she
knew. Eventually she made her escape and managed to walk home.

Canning's plight aroused the sympathy of her friends and neighbours
and a collection was made to help identify her assailants and bring
them to justice. The clue of the Hertford stage drew suspicion to a
lodging house for the vagrant poor, where prostitutes frequently lodged,
at Enfield Wash, eleven or twelve miles from where Canning said she
had been seized. A search party with the girl among them duly visited
the house. All there said they had never seen her before. But a strikingly
ugly old Gypsy woman lodging in the house, Mary Squires, was identified by Canning as the woman who had taken her stays from her.
Squires was duly committed on suspicion of theft to the New Prison,
Clerkenwell, by one of the Enfield justices.

Canning's sensational story, so incredible in many of its details, reached Grub Street and became the talk of London, indeed the nation. It now gained credence from the committal of Squires. Canning's friends were sure that others were involved, notably 'Mother' Wells, the lodging-house keeper, and so instructed a lawyer to ensure that justice was done. This was one Salt, an attorney who had instructed Fielding as counsel on previous occasions and who now asked him for advice on how 'to bring the offenders to justice', which the magistrate duly gave. At Salt's request he also took charge of the investigation and brought the witnesses to Bow Street. There he heard Canning swear to the 'information' drawn up for her by Salt charging Squires with theft. And he examined two further witnesses. Virtue Hall was a young prostitute who had lodged at the Enfield house over the weeks in question and denied vehemently that Canning had been there. Under a long examination, apparently with Salt in the room, Hall stuck to her story until, exasperated, Fielding told her he would commit her to Newgate and, in her hearing, advised Salt to prosecute her as a felon, 'together with the gipsy woman'. Hall then broke down in tears and Fielding 'recommended to Mr. Salt to go with her and take her information in writing'. When she returned Salt had produced a written statement for her to swear that corroborated Canning's story in every salient point.

The second witness, Judith Natus, an older married woman, swore she occupied the attic room with her husband during the weeks Canning said she had been kept there. Natus would not change her story and Fielding warned her severely of the perils of perjury and sent her on her way. Her evidence, vital though it was, did not reach the Old Bailey jury in February 1753 – an angry crowd, it was said, had obstructed any witness hostile to Canning from attending the trial. On the evidence of Elizabeth Canning, shored up by Virtue Hall, Mrs Wells was convicted of harbouring a thief, burned in the hand and imprisoned. Mary Squires, the friendless Gypsy some seventy years old, was sentenced to death for stealing the girl's stays.

Not quite friendless, it's true to say. Others thought Canning's story less believable than did Fielding, whose credulousness seems to have increased with age: he found Christianity after many years spent amusingly decrying its enthusiasts, began to profess a belief in ghosts and in 1752 put his name to a book of cases where the identity of murderers had been revealed by divine intervention.[5] For the Lord Mayor of London and chief magistrate of the City, Sir Crisp Gascoyne, Canning's story was frankly incredible. 'I cannot comprehend', he later wrote, how any magistrate could have believed Canning's story when set beside the original evidence of Hall and Natus, though he was too polite to dwell on Fielding's conflicting financial interest in advising Salt in the first place. When, after Squires's conviction, incontrovertible evidence arrived from Dorset that over the time in question the old woman had been peddling linens in Abbotsbury, where she was a frequent visitor, Gascoyne oversaw an investigation that proved the Gypsy innocent and Canning – for whatever reason – a potential perjuror.[6]

Just as striking, Virtue Hall, under no charge and after the trial was over, was lodged at the Gatehouse Prison in Westminster, where Salt's brother was keeper and where she was hidden away from anyone curious to speak to her about Canning. But rumours that she was uneasy in her mind reached Gascoyne, who summoned her to the City. When eventually he and a witness were able to interview her alone she freely confessed that her evidence in support of Canning was false: '*Justice* Fielding *and his Clerk frighten'd me, and made me swear it . . .*'[7]

Squires was duly pardoned, but not before Fielding unwisely exposed his shabby handling of the whole affair in a pamphlet, the dual purpose of which was to salvage his reputation as the protector of 'injured Innocence' (Canning) and to do his utmost to send an old woman, 'the Gipsy Woman', one of 'a Set of horrid Villains', to the gallows for a crime she plainly did not commit. In the event Canning was convicted of perjury and transported to America in August 1754. By then Fielding was nearing the end of a long decline in health, suffering from a gross dropsy, probably caused by cirrhosis of the liver. He handed over his public duties to his brother John in January 1754 and in October he died in Lisbon, just forty-seven years old.[8]

John Fielding was Henry's half-brother, born to Edmund's second wife in 1721, so fourteen years younger than his celebrated sibling, whom he revered. Little is known of his upbringing, but as a youngster he developed eye trouble and when he was nineteen botched operations left him entirely blind. 'The Blind Beak', the magistrate sitting with a black bandage over his eyes and sifting truth from lies solely through aural finesse, has endowed John Fielding with much heroic glamour, and understandably so. He followed Henry on to the Westminster bench in August 1751 and Middlesex in January 1754. That month he took over from Henry as court justice and by June had moved into 4 Bow

Street. It was his town residence for the rest of his life, though he died in his country villa at Brompton just before his fifty-ninth birthday in September 1780.[9]

John Fielding's twenty-six years in office – he became Sir John in 1761 – added greatly to his brother's legacy. Their central achievement was to establish thief-taking – the detection of crime and apprehending offenders – on a sounder basis than ever before. It is this that justifies the claim that the Fieldings were the founders of professional policing in London.

Thief-taking had a history both long and vexed. The system of rewards for apprehending thieves, put on a statutory basis from 1693, had encouraged a private trade in bounty hunting, a business none too scrupulous about matching a thief to a crime: a £40 reward, sometimes more, was as valuable when based on a trumped-up charge as on sound evidence. Any thief-taker, though, would have to share the reward with at least one other person. Where thieves were taken in the act or later discovered, it was for the victims to bring prosecutions against them, an often inconvenient, costly and sometimes risky venture. To lighten the burden, prosecutors shared in the reward on conviction, and could claim a 'Tyburn Ticket' releasing them from the obligation to serve as a parish constable: these tickets could be sold to a third party and so might supplement the reward. Many victims, however, were more concerned to secure the return of their property than to prosecute the thief. A common solution was to advertise a reward for their return in the newspapers:

Taken or Dropt from a Hackney Coach at the Cross-Keys-Inn in Grace-Church-street on Wednesday the 29th of December last, about 6 a Clock in the Evening, a Trunk with the several things following, viz . . . Whoever shall bring the said Trunk and goods, or make discovery thereof, so as the same be had again, shall receive 4 Guineas of Mr. John Jones at the King's-Head, a Powder-Shop, in Cheapside, without being ask'd any Questions.[10]

By the early years of the century some enterprising law officers in the City were combining the trade of thief-taker with the role of inter-mediary between thieves and victims anxious for the return of their property and no questions asked. It was Jonathan Wild, a buckle maker from Wolverhampton, in London from about 1707, who perfected this trade by means of dauntless courage, administrative flair and merciless rapacity. He was given some official status by the City authorities as deputy to one of the Under-Marshals, which enabled him to make arrests with impunity. From an office at Little Old Bailey, open from 1717, he advertised in the press his ability to facilitate the recovery of stolen goods. These he did not handle himself, though he seems to have had others run 'warehouses' on his behalf in various parts of London where stolen goods could be kept safe pending return to the owners or shipment to the Continent. The Old House in Chick Lane, demolished more than a century later, was said to be one of them.

Wild's office became the natural point of enquiry for any Londoner whose goods had been stolen. His comprehensive penetration of the London underworld through his own extensive knowledge and his paid agents enabled him rapidly to identify the thief concerned and strike a bargain profitable to villain, victim and of course himself. Those thieves who failed to cooperate or who were worth more to him dead than alive risked arrest by Wild and his thief-takers, who then shared in the reward.

For much of the period from 1717 Wild was most often seen as a public benefactor, despite the encouragement to crime his system plainly gave. But his reputation for ruthlessness in swearing away the lives of those who crossed him, especially his role in hanging the popular prison-breaker Jack Sheppard in 1724, made the trade of thief-taker notorious. In 1725 Wild was charged with offering to secure some stolen lace while making no effort to identify and take the thieves. He was convicted and in May hanged at Tyburn in front of a hostile crowd. The young Henry Fielding watched him die. In pleading for his life, Wild had submitted to the Old Bailey jurors a list of some seventy-five thieves he had 'brought to Justice'. Some months later a French visitor noted how 'Many persons consider that more harm than good was done by the execution of this famous thief, for there is now no one to go to who will help you to recover your stolen property; the government has certainly got rid of a robber, but he was only one, whereas by his help several thieves were hanged every year.'[11]

Something of the gap in crime detection that Wild had selectively filled had to await a more active magistracy in Westminster and Middlesex. It came in the shape of a superannuated army officer, Colonel Thomas de Veil. He was appointed as a justice to both commissions of the peace in 1729, opening an office in Leicester Fields. He was physically courageous, a pertinacious investigator of crime and intolerant of malfeasance on the bench. He lived in some style, though his money seems not to have come from propagating fees as a 'trading justice' keen to make money from justicing business, but from public sinecures and family resources. Drink and women were his main weaknesses, and rumours abounded of judicial leniency for favours received by young women appearing before him. His strengths, however, proved of acknowledged use to government. De Veil frequently provoked the unpopularity of the London crowd by his energetic prosecution of the Gin Act of 1736 and the protection he gave the hated 'common informers' who trapped gin sellers into conflict with the law. He became indispensable to government as court justice, both adviser and executive in support of government interests, and was knighted in 1744. That same year the City authorities obtained his assistance in suppressing the thieves and robbers of Black Boy Alley. By then, from 1740, he leased 4 Bow Street, quickly making it the intelligence centre of metropolitan crime detection. It was there that he died in 1746, shortly after a stroke during the examination of a prisoner.[12]

It was on these foundations of de Veil at Bow Street that Henry and John Fielding built their improved system of crime detection from 1749. It relied initially on a changed approach to the thief-taker, whose image had been so tarnished by the rapacious career of Jonathan Wild. Some details of the origins of these new professional thief-takers remain obscure but, as described by the Fieldings, in 1750 the most active of the parish constables of Westminster were organised under Henry's leadership to break up a gang of street robbers in a year of genuine alarm about crime in the metropolis. Some of them, at least, were due to relinquish their office with the annual election of new constables in 1751. But six or so were persuaded to remain available for duty as thief-takers under Fielding's direction. How they were paid is a mystery, but some may have been employed as 'deputies' for those ratepayers elected as constable but unwilling to serve in that dangerous and unpopular office; some may have been paid a retainer from government funds available to Fielding; and all presumably relied on fees arising from rewards. Despite the new arrangements crime failed to abate and in 1753 the government asked Fielding for a plan to break up the worst of the criminal gangs of London. Fielding asked for money to put his band of thief-takers on a reasonable retainer; and, equally important, cash was made available to bribe gang members to peach on their fellows. Fielding claimed his efforts brought great success, and certainly there were many convictions at the Old Bailey for street robbery in 1753, twenty-nine, including two for murder.[13]

In 1755, after Henry's death, these arrangements were put on a more permanent footing with four 'pursuers', an orderly and clerk funded from the public purse. The pursuers or thief-takers were most often called 'Mr Fielding's men' – or 'Fielding's cursed crew', depending on one's point of view. They were paid just £10 a year, a retainer that once more must have been supplemented by reward money and other earnings: John Cross, in 1780, described himself as a mason by trade, a broker and an officer – 'I belong to Sir John Fielding'. By the 1770s they were also called 'officers', 'peace officers', 'constables' or 'runners'; 'Bow Street runner' had some limited currency by 1785.[14]

Even so, the name of thief-taker took time to drag itself from the public opprobrium sticking to it from Wild's day. Bad memories were revived during the Fieldings' first reforms when the horrifying manoeuvres of Stephen McDaniel, a thief-taker of Irish origins, came to light in 1754–6. He and his 'crew' sought out simple-minded dupes to commit robberies they were assured were easy pickings. In fact, victim, accomplices and the receiver of the stolen goods were all members of the gang (which included a woman, Mary Jones) and all shared in the reward on conviction. In this way they procured the executions of at least three young men and were finally detected trying to prosecute two more. One of the gang, Thomas Blee, turned evidence, enabling the High Constable of Blackheath to prevent another tragic miscarriage of justice. McDaniel and three others were convicted of murder. During these proceedings it emerged that Blee had sworn an information against McDaniel before Henry Fielding, who had refused to accept it: had he done so, one life at least would have been saved. McDaniel was known to the Fieldings as a thief-taker but was not apparently used by them, though the gang was well known to Mr Fielding's men. It was all a murky business that threatened to abort the rehabilitation of thief-takers as a main plank of the reforms at Bow Street. That may have been one reason why the crown remitted the death sentence against McDaniel and the others, substituting imprisonment and the pillory.[15]

After 1756 and until the end of the century the reputation of Mr Fielding's men escaped significant scandal and gained much public respect. But if the reformed thief-taker, with all the cunning and heroism it took to confront London's violent underworld, was one foundation of improvement, John Fielding recognised from the outset that it would not be enough on its own. Quick communication, just as in the bustling world of trade in the City, was essential to circulate descriptions of robbers and the goods they had stolen. Grub Street and the burgeoning business of print were duly enlisted in aid. The *Public Advertiser* urged victims to bring information to Mr Fielding at Bow Street, where something like a register of crime and criminals began to be compiled. From 1772 weekly circulars were issued by Bow Street to local magistrates and parish clerks in the environs of London. From 1773 Fielding established night-time patrols of parish constables led by a Bow Street officer for districts where crime was a particular problem: ten years earlier he had persuaded the Treasury to fund a Horse Patrole to protect the main suburban roads from highwaymen, but the money was withdrawn after about a year in 1764.[16]

This was all good work. But lest we should think Sir John Fielding the paragon of wisdom that he and many others would have us believe, we might note that it was he who enthusiastically suppressed opera at Mrs Cornelys's Carlisle House in 1771, partly on the grounds that there was a surfeit of entertainment in London. And in 1772–3 he entered into a preposterous dispute with the London theatres over a revival of *The Beggar's Opera*, which he claimed 'undoubtedly increased the number of thieves': he drew down the scorn of Samuel Johnson for a proposition based on 'more speculation than life requires or admits'.[17]

Some reforms were also brought about by consensus rather than solely at Fielding's urging, though his views were no doubt influential. One of the most important concerned the organisation of the magistracy in Westminster and Middlesex, and both benches pressed for the change. Outside Bow Street, magistrates generally bore a bad name as 'trading justices'. They were said to maximise their profits from fees at the expense of poor litigants, whose disputes they encouraged, and sometimes corruptly granted liquor and other licences for backhand payments. Modern research suggests that not all could be tarred with this brush, but the lack of any government salary for magistrates, and the irregularities inherent in the fee system, exposed them to the easy charge of venality. By contrast de Veil and the Fieldings were salaried as court justices from 'secret' funds at some £300–400 a year; fees at Bow Street went not to the magistrates but were pooled to fund the office.[18]

In 1763 such a system was extended. Westminster was divided into three districts with magistrates' offices at Bow Street, Litchfield Street (Soho, where Saunders Welch presided, formerly High Constable of

Holborn and a great friend of Henry Fielding) and Westminster Guildhall in King Street, near the Houses of Parliament. Two Middlesex offices were established at Hyde Street, Bloomsbury, and Worship Street, Shoreditch, and one south of the river in Southwark. Justices were available throughout the day on a rota. As at Bow Street, the magistrates were uncoupled from the fee system, with fees pooled to meet all running costs, and some at least were paid a salary from secret funds. A few thief-takers or 'peace officers' were also attached to each office.

This was real progress. And a more wide-ranging reform emerged from these 'Rotation Offices' along the same lines. In 1792 a system of salaried or stipendiary magistrates was extended to the whole metropolis. The seven offices were made eight: Bow Street, Great Queen Street (now Queen Anne's Gate) and Great Marlborough Street in Westminster; Hatton Garden, Worship Street, Lambeth Street (Whitechapel) and High Street Shadwell in Middlesex; and Union Hall, Southwark. Three salaried magistrates were attached to each and so were six officers or constables at 12s a week, rewards still a significant element in their pay. At Bow Street the night-time patrol was now sixty-eight men strong and organised by parishes or districts: occasionally a major fracas or public event could bring them all out as a body. And finally a special police office for the River Thames was opened in midsummer 1798 at Wapping New Stairs, with stipendiary magistrates, eight constables for investigating crime and a staff of sixty-two surveyors and others for the prevention of theft on the river. When the new police arrested coalheavers taking home their sacks of coals, long considered a perk of the trade, hundreds descended on the office a few months after it opened with the intent of destroying it and everyone in it. There were shots and at least one death on each side until the men's anger eventually subsided.[19]

The reforms begun so tentatively under Henry Fielding in 1749 had developed a metropolitan police by the end of the century of considerable sophistication. The runner had become a resource even for the nation at large, as requests for assistance from prominent victims of crime up and down the country were directed towards the chief magistrate at Bow Street. In the metropolis the mechanics of thief-taking was now on a much-improved footing, though reliance on rewards and the necessarily shifty dealings between thieves, informers and peace officers laid the system open to ready abuse.

Despite those flaws there is no doubting the heroism of the thief-takers and the extraordinary ferocity of the opposition they routinely encountered. We might choose one instance from many. In August 1783 one of the last transport ships taking convicts to America left the Thames. There was a mutiny among the transports, who locked up the crew and captured the ship, running it aground at Rye in Sussex. Many escaped and some made their way back to London. There was a general hue and cry and information reached Bow Street that some of the men were hiding in a house in Onslow Street, Clerkenwell, near Saffron Hill. Three officers armed with cutlasses forced their way in and found five transports. Two ran upstairs and escaped by letting themselves down from the windows.

But the others, arming themselves, one with a poker, another with a shovel, and a third with a clasp-knife, having a blade above six inches long, as with one voice cried out, 'Cut away; we shall be hanged, if taken; and we will die on the spot, rather than submit.' All expostulation proving fruitless, the Officers attempted to seize them, upon which a dreadful contest ensued. Redgrave had the fore-part of his head laid open to the length of five inches, and received three deep wounds from the right-eye down to the cheek; besides which one of the villains aimed a thrust at his gullet with a knife, which being square at the end, its entrance was impeded by the collar-bone. Season received a terrible wound a little above the temple from a large poker, after which he closed with the man who struck him, and throwing him on the bed, wrested the poker from him, and at this instant Isaacs having obliged another to drop his weapon by striking him on the hand with a cutlass, the villains said they would surrender, and go quietly to prison.[20]

The three men were hanged at Tyburn that same month.

All this was classic thief-taker business, and the main object of the reforms since 1749 had been to provide Londoners with a more effective response to the rise in crime, but the magistrates and runners also had an important role in upholding public order in London, stiffening the backbone of the parish police. And that, almost everyone agreed, was much needed.

'Pluck Off Your Hat Before the Constable': The Parish Police

From time immemorial the ratepayers of each parish in London had been responsible for organising a 'nightly watch and ward'. At the

beginning of the eighteenth century the organisation of the watch fell
to parishes in Middlesex and Southwark, to wards in the City of London
and to the Court of Burgesses of Westminster. There were numerous
local differences but in general arrangements worked along these lines:
watchmen were paid by the night to patrol a district of some hundred
or so houses; they were recruited and supervised by the beadle, generally the only salaried official of the parish; payments for watchmen
and beadle were funded from a rate raised annually among the ratepayers, generally main tenants or householders; watchmen and beadles
had the power of arrest, but the interrogation of prisoners and the
decision to bring them on a charge before the magistrates fell to the
constable. He was elected for one year only from among the ratepayers
and was paid no salary. The watchman was generally the first to be
called to the scene of a crime; any suspected person was brought to
the watch-house erected by every parish or City ward, there to be
examined by the 'constable of the night'. Though constables were available to victims of crimes committed in the daytime, this essentially was
a police that operated only in the hours of darkness.[21]

Even so it was extensive, especially in the square mile of the City of
London. A reorganisation of the nightly watch in 1705 required twenty-
five City wards (not including Bridge Without, Southwark) to arrange
for 583 watchmen to be on the streets each night. The duty to watch
had nominally fallen on householders but the 1705 arrangements recognised that most would pay for men to do that unpleasant job in their
stead and so rates were levied to pay for the service on behalf of the
ward as a whole. A constable would also watch each ward by night.
Constables carried a staff of office and a wooden truncheon emblazoned
with the king's arms, and in the City they were obliged to fix the king's
arms and those of the City above their doors or at the end of the alley
where they lived so they could be fetched in an emergency. The task
of constable was onerous, sometimes costly and occasionally dangerous
and many ratepayers, once elected, chose to employ a 'deputy' or
'substitute' to perform their duties on their behalf. Even by the early
years of the century it was customary for some of these deputies to
serve for several years, in effect forming a kernel of professional policing
within the parish. Deputies were more common in the wealthier City
wards; in the poorer districts larger numbers of elected constables would
share the duties between them. These, with constant refinements as to
the collection of rates and numbers employed, remained the basis of

City policing throughout the century. By mid-century the watch had grown in numbers to around 900 men; and the professionalisation of the constable strengthened: by 1778 two out of three in the City were paid deputies.[22]

Similar arrangements were in place in the suburban parishes of Middlesex. As new parishes were formed with the growth of London – seven new Middlesex parishes were established between 1729 and 1746 – the opportunity arose to petition Parliament for powers to employ their own watch and ward. In this way and others, the numbers of suburban watchmen, beadles and constables increased during the first half of the century. Even so, around 1755 fewer than 250 watchmen were available for that enormous and turbulent area from Whitechapel, through Shoreditch, Clerkenwell and St Giles to Marylebone. South of the river, Southwark and Lambeth, with ten parishes between them from 1733, employed some ninety-two watchmen around 1755.[23]

The arrangements in the City of Westminster had different beginnings, outside the parish structure altogether. From 1585 a Court of Burgesses, its members appointed for life by the High Steward for Westminster, was responsible for watching the city's streets, appointing constables, beadles and watchmen. But as the numbers of houses and residents grew the authority of the Court declined. In 1735 the wealthy parishes of St George Hanover Square (newly created in 1729) and St James's successfully obtained their own powers to watch and ward their streets, and the next year four of the largest remaining Westminster parishes did the same. This parish revolution reconstructed policing in Westminster along lines already existing in the City and suburbs. By around 1755 the nightly watch in Westminster comprised 236 watchmen, thirty-one beadles and fifty-seven constables. In all, at that time, London was watched at night by a parish police of some 1,300 watchmen, 134 beadles, 420 constables and 227 headboroughs (assistant constables), some 2,100 men in all.[24]

This was a large force but in general it had only a poor reputation. The magistrates of Westminster, Sir John Fielding at the helm, led an attack in 1770 on the city's watch as insufficient and too parochial – watchmen were said not to intervene beyond their boundaries, even on the other side of the street – but the magistrates were petitioning for the organisation to be put in their own hands and their evidence must be read accordingly. Grub Street writers commonly assailed the watch for being in the pay of prostitutes and thieves, or turning thieves themselves, or being drunk on duty, or too aged and infirm for the responsibilities given them, parishes often reluctant to pay more than a pauper's pittance of around a shilling a night. There was occasional truth in all of this, drink in particular an occupational hazard: two watchmen of St George Bloomsbury were found frozen to death 'on their posts' in January 1795, having fallen asleep after drinking to keep out the cold. And even in the City, best-policed by far of all the London districts, the watch was said to be 'very insufficient, for want of stouter and better conducted Men' in 1754.[25]

Even so, the evidence given to the Old Bailey in many hundreds of cases shows the nightly watch to have been surprisingly effective at responding to alarms and cries for help, and there are many instances of heroism and self-sacrifice in the performance of the watchman's duties. A watchman of Goodman's Fields, Whitechapel, told the Old Bailey in February 1750, 'I heard the prosecutor cry out, Watch! Stop Thief! &c . . . I pursued the prisoner, and going to strike him, he said don't abuse me, I'll stand; I'll stand still.'[26] In October 1750 James Clayton was making water against a wall in Featherstone Buildings, Holborn, when he was robbed of his hat and wig by three men. When he called 'Watch!' they cut him on the head with a hanger or short cutlass and fired a pistol so close to his face he was thought to be powder-burned for life. George Wood, the watchman, heard the cry and set off in pursuit: 'I never lost sight of the prisoner from the pistol going off till he was taken, I still calling out, *watch, thieves, murder,* as I ran; he fell down near the White Hart Door in the lane: I was within about two yards of him when he fell . . .'[27]

In these cases and many more like them the watch operated with the common consent of victims and any householders who were not acquaintances or confederates of the thieves. To that extent the parish police was a communal resource and one that many wished to assist. 'I keep the George ale-house' in Mansfield Street, Goodman's Fields: 'I heard the cry, Stop Thief! &c. I went to my door, and the watchman and I took hold of the prisoner together, and brought him into the house. He own'd he gave the prosecutor a knock on the pate, and took his hat and wigg.' And this ready mutual aid of passers-by and neighbours was often the only recourse to victims of crime in daylight, when all who could were expected to take part in a general hue and cry: when a washerwoman in Islington challenged a man about the theft of a pair of breeches drying on her pailings, 'he said, damn you, you old bitch, what is that to you, he run away, and I cried stop thief, he was taken in about a quarter of an hour'.[28]

Sometimes, extraordinary though it may seem, ordinary citizens could effect an arrest even in the most dangerous of places. Richard Coombe, a carpenter, went through Black Boy Alley one Saturday night in 1753 on his way to get payment for work done during the week. In a dark spot he was attacked by a knot of men and women standing in the alley and had his pocket picked. He pursued a man and woman who ran into the Black Raven alehouse in Chick Lane. His cries brought a shoemaker, an ironworker and a wheelwright to his aid: 'I went up to the prosecutor, and said, are you actually robbed? he said yes, of 11s. and upwards, then I said, I'll assist you.' Despite resistance from the thieves and many drinkers in the Black Raven they made their arrests and took the couple 'to the constable, at the Butchers Arms, in Smithfield'.[29]

On the other hand, in difficult areas like this or when dealing with individuals made savage by drink or arrogance, all hell might descend on the parish police. 'I was a Headborough last Year for St. Giles's Parish,' Robert Rhodes told the Old Bailey jury in 1741. He was called out of his shop one February night to arrest on a justice's warrant Thomas Robinson, whom Rhodes found drinking in the White Horse alehouse, Drum Alley, Drury Lane, an Irish house. Robinson refused to go with him, 'and in a little Time, a great many People came with Clubs, Sticks and Hangers' and 'took him from me, and beat me'.[30]

There could be much worse. There were a dozen or so trials reported in the Old Bailey Proceedings across the century for the murder of watchmen: by drunken gentlemen armed with swords, by smugglers and thieves, by drunken journeymen and affronted householders. And no doubt the deaths of watchmen and constables from wounds received on duty amounted to many more than this.

The most notorious case of the century involved some young men of Irish origin on Christmas Eve 1769. They had become ferociously drunk at public houses in Westminster, assaulting any man they could find in the streets, knocking them to the ground with sticks and iron bars. On Westminster Bridge, patrolled by two watchmen at either end and a watchman and constable in the middle, they got into a row with the watch. John Bigby, a bricklayer's labourer standing in for a regular watchman, called for assistance using 'the watch word YO-I!' but was hit over the head with a long iron poker. His skull was fractured along seven inches and he died soon after. Four men were charged and tried in February 1770. Two were acquitted; but Matthew and Patrick Kennedy were convicted and sentenced to death.[31]

The brothers were fashionable and well connected. Their sister was Kitty Kennedy, a courtesan whose protectors included at one time or another Lord Bolingbroke's younger brother, the Earls of Carlisle and Fife, Viscount Palmerston and Lord Robert Spencer. Numbers of wealthy admirers of Kitty and their friends, including George Selwyn and Horace Walpole, agitated with the King and Privy Council for the brothers' lives. Both were eventually saved from the gallows and transported. There was one last hitch when John Bigby's widow was funded by radicals outraged at one more instance of aristocratic insouciance to challenge the reprieve in the courts, but she was bought off for £350.[32]

It was inevitable, though, given the violence inherent in personal and social relations in London for much of the century, and given the ignorance of many of the poorer sort about their rights, that individual watchmen and constables would abuse their powers. Charges against watchmen for assault, even murder, are occasionally found in the Old Bailey Proceedings: two were convicted of the manslaughter of a truculent drunk in Westminster in 1779, for instance.[33] And the figure of the tradesman-constable exulting in his power was an object of snobbery and satire throughout the century:

Pray Mr. *Lickspiggot*, why so Prodigal in your Office, now you are chosen by the *Wardmote* to be a *Midnight Magistrate* . . . a Prince of *Darkness* . . . But why so very Humble in the Day, and so Tyrannical at Night . . . 'Tis strange that a Painted *Staff* and a Wooden *Chair* should change a Tunbelly'd *Tapster* into an Emperour of the *Moon* . . . and that the Mornings Tone of *Your Servant Master*, and you're *wellcome Sir*, should at Night, be turn'd into the Austere Language of *Who comes there? Pluck off your Hat before the Constable*.[34]

Constables had the power to charge or release persons taken by the watch and there were many insinuations, and some hard evidence, to show that petty offenders could be forgiven for a half-crown or a round of beer for the watch-house. Justice was probably not much compromised by this self-interested lenience. Far worse were false arrests and trumped-up charges against poor men and women, the better sort always able to look after themselves with friends and legal advice: in October

1785 a Westminster constable was sentenced to the pillory and imprisoned for perjury, trying to swear away the life of a man to share a reward of £80 with the prosecutor in a case reminiscent of McDaniel thirty years before. And an overzealous and hard-hearted constable, motivated as some were by religious fervour, must have been a terror to the poor, especially women out at night.[35]

There were also a few dreadful cases of neglect, the watch-house the last resort for the sick and destitute found in the street at night. A dying man brought from an alehouse to Hatton Garden watch-house in August 1789 was declared 'an impostor' by Wade, the keeper, who ordered him to be carried out and laid in the open street, just outside the constable's jurisdiction, where he later died.[36] But the most terrible instance of abuse of power and inhuman neglect by the London parish police during the whole century took place at St Martin's watch-house in July 1742. The High Constable of Westminster conducted a round-up of women found in the streets late one night, mostly prostitutes though with some respectable working women just going about their business whose stories were not accepted by the watch. Twenty-eight were sent to St Martin's round-house, where William Bird, the keeper, forced them into a cellar known as 'the Hole' beneath the watch-room. It was said to be some six and a half feet square and less than six feet high, with a window that was kept close shut. The night was sweltering. But Bird denied the women both air and water.

We cried out Fire and Murder; that there were People in Labour, For God's Sake have Mercy upon us, or we had better be hanged out of the Way . . . We could but just stand upright in the Hole. I had but three half-pence in the World, and I offered that for a little Air . . . I staid the last in the Hole except three besides the dead Women. There were five or six in Fits, – that was owing to the Heat of the Place . . . I went down about twelve o'Clock, and there was a continual Cry from that Time till ten o'Clock in the Morning. The Skin of my Face rose in Blisters, and all came off.[37]

'He said twice that we might die and be damned', another woman recalled, and four women, one of whom was pregnant, did indeed die of suffocation and thirst. Bird was sentenced to death for murder but was respited and transported. The respite proved short-lived. Bird had a grisly end, dying himself of thirst, denied water by the captain of the aptly named *Justitia* transporting him to America. Horace Walpole, commenting on the tragedy in the round-house, told a friend that 'the greatest criminals in this town are the officers of justice'.[38]

The events of that night in St Martin's roundhouse aroused fury in the local population. On the Sunday night following, it was reported that 'the mob' had demolished it and though 're-building every day' was 're-demolished every night'. Indeed, the watch-house elsewhere was an occasional target of collective attack when the officers of the watch were thought to have abused their power. Sailors pulled down the Greenwich watch-house in May 1774 and released a number of their mates arrested for pilfering from gardens; and when a servants' hop was broken up and arrests made by a justice and fifty constables in June 1792 the watch-house at Mount Street, Mayfair, was besieged by a large crowd for much of the next day, broken into and badly damaged.[39]

There, and in similar moments, the civil power proved unequal to the task of controlling the London crowd and the watch, peace officers and magistrates had to be rescued by military force. In the last resort London's peacekeepers were soldiers, at least in Westminster and the suburbs, if not generally in the City. We have witnessed the involvement of troops in putting down industrial riots in Spitalfields and elsewhere in the 1760s and we shall see in the following chapters how indispensable they were in moments of religious or political turbulence. But the 'last resort' might in fact be invoked pretty quickly, even on routine occasions of potential or actual disorder. Soldiers were frequently called out from their public-house billets and their barracks at the Savoy, St James's Park and Horse Guards to prevent or put down looting during fires, to guard against possible rescues during executions at Tyburn or to control large public events – the Horse Guards meting out violent treatment to the crowds at the coronation in September 1761, for instance. And they were summoned in support of the magistrates in the suppression of crime, rounding up thieves in Black Boy Alley in 1744, putting down gaming houses in Westminster, and so on.[40]

Soldiers were also the almost inevitable companions of customs officers when dealing with the many gangs of smugglers who came from the coast to do business in London and who would not take kindly to interference. There was a pitched battle with shots fired on both sides in Buckridge Street, St Giles, when 'musqueteers' from the Savoy, customs officers and Mr Fielding's men recovered just eight pounds of smuggled tea in September 1775. A raid with soldiers on the Fleet Prison three years later recovered far larger hauls of tea, coffee, chocolate and lace: the goods were hoisted over the walls and warehoused by the prisoners for a fee. And in May 1778 there was an astonishing encounter on Blackfriars Bridge when a baggage train of thirty-two mounted smugglers bringing goods into London, quite possibly to the Fleet, were ambushed by three customs officers and a sergeant and twenty-two dismounted Horse Grenadiers. But not expecting resistance, their muskets weren't loaded and the smugglers charged and galloped through them, braving the bayonet cuts to legs and horses and trampling several soldiers on the way.[41]

Besides the army, the civil power also had available in the early years of the century the City's trained bands, a citizen force of armed middling-sort volunteers. And from 1757 the various companies of militia formed in an invasion scare during the Seven Years War, and doubled in size after another panic in 1779, became available to support the military and give it local legitimacy. Most notable among the metropolitan militias was the London Military Foot Association. And the City's Honourable Artillery Company, formed in 1537, with its extensive drill ground west of Moorfields, was a continuous resource for the citizens, readily used in 1780 and after. The City of London Light Horse Volunteer force, in true cit fashion, was famous 'for the beauty and value of its horses', which 'could not be surpassed in Europe; and . . . the wealth of its members, could not be matched by the whole world'.[42]

Around these numerous armed forces available to shore up the civil power in London were vigilante associations, flaring and dying like fireflies, to protect vulnerable neighbourhoods from the terrors of the night. Much enforcement of the criminal law depended on neighbours helping neighbours and we have seen instances of its effective operation. It was a logical further step to band together to prevent crime happening in the first place, the citizen's courage emboldened by the right to bear arms. Wealthy householders could afford to be vigilantes by proxy. So we hear of the inhabitants of Stoke Newington in the 1750s raising subscriptions for an armed patrol on the London road to protect foot passengers by night, with another in Kentish Town around the same time. The proprietors of Bermondsey Spa and Sadler's Wells paid for similar protection to encourage customers to venture out from London, probably in the 1780s. 'The inhabitants of Moorfields' established armed patrols in 1782 'to clear it of thieves', and fifteen gentlemen agreed to patrol the streets of St Pancras by night to preserve local women from the attentions of the 'London Monster' in May 1790. And in the fearful years from 1793 a rash of parochial associations were busy equipping householders with twenty-six-inch staves to be available to the magistrates as 'Extra-Constables' in St Giles and Bloomsbury, St Margaret Westminster and doubtless elsewhere, 'for the Purpose of preserving Tranquillity in the Metropolis'.[43]

How much deterrent effect these preventive forces had on crime is a debatable point. Even so, the forces of law and order were responsible for apprehending thousands of thieves and disorderly persons and others more innocent each year in the metropolis. Very many, for a time at least, would be given some taste of the London prison system. It was a foul and bitter taste indeed.

'Hell in Epitome': Prison

Of all the miserable places in which to live and die in eighteenth-century London none was more terrible than the prison. Yet prison, in one way or another, touched the lives of a large minority of Londoners and hung like a pall over the prospects of many more.

It is indeed difficult to exaggerate the significance of the prison in the life of eighteenth-century London. Next to churches, prisons were the most important public buildings in the metropolis. They were rebuilt before churches or almost any other public institution after the Great Fire and were the only new City buildings to be awarded parliamentary subsidy.[44] There were, too, so many of them. Daniel Defoe thought there were more prisons in London 'than any City in Europe' in the 1720s. He listed twenty-two 'public gaols', added 'Five Night Prisons, called *Round Houses*' and ended his list '&c'. Southwark in Defoe's day, for instance, was a veritable township of prisons. As you walked from St George's Church north towards London Bridge along the Borough and looked to your right, you came immediately upon the White Lyon Prison. It originated, as its name suggests, in an inn some time in the sixteenth century and had been recently rebuilt as the New Gaol for Southwark felons. Next door was the Southwark House of Correction or Bridewell for vagrants, night-walkers and turbulent apprentices. Then, a few doors on, the King's Bench, for political prisoners and better-off debtors. Then, almost without pause, the Marshalsea, its buildings a mix of fifteenth- and sixteenth-century gabled houses and a rather grand Jacobean courthouse. A few hundred yards to the north of that was the Borough Clink, ruinous and little used except for a few miserable debtors; it was the prison of the Clink Liberty, nominally in the jurisdiction of the Bishop of Winchester.

Around these often ancient institutions both north and south of the river clustered a dense penumbra of private prisons where those under arrest were held awaiting bail or commitment to prison proper. For political prisoners and prisoners of conscience there were the King's Messengers' houses, the Serjeant at Arms Officers' houses and the Black Rod Officers' houses. For seamen there were the Admiralty Officers' houses. Most numerous of all there were, Defoe thought, 119 'Spunging Houses' run by licensed bailiffs for debtors under arrest, where 'the bailiffs sponge upon them or riot at their cost', as Samuel Johnson put it.[45]

Prison was the first line of punishment not only for transgression of the criminal law. Just as important, prison helped discipline the circulation of capital in eighteenth-century London. It was the apex of terror facing all borrowers who could not pay their debts – every journeyman or apprentice owing money to his master, every customer in debt to a tradesman, every tradesman in hock to a supplier, every lodger and householder behind with their rent, all knew that continued default might land them in gaol. In the Marshalsea Court very small debts could be proceeded against – a shilling was common, sometimes less. But such was the rapacious industry battening on the debtor that when fees were added on – in an example from as late as 1783 – a debt of 1s 6d could grow nearly twenty-fold to £1 5s 6d. It is unsurprising, then, that most inmates of London's prison system on any one day were debtors: of 1,500 counted in 1779, 945 were locked up for their debts.[46]

Among those we have met so far in this narrative very many had experience of London's prison system from the inside. Daniel Defoe was in Newgate for a political offence in 1703 and for some time was a debtor in the Fleet. Richard Steele, a chronic debtor, was locked up in spunging houses in 1709 and 1710. Jonathan Wild was a debtor in Wood Street Compter in the City from around 1708 till 1712 and William Hogarth's father was a debtor forced to live in the streets around the Fleet – the 'Rules' – around the same time. Robert Dodsley was held in a spunging house by the Gentleman Usher for a libel in 1739. Charlotte Charke, the actress and memoirist, was in a spunging house at least twice around 1741–2, while Laetitia Pilkington was in the Marshalsea for debt, also in 1742. Edmund Fielding died in the Rules of the Fleet in 1741 and his son Henry was imprisoned in a spunging house and possibly the Fleet not long before. John Cleland was imprisoned in the Fleet for debt in 1748–9, where he wrote much of *Memoirs of a Woman of Pleasure*, popularly known as *Fanny Hill*. Samuel Johnson, we will recall, was held in a spunging house in 1756 and again in 1758. Lucy Cooper, the courtesan, was in the Marshalsea for debt and Oliver Goldsmith was in a spunging house, both in 1764. Mary Robinson, who became the beautiful Perdita, joined her husband in the Fleet when he was imprisoned there for debt in 1775. Simon Place, Francis's father, was a spunging-house keeper for Marshalsea Court debtors until such places were done away with around 1780. In the King's Bench Prison were Tobias Smollett for a criminal libel in 1760–61; John Wilkes, who was also held for a time in the Tower of London, for various libels from 1768 to 1770; the Rev. Henry Bate Dudley, newspaper proprietor, for a libel in 1781–2; William Combe, the hackney writer, for debt in 1785–6; Colonel George Hanger, soldier-memoirist, for debt in 1798–9. And we will remember that Teresa Cornelys died in the Fleet, after numerous spells of imprisonment for debt, in 1797.

Prison, of course, became familiar not just to those who suffered in it. Countless numbers were called upon to bail friends or relatives from the spunging house or visit them in their cells or the prison's common yard. And such was the influence of prison on London life and times that it developed a sort of fascination, even a perverse glamour. Many were drawn to visit prisons, especially Newgate, as one of the shows or 'Lions' of London, for the Gothic sensation of the fearful sights to be seen there. A kind of fan club revolved around Richard Akerman, the famously humane keeper of Newgate, which met frequently with their hero in the chair at the Globe Tavern, Fleet Street, in the 1780s – James Boswell was a fawning habitué. And vicarious thrills of prison life could be had from many a writer's pen and an artist's pencil. Hogarth painted an examination of a witness in the Fleet and the murderess Sarah Malcolm in her Newgate cell and Sir James Thornhill memorably captured Jack Sheppard in Newgate just days before his execution. The novels of Defoe, Richardson, Fielding, Smollett, Charlotte Lennox and others abound in scenes from the spunging house and the prison world. Poets frequently addressed their audience from the Fleet, the Marshalsea and the King's Bench. And Newgate could take over the playhouse, most notably of course in John Gay's *The Beggar's Opera* of 1728, the greatest stage hit of the century, frequently and controversially revived, as we have seen.[47]

Of the seventeen London prisons extant in 1785 at least nine, including Newgate, accommodated debtors. Prison for debtors, as indeed for felons, was an experience sharply divided by rank. There was a hierarchy even among the main debtors' prisons. The Marshalsea, old and worn out across the whole century, was said in 1718 to be 'Hell in Epitome' and accommodated the poorest debtors; those better off, even if reasonably lodged there, frequently secured removal by writ of habeas corpus to the Fleet, by Fleet Market, or the King's Bench, most comfortable of all and completely rebuilt on a new site in St George's Fields, Southwark, in 1755–8. They were all tiny enclosed worlds for 300–500 hundred men and women, frequently with family members in addition, where half the trades of London were plied by debtors for debtors, often – extraordinary though it may seem – on credit: barbers, coffee shops, tailors, chop houses, chandlers' shops and so on.[48]

Facilities like these, a room and bed generally both shared with another debtor 'chum' and reasonable courtesy from turnkey and keeper were all available to prisoners who had managed to hide some money from creditors or who were supported by the charity of friends. These were the prisoners on the 'Master's Side' of the gaol.[49] The intimate and mutually beneficial relationship between the keeper and those prisoners with money led to a certain autonomy among long-standing debtors. Something like a prisoner republic emerged in all debtors' prisons, where the prisoners demanded 'garnish' or an entrance fine from new arrivals for drink and food and where the prisoners' rules of conduct could become as important as the keeper's.

At the King's Bench a scandal arose in 1779 over prisoners abrogating the keeper's power to dispose of property, evicting prisoners from their rooms and awarding new tenancies, even inflicting corporal punishment. One prisoner styled himself 'Marshall' and 'Lord Chief Justice' and another his 'Deputy'. They inflated room rents and gaol fees, gave the real keeper his dues and pocketed the rest. The arrangements seem to have been in place many years and were plainly tolerated by the keeper as an informal scheme of delegation which secured him both his profits and an easy life.[50]

It was this profit-making foundation of the London prison system that was productive of so many evils throughout the century. Those in charge of the gaols were not paid officials. On the contrary, they paid as much as £5,000 for the privilege of 'farming' the prison on a franchise, profiting from the fees that all prisoners had to pay on entry and delivery and, if they were able, from rent for bed and board. A celebrated parliamentary inquiry into the Fleet and other prisons, led by Colonel James Oglethorpe in 1729–30, uncovered appalling exploitation of debtors to extract their fees and other payments through starvation, neglect, torture, even murder. Its findings horrified the nation. The plight of the poorest prisoners on the 'common side' who, in the absence of help from their friends, relied solely on passing charity and bequests, was terrible beyond belief. In the Marshalsea in the early months of 1729 the Committee found that several were dying every day from sickness and malnutrition in close rooms where prisoners were stacked on shelves, one tier above another. Thomas Bambridge and William Acton, deputy keepers of the Fleet and the Marshalsea, among others, were prosecuted for murder and some lesser offences; all were acquitted in controversial circumstances.[51]

This reticulum of terror with the debtors' prison at its centre explains why arrest for debt could occasionally be so violently resisted, particularly in the early years of the century. A bailiff or 'catchpole' was an object of loathing in every poor district. A pamphlet of 1723 enthusiastically recounted the murderous assaults made on them, including the gory end of Harry Boyte, a bailiff of the Marshalsea Court, run through the breast with a red-hot iron wielded by a smith in Shoe Lane in 1722.[52] In certain parts of London collective resistance to bailiffs had long been a matter of local pride. Numerous places over many generations had claimed immunity for their residents from arrest for debt, but these had been suppressed by an Act of 1696. Creditors were now able to secure an arrest by the overwhelming force of arms of the sheriffs, though no doubt suppression did not become effective overnight.

The largest of these areas was the Mint, in Southwark, and despite the new law its residents continued to persist in their traditional claims, setting all authority at nought. It comprised some nine or so streets, including Mint Street and Suffolk Place, with a maze of interconnecting courts and alleys, at various places protected by strong gates. Parliament was told of riots in the Mint in 1706, when 'a great Number of Minters, armed with Clubs and Staves' fought off bailiffs and constables trying to execute arrest warrants for a local publican. Two or three days later the Minters went in search of the offending creditor in order that he 'be pumped, and undergo the Law of the *Mint*', enforced by their own beadles and constables in this independent republic of penury. Their favoured punishment for bailiffs and creditors was to empty the contents of a chamber pot over their heads, throw them into the 'black Ditch' or open cesspool and then roll them in 'a great Heap of the same Filth'. A landlord subjected to all this related how 'his Head was bruised and broken in several Places, his Ears filled with the said Filth, he almost lost both Sense of Sight, and Hearing'.[53]

In 1723 there was said to be 'several Thousands' of insolvent debtors who had crowded into the Mint, so many that the rents were three times their previous value. The House of Commons inquired once more into its abuses and decided a new law was required finally to suppress such an insolent nuisance, summoning all its members who were merchants and 'gentlemen of the long robe' to help in the drafting. The Mint in Southwark Act 1722, the year the session opened, at last proved sufficient to stifle this extraordinary affront to the rule of law in London. In 1724 a 'New Mint' sprang up in Wapping but was quickly put down with some bloodshed. Even so, a collective culture of lawlessness continued to feature in places like the old Mint for decades, even generations, to come.[54]

Those fighting for their freedom in the Mint knew just how terrible the alternative of imprisonment in the nearby Marshalsea and elsewhere could be, and for the poorest prisoners in the criminal system conditions were hardly, if at all, better. All prisons, including Newgate, offered privileges to convicted felons with money. But for the large majority without significant resources imprisonment even for a term of months could prove a death sentence.

We are privileged indeed to have a prisoner's-eye view of life in the Clerkenwell House of Correction or Bridewell from Jacob Ilive, there in 1756–8 for publishing a blasphemy. The four Bridewells in Middlesex, the City, Westminster and Southwark were used mainly for punishing petty offenders for crimes of disorder, often with corporal punishment combined with short stints of imprisonment. More serious offences, like Ilive's, were punished with hard labour, usually beating hemp. At fifty-three such strenuous work was a great burden to him and the daily task had to be reduced. But far worse torment was to see his fellow prisoners dying around him 'for Want of Food'. Even for those

getting food of sorts, conditions were deadly. Five or six men – sometimes up to eleven – might be kept at night in a cell nine feet by six.
They lay generally on the bare boards without bedding. Where there
were beds they were shared by two, sometimes three prisoners. Ilive
earned money by correcting the press for a local printer and could
afford a cell with a bed and mattress. It cost him a shilling to the gaoler
the first night and sixpence a night thereafter, with a candle a penny
more. At the bedhead was a wooden 'Piss-Bowl' which stank so in the
confined room – the only air on a hot summer's night from a grating
ten inches by eight – that it 'made my Head ach egregiously'. The 'thin
flock Mattress . . . swarmed with Lice, Fleas and Bugs; insomuch that
my Body was greatly whaled [wealed]'. After twenty-six nights, when
he was moved, he was 'almost eat up as it were with Vermin'.[55]

Overcrowding, filth and the ubiquitous body louse produced endemic
sickness among the prisoners, and often those who supervised them.
Epidemics of 'gaol fever' – louse-borne typhus, as later generations
recognised it to be – were commonplace in the London prisons and
remained so into the 1770s. Occasionally outbreaks of gaol fever burst
through the prison walls, as from Newgate in the 'Black Assize' of April
1750. There was an unusually large number of prisoners to be tried
that session and Newgate was crowded. They brought gaol fever with
them into the packed Old Bailey courtroom and it carried off four
judges, including the Lord Mayor and an alderman, lawyers, clerks,
jurymen, witnesses and spectators, around fifty persons in all. The
authorities improved ventilation in Newgate as a consequence and in
1752 a windmill was fitted to the roof: it was said that seven of the
eleven carpenters who fitted it fell sick with the fever, which then spread
among their families.[56]

Some years later, when Luke Hansard was finding his way round
London, he asked a passer-by, 'what place that was with the Windmill
upon it? – I was archly told, it was the *Windmill Tavern*, and to take
care I did not get into it.'[57] To his consternation he found that to
continue along the street he had to enter its arch, for at that time
Newgate was still the old gaol rebuilt in 1673 and centred on the
ancient gate in the City wall. The prison occupied the rooms over the
gateway, some sixty feet high, and blocks of four-storey buildings
adjoining on either side of Newgate Street. The main part of the prison,
its entrance, lodge and 'condemned hold', a dungeon twenty feet by
fourteen, were on the south side of Newgate Street, stretching back

into Old Bailey near the Sessions House. Newgate housed numerous citizen-debtors but its primary function was the main gaol for felons in London, Middlesex and Westminster, including those on remand awaiting trial. Convicted felons served their sentences here – sometimes moving to other prisons if overcrowding required it, as in Ilive's case – or were kept pending transportation or execution.

Newgate was worn and inconvenient and highly insecure, and that was the position with most of the London gaols throughout the century. As a consequence escapes were rife, despite the personal liability of keepers to creditors should a debtor escape and to prosecutors should a man or woman on remand get away. A favourite way out of old Newgate was to break through the floor into the common sewer. Seven men awaiting transportation broke out this way one night in 1736 and another managed to do the same later that year. But it was a dangerous venture and in one search of the sewer two bodies were found of men who had suffocated during an earlier attempt.[58]

The most extraordinary prison escapes of the century were made by just one man, Jack Sheppard. He was born in White's Row, Spitalfields, in 1702, his father a carpenter. Educated at the City's workhouse school, he was apprenticed to his father's trade. By 1723, just before his time was out, he turned to crime, it seems to cut a better figure with his girlfriend, a woman of the town. He became a housebreaker and not a very successful one, at least for any length of time. In April 1724 he was arrested in an alehouse in Seven Dials and committed for trial.

Now began the series of escapes that made Jack Sheppard's name immortal: from the St Giles Round-house that same month; from Clerkenwell New Prison in May; in August from the condemned hold at Newgate, after an arrest and trial for highway robbery in which Jonathan Wild had played a part; and most spectacular of all from 'the Castle' at Newgate in October 1724.

This last feat defied belief. Sheppard was held in what was thought the strongest room of the prison. He was fettered hand and foot, his leg chains stapled to the floor and secured by a horse-padlock. Somehow he freed his wrists from his handcuffs, picked the padlock with a nail, broke the fetters from his legs by twisting and prising apart the weakest link and tied the loose chains to his legs with rags. He used the heavy padlock to break through the brickwork of the fireplace and dislodged from the chimney a stout iron bar that had been placed there to prevent escapes. He climbed the flue until he was above the ceiling and then broke through into the disused room over the Castle. Its door had not been opened for seven years, but he picked the lock and found himself in a passage leading to the prison chapel. The chapel door was bolted on the inside, so he used the iron bar to break through the stone wall at the side of the doorframe. In the chapel he had to negotiate two locked gates and then met his final obstacle: an iron-bound door of formidable construction which opened on to the roof of the prison. Unable to pick the lock, he levered it off its fastenings and eventually wrenched it to one side. He was now on the leads above Newgate itself. But he had no means to lower himself on to the roof of the house adjoining. So he had to return through chapel, room and chimney to his cell for his blanket, make his way up again to the leads, fashion a rope and ease himself on to the parapet of the house next door. There he forced a window and entered an empty garret. After resting some time he crept down the staircase and exited into Giltspur Street.

Sheppard's sensational escape was the wonder of the town and a humiliation for the City gaolers. His triumph, though, was short-lived – probably because he lacked the resources or wit to drag himself away from his old haunts. Just over a fortnight later he was recognised and taken by the watch at a brandy shop in Drury Lane. He was hanged at Tyburn on 16 November 1724.[59]

As the prisoner-republic at the King's Bench and the superhuman achievements of Jack Sheppard both show, the London prisons of the eighteenth century were difficult places to control. There were mutinies by prisoners, sometimes accompanied by great violence on both sides, at the Fleet in 1731 and 1772, at the King's Bench in 1771, 1784 and 1791, at the New Gaol, Southwark, in 1775 and the New Prison, Clerkenwell, in 1781, and at the Marshalsea in 1749 and 1768. A complete catalogue of prison riots would doubtless be much longer.

There were also riots in Newgate in 1777 and in 1792, both in a brand-new gaol of which Lord Mayor William Beckford had laid the foundation stone in May 1770. Designed in a stark and monumental classicism by George Dance the Younger, the City's architect, it stretched from the south side of Newgate Street, where the old gate had been demolished in 1767, along Old Bailey to the courtyard of the Sessions House. Escapes still took place though, including once again into the common sewer in 1785, by two men under sentence of death who had to be rescued by the gaolers.[60]

The physical condition of Newgate was vastly improved by the rebuilding. But the plight of the prisoners remained abject in all the London gaols. The Oglethorpe Committee of 1729–30 had probably done something to mitigate the worst criminality of prison keepers and their deputies, if only through fear of exposure and prosecution. But, as Ilive shows in Clerkenwell and recurrent gaol fever indicates elsewhere, starvation, sickness and deplorable living conditions remained the lot of poor prisoners. That was the case in both criminal and civil justice systems. In the early 1770s there was renewed pressure for reform, largely stimulated by the efforts of John Howard. He was a pious dissenter and a Londoner, born in 1726 in either Hackney or Enfield, his father a prosperous upholsterer in the City. When he was eighteen he inherited a substantial estate, including land in Bedfordshire, where he became High Sheriff in 1773. Part of his duties included oversight of Bedford Gaol and until his death in 1790 all his energy and much of his fortune were spent investigating prison conditions in Britain and across Europe and then publishing his findings. Under his influence some relief was obtained for innocent prisoners acquitted in the courts but held in gaol till their fees were paid; and some provision was made in principle for medical care and aid for the sick, though in practice the law was a dead letter for some years to come.[61]

The need for reform was vividly pointed up in a survey by Dr William Smith, a medical man of Red Lion Square, commissioned by the Westminster Charity and conducted around 1775. Some fifty years after Oglethorpe, Smith revealed a continuing catalogue of horrors:

Besides the dangers attending the visitation of gaols, few, accustomed to any degree of cleanliness, could bear the stench of such places, or stand the shock of such misery. Vagrants and disorderly women of the very lowest and most wretched class of human beings, almost naked, with only a few filthy rags almost alive and in motion with vermin, their bodies rotting with the bad distemper, and covered with itch, scorbutic and venereal ulcers; and being unable to treat the constable even with a pot of beer to let them escape, are drove in shoals to gaols, particularly to the two Clerkenwells and Tothil-fields; there thirty, and sometimes near forty of these unhappy wretches are crouded or crammed together in one ward, where in the dark they bruise and beat one another in a most shocking manner.

In the morning, before the turn-keys attempt to open the doors of the different wards, which are . . . like the black hole in Calcutta . . . , they are obliged to drink a glass of spirits to keep them from fainting, for the putrid steam of myasma is enough to knock them down. They are very frequently seized with such violent reachings, that nothing will lie upon their stomachs.[62]

Even at the end of the century and in a brand-new prison, things were little better. Cold Bath Fields House of Correction replaced Clerkenwell's worn-out New Prison in 1794. It became quickly known throughout plebeian London as the 'Bastille'. One of its terrors was the cold. When Colonel Despard was held there in 1798 on suspicion of treason he was confined alone for seven months in 'a damp cell, seven feet square, without either fire, candle, chair, table, knife, fork, or glazed window and without any book to read'; his legs became 'ulcerated with frost' before he was at last removed to a room with a fire.[63] In the Southwark Compter debtors were entirely without 'bedsteads, bedding, *nor even straw to lie upon!*', having 'to sleep in their clothes upon the dirty boards'. The King's Bench Prison had no medical attendance even thirty years after the Act of 1774 that Howard had inspired. At Newgate visitors noted the filthy state of the 'poorer females, particularly convicts, crowded like sheep in a pen' and 'covered (scarcely covered) with rags'. And so on. The fundamental problem of the London prison system, its farming out to men whose duty and humanity had always to be tempered by the need to screw profit from the prisoners, remained untouched until the century to come.[64]

Reformers in these years had only intermittently turned their attention to the condition of the London prisons. The savagery of the penal code, however, the increasing numbers of crimes attracting the death penalty and the way that sentence should be carried out had long been matters of debate and controversy.

'Low Lived, Blackguard Merry-Making': Public Punishments

In eighteenth-century London rising wealth and luxury provided increased opportunity and incentive for crime. Yet traditional policing, even after innovations, proved unable to safeguard citizens or their property. The only deterrent seemed to be to punish offenders so harshly that they would or could never reoffend and that others would take warning from their suffering. And suffering was amplified and deterrence stiffened by punishment taking place in public, where neighbours and even casual passers-by could witness the miscreant's shame, mortification and agony.

Whipping, for instance, was a common punishment for men and women convicted of disorderly behaviour and petty theft. Most sentences were carried out in private in the Bridewells or Newgate, but frequently the whipping was in public, where the offender was tied to a post or, more commonly, to a 'cart's tail', or 'cart's arse' as the vulgar had it, and whipped through streets close to where the offence was committed. Both men and women were whipped on their naked backs. The public whipping of women was uncommon after the 1750s, and a declining proportion of men sentenced to be whipped had to endure the humiliations and dangers of a public punishment. Even so, the numbers of public whippings in London peaked as late as the 1780s. The American loyalist Samuel Curwen met a 'great crowd' in Old Bailey in September 1780 and learned that two pickpockets were to be whipped:

the first seemed like an old offender, and was moderately lashed; the mob said he had bought off the minister of justice; he writhed but little. The other was young, distress painted strongly on his countenance; he cried loudly; his back seemed unused to stripes; from this time it will carry the marks of legal vengeance, and proofs of his folly and wickedness.[65]

The crowd was expected to take a larger share in the punishment of those sentenced to stand in the pillory. In general this was a punishment reserved for crimes of special odium to the system of justice (most commonly for perjury), to morality (occasionally for running brothels and bawdy houses, more commonly for sodomy), to government (publishing libels) and to religion (blasphemy). The behaviour of the crowd could not always be predicted and sometimes the will of the authorities was frustrated by its active sympathy. When Daniel Defoe stood in the pillory at Cheapside, Fleet Street and elsewhere in 1703 he was received with acclaim and his friends used it as an opportunity to sell his books to the crowd. Other writers and publishers might receive similar favours: when John Williams, publisher of the *North Briton* in volumes, was pilloried in February 1765 at New Palace Yard for reprinting Wilkes's libel on George III, he was greeted by 'the repeated acclamations of upwards of ten thousand people' and a collection on the spot raised over 200 guineas for him. Less predictably, when two elderly men – one over sixty, the other over seventy – were pilloried for perjury outside Westminster Hall in June 1763 'their tears and grey hairs drew such compassion from the people, that instead of pelting they collected money for them'.[66]

More frequently the pillory provoked the response the law expected and the crowd added corporal punishment to public shame in a chaotic combination of execration and excrement. Street dung, the contents of cesspits, dead cats and dogs, rotten fish and vegetables, all were the staple ammunition of the London crowd against unpopular offenders exposed in this way. But where the crime was especially odious a crowd at the pillory could readily become more murderous, throwing stones and brickbats calculated to injure, even kill. Just two months before that kindly scene outside Westminster Hall a man convicted of sodomy was killed in the pillory at Bow.[67] Death in these circumstances was most commonly from skull fractures or strangulation, the offender knocked unconscious and his neck left hanging in the block. Like the poor man at Bow, it was most often men convicted of 'unnatural offences' with other men who most frequently provoked the fury of the crowd. One of the worst instances of the kind took place in April 1780 at St Margaret's Hill, near Southwark town hall. Two men convicted of 'sodomitical practices at the Magdalen Coffee-house' stood in the pillory. William Smith, a coachman, who had complained the pillory was too high for him, was knocked out and strangled 'till he appeared black in the face, the blood gushing from his ears'. Edmund Burke took up the case with the Attorney General and in Parliament some members unsuccessfully moved for the pillory's abolition; Burke was libelled in the *Morning Post* as a friend to sodomy for his pains. The under-sheriff of Surrey was subsequently charged with negligent lenity towards the crowd but acquitted.[68]

The resentment of the crowd was perhaps never higher in the century than when Stephen McDaniel and three of his gang of thief-takers were set in the pillory in March 1756. The sentences were carried out over two days. McDaniel and John Berry were pilloried at the end of Hatton Garden and harshly treated; despite considerable protection from the constables McDaniel was badly cut on the head and Berry, 'who was weak before, was scarce able to survive'. But a few days later, the officers of justice, who must have known they were passing something like a death sentence on the two thief-takers, decided that the pillory for James Salmon and James Eagan, otherwise Gahagan, was to be erected in Smithfield on a market day, the concourse filled with drovers, inured to cruelty for their daily bread. Sure enough, they were stoned and pelted with bones. According to the *British Spy*, reporting from the inquest:

Eagan had one of his Eyes cut out soon, [and] after some Time one particular Bone was flung at him, which struck him on the Fore Part of his Head and Face, by which he had his other Eye beat out, and with his struggling, through the Pain, got his Hands out of the Pillory; then being much stupefied with the Blow . . . his Legs gave Way under him, he soon appear'd as if he was dead, but was continu'd in the Pillory till the Time was expir'd, which was near Half an Hour.[69]

Two days later it was reported that Salmon 'could not see out of either of his Eyes, and his Head were swell'd as big as two'; he was not expected to live.[70] Of all the punishments to strike fear into the criminal's heart, death in the pillory was the most terrible. These events were not frequent by any means, but they were still happening through to the end of the century and beyond.

Some punishments did not have this public dimension. Branding did, for though not carried out in public it displayed itself every time an offender opened his or her hand. But imprisonment, increasingly used as the century grew older, and transportation to America until 1783 and to Australia from 1787, were punishments carried out more or less in private. Their deterrent value was questioned by many as a consequence, especially when, as in the case of transportation, they seemed such lenient alternatives to capital punishment. From 1776 the deterrent value of imprisonment was strengthened by the use of two hulks moored on the Thames at Woolwich, where convicts performed severe hard labour on inadequate food lifting ballast from the river. The first to be ready was the *Justitia*, on which William Bird the round-house keeper perished. There was, though, a public shaming aspect here: parties from London of the middling sort and above took boats to watch the convicts at work as a sightseeing treat.[71]

The most public punishment of all, of course, was the death sentence. An execution was the best free show in London. It was an entertainment as attractive to the man of leisure as to the most ragged urchin in the London streets. James Boswell and the aristocratic George Selwyn famously made a point of attending every execution they could and getting as close to the agony as possible. 'I got upon a scaffold very near the fatal tree . . . I was most terribly shocked, and thrown into a very deep melancholy,' Boswell recorded in 1763; but nearly thirty years on frequent exposure had dulled his feelings: 'I have omitted to mention', after retailing a very full day's socialising in May 1790, 'that I this morning saw three men hanged before Newgate.'[72]

Executions were frequent events in eighteenth-century London, although just how frequent is impossible to measure accurately. There were ten or so hanging days a year whenever the sessions calendars were reasonably full. In London and Middlesex in the fifty-one years from 1749 to 1799 1,696 men and women were executed, almost entirely for crimes against property. Numbers varied widely year on year, as low as six in 1759, for instance, and as many as 108 in 1782; but from 1749 to 1754 and from 1764 to 1787 over fifty a year were put to death. None of these figures includes executions south of the river. Until November 1783 most London hangings were held at Tyburn, at or close to where Marble Arch stands today, involving a long procession from Newgate by cart, hearse or hurdle, a painful refinement for coiners and others dragged over the pitiless holes and ridges in the London streets. Death from hanging at Tyburn was mostly by strangulation, offenders placed in a cart while the noose was fastened to a tripod-shaped structure, the 'Fatal Tree', and the cart driven away from under their feet. Friends sometimes pulled the legs of those dying hard to shorten their agony. Executions were then moved to Old Bailey, in the wide triangular roadway next to Newgate, and effected by an 'improved drop', a trapdoor opening below the offender in an effort to shorten suffering by breaking the neck, not always successfully. The first execution at Newgate was on 9 December 1783, nine men and one woman hanged before a 'vast Crowd of People . . . drawn together by the Novelty of the Sight'.[73]

There were many other places of execution in London. A gallows could be erected in any open space, even a roadway, near the site of a crime thought specially heinous: we have seen instances in Spitalfields, the Mint and elsewhere, and in most years there were exemplary displays of this kind. Tower Hill was the place for beheading any high-born offender convicted of treason. In 1716 and 1746, when the Jacobite lords were beheaded, multitudes turned out to watch, even clinging to the spars and rigging of ships in the port: George Selwyn seems to have acquired one of the heads in 1746, paying just a guinea.[74] South of the river Kennington and Putney Commons were the most popular places for a hanging.

Wherever or whenever, a hanging day was a holiday for Londoners. No master could keep his apprentice or journeyman at the bench when 'Tyburn Fair' or a 'Hanging Match' was under way, and there was similar excitement among all classes, especially when the offender was of the quality. When three gentlemen forgers were executed at Newgate in June 1798, 100,000 people were said to be watching. Windows were removed from the houses to make more room, even the tiles from the roofs, which were said to be 'canopied with heads': 'a great proportion were women, and many of them with the appearance of ladies'. In general, though, especially along the procession to Tyburn, the flavour was plebeian, as Francis Place remembered:

Within my recollection, a hanging day was to all intents and purposes a fair day. The streets from Newgate to Tyburn were thronged with people, and all the windows of the houses were filled. The friends and acquaintance of those going to be hanged used to follow the carts in which the criminals were seated, and if any one bore his fate with indifference or bravado he was occasionally applauded. People used to wait the coming of the carts in different places, some holding a pot of beer in their hands, others, a measure of gin, to treat the criminals, for which purpose the carts occasionally made a stop. Others, threw oranges and apples to them. Pye men, and others with gingerbread nuts, and other things bawld about as they do now in the Old Bailey, but to a hundred times the extent, and in much greater variety. Songs were sung and the ballads sold at the corners of the streets all along Holborn, St Giles's and Oxford Street. These songs were either bawdy songs or songs commemorating the acts and deeds of highwaymen, and other thieves. Carts were placed along the middle of the streets and the people paid a trifle for permission to sit or stand in them to see the culprits pass.[75]

We might recall from the execution of Elizabeth Brownrigg that the crowd was not always a passive spectator. Jonathan Wild was badly pelted in the cart to Tyburn and no doubt many others were too. In the bitter January of 1767, so cold that birds fell dead from the skies, John Wilkinson, a journeyman shoemaker, was hanged in Moorfields for the murder of his wife. He had starved her to death. It was thought some 80,000 turned out to watch, 'a great number of whom were women'. 'It was with difficulty that the resentment of the populace was restrained; for they were prepossessed that the punishment of hanging was too mild for so heinous a crime. He seemed apprehensive of being torn to pieces, and hastened the executioner to perform his office.'[76]

The idea that hanging was too good for some was actively sanctioned by the criminal law. Women convicted of 'petty treason', for the murder of their husbands and for coining offences were occasionally sentenced to be burned to death. It was a punishment mitigated in practice throughout the century by the hangman strangling the woman with the rope that held her neck to the stake before the flames reached her. But on one notorious occasion at least, in November 1726, the hangman's hands were scorched while he was trying to dispatch Catherine Hayes for arranging the murder of her husband and she died by burning. The law was repealed in 1790 but the last burning outside Newgate took place just a year before, for coining. Men convicted of similar crimes were sentenced only to hang, though some coiners additionally had their bowels and heart removed and burned on the gallows.[77]

The public shaming of a hanged criminal was also frequently continued after death. We might recall the heads of traitors fixed on spikes at the top of Temple Bar for much of the century, and men convicted of treason were often decapitated after hanging even into the nineteenth century. Sentences for other offences frequently required that a hanged man's body should be suspended high in an iron cage or gibbet for the birds and flies to reduce it to a skeleton. So highwaymen were often gibbeted on the heaths and commons about London as a warning to their kind. It was a punishment feared and resented: gibbets near the Edgware Road were cut down one night in 1763 by the friends of the hanged men.[78]

More frequently still the bodies of those hanged at Tyburn and elsewhere were given to the surgeons for public dissection, great crowds attending at Surgeon's Hall to see the mutilated corpses of notorious offenders, men and women both. This was considered an awful further punishment and not just among those of the poorer sort, who saw it as a damnable impediment to the afterlife. The surgeons' men might be frustrated in their efforts to take a body from the gallows, sometimes because friends thought that resuscitation might be possible – odd cases of revival after hanging did indeed occur.

At one level, these violent disputes with the surgeons' men at Tyburn were but a further expression of the superstitions attaching to these great public festivals of death. Children were sometimes lifted up so that a hanged man's fingers – even still in the throes of death – might touch and cure a wen or facial impairment, and there are reports of women, perhaps with cancers, doing the same. Ropes used in hangings were sold by the inch as keepsakes and charms. Offenders who cheated the gallows by killing themselves in their cells might be hauled in a shroud on a hurdle and buried at a crossroads near the scene of their crime, a stake driven through their hearts – great crowds turned out to watch such a spectacle on Holborn Hill in December 1793, for instance.[79]

But violent resistance to the surgeons' men could also be a sign that the crowd sympathised with the offender and disapproved of the execution. Jack Sheppard's body was taken away on the shoulders of the crowd in November 1724 to keep it from the surgeons, and rioting broke out when it was rumoured they had secured it after all; he was eventually buried in St Martin-in-the-Fields' burial ground at an unknown gentleman's expense.[80] Sometimes friends might mount a rescue attempt though these were rare, generally confined to men like sailors or journeymen with close work ties to the man to be hanged, and never – it seems – successful. Sometimes, as we saw at the executions of Spitalfields weavers in December 1769, a violent crowd could make things very hot for the sheriff and constables carrying out the hanging. Disapproval could also be expressed where a hanging victim was very young, just fourteen or fifteen, or where it seemed the crime was unworthy of such a merciless penalty, or where a prosecution was deemed malicious in some way. When Cornelius Saunders was hanged for a theft at Tyburn in August 1763 his body was carried to Spitalfields and laid at the door of the prosecutor, a Mrs White of Lamb Street; her house was broken into, her furniture and 'salmon tubs' pulled into the street and burned, and soldiers trying to put out the flames were kept away by volleys of stones. There were similar cases elsewhere in London in 1764, 1774 and doubtless at other times too.[81]

None of this, of course, should be taken as signifying revulsion against public hanging in principle as a just measure of retribution. A hanging day was an indispensable public pleasure, free to the very poorest, as exciting and unpredictable as Bartholomew Fair. It was literally awesome, potentially resonant of pity or righteous anger and inviting contemplation on the great mysteries of life and death. It was, though, controversial, its 'low lived, blackguard merry-making', as

Francis Place called it, giving unwonted opportunity for mischief by thieves, whores and 'the mob'.

Henry Fielding thought the public display of executions diminished their deterrent effect by making the criminal a celebrity and nurturing the worst instincts of Londoners: 'I hate the mob', he once wrote, and here was one more chance for the 'fourth estate' to rule the metropolis, if only for a day. He thought executions would be more terrible if carried out in private. On the other hand, Samuel Johnson seems to have considered the procession to Tyburn gratifying to the public and a support to criminals in their last moments; he lamented its abolition in 1783, and Boswell agreed.[82]

There was little debate until the end of the century on the abolition of the death penalty itself, although there was frequent disquiet over its application to convictions for thefts of small value. Henry Fielding was a vociferous defender of the death penalty even here, thinking it right that 'one man is sacrificed to the preservation of thousands'.[83]

It is striking, though, that among those reformers wishing to mitigate the death sentence for minor offences or abolish it altogether no clergyman made a prominent figure. In eighteenth-century London, church and gallows were so closely fettered that there was little questioning on religious grounds of the death penalty, its indiscriminate reach across so many venial sins, or the public martyrdom that was indispensable to it. Newgate and the Old Bailey Sessions House lay in the shadow of St Paul's Cathedral. The great bell of St Sepulchre's, Newgate's parish church, tolled from six till ten on the morning of every execution. The carts, hearses and hurdles stopped there on the way to Tyburn and an intercessionary prayer was read to those about to die. In the cart with them, though not always if the crowd was very hostile, the Ordinary or chaplain of Newgate urged repentance; a Methodist preacher was often alongside him to lead the prisoners in a hymn. And it was the Ordinary who published an account of the prisoners' lives and crimes, as they were relayed to him in the condemned hold and the prison chapel, spelling out their final disposition to salvation and their hopes of redemption in the afterlife.

The Ordinary's task was not without its difficulties. As if lice and fleas and stench and threats were not enough, there was that complex response of the London poor to matters religious – from blind faith and utter ignorance to scoffing scepticism – which he had daily to contend with. When the Rev. John Trusler visited Newgate to see his friend the Ordinary in 1776 he was invited to preach to the condemned prisoners in the chapel. Trusler was an effective orator and

I had the satisfaction to think that I spoke Conviction & to learn afterwards that what I urged was attended to by three or four of them . . . but one of these fellows was so hardened that as soon as my back was turn'd he put his finger in his Cheek and drawing it out forcibly made the noise of a pop-gun & winking to his Comrade cried 'Twig the Parson'.[84]

Trusler's frank account brings us to the very heart of that vexed interface between religion and power in eighteenth-century London.

Jonas Hanway

XII

JONAS HANWAY'S LONDON –
RELIGION AND CHARITY

Fear of God and Proper Subjection: Charity

You are not unacquainted that Queen *Anne* promoted the building of a number of *new churches*; these will become useless, unless we now add a number of *new workhouses*, as well as *new prisons*.[1]

It was Jonas Hanway who in 1775 most clearly articulated this trinitarian unity of religion, industry and discipline as the only solution for the ills of the nation, especially of London, 'the common sewer of the iniquity of the British empire'. Hanway expressed his trinity in a single word, 'Police'. And its driving force, embodied in his own practice as the most indefatigable moral meddler of the age, was charity.[2]

Jonas Hanway was born in Portsmouth around 1712, his father a victualling agent for the Royal Navy who died in a riding accident when Jonas was just two. The tragedy deprived the boy of a gentleman's education. But the next best thing was a merchant's apprenticeship and at seventeen, probably through the influence of his father's brother, an army officer who lived in Oxford Street, young Jonas was shipped to London and then to 'the English Factory' at Lisbon. He was there from 1729 to 1741, becoming fluent in French and Portuguese and mastering the merchant's art. In 1743, after a short spell once more in London, he joined the Russia Company and sailed for St Petersburg. From there he travelled by land and sea to Persia, where he fell foul of bandits and suffered great privations. Till then he had been noted for his good looks and was known as 'the "*Handsome Englishman*"' in Lisbon. But Persia stripped him of his 'plumpness' and he became spare though sprightly for the rest of his life.³

When Hanway returned to London at the end of 1750 he was unknown beyond the Portugal and Russia merchants. But in 1753 he published an account of the British trade to Russia and Persia and his own experiences in it that established his reputation as a traveller and – more fatally – as a writer. Its success unleashed an egomania in ink whose main characteristic was a tendency to pronounce on everything that seized his restless attention. 'Writing was his favourite employment, or rather amusement', and to make the most of his fun he employed resident clerks who had to be ready in a moment to capture his rapid dictation. Theirs was a distasteful task, forbearance and humility not strong elements in Hanway's character: 'his impatience, and the natural turn of his temper, seldom satisfied, not infrequently petulant, and always expressing his disapprobation in terms which had the appearance of ill nature, were the cause that but few of the youths he took under his care remained with him any length of time'.⁴

Even so, Hanway's bachelor household in Red Lion Square became a manufactory of homilies in tracts, pamphlets, supplications, prospectuses and multi-volume manuals for avoiding sin and propagating virtue that was unrivalled in his times. His panoptic gaze found inexhaustible fuel for moral reflection: how to make public executions more '*decent* and *awful*'; rendering transportation more terrible by sending convicts to Africa and Asia rather than America; replacing *The Beggar's Opera* with plays of '*moral* and *christian* philosophy'; proposing solitary confinement for prisoners to allow reflection on their sins and prevent contamination of the innocent. He wrote a pamphlet, we might recall, on how best to improve Westminster's streets and corresponded with the City of London's street commissioners to explain how they should lay their pavements.⁵ He wrote on a citizen's duty at a time of war and under threat of invasion; on how to recruit seamen; against the naturalisation of the Jews as 'not consistent with the *christian* religion, and repugnant to the constitution of *Great-Britain*';⁶ on the reclamation of prostitutes; on the duties of the poor law authorities; on the proper conduct of apprentices; against the custom of vails giving; on the management of the public funds; on the usefulness of music; for the relief of sufferers in foreign disasters; on the advantages of a preventive police; for the relief of

London's black poor; on the management of Sunday schools; against the adulteration of bread and the evils of tea drinking. He offered popular explanations of Christian theology and moral guidance to selected audiences like soldiers and sailors. Though unmarried, childless and a citizen merchant, he felt no inhibition in offering advice as a farmer to his daughter: in three volumes, some 700 pages in all, and with a disquisition on prayer so lengthy and turgid it must have curdled milk in the pail. In sum, few men have so freely exercised their right to offer their advice on so much – in some eighty-eight publications from 1753 until his death, brought on by an enlarged prostate, in September 1786.

Nor did his energies end in his study. Though ever anxious about his health – he wore flannel next to his skin and three pairs of stockings to keep out the cold – he was a restless pedestrian in the London streets. Blithely unconcerned by the astonished looks and ribald comments of the Londoners around him, he dressed as if expecting an immediate summons to St James's Palace – in dress clothes of full fashion, a large French bag wig, a gold button on his hat, an ermine-lined coat and waistcoat, and a small gold-hilted sword. Wary of a soaking, he habitually carried an umbrella, in the 1750s usually resorted to only by maidservants; Hanway is often credited with establishing that prudent habit among gentlemen in London during the years that followed.[7]

And yet, for all Jonas Hanway's preposterous pretensions, it is impossible to deny his extraordinary achievements in practical philanthropy in the second half of London's eighteenth century. For his energies found their most productive outlet in creating institutions that combined Christian charity with political ends. Of these ends two stand out: helping to find solutions to the problems of disorder in London's streets and helping to satisfy the manpower needs of an increasingly aggressive imperialist nation state. In proposing and building these institutions, Hanway found much personal gratification and holy pride. These mixed motives of charitable obligation, utilitarianism and self-love were impossible to disentangle in almost all philanthropy of the time and it is no cause for special condemnation in Hanway's endeavours. What was remarkable, though, was the success of his interventions, especially in seeking to improve the lot of poor children and young people in the metropolis.

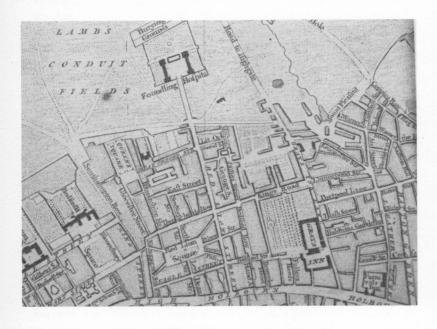

Bloomsbury, *c.*1761

From the outset of the eighteenth century, initiatives to aid and civilise the London child had been at the forefront of metropolitan philanthropy. Earliest and most extensive was the charity school movement, emerging in the 1690s and driven forward by the Society for Promoting Christian Knowledge, founded in 1699. Charity schools were parish-based and relied on subscriptions and bequests from parishioners. For most of the eighteenth century, until the Sunday school movement from 1785, they were the only educational provision for the poorest children in the capital. Their great period of growth was the twenty-five years after the accession of Queen Anne in 1702, and London led the nation in the numbers of foundations and children educated. At the end of the century there were 179 charity schools in the metropolis, teaching 7,108 children, boys outnumbering girls by about two to one.[8]

Alongside a religious purpose to the learning children received, the schools were envisaged as fruitful tools of industry and discipline. It was industry of a quite specific type: the lowest and most menial manual labour. For such a life, Hanway thought, the ability to read was desirable, but 'I do not think it necessary that above *one* in *ten* of the common people should be taught to write', and many shared this view right through the century. Schools and teachers in fact often went further, teaching their children to write and use numbers, but their efforts were observed with great concern. In 1724 the Bishop of London told the charity-school teachers that no school should tolerate 'fine Writing' or fine needlework or 'fine Singing'; and they were to avoid 'teaching the Children to *value* themselves upon these Attainments', or imparting any learning that might 'set [the children] above the meaner and more laborious Stations and Offices of Life'.[9]

The reading thought best to equip children for a life of manual labour was entirely religious, the Bible and Book of Common Prayer in particular. There was a public examination of the scholars' understanding of the catechism weekly or monthly in the parish church, including its obligation 'To submit my self to all my Governours, Teachers, spiritual Pastors and Masters. To order my self lowly and reverently to all my betters.' Charity-school children were frequently clothed in uniforms or badged to distinguish them from their neighbours. All were frequently reminded 'that whatever Attainments they gain there, are all the Effects of Charity', for which they were to be 'thankful to God, and grateful to their Benefactors'.[10]

Not all thought these most active and far-reaching philanthropic institutions in London had an entirely beneficial effect on their scholars. William Hogarth's Tom Nero, the villain of *The Four Stages of Cruelty* (1751), wears the cap and badge of St Giles Charity School, for instance. And the schools could only impact on a small minority – just 171 children in the teeming united parish of St Giles and St George Bloomsbury in 1799. Even so, the numbers of charity-school children established in the 'laborious Stations' of metropolitan life across the century were impressive: over 20,000 boys apprenticed, over 20,000 put to service, some 1,661 sent to sea, more than 42,000 in all; and over 15,000 girls put to service, with a further 5,000 and more apprenticed.[11]

The utilitarian purpose of another great charity for children, the most famous and prestigious of the age, was less nakedly visible than in the charity schools but it was there nonetheless. The London Foundling Hospital was begun by Thomas Coram, a venerable sea captain in the merchant fleet with shipbuilding experience in America. Coram and Hanway could hardly have presented a starker contrast. Coram, self-effacing, modest, unpolished in fine company and clumsy with his pen, had for many years just one charitable enterprise in view. It arose from his own lamentable experiences in the streets of London. It was said of him that, while living alongside the river, probably Rotherhithe, around 1720, 'he used to come early into the city, and return late, according as his business required his presence; and both these circumstances afforded him frequent occasions of seeing young children exposed, sometimes alive, sometimes dead, and sometimes dying, which affected him extremely . . .'[12]

Coram's proposal to establish a rescue-home or 'hospital' for abandoned babies was some two decades in the making. It took so long because it was fraught with anxieties. Just as the great fear for the charity schools was raising children above their station so a hospital for foundlings was suspected of fostering feckless morals among single women, whose illegitimate children could be farmed out to the charitable to raise. On the other hand the loss of life and labour in the kennels and waste grounds and dunghills of London was a missed opportunity for a nation in competition, often at war, with neighbouring states like France, Holland and others who had already made provision to save the unwanted infants of the poor.

Humanity, tempered but by no means adulterated with these sentiments of national interest, secured Coram his hospital. His masterstroke was to encourage a petition among aristocratic women – as a class no strangers to the complications of bastardy – that helped persuade George II to grant Coram's scheme a royal charter in November 1739. Established first at a house in Hatton Garden in March 1741, the Foundling Hospital moved in 1745 to a purpose-built palatial mansion in Lamb's Conduit Fields beyond Bloomsbury. By 1753 it comprised two wings linked by a pedimented chapel. Its courtyard lay open to London, as if in welcome to the city's poor.[13]

The Foundling Hospital became the most fashionable charity in the capital. It retained the support and interest of the wealthy women who had been instrumental in its establishment. It enlisted, through Thomas Coram's efforts, the help of wise-headed City merchants to manage the finances and the services of the most sought-after medical men in London to supervise the children's care. Their frequently piteous state on admission, and the tiny charms or mementoes left with them by their anonymous mothers, aroused the consciences of well-off Londoners in a sentimental age. Richly dressed crowds packed the chapel to see the children baptised, crammed the tables at the annual 'Ladies' Breakfasts' in May, and filled the audiences at concerts where Handel gave his services free of charge – he had donated an organ to the Hospital in 1750 – and where the *Messiah* was a perennial favourite. Music won the Hospital a special place in London's entertainment world, and so did art. Hogarth was a friend of Coram's and famously painted his portrait in 1740. He also designed the Hospital's coat of arms and was one of its founder-governors. When the first wing of the new Hospital was opened, Hogarth proposed to his fellow artists that they donate paintings to be displayed there. His scheme had several purposes – to beautify the Hospital for the children, to attract more wealthy patrons keen to see the art and to advertise the artists' skills to win them commissions. By the end of 1746 fifteen artists had presented pieces and joined Hogarth and John Michael Rysbrack as governors: they included Francis Hayman, Joseph Highmore, Thomas Hudson and Allan Ramsay.

Enlightened self-interest among London's artists, the gratifying compensations of fashionable charity on display in the Hospital's public festivals of benevolence and the usefulness of a venture that saved lives for the nation were combined with a sharp religious discipline imposed on the foundlings themselves. Those who survived the perils of infancy were treated much like charity-school children. They were taught "'to undergo with Contentment the most Servile and laborious Offices"' below '"a level with the Children of Parents who have the Humanity and Virtue to preserve them, and the Industry to Support them"'. And just as in the schools, subjection to the obligations of the Christian religion was the preferred way to secure 'Contentment' in a life of manual labour. When the Hospital put children out to apprenticeships they were accompanied by a printed instruction to employers to hear the children's prayers morning and evening and to ensure they attended church on Sundays, '"As it is of the greatest moment to breed up Children in the Fear of God, as the best means of keeping them in Proper Subjection to their Masters, Mistresses, and Superiors, and as Praying is the most effectual means to promote such Fear, and to inforce obedience to the Laws of God . . ."'[14]

Inevitably, Jonas Hanway eventually took his place as a life governor of the Foundling Hospital in May 1756. Elected a vice-president in 1771, he continued to play some part in the work of the Hospital until his death, though his job at the Navy Victualling Board, to which he had been appointed a commissioner in 1762, left him little time for the Foundling Hospital, especially during the years of the American War. But by then Hanway had made his own interventions to aid the neglected children of London.[15]

We shall look in a moment at his important representations on the plight of orphans and abandoned children in the care of London's parish authorities, but the other work for which Hanway is usually best remembered was his foundation of the Marine Society in June 1756. Jonas Hanway was of no great originality of mind. He was at his best in taking forward ideas and ventures first proposed by others. In this case, the charitable objective of apprenticing poor boys as sailors had a long history. The Stepney Society had recruited boys for the merchant service from 1674; the annual charitable 'Cockney Feasts' in Stepney and elsewhere were continuing this work into the 1730s at least, and so had the charity schools on a small scale, as we have seen. In the 1750s the idea was revived by John Fielding as some solution for that '"vast number of wretched boys, ragged as colts, abandoned, strangers to beds, and who lay about under bulks and in ruinous empty houses, in Westminster and its environs"'.[16]

With others' help Fielding raised funds to clothe and equip some few hundred boys for enlistment in the navy on the eve of the Seven Years War, from January 1756. The dual benefits to boy and nation were, in theory at least, plain to see. Hanway's Marine Society put this venture on a more permanent subscription basis and opened its benefits to men among the vagrant poor as well as boys. By May 1758 the Society had raised nearly £8,000 and clothed 1,180 men and 1,126 boys. The London theatres and pleasure gardens put on benefit nights to swell the Society's coffers, George II gave a well-publicised £1,000, London's merchant companies donated substantial sums, and by May 1759 there were 1,500 individual subscribers on the Society's books. At the close of the war in 1763, 10,625 boys and men had been fitted out for the navy at a cost of over £23,000. And in its first half century over 25,500 boys and 36,000 men were clothed for the sea.[17]

In a later, though less successful, venture Hanway plied his restless pen on behalf of the 'climbing boys' employed by master sweeps to clean house flues in London. They were often vilely mistreated, sometimes crippled by the rigours of their work, at risk from heat exhaustion and suffocation and from cancer of the scrotum, an industrial disease peculiar to their calling. Hanway's plea for protection and reform would not bear fruit till long after his death. But the boys' plight seems to have moved him greatly and this unfashionable but deeply felt campaign, pursued actively from 1773 till his death, shows Hanway at his least vain and most humane.[18]

Hanway and Fielding, so close was the work of philanthropist and police officer at the time, were also involved in two further complementary ventures aimed at children and young people. Both were also established during this uneasy opening period of the Seven Years War. Fielding began a pamphlet debate in February 1758 over the need to preserve orphaned or abandoned girls from the perils of the London streets and to rescue those young prostitutes who had already 'fallen'. Other contributions appeared along similar lines, among them one by Saunders Welch, Fielding's fellow magistrate, and another by Robert Dingley, a fellow merchant-philanthropist of Hanway's in the Russia Company. This propaganda led with remarkable swiftness to the foundation of two separate institutions that same year.

The Female Orphan Asylum – often just 'the Asylum' – was the 'preventive' part of Fielding's original plan. It gave a home to girls aged between nine and twelve whose parents were both dead; but not all girls, we might recall, for 'No negro or mulatto girl can be admitted', and 'no diseased, deformed, or infirm child is received'. Once allowed in, its 180 or so girls – or 'objects', as the rules described them – were bred to domestic service and placed 'in reputable families in Great Britain' on seven-year apprenticeships. Daily prayer reading and Sunday sermons maintained the rigorous piety required in the charity schools and elsewhere.[19]

Hanway played no part in Fielding's venture but he was instrumental in implementing the rescue side of the magistrate's proposals. The Magdalen Hospital, as it was eventually known, was established by Dingley with Hanway's help in buildings in Goodman's Fields, Whitechapel, to give a home to repentant prostitutes from the streets of London. From 1772 it moved to purpose-built premises just a stone's throw from the Asylum on the London side of St George's Fields, Southwark. The Magdalen was fashionable but controversial. It catered for eighty or so 'penitents' at any one time, including some who had 'never been in public prostitution' but had been seduced and deserted by their lovers and abandoned by their families. Girls diseased or pregnant were not admitted. Those taken in were taught to read and schooled for domestic service or the needle trades. Most were twenty or under when discharged. Of 3,775 who left the Hospital between 1758 and 1806, 2,468 were reconciled to their friends or found work: 'A very considerable number are since married, and are, at this moment, respectable members of society . . .' Religion made up a good part of life in the Magdalen. The penitents were attended by the Hospital's chaplain daily. And Sunday sermons in the chapel became as much a resort of the fashionable as events at the Foundling Hospital, many preening and prurient beaus (like James Boswell) among them. We shall see a little more of the Magdalen's Sundays in a moment.[20]

'Hospital' still retained its old and wide meaning as a place of sanctuary and succour for the vulnerable and that, of course, included places for the reception and treatment of the sick. But at the beginning of the eighteenth century there were just two such places in London: St Bartholomew's Hospital at Smithfield in the City and St Thomas's in Southwark. They were ancient institutions, by 1700 barely fit for purpose in a city growing dynamically in wealth and population: St Thomas's was rebuilt between 1693 and 1720; and we might recall that James Gibbs was actively involved in the reconstruction of Bart's from the 1720s on. Despite these efforts, accommodation for the sick poor in London was plainly inadequate, with Westminster and the inner suburbs having no hospital provision at all.

That would soon change. By 1765 London led the nation in

establishing a voluntary hospital movement that would endure for almost 200 years. It all began in a meeting of a dozen wealthy men at St Dunstan's Coffee House, Fleet Street, in December 1719. Their leader was 'Good' Henry Hoare, a banker at the sign of the Golden Bottle in Fleet Street, a devout follower of the established church. Money was subscribed to open an infirmary in the parish of St Margaret's and in May 1720, at a house in Petty France, near St James's Park, the Westminster Hospital received its first patient, a young man with '"evil in his joints and scurvey"'; he was discharged a month later, happily cured. This was the first hospital in England founded and maintained by voluntary subscription, annual subscribers becoming governors and permitted to nominate patients to the hospital. These arrangements were used by all the Westminster's successors, often with the refinement of a 3- or 5-guinea annual payment to qualify a subscriber as a governor, and often limiting the number of inpatients any governor could introduce to two at any time.[21]

Eventually run on these lines but with a very different beginning was Guy's Hospital. It was built by Thomas Guy, a dissenting City bookseller who had grown rich printing and selling Bibles and who made a vast fortune by offloading his South Sea stock shortly before the bubble burst. He had been a governor and benefactor of St Thomas's from 1708 and continued to fund it lavishly, helping with its rebuilding. It was from this experience that Guy discerned the need to build a hospital for those discharged as incurable from St Thomas's, though by his will he provided that it could duplicate as a general hospital should the need arise. 'Mr Guy's Hospital' was built adjacent to St Thomas's on land bought from the ancient hospital. It opened in 1725, shortly after Guy's death at his home on the corner of Cornhill and Lombard Street the previous December.[22]

There then followed three grand projects. In 1733 St George's Hospital was created as a breakaway from the Westminster, its founders taking the recently vacated Lanesborough House at Hyde Park Corner and with it all the older hospital's medical staff and many of its subscribers, lured by the social and other advantages of a new institution at the polite end of the town. But on the other side of London, there had been no provision for the sick poor east of the City. That was remedied by the London Hospital, founded by subscribers at the Feathers Tavern, Cheapside, in September 1740, its leading light the young surgeon John Harrison. It was set up first near Moorfields, moving to Prescot Street, Goodman's Fields, in 1741. A new hospital was built in Whitechapel Road and opened in September 1757. And for the northern suburbs the Middlesex Hospital was opened at the edge of London in 1745, at first in Windmill Street, Tottenham Court Road, and finally in a new building in the Marylebone Fields at Mortimer Street, completed in 1775.

These were all general hospitals. But immediately after the Middlesex there was a second wave of specialist-hospital building in London, in which maternity care – once more of prime usefulness in saving lives for the nation – led the way: the British Lying-In Hospital for married women, Brownlow Street, Long Acre, 1749; the City of London Lying-In Hospital, for married citizens, Aldersgate Street, 1750, moving to City Road in 1773; the Queen's Lying-In Hospital, 1752, at first on the Uxbridge Road and later moving to the New (Marylebone) Road around 1794; the Westminster Lying-In Hospital, 1765, located near the bridge and opening its wards to unmarried as well as married women; and the General Lying-In Hospital, established that same year south of the river in Lambeth, on the Westminster Bridge Road.

Other specialist infirmaries included the Middlesex County Hospital for Smallpox, founded in Windmill Street in 1746 and, after numerous moves forced by the anxieties of nervous neighbours, settling in 1767 at St Pancras on a site where King's Cross Station now stands; and the Lock Hospital, also 1746, at Hyde Park Corner for men, women and children suffering from venereal diseases, excluded from treatment in most general hospitals at that time – over the years it also became a reformatory for prostitutes along the lines of the Magdalen. Finally, among the more important of these specialist healing institutions was St Luke's Hospital for Lunatics, established in 1751 at Windmill Hill, Upper Moorfields, and moving to purpose-built premises in Old Street in 1787; it supplemented the accommodation at Bedlam nearby, and offered some alternative to the many private madhouses that clustered in Shoreditch and Hoxton. All these institutions were augmented from 1769 by the movement to build dispensaries for the poor, where free or cheap medicines and medical advice, sometimes treatment, could be offered in people's homes.[23]

By any standards these were extraordinary achievements. All were run on the basis of annual subscriptions and benefactions. In every case except Guy's, the subscribers had raised the large amounts of capital needed for land acquisition and new buildings, in addition to the revenue needed to run and maintain them. All encountered setbacks, not least because there were so many projects plucking at the purses of the benevolent. The popularity of hospitals as charitable causes had waned by the end of the century, and ward closures and neglect of sanitary conditions were common. Even so, these brand-new London hospitals were an enduring testimonial to the philanthropic imagination of the age.[24]

If, on the face of it, the hospital movement in eighteenth-century London seems a monument of selfless secular humanitarianism, then appearances would be deceptive. Utilitarianism – saving lives for the nation and restoring men and women to useful labour – was an explicit and universal objective. The medical professions, so indispensable to the lives of the rich and so susceptible to the lures of vanity and wealth, gained reputation and experience from their hospitals, even if the work was not without its dangers. And the hospital governors benefited directly from the considerable power they wielded. Indeed, the hospitals were playgrounds of patronage. Governors were solicited for admission tickets by the poor and parish authorities; they were able to remove sick servants from their households and the homes of their friends and have them treated at the subscribers' collective expense; and they were able to influence the filling of many hospital jobs, from cooks and porters to surgeons, physicians and apothecaries, sometimes to gratify wider objectives:

The hospital of St. Thomas, and that of Guy, in Southwark, were both under the government of dissenters and whigs; and as soon as any one became physician of either, his fortune was looked upon as made . . . The same advantage attended the election of a physician to the hospitals of Bethlehem and St. Bartholomew, which are of royal foundation, and have been under tory government. By cultivating an interest with either of the two parties, the succession of a young physician was insured.[25]

More surprisingly, perhaps, the hospitals played their part, and not an insignificant one, in disciplining the London poor. The rhetoric and practice of a demanding Christianity underpinned all they did, with unabated stridency till past the century's end. At the Westminster, for instance, 'A clergyman constantly and carefully visits and instructs the patients in their religious duties, and, at their discharge, some pious tracts are given to them.' A rule adopted in 1721 required all patients on discharge to appear before the governors to give thanks to God and the hospital for their cure, and to proclaim it publicly in their parish church. The London Hospital imposed a similar obligation and kept a blacklist of those who failed to comply that barred them from any further treatment. At Guy's, patients caught swearing lost a day's diet and were discharged on a third offence; and bringing in gin or brandy, or gaming or indecency could lead to immediate expulsion. Smoking, gaming, liquor and talking in bed after 9 p.m. were all outlawed at the Middlesex. And so on.[26]

This was indeed, as many contemporaries called it, an age of benevolence, with thousands of individuals supporting their 'pensioners', subscribing to charities or making charitable bequests in their wills. Jonas Hanway, not a hugely rich man and hence not an extravagant giver in his lifetime, left almost all his wealth of less than £2,000 at death 'to sundry orphans and poor persons, whom he had befriended in his lifetime', including Mercy Draper, a blind musical prodigy from the Foundling Hospital who had become disordered in her mind.[27] But we should not forget that benevolence for the poor in the charitable institutions of eighteenth-century London always came at a price.

A final period of philanthropic endeavour emerged from the mid-1780s and gathered strength through the century's end. There continued to be an aggressive Christian proselytising about it that required subjection, obedience and gratitude from all who received its bounty. Links with the past were strong. Sunday schools, proliferating in London from 1785, had much of the charity schools about them, for instance. And the Philanthropic Society, a reformatory home for delinquent children established in 1788 in Bethnal Green, moving later to that constellation of charitable institutions near St George's Fields, saw itself as a system of 'police' just as Fielding's Asylum and the Magdalen had been.[28]

But something of a new tone accompanied these developments, less harsh and utilitarian than much that had gone before. It was best, most humanely, expressed in the work of Sir Thomas Bernard. He was born in Lincoln in 1750, brought up in Massachusetts and called to the Bar at the Middle Temple in 1780. He married well two years later and was able to retire, devoting his life and part of his fortune to works of benevolence. A governor of the Foundling Hospital, he became its treasurer from 1795. A year later, with evangelicals like William Wilberforce, he formed the Society for Bettering the Condition and

Increasing the Comforts of the Poor. Bernard encouraged, for the first time, an active spirit of curiosity about the lives, needs and feelings of the poor. 'Let us therefore make the inquiry into all that concerns the POOR, and the promotion of their happiness, a SCIENCE,' he wrote in 1797.[29]

The Society became a coordinating organisation for a range of local ventures nationwide that put this idea of service into action. In London in the very last years of the century its supporters established over forty soup kitchens feeding 10,000 families in Spitalfields and elsewhere; helped climbing boys; assisted patients discharged from hospital with clothing, furnishings and so on; and set up industrial schools where children were trained in 'virtuous and industrious habits' to make them 'useful and valuable members of society'. There was now, too, more of self-help about these initiatives, like a 'female benefit club' or friendly society at High Cross, Tottenham, in 1798, which tried to provide something like an old age pension to its members.[30]

Even so, the impertinence of rank fortified by religion undermined Bernard's notion of personal service. It continued to exact a pound of flesh for each half-guinea of charity expended. As at Clapham, that thriving nest of evangelicals, where in February 1799 lady and gentleman subscribers resolved to police their poorer neighbours by '*the discovery and relief of cases of real distress, the assisting and rewarding of honest industry, the detection of fraud and imposture, the discouragement of idleness and vice, and the employment of children at an early age*, so as to improve both the condition and the morals of the poor'.[31]

In this way a pious laity began taking on themselves tasks that had long been the responsibility of the parish authorities in London.

Nurseries of Religion, Virtue and Industry: Governing the Poor

For Jonas Hanway it was 'the poor's laws' that were '*the foundation of our police*', and though based on statute and case law rather than voluntary action, a great mechanism of '*parochial charity*'.[32] In London the mechanism was driven by some 197 parishes and other bodies, sometimes joined together for the purpose of administering to the poor. In general, parish duties were carried out by churchwardens or overseers of the poor, elected annually, assisted by the beadle, the one full-time salaried officer employed by most parishes. In some cases there were local acts establishing named individuals as 'governors of the poor' to whom the overseers reported, rather than leaving these expensive functions to the parish vestrymen: Jonas Hanway himself was a governor of the poor of the united parishes of St Andrew and St George the Martyr, Holborn, from 1766.

For Hanway, the religious and secular functions of the parish were indivisible. They were the very foundation of order in society, implying 'the influence of the *clergy*; the power of the *lord of the manor*; the authority of the *justice of the peace*; the affluence and benignity of the *gentleman*, and the benevolence of the *philosopher*'.[33] Benevolence, though, was something Hanway found wanting in much parish administration. Poor relief raised vexed questions of morality and equity, with – as many saw it – the illegitimate children of feckless parents raised at the ratepayers' expense and the work-shy kept idle on a pension, questions that grew more pointed as the cost of the poor rose during the course of the century. The care of parish children and how best to discipline the idle poor became the great questions for the London poor law for much of this period.

It was a fundamental objective of all parishes to keep as low as possible the numbers receiving 'parochial charity'. In the case of children, considerable care was taken to avoid the cost of an illegitimate child falling on the ratepayers. Enquiries were set on foot to identify the mothers of abandoned children and, if found, determine whether the father could first be identified and second made to pay for the child's care:

Whereas there were 2 Female Children left in the Parish of St. Gregory's by St. Paul's, London, one on the 14th the other on the 15th of this Instant February [1709], each of them near 2 Months old, one of them in a Hand-Basket bedded with Cotton, with a Note telling its Name to be Cunstable but not Baptized, with a Pair of Mittens on its Hands, a new Pair of Yellow Shoos on its Feet, and other Necessaries, with a Bottle of Cordial. If any Person can give an account either of the Parents or those that left either of the said 2 Children, so as the Church-Wardens may speak with them, they shall receive for each Childe so discover'd the Sum of 40s. to be paid by the Church-Wardens of the said Parish.[34]

Once a parish accepted a child into its care, then the chance of an early death was very high. Most babies were put out to nurses wet or dry, sometimes to poor women in the same parish but often to women in country districts where the air was thought to be kinder to their charges. Nonetheless, most parish children died before reaching the age of one or two years old and never troubled the parish authorities further. These facts were well known. But it was Hanway who from 1760 raised the issue into a national scandal, lamenting the avoidable waste of life in a country at war and with an empire to lose. He claimed to show that in St Martin-in-the-Fields from 1749 to 1756 158 out of 312 infants in the care of the parish had died (50.6 per cent) but that in the united parishes where he would later become a governor 222 out of 284 had died, or 78 per cent. He computed that 1,000–1,200 parish children were dying each year in London and had been for fifty years past.[35]

In 1762 Hanway was instrumental in having the MP for Maidstone, Rose Fuller, introduce a measure in Parliament requiring London parishes to keep registers of the infant poor in their care so that mortality could at least be accurately ascertained: 'The common people,' wrote Hanway, 'have understood the tendency of the design so well that *they* call it *an act for keeping children alive.*' More importantly, Hanway's own act of 1767 required all London's parish children under six to be sent to the country to be nursed at not less than 2s 6d a week, with a reward of 10s for successfully rearing an infant less than nine months old.[36]

It seems likely that Hanway exaggerated the neglect and culpability of the parish authorities, though it was undoubtedly true that many London workhouses were deadly places in which to try to rear babies. One reason for exaggeration was his long-held belief that the Foundling Hospital should be given the role of rearing London's poor children, at least from parishes outside the City. Some had already contracted with the Hospital to take their children even before Hanway's act and numbers of others did after. But in fact the Hospital's own record here suffered from the same general context of ignorance, poor hygiene and unsatisfactory rearing methods that blighted the lives of parish infants and – as we have seen – many children of the middling sort and above. Hanway praised the Foundling Hospital for losing only two out of three children before reaching the ages of '8, 9, or 10 years old', and for many periods it did better than that. But the Foundling Hospital did not take all infants, where the parish could refuse none. Those babies deemed to be diseased on medical inspection were refused admission to the Foundling Hospital. When 'general reception' of all babies, whatever their condition, was required from 1756 to 1760 in exchange for extensive funding from Parliament, then from June 1758 to March 1760 mortality jumped to 71 per cent. These were figures almost as bad as Hanway had found in the London parishes, and in a new-built institution with access to the best medical advice to be had.[37]

Nor was the Hospital immune from the risks of sending apprentices to masters and mistresses who might neglect or abuse them. Saving a life for the nation was of no use if it were to wilt, even perish, at the first step on the ladder of servile employment. Hanway's act of 1767 was passed with the Metyard and Brownrigg cases of dreadful mistreatment of London's parish apprentices still fresh in the public mind and it sensibly provided for adjustments in the way children should be put out to work. It required that fees be raised to attract better employers, that half the fee only should be paid after three years and that indentures should end when the apprentice reached twenty-one, though compliance with these regulations was almost certainly uneven.

It is clear, however, that the Foundling Hospital faced similar problems to the parishes. It had even apprenticed a girl to the Brownriggs but she luckily ran away and the Hospital refused to send her back. But luck ran out on some others. Sarah Butterworth, put out to a Manchester weaver, was brutally murdered in 1771 and there were numerous complaints of sexual and physical assaults, of overworking and neglect.[38]

Apprenticeships determined as far as possible that children raised by the parish and saved for the nation would not remain workless or impose a future burden on the ratepayers. That problem of the idle poor, those considered able but unwilling to work, was a constant aggravation to the parish authorities in London throughout the century. The vagrant class of wandering casual poor, among which were many of London's beggars, comprised one constant element. They were objects of repression, dealt with by arrest, perhaps a whipping and hard labour in Bridewell, and then by passing them to parishes where they could claim a settlement.

As a House of Correction since Tudor times Bridewell, at the City end of Blackfriars Bridge, was used as a place to punish those committing minor misdemeanours like vagrancy, prostitution, assaults, petty thefts and street disorders. Besides the whippings for which it was notorious, hard work was at the heart of its corrective policy. Vagrants and the disorderly poor were set to work beating hemp for rope making, lack of effort rewarded by further beatings. But over time it also became a place for the City to apprentice some hundred or so children who were accommodated in Bridewell and put to work under twenty 'Arts masters', 'decayed tradesmen, such as shoemakers, taylors, flax-dressers, and weavers'. Boys satisfactorily completing their apprenticeships were entitled to freedom of the City and sent into the world with a £10 dowry. The 'Bridewell Boys' could occasionally be an unruly element, but they were also the backbone of the parochial fire fighters in the City, and some former apprentices were said to have risen over the years to become among Bridewell's 300 governors.[39]

It was from Bridewell that the idea of the workhouse emerged, a place where the able-bodied poor would have to live and work in exchange for the relief given them by the parish. The first was the London Workhouse in Bishopsgate Street, established in 1699 for poor children, vagrants, rogues and sturdy beggars, adults treated much as they would have been in Bridewell. Orphaned or abandoned children were taken from the City streets to the workhouse when they had no apparent parish of settlement. There they were 'taught to read, write, and cast accounts' and put out as apprentices. And they were brought up in the Church of England and taken to St Helen's Bishopsgate every Sunday.[40]

The workhouse idea caught on, if only hesitantly. In 1723 Sir Edward Knatchbull's act gave all parishes the right to rent or build workhouses, and for smaller parishes to 'unite' to share that task where necessary. There followed a spate of workhouse building in London such that, as early as 1725, workhouses were fully operational in City parishes like St Giles Cripplegate and in the crowded inner suburbs like Whitechapel, St Giles-in-the-Fields and others, and more were planned in Westminster at St Martin-in-the-Fields and St James's. The work to which the poor were set was picking oakum or 'junk', teasing apart the tarred and knotted ends of rope to make them usable once more, and winding yarn for sack and sailmakers. Profits from the labour were used to offset capital and running costs – oakum, for instance, was bought in for 5s a hundredweight but sold on when picked for 12s. By 1732 there were at least thirty-eight workhouses in London and by 1776 some eighty-six. They were supplemented by 'poor farms', where

parishes without a workhouse could send their poor to be managed by
a contractor, often in old converted mansions in the outer suburbs north
and east of the City, with a few south of the river. Parishes with work-
houses also sent their truculent inmates to be farmed in this way.[41]

Under the pressures of fluctuating economic circumstances and the
widespread local unemployment they caused, the work element of the
workhouse tended to fade away so that by the 1770s and 1780s work-
houses were predominantly a shelter for the aged, the incapacitated
and the young. The able-bodied and their families were relieved at home
with a dole that in effect became a supplement to wages or a substitute.
This was a state of affairs explicitly sanctioned by Thomas Gilbert's
act of 1782, which effectively removed the able-bodied from the general
workhouse.[42]

By the end of the century the parish workhouse had elements, if not
of generosity, then certainly of humanity. The beginning of an infirmary
system for the sick poor, as part of or separate from the parish workhouse, had become a common feature in London, bypassing the need
for a charitable governor's introduction to the London hospitals. Around
1797 St Martin-in-the-Fields parish workhouse at Castle Street, Leicester
Square, housed 473 adults and 100 children, twenty-five of them infants.
Each adult had fourteen ounces of bread and a quart of beer a day;
lying-in mothers had porter; there were three beef days a week and a
pound each of plum pudding on Saturdays; and there were treats –
'baked mutton with potatoes once in six weeks; pease and beans with
bacon, and mackerel and salmon, once in the season; grey pease and
bacon, on Shrove Tuesday; bunns on Good Friday; roast beef on
Christmas-day; pork and pease-pudding on New-Year's-day; plum cake
on Holy Thursday'. Robert Blincoe, orphaned or abandoned by his
parents at the age of four to the care of the overseers of St Pancras in
the parish workhouse, felt himself 'well fed, decently clad, and comfortably lodged, and not at all overdone as regarded work'; his troubles
began when he was sent to a cotton mill near Nottingham aged seven,
around 1799. Hundreds, probably thousands, of London's workhouse
children were similarly indentured to mill and factory owners in the
Midlands and North from the 1780s into the early nineteenth century.[43]

Abuses within the institutions themselves were not uncommon. There
was terrible oppression of the child silk-winders at Aldgate workhouse
in the 1750s, with the pauper-woman aged seventy-seven in charge of
their work beating them mercilessly and killing a boy in July 1755. In

April 1768 a lunatic confined in the general workhouse at Bow, Poplar, cut off an attendant's head, 'entered the ward where the poor lay, and cut and mangled in a dreadful manner the helpless wretches as they lay in bed' – he had to be shot several times before he could be disarmed. At the Shoreditch workhouse the master made a profitable trade in dead bodies with his son-in-law, a surgeon, until they were exposed in 1785.[44] And so on.

The restrictiveness of workhouse life, the stigma frequently attached to inmates by a uniform or badge, and the often unsatisfactory accommodation provided were spurs to a kinder alternative at least for the deserving aged: the building of almshouses. These were provided by rich citizens and City companies for their decayed workers and dependants. Many almshouses pre-dated the workhouses, but from the late 1720s others followed for weavers, brewery workers, merchant seamen and others. By 1785 there were ninety-three almshouses in the metropolis for nearly a thousand aged men and women.[45]

Once more, 'parochial charity' and alms for the elderly all came at the price of religious obeisance. Workhouses were to be 'Nurseries of Religion, Virtue and Industry, by having daily Prayers and the Scriptures constantly read', their inmates '*content* and *thankful*, and do their Duty, that is, all they can do, in that State of Life wherein it has pleased God to place them'. It was customary for the workhouse poor to attend the parish church on Sundays, as at St Botolph's Without, Bishopsgate, 'where the old people set in the middle Isle, and the Children in the Gallery, that the Parishioners may see the good Order observed by them'.[46]

But one captive audience did not a congregation make.

'To Resest ye World ye Flesh and ye Devell': Religion

The polite ranks of eighteenth-century Londoners, so influential in the metropolitan culture, were not generally noted for their piety. But it would be an oversimplification to claim that the London rich were consistently irreligious. The nobility and gentry took a strong lead in such matters from the court. Till the death of Queen Anne in 1714 the court was pious and so, at least on the surface, were its lawmakers and courtiers. This was the time of the Fifty New Churches Act, which attempted to root religious observance in the suburbs of London, with uneven success. The courts of the first two Georges, on the other hand, were pious in public but far less so in private. George II, his Queen, his first minister, Sir Robert Walpole, and the chief courtier, Lord John Hervey, all (according to wicked Lord Hervey) thought religion a sham and observance the comfort of 'idiots'.[47] From 1760 the court of George III slowly restored much piety and provided a sympathetic climate for the rise of polite evangelicalism in the last two decades of the century.

Woven through this broad pattern were individuals and families who were deeply pious within the framework of the national church, and the large majority who paid constant lip service to its forms, not because they believed but because they acknowledged religion as one of the foundation stones of order in society. So Sunday churchgoing was an obligation obeyed by most of the London rich. But it was observed in a manner infuriating to the pious and amusing to many chroniclers of London life:

I live with an Uncle at the polite End of the Town, where, my Parents us'd often to tell me, I might meet with daily Opportunities to improve myself . . . But in this our great Parish-Church, where we abound with Lords, Ladies, and other great Folks, near three Parts in four demonstrate their *Politeness*, by the Sourness of their Countenance; and their Decency in their Loquaciousness during divine Service. Look when you will, you will find Heads and Tongues in a continual Motion. Pews are not able to part them: For I have seen venerable Ladies, of Quality too, whisper distinguishably loud over a Pew in the Middle of the Church. The young Ones are equally *polite*, tho' in a different Way. They enter with Countenances somewhat more than cheerful . . . But that may proceed from their vast Zeal to pay their Addresses to their numerous Acquaintance in the Congregation.[48]

'Martha Meanwell's' tongue-in-cheek complaint to the *Grubstreet Journal* in December 1733 that Sunday churchgoing was just one more of London's public entertainments was a common jibe into the mid-1760s and perhaps beyond. And churchgoing among the rich on any other day than Sunday was a minority taste indeed, 'enthusiasm' a rapid route to loss of caste in polite society. William Hutton, a dissenter from Birmingham, attended prayers at Westminster Abbey, read by the Sub-Deacon and Chapter, when 'the whole congregation, during a considerable part of the service, consisted solely of myself', and that was in 1784. On the other hand there were not a few who were devout among the wealthy, certainly in the second half of the century: in the aristocratic suburb of Marylebone, rich subscribers and benefactors were found for not only James Gibbs's Oxford Chapel in Vere Street in the 1720s, but no fewer than seven more dotted around the parish between 1766 and 1795.[49]

Throughout the metropolis as a whole, however, the backbone to Protestant worship in London was provided by that medley of ranks comprised in 'the middling sort of people'. Sunday church- or chapel-going seems to have been common among respectable tradesmen like master artisans, shopkeepers and professionals. When complaints arose late in the century of empty City churches on Sundays, they denoted less a falling off of the habit than the weekend migration of citizens to their country boxes. Star preachers, of whom there were many, could always still draw a City crowd, as on one Sunday in August 1772 at St Andrew-by-the-Wardrobe, Blackfriars: 'Attended wth a Croud & Church full both wthin and wthout, who came together to have ye Pleasure of Hearing a young Divine . . .' The connection between parish and local government – churchwardens included among the overseers of the poor, constables and surveyors elected annually at vestry meetings which the clergyman had the right to chair – was the foundation of civic life in Westminster and the suburbs. And though the link was not so strong in the City, and weakened as suburbanisation took a stronger hold, the ordering of precedence by pew still symbolised a hierarchy based on wealth and public office-holding.[50]

The middling sort also comprised the large majority of London's Protestant dissenters. '*England* is properly the country of sectarists,' Voltaire wrote after his visit of 1729–31. 'An *Englishman*, as one to whom liberty is natural, may go to heaven his own way.' The dissenting way was to reject the authority of bishop and rector and to construct a church that best satisfied its members' spiritual needs. But usurpers of power might arise in any congregation and the dissenting communities in London proved notoriously fissiparous, with frequent movement of believers between the various sects. There was frequent movement, too, between dissenters and the established church, some attending both church and chapel, with some large defections from dissent to orthodoxy at the end of the 1720s, for instance. It seems likely that dissenting communities in London, at least as represented in numbers of meeting houses, declined somewhat over the course of the century. In the 1750s, though, their vitality was charted by William

Maitland, who listed the addresses of thirty-three Anabaptist meeting houses, twenty-eight Presbyterian, twenty-six Independent, twelve Quaker, three Nonjuror and two Muggletonian, 104 in all. In addition there were twenty-one French chapels in the Huguenot districts and eight German, Dutch and others. Of the English dissenting meeting houses in London, most were in the City, especially its eastern parts, in the inner eastern and northern suburbs (with a notable cluster in Holborn), and south of the river in Southwark; but there were also some in Westminster and in outer suburban villages and towns like Islington, Stoke Newington and Hackney, famed for its dissenting schools and academies.[51]

The plebeian locations of many of the dissenting meeting houses indicate that Protestant dissent found adherents among the lower ranks of the middling sort and among the journeymen and their families. There were also many rich dissenters, the Quakers especially prominent among the great brewing families and among West Indian sugar planters with slave-holding estates: John Coakley Lettsom, the physician-philanthropist, inherited slaves in the Virgin Islands whom he emancipated on reaching his majority; and John Howard's father, a strict dissenting City carpet warehouseman, left his son a large fortune in property and land, and so on.

These were truly zealous men, but zeal might also be found among the poorer sort of dissenter to whom dissent's rejection of temporal authority and high valuation of an independent spirit were great attractions. We might cite Samuel Kevan, the Scottish slater who arrived in London in 1784 aged twenty-one. His religious affiliations led him to a meeting of 'Scotch Presbyterians' in Swallow Street, Piccadilly, but he also found occasional solace in other congregations, even in the established church. With a room of his own in Tooley Street, Southwark, 'my grand object was to obtain information – There were two or three Grand points of pursuit – Better acquaintance with the Bible . . . Better information on the Arminian & Calvinistic dispute, The Baptist controversy – The History of the church and reformation of Scotland; and being without any near associates, Books was my only resource –'[52] His reading seems to have led him back to his strict North British Presbyterian roots.

In 1795, as we have seen, Kevan married his Southwark employer's widow. She was a Baptist, an Excellent Woman, but my Situation as it respected a religious profession, was extreamly Awkward. I was attached to a people at a vast distance, and it was a Maxim, that, hearing Minister's of a different persuasion was <u>criminal</u>. consequently in every Sermon I heard I had incurred new Guilt, a new challenge of conscience – while my wife was full in Opinion that to omit public worship entirely was a real, & serious Sin – There lay my Pinch . . .[53]

In general, with give and take on both sides, they managed to rub along well enough. But when Kevan's first son, Samuel, died at five months in February 1797, he did not attend the funeral because of his distaste for an alien service and preacher: 'I always think on this with regrate,' he wrote a long time after.[54]

Kevan was a journeyman and dissent had a strong resonance among the most serious-minded and aspiring of his class, and among the artisans with whom the journeymen were so closely connected. Other plebeians could be found as devout as Kevan, even – though much more rarely – in the established church. William Woodman was a cockney citizen, almost certainly a wig maker, earning a comfortable wage of £50–70 a year. He lived at home with his parents, or probably just his mother, during 1707–9, a period for which some of his diaries and accounts survive. He was an active churchgoer, patronising at least thirteen churches, mostly in the City but as far afield as 'Hackny', 'Chelsy' and 'Iselton' (Islington). He was a young man and he loved a drink. But he suffered sadly for his sins when it came to his 'dewoshans':

here did I macke my Solom vous of a mendment to stand upone my gard to resest yᵉ world yᵉ Flesh and yᵉ Devell and with open harte and mynd to folo yᵉ my God here did I all so onfer yᵉ my Self Body and Soul to thy Sarvcs and I must humlly be sche [beseech] yᵉ to Except thes my ofring for Jesus Christs Sacke and Sche my parding and protect thy one Amen.

       This is yᵉ copey of my agreement and Recekinashon of my Self to my God thrue yᵉ words of Christ.
              Witness my name Wᵐ Woodman.[55]

But just five days later he stumbled once more: 'Give waye to Sin to Lust in my flesh . . . have marcy one mee o Lord Lett not Sin prewall I be sche yᵉ Amen.'[56]

Even among the very poorest, those far too ragged or dirty ever to attend church or chapel, some sense of religion was often strongly present. A devout Catholicism was widely prevalent among the Irish poor. And something of the trappings of religious belief was widespread even among the poorest cockney and provincial Londoners. Jacob Ilive noted how the poor prisoners at Clerkenwell House of Correction in the 1750s

can scarce speak a Word without Swearing, Blasting or Profaning the Sacred Name of GOD. Yet they are great Believers, every one of them implicitly believe all the Articles of the Christian Faith; they believe also in Devils, Demons, Spirits, Angels and Saints. They hope they shall live, they say, to repent of their Sins, and they doubt not, but they shall be saved, as well as the Thief on the Cross, or as *Mary Magdalene* was, thro' the Merits, Intercession, Death and Blood of the Blessed JESUS.[57]

The poor were not the only ones to believe in devils, demons and angels. Even in an age that congratulated itself on its enlightenment this widespread penetration of religious ideas tended to credulousness, superstition and a ready belief in the miraculous intervention of the divinity. Astrologers, occultists and fortune-tellers were popular throughout the century, even though risking severe punishment in the courts. Ghosts caused sensations at Sherrard (now Sherwood) Street, Golden Square, in July 1755, most famously at Cock Lane, west of Smithfield, in 1762 – Samuel Johnson was instrumental in uncovering the hoax – at Stockwell ten years later, and doubtless on other occasions. Fast days were held and generally observed as a sacrifice to preserve the nation from plague, the French and other evils. Two earthquakes that shook London a week apart in March 1750 provoked prophecies a month later by a Swiss Life Guardsman of a general destruction of the capital that caused an exodus to the fields; a subsequent pamphlet by the Bishop of London called for 'Repentance' by the sinful Londoners to divert 'the Displeasure of the Almighty'. The Lisbon earthquake of November 1755 armed the clergy for war once again, with a public fast and ban on masquerades, God 'hating dominoes', as Horace Walpole put it. Even Hester Thrale, so sensible in so many ways, was constantly alert for heavenly signs and portents. And as late as March 1795 many thousands left town for the fields when Richard Brothers, a mad naval lieutenant calling himself the 'Nephew of God', prophesied London's destruction by an earthquake, in punishment for metropolitan wickedness.[58]

Superstition and credulousness were strong elements in the appeal of Methodism for the London poor. This was an evangelical movement within the established church that had many of the oppositional overtones of dissent. Its leading lights were George Whitefield and John Wesley, both clergymen, the latter an authoritarian leader whose detailed control over 'the Methodist Society' contrasted strongly with practice in the dissenting sects. Outside London, Methodism found great resonance among labouring communities, Wesley pursuing his mission throughout Britain, Ireland and America with energy exhausting to behold. But, though originally from Lincolnshire and a restless traveller, Wesley made London his home. He was 'reborn' in a meeting room of one of the church's religious societies at Aldersgate Street in May 1738. By then George Whitefield, an even more charismatic and emotional preacher than Wesley, had already made a mark in London. From late 1738 they were both controversially active in the metropolis.

Controversy lay in style and content. Their message of personal salvation through sudden conversion to faith, open to all irrespective of previous religious practice and piety, upset many among the orthodox clergy. Barred from some pulpits, Whitefield and Wesley preached in churchyards and open spaces. This 'field-preaching' drew crowds of many thousands, at first out of curiosity, later with a core of believers among them. Among their favourite venues were Moorfields, Kennington Common, Blackheath and Hackney, and their most popular meeting houses were in plebeian districts like Smithfield, Spitalfields, Deptford and Hoxton. Wesley's preaching was often accompanied by disorder. The extraordinary gestures and acclamations and rolling-eyed fits of the 'saved' provoked the sceptical to exasperated violence, among them many of the poor labourers whom Wesley was most anxious to reach. The 'rabble' let loose an ox among an open-air meeting at Charles Square, Hoxton, in July 1741; they stoned the meeting room at Long Lane, Smithfield, in January 1742 so badly that rocks and tiles fell 'among the people, so that they were in danger of their lives'; a few days later a congregation at Chelsea was smoked out with 'wild-fire'. These struggles were most frequent in the early years of the agitation, but even as late as March 1760 a Methodist preacher was nearly beaten to death by a crowd at Kingston.[59]

London Methodism put down stronger roots when Wesley leased a disused ironworks that had made cannon in the Civil War in the fields south of Old Street. By September 1740 he had converted 'the Foundery' to make a chapel seating 1,500 and a small charity school, with a home for himself over the shop, as it were. From around 1740, through all his travels, he constantly returned to London and made a point of trying to spend the end and beginning of every year there. When the Foundry's lease expired the Methodist Society was rich enough to buy land and build a new chapel in City Road, with a house for Wesley adjoining. The chapel was opened in front of enormous crowds in November 1778.

Similarly, George Whitefield, with whom Wesley had split in 1741 over a doctrinal matter, built a wooden 'Tabernacle' that same year north of Moorfields and close to the Foundry, followed by a more permanent chapel on the west side of Tottenham Court Road in November 1756. A Gloucestershire man by birth, Whitefield made London his home, his wife and family staying there during his inter-minable travels – he died in Massachusetts in September 1770.

Both preachers especially directed their propaganda of new birth through faith at the plebeians and lower middling sort whom the established church had failed to reach. There were numerous attractive elements to their teachings. The promise of salvation in an afterlife had much to offer those whose lives were so hard, and often so miser-able, in reality. But there was also something essentially egalitarian in the Methodist message, Wesley in particular expressing a partisan love for the poor and disdain for the rich that can only have endeared him to his London congregations. Nor did his ready belief in devils and witches alienate him from poor Londoners as superstitious as he, though Wesley lost some of his flock by disowning George Bell, a corporal in the Life Guards, who impertinently foretold the end of the world on 28 February 1763 without his leader's authority, causing some panic in the capital. And there was a strong element of mutual self-help among the Methodists that contradicted the frequent criticism that they were only concerned with faith and not good works, among their own people at least. Each winter Wesley was active in raising cash, clothing and coals for the sick poor among his followers, as here in February 1753:

I found some in their cells under ground, others in their garrets, half starved both with cold and hunger, added to weakness and pain. But I found not one of them unemployed who was able to crawl about the room. So wickedly, devilishly false is that common objection, 'They are poor only because they are idle.' If you saw these things with your own eyes, could you lay out money in ornaments or superfluities?[60]

Even in his mid-eighties, indeed not long before his death in London in March 1791, he would go 'a-begging for the poor', and it seems that at any time around one in ten, say 200, of his Society members were in crying need and were relieved by their fellows in this way.[61]

This collective assistance among Methodists, mirrored in the dissenting sects, was a powerful incentive to membership, like many another of those societies in London we have already noted as easing the pathways through a metropolis of strangers. Religion could be the most effective Freemasonry of all. The Quakers, in particular, helped their brethren rich and poor through all the vicissitudes of life, providing a workhouse for their needy at Clerkenwell from 1702 and, at the other end, assisting their brightest sons, like John Coakley Lettsom, with contacts and support from the West Indies through Lancashire and Yorkshire to London, so that he might train as a physician with a fellow Quaker. And similarly among the Methodists, James Lackington, a journeyman shoemaker from Somerset, found his first London lodging with a 'holy brother' in Whitecross Street in 1773, and was helped to his first shop by 'one of Mr. Wesley's people' a year later.[62]

When Lackington first came to London it took him 'several weeks' to overcome his fears for his immortal soul there: 'I really was struck with horror for the fate of it; more particularly on Sundays, as I found so few went to church, and so many were walking and riding about for pleasure, and the lower class getting drunk, quarrelling, fighting, working, buying, selling &c.'[63] And despite the age of benevolence and the penetration of religion deep into the tissues of every public institution in London, it was the irreligion of the metropolis, as displayed in its lax observance of 'the Lord's Day' and in the general impoliteness of its streets, that most disturbed the pious conscience.

Some bravehearts went to war on the matter. From around 1690 there emerged local networks of puritans who combined with the parish authorities – churchwardens, constables and the watch – to construct what has reasonably been called a religious police. It seems to have begun in the Tower Hamlets in a society to suppress bawdy houses, with a second along the same lines in the Strand a year later, in 1691. Inevitably these local initiatives waxed and waned according to the zeal and capacity of the enthusiasts who joined them, but the Societies for

Promoting a Reformation of Manners, as they became known, were nourished from 1691 by Queen Mary's public support, which swept up noble courtiers, rich citizens and gentry, lawyers, churchmen and dissenters in a common cause. By 1701 there were local societies of tradesmen, of 'reforming constables', of local householders and – the '*Corner-Stone*' – a body of informers, paragons 'of *Zeal* and *Christian Courage*', who did the difficult work of bringing transgressors before the justices and were rewarded with half the fines. The Societies' main targets were 'Night-Walkers' and 'Gangs of detestable *Sodomites*', persons swearing and blaspheming in public places, the keepers of bawdy houses and gaming houses, drunkards and those not observing the Sabbath, especially poor shopkeepers. The informers and reforming constables met great abuse. At least two constables were murdered by resentful sinners: John Cooper at May Fair in 1703 and John Dent, trying to arrest a prostitute in Covent Garden in March 1708. And no informer was ever a popular figure in London, as we have seen. Even so, the numbers of prosecutions claimed by the Societies were staggering: 84,710 from 1690 to 1722; by the final year of their coordinated activity, around 1738, 101,683, all for 'Debauchery and Profaneness' of one complexion or another, and all in the metropolis alone.[64]

The decay of the Societies in the late 1730s did not mean that the activities of the religious police were allowed to lapse. Some church-wardens vigorously acted against Sunday trading – the main shopping day for the very poorest in London, we might recall – and tried to enforce church attendance as the law required: Nehemiah Rule and Edward Barnard, Hackney churchwardens, brought scores of Sunday trading charges before the magistrates in 1752, for instance. Indeed, every year saw prosecutions somewhere in London of the kind the Societies had made their own – against swearing, blasphemy, lewdness, gaming and so on. From around 1785 the Societies were revived in the era of polite evangelicalism, encouraged from 1787 by an active new Bishop of London, Beilby Porteus, and by another royal proclamation from a pious monarch, George III, 'for the preventing and punishing of Vice, Profaneness, and Immorality'.[65]

Almost all this religious policing was the work of a pious laity, aided but rarely led by ministers of the established church. There were doubt-less numerous individual instances of devoted service and religious zeal among the clergy; and many clergymen were highly educated, even learned, and eloquent theologians in print and pulpit. Yet as a class the clergy were not popular and not deeply respected, and the example of the eighteenth-century clergy, especially in London, was not inspiring to the Christian enthusiast.

One cause of unpopularity was plurality of livings – two or more parishes, often widely separated, in the care of a single clergyman: the vicar of St Leonard's, Shoreditch, for instance, lived in South Molton, Devon, and from 1780 to 1799 never visited his troublesome London parishioners 'but to receive their Easter offerings'. The burden of tithes to maintain the church and keep the minister seemed yet another undesirable tax on ratepayers already hard-pressed by the cost of poor relief, paving, lighting and the nightly watch, and it was especially resented among dissenters.[66]

Nor were clergymen always impeccable in their personal behaviour. The Rev. Laurence Sterne, the comic novelist, met Samuel Johnson just once, 'when his only attempt at merriment consisted in his display of a drawing too indecently gross to have delighted in a brothel'; one vicar at the west end of the town was 'so drunk' at the christening in 1764 of a boy called Alfred 'he had like have named it Hiccup!'; 'Pastor' John Ferdinando Lloyd was executed for a violent robbery at a tailor's in King Street, Soho, in August 1783; the Rev. Benjamin Russen, master of a Bethnal Green charity school, was hanged for a rape on a ten-year-old girl in December 1777; and the Rev. James Hackman was hanged for assassinating Martha Ray, Lord Sandwich's mistress, in April 1779, as we have seen.[67]

Besides such isolated but not infrequent cases, a large business was built up by some of the poorer clergy in London in irregular marriages without licence or banns, most notoriously by debtor-clergymen living in the Rules of the Fleet Prison. They were assisted by clerks or 'plyers' who touted for business in the streets and public houses thereabouts. These Fleet marriages proved hugely popular among the very poor for cheapness – at half a crown and a bottle of wine – and for convenience: not a few proved bigamous. Thomas Pennant recalled walking along Fleet Market

in my youth, on the side next to this prison, [when] I have often been tempted by the question, *Sir, will you be pleased to walk in and be married?* Along this most lawless space was hung up the frequent sign of male and female hand conjoined, with, *Marriages performed within*, written beneath. A dirty fellow invited you in. The parson was seen walking before his shop; a squalid profligate figure, clad in a tattered plaid night-gown, with a fiery face, and ready to couple you for a dram of gin, or roll of tobacco.[68]

Similar arrangements were to be had in the chapel of the Savoy Palace. But all these abuses 'by a Sett of drunken swearing Parsons' were outlawed from March 1754 by Lord Chancellor Hardwicke's Clandestine Marriages Act of the previous year. The Rev. John Wilkinson, chaplain at the Savoy, and his deputy were both transported for fourteen years for continuing the trade; some 1,400 of their marriages were declared null and void.[69]

Throughout the century it tended to be the eccentric, the deplorable and the disgraced among the clergy who seized the popular imagination and did much to tarnish both church and religion. Of the eccentrics we might take John 'Orator' Henley. Bred to the church in Somerset, in London from 1720, he held down clerical appointments in the City and Bloomsbury, combining preaching with an active career in hack writing for the disreputable bookseller Edmund Curll. From 1725, dissatisfied with the slow pace of his advancement, he split from the established church and founded around 1726 his 'Oratory', where he charged for admission those attracted by his lively strand of dissent. The Oratory, most famously at Portsmouth Street, Clare Market, and then in the disused Lincoln's Inn Fields Theatre nearby, became a place of disorder and riot, Henley's clerk wielding a club to secure the pulpit from invasion, the congregation brandishing staves for and against the theatrical Orator, his tongue loosened by addiction to drink. The Oratory was one of London's more boisterous Sabbath entertainments until Henley's death in 1756.[70]

As in Henley's case, the clerical connection with Grub Street was extensive, occasionally notorious, an alliance of God and Mammon plain for all to see. Joseph Brasbridge, the City silversmith, had his press advertisements drawn up by the Rev. Dr Cosens, 'an elegant writer and admired preacher in his day'. Lord Sandwich's chaplain Dr James Scott shamelessly puffed his employer in the newspapers. The Rev. Charles Churchill was a journalist and satirical poet so vindictive he was known as 'the Clerical Bruiser'. And the Rev. John Trusler, whom we last met visiting the condemned in Newgate, made a handsome living from around 1766 by hunting out old and scarce sermons, adapting them for the modern pulpit and selling them direct to cler-gymen through the post office in weekly numbers at a shilling a go; to complete the illusion that they were his purchasers' own work they were printed in copperplate script – 'they found a ready sale'.[71]

Most infamous of all the Grub Street clerics was the Rev. Henry Bate Dudley. 'He was constituted, both in mind and body, for the army or navy, rather than for the church,' recalled a close acquaintance. His propensity for fist fights and pistol duels earned him the title of the Fighting Parson: he made a considerable name for himself in 1773 by defending an actress taking the air at Vauxhall Gardens from the unwelcome attentions of some impertinent rakes. Fearing no man, he helped establish a new tone in London journalism of muck-raking scandal aimed at public figures, at first as editor of the *Morning Post* from 1775 and then in his own *Morning Herald*, set up as the *Post*'s rival from 1780. The *Herald* quickly became the best-selling newspaper in London, Bate Dudley's finances supplemented by secret payments for his press support of an unpopular government. He was immortalised as Snake in Sheridan's *School for Scandal* (1777).[72]

The whiff of clerical hypocrisy, brought daily to the nostrils of the London public through gossip and the papers, was never more pungent than in the case of Dr William Dodd. Like Bate Dudley, bred to the church, Dodd reached London from Lincolnshire via Cambridge when he was appointed curate at West Ham in 1752 at the age of twenty-three. There soon followed lectureships at City churches, even St Paul's, his handsome, fashionable figure combining with an emotional preaching style that even Horace Walpole found not unpleasing. Dodd had voluptuous appetites for polite entertainments, good food and drink, for dress (he was often known as 'the Macaroni Parson') and especially for the flesh – he kept a mistress in a house close to his marital home for a while. But his extravagantly expensive style of living was never matched by his income. He supplemented it, inevitably, in Grub Street with a litter of publications, including a novel, a Bible and a commentary in sixpenny weekly parts, and with a journal, the *Christian Magazine*, where he anonymously puffed his own sermons. Still his debts mounted, and he became greedy of appointments. He became a royal chaplain to George III and even built his own chapel near Buckingham House, the Queen's palace, to display his preaching talents. But the most prestigious of his sinecures was as chaplain to the Magdalen Hospital from 1761. It was a gratifying position for a voluptuary:

> See Talbot now, – who drank in pomp of sin,
> Thro' wretched want, a sad, bad Magdalene.
> Kindling new passions in her Nun's attire,
> Till D[od]d and D[ing]l[e]y are themselves on fire.[73]

Dodd's Sunday sermons at the Magdalen became an entertainment for polite society. His 'eternal bray' was witnessed by Alexander Carlyle, a Scottish cleric, in February 1769.

It being much the fashion to go on a Sunday evening to a chapel of the Magdalene Asylum, we went there on the second Sunday we were in London, and had difficulty to get tolerable seats for my sister and wife, the crowd of genteel people was so great. The preacher was Dr. Dodd, a man afterwards too well known. The unfortunate young women were in a latticed gallery, where you could only see those who chose to be seen. The preacher's text was, 'If a man look on a woman to lust after her,' etc. The text itself was shocking, and the sermon was composed with the least possible delicacy, and was a shocking insult on a sincere penitent, and fuel for the warm passions of the hypocrites. The fellow was handsome, and delivered his discourse remarkably well for a reader. When he had finished, there were unnecessary whispers of applause, which I could not help contradicting aloud, and condemning the whole institution, as well as the exhibition of the preacher, as *contra bonos mores*, and a disgrace to a Christian city.[74]

In 1774 polite society was scandalised to learn that Dodd's wife had sought to bribe the Lord Chancellor to give her husband the wealthy living of St George's, Hanover Square, and Dodd was struck from the list of the King's chaplains. The Dodds were mercilessly paraded as Dr and Mrs Simony in Samuel Foote's *The Cozeners* that same year.

Far worse was to come. As one of his many jobs Dodd had been tutor to the young Earl of Chesterfield some years before he succeeded to the title. To avoid further embarrassment from the Simony affair, Dodd fled to the Earl's house in Geneva, where he was kindly received. By 1776 Dodd was back in London. But early in 1777 he was desperate for money once more – mad for money might be a better way of putting it, for on 1 February he forged the Earl's signature on a bill of exchange and obtained £4,200. Within days the forgery was discovered and Dodd arrested. He quickly confessed and, his friends anxiously responding to his predicament, he was able somehow to repay the money. But he no

longer had a friend in Chesterfield, whose resolution not to compromise
was fortified, it seems, by his lawyers and the Lord Mayor, Sir Thomas
Hallifax, who remanded Dodd to Newgate to await his trial on a capital
charge. At the hearing in the Guildhall, it is said that Dodd begged
Chesterfield on his knees to withdraw the charge and 'moved everyone,
but the polished statue to whom he addressed himself'.[75]

At the Old Bailey on 22 February Dodd was convicted and sentenced
to death. The jury recommended mercy and, despite the cavortings of
the Macaroni Parson over a number of years, his desperate plight
brought most of the press and many in the metropolis behind him.
Petitions for clemency were energetically pursued, one signed by 23,000,
Bate Dudley and other supporters, 'with a long roll of parchment, pens,
and ink-bottles in their button-holes, going from house to house in
Soho-square, to obtain signatures'. Among many who visited Dodd in
his spacious Newgate quarters was Samuel Johnson, who drafted for
him *Dr. Dodd's Last Solemn Declaration*. It acknowledged that his life
for some years had been 'dreadfully erroneous'. Johnson had written
'hypocritical': but, 'With this he said he could not charge himself.'[76]

Dodd was executed in front of a huge and largely sympathetic crowd,
estimated to be 40,000 strong, at Tyburn on 27 June 1777. He had
pinned his last hopes on friends enlisting the best medical help to revive
him from the scaffold. But after hanging his allotted hour, despite all
his surgeons' best efforts in the mourning coach, there would be no
reprieve for 'the Unfortunate Dr Dodd'.[77]

Why did the royal prerogative not extend mercy to William Dodd?
We have seen other instances where polite criminals, guilty even of
murder, were reprieved on the supplication of persons of quality, and
here the King himself was minded in favour of a man he had appointed
as one of his own chaplains. But it was said to be the intransigent Lord
Mansfield, Lord Chief Justice, who in the end successfully pleaded the
constitutional necessity of hanging a clergyman of the established church
for such a crime as forgery, so unsettling to the business of the nation
and committed at such an unsettling time.[78] For in 1777 the American
War, single-mindedly pursued by the King, was deeply unpopular in
much of the nation, especially in the City of London, whose Corporation
(the Lord Mayor notwithstanding) had petitioned vociferously for
Dodd's reprieve. And religion and politics in London had long been
inextricably mixed.

'No Hanoverian,
No Presbyterian': Religion and Politics, 1700–59

Religious tolerance lay only skin deep in London for much of the first fifty years or so of the eighteenth century. In 1714 old men and women could still remember the travails of civil war, when puritans in City and Parliament battled a monarch whose indebtedness to Catholic Europe seemed likely to re-establish the papacy in England. People only in their middle age had witnessed a king flirting with Catholicism removed by the threat of force of arms in a Glorious Revolution that established a Protestant succession. But the settlement of 1688–9 was still so fresh as to feel contingent and fragile and for the first fifty years of the eighteenth century there were moments when it might possibly have been undone. Religion and politics, then, were enmeshed so tightly they could not be disentangled. Politics seemed not just a party struggle over temporal power or the spoils of office but a war for the very soul of the nation. Though the two Stuart uprisings of 1715 and 1745 would shift events dramatically elsewhere, this was a struggle waged largely in London. Church, Parliament, City, court and Londoners – or, rather, factions within each of them – were all protagonists at one time or another.

There were some unlikely alliances. It was a notion popular among Londoners of all ranks as the century opened that the established church and nation were so entwined that a threat to one meant a threat to both. Within the church itself that view was propagated by the High Church faction, closely allied to land, the universities, high rank and the Tory party. It showed itself in a flowery ritual and a loyalty to the Stuart cause that was, or came close to, Jacobitism, the desire to restore James II or his successors to the throne. For much of the reign of Queen Anne, High Church and the Tory party were in the ascendance. Their Low Church opponents espoused the Whigs, trade and the City, and had a spartan approach to church ritual and a tolerance of fervent preaching that drew them close to the dissenters. For the High Church party, on the other hand, dissenters were loathed as much as, perhaps more than, papists. In the High Church view of the nation, the church was in danger most of all from those who dissented from its authority and so, by inference, from monarchy, hierarchy and all that kept society together. All this took a new twist in 1707 when, during a Whig inter-regnum in the administration, the Act of Union with Scotland brought accusations of Scotch Presbyterian influence penetrating every byway of London life. How these politics played out among Londoners was not always consistent. Daniel Defoe, a prominent dissenter himself, was prosecuted in 1703 for a satirical pamphlet lampooning the High Church party's position on dissent. He was imprisoned in Newgate and pilloried; but the London crowd, as we have seen, sympathised more with the independent individual oppressed by a bullying state than with the injured sensibilities of churchmen and fêted him for his courage while ignoring his opinions.

Something similar in reverse was played out in the first great popular disturbances of the century – the Sacheverell Riots of 1710. Dr Henry Sacheverell, chaplain of St Saviour's, Southwark, by all accounts owed more to good looks and oratory than to learning or piety. On 5 November 1709 he preached a sermon at St Paul's to the Lord Mayor and City Corporation attacking any toleration of dissent, warning that the church was in imminent mortal danger, and abusing the Whig ministers as its false friends. It infuriated the Low Church party and its allies in government. Unwisely, ministers arranged for Sacheverell's impeachment by Parliament for publishing a scurrilous and seditious libel. His trial began at Westminster Hall on 27 February 1710.

Many Londoners thought that not just one outspoken clergyman but the whole church was under attack by the forces of Presbyterianism. Prayers were said for the relief of the martyred Sacheverell in pulpits up and down the metropolis and beyond. Each day his coach was escorted to and from his lodgings at the Temple 'by a most furious and insolent mob', who demanded that hats were doffed to Sacheverell and allegiance shown to church and nation.[79] 'High Church and Sacheverell!' was the battle cry and on the third day battle was joined in earnest. From the Temple a crowd

ran from thence like so many enraged Furies, to the Meeting-house of Mr. *Burgess*, a Presbyterian Minister, in *New Court*, *Little Lincoln's-Inn-Fields*, which they instantly breaking open, stript it of its Doors, Casements, Sconces, Wainscot, Pews and Pulpit, which they carried into *Lincoln's Inn-Fields*; and, whilst they were erecting the same into a Pile, a Party was sent to surprise *Burgess* at his House, in order to have burnt him in his Pulpit on the Top of the said Pile: But *Burgess* providentially escaping out at a back Window, luckily got off without being made a Holocaust to Party Zeal.[80]

Over several days other meeting houses were 'pulled down' and their contents burned in Drury Lane, Kirby Street (Hatton Garden), Blackfriars, St John's Square (Smithfield) and elsewhere. Force was met with force, the City's trained bands called out by beat of drum to preserve the chapels, and the Horse and Foot Guards to protect the Bank of England. The houses of the Lord Chancellor and other notable Whigs were threatened and John Dolben, a Member of Parliament active in the impeachment and a mortally sick man, had to swear he was someone else to avoid being hanged from a tree.[81]

Yet in the long run it was Jacobitism that proved far more important than anti-dissenter prejudice in dividing Londoners. High Church, Tory and Jacobite were seen by many as equivalent terms for the first quarter of the century and beyond. Jacobite hopes of the restoration of a Stuart monarchy rose sharply with the long-approaching demise of Queen Anne, but were dented by the proclamation of the Hanoverian Prince George as king on 1 August 1714. He was received in London with great processions and rejoicing on 20 September. But he was not welcomed by all and the hopes of a Stuart revival were not entirely dashed. As news reached London of James II's son planning an invasion from France 'the City Rabble', whether in instinctive opposition to foreigners or stoked by Jacobite incendiaries, took to the streets. On 28 May 1715, the King's birthday, official celebrations provoked extensive rioting in the eastern part of the City around Cheapside. 'Gentlemen' drinking George's health were assaulted, windows broken, threats made to pull down houses illuminated for the King, and constables and watchmen knocked down and beaten. The political objectives of these disturbances were evidenced in the rioters' cries: 'no *Hanoverian*, no *Presbyterian*; *High-Church* for ever; *High-Church* and *Ormond* [a Jacobite soldier-politician soon to flee to France]; *High-Church* and *Sacheveral*; a *Second Restoration*; no King *George*, but King *James* the 3d . . . and the Race of the *Steuarts* for ever'. The Riot Act, requiring a crowd to disperse on pain of death once a magistrate had read a statutory proclamation, was made law that July.[82]

Two months later the Jacobite rebellion of September 1715 and its bloody aftermath the following year once more set Londoners at one another's throats. Supporters of the Hanoverian succession organised themselves around City alehouses to drink the King's health from mugs decorated with his portrait. Each 'Mug-House' was equipped with 'a great Number of Ashen Cudgels, not unlike Quarter-Staves', used to quell any expression of Jacobitism in the streets. In July 1716 a furious Jacobite crowd attacked a prominent mug-house run by Robert Read in Salisbury Court, Fleet Street. The crowd was armed with pickaxes, stones, bottles and hundreds of sticks given out by sympathetic shop-keepers along the way from St Giles through Holborn to Fleet Street. Among its number were noted a watchmaker, a servant to rebels awaiting trial in Newgate, a brewer's assistant, numerous apprentices, women who used their iron-shod pattens as weapons, and one man who told the Old Bailey he 'had no Friends in the World' to give evidence on his behalf. Read defended his house with a blunderbuss and other firearms and one of the crowd was shot dead. At least five men were later executed under the terms of the new Riot Act.[83]

Jacobitism remained a force in London. Rumours of plots and repres-sion of anti-Hanoverian behaviour marked the years that immediately followed the '15. Jacobite printers and publishers were fined and impris-oned and some were publicly whipped; journeymen 'reflecting on King George' in public places were fined, pilloried or whipped along the streets; soldiers were flogged for drinking the Pretender's health; Augustin Moor, a chairman, was whipped from Somerset House to the top of the Haymarket for spitting three times towards the face of the Princess of Wales and saying, 'He'd make as good a Princess of a Cobler's Wife', and so on. The discovery of a Jacobite conspiracy involving Bishop Atterbury in 1722 divided the London clergy once more, with prayers offered up on behalf of the traitorous bishop in many metropolitan pulpits. There was then a lengthy period of quiet, punctuated by rumours of 'seditious Discourses going forward in certain Jacobite Coffee-houses, and other private Publick-houses in the dark Corners of the Town', and by punitive action against Roman Catholics in London which helped keep the Jacobite fear alive.[84]

But in the 1740s another Stuart resurgence around the grandson of James II, the Young Pretender, seemed once more a possibility. Invasion fears in 1744 brought many arrests in London, with royal proclama-tions and loyal addresses to the King from the citizens and others. In August 1745 another invasion panic took hold and soon it became clear that a force from France had landed in Scotland and that the Scottish Jacobites had rebelled once more. The City's trained bands were mobilised, local tradesmen and others formed themselves into military associations – the 'Hanover and Cripplegate Grenadiers' were one of them – the 'compleatly clothed' gentlemen of Fleet Street shouldered arms, London parishes raised subscriptions that turned out soldiers for the King at £5 a noddle, and 3,000 men were armed by the Spitalfields silk manufacturers, no friends to a Catholic invasion from France. That December, as the rebels approached Derby, just 126 miles from Charing Cross, a proclamation offered a reward of £100 for every Catholic priest arrested in London. The guards were ordered to form a camp at Finchley – among such fright and chaos that Hogarth made the departure of a regiment from Tottenham Court into one of his most memorable satires – and other regiments marched through the capital for the Kent and Sussex coasts. The militias were to be alerted to any 'tumult or insurrection' in London with cannon-fire from the Tower and St James's Park. And there was a general fast to entice God to the side of George II. In the event the rebels got no closer to London than Derby and the '45 would be the last great Jacobite spectacular. But no one knew that at the time, none less than the Jacobites. A plot to kidnap the royal family and replace them with Stuarts was thwarted in 1752. And whispers that the Young Pretender was secretly in London recruiting insurrectionaries continued well beyond the 1750s.[85]

The terrors of 1715 and 1745 made life even more difficult for the few thousands of Roman Catholics living in London. There they were theoretically subject to specially draconian restrictions that applied nowhere else in the nation. The century had opened with a proclama-tion in 1700 'banishing all Papists and other Malcontents from the Cities of *London* and *Westminster*' on the discovery of caches of arms and ammunition. An act of Parliament in force that same year for Further Preventing the Growth of Popery made anyone keeping a Catholic school liable to life imprisonment, disinherited Catholics from owning land and so on. Persecution was screwed tighter in 1714, 1715 and 1722.[86]

Not all Catholic worship was forbidden. For convenience sake, the ambassadors of some friendly foreign courts in London were allowed chapels that provided some succour to their religious brethren from England and Ireland: the Portuguese ambassador's chapel at Warwick Street, Golden Square, later moving to South Audley Street, Mayfair; the Imperial ambassador's at Hanover Square; the Venetian ambassador's at Suffolk Street, Haymarket; and, 'finest and most frequented' of all, the Sardinian envoy's chapel in Duke Street, Lincoln's Inn Fields. There was also by 1760 a long-tolerated Catholic 'Meeting-House' in Butler's Alley, Grub Street. We shall encounter many of these places again.[87]

Despite these and other small acts of tolerance, continued affronts remained the lot of Roman Catholic Londoners in the first half of the century. Insults were graved in stone. The base of the Monument commemorating the Great Fire of London carried throughout the century a 'deeply engraven' inscription blaming the Fire on 'the Treachery and Malice of the Popish Faction . . . for the extirpating the Protestant Religion and English Liberties, and to introduce Popery and Slavery'. The London calendar kept many days in ways designed to offend Catholic neighbours. Guy Fawkes Night involved 'processions in carts of the Pope and the Devil' to be burned on bonfires; and unlit windows risked a volley of stones as denoting houses of Jacobites or papists. Less than two weeks later on 17 November, the anniversary of Queen Elizabeth's birthday, 'the Pope, Devil, Cardinals' were again burned in effigy. Celebrations for and against the Stuart cause marked 30 January, the anniversary of Charles I's execution, which some called 'martyrdom' and others a triumph of puritan justice. Those of the latter conviction feasted traditionally on calves' heads as substitutes for the King's; the antics of one such so-called 'Calves' Head Club' at Suffolk Street in 1735, close to a Roman chapel, brought on a riot that had to be quelled by the Foot Guards.[88]

Around that time there were sustained efforts to persecute the London Catholics. A scare had evolved from 1734 when the press reported at least thirty mass-houses in London, perhaps twice that number, and some 300 priests. Sermons and dissenting lectures against popery stoked the fire in pulpits across the capital, leading to a fierce riot against a preacher at Henley's Oratory in July 1738 that had again to be put down by the guards. Some mass-houses used by the Irish poor were suppressed by the justices, there was violent anti-Irish rioting in 1736, as we have seen, and an attack in May of that year on the Sardinian ambassador's chapel. Anti-popery was also an element in some of the great charitable institutions for which this half-century in London's history was so renowned: from 1741, Roman Catholics were excluded from treatment as incurables at the Westminster Hospital and no priest could visit its wards; when the hospital's cook was found to be a Catholic a year later she was promptly dismissed.[89]

Anti-Catholic feeling, so closely linked with political fears of Jacobitism, was an important strand in the world view of many Londoners of all ranks and was especially strong in these first fifty years or so of the century. Given the continued existence of a Jacobite 'court' on the Continent, some of these fears were reasonable enough. Yet although the London dissenters were indefatigable opponents of the Pretender and the Catholics, their very minority status, their cliquishness, their separate forms and places of worship, so often allied with a belief that they had been specially chosen for salvation by God, and a marked republicanism shared by more than a few all combined to make them objects of suspicion and enmity among many Londoners of the plebeian sort and above. There seem to have been few attacks on dissenting meeting houses in London after the High Church agitations around the accession of George I. But the Quakers' instinctual opposition to war made them targets during the Seven Years War and perhaps at other times: there were attacks on Quaker-owned shops in the City in February 1756 for remaining open on a fast day; and a Quaker woollen draper had his windows and shutters broken for not illuminating during a night of public celebration in June 1759.[90]

But dissenters had worse than this to bear in the disabilities imposed on them by law. The Test Act of 1673 required all elected office holders, including parish officers, to take the sacrament of the established church. Some dissenters, like the Presbyterians, expelled from the church during the Restoration, could take the sacrament with a clear conscience, while others compromised their religious principles in doing so. All were criticised for adopting what became known as 'occasional conformity'. In general, the dissenters deeply resented the requirement and agitated against it throughout the century, without success. Where dissenters refused to comply, then fines became a source of income for public authorities, dissenters deliberately persecuted by election to a public office that it would be impossible for them to accept and expensive to decline. Dissenting ministers were exempt from election in this way by the Toleration Act of 1689, but that didn't stop the vestry of St Olave's, Southwark, electing a prominent Baptist minister to be collector of assessments for building a new church and sending bailiffs to seize his furniture when he refused; he successfully sued the vestry for trespass in 1744. A long-running dispute between the City and rich dissenters, whom the Corporation persisted in electing as sheriffs in anticipation of a substantial fine of £400 on refusal, was not finally decided in the dissenters' favour till 1767.[91]

So religion penetrated all significant political discourse among Londoners in this first half of the eighteenth century, whether the daily workings of local government or the most important questions of national sovereignty and security. It continued to have loud resonance in the years to come. But there would then be other elements in London politics which followed different fault lines than those of warring sects. The most important lay between the City of London on the one hand and the court of St James's, and its administration in Parliament, on the other. For generations, that vexed relationship too had been overlaid by religion. By 1760 those religious antagonisms had faded. Yet London politics in the second half of the eighteenth century would become more ferocious than ever. And much of the drama would begin with just one man.

John Wilkes

XIII

JOHN WILKES'S LONDON – POLITICS AND GOVERNMENT

'Wilkes and Liberty!' 1760–68

WHAT are we to make of John Wilkes? Here was a man whose wit and charm won him many loyal friends but whose friends could not trust him with their money or their wives and mistresses. Among the dominant features of his complex character – uxoriousness and lust; recklessness to the point of dishonesty with money entrusted to him; an unflagging belief that as a gentleman the world owed him a plump living with no need to work for it; unalloyed pleasures in books, languages and classical learning; selfless doting on his daughter Polly, the priceless jewel of his existence – one stands out more than any other: indomitable courage. He would be bullied by no man, not even his king. In the titanic struggle – for such it proved to be – between George III, his ministers and a large majority of Parliament on one side and John Wilkes on the other, Wilkes became a lightning rod for the resentments of the age. Behind him stood, first, a parliamentary opposition worried by an excess of monarchical arrogance that risked undermining the Glorious Revolution; second, the middling sort neglected by a corrupt administration and a parliamentary system incapable of representing their interests; and, behind all of them, the mass of unfranchised Londoners galvanised as never before in the cause of one injured individual who epitomised every cruel injustice of society at large. From 1763 to 1771 John Wilkes dominated the popular discourse of his time as few men or women have ever done before or since. Single-handedly he advanced the cause of liberty, the rule of law and the widening of democracy in ways that have proved irreversible. Yet it is hard to avoid the conclusion that he did so less to further the ends of liberty than to advance the material interests of John Wilkes, Esq.[1]

He was born probably in 1725, though he himself always gave the year as 1727, in St John's Square, Clerkenwell. His father, Israel, was a prosperous citizen manufacturer who had built a distillery and dwelling house abutting the north wall of St John's Church in the early years of the century.[2] Israel was a follower of the established church but his wife, Sarah, was a dissenter. Wilkes would observe the forms of his father's religion while consistently advocating religious toleration: his mother was an influential supporter of her son throughout her long life and there was much of the obstinate uncompromising dissenter in Wilkes's character.

John Wilkes was his parents' favourite son. Though marred by a jutting jaw and a disabling squint that focused his eyes just a few inches from his nose, the boy was brilliant, amusing and ingratiating. He was marked out not for the distillery but for a career as a gentleman. Sent to board at a school at Hertford and then to a clerical tutor in Oxfordshire, Wilkes developed a love of the classics that never left him – late in life he published new editions of two Latin and Greek texts, the first of which at least won him credit among scholars. In 1744, entered at Lincoln's Inn though not a student there, he enrolled at the university in Leyden, a finishing school for many English (and even more Scottish) gentlemen. There he developed a passion for the company of women that lasted into old age. Despite a 'horrid' countenance, as Horace Walpole called it, Wilkes boasted that it '"took him only half an hour to talk away his face"', and that he could outmanoeuvre the handsomest man in England for a lady's favours if he could be given a decent start in the wooing.[3] By his middle years Wilkes's teeth were uneven, bad or missing and he talked with such a lisp that he was at first hearing difficult to understand. But at no time did he lose the ability to talk away his face.

In 1747, keen to advance his fortunes, Wilkes's parents arranged for him to marry the daughter of a wealthy dissenting widow from Buckinghamshire who had a house in the City and worshipped at the same chapel as Sarah. It was an ill-made match. Mary Meade was older than Wilkes and could not satisfy his demanding ideals of beauty or sensuality. On the other hand she brought Wilkes land and property that endowed him as Lord of the Manor of Aylesbury. Exploiting his wife's bounty to the full, Wilkes entered the lists of country gentlemen with all their elegant amusements and undemanding obligations. He became a rake in London and a squire in the country. He was appointed a Buckinghamshire magistrate and was High Sheriff for the county in 1754–5. And through his connections he became a rake in the country too. He helped found the 'Monks of Medmenham' at a disused abbey near Marlow, bought by Sir Francis Dashwood and turned over, as far as we can tell, to feasting, sexual licence, even orgies; the brethren included Lord Sandwich, whom we have already met.

Bred a Whig and now a prosperous country gentleman, Wilkes developed political aspirations, standing unsuccessfully for the parliamentary seat of Berwick-upon-Tweed in 1754 and losing much money in the process. Relations with his wife, who could see her fortune being squandered and her domestic life a mockery, deteriorated such that in 1756 they formally separated. Wilkes agreed to pay her £200 a year; when he tried soon to renege on his promise the courts defended Mary, Lord Mansfield requiring the agreement to be enforced. In line with custom and law, Polly, their six-year-old daughter, came to live with her father at his lodgings in St James's Place.

In 1757, with the help of extensive bribery, Wilkes was elected MP for Aylesbury. Over the next few years his profligacy both private and public landed him in money difficulties that would dog him for many years to come and which from time to time became critical. He had no compunction in 'borrowing' from friends or misappropriating public or charitable funds entrusted to him. He became a governor of the Foundling Hospital in 1758, was treasurer of its Aylesbury branch hospital during the period of general reception and pocketed funds in his trust: his friends would eventually pay what was owed, but only many years later. And appointed an officer in the Buckinghamshire militia in 1759, he squirrelled away money intended for uniforms and recruitment, contriving to cover his tracks in the accounts.[4]

These difficulties had only marginal repercussions on Wilkes's political career. It flourished under aristocratic Whig patronage and with the crucial encouragement of William Pitt, hugely popular because of his aggressive management of the nation during the Seven Years War. All that changed with the accession of George III. A new policy edging towards peace forced Pitt's resignation and Wilkes became an active member of the opposition in Parliament. An ineffective speaker in the House of Commons, his eyes and teeth working against him, he found

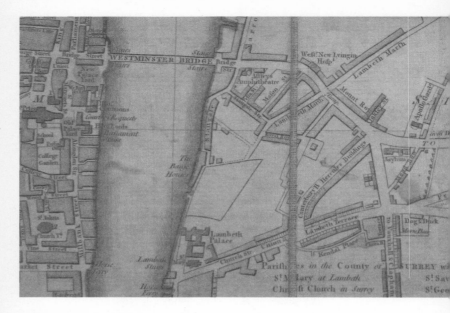

new opportunities for action in the brilliance of his pen. The King and his ministers, headed by the unpopular Scot Lord Bute, had established Grub Street journals to press the government's case before the reading public. One of them was the *Briton*, edited by Tobias Smollett, another Scot. On 5 June 1762 John Wilkes published the first number of an anti-government paper. In a caustic comment on the new dimension in British politics it was called the *North Briton*.

The *North Briton* at first kept up the pretence of being a Scotch paper delighted with its countrymen's success in procuring every powerful position in the new king's realm. It was written by Wilkes, with some help from a new friend, Charles Churchill, 'the Clerical Bruiser', and it all had a knockabout humour that can still raise a smile. Arguments used in the government press were rebutted with vigour in the *North Briton*, every government pamphleteer and supporter excoriated less with abuse than with a knowing wink. Samuel Johnson was mercilessly teased for having described a pension in his *Dictionary* as 'pay given to a state hireling for treason to his country' and then accepting one from Lord Bute worth £300 a year: in the *North Briton* he would ever be 'Pensioner Johnson'. No one

Westminster to St George's
Fields, 1790

was immune. *North Briton* No. 17 turned angrily on Wilkes's old friend William Hogarth, now an elderly and ever-prickly man, for wielding his pencil in the interests of government. In all this, Wilkes contemptuously rejected the publishing convention of disguising names with asterisks and dashes to avoid a libel suit. And his wide reading in English history and the classics gave him a store of parables with which the overweening tendencies of King and administration might be readily compared. It all proved hugely popular and influential, less thorn than dagger in the side of government. As such it was also hugely dangerous to the person of John Wilkes. A satirical thrust at the horsemanship of the Earl of Talbot, Lord Steward of the Household, brought about a duel in August 1762 in which Wilkes's cool head and good-humoured courage won him many admirers when the facts were later made known. On this occasion the duel proved harmless to both parties.

On 8 April 1763 Lord Bute abruptly stepped down as prime minister. Wilkes at first thought his work was done. But on 19 April the King's speech at the closing of Parliament extolled the virtues of peace and the relinquishment of territory and advantage won by seven

years   of war and sacrifice. It infuriated the opposition. After a gap
in publication of the *North Briton*, Wilkes brought out No. 45 on St
George's Day, Saturday 23 April 1763. It opened by exposing the
fiction of the 'King's speech', itself an affront to the pious appearances
of protocol: 'The *King's-Speech* has always been considered by the
legislature, and by the public at large, as the *Speech of the Minister*.'
Thus pretending to distance himself from an outright and possibly
treasonable attack on the King in person, Wilkes trained his fire on
George Grenville and the other ministers hired to do the royal bidding:

This week has given the public the most abandoned instance of ministerial
effrontery ever attempted to be imposed on mankind. The *minister's speech* of
last Tuesday is not to be parallelled in the annals of this country. I am in doubt,
whether the imposition is greater on the sovereign, or on the nation. Every
friend of his country must lament that a prince of so many great and amiable
qualities, whom England truly reveres, can be brought to give the sanction of
his sacred name to the most odious measures, and to the most unjustifiable
public declarations, from a throne ever renowned for truth, honour, and unsullied virtue.

Bold Wilkes must have known he had invited a martyr's crown. But
he had determined it should not be placed on his head; or, if it was,
then only after a most ferocious struggle. In the event it was a struggle
made easier for Wilkes by the hubris of his opponents, whose contempt
for the rule of law made even the country's highest judges his reluctant
allies – for a time at least.

Wilkes was widely known to be the author of No. 45 but, like all
political journalism of the time, the *North Briton* was anonymous. It
was an indispensable precaution. He could not be arrested as the author
without proof that he was indeed so. To gain the proof it needed, the
government issued on 26 April 1763 a 'general warrant' instructing the
King's Messengers to seek out and arrest the 'Authors, Printers &
Publishers of a seditious and treasonable paper intitled, the North Briton
Number 45'.[5] There followed moments of high drama heavily larded
with farce. Some forty-nine men were arrested over three days, from
master printers through journeymen and servants to the inky boy-'devils'
who scuttled about their workshops. Masses of papers were seized in
the hope of finding something to incriminate Wilkes, whose arrest was
left till last.

On 30 April, at his house at 13 Great George Street, the Messengers arrived with that same general warrant to arrest John Wilkes. He disputed their right to do so almost at swordpoint. But he agreed to be taken by a Westminster constable whom he knew. A hundred yards separated Wilkes from the Secretaries of State who had procured his arrest. Wilkes, a great walker, demanded to be taken there in a chair. When he arrived he refused to answer a single question: 'I thank God I am in a country where there is no torture, and if there was, I hope I have firmness enough to endure it.'[6] He protested the illegality of the general warrant and said he would sue both secretaries for unlawful arrest. Meanwhile 13 Great George Street was ransacked for evidence that Wilkes was the author of No. 45. Locks were picked, drawers opened, a sack filled with papers taken away.

Wilkes was imprisoned in the Tower of London, where cavalcades of carriages daily choked the streets in visits to see the hero of the hour. He promptly began proceedings claiming that as a Member of Parliament he was protected by privilege from arrest for a seditious libel. To the King's consternation the judges agreed. On 6 May Wilkes walked free from the court at Westminster Hall. Watching him at the hearing that day sat William Hogarth, pencil in hand. Two days later his famous engraving of Wilkes appeared in the printsellers' windows, price a shilling. It was a satire so breathtakingly true to the character of Wilkes, mischievous, lascivious, self-interested, insouciant, that it was designed to do him irreparable harm. But Wilkes's private vices rarely damaged his public reputation as the champion of liberty, and the hugely popular print found as many purchasers among his supporters as among his enemies.

Wilkes had described those supporters as the 'middling and inferior set of people, who stand most in need of protection', and it was they who mostly made up the huge cheering crowds that had accompanied his journeys from the Tower to the hearings at Westminster Hall. On his triumphant release from custody that 6 May 1763, 'Wilkes and Liberty!' became their cry.[7] That night there were bonfires, illuminations and fireworks across London. It proved to be just the beginning of Wilkes's victories in the courts of law regarding the events of 30 April. He triumphed over general warrants, winning £1,000 damages against the government for trespass in December 1763; at his instigation, some of his printers would win damages for false imprisonment in 1764; in November 1765 the Court of King's Bench under Lord Mansfield effectively ruled general warrants unlawful; and in November 1769

Wilkes won £4,000 damages for his treatment by the Secretaries of State more than six years before.[8]

Yet on his release from the Tower in May 1763 Wilkes would make the biggest mistake of his political life. Unable to find any printer prepared to take on his work, he set up a press at 13 Great George Street and hired journeymen to help him on a number of projects, one of which was to reprint the *North Briton* in volume form. In a fatal moment he instructed his men to set an obscene poem, written some years before for the Monks of Medmenham by Wilkes or his friend Thomas Potter, a notorious rake; more probably by both. The *Essay on Woman* was a satire on Alexander Pope's *Essay on Man* of 1733–4, later reissued with notes by William Warburton, Bishop of Gloucester. Wilkes gave strict instructions that no more than twelve copies should be run off and that no text should leave Great George Street. In fact no complete copy seems ever to have been printed at his house, though proof sheets of some pages were. One of these was secretly removed by a journeyman. The introduction to the poem not only put into Warburton's mouth obscene and blasphemous remarks but also made crude allusions to the chastity of the Bishop's wife. The missing sheet came eventually into the hands of government. And by mid-July the volumes of the reprinted *North Briton*, including No. 45, were in the booksellers' hands.

At the opening of the new parliamentary session on 15 November 1763, Wilkes knew he faced a ferocious battle in both Houses of Parliament. Frustrated by the unwillingness of the courts to silence Wilkes, the King sought to influence a more malleable tribunal, the House of Commons. In an extraordinary personal intervention in its business, the King by royal message complained of No. 45, 'that most seditious and dangerous libel', pointing out that Wilkes had escaped punishment because of his privilege as a member and now putting the matter before his peers. Led by Lord North, the House duly condemned the paper as 'a false, scandalous, and seditious libel' showing 'insolence and contumely' towards the King, alienating his subjects and inviting 'traitorous insurrections against His Majesty's Government'. Wilkes jumped up to object to the word 'false', inviting North to say just what in it was untrue, but North chose not to answer.[9]

At the same time, in the House of Lords, Wilkes was accused of publishing an obscene and blasphemous libel that violated the privilege of one of its members, Bishop Warburton. The accusation was laid by

Lord Sandwich, a Medmenham Monk, a former friend of Wilkes and one of the greatest rakes in England. He read to an astonished House from the sheet stolen by the printer:

> Awake, my Fanny, leave all meaner things,
> This morn shall prove what rapture swiving brings.
> Let us (since life can little more supply
> Than just a few good Fucks and then we die)
> Expatiate free o'er that lov'd scene of Man;
> A mighty Maze! for mighty Pricks to scan.[10]

Amid great disorder there were cries that Sandwich should stop, others that he go on. He went on. Sandwich then called witnesses to prove that Wilkes was the author, or at least the printer and publisher. Lord Mansfield intervened to ask that Wilkes be heard in his own defence and the House adjourned. That evening, as Sandwich left the House, he was booed in the streets for his treachery. He attended a performance of *The Beggar's Opera* that night and there were hisses in the audience as Macheath expressed surprise that his friend Jemmy Twitcher had given king's evidence against him. Sandwich would be known as Jemmy Twitcher for the rest of his days.

That momentous 15 November had yet further trouble stored up for John Wilkes. Samuel Martin, a former Secretary to the Treasury whom Wilkes had vilified in No. 40 of *North Briton*, rose in the Commons to call the anonymous author of that paper a 'cowardly rascal, a villain, and a scoundrel'.[11] Next day Wilkes and Martin fought a duel with pistols in Hyde Park. Wilkes was shot in the abdomen, the ball resting in his groin. Evidence later materialised which led many to conclude this was in fact an assassination attempt, Martin paid by secret government funds to be the murderer. For some time Wilkes's life lay in the balance. Despite his incapacity, both Houses of Parliament continued to move against him. Shaken by his injury, keen to see his beloved Polly, who was living in Paris, probably convinced that nothing he might do could save him from the remorseless antagonism of the King and his supporters in Parliament, he fled secretly to Paris on Christmas Eve 1763.

Wilkes would remain in exile on the Continent for more than four years. In January 1764 he was expelled from the House of Commons. In February he was tried in his absence before Lord Mansfield for publishing libels in No. 45 and the *Essay on Woman*, no attempt deemed necessary to prove him the author of either. He was convicted but not sentenced until he could come before the court. Summonses to require his appearance were not answered and in November 1764 Wilkes was declared an outlaw from his country. Those legal actions he had brought against government ministers were promptly stayed.

Despite his absence Wilkes remained a power in the land. The King's ministers sought an accommodation with him, offering bribes – even a pension – to keep him permanently abroad. He refused them and kept in touch with those of the opposition not alienated – as was William Pitt – by the *Essay on Woman*. He even made clandestine trips to London which were known to government, though no move was made against him for fear of reigniting support in the metropolis.

By the end of 1767, however, there were forces tending strongly towards a return to England, despite all the dangers that had in store for Wilkes's liberty. His financial difficulties were putting him under constant threat of arrest in Paris. And in England the impending dissolution of Parliament in the New Year offered some hope of a political shift that might favour his remaining friends among the Whigs. It also marked an end to his expulsion as an MP. If he could win a seat in the general election he would embarrass his enemies and stifle his creditors, privilege rendering members immune from a debtor's arrest. Signalling his intentions to his friends and the London papers, he returned permanently to the capital in early February 1768. He immediately announced himself a parliamentary candidate for the City of London.

'Life-Blood of the State': City versus Court, 1768–79

It seemed a wise choice. The Corporation of the City of London was the greatest municipal democracy in the country. Its rights and privileges were of great antiquity, its wealth in land, tolls and taxes immense, its status in the nation of unchallengeable independence. It could close its gates on king and Parliament and ritualistically did so in many official ceremonies. Its aldermen were frequently among the wealthiest commoners in England. They and the Lord Mayor had the right of access to the monarch, its Common Council the right to be heard before the bar of the House of Commons to ask for the City's grievances to be redressed.

All this power rested on a democracy with two main strands. Some 22,000 ratepayers, one in seven or eight of the City's population, had the right to attend their local Court of Wardmote to choose the alderman, deputy alderman and Common Councilmen for their ward. And some 8,000–10,000 higher-ranking freemen of the City companies, those who had paid an extra fee to don the company livery, elected at the Court of Common Hall candidates for the City's sheriffs and Lord Mayor from among the aldermen, and could directly elect the City's most important salaried officials when positions fell vacant. The livery and other freemen (perhaps 20,000 in all) also had the right to vote for the City's four MPs. The government of City business fell mainly on the Court of Common Council – some 200 common councilmen plus the aldermen and Lord Mayor. And the Court of Aldermen, twenty-six of them for twenty-six wards and the Borough of Southwark, comprised the City's magistrates and governed its prisons and courts of law, including the Old Bailey. The real or potential participation of so many citizens in the governance of the City gave its elected bodies, its magistrates and chief citizen, the Lord Mayor, unparalleled legitimacy and authority.[12]

Frequently, throughout the eighteenth century, the City Corporation had adopted a tone of strident opposition to the government of the day and, by implication, to the monarch whose government it was. At least, the majority within the Corporation, for often the City's governors and their citizens were not of one mind. The key division was class. Sir Robert Walpole's long administration, for instance, had large support among most of the wealthy Court of Aldermen in the early 1720s but very little among the Courts of Common Council and Common Hall. Some bitterly contested shrieval and aldermanic elections in 1723 ended in the success of anti-Walpole candidates in dubious circumstances. With limited City support, and then only among its wealthiest citizens, Parliament passed a City Elections Act that was the most impertinent intervention in the citizens' affairs since the reign of James II: it confirmed in statute a long-standing but controversial claim by the aldermen that they should have a veto on the legislative actions of the Common Council.

There followed a period of some quiet. But Walpole's proposal to place an excise, or purchase tax, on tobacco and wine, while reducing the land tax for country gentlemen, provoked fury in the City. The citizens viewed it as the thin end of a 'general excise' wedge soon to apply to all commodities, and smacking of the internal customs duties common on the Continent. The popular clamour against excise in London spread to all parts of the nation, so that 'the universal cry of the kingdom was "No slavery, no excise, no wooden shoes"'. Rioting in April 1733, 'fomented by the upper sort of citizens, and put in practice by the inferior', involved physical assaults on Walpole and his parliamentary supporters. He and the Queen, whose favourite he was thought to be, were burned in effigy in the City. The turbulence was such that Walpole withdrew his bill, to illuminations, bonfires and joyous rioting all over London and beyond. A few years later and the City's merchants and Corporation exploited the loss of British shipping to Spanish privateers to force Walpole's reluctant government into the War of Jenkins' Ear, instrumental in the Prime Minister's downfall in 1742. In 1746 the aldermanic veto was repealed by Parliament.[13]

Aggressive mercantilism assured the City's wholehearted support for the Seven Years War and for William Pitt, architect of many victories, especially in the Americas. Pitt was adored in the City and was given its freedom. But he resigned in October 1761 over the new King's refusal to declare war on Spain. With his removal the weight of City opinion shifted decisively against the King and Lord Bute.[14]

Pitt's leading ally, indeed his City spokesman since 1756, was Alderman William Beckford, he of the terrible eye. As we have seen, Beckford entered Parliament in 1747 as MP for Shaftesbury, speaking in the West Indian and American interests for some years before he busied himself with City politics. His independent wealth made him immune to government influence and his trading background was inimical to aristocratic privilege. From 1751 he leased 22 Soho Square, his town house for the rest of his life, in an unfashionable location away from the new smart suburbs further west. The following year he entered City politics as a freeman of the Ironmongers' Company and was elected alderman for Billingsgate Ward in July 1752. In 1754 he became one of the City's MPs and was elected Lord Mayor in 1762–3.[15] It was during his mayoralty that the Peace of Paris was signed, to the dismay of most in the City. The Court of Common Council refused to present the customary address to the King in grateful thanks for the peace, though the Court of Aldermen did so; it was carried to St James's Palace by just eight aldermen, their tiny cavalcade sarcastically saluted through the City with muffled mourning bells. Lord Mayor Beckford did not accompany them, claiming an indisposition.[16]

That was on 12 May 1763. Two weeks or so before, John Wilkes had articulated the citizens' anger in *North Briton* No. 45. Beckford had been generously praised in No. 39 for his opposition to the peace preliminaries. But his vulgarities of speech had been condescendingly satirised and Beckford would be a supporter of Wilkes without any close bond between them. They shared, however, a platform of regard for the 'middling and inferior set of people' against the interests of landowners and aristocrats. Just before Wilkes fled the country Beckford had written him a letter offering support and assistance, and in February 1764 he had argued and voted in the House of Commons against general warrants.[17]

There was no doubt, then, that the City of London would provide for Wilkes on his return from exile not only an enthusiastic popular following but the safest bastion in the nation from which to pursue his quarrels with the King and his ministers. Through February 1768 collections were made by his City friends to defray his election expenses. On 10 March he became a citizen of London, made free of the Joiners' Company by redemption, paying just 31s for the privilege.[18] When a public subscription list was opened to reassure his London creditors that their money would be forthcoming without the need to arrest him, Wilkes felt confident enough to put his name forward as a candidate. There were seven in all for the four seats, including the popular radical City aldermen William Beckford and Barlow Trecothick, an American merchant. There was noisy clamour at the hustings for John Wilkes, but householders and lodgers were noisier than the freemen, who alone held the vote, and Wilkes came bottom of the poll with 1,247 votes out of nearly 18,000 cast. Undaunted, hardly expecting to win against established City men whose votes had already been assured, Wilkes offered himself as a candidate for Middlesex, where the poll to elect two MPs for the county would open five days later on Monday 28 March 1768.[19]

In many ways, Middlesex was a better choice for Wilkes than the City. It was the most important county in England. Many citizens held freeholds in Middlesex and could offer Wilkes their votes untrammelled by City loyalties. And it comprised not just wealthy rural parishes and market towns but those City suburbs that had become a byword for poverty and the trading classes of the 'inferior sort', from Wapping to Whitechapel in the east, from Shoreditch to Clerkenwell in the north, with Holborn and St Giles in the west. These were populations suffering most from the immediate economic disruption of a terrible winter and from high prices and unemployment. We have already glimpsed the violent disputes between workers and employers in these very same districts that moved in furious counterpoint to the political agitations that Wilkes would now introduce to the metropolis.[20] And Wilkes would be the only opposition to two court candidates who had little purchase on the affections of the middling sort of Middlesex freeholder.

The five days were spent in consummate planning at the considerable expense of Wilkes's many friends. On the morning of the poll a caravan of 250 coaches decked in blue Wilkite favours joined a stream of voters and well-wishers pouring from London to Brentford, the county town ten miles to the west of the metropolis where the poll was held. Thousands of handbills and placards had been distributed. Weavers from Spitalfields and Bethnal Green took it upon themselves to harass the supporters of Wilkes's opponents making the same journey. Great crowds booed and jeered the court candidates at the hustings and cheered for Wilkes. Though the result was not announced till the next day it was clear from the polling books that Wilkes had been elected. His elated supporters rioted through London on their return, compelling illuminations on pain of broken windows, chalking 'No. 45' on coaches and doors, assaulting those who would not join in the cry of 'Wilkes and Liberty!' An attempt was made to storm the Mansion House, where Lord Mayor Harley had proved a vocal opponent of Wilkes, and Lord Bute's windows in Berkeley Square lost every pane. Next morning the result was confirmed. Wilkes headed the poll with 1,292 votes, his opponents recording 1,634 between them. Jubilant rioting continued in London that day too; heard among the cries were 'No King' and 'No regal Government'.[21]

John Wilkes's eruption once more into metropolitan and national politics shocked the King and his ministers to their very bowels. Their hopes lay in the court proceedings against him, unfinished from four years before. Wilkes had publicly promised to appear before the Court of King's Bench and Lord Mansfield at the beginning of the law term on 20 April and duly did so. After a technical hitch that further embarrassed the crown and its law officers, Wilkes was committed to the King's Bench Prison on 27 April to await sentencing. He was put in a hackney coach with three court officers as escort for the short journey across Westminster Bridge to the prison in St George's Fields. But on the bridge a vast crowd stopped the coach and unhitched the horses.

Wilkes told the officers to make their escape as he could not answer for their lives. And, drawn by his supporters, so many and so agitated that no civil or military force dared interfere, Wilkes was dragged in his coach through Westminster, beneath Temple Bar and across the City to a tavern in Spitalfields for a jubilant celebration of his rescue. Hours later, when darkness and some quiet had descended, Wilkes slipped out of the public house in disguise, crossed the river and gave himself up to the keeper of the King's Bench Prison.

There followed months of high drama on the streets of London and sordid manoeuvrings in St James's Palace and the House of Commons. At the King's Bench Wilkes was a celebrity prisoner, showered with gifts from London, the nation (perhaps not from Scotland) and America. The huge quantities of food and drink he received were such that all prisoners ate well during his stay. Every day, crowds of supporters shouted encouragement from St George's Fields. Fearful of an attempt to rescue Wilkes, the Secretary of State told the Surrey magistrates that there were troops at their disposal and ordered their engagement should the need arise.

On 10 May 1768 Parliament was opened by the King. The crowds at St George's Fields had swollen with huge numbers expecting to haul Wilkes in triumph to take his place in the Commons as member for Middlesex. But the gaol stayed shut, defended by magistrates, constables and 100 armed redcoats of the 3rd Regiment of Foot – with inept planning, or as a studied insult, a Scottish regiment. Early in the afternoon a row between a soldier and a Wilkite sparked a rain of stones, sticks and rubbish on the soldiers and peace officers. The Surrey magistrates read the Riot Act but the violence intensified and the soldiers were ordered to fire. Two volleys of musketball were shot into and over the crowd. Seven died that day, including a woman orange seller and a man driving a haycart, unluckily hit by a ball fired over the people's heads. Worst of all, William Allen, son of a farmer at work in his father's stables nearby, was mistaken for a ringleader and appears to have been shot in cold blood. The 'St George's Massacre', as it immediately became known, for a time elevated 'Wilkes and Liberty' into a life and death struggle between the people of London and their oppressors.

The deaths that day would have repercussions in the law courts for months to come. Magistrates and soldiers were accused of wilful murder but acquitted, the guardsman who killed William Allen absconding or sent into hiding. Despite the public anger, Wilkes was brought up to

Westminster Hall on 18 June, where Lord Mansfield pronounced a sentence of two years for the convictions for libel in 1764. Less the time already spent in gaol, he had twenty-two months to serve.

Though out of sight and unable to take his seat in the Commons, Wilkes was not out of the mind of public or Parliament for a single moment. In December 1768 he published with an anonymous introduction a letter that had fallen into his hands from Lord Weymouth, the Secretary of State, urging the magistrates to use firepower in St George's Fields some three weeks before the massacre. The House of Lords condemned the publication as a breach of privilege. That same month, Serjeant John Glynn, a radical barrister with strong City connections and Wilkes's lawyer, though no unequivocal admirer of his client, was chosen MP for Middlesex on the death of the member elected with Wilkes some seven months before. At the hustings in Brentford, Glynn's court opponent hired a gang of Irish chairmen, led by a giant of a man, Edward MacQuirk, who bludgeoned one of Glynn's supporters to death. MacQuirk and an accomplice were sentenced at first to death, then respited for transportation and finally pardoned by the King.

After weeks of tortuous proceedings in which Wilkes petitioned the House in person, accompanied by crowds of supporters from the King's Bench to Westminster and back again, the Commons expelled him in February 1769 for a seditious libel on Lord Weymouth and those previous libels for which he was now imprisoned. His seat in Middlesex thus became vacant. Though unable to attend the hustings he was re-elected on 16 February, only to have the House of Commons resolve that he was incapable of being elected MP. A month later, on 16 March, Wilkes was elected again, for the third time, with the same result. Each re-election had provoked jubilant rioting in London. And when six days later a cavalcade of City merchants in 130 coaches attempted to present a loyal petition to the King it was so mercilessly pelted with stones, mud and filth that only twenty-two battered chariots reached St James's Palace.[22]

But now the court had come up with a rival candidate nearly as pugnacious as Wilkes himself. Col. Henry Lawes Luttrell, a short stocky fearless bull of a man, was another notorious rake. His candidature infuriated the Middlesex freeholders and their disenfranchised compatriots. Bets were taken on whether Luttrell would live to see the contest to a conclusion.[23] He did, testimony to his own courage and to the chivalry of Wilkes's leading supporters, who may well have saved his life when he was mobbed on the way to the poll. But Wilkes was elected a fourth time on 13 April 1769, polling 1,143 to Luttrell's 296.

Two days later the House of Commons, egged on by an enraged King George, showed how low it could bend the knee. With Wilkes 'incapacitated' from standing, it ruled that every vote cast for him was void, ignored the plain wishes of the Middlesex freeholders and concluded that Luttrell was duly elected. To the opposition, it raised the possibility of the House of Commons selecting its own members if the voters' choice were incompatible with government's wishes.

There followed a nationwide revulsion against Parliament's treatment of Wilkes and its cynical disregard of the Middlesex freeholders' rights. Scores of petitions with tens of thousands of signatures were submitted to the King, praying for the relief of property-owners everywhere against Parliament's disenfranchisement of the Middlesex voters. Among the earliest and most vocal of all were the petitioners of the City, Middlesex, Westminster and Southwark, soon followed by counties across England. It was an agitation that spread from the grievances of Middlesex into a wider movement for parliamentary reform, especially in the metropolis. Many, perhaps most, of Wilkes's supporters had no vote at all and it began to be clear that a wider franchise and a more equal representation of urban areas – the tiny adjoining Dorset boroughs of Weymouth and Melcombe shared as many MPs as the City of London – would deliver a distinctively different House of Commons.

On 20 February 1769, meeting first at the London Tavern in Bishopsgate Street, the Society of Supporters of the Bill of Rights, later known as the Bill of Rights Society, was formed to raise funds to pay Wilkes's debts. Though thousands of pounds were collected, the debts proved bottomless. But the Society also took the first steps in petitioning the King after Luttrell's selection and in widening the dispute from Middlesex to attack government more generally in the interests of reform. The most vocal spokesman of the Bill of Rights Society was John Horne, vicar of Brentford, who later adopted the name of John Horne Tooke and fell out with Wilkes over money and policy.

Several City aldermen were among the Society's founders. And by that February of 1769, John Wilkes, up to his squint in debt and with no visible means of support, had himself joined the ranks of the richest men in the City of London. He was chosen alderman for the ward of Farringdon Without, one of the largest and poorest of the City wards, containing Smithfield Market, part of Chick Lane, Fleet Ditch and the Fleet Prison. Wilkes himself was still in prison when elected alderman in January 1769. Doubts were cast on the legitimacy of the election and it had to be re-run, but the householders of Farringdon Without would have no other representative. Wilkes was now one of the City's own.[24]

On 24 June 1769 the 'Livery in Common Hall assembled' delivered a 'remonstrance' to the King that was outspoken to the point of intemperance, accusing his ministers of corruption and illegality and calling for their dismissal. It was received by the King in silence and lay unanswered. Frustration in the City was such that William Beckford, 'feeble' and 'worn out' though he proclaimed himself to be, was chosen by the Livery and aldermen as Lord Mayor for the second time, a rare honour, in October 1769.[25]

In March 1770 the question of the unanswered remonstrance was revived by the Livery. This time a second petition to the King was prepared by the City Corporation as a whole and 'a bolder declaration both against the King and parliament', in the words of Horace Walpole, had never been seen. It reiterated the Livery's former complaints and called for an immediate dissolution of Parliament. The King waved away the remonstrance as 'disrespectful to me, injurious to parliament, and irreconcilable to the principles of the constitution'.[26] This out-of-hand dismissal seemed to strike a blow not just at the City but at the people of England. 'Junius', whose identity still remains uncertain and who had been the most able newspaper critic of the King and his ministers in the cause of liberty and reform, thought that:

At such a moment, no honest man will remain silent or inactive . . . The noble spirit of the metropolis is the life-blood of the state: from that point it circulates with health and vigour through every artery of the constitution. The time is come, when the body of the English people must assert their own cause: conscious of their strength, and animated by a sense of their duty, they will not surrender their birthright to ministers, parliament, or kings.[27]

Into this 'alarming crisis' stepped John Wilkes, freed at last from the King's Bench Prison on 17 April 1770. A week later he took his seat as alderman to enormous crowds gathered at the Guildhall. There would now follow two moments of extraordinary drama between City and Crown.

Deep resentment in the City at the King's repulse led to preparations for another remonstrance, with Alderman Wilkes on the drafting committee. When finished it was considered more diplomatic and conciliatory than the earlier petition and was presented to the King by Lord Mayor Beckford on 23 May. But the King's reply was briefer and even more dismissive. Once he had spoken the audience was at an end. To the astonishment of the King, his courtiers, the citizens and probably Beckford himself, the Lord Mayor again stepped towards the throne. He expressed his sorrow that the citizens had incurred their monarch's displeasure but angrily denounced the King's advisers.

Permit me, Sir, to observe that whoever has already dared, or shall hereafter endeavour, by false insinuations and suggestions, to alienate your Majesty's affections from your loyal subjects in general, and from the City of London in particular, is an enemy to your Majesty's person and family, a violator of the public peace, and a betrayer of our happy Constitution, as it was established at the Glorious Revolution.[28]

Those at least were the words as recollected that evening, probably embellished by the pen of Parson Horne, and immediately released to the newspapers. They were also engraved on the base of a memorial statue to Beckford, designed by John Francis Moore, erected later in the Guildhall and still to be seen there. For Beckford, elderly and sick, would not live to the end of his second mayoralty, dying less than a month later from what was thought to be rheumatic fever on 21 June 1770; he was about sixty years old.[29]

The second drama took longer to play out, had far larger consequences and seems to have been brought about entirely through the machinations of Alderman Wilkes, now of course one of the City's twenty-six magistrates. He had already infuriated government by refusing to accept 'press warrants' by which young men were arrested and forced to serve in the Royal Navy: he declared the warrants illegal in the City, a view long-held by some other aldermen before him, though not one shared by leading counsel. Nonetheless, men coming before him were set free, and disputes between the Admiralty and the City magistrates on this point rumbled on through the 1770s and were resurrected once more between 1788 and 1790.[30]

But this second issue concerned the freedom of the press, a matter genuinely – even for Wilkes the word is not too strong – close to his heart. He had gone out of his way to name the targets he had attacked in the *North Briton*. In defiance of the draconian libel laws he had preserved the anonymity of authorship even at the risk of his own life and then of his freedom. And it was an issue, as he well knew, that could embroil the City and Parliament in a mighty struggle. So it proved.

Parliament had long prevented newspapers and magazines reporting any of its proceedings as an indignity and a breach of privilege, constraining members' rights to speak their minds and inevitably involving error and misconception. In fact some compromise had allowed parliamentary business to be reported in the press without drawing down the wrath of the House of Commons by partly anonymising members' names and not claiming to report direct speech. At the instigation of John Wilkes, these conventions were breached in early 1771 by City newspaper publishers, who reported speeches and gave the speakers' names in full. This was objected to by a member. Two printers were ordered to attend the bar of the House of Commons but they ignored the summons. On 20 February a proclamation offered a £50 reward for their arrest.[31]

The vengeful vanity of the House of Commons was now transformed into farce, with Wilkes the chief comedian. With his connivance, one of the printers, John Wheble of the *Middlesex Journal*, contrived to get himself arrested by his journeyman and brought before Wilkes at the Guildhall. Wilkes found no charge made out against him and invited Wheble to charge his journeyman with unlawful arrest. He straight away told the Secretary of State of his actions and sent a printer's devil to the Treasury to claim the £50 reward for Wheble's man. That same evening, 15 March 1771, the other printer, John Miller of the *London Evening Post*, was arrested by a King's Messenger; but Miller had a City constable at hand who seized the Messenger and brought him to the Mansion House on a charge of unlawful arrest. Lord Mayor Brass Crosby, ill with gout, gave judgement from his bed, Aldermen Wilkes and Richard Oliver at the bedside. All three magistrates were Members of Parliament – or, rather, two were, Wilkes elected but incapacitated. The arrest warrant of the Speaker of the House of Commons was ruled inoperable within the City of London and the magistrates bound over the Messenger to appear before them on a charge of assaulting a citizen of London. The Deputy Serjeant at Arms, sent to the City hotfoot from the Commons, had great trouble keeping his Messenger out of Newgate.

As expected, there was a furious response from the Commons and from the King and his ministers. Crosby and Oliver were ordered to appear at the bar of the House – 'That Devil Wilkes', as the King called him, considered too troublesome to meddle with.[32] Crosby levered himself from his sickbed, his mayoral coach escorted to Parliament by huge cheering crowds. He was so ill that his examination could not be concluded and the matter was adjourned until 25 March. On that day a bitterly divided House of Commons, many members leaving the chamber in shame at this display of tyranny, sentenced the Lord Mayor of London and Alderman Oliver to be imprisoned in the Tower till the end of the parliamentary session. Oliver, asked if he wished to say anything in his defence, answered the House, 'I know the punishment I am to receive is determined upon. I have nothing to say . . . I defy you.'[33] In and around these dramatic events the London crowd proved equally tempestuous: they destroyed Prime Minister Lord North's coach, pulled him from it and cut off his hair, his life saved by members of the House who rallied round him.

The two citizens were not released from custody until 9 May 1771. Wilkes, fearing arrest, moved from his house at 9 Prince's Court, Great George Street, to the safety of the City. In fact, the Commons was becoming more circumspect. No attempt was made to arrest Wilkes and proceedings against the printers were quietly dropped. But the City remained defiant. Its remonstrances to the King continued. It permanently distinguished Brass Crosby's mayoralty by inscribing to his memory the obelisk erected at the crossroads in St George's Fields (now St George's Circus).[34] And John Wilkes's star continued to rise east of Temple Bar. In July 1771 he was elected one of the two sheriffs for London and Middlesex for the coming year. During his term he acted to free prisoners on trial at the Old Bailey from their chains and to stop the turnkeys charging for admission to the courtroom during trials. And he urged more stringent application of the regulations against the cruelty of drovers and market men to the animals brought to Smithfield. All these abuses proved harder to stop than Wilkes had hoped, but his humane intentions in the cause of liberty were clear enough.

In 1772 and 1773 Wilkes stood for Lord Mayor, heading the poll of the Livery both times but overlooked by the Court of Aldermen in favour of the second candidate. But in October 1774 Wilkes so arranged things that the Wilkite Alderman Frederick Bull, who had just retired as Lord Mayor, came second in the poll and could not be chosen for a second term without a gross affront to precedent. Wilkes's election was now inevitable. Lord Mayor Wilkes had the horses unhitched from his coach at the Guildhall and was drawn by the citizens to the Mansion House, the joy so irrepressible that one man lost his life in the crush. That same month a general election saw Wilkes elected once more for Middlesex; the incapacitation only endured till the end of the previous Parliament and this time Wilkes was allowed to take his seat without resistance. A few weeks later the House of Lords threatened to send a King's Messenger to the City to arrest a printer who had reported their proceedings. Lord Mayor Wilkes let it be known that Black Rod himself would be arrested if he tried to take the man. Once more the case was quietly allowed to die. From the time of these events of 1771 to 1774, entirely instigated by John Wilkes, it was said a few years later that 'the debates in both houses have been constantly printed in all the London newspapers, and copied into all the provincial ones . . .'[35]

Wilkes had pitted himself against King and Parliament on matters of great constitutional importance affecting the rights of the individual, of the press and of parliamentary constituents to choose their own representative. He had presided over three years and more of domestic political turbulence not experienced in England for over a century. On every issue this extraordinary man had won the day. But the question of the reform of Parliament which the Wilkite agitations had opened up would prove less tractable. And there would be more tumultuous battles to come.

Not a Prison Standing: The Gordon Riots, 1780

Side by side with the struggle for the rights of existing voters that had begun in 1769, the movement to reform Parliament and widen the franchise began to clarify its aims. It was very much a metropolitan initiative, and driven from east of Temple Bar. William Beckford had been influential in articulating a three-point programme of annual parliaments (they lasted then for seven years), equal representation and the exclusion of officials on the government payroll from becoming MPs. Each year the radical MP Alderman John Sawbridge presented a motion to the House of Commons calling for shorter parliaments, though without success. And it would be Alderman Wilkes himself who became the first parliamentarian to propose adult male suffrage to the

House of Commons in a motion on 21 March 1776 – the House laughed him out of court, his sole supporter faithful Alderman Bull.[36]

Wilkes was also involved in the agitation for parliamentary reform that centred on the waste of public money in sinecures and pensions. It originated in petitions from Yorkshire at the end of 1779 and spread quickly to Middlesex and other counties. And it was voiced brilliantly in Parliament by Edmund Burke and at assemblies in Westminster by Charles James Fox. Through February and April 1780 the London press reported accounts of City petitions and meetings of the Westminster committee for parliamentary reform at Westminster Hall – 6,000 at one in April it was said – where speeches extolling the rights of the people to change their government and their constitution, even to a republic if they wished, were heard to loud applause. Tempers that spring were raised very high. John Dunning's famous motion that 'the influence of the Crown has increased, is increasing, and ought to be diminished', passed the House of Commons on 6 April by a majority of eighteen. In May it was reported that a Middlesex justice had ordered a brigade of guards to be held in readiness should there be trouble at the presentation of a reform petition. If 'we are thus watched', Fox told the Commons, 'it is time for the people to arm themselves; I shall go armed in future to popular assemblies, when I know that orders to watch me are issued to the Guards'.[37]

Other reasons for discontent had also been accumulating over many months. The American War proved bitterly unpopular in London, repression of the colonists having many echoes of the King's tyrannous personal rule so much in evidence since 1763. The independence of America was seen greatly to weaken the kingdom and the conduct of the war against France and Spain proved lamentably incompetent. In February 1779 a crowd, said to have been organised by Fox, celebrated the acquittal of the popular Admiral Keppel at a Portsmouth court-martial by enforcing an illumination in London. Keppel's opponents had their windows broken and their furniture piled in the streets and burned. An attack on the Admiralty put Lord Sandwich, then First Lord, in fear of his life – he and Miss Ray escaped through the back garden. Keppel was promptly given the freedom of the City of London. Disasters and disgraces abroad mounted through the rest of the year, with Plymouth dockyard at risk of bombardment from a French and Spanish fleet and West Indian colonies falling like skittles to the French.[38]

By late 1779 into early 1780 Lord North's administration was loathed by Londoners of all classes. And now an unexpected but terrible fire-brand was thrown into this flammable discontent.

The widespread prejudice against Roman Catholics in the metropolis had not vanished with the defeat of the rebellion of 1745 or the dying away of its aftershocks. From 1763 Richard Terrick, Bishop of London, led a crusade against what he considered the growth of popery, and a crusading puritan constable, William Payne, suppressed City mass-houses and pursued and charged Catholic priests through the rest of the decade. On the other side of the divide some Catholics felt sure they had seen the Young Pretender in London in early 1773, recruiting to his cause, and many Londoners once more clandestinely drank his health. Parliament's decision to tolerate Catholicism in Quebec in 1774 led to petitions to the King from the City pleading that he refuse to sign the act and there was rioting when it passed into law. City radicals were prominent among the anti-Catholic ranks, led especially by Alderman Bull, though John Wilkes, always tolerant in matters of reli-gious affiliation, would have nothing to do with the protests. Public restiveness over Catholicism and its old associations with superstition, Jacobitism and papal tyranny continued to exercise Londoners of the middling and inferior sorts: anti-Catholic motions frequently cropped up in the numerous London debating clubs from 1776, for instance.[39]

Matters turned more serious during 1779. The previous year a measure affecting Irish Catholics had removed some disabilities, and a bill was introduced to the House of Commons by Sir George Savile proposing similar relief for Roman Catholics in England. The Catholic Relief Act of 1778 passed with little public attention or disquiet. But in 1779 an attempt to extend its provisions to Scotland had far different results. Fierce anti-Catholic rioting broke out in Glasgow and Edinburgh, so severe that Scottish Catholics petitioned Lord North to withdraw the measure, which he duly did. Meanwhile in London, at the beginning of that year, a Protestant Association was formed to support the North British agitation and to begin a movement for the repeal of Savile's act in England. From November 1779 its new president was a member of the Scottish peerage and of the House of Commons. His name was Lord George Gordon.

Gordon was then twenty-nine years old, a former naval lieutenant, MP for a Wiltshire constituency and the third son of a duke. He had been a fanatical leader of the Scottish opposition to Catholic relief and was widely considered mad – or at least unhinged in matters of religion.

He wore his hair long and lank like a puritan of the previous century. His speeches were wild and unbalanced. In all he made a striking martyr-like figure in the Protestant cause.

From the end of 1779 petitions trickled into Parliament from 'his Majesty's loyal Protestant Subjects' for the repeal of the 1778 act 'in favour of Popery in England'. One of the earliest came from the Cities of London and Westminster and was presented in January 1780. This well-organised agitation by the Protestant Association continued through the next few months. It won support among Protestants of many complexions. John Wesley, while repudiating 'persecution', wrote to the papers to congratulate the Association on its 'kind and benevolent design'. But the House of Commons, frequent witness to Gordon's absurd antics, dismissed him with derision. He did, though, give them warning enough of what was to come. In March 1780 he told the Commons 'he had 160,000 men in Scotland at his command, and . . . if the King did not keep his Coronation Oath, they would do more than take away his Civil List Revenue, they were determined to cut off his head': the House politely called him to order. Two months later, on 30 May, Lord George Gordon announced he would present the petition of the Protestant Associations of London, Westminster and Southwark to the House on Friday 2 June 1780.[40]

The arrangements for that memorable Friday were as minutely planned as much of the Association's propaganda over the past months. Advertisements and handbills called for a mass turnout of supporters at St George's Fields to carry and escort the petition, signed by some 44,000, to the House of Commons. Blue cockades were handed out in their thousands for people to wear in their hats – both St George's Fields and the cockades reminiscent of that earlier agitation involving John Wilkes, also in the name of liberty. The weather was oppressively hot and thundery and had been for some days past. Even so, some 50,000–60,000 were said to be in the fields when Lord George Gordon arrived around 11 a.m. to address his supporters, including 'a Scots division' who clustered close to their leader. From the fields contingents marched to London, the largest by way of London Bridge, 'through Cornhill and the city', 'with banner, flags, pennants, &c.', many singing hymns, the petition carried in front like an offering. Smaller marches made their way over Blackfriars and Westminster Bridges, Lord George among the last.[41]

Around 3 p.m. the columns met with 'a general shout' outside the

Houses of Parliament, swirled in great numbers into Palace Yard, burst into Westminster Hall, where the courts were sitting, and into the approaches to both Houses. The crowds contained many of the middling sort in their Sunday best. But Samuel Romilly, then a law student, in Palace Yard to attend a debate at the House of Lords on parliamentary reform, thought many were of 'the lowest rabble'. Worse, they were furious. Bishops and other members of the House of Lords were attacked in their carriages and punched, kicked and abused – at least two had the watches picked from their pockets. Lord Mansfield, who had recently treated leniently a Catholic priest coming before him, had the windows of his coach pushed in and had to be rescued by other members from what might have proved a dangerous assault. Eventually a trickle of peers made their bedraggled way into the chamber.

In the House of Commons, where members were already assembled, a noisy crowd clamoured in the lobby, where Gordon addressed them from a gallery on the progress of the debate on whether to receive the Protestant Association's petition. He was heard to tell them that the 'Scotch . . . had no redress until they pulled down the mass-houses'. In the chamber, many MPs were armed with swords and were poised to draw them. One told Gordon that should any of his 'rascally adherents' come through the door into the chamber, 'the first man of them that enters, I will plunge my sword, not into his, but into your body'. That evening, amid utter confusion, magistrates and constables incapable of regaining order even with parties of Horse and Foot Guards, the peers were able to escape from around 8.30. In the Commons, which dispersed somewhat later, Gordon lost the vote to receive his petition, mustering just nine supporters, chief among them Alderman Frederick Bull. In Bull's ward of Queenhithe the constables were wearing blue cockades.

That same evening groups among the crowds moved northwards away from Parliament and towards Holborn. In Duke Street, Lincoln's Inn Fields, they forced their way through the Sardinian ambassador's residence, broke into the chapel, tore out everything movable, made a bonfire of it in the Fields and set the chapel alight. Fire engines were called out but were attacked by the crowd until soldiers arrived to protect them. Many of the troops were thought to be on the rioters' side. Eventually, around midnight, the crowds in the Fields dispersed. Other rioters had broken into the Bavarian chapel in Warwick Street, Golden Square, sacking it and the ambassador's house nearby. Attacks on the Portuguese chapel in South Audley Street and a mass-house in Ropemaker's Alley, Moorfields, were frustrated by companies of guards. In all these places many arrests were made.

Next day, Saturday 3 June, those arrested and held overnight in the gaols were taken before the justices and released or returned to prison to await trial. Crowds of sightseers visited the ruined chapels. Rumours of fresh attacks reached the ears of Lord Stormont, Secretary of State, and magistrates, constables and troops were made ready across the metropolis. That evening crowds assembled outside the mass-house near Moorfields but no damage was done until the morning of Sunday 4 June, when the windows were broken. From Sunday evening through to Monday morning the attack was urged with greater violence, the chapel broken into, the altar and pews and vestments dragged into the narrow alley and burned; a nearby Catholic school and the dwellings of local Catholics were also stoned and sacked.

By Monday 5 June both Lord Stormont and prominent Roman Catholics who had sought assistance from the Mansion House were alarmed by the attitude of Lord Mayor Brackley Kennett, the City's chief magistrate, who made plain his sympathy with the rioters. Kennett proved unable or unwilling to mobilise the City marshals, constables and nightly watch and resisted using the troops at his disposal. Amid continuing rioting the Court of Aldermen eventually ordered the City marshals to swear in special constables and take men to Moorfields. But trouble was by now moving beyond the City into Wapping, where some Irish mass-houses were attacked. And on this Monday came the first signs of a shift in the rioters' quarry when the house of Justice Rainsforth, especially active in making arrests, was wrecked in Clare Street, Clare Market. There were attacks too on Sir George Savile's house in Leicester Square for his role in proposing the Catholic Relief Act. Edmund Burke, his seconder, had his house in Charles (now Charles II) Street, St James's Square, protected by soldiers but had to draw his sword to fend off angry rioters who surrounded him in the street.

On Tuesday 6 June the rioters' efforts gathered strength, despite large numbers of Horse and Foot Guards arriving in London from all directions. That morning a crowd of 500 or so with drums, fifes and flags gathered outside Lambeth Palace, the Archbishop of Canterbury's London residence, which had to be protected by the guards. Nearby, in St George's Fields, where it all began, crowds assembled once more to march on Parliament. Cockades and colours were still in evidence but now many 'were armed with poleaxes, cutlasses, bludgeons, &c.'[42] Crossing Westminster Bridge, they attacked MPs considered unsympathetic to repeal and any minister of Lord North's government they could lay their hands on. Lord Sandwich – shades of Wilkes here too – was especially badly treated, his face cut by glass when his carriage windows were smashed. The poet George Crabbe, walking away from Parliament, noted in his diary the first disconcerting signs of what proved now to be nothing less than an uprising of the London poor: 'In my way I met a resolute band of vile-looking fellows, ragged, dirty, and insolent, armed with clubs, going to join their companions. I since learned that there were eight or ten of these bodies in different parts of the City.'[43]

For the next two nights London was submerged in the throes of civil war. By the early evening of 6 June the riot had decisively made that shift heralded by the attack on Justice Rainsforth's house the day before. First, the eyewitness accounts agree on the distinctively more ragged character of the rioters themselves. Second, there was a marked increment in the violence of the crowd and the destruction it was prepared to cause. Third, there was more attention paid to the spoils of war in theft, extortion and looting. Last, the rioters' primary target was no longer the institutions of Catholic London or the homes and businesses of Catholics and their supporters, though cries of 'No Popery' were frequently heard and such attacks continued to be made. Now the fury of this crowd turned itself most of all against the institutions of justice, cruellest symbols of class oppression in eighteenth-century London.

There were attacks that Tuesday night on, among others, Lord Mansfield's house in Bloomsbury Square, where his furniture and irreplaceable library of books and manuscripts were dragged into the square and burned; on Lord North's house, 10 Downing Street; and on the houses of prominent Roman Catholics north of the City. Justice Hyde, active that afternoon in defending Lord Sandwich and others on their way to Parliament, promptly had his town house in St Martin's Street, and later his country house near Cross Street, Islington, wrecked for his pains.[44] The crowd then moved to Sir John Fielding's office and house at 4 Bow Street, where furniture, wainscoting and all the papers of the office, including its cache of criminal records built up over thirty years, were dragged into the street and burned.

That night, too, the hated London prisons became the main target of the rioters – first to release the prisoners, including those arrested

33. *Box-Lobby Loungers*, 1786 (Thomas Rowlandson). The theatre was one of the great attractions of London and chief entertainment of the Londoners. The theatre was also the place to be seen, as here, the box lobby filled with bucks and expensive women of the town.

34. *EO, or 'The Fashionable Vowels'*, 1781 (Thomas Rowlandson). Gambling was a vice of all classes, and EO tables were popular in rich drawing rooms and gaming houses. Fortunes could be lost on cards and the tables, Charles James Fox at one time owing £130,000 (more than £30 million at current prices).

35. *Nosegay and Memorandum Book Seller,* c.1760 (Paul Sandby). Some women combined prostitution with street selling as a more polite way of approaching men. Prostitutes came in many forms but it's clear from Sandby's drawing 'from the Life' that some at least had allure and youth on their side.

36. Covent Garden Ladies, c.1779. The Covent Garden Piazza and the taverns and coffee houses around formed the centre of smart prostitution in London. Here were the bawdy-house and brothel haunts most favoured by high-ranking rakes.

37. A Coffee House Duel, c.1781. The sword had long been a badge of high rank but by the 1780s it had become less commonly worn in the daytime. For a night in the theatre or tavern, however, swords were a normal accessory and frequently drawn to settle a row.

38. *St Giles's Courtship*, 1799 (Thomas Rowlandson). The public house was the plebeian Londoners' favourite place for fun, relaxation, tippling and love-making, celebrated here by the century's greatest chronicler of the capital's pleasures.

39. *Smithfield Sharpers*, 1787 (Thomas Rowlandson). London was thought to be a terrible place for innocent countrymen, too frequently gulls for the wily Londoners. Confidence tricksters of one form or another were the London villains most warned against by printed guides to the metropolis.

40. *Housebreakers*, 1788 (Thomas Rowlandson). Being broken in upon at night by armed burglars was one of the Londoners' worst nightmares. Householders frequently owned guns, here a blunderbuss, and when travelling by coach one or more pistols were essential accessories for peace of mind.

41. Newgate Prison, *c.*1796 (Thomas Malton). Newgate was rebuilt in the 1770s to a design by George Dance the Younger. Never large enough for its purpose it was the main gaol for persons charged or convicted of offences committed in London and Middlesex, and for debtors within the City of London.

42. The Fleet Prison, *c.*1808 (A.C. Pugin and Thomas Rowlandson). The three main debtors' prisons in London were tiny townships, complete worlds of their own making, where better-off debtors could live in comfort but the poorest might starve to death.

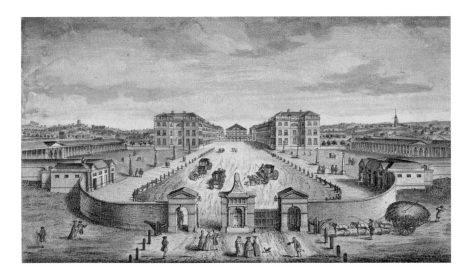

43. The Foundling Hospital, c.1753. This was the Londoners' favourite charitable enterprise, established in 1741 to receive abandoned babies delivered by desperate mothers or found on the streets. The central chapel housed an organ donated by Handel, and the hospital displayed art by London's greatest painters and sculptors.

44. Sacheverell Riots, 1710, the attack by 'a High Church mob' on Mr Burgess's dissenting meeting house in Lincoln's Inn Fields. Burgess narrowly escaped with his life. Other chapels were burned out and the riots had to be put down by military force of arms.

CREDULITY, SUPERSTITION, & FANATICISM.

45. *Credulity, Superstition and Fanaticism*, 1762 (William Hogarth), an attack on the religious excesses of the age, notably the credulous ecstasy demanded of the Methodists by Wesley and Whitefield. The Cock Lane Ghost and Mary Toft, said to have given birth to rabbits in 1726, also figure in the satire.

46. Old Broad Street, City, 7 June 1780 (Francis Wheatley). The Gordon Riots began as an attack on Roman Catholicism in London and ended as an uprising of the London poor, their main target the prisons and police offices of an unfair just system. The riots were suppressed by overwhelming military might.

47. Burning of the Albion Mills, Southwark, April 1791. Londoners dance on Blackfriars Bridge to celebrate the destruction of these giant flour mills, said to be hoarding supplies to force up the price of bread. Arson was suspected, another source of official anxiety in this politically turbulent decade.

in the riots since 1 June, and then to destroy the prisons themselves. At 7 p.m. word ran quickly through the crowd to move to Newgate, a brand-new gaol barely out of the hands of the contractors. With its great stone walls it was a daunting obstacle. But the weak point was the house of the keeper, Richard Akerman, brick-built and linking the prison's two wings. Men with paving mattocks, sledgehammers and pickaxes, iron crows and bars, chisels and bludgeons broke down the doors and window shutters, stormed the house, threw Akerman's belongings into the street and burned them. They then fired the house, broke into the prison and set that alight too. Soon a fierce blaze spread to everything combustible in the prison itself, so fierce that some of the new-laid stone vitrified. The prisoners were led away to freedom, those awaiting execution still in their chains. George Crabbe, one of many eyewitnesses who recorded the drama of this, London's Bastille Day *avant la lettre*, wrote to a friend: 'I must not omit what struck me most. About ten or twelve of the mob getting to the top of the debtors' prison, whilst it was burning, to halloo, they appeared rolled in black smoke mixed with sudden bursts of fire – like Milton's infernals who were as familiar with flame as with each other.'[45]

   As the rioters drifted away from the empty burning gaol they called on the citizens to light up their windows in celebration of Newgate's destruction. And later that night, among the drinkers at the Bell public house, St James's Market, Thomas Haycock, a tavern waiter by calling, boasted how he'd been active in the destruction: 'I asked him what could induce him to do all this? He said *the cause*. I said, do you mean a religious cause? He said no; *for he was of no religion*. He said, *there should not be a prison standing on the morrow in London*'.[46] Haycock would be proved nearly right, though a little premature. Prisoners were freed that night from the two gaols in Clerkenwell but the buildings were not set ablaze, in one case at least because it was so closely confined among poor houses. And the Fleet Prison was broken open and the debtors given time to get their goods away before it was put to the torch.

   In all or many of these events the soldiers brought to relieve London looked on as fires burned and the gaols were emptied. Their officers would not order their men to fire on the crowd without instructions from the magistrates to do so. Magistrates, though, were not always readily to be found; and those that were remembered the St George's Fields Massacre and its aftermath and were understandably cautious too. The first shots were, however, fired this night in Bloomsbury Square and six or seven rioters were said to have been killed under the command of an officer who, by a twist of fate, was Lord George Gordon's brother-in-law.

The next day and night, 'Black Wednesday', 7 June, witnessed London's most terrible crisis in the modern period, not exceeded until the wartime blitz 160 years later.

As the day opened gangs armed with iron bars and bludgeons roamed the streets, knocking door to door and demanding money 'for the true religion' or 'the poor mob'. Damaged or destroyed buildings were systematically looted by rioters and by those taking advantage of the confusion, and in the hours of darkness many houses at random were broken into and plundered. Rumours of more rioting to come swept the town. Facing the prospect of a general insurrection and the destruction of the prisons and even the Bank of England, the City, at a Court of Common Council with Lord Mayor Kennett in the chair, resolved not to deploy force but instead to petition the House of Commons to repeal the Catholic Relief Act. At last, though, there was more urgency in Westminster. An emergency meeting of the Privy Council that morning, at the personal urging of the King, announced that the military had been given orders to shoot to kill without the need for magistrates first to read the Riot Act.

Troops, however, could not be everywhere. The London poor seemingly could. Attacks on prominent Roman Catholics resumed through the afternoon and into the evening. Notable among them was the burning of Langdale's distilleries in Holborn, their great vats of alcohol sending flames and smoke into the sky that were visible thirty miles from London. The fire spread and consumed numerous houses and businesses around. But the rioters' main targets were once more the machinery of judicial oppression. Justice Wilmot's police office at Worship Street, Shoreditch, was demolished and his house in Bethnal Green ransacked. Samuel Johnson

walked with Dr. Scot to look at Newgate, and found it in ruins, with the fire yet glowing. As I went by, the Protestants were plundering the Sessions-house at the Old Bailey. There were not, I believe, a hundred; but they did their work at leisure, in full security, without sentinels, without trepidation, as men lawfully employed, in full day. Such is the cowardice of a commercial place.[47]

Great destruction was wreaked in Southwark. The King's Bench Prison was set on fire and burned out; the ancient Borough Clink was burned to the ground and never rebuilt; the Southwark New Prison was emptied of prisoners; the Marshalsea was attacked but saved by the military; the round-houses in Borough High Street and Kent Street pulled down and fired. And on the last night of the riots, 8–9 June, it was said that twenty spunging houses in Southwark were destroyed. The London gaols still standing were filled with those taken in the riots, mostly 'wretched' persons. All were heavily guarded by soldiers, as were the sheriffs' offices in the City and those police offices that had escaped destruction. And old grudges seem to have been settled under the guise of religious enthusiasm: a public house pulled down in Whitechapel was owned by a Roman Catholic who was also a Marshalsea Court officer or bailiff, his house a resort of thief-takers who 'lived "by the price of blood"'.[48]

The ferocious destruction on that night of Black Wednesday, with London ablaze at all points of the compass, now provoked a furious revenge from the military, including the London militias, unevenly supported by the civil power of magistrates and constables. Many rioters were shot dead on Blackfriars Bridge while they were setting the toll houses alight. Musket volleys and charges with fixed bayonets cleared crowds from around the burning Fleet Prison. In the City makeshift rope barriers were made in the main streets to hold off the rioting crowds and there were many casualties from musket balls in Poultry and the great streets around the Bank and Royal Exchange. About 11 p.m. there was a concerted attack on the Bank of England led by a man on a great drayhorse festooned with chains struck off the condemned prisoners from Newgate. Among the Bank's defenders was Alderman John Wilkes, City magistrate and former Colonel of the Buckinghamshire Militia, fearless as ever and in charge of London militiamen. Wilkes's soldiers killed rioters in Cheapside, Pig Street and near the gates of the Bank. Many looters ransacking houses in Broad Street, City, were shot dead, the moment captured by Francis Wheatley in a memorable painting, quickly engraved for sale in the printshops. The chaos, confusion and terror of that night and the early hours of Thursday morning witnessed the bulk of the deaths in the riots: in all, some 210 rioters shot dead in the streets; another seventy-five or so dying in the hospitals; unknown others dead from drinking neat liquor at Langdale's and elsewhere or dying at home from their wounds. Thirty years later and Londoners still recalled this moment with shuddering disbelief:

No mind can form the smallest conception of the horror of the scene; the prisons, the toll-gates on Blackfriars-bridge, the houses in every quarter of the town, and particularly the middle and lower part of Holborn, were one general scene of conflagration. Sleep was vanished from every part; the firing of the soldiers' muskets, the shouts of the rioters, the cries of the distressed, and the confusion of the people, who were every where carrying off beds, furniture, and goods, is more easy to be imagined than described.[49]

Next day almost every shop in the metropolis was shut as Londoners held their breath in fear of the rioters' return. Skirmishes between troops and looters went on through Thursday. Some armed men exchanged musket-fire with the military at Fleet Market. There were many break-ins, with large quantities of silk stolen from a prominent manufacturer's in Pearl Street, Spitalfields, for instance. Searches by soldiers, peace officers and magistrates for those identified as ringleaders scoured the criminal districts of London like Black Boy Alley and Chick Lane. Yet by no means all of those later charged were of this desperate class. Most were journeymen wage earners, a number were domestic or public-house servants, a few were apprentices and young boys; others were, indeed, of the marginal poor – a street seller of garden stuff, a barker at a second-hand clothes shop in Monmouth Street, a former workhouse inmate given a chance as an ostler, two casual porters, one of them 'almost an idiot', and a few women, one of them black, whose occupations have not come down to us.[50]

As darkness descended on the evening of Thursday 8 June so the fears of another night of riot and destruction mounted once more. But in fact the rioters' strength had been exhausted in the excesses of Black Wednesday and cowed by the remorseless military now visible in force throughout the metropolis, aided by citizens armed in volunteer associations that patrolled their neighbourhoods for many nights to come. London resembled a city recovering from the ravages of invasion and remained under something like military occupation for much of the summer to come. But despite disturbances south of the river on that Thursday night and Friday morning, and despite some threats against the London police offices, the riots were effectively over. Their repercussions, though, would last far longer.

'I Would Have No King':
Revolution and Democracy, 1780–99

The immediate aftermath of the Gordon Riots was filled with recrimin-
ation and retribution. Their cost was enormous. Besides the great loss
of life, at least £180,000 was claimed in material damages from insurers
and the authorities. It is said that the riots 'destroyed *ten times* more
property than was destroyed in Paris during the entire French
Revolution'. Langdale the distiller alone lost property worth over
£50,000 and lawsuits by his insurers to recover damages from the City
Corporation dragged on in the courts for five years to come. Large
losses were indeed recovered from the City for its negligent failure to
protect businesses and homes from the rioters.[51]

Theories that the riots had been deliberately fostered by a conspiracy
against King and government by the opposition, or against the nation
by the Americans and their allies, circulated freely and were widely
believed. The role of the City's governors made the first more credible,
the Lord Mayor and some other aldermen vocal in the Protestant cause
and eager to pursue old struggles against the court, its hated government and all their measures. The inaction of Brackley Kennett looked
to be as much motivated by hostility to Westminster as by the 'timidity
and imbecility' of which he was widely accused, and perhaps it was.
After the event, the City disowned its chief magistrate's dishonourable
conduct; he was charged with criminal neglect, tried before Lord
Mansfield and found guilty in March 1781, but died before he could
be sentenced, perhaps by his own hand.[52]

Revenge against those few rioters to be seized and convicted was swift
and condign. Ninety-six were charged with riot, some as young as thirteen
or fourteen, but acquitted by juries north and south of the river. At the
Old Bailey thirty-five were sentenced to death, often for looting, and at
Southwark twenty-four. In all some two dozen were hanged near the
places they had committed their crimes. The executions passed with no
disturbances.[53] Lord George Gordon was committed to the Tower of
London and tried for treason but acquitted in February 1781. His
successful defence, brilliantly led by Thomas Erskine, made the point that
none among those convicted for riot had been among the 44,000 signing
the Protestant Association's petition. A free man, Gordon contemplated
standing for Parliament in the City, where he had found so much support.
But in 1787 he was sentenced to five years' imprisonment for publishing

libels, including one on the French queen; unable to find sureties for his subsequent good behaviour he could not free himself from Newgate and died there in 1793. By then he had converted to Judaism and grown a long beard, convinced he would lead the Jews back to their promised land – perhaps from St George's Fields. The mad Lord George Gordon proved only the second man of the century to unite in a single political movement large numbers of Londoners from all corners of the metropolis. The first, of course, was John Wilkes.

Fear of the London poor, what contemporaries termed 'the mob', had caused tremors throughout the century. But after 1780 that fear had become a terror that none wished to see repeated. The riots had almost certainly some effect on the changed tone of that spirit of enquiry into the lives of the poor we noticed emerging from the mid-1780s. Terror was then redoubled by the French Revolution of 1789 and the murderous events that unfolded over the next four years. How to stifle a rising of the English poor became one driving force of evangelicalism. In the House of Commons some saw the need for an alliance between the aristocracy and the upper reaches of the middling sort to satisfy moderate desires for parliamentary reform. William Pitt the Younger, favourite of George III and shortly to become prime minister, was among those proposing more frequent elections and more equal representation each year from 1782 to 1785, sometimes supported by reform petitions from all parts of the metropolis.[54] By then the leadership of a popular reform movement had shifted decisively westwards from the City, its own leading men so generally discredited by the debacle of June 1780. And by the early 1780s it centred on Westminster and the burly unkempt patrician figure of Charles James Fox.

Fox was thirty-one in 1780 and had been an MP since 1768 at the age of nineteen, too young by law to stand for Parliament but all obstacles smoothed away by his father, Henry Fox, a consummate politician and government minister. The young Fox adored his father and during his lifetime supported the ministry. But from 1774 he drifted into opposition, his popularity, intellectual brilliance and eloquent facility in debate assuring him appreciative attention in the highest Whig ranks. Fox's background – he was a direct descendant of Charles II – could hardly have been more different from that of John Wilkes. But politically there was one close parallel. For by 1780 Fox had become as convinced as ever Wilkes had been that the King was developing a personal, despotic and unconstitutional rule to match royal dictators on the continent of Europe. In the general election of September 1780, Fox was elected MP for Westminster with acclamation, and was 'carried triumphantly through the whole town'.[55]

Westminster elections had long had the reputation of being rancorous and frequently violent. But apart from a radical moment in 1769 on the tail of the Wilkite drama, Westminster had been classed among 'the most obsequious boroughs' in sending aristocratic government supporters to Parliament.[56] Now, with the election of Fox, it became the lodestone of the parliamentary reformers and of all those opposing the unpopular war against the Americans. The Foxite colours of buff and blue copied those chosen by George Washington for his troops. And popular radicalism was assisted in Westminster by a wide parliamentary franchise extending to the lower ranks of the middling sort: some 20,000 ratepayer householders by the end of the century had the right to vote.

In March 1784 the King dissolved Parliament three years earlier than necessary, calculating a political advantage from the end of the American War that would restore the parliamentary losses suffered by the government four years before. In general the tactic proved successful. But in Westminster the general election led to the most ferocious and hard-fought hustings of the century in London.

Westminster was littered in a deluge of handbills arguing for and against the King and his government. Artists, engravers and printsellers pronounced Fox 'The Champion of the People' wielding the shield of truth and the sword of justice – or Carlo Khan, a fat lascivious Oriental despot-in-waiting. Ballad-sellers sang new-minted election songs in the streets. Noisy meetings at Westminster Hall brought together more 'motley a groupe' than was ever seen, it was said, in England before – 'Lords, Chandlers, Baronets, Glaziers, Knights, Shoe-boys, Pickpockets, &c. &c. &c. mixed among a considerable number of the Electors', Westminster's tradesmen and lodging-house keepers.[57]

The poll was conducted over forty days through April into May. Canvassing was spiced by the Duchess of Devonshire and other ladies campaigning for the fascinating Fox, notoriously offering kisses to the householders for their votes – from 'Devon and Co's Crimson Pouting Warehouse, Piccadilly', as one government handbill had it. Encounters on the hustings between the court candidates, Admiral Lord Hood and Sir Cecil Wray, and Charles James Fox for the opposition were so fractious that the hustings themselves on occasion gave way, with 'noblemen and gentlemen thrown down and trampled on'. Crowds in the streets and at the hustings were frequently violent. On Saturday 1 May a riot outside the court candidates' headquarters at Wood's Hotel, Covent Garden Piazza, was said to involve 'a desperate banditti of Irish Chairmen and Pickpockets' who bludgeoned everyone leaving the hotel and then tried to break in. Weapons included wheel-spokes, marrow bones and cleavers, and many government supporters and peace officers were badly hurt. On the other side, men 'habited like sailors' on behalf of Lord Hood assaulted Fox's supporters in the streets and attacked his headquarters at the Shakespeare Tavern, also in the Piazza. When the 'sailors' made an appearance at the hustings, 'The honest mob then assembled, no longer able to endure the insults of these desperadoes and assassins, fell upon them and soon routed them; several had their skulls fractured, others were afterwards picked up with arms, legs, and ribs, broken.' These Foxite supporters were 'Chairmen, Butchers, brewers, and others of the common people', and must have included many non-electors and many Irish, Fox a prominent parliamentary advocate of their country's freedoms.[58]

Hundreds of constables were brought into Westminster from all over the metropolis to keep order. But on 10 May, in the worst riot of the campaign, Nicholas Casson, a constable from the Tower Hamlets, was beaten to death near the hustings at Covent Garden in a violent Foxite crowd in which 'Irish chairmen, Welch porters' and others 'armed with sticks and bludgeons' were prominent. Four men were tried for the murder and acquitted and no evidence was offered against three more. Thomas Erskine was prominent among the defence counsel. Lord Hood and Charles James Fox were eventually elected in a very high poll where nearly 19,000 votes were cast.[59]

Parliamentary reform was part of Fox's programme in the Westminster election, though in private life and in the shadow of the Gordon Riots he was but a queasy democrat.[60] With the court party ascendant in Parliament after the general election of 1784, the cause of reform in London would stumble. And then move into other hands.

It was the inspirational effect of the victorious Americans and, even more important, the example of the 1789 revolution in France that renewed interest in the reform of Parliament, from 1791 in particular. This was very much a London movement. It found polite expression in the revived pamphlet propaganda of the Society for Constitutional Information and in the Society of the Friends of the People, formed in April 1792, whose meetings and influential membership put the case once again for more frequent parliaments and equal representation for the growing urban areas of the nation. Among its members were the young Charles Grey, who led the reformers in Parliament, and that old City radical Alderman John Sawbridge, MP. Charles James Fox, however, was not a member.[61]

Around the same time a quite new movement began among the barely franchised ranks of plebeian Londoners of the clerk, small-trading, artisan and labouring classes, who saw in reform not just an end to parliamentary corruption but the means of securing a more equal distribution of the nation's resources. The London Corresponding Society (LCS) was begun by Thomas Hardy, the Scottish shoemaker who had settled in London at the age of twenty-two in 1774 and who by 1792 was a master with his own shop in Piccadilly. The Society's first meeting was at the Bell in Exeter Street, Strand, in January that year. In April the LCS announced its programme, including manhood suffrage, equal representation in Parliament and an end to bribery at elections; it emphasised that all its ends were to be achieved by peaceful means, mainly by corresponding with like-minded bodies elsewhere in the kingdom.[62]

From the outset the plebeian reform propaganda was met with suppression from government led by that erstwhile reformer William Pitt the Younger. For King and Parliament the times were menacing. The example of France, its king and queen insulted and under arrest, its government at war that same month of April 1792 in a struggle that threatened the balance of power in Europe, shook the security of monarchs everywhere. Yet revolutionary France had much support among the reformers, with addresses even from the respectable societies in London applauding the Jacobin regime in Paris. On 21 May 1792 George III issued a proclamation against 'wicked and seditious writings, printed, published, and industriously dispersed, tending to excite tumult and disorder'. Prosecutions against the London pamphleteers were revived with all the vindictiveness of the age of Wilkes and Crosby. Among many others Tom Paine was arrested, bailed, prosecuted as the author of *The Rights of Man* (1791), tried in front of a special jury and convicted in his absence – he had fled to France – despite Thomas Erskine's eloquent defence. Erskine was a prominent member of the Society of the Friends of the People and outside the Guildhall at the trial's end he was greeted by large crowds shouting, '"Paine for ever!"; "Erskine and the Rights of Juries!"; and "Paine and the liberty of the press!"'[63]

No formal moves were made against the LCS at this time but by

October 1792 the activities of the London Jacobins were becoming penetrated by an astonishing network of government spies reporting on their meetings. By then the LCS had spawned some sixteen 'divisions' in London, nine or so in Westminster and the rest in Bloomsbury, the City and Southwark. The divisions each had a few dozen members and met in hired rooms in public houses. Yet these small numbers, combined with the excitement over Paine's trial and anxieties over events in France, triggered a government panic at the end of 1792 that seemed to anticipate another insurrection in London along the lines of the riots of a dozen years before. Debating societies were put down by the City magistrates, not without some tumult in the streets, and the Corporation adopted loyal resolutions for king and constitution. The London Militia and the Honourable Artillery Company were kept on alert at a moment's readiness. The Tower of London was barricaded with barrels filled with mud and boulders, trenches were dug and cannon mounted on the walls. The Bank of England had its military guard – in place ever since the Gordon Riots, to the great displeasure of the City authorities – doubled in strength. Troops were moved into villages in the environs. The panic had abated by the New Year, but in Europe matters took another turn for the worse. Louis XVI was guillotined on 21 January 1793 and Britain declared war on France on 1 February.[64]

In such a climate, agitation for the reform of a corrupt and unrepresentative Parliament began to seem like – or could be represented as – treason. Undaunted, the LCS continued to flourish. By January 1793 it had at least thirty-one divisions, some more active than others, with around 650 members. Francis Place, who joined the Society in the following year, described their meetings as models of sobriety and order: 'Eating – drinking – & smoaking were forbidden either in a division or a committee. No man in liquor was permitted to remain . . . and habitual drunkenness was sufficient cause for expulsion.' The divisions collected subscriptions to buy books and pamphlets, and part of each meeting was given up to readings and debate. There were Sunday evening parties in those members' homes large enough to receive them for more 'readings, conversations and discussions'. Not all proved peaceful, however, and doctrinal splits, tactical disagreements and the mischief of spies dogged the LCS throughout its short existence.[65]

Government repression of the London democrats continued throughout 1793 and 1794. It was frequently counterproductive. John Frost, an attorney, was allegedly overheard in the Percy Coffee House,

Rathbone Place, in May 1793, saying, 'I am for equality; I see no reason why one man should be greater than another; I would have no king, and the constitution of this country is a bad one.' He was sentenced to the pillory and five months in Newgate. But when he was released in November, sick and swaddled in blankets, 'the multitude took the horses out of the carriage, and drew him along the streets, stopping at every marked place, particularly St James's palace, Carleton-house, Charing-cross, &c. to shout and express their joy'.[66]

In May 1794 the government moved against the LCS, arresting its leaders and seizing papers on warrants alleging high treason. The Piccadilly shop of Thomas Hardy, held in the Tower, was attacked by a crowd celebrating Lord Howe's naval victory in the following month. But the tables were turned when Hardy and his fellow 'conspirators' John Horne Tooke and John Thelwall were acquitted by juries in separate trials at the end of 1794. Poor Hardy, whose wife had miscarried and died while he was in prison, heard the crowd outside the Old Bailey receive news of his acquittal with 'loud and repeated acclamations'. He tried to leave

in private, and proceeded in a hackney-coach down Snow-hill; but the people soon recognized him – they followed his coach, huzzaing, and imploring blessings on the twelve men who had acquitted him; and, though the coachman drove fast, they overtook the coach in the Strand, and taking the horses out, drew it along Pall-Mall, and up St. James's-street, to Mr. Hardy's late residence in Piccadilly.[67]

Despite these persecutions by government and the suspension of habeas corpus after the LCS arrests in May there was frequent expression of opposition to the crown and sympathy for the people of France in what many still saw as their struggle for liberty. Through late 1794 into early 1795 there were violent attacks on recruiting or 'crimping' houses where it was thought young men were being inveigled or forced into the army. Houses were 'pulled down' or damaged in Holborn, Charing Cross, Finsbury and especially Southwark; Pitt's windows in 10 Downing Street were broken in the spillage from one such fracas. Later in 1795 the LCS, then at its maximum membership of 3,000 or so in some seventy divisions, felt confident enough to call for mass meetings. Such was the unpopularity of the King and his ministers, and so angry the discontent of the people suffering from the high prices of food and other commodities during the war with France, that the demonstrations attracted huge numbers. In two meetings in October and November in Copenhagen Fields, south-west Islington, vast crowds estimated at 100,000 and more listened to speeches from 'rostra' or 'tribunes' spread out across the fields.[68]

These meetings went off peacefully. But as the King passed through the Mall in his coach to open Parliament on 29 October, he was beset by a hostile crowd. George was 'violently hissed and hooted, and groaned at the whole way'. During the melee his carriage window was holed, perhaps by a stone, perhaps by a ball-bearing fired from an airgun, and the coach was mobbed. There were cries of 'Bread! Bread! Peace! Peace!' and a man was arrested for calling out 'No King'. In December 1795 the government forced through Parliament a Seditious Meetings Act, to considerable popular protest. It made further meetings of the kind organised that winter unlawful.

There was an immediate effect on the LCS. According to Place, 'the numbers of members rapidly declined and the whole labour and expense fell upon a comparatively small number'. By the second half of 1796 membership had fallen to a thousand and in 1797 around 600; Place himself resigned from the Society that June. In April 1798 the government arranged the wholesale arrest by Bow Street officers of the whole General Committee of the LCS, some thirty-four men in all. Habeas corpus was again suspended, allowing them to be held for lengthy periods without trial. From early 1799 the LCS ceased to exist.[69]

Occasional disturbances on the streets of London continued throughout the late 1790s – the window of the King's coach was broken once more by a crowd in February 1796, for instance. As the LCS fell away the vacuum was filled by a host of backstreet atheist societies in the plebeian suburbs of Bethnal Green, Shoreditch, Clerkenwell and elsewhere, taking Paine's *The Age of Reason* (1794) for their text, and setting up a propaganda against field-preaching Methodists and others.[70] The paper war still raged on: for and against the French Revolution and parliamentary reform, on the rights of the British people to select their government and of women to establish an equal place in civil society. But the real departure of the 1790s lay in the penetration of political ideas and debate deep into the ranks of Wilkes's 'inferior sort of people'. And in creating a movement that did not merely vent its frustrations in the streets but sought also to channel them through rational meetings, propaganda and print.

What of John Wilkes in these momentous times for metropolitan democracy? He was ploughing another furrow. From 1779 he was able single-mindedly to pursue what had always been his primary interest: John Wilkes himself and his daughter, Polly. That November, after numerous setbacks met with his usual obstinate refusal ever to accept defeat, Wilkes was elected chamberlain (or treasurer) of the City of London by the Livery who had been so loyal to him. He had long considered it a 'safe port' because of its emoluments of some £1,500 or £2,000 a year.[71] Despite many reservations among the citizens of entrusting the City's cash to a chronic debtor who had not shrunk from embezzlement in an emergency, Wilkes by all accounts proved prudent, honest and hard-working. He walked to the Guildhall from his home first at Prince's Court and later Grosvenor Square, or from his country villa at Kensington Gore, several days each week, instantly recognisable by his beau's garb, 'either a scarlet or green suit, edged with gold'.[72]

He retained his aldermanship and his seat for Middlesex. Every year from 1775 in the Commons he moved that the record of his incapacitation be expunged from the records. In 1782 he won his point and the records were amended accordingly. From that year, his purpose gained, Wilkes voted with the government benches and became a loyal supporter of the King and his ministers. In 1784, standing as a court candidate for Middlesex, he narrowly avoided defeat. But in 1790, after a hostile meeting of the freeholders in Hackney, he declined to stand and walked away from the election. He was not among those reformers who subscribed to the Society of the Friends of the People in 1792: indeed, for a decade or so he had not been a reformer at all. These same fraught years of the 1790s showed Wilkes and the City in step once more, the citizens generally tacking loyally west towards the King and his ministers.

John Wilkes died on Boxing Day 1797, aged seventy-two or thereabouts, from what seems to have been some sort of wasting disease. Unrealistic as ever about money, he left in his will numerous generous legacies, but the funds were unable even to satisfy his many creditors.

So what *are* we to make of John Wilkes? He wrote his own epitaph – 'A Friend to Liberty' – still to be seen on the memorial tablet in the Grosvenor Chapel, South Audley Street. But perhaps the truest assessment comes to us from Sir Nathaniel Wraxall, friend and admirer of the man he called the 'most interesting individual of the age in which he lived':

He was an incomparable comedian in all he said or did, and he seemed to consider human life itself as a mere comedy.[73]

AFTERWORD

How much progress had there been in healing London's great divisions during the course of the eighteenth century?

Perhaps most advance had been made in unifying the separate parts of the metropolis. Maps at the century's end still commonly describe 'The Cities of London and Westminster and the borough of Southwark', but the whole was fast becoming a single London. The great achievements were the bridges, London Bridge cleared of its buildings and Westminster and Blackfriars Bridges entirely new. Southwark and Lambeth were not just better connected to the great metropolis north of the Thames, but better integrated too. The south bank now provided wealthy residences for citizens along the Dover and Brighton roads; south London manufacturers had easier access to markets north of the river; and workers could sell their labour in a wider pool. On the north side, connections between London and Westminster were opened through Parliament Street and an enlarged Charing Cross; the City's streets were widened at various points, not least through the removal of the City gates; and the New Road connected the residents of Marylebone and the new western suburbs to the City more easily than ever before.

The City and Westminster had grown closer in other ways too. From the 1780s, the political antagonisms that had long made the citizens the natural enemies of the crown and its ministers were mitigated. The anxieties and humiliations of the Gordon Riots, and then the French Revolution and its wars, loosened the City's old attachments to democracy and brought merchants and courtiers into a loyal alliance that would in general prove of lasting stability.

Other political fractures among the Londoners proved less easy to bridge. The struggles between masters and workers did not return to the ferocity of the late 1760s, but the combination of low wages, uncertain employment and high prices remained an enduring injury to London's workers, especially painful once more from the 1790s. Power was much on the masters' side, bolstered by penal laws against combinations of workers that threatened prosecution and imprisonment and stifled much nascent trade unionism. There would be many years before the balance was redressed. Similarly, the plebeian movement for parliamentary reform remained suppressed by force of law, and agitation among the middling and polite classes for more equal representation would not bear fruit until 1832.

Intolerance of minorities like the Irish and the French showed little or no sign of abating during the century. Religious discord would never again disturb London, as it had in the first half of the eighteenth century, or be made the excuse for insurrection, as it had in 1780. But disabilities still attached to dissenters and Roman Catholics, though some relief was given the latter in an act of 1791 which permitted more open places of worship: we might recall that a chapel occupied part of what had been Carlisle House from the following year. None of this was accompanied by the turmoil of a dozen years before. But dissenters and Catholics would have to wait another generation for the penalties and restrictions finally to be removed.

There was no doubt some softening of manners in the streets and public places of London as the eighteenth century neared its close. But this was a phenomenon hard to measure and the evidence tells us that London remained a city where politeness and impertinence rubbed uneasily against each other. The events of June 1780 remain a great corrective to any facile notion of a revolution of manners affecting all classes by the last quarter of the century. It would not be until the 1820s and 1830s that a discernible shift in manners began to affect the behaviour of the poorest Londoners.

For those poorest, the impact of self-help organisations and of evangelical and other educational movements did not make inroads on ignorance until the early years of the nineteenth century. On the other hand there is some evidence of a more humane and generous approach to the operation of the poor law by the 1780s and 1790s, with workhouses less harsh and out-relief given extensively during times of crisis; and similarly a new tone in the organisation of much charity must have made lives more free from hunger and cold at the end of the century than at the beginning.

The wide disparity between what London's wealth and pleasures offered on the one hand and what could be accessed by the general run of Londoners on the other meant that crime continued to be one of the great problems of the age. The arrangements for a detective police had certainly improved by the 1790s, though the preventive police in watch and ward offered but patchy security for Londoners, and that largely confined to the hours of darkness. Accordingly, an extensive machinery of repression through prisons and punishment continued in operation. Some elements of the latter had been humanised with the abolition of Tyburn shows, burnings and some whippings. But the London prisons remained a shameful feature of the justice system, still based largely on the fee system and wardens' profits until well into the nineteenth century.

The separation between men and women in London's public spheres had never been complete. Theatres, pleasure gardens, coffee houses (many were run and staffed by women), public houses, the Thames and the London streets had always been spaces shared to some extent by men and women both, even if the power relations had never been equal, greatly distorted as they were by prostitution. Women's debating societies had developed alongside men's, and women had throughout the century made their voices heard in Grub Street. By the end of the century those voices had begun to claim for women a role in democracy and society that would reverberate throughout the century to come; but it would take many generations before their claims were met.

Any balance sheet, then, of the resolution of London's multilayered divisions must necessarily contain many entries on the debit side. There would be much work still to do.

ACKNOWLEDGEMENTS

London in the Eighteenth Century was some six years in the making, and during that time I incurred many debts – I mean of gratitude. For access to original manuscripts and rare publications I need to thank staff at the British Library and London Metropolitan Archives, and the Bodleian Library at Oxford. I have received generous assistance from Jeremy Smith, keeper of the Guildhall print collection of the Corporation of London, now held at the LMA; I am grateful for the Corporation's permission to reproduce some items from this invaluable collection here. In the summer of 2008 I was Charles J. Cole Fellow at the Lewis Walpole Library of Farmington, Connecticut, a department of Yale University. The Library is a treasure trove for the historian of eighteenth-century England and this book would have been much the poorer without my visit, so I owe a special thanks to Maggie Powell, Sue Walker and other staff at LWL. The Library has additionally kindly given permission to publish images they copied for me. Tina L. Skoczylas, of Plymouth, Connecticut, also helped me make the most of a memorable stay.

Without the Internet, even six years would have been far too short. Most books and pamphlets published in English during the period, almost all the surviving newspapers, and all parliamentary journals and reports are available online through university libraries. Other publicly accessible websites have put similarly invaluable sources within the reach of every researcher, amateur or professional. All of this information is digitally searchable. Material that a diligent lifetime could not have uncovered is now instantly available on any home computer. It all represents an extraordinary outpouring of public generosity, most of it freely available to the user.

One of the most selfless and inspiring of these projects has been the Old Bailey Proceedings Online, which expanded into the Plebeian Londoners Project while I was writing this book. I would like to thank Tim Hitchcock, one of the project's initiators, for his unfailing generosity in providing me with much archive material in advance of its finally going online – as well as being an inexhaustible fount of knowledge for plebeian London during this period.

Other historians have been generous too. In a profession often sneered at for backbiting and pettiness, I should put on record my own experience of an overwhelming readiness to help, to discuss, to offer short cuts, to share sources and even unpublished writings. Among many, I'd like to mention here Vic Gatrell, historian of both the tragedy and the comedy of eighteenth-century London life, and John Seed, chronicler of the London dissenters. Both read chapters in draft and saved me from many a howler, in their own specialisms and beyond. Sally Alexander has, in the culmination of what has now been a fifteen-year undertaking, read nearly every chapter of three big books and has given me huge support and encouragement. Something of the same task, over that same period, has been shouldered by Andrew Williams, and I'm very grateful for all his help. Needless to say, the mistakes that have inevitably slipped through these safety nets are all my own doing.

I don't have space to do justice to the two friends to whom I've dedicated this book. Paul Wilsdon-Tagg has made me laugh more than any man I know – sometimes intentionally. And John Hodgkins has sold me books for more years than I care to admit to: an expert on all things Johnsonian, he allowed me to *borrow* books from his own collection *and from stock* – no greater love hath any bookseller!

Maggie Hanbury has been my friend and agent for (she'll blush to hear it) more than thirty years. It was she and Will Sulkin, commissioning editor at Random House, who suggested that I write a book on eighteenth-century London. Fools rush in, and I said, 'Why not?' So without them it wouldn't have been written – I just hope they're pleased with themselves. Jörg Hensgen at the Bodley Head has been his usual model of enthusiastic efficiency; and Lesley Levene, the copy-editor from heaven, has once more covered up my slips time without number.

Finally, I must thank Rosie Cooper, who has looked on my writing with pride while deploring the constant stream of book parcels that

I struggled to hide, could not always afford and never quite had the room for. Books would appear in surprising and not-always-welcome places, and though Rosie tried to impose a one-in one-out policy it was one I could never entirely sign up to. Despite all that, and despite many difficulties that she personally encountered during the writing of this book, she has given me the love and peace of mind to do what I do.

Illustrations

For the images appearing within the text I would like to extend my thanks to The Lewis Walpole Library, Yale University, for permission to reproduce the images on pages 16, 21, 124, 164, 248, 344, 424 (Sir John Fielding), and 466.

For the images appearing in the plate sections I would like to extend my thanks to: The Lewis Walpole Library, Yale University, for permission to reproduce images 1, 4, 5, 9, 17, 21, 22, 23, 26, 27, 29, 30, 35, 36, 37, 41, and 43; and the City of London Corporation (London Metropolitan Archive) for permission to reproduce images 2, 3, 7, 8, 10, 18, 19, 20, 31, 32, and 46; all other images from the author's own collection.

NOTES

Introduction: London 1700–1708

1. Hatton, *A New View of London*, 1708, I, p. i. • 2. Stow, *Remarks on London*, 1722, n.p. [p. v]. On the extent of London see Chamberlayne, *Magna Britannia Notitia*, 1710, p. 218. He ends in the west at Tothill or Tuttle Street, but contemporary maps show solid building along the riverbank pretty much to the horse ferry at Millbank to Vauxhall and just beyond. • 3. *The Spectator*, 12 June 1712: the Temple was the lawyers' quarter, and Smithfield the cattle and horse market for London. For the divisions of London, not dissimilar to that given here, see Strype, *A Survey* . . ., 1720, I, Book II, pp. 1–2. • 4. For some contemporary ranges see Hatton, *A New View of London*, I, pp. iv–v, and Strype, *A Survey* . . ., II, Book V, p. 449. For the eighteenth-century controversies over London's population see Glass, *Numbering the People*, 1973, pp. 16–67. M. Dorothy George and John Summerson are the two eminent historians: see George, *London Life* . . ., 1925, pp. 23–4, and Summerson, *Georgian London*, 1945, p. 9 (adopting George's figures). For the emerging consensus see Wrigley, 'A Simple Model of London's Importance in Changing English Society and Economy 1650–1750', 1967, which gives 575,000 for 1700 and 675,000 for 1750; Roger Finlay and Beatrice Shearer in Beier and Finlay (eds.), *London 1500–1700*, 1986, p. 39, give 490,000 for 1700 and 675,000 (following Wrigley) for 1750; Earle, *The Making of the English Middle Class*, 1989, p. 17, gives around 500,000 for 1700; Spence, *London in the 1690s*, 2000, pp. 64–6, gives around 550,000 for 1700. For an overview see Harding, 'The Population of London, 1550–1700', 1990, and Schwarz, *London in the Age of Industrialization*, 1992, p. 125ff. You pays your money . . . The one in ten and one in six estimates, oft-repeated, are in Wrigley, 'A Simple Model of London's Importance in Changing English Society and Economy 1650–1750', pp. 45, 49. • 5. The best account of post-Fire reconstruction remains Reddaway, *The Rebuilding of London*, 1940. See also Bell, *The Great Fire of London in 1666*, 1920, Chs. XIII–XVII; and Baker, *London*, 2000. • 6. The best account of this period in London's growth remains Brett-James, *The Growth of Stuart London*, 1935, but see also McKellar, *The Birth of Modern London*, 1999. See Defoe, *A Tour* . . ., 1724–6, I, p. 331. Defoe mistakenly believed that 4,000 *more* buildings had been rebuilt in the City than were destroyed, precisely the reverse of the truth (p. 328). • 7. The 'fairest city' is in Chamberlayne, *Magna Britannia Notitia*,

p. 217; Westminster Abbey is in Ralph, *A New Critical Review* . . ., 1736, pp. 33–4; on the change of brick from red to grey see Summerson, *Georgian London*, p. 63. Smoke-staining of London buildings is a vexed question. According to Pollnitz, *The Memoirs* . . ., 1737, II, p. 431, London was blackened by coal smoke to 'a dark Hue'; but the paintings of London even from the late century have pinks and reds distinctively showing through: see Phillips, *The Thames about 1750*, 1951, p. 32. • **8.** On Wren and the City see Summerson, *Georgian London*, p. 45, and Bradley and Pevsner, *The Buildings of England: London 1*, 1997, p. 73ff. For St Paul's see Keene, Burns and Saint (eds.), *St Paul's*, 2004. For a stranger navigating by means of the dome see Anon. [An Irish Clergyman], 'Journals of Visits to London in 1761 and 1772', f. 24, August 1761. The claustrophobia is in Ralph, *A New Critical Review* . . ., pp. 13–17. • **9.** On the Bermudas see Macmichael, *The Story of Charing Cross and Its Immediate Neighbourhood*, 1906, pp. 143–4. On Turnmill (sometimes Turnball) Street see Hawkins, *The Life of Samuel Johnson*, 1787, p. 136, and George, *London Life* . . ., pp. 82–5. Pissing Alley is in Strype, *A Survey* . . ., II, Book IV, p. 117. • **10.** For Southwark see ibid., pp. 27–31; for Westminster see ibid., Book VI, pp. 63–6, and Walcott, *Westminster*, 1849, p. 24. • **11.** Stow, *Remarks on London*, n.p. [p. iv]. For the Great Storm see Defoe, *An Historical Narrative* . . ., 1769, p. 70. For ruined houses and dubious property rights more generally see George, *London Life* . . ., pp. 73–5. • **12.** Ward, *The London-Spy*, 1703, pp. 151–2. See also Van Muyden (ed.), *A Foreign View of England* . . ., 1902, pp. 67–8, December 1725. There is a good illustration of the squat wooden posts in Hogarth's *Rake's Progress*, 1734, Plate 4. • **13.** Swift, 'A City Shower', 1710, lines 61–3. See also Gay, *Trivia*, 1716, Book I, lines 171–4; Book II, lines 297–300; Book III, lines 335–8. • **14.** Swift, *Journal to Stella*, 1948, I, p. 87; II, p. 380. Billingsgate is in Ward, *The London-Spy*, p. 40. Whitechapel and the tide ditches are in Defoe, *Due Preparations for the Plague*, 1722, pp. 29–30. For the Thames-side laystalls see Phillips, *The Thames about 1750*, pp. 64, 70–71, 82. On the Clerkenwell Mound see Pinks, *The History of Clerkenwell*, 1880, p. 283. Mandeville, *The Fable of the Bees*, 1714, Preface, n.p. [pp. ix–xi]. On the flies see Hunter, *The History of London* . . ., 1811, II, p. 585. • **15.** Ward, *The London-Spy*, pp. 275–6: 'Fats' may be some misreading for 'Vats'. For the smoke see Pollnitz, *The Memoirs* . . ., II, pp. 431–3; Le Blanc, *Letters* . . ., 1747, I, pp. 261–2; Anon., *The Foreigner's Guide*, 1729, p. 132. The advertisement is in *Daily Journal*, 18 March 1730. See also Cynthia Wall, '"At Shakespear's Head, Over-Against Catharine-Street in the Strand"' 'Forms of Address in London Streets', in Hitchcock and Shore (eds.), *The Streets of London*, 2003, pp. 10–26. • **16.** On taking the wall see Boswell, *The Life of Samuel Johnson*, 1799, I, pp. 104–5. On the boisterous chairmen see Van Muyden (ed.), *A Foreign View of England* . . ., pp. 167–9, October 1726; see also Swift, *Journal to Stella*, II, p. 198. • **17.** On lighting at this time see Griffiths, *Lost Londons*, 2008, pp. 343–4; Miège, *The New State of England*, 1703, Part I, p. 155; Malcolm, *Anecdotes* . . ., 1810, II, pp. 380–81. • **18.** Percival MS, 'Observations made by Mrs Percivall when in London Anno 1713 or 1714 in Letters to a Friend', pp. 35–6, 43–4. • **19.** The plying places are in Hatton, *A New View of London*, II, pp. 622, 794–5. The boat almost sucked under is in Quarrell and Mare (eds.), *London in 1710* . . ., 1934, p. 26. The accidents are in *HR 1718*, Chronological Register, p. 18, 13 and 15 April 1718. • **20.** For the rats see Wilkinson, *Memoirs* . . ., 1790, I, p. 194. Ward, *The London-Spy*, p. 156. On Thames water for drinking see Phillips, *The Thames about 1750*, pp. 58–9. The best in the world is said many times but see, for instance, Defoe, *A Tour . . .*, I, pp. 351–3. • **21.** Anon., *The Foreigner's Guide*, pp. 166–8.

1 *James Gibbs's London, 1708–54*

1. The definitive biography is Friedman, *James Gibbs*, 1984, but see also Little, *The Life and Work of James Gibbs*, 1955, and Summerson, *Architecture in Britain*, 1953, Ch. 21. • **2.** Little, *The Life and Work of James Gibbs*, pp. 29–30. • **3.** On the rise of Palladianism see Summerson, *Architecture in Britain*, Ch. 20; for some of its impact on London see Barnard and Clark (eds.), *Lord Burlington*, 1995; Campbell (ed.), *A House in Town*, 1984, pp. 11–17. • **4.** See *HCJ*, 16, p. 495, 14 February 1711, for the Greenwich petition; p. 542, 10 March 1711, for church provision and population figures; pp. 580–83, 6 April 1711, for the report of the committee on the Greenwich and other petitions. See also Port (ed.), *The Commissions . . .*, 1986, Introduction. • **5.** Downes, *Hawksmoor*, 1959. On Gibbs's election see Port, *The Commissions . . .*, pp. 24–6; Friedman, *James Gibbs*, pp. 9–10; Little, *The Life and Work of James Gibbs*, pp. 32–3. • **6.** The steeple's origin is described in Birch, *London Churches . . .*, 1896, pp. 154–5. Mar is cited in Friedman, *James Gibbs*, p. 10. • **7.** Friedman, ibid., says Gibbs was sacked in December 1715, but the commission seems formally to have dismissed him on 5 January 1716: see Port, *The Commissions . . .*, p. 45. On Lord Burlington's role see Barnard and Clark (eds.), *Lord Burlington*, pp. 274–5. • **8.** McMaster, *A Short History of the Royal Parish of St. Martin-in-the-Fields*, 1916, pp. 75–89. His reference to full Masonic rites may be misleading. From information kindly given to me by Martin Cherry, the librarian at Freemason's Hall, there appears to have been no connection between the stone-laying and Freemasonry, and there is no evidence that Gibbs was a Freemason. See also Friedman, *James Gibbs*, pp. 55–72, which wrongly gives 1717 as the date of the enabling act which paved the way for rebuilding, rather than 1720. The correct date is given in SOL, *XX*, 1940, Ch. 3. • **9.** Ralph, *A New Critical Review . . .*, 1736, p. 22. The endorsement is by Summerson, *Architecture in Britain*, p. 211. • **10.** Walpole, *Anecdotes . . .*, 1782, IV, pp. 92–3. • **11.** Moore, *The History of St. Bartholomew's Hospital*, 1918, II, p. 854. See also Bradley and Pevsner, *The Buildings of England: London 1*, 1997, pp. 331–5. • **12.** Act II, Scene i. The play was published in 1704. • **13.** See Wheatley and Cunningham, *London Past and Present*, 1891, II, pp. 186–8. • **14.** See the plan of 1708 reprinted in Clinch, *Marylebone and St. Pancras*, 1890, opp. p. 4. • **15.** HMC, Portland MSS, V, 1899, p. 550. See also Friedman, *James Gibbs*, p. 205ff., and Little, *The Life and Work of James Gibbs*, pp. 46–54. • **16.** On this development see John Summerson, 'Henrietta Place, Marylebone, and Its Associations with James Gibbs', *LTR*, 1958, pp. 26–36. • **17.** On Palladianism in practice see Bradley and Pevsner, *The Buildings of England: London 6*, 2003, pp. 27–8; and on the palace-front see, for instance, Frank Kelsall, 'Nos. 54–64 Strand: An Account of the Post-1737 Development of the Site', *LTR*, 1980, pp. 93–112. • **18.** On the London speculative builder see Summerson, *Georgian London*, 1945, pp. 22–8, 53–4, 61–2. • **19.** For the Grosvenor Estate see SOL, *XXXIX*, 1997, and *XL*, 1980. See also Dasent, *A History of Grosvenor Square*, 1935, for the square and its inhabitants. His comment that 'The foundations of Grosvenor Square were well and truly laid in an age when jerry-building was practically unknown' (p. vii) is wishful thinking. For the women inhabitants see Schlarman, 'The Social Geography of Grosvenor Square', 2003, pp. 8–28. • **20.** Climenson (ed.), *Elizabeth Montagu . . .*, 1906, I, pp. 230, 239, 253–8, 270, 278. For the Berkeley Square district see Johnson, *Berkeley Square to Bond Street*, 1952. • **21.** Lewis, Smith and Lam (eds.), *Horace Walpole's Correspondence . . .*, 24, 1967, p. 228, HW to Sir Horace Mann, 16 July 1776. • **22.** The key maps here are those engraved for Strype, *A Survey . . .*, 1720, and published in 1720 and the great map prepared by John Rocque, 1739–46, and published in 1747. The maps in Maitland, *The History and Survey . . .*, 1756, are often very fine but seem to rely on a re-presentation of Strype's maps with only the most obvious changes in the street plan taken into the new versions. Figures for numbers of houses in London parishes for this period are unreliable, but for what they're worth they are helpfully set out in George, *London Life . . .*, 1925, pp. 412–15. For growth in Clerkenwell in this period see SOL, *XLVI*, 2008, pp. 9–10 and passim. • **23.** On Spitalfields in this period see SOL, *XXVII*, 1957, pp. 4–5 and passim. On growth in Mile End Old Town, see Morris, *Mile End Old Town*, 2007, pp. 5–6. On wooden vernacular building despite the fire regulations see Guillery, *The Small House in Eighteenth-Century London*, 2004, Ch. 1 generally and for the East End Chs. 3 and 5. For the London Building Act of 1707 and subsequent legislation in this period see Knowles and Pitt, *The History of Building Regulation in London*, 1972, Ch. V. On Bethnal Green see VCH, *A History of the County of Middlesex*, XI, 1998, p. 87ff., and HCJ, 24, p. 391, 25 January 1743. • **24.** HCJ, 23, pp. 44–5, 2 March 1738. • **25.** The leading pessimists in this regard are George, *London Life . . .*, followed by Summerson, *Georgian London*, pp. 8–9; they have had recent scholarly support from Schwarz, *London in the Age of Industrialization*, 1992, Chs. 3 and 5; see also Landers, *Death and the Metropolis*, 1993, pp. 41–3, 54ff. • **26.** The existing-foundations proposal is in HCJ, 16, p. 209ff. (15 November 1709–4 March 1710). The kind of monster is in Tucker, *Four Letters . . .*, 1783, pp. 44–5. The wen is in Gwynn, *London and Westminster Improved*, 1766, p. 16. • **27.** Defoe, *A Tour . . .*, 1724–6, I, p. 6. • **28.** Colman and Thornton, *The Connoisseur*, 1757, I, pp. 255, 258, no. XXXIII, 12 September 1754. • **29.** On Stratford see Macky, *A Journey Through England*, 1722, p. 24. On Middlesex see Anon. [P. Cox?], *A Compleat History of Middlesex . . .*, 1730, p. 1. VCH, *Essex*, VI, 1973, pp. 44–6, 175–8, 241, 318–19, 339; *Middlesex*, IX, 1989, pp. 9–11 (Hampstead); *Middlesex*, X, 1995, p. 13 (Hackney); *Middlesex*, XII, 2004, pp. 26, 35–6 (Chelsea). For south London see Cherry and Pevsner, *The Buildings of England: London 2*, 1983, pp. 44–7. On the 'great increase of the Inhabitants' of Putney see HCJ, 16, pp. 545–6, 13 March 1711. • **30.** On Hampstead see Matthews (ed.), *The Diary of Dudley Ryder*, 1939, p. 90, 3 September 1715. On Kingsland see HCJ, 17, pp. 310–11, 4 May 1713. On Kensington see HCJ, 18, pp. 356–7, 13 April 1717. On Hyde Park Corner see HCJ, 20, pp. 410–11, 16 February 1725. • **31.** London was 'up' generations before the railway age: see, for instance, Swift, *Gulliver's Travels*, 1726, Part I, Ch. I, when Gulliver 'went down' from London to his father in Nottingham. • **32.** Morris, *Observations on the Past Growth . . .*, 1751, p. 19. • **33.** Summerson, *Georgian London*, p. 40. • **34.** Devonshire Square is there still, but the earliest remaining houses are thought to date from 1740. See Bradley and Pevsner, *The Buildings of England: London 1*, p. 479. • **35.** Harding, 'The Population of London, 1550–1700', 1990, p. 123. • **36.** On Horsleydown see HCJ, 22, pp. 45–6, 19 February 1733. On St Margaret see HCJ, 22, p. 397, 28 February 1735. On St Botolph see HCJ, 24, p. 372, 11 January 1743, and pp. 385–6, 21 January 1743. On Bethnal Green see *HCJ*, 24, p. 369, 10 January 1743, and p. 441, 25 February 1743. On the lodging houses see Henry Fielding, *An Enquiry . . .*, 1751, pp. 140–41. • 37. There were London Building Acts in 1667, 1707, 1708 and 1724, with others after 1760. Toynbee and Whibley (eds.), *Correspondence of Thomas Gray*, 1935, I, pp. 421–2, II, pp. 653–4. • 38. For Limehouse see *HCJ*, 18, pp. 511–12, 21 and 23 March 1717. For St Katherine's see *GM*, 1735, pp. 48–9; Upper Shadwell, *GM*, 1736, p. 550; Horsleydown, *GM*, 1745, p. 274; Battle Bridge, Southwark, *GM*, 1749, pp. 377–8; Cornhill, *GM*, 1748, pp. 138, 148–9. The Swedish visitor was Kalm: see *Kalm's Account of his Visit to England . . .*, 1892, pp. 88–9. • 39. Maitland, *The History and Survey . . .*, II, p. 902. • 40. Cited in Downes, *Hawksmoor*, pp. 241–2. • 41. For Jackanapes Alley see *HCJ*, 13, p. 162, 31 January 1700; for Hemmings Row see *HCJ*, 13, p. 506, 24 April 1702. For the Westminster gates see *HCJ*, 15, p. 103, 22 January 1706; the Holbein Gate at Whitehall was demolished in 1759 – Vanbrugh had successfully campaigned to save it as an antique treasure in 1714. The first of several Commons committees on the Westminster streets seems to appear at *HCJ*, 16, p. 58, 13 January 1709; the common sewers are at p. 141, 7 March 1709. The bill can be found at *HCJ*, 13, p. 342, 1 March 1710. See also the report of the committee on obstructions in the Westminster streets in *HCJ*, 19, p. 92, 9 February 1719, and pp. 118–19, 3 March 1719. • 42. Cited in Maitland, *The History and Survey . . .*, I, p. 615. • 43. Anon., *Reasons against Building a Bridge . . .*, 1722, pp. 13–14. • 44. *HCJ*, 19, pp. 694–5, 15 December 1721. • 45. Anon., *Reasons against Building a Bridge . . .*, pp. 6–7, 21. • 46. *HCJ*, 22, pp. 59–60, 26 February 1733. • 47. The idea of a Mansion House had been mooted since at least 1670: see Perks, *The History of the Mansion House*, 1922, Ch. X. Batty Langley, writing in August 1734, is cited ibid., p. 166. See also Jeffery, *The Mansion House*, 1993, for the definitive study. • 48. The attics were removed by about 1843. The judgement of posterity is in Bradley and Pevsner, *The Buildings of England: London 1*, p. 92. • 49. *HCJ*, 15, p. 272, 1 February 1707; *HCJ*, 22, p. 264, 2 March 1734, p. 442, 2 April 1735, and p. 444, 3 April 1735. • 50. *HCJ*, 20, p. 590, 25 February, and p. 595, 2 March 1726. For the residents see Dasent, *The History of St James's Square . . .*, 1895, pp. 52–4 and Appendix A. • 51. *HCJ*, 22, pp. 568–71, 16 February 1736. • 52. 10 Geo. 2 c.16. See *HCJ*, 22, p. 547, 4 February 1736, pp. 568–71, 16 February 1736, pp. 612–13, 5 March 1736, and pp. 641–2, 22 March 1736. See also Anon., *Reasons for erecting a Bridge . . .*, n.d. [1736]. • 53. *HCJ*, 22, pp. 568–71, 16 February 1736. • 54. The best summary of these complex affairs is in SOL, X, 1926, pp. 1–60. • 55. Maitland, *The History and Survey . . .*, I, p. 682; Grosley, *A Tour to London*, 1772, I, p. 27. See also SOL, *XXIII*, 1951, pp. 66–7. • 56. Friedman, *James Gibbs*, pp. 18–20; Little, *The Life and Work of James Gibbs*, Ch. VIII.

2 Robert Adam's London, 1754–99

1. Swarbrick, *Robert Adam and His Brothers*, 1915; Bolton, *The Architecture of Robert and James Adam*, 1922; Summerson, *Architecture in Britain*, 1953, pp. 261–70; Fleming, *Robert Adam and His Circle*, 1962; Harris, *The Genius of Robert Adam*, 2001; *ODNB*. The letter to Nelly is cited in Fleming, *Robert Adam and His Circle*, pp. 351–2. • 2. For the meeting with Bute see Carlyle, *The Autobiography . . .*, 1910, pp. 375–6. The best coverage of this early period is in Fleming, *Robert*

Adam and His Circle, Ch. 7. • **3.** Cited in Swarbrick, *Robert Adam and His Brothers*, pp. 66–7. • **4.** See esp. Summerson, *Architecture in Britain*, pp. 262–4. • **5.** See, for instance, the case of Stratford Place, Oxford Street, considered for generations an Adam development until it was established in 1920 that the brothers had no hand in the project. See Arthur T. Bolton, 'Stratford Place', *LTR*, 1920, pp. 78–86. • **6.** Harris, *The Genius of Robert Adam*, p. 157, and *AR 1782*, Chronicle, p. 218, on the death of Robert Child. • **7.** James and Robert had lived together in London in 1758 but it was not until James returned from his Grand Tour in 1763 that the London architectural partnership can be said to have begun. See Fleming, *Robert Adam and His Circle*, p. 245ff. • **8.** Anon. [An Irish Clergyman], 'Journals of Visits to London in 1761 and 1772', ff. 121–2, 26 August 1772. • **9.** Wheatley, *The Adelphi and Its Site*, 1885; Bolton, *Architecture of Robert and James Adam*, I, pp. 115–18 and II, Ch. XVIII. See also Bradley and Pevsner, *The Buildings of England: London 6*, 2003, pp. 326–30: the Adelphi was transformed in the 1870s and the Royal or Adelphi Terrace destroyed in 1936. The fogs are in King, *The Complete Modern London Spy . . .*, 1781, p. 31. • **10.** From analysing Middlesex deeds registrations and other data, Schwarz, *London in the Age of Industrialization*, 1992, pp. 79–85, tells us that 1761–7 witnessed a building boom, 1767–75 was stagnant and 1776–80 was a slump. If that's true, then the Adam speculations would be very much against the grain. In reality they appear not out of step with activity on the ground. • **11.** Bolton, *The Architecture of Robert and James Adam*, II, Ch. XXII. • **12.** Dates for Clerk's house are given as early as 1768 (Cherry and Pevsner, *The Buildings of England: London 3*, 1999, p. 643); but I've followed Bolton, *The Architecture of Robert and James Adam*, II, p. 99, which gives 1779. On Clerk the bore see Carlyle, *The Autobiography . . .*, p. 473ff. • **13.** On Portland Place see Bolton, *The Architecture of Robert and James Adam*, II, p. 102ff. • **14.** See ibid., Ch. XXI and Cherry and Pevsner, *The Buildings of England: London 3*, pp. 650–53. • **15.** See Bolton, *The Architecture of Robert and James Adam*, II, pp. 112–16; Cherry and Pevsner, *The Buildings of England: London 4*, 1999, pp. 335–6. • **16.** *AR 1799*, Chronicle, p. 39; Smith, *A Topographical and Historical Account . . .*, 1833, pp. 214–15. • **17.** Massie, *An Essay . . .*, 1754. • **18.** *HCJ*, 27, p. 134, 1 February 1755, pp. 158–60, 14 February 1755, pp. 348–9, 13 January 1756, and pp. 514–22, 12 March 1756. • **19.** *HCJ*, 27, pp. 514–22, 12 March 1756. • **20.** See Home, *Old London Bridge*, 1931, pp. 264–77. • **21.** See Ward, *The Man Who Buried Nelson*, 2007, Ch. 5. For the inscription see Birch, *City Latin*, 1761, pp. 2–3. • **22.** 33 Geo. 2 c.30, the London Streets (City) Act 1759, bearing the date of the start of the session. See Noorthouck, *A New History of London*, 1773, pp. 397–9 and n. Hughson, *London*, 1805–9, I, pp. 446–50, usefully sets out what was and was not completed. See also Gomme (ed.), *The Gentleman's Magazine Library . . .*, 1904–5, I, pp. 227–9. And there is a good description too in Hunter, *The History of London . . .*, 1811, II, pp. 754–6. • **23.** Spranger, *A Proposal or Plan . . .*, 1754, Preface, n.p. [p. iv]. His *Proposal* also extended to some parishes in Middlesex. • **24.** Hanway, *A Letter to Mr. John Spranger . . .*, 1754. • **25.** 2 Geo. 3 c.21 London Streets Act 1762, subsequently explained and enlarged by 3 Geo. 3 c.23, 4 Geo. 3 c.39, 5 Geo. 3 c.50 and 6 Geo. 3 c.54. The best account of these events remains Webb, *English Local Government*, 1922, pp. 276–88; see also George, *London Life . . .*, 1925, pp. 99–102. • **26.** *AR 1765*, Chronicle, p. 110. • **27.** Massie, *An Essay . . .*, p. 12. Grosley, *A Tour to London*, 1772, I, pp. 35–6 and n. His stay in London was in 1765 and his equally severe strictures on the Strand presumably pre-dated July. • **28.** 6 Geo. 3 c.26, London Paving and Lighting Act 1766. See

Entick, *A New and Accurate History . . .*, 1766, III, pp. 264–90; Noorthouck, *A New History of London*, p. 436ff.; Hughson, *London*, I, pp. 546–64. • **29.** City of London Commissioners of Sewers and Pavements: Proceedings 1766–7, pp. 1–69, 17 May to 16 July 1766. • **30.** City of London Commissioners of Sewers and Pavements: Proceedings 1765–9, ff. 40–41, 18 April 1766. • **31.** Defoe, Richardson and another, *A Tour . . .*, 1769, II, p. 163; Grosley, *A Tour to London*, I, pp. 35–6n. Meister, *Letters . . .*, 1799, pp. 182–4. • **32.** Hunter, *The History of London . . .*, II, pp. 754–6; Bradley and Pevsner, *The Buildings of England: London 1*, 1997, pp. 95–6. • **33.** Harris, *Sir William Chambers*, 1970. • **34.** Ibid., Ch. 7; Bradley and Pevsner, *The Buildings of England: London 6*, pp. 318–25. The riverside walk and indeed the courtyard of Somerset House were out of bounds to Londoners for much of their history, but not in the eighteenth century and happily not at present. • **35.** Maitland, *The History of London . . .*, 1739, pp. 519–20, gives 11,975 houses (11,484 inhabited) in 1737; the number in the 1801 census was 8,638, a reduction of 27.9 per cent. • **36.** Noorthouck, *A New History of London*, p. 425. The 'houses' of course had shops on their ground floors. • **37.** Dawe and Oswald, *11 Ironmonger Lane*, 1952, p. 84ff. • **38.** *New AR 1794*, Principal Occurrences, pp. 39–40. • **39.** Knowles and Pitt, *The History of Building Regulation in London*, 1972, pp. 44–53. • **40.** Hutton, *A Journey to London*, 1818, pp. 10, 13–14, 16–17. Hanway, *The Defects of Police . . .*, 1775, p. 251. • **41.** Stuart, *Critical Observations . . .*, 1771, esp. pp. 11–20, 44–6. On Stuart see Soros (ed.), *James 'Athenian' Stuart*, 2006. Gwynn, *London and Westminster Improved*, 1776. • **42.** *AR 1758*, Chronicle, p. 101. • **43.** *AR 1774*, Chronicle, p. 143. • **44.** King, *The Complete Modern London Spy . . .*, pp. 106–8. • **45.** *HCJ*, 27, p. 344, 18 December 1755; pp. 472–7, 25 February 1756. See also *GM*, 1755, Supplement, pp. 577–8. • **46.** On the City Road see *AR 1761*, Chronicle, p. 129. On the Duke of Bedford's private road see Thomson, *The Russells of Bloomsbury*, 1940, p. 367; and Little and Kahrl (eds.), *The Letters of David Garrick*, 1963, I, p. 324, 8 March 1760. • **47.** Gwynn, *London and Westminster Improved*, pp. x–xi. • **48.** *AR 1764*, Chronicle, p. 82; *AR 1769*, Chronicle, p. 86; *AR 1776*, Chronicle, p.178. • **49.** 'The Structu-Mania. An Epistle from Squire Quoz in Town, to his Uncle Quiz in the Country', *Attic*, I, pp. 247–8, April 1790. See also Malcolm, *Anecdotes . . .*, 1810, II, pp. 390–91; George, *London Life . . .*, pp. 73–4. • **50.** Anon. [An Irish Clergyman], 'Journals of Visits to London in 1761 and 1772', ff. 107–8, Saturday 15 August 1772. • **51.** Cherry and Pevsner, *The Buildings of England: London 3*, pp. 630–58. • **52.** Williams, *Memoirs of the Life and Correspondence of Mrs Hannah More*, I, 1835, p. 241, describing Mrs Elizabeth Montagu's house. • **53.** VCH, *A History of the County of Middlesex, XII*, 2004, pp. 47–51. Virtually none of this survived; it was redeveloped as part of the Cadogan Estate from the 1870s. • **54.** SOL, *XXIV*, 1952, Ch. 12. • **55.** See Thomson, *The Russells of Bloomsbury*, pp. 354–5. • **56.** See Olsen, *Town Planning in London*, 1964, pp. 43–51. See also Eliza Jeffries Davis, 'The University Site, Bloomsbury', *LTR*, 1936, pp. 19–139, esp. pp. 76–8. On the addresses of members of the House of Lords etc. see Barfoot and Wilkes, *The Universal British Directory . . .*, 1793, pp. lxxi–lxxxvi. • **57.** Olsen, *Town Planning in London*, pp. 74–96. • **58.** See Morris, *Mile End Old Town*, 2007, pp. 5–6, 13. The 1801 Census for London and Middlesex is usefully tabulated in Brayley and others, *London and Middlesex*, 1810–16, I, pp. 41–54. On Limehouse see Lysons, *The Environs of London*, 1792–6, III, pp. 238–9. On Bethnal Green see VCH, *A History of the County of Middlesex, XI*, 1998, p. 95. • **59.** See SOL, *XXIII*, 1951, Chs. 18 and 20. • **60.** See SOL, *XXII*, 1950, Ch. 22; VCH, *The Victoria History of the County of Surrey, IV*, 1912,

p. 132; Cherry and Pevsner, *The Buildings of England: London* 2, 1983, p. 52.
• **61**. Maitland, *The History and Survey* . . ., 1756, II, p. 1366; Lysons, *The Environs of London*, II, pp. 450–516; VCH, *Middlesex*, X, 1995, pp. 13–14, 96, 120.
• **62**. Lysons, *The Environs of London*, I, p. 81; Manning and Bray, *The History and Antiquities of the County of Surrey*, 1804–14, III, pp. 397–8. See also VCH, *The Victoria History of the County of Surrey*, IV, pp. 25–6; Dyos, *Victorian Suburb*, 1973, pp. 29–39. • **63**. Wimsatt and Pottle (eds.), *Boswell for the Defence*, 1960, pp. 30–35. The news of the bank crash is in Welch, *Modern History of the City of London*, 1896, p. 41. The stage coach numbers are in *AR 1775*, Chronicle, p. 191. On journey times generally see Blanning, *The Pursuit of Glory*, 2007, p. 11. The boat journey is in Yearsley (ed.), *The Diary of the Visits of John Yeoman*, 1934, pp. 22–3, 2 April 1774. • **64**. Young, *The Farmer's Letter* . . ., 1768, pp. 334–52. Smollett, *The Expedition of Humphry Clinker*, 1771, I, Matthew Bramble to Dr Lewis, 29 May; the encroachments are in Tucker, *Four Letters* . . ., 1783, pp. 47–8.
• **65**. Lewis, Smith and Lam (eds.), *Horace Walpole's Correspondence* . . ., 24, 1967, p. 228, HW to Sir Horace Mann, 16 July 1776. Lewis and Wallace (eds.), *Horace Walpole's Correspondence* . . ., 11, 1944, p. 249, HW to Mary Berry, 15–18 April 1791. • **66**. Moritz, *Travels of Carl Philipp Moritz* . . ., 1924, p. 93. • **67**. *AR 1798*, Chronicle, p. 84. See Olsen, *Town Planning in London*, p. 109; Chancellor, *The Private Palaces* . . ., 1908, pp. 88–94. • **68**. Smith, *A Book for a Rainy Day*, 1845, pp. 22–3. • **69**. On Tomlin's New Town see Lysons, *The Environs of London*, III, pp. 336–7; Robins, *Paddington*, 1853, pp. 190–91. Holcroft, *Memoirs* . . ., 1816, III, p. 44, 7 October 1798. Lewis, Wallace and Smith (eds.), *Horace Walpole's Correspondence* . . ., 35, 1973, pp. 389–90, HW to the Earl of Strafford, 28 July 1787. • **70**. Archenholtz, *A Picture of England*, 1797, pp. 131–2; Wendeborn, *A View of England* . . ., 1791, I, pp. 262–3; Hutton, *A Journey to London*, p. 10.
• **71**. Willan, *Reports on the Diseases in London*, 1801, pp. 256–7. • **72**. I have used the figures for 'Summary of the Population of the Metropolis of London' in Brayley and others, *London and Middlesex*, I, p. 54, and later reworkings of the London census data published by the London County Council in the twentieth century. • **73**. Parker, *A View of Society and Manners* . . ., 1781, II, p. 146; Pennant, *Some Account of London*, 1805, p. 151; Concanen and Morgan, *The History and Antiquities* . . ., 1795, pp. 257–8; Walpole, 'Additional Notes' MS, p. 10. • **74**. Gwynn, *London and Westminster Improved*, p. 20; Southey, *Letters from England*, 1807, pp. 408–9. Middleton, *View of the Agriculture of Middlesex*, 1798, p. 301, says 99 per cent of London night soil found its way into the Thames, but before the popularisation of the WC this seems an incredible proposition. • **75**. Yearsley (ed.), *The Diary of the Visits of John Yeoman*, pp. 40–41. • **76**. *The Times*, 19 February 1788; Pickett, *Public Improvement*, n.d. [1789]; see also Pickett's scrapbook, 'Manuscripts and Publications', 1782–96. • **77**. Lewis and Wallace (eds.), *Horace Walpole's Correspondence* . . ., 11, 1944, p. 249, HW to Mary Berry, 15–18 April 1791.

3 *Samuel Johnson's London – Britons*

1. On the mob see Napier (ed.), *Johnsoniana*, 1892, p. 343; for the linen see Boswell, *The Life of Samuel Johnson*, 1799, I, pp. 396–7. • **2**. Murphy, *An Essay on the Life* . . ., 1792, p. 7. • **3**. Boswell, *The Life of Samuel Johnson*, I, pp. 101–2.
• **4**. Ibid., III, pp. 534–6. • **5**. Ibid., III, p. 378; II, p. 120; III, p. 378. • **6**. On

Savage and Johnson see ibid., I, p. 162ff.; Johnson, *Life of Savage*, 1744. For the friend see Boswell, *The Life of Samuel Johnson*, II, p. 119. On the sleeping children see Napier (ed.), *Johnsoniana*, p. 342. On the prostitute see Boswell, *The Life of Samuel Johnson*, IV, pp. 321–2. Mrs Thrale's judgement is in Piozzi, *Anecdotes . . .*, 1786, p. 84. • 7. On Levett see Hawkins, *The Life of Samuel Johnson*, 1787, pp. 396–401. For Johnson's love of Levett see his moving poem 'On the Death of Dr. Robert Levet', 1783: I have followed Hawkins's spelling of the good doctor's name. For the ménage in general see Boswell, *The Life of Samuel Johnson*, III, Appendix D, pp. 462–4; and the *Times Literary Supplement*, 18 and 25 December 2009, pp. 19–21, for an interesting article on Mrs Desmoulins. • 8. 'Nests' is Mrs Thrale's derogatory term: Piozzi, *Anecdotes . . .*, p. 85. • 9. The estimate of annual migration is in Wrigley, 'A Simple Model of London's Importance in Changing English Society and Economy 1650–1750', 1967, p. 46. Bland's survey is in *AR* 1782, Chronicle, pp. 229–30. • 10. The City beggars are given in Hitchcock, *Down and Out . . .*, 2004, p. 6. The later sample is in *Reports from the Committees on the State of Mendicity . . .*, 1815–16, First Report, pp. 90–94. Some results from 1796 are given in Colquhoun, *The State of Indigence . . .*, 1799, pp. 12–13n. The apprentices are in Earle, *The Making of the English Middle Class*, 1989, pp. 3–5. For the bulk of migration probably coming from close to London see the discussion in Landers, *Death and the Metropolis*, 1993, pp. 41–9. And the general picture of migration is given in Colquhoun, *An Account of a Meat and Soup Charity*, 1797, p. 5. • 11. St Clement Danes Poor Law Examinations as to Settlement, WCCDEP358110031–84, 1752–3; I am very grateful to Tim Hitchcock for making this material available to me in advance of online publication. See also Hitchcock and Black (eds.), *Chelsea Settlement and Bastardy Examinations*, 1999. Rossell, *The Ordinary of Newgate's Account . . .*, 1746. • 12. Anon., *The London and Westminster Guide*, 1768, p. xii, quoting 'an eminent civilian' whom I've not identified. The Mahometans are in Archenholtz, *A Picture of England*, 1797, pp. 305–6. • 13. *ODNB*, aldermen alive in 1750; of merchants alive in 1750, with any life event in London, seventeen out of sixty-seven were London-born. • 14. The fruit-women are in Middleton, *View of the Agriculture of Middlesex*, 1798, p. 382. On the milkmaids see Nelson, *The History, Topography, and Antiquities . . .*, 1811, p. 110. • 15. The 'waggon loads' are cited in Hill, *Servants*, 1996, p. 4. The Welsh servant is in Grosley, *A Tour to London*, 1772, I, p. 82. Brady and Pottle (eds.), *Boswell in Search of a Wife*, 1957, p. 323, 22 September 1769. • 16. On the Welshmen see Anon., *A Trip from St James's . . .*, 1744, p. 2, and Anon., *Hell upon Earth*, 1729, pp. 4–5. On the vagabonds see Henry Fielding, *A Proposal for Making an Effectual Provision . . .*, 1753, p. 64. On the vagrant children see *HCJ*, 21, p. 921, 12 May 1732. On the Scots see Anon., *A Trip from St James's . . .*, p. 2. • 17. Lecky, *A History of England . . .*, 1877, I, p. 565. • 18. Matthews (ed.), *The Diary of Dudley Ryder*, 1939, pp. 88, 227. • 19. Wheatley and Cunningham, *London Past and Present*, 1891, III, p. 359 records the penultimate head falling in March 1772 and the last 'shortly after'. • 20. Carlyle, *The Autobiography . . .*, 1910, pp. 198–9. • 21. Pottle (ed.), *Boswell's London Journal*, 1950, pp. 71–2. • 22. Transcribed from memory into a commonplace book: Gulston, 'The Effusions of Fancy and Fun Compiled by Joseph Gulston 1784', p. 41. • 23. Smollett, *The Adventures of Roderick Random*, 1748, I, Ch. XVII. • 24. Carlyle, *The Autobiography*, pp. 361–2. • 25. Hardy, *Memoir of Thomas Hardy*, 1832, p. 4. Hardy writes of himself in the third person. • 26. Kevan, 'Autobiographical Memoir and Diary', f. 14. • 27. Edgeworth, *Memoirs . . .*, 1821, I, pp. 349–51. • 28. *Reports from the Committees on the State of Mendicity . . .*, First Report, p. 94. • **29.** Wilkinson, *Memoirs . . .*, 1790, IV, p. 102. 'Bow bell' was frequently used in the singular, but there was a peal of bells, increased to ten during the reign of George III: see St Aubyn-Brisbane, *If Stones Could Speak*, 1929, Ch. XXXV. • **30.** On freedom of the City see Webb, *English Local Government . . .*, 1908, II, pp. 575n., 583–4. • **31.** Uglow, *Hogarth*, 1997, pp. 3ff., 31. Allan, *William Shipley*, 1968, pp. 20–24. Argent (ed.), *Recollections of R. J. S. Stevens*, 1992, pp. 1–6. Sutherland, *A London Merchant*, 1933, pp. 1–4. • **32.** The law of settlement was complex and much disputed. See Shaw, *Parish Law*, 1753, pp. 255–71. See also Marshall, *The English Poor . . .*, 1926, Chs. V and VI. • **33.** St Clement Danes Poor Law Examinations as to Settlement, WCCDEP358020191–331. On St Clement's as a 'casualty parish' see Hitchcock, *Down and Out . . .*, p. 142. • **34.** Holcroft, *Memoirs . . .*, 1816, II, pp. 69–82. Foote, *The Commissary*, 1765, Act II. There is some non-fictional reportage of these aldermanic irregularities, but see also Knox, *Winter Evenings*, 1790, I, p. 503. • **35.** Wilkinson, *Memoirs . . .*, IV, pp. 99–102. • **36.** The watermen are in Van Muyden (ed.), *A Foreign View of England . . .*, 1902, p. 94, December 1725. Pelting with mud is in Casanova, *His Life and Memoirs*, 1933, II, p. 180 (1763). The fighting is in Van Muyden (ed.), *A Foreign View of England . . .*, pp. 180–81, February 1727. Anon., *The London and Westminster Guide*, pp. xxii–iii. And the American is in Price (ed.), *Joshua Johnson's Letterbook*, 1979, p. 18, 1 December 1771. • **37.** Archenholtz, *A Picture of England*, p. 38. • **38.** On the significance of dress in this period see Styles, *The Dress of the People*, 2007. For the German resident see Wendeborn, *A View of England . . .*, 1791, I, pp. 265–6. On the toupees see Defoe, *Augusta Triumphans*, 1728, p. 42. Smollett, *The Expedition of Humphry Clinker*, 1771, I, Matthew Bramble to Dr Lewis, London, 29 May; kibes are blisters. • **39.** Steele, *The Funeral*, 1702, Act I, Scene i. On the coats of arms see also Warburton, *London and Middlesex Illustrated*, 1749, defending the 509 citizens' coats of arms with which he'd decorated a map of London. • **40.** The attacks on the cits come from Burney, *Evelina*, 1778, I, Letter XLI; Burney, *Camilla*, 1796, I, Chs. IX and XXXVII. The gold is in Colman and Garrick, *The Clandestine Marriage*, 1766, Act I. The gluttony is in Ward, *Miscellaneous Writings . . .*, 1718, III, p. 97. • **41.** Anon., *A Trip from St James's . . .*, pp. 4–5. • **42.** Knox, *Winter Evenings*, I, pp. 91–2. • **43.** Saxby, *Memoirs . . .*, 1806, pp. 1–8. • **44.** Potter, *Life and Adventures . . .*, 1824, p. 62. • **45.** Cumberland, *Memoirs . . .*, 1807, I, p. 185. • **46.** D'Arblay, *Diary and Letters . . .*, 1854, V, pp. 255–9. On Montagu House see Chancellor, *The Private Palaces . . .*, 1908, Ch. XV; Soros (ed.), *James 'Athenian' Stuart*, 2006, pp. 248–56. • **47.** See Trusler, *The London Adviser and Guide*, 1786, p. 1. • **48.** Anon., *Reasons for a Pound-Rate . . .*, 1727, p. 1. • **49.** Wales, *An Inquiry . . .*, 1781, p. 19. • **50.** Blanchard (ed.), *The Correspondence of Richard Steele*, 1941, p. 20; Toynbee and Whibley (eds.), *Correspondence of Thomas Gray*, 1935, I, pp. 375–6n.; Pottle (ed.), *Boswell's London Journal*, p. 50, 26 November 1762; Ryskamp and Pottle (eds.), *Boswell*, 1963, p. 89, 22 March 1775. For Sterne see Cross, *The Life and Times of Laurence Sterne*, 1925, pp. 97, 163; and Macdonald, *Memoirs . . .*, 1790. • **51.** Smith, *A Book for a Rainy Day*, 1845, pp. 125–6. • **52.** Norton (ed.), *The Letters of Edward Gibbon*, 1956, I, pp. 114, 202, 248, 263, 349, 353, 364; III, pp. 357–8. • **53.** *The Museum*, 1771, II, pp. 13–14 (July 1771); *Town and Country Magazine*, August 1769, p. 397. • **54.** Thale (ed.), *The Autobiography of Francis Place*, 1972, pp. 104, 111, 124–7, 129, 138, 151, 173. For a general discussion on the housing of London's 'poorer sort' see George, *London Life . . .*, 1925, pp. 92–6. • **55.** Taylor, *The*

Ordinary of Newgate's Account . . ., 1747, pp. 37–43; OBP t17470604-19. • **56.** Kevan, 'Autobiographical Memoir and Diary', f. 15. • **57.** Ibid., f. 35. • **58.** City of London Police MSS, *Proclamation, Barber Mayor, 28 November 1732* (CLA/048/PS/01/044). *AR 1771*, Chronicle, p. 76. Nelson, *The History, Topography, and Antiquities* . . ., pp. 85–6n. • **59.** *Lloyd's Evening Post*, 21 November 1763; *AR 1763*, Chronicle, p. 110; Malcolm, *Anecdotes* . . ., 1810, I, pp. 58–64; George, *London Life* . . ., pp. 171–2; Hitchcock, *Down and Out* . . ., pp. 30–31 and Ch. 2 more generally for much detail on homelessness in eighteenth-century London. • **60.** Lettsom, *Medical Memoirs* . . ., 1774, pp. xi–xii. Willan, *Reports on the Diseases in London*, 1801, pp. 254–5. Colquhoun, *An Account of a Meat and Soup Charity*, 1797, p. 4n. The final case is in *AR 1784*, Chronicle, p. 185. • **61.** On London's excess mortality see Wrigley and Schofield, *The Population History of England*, 1981, pp. 166–7. • **62.** Creighton, *A History of Epidemics in Britain*, 1894, II, p. 648. Landers, *Death and the Metropolis*, pp. 98–101. • **63.** For the gin thesis swallowed neat see George, *London Life* . . ., Ch. I. For a survey of the available data see Landers, *Death and the Metropolis*. For typhus see Creighton, *A History of Epidemics in Britain*, II, pp. 66–81; for smallpox see ibid., pp. 461, 531, 535 and Ch. IV generally; for infantile diarrhoea being worse in the first half century see ibid., p. 756. See Landers, *Death and the Metropolis*, pp. 151–2, on infant care. Dr Price's actuarial tables are in *AR 1772*, Appendix to Chronicle, pp. 204–6. • **64.** For 1710 see Creighton, *A History of Epidemics in Britain*, II, p. 58; for 1722 see Maitland, *The History and Survey* . . ., 1756, I, p. 531; for 1743 see Lewis and Smith (eds.), *Horace Walpole's Correspondence* . . ., *18*, 1955, pp. 282–3, 293, July 1743; for 1760 see Lewis, Smith and Lam (eds.), *Horace Walpole's Correspondence* . . ., *21*, 1960, p. 427, 1 August 1760; for 1799 see Creighton, *A History of Epidemics in Britain*, II, p. 140. • **65.** Cumberland, 'Cumberland Papers Vol. I: Correspondence 1748–1777', ff. 132–3, 8 December 1774, to his brother Richard in Cambridge. • **66.** On stories of highwaymen see Black (ed.), *The Cumberland Letters*, 1912, pp. 58–9; on coach manners and a taciturn Samuel Richardson see Hawkins, *The Life of Samuel Johnson*, pp. 384–5n. • **67.** *Town and Country Magazine*, July 1790, p. 314. • **68.** The wild beasts are in Anon., *A Trip through the Town*, 1735, p. 1. The authorship of *The Art of Living in London* is disputed. On taking the wall see Legg, *Low-Life*, 1764, pp. 6–7; Boswell, *The Life of Samuel Johnson*, I, p. 110. • **69.** For the City of Bristol see *The Post-Man*, 30 January–1 February 1705. For the Angel Inn see Strype, *A Survey* . . ., 1720, II, Book IV, p. 118. The Notts club is in Jesse, *George Selwyn* . . ., 1843, I, p. 355. • **70.** *AR 1798*, Chronicle, pp. 15–16. See also Highmore, *Pietas Londinensis*, 1810, pp. 906–12. The Welsh Charity School on Clerkenwell Green is now the Marx Memorial Library: see Andrew Rothstein, *A House on Clerkenwell Green*, 1972. • **71.** For Downing Street see Pottle (ed.), *Boswell's London Journal*, p. 50, 26 November 1762, and p. 207; for the barber and shoe-black see Ryskamp and Pottle (eds.), *Boswell*, p. 262, 17 March 1776, and p. 103, 27 March 1775; for Drummond see Smyth (ed.), *Memoirs and Correspondence* . . ., 1849, I, pp. 393–4, 13 April 1773. For London the capital of Scotland see Ryskamp and Pottle (eds.), *Boswell*, pp. 95–6, 25 March 1775. For the manners see Danziger and Brady (eds.), *Boswell*, 1989, p. 105, 28 August 1790. • **72.** Carlyle, *The Autobiography* . . ., pp. 204–5, 356: he says Savile Row or Sackville Street, but the latter seems more likely according to Bryant Lillywhite (see below). Coleridge, *The Life of Thomas Coutts Banker*, 1920, I, pp. 65–6. Somerville, *My Own Life and Times*, 1861, pp. 140–65. Norton (ed.), *The Letters of Gibbon*, II, p. 2, 29

January 1774. For the British Coffee House see SOL, *XVI*, 1935, pp. 148–9; Lillywhite, *London Coffee Houses*, 1963, pp. 132–5, gives the first Scottish association in 1715 and the St Andrews Lodge of Freemasons meeting there in 1826; Carlyle, *The Autobiography*, pp. 354–5n., tells us Mrs Anderson was hostess there in 1758, when her husband seems to have been the ratepayer according to the Survey of London. • **73.** On the Scottish Corporation see Taylor, *A Cup of Kindness*, 2003, esp. Ch. 14. *The World*, 4 December 1787. For the cost of the tickets see the Caledonian Society advertisement for the previous year's ball at the same venue in *Morning Herald*, 25 November 1786. • **74.** For Freemasonry generally see Clark, *British Clubs and Societies*, 2000, Ch. 9. • **75.** Henry Fielding, *History of Joseph Andrews*, 1742, Book I, Ch. VI. Legg, *Low-Life*, pp. 55, 60. • **76.** For a general discussion of metropolitan loneliness and disconnectedness in this period see Byrd, *London Transformed*, 1978, p. 24ff. Lewis and Smith (eds.), *Horace Walpole's Correspondence . . .*, *18*, 1955, pp. 315–16, 3 October 1743. • **77.** On the loneliness of radicals see Barrell, *The Spirit of Despotism*, 2006, pp. 73–4. • **78.** Parker, *A View of Society and Manners . . .*, 1781, I, pp. 23–4.

4 *Ignatius Sancho's London – Citizens of the World*

1. Edwards and Rewt (eds.), *The Letters of Ignatius Sancho*, 1994, p. 168, to John Rush, May 1779. • **2.** *London Morning Penny Post*, 17 May 1751. • **3.** For Sancho's life see *ODNB*; Edwards and Rewt (eds.), *The Letters of Ignatius Sancho*, pp. 1–29; Gerzina, *Black London*, 1995, p. 59ff.; King, Sandhu, Walvin and Girdham, *Ignatius Sancho*, 1997; Dabydeen, Gilmore and Jones, *The Oxford Companion to Black British History*, 2007, pp. 428–9; see also Nichols, *Literary Anecdotes . . .*, 1812–16, VIII, p. 109n.; Smith, *Nollekens and His Times*, 1829, I, pp. 26–7n. His description of his old age is in Edwards and Rewt (eds.), *The Letters of Ignatius Sancho*, p. 227, to Mrs H—, 20 May 1780. • **4.** Ibid., pp. 163–4, to William Stevenson, 11 March 1779 (for the death of Kitty); the fate of Sancho's children is not entirely clear: of seven known to posterity, two lived to adulthood and three died before the age of ten. See ibid., p. 85, for the letter to Sterne, July 1766. • **5.** Ibid., p. 56, 11 October 1772. • **6.** Ibid., p. 104, to John Rush, 27 August 1777. • **7.** Nichols, *Literary Anecdotes . . .*, IX, pp. 682–3; Johnson gives 'ridicule to the face' as this meaning of 'smoke' – it could also mean discover, find out. • **8.** Myers, *Reconstructing the Black Past*, 1996, Ch. 2. • **9.** See, in general, Dabydeen, *Hogarth's Blacks*, 1985, p. 18; Norman, *London Signs and Inscriptions*, 1893, pp. 24–5; for Ludgate Hill see F. G. Hilton Price, 'Signs of Old London', *LTR*, 1903, pp. 70–108; Cumberland, *The West Indian*, 1771, Act I, Scene ii. • **10.** See Fryer, *Staying Power*, 1984, pp. 44–50. • **11.** For Jack Beef see Yorke (ed.), *The Diary of John Baker*, 1931, p. 15. On Somerset and the judgement see *ODNB* and Braidwood, *Black Poor . . .*, 1994, pp. 18–22. For the 1774 case see Welch, *Modern History of the City of London*, 1896, pp. 43–4. Flavell, *When London was Capital of America*, 2010, Ch. II. • **12.** For Frank Barber see *ODNB*; Gerzina, *Black London*, p. 43ff. For Alamaze see *Bon Ton*, 1791, pp. 60–61 (April), 173–4 (July) and 220 (August). For Jarbe see Casanova, *His Life and Memoirs*, 1933, II, pp. 179–80. For Reynolds's servant see Northcote, *Memoirs of Sir Joshua Reynolds*, 1813, pp. 117–19. For Clements see Smith, *Nollekens and His Times*, I, p. 34. For Pleasant see OBP t17801206-2, trail of Michael Daniel, 6 December 1780: guilty, death. • 13. The visitor to Johnson met by the 'Africans' was the Reverend Ben Turner, cited in Nichols, *Illustrations . . .*, 1817–58, VI, p. 148. Ruth Crook's funeral is in *Lloyd's Evening Post*, 5 September 1763. For the balls and other gatherings see Fryer, *Staying Power*, pp. 68–70, 124–5. • 14. For Gilbert see Foreman, *Georgiana Duchess of Devonshire*, 1998, p. 240n.; Equiano, *The Interesting Narrative . . .*, 1789, pp. 125–6, 135–6; for Soubise see *ODNB* and Angelo, *Reminiscences . . .*, 1828–30, I, pp. 446–53; Guy is in OBP t17360908-39, trial of Sarah Jones and Mary Smith: acquitted – they said Guy had given them the money; and for Commins see OBP t17820515-20, trial of Thomas Lee: not guilty, mistaken identity. • 15. For black musicians generally see Fryer, *Staying Power*, pp. 79–88; King-Dorset, *Black Dance in London*, 2008, pp. 112–15. For black musicians in art see Dabydeen, *Hogarth's Blacks*, pp. 18, 129. For Douglas see Ginger (ed.), *John Grano*, 1998, p. 21. For Lincoln see Edwards and Rewt (eds.), *The Letters of Ignatius Sancho*, pp. 35–6. • 16. Ward, *The London-Spy*, 1703, p. 244; *GM*, 1751, p. 571; Dabydeen, Gilmore and Jones, *The Oxford Companion to Black British History*, pp. 161–2. • 17. For Lord Pembroke see Ryskamp and Pottle (eds.), *Boswell*, 1963, p. 118, 3 April 1775; Allingham is in OBP t17820515-27; for black prostitutes more generally see Fryer, *Staying Power*, pp. 76–7. Smith, *Vagabondiana*, 1817, p. 34. • 18. For the City Corporation see Fryer, *Staying Power*, pp. 74–5; for the orphans see Highmore, *Pietas Londinensis*, 1810, pp. 600–608; Thomas is in *AR 1770*, Chronicle, p. 161; the poor black is in Blizard, *Desultory Reflections on Police*, 1785, p. 46. Black people do not seem to have been unduly picked on by press gangs: see Nicholas Rogers, *The Press Gang*, 2007, pp. 91–5. • 19. OBP t17810425-37, trial of Sarah Robinson and Elizabeth Clarke. • 20. Hoare, *Memoirs of Granville Sharp*, 1828, II, p. 4. • 21. Equiano, *The Interesting Narrative . . .*, pp. 171–2; Hoare, *Memoirs of Granville Sharp*, II, pp. 3–20; see also the excellent Braidwood, *Black Poor . . .*, passim but esp. pp. 63–79; and Carretta, *Equiano the African*, 2006, Ch. 10, which gives one count of 459 sailing, comprising 344 blacks and 115 whites. • 22. On the Orchard House see OBP t17671021-23, trial of Thomas James, a lascar, sentenced to death for a burglary there. Charles Eyloe, the prosecutor, said, 'I live at the Orchard-house, Blackwall, where the East-India company send their people to board.' It was still used 'by contract' in 1787: see Pennant, *A Journey from London to the Isle of Wight*, 1801, I, p. 28. For the lascars generally see Visram, *Asians in Britain*, 2002, pp. 15–37. For the vandalism in St Paul's see *AR 1769*, Chronicle, p. 131. • 23. *London Chronicle*, 3–5, 5–8, 8–10 and 10–12 February 1780; *AR 1784–5*, Chronicle 1785, pp. 242–3. For numbers see Myers, *Reconstructing the Black Past*, pp. 104–6. • 24. Wimsatt and Pottle (eds.), *Boswell for the Defence*, 1960, p. 35, 21 March 1772; Reed and Pottle (eds.), *Boswell Laird of Auchinleck*, 1993, p. 314, 9 April 1781. Hickey, *Memoirs*, 1913–25, II, pp. 275, 281. OBP t17950916-2, trial of Susannah. • 25. Gwynn, *Huguenot Heritage*, 1985, Chs. 1 and 2. The wider French community in modern London has yet to find its historian. • 26. On Soho see SOL, *XXXIII*, 1966, pp. 6–8. For charitable relief see Le Committé François, *Estat de la Distribution . . .*, 1707. • 27. On the anxieties of English weavers before 1700 see SOL, *XXVII*, 1957, pp. 4–5; on the drop of blood see Gwynn, *Huguenot Heritage*, p. 155, and for the artisan industries pp. 71–3. • 28. For the churches and charities see ibid., pp. 165–6, 171–2; see also for the charities Highmore, *Pietas Londinensis*, pp. 254–64. On the Camisards see Calamy, *An Historical Account . . .*, 1829, II, pp. 71–7. • 29. On the equation between the French and luxurious decline see, for instance, Anon., *Hell upon Earth*, 1729; for the events of 1738 see *HR Year 1738*,

p. 278ff., and Anon., *Memoirs of the Life and Times of Sir Thomas Deveil . . .*, 1748, pp. 42-4. For 1749 see *GM*, 1749, p. 519. For the footmen's riot see Anon., *Memoirs of the Life and Times of Sir Thomas Deveil . . .*, p. 60ff. Foote, *The Liar*, 1762, Act I, Scene ii. For French and other servants in the period see Horn, *Flunkeys and Scullions*, 2004, p. 73ff. • 30. Grosley, *A Tour to London*, 1772, I, pp. 91-2. • 31. Whistler, *Sir John Vanbrugh*, 1938, p. 85. • 32. Smith, *Nollekens and His Times*, II, p. 130ff. • 33. On Gibbs and Rysbrack see Whitley, *Artists and Their Friends . . .*, 1928, I, p. 79. • 34. Harris, *The Genius of Robert Adam*, 2001, p. 2. • 35. Grosley, *A Tour to London*, I, p. 103. • 36. Samuel Johnson, *London*, 1738, lines 94-5; 'shore' here means sewer. • 37. On the German hotels of Suffolk Street see Quarrell and Mare (eds.), *London in 1710 . . .*, 1934, p. 12; Roche, *Sophie in London . . .*, 1933, p. 85. • 38. On the Palatines see *HCJ*, 16, pp. 456-7, 15 January, and pp. 596-8, 14 April 1711; see also Panayi (ed.), *Germans in Britain . . .*, 1996, pp. 29-31; Strype, *A Survey . . .*, 1720, II, Book V, p. 43; Noorthouck, *A New History of London*, 1773, pp. 294-5. • 39. For Germans and Dutch in London sugar refining see Campbell, *The London Tradesman*, 1747, p. 273; see also Morris and Cozens, *Wapping*, 2009, pp. 136-7. Susanne Steinmetz, 'The German Churches in London, 1669-1914', in Panayi (ed.), *Germans in Britain . . .*, pp. 52-7. For the Moravians see *GM*, 1750, p. 282, June 1750, and for their continued residence Lysons, *The Environs of London*, 1792-6, II, pp. 169-70. On the Hackney market gardeners see VCH, *Middlesex*, X, 1995, p. 94. • 40. For the Palatines see Noorthouck, *A New History of London*, pp. 427-8; for the Corsicans see Brady and Pottle (eds.), *Boswell in Search of a Wife*, 1957, p. 319ff.; and for the Americans see George Atkinson Ward (ed.), *Journal and Letters of the Late Samuel Curwen*, 1842, passim. • 41. Lewis and Wallace (eds.), *Horace Walpole's Correspondence . . .*, 11, 1944, I, p. 74, HW to Mary Berry, 2 July 1790; the reception in the London streets is in Copeland and others (eds.), *The Correspondence of Edmund Burke*, VII, 1958-78, pp. 208-10, to the Bishop of St-Pol-de-Léon, post 13 September 1792. The sufferings of the pregnant women and others is in *Address from the Committee for the Relief of the French . . .*, 1796, n.p. [p. 1]. Botany Bay is in Palmer, *St Pancras*, 1870, p. 59. Lewis, Smith and Bennett (eds.), *Horace Walpole's Correspondence . . .*, 31, 1961, p. 386, HW to Hannah More, 23 March 1793. • 42. For Rewbrey see OBP t17000828-63; for Finch see Lysons, *The Environs of London*, IV, pp. 301-2, and for Bridget see I, p. 107; for Boswell (no relation) see *AR 1773*, Chronicle, pp. 142-3, 20 October 1773. • 43. For Stoke Newington see Andrews, *The Eighteenth Century . . .*, 1856, p. 58. The turkeys are in Legg, *Low-Life*, 1764, p. 35; Wyndham (ed.), *The Diary of the Late George Bubb Dodington*, 1784, p. 80, 28 June 1750; Greig (ed.), *The Farington Diary*, 1922, p. 235, 29 August 1798. • 44. See Endelman, *The Jews of Georgian England*, 1979, pp. 119-21, 170ff.; the overview in Lipman, *Social History of the Jews in England*, 1954, Ch. 1, remains useful. • 45. For the list of merchants see Maitland, *The History and Survey . . .*, 1756, I, pp. 634-5. For the German visitor see Kielmansegge, *Diary of a Journey to England*, 1902, pp. 28, 170. • 46. On Salvadore see Andrew and McGowen, *The Perreaus and Mrs Rudd*, 2001, pp. 106-7. For Gideon see Nichols, *Literary Anecdotes . . .*, IX, pp. 642-3; Nichols, *Illustrations . . .*, VI, pp. 277-84; the smelling salts are in *ODNB* (Edgar Samuel). For da Costa see *AR 1764*, Chronicle, p. 78 and *ODNB*. • 47. Carlisle is in Jesse, *George Selwyn . . .*, 1843, III, p. 59. The shabby old fellow is in Anon., *A Sunday Ramble*, 1774, pp. 36-7. Burney, *Cecilia*, 1782, Book III, Ch. III. Moses Manasses is in Foote, *The Cozeners*, 1774, Act 1, Scene i. Fox is in Wheatley (ed.), *The Historical and*

Posthumous Memoirs . . ., 1884, II, p. 7, spelling error silently corrected. There is a slightly different version in Jesse, *George Selwyn* . . ., II, p. 222. • **48.** For the suburban presence see Defoe, *A Tour* . . ., 1724–6, I, pp. 382–3 for Highgate; for Hackney and Stamford Hill see VCH, *Middlesex, X,* p. 145; and for Stoke Newington see VCH, *A History of the County of Middlesex, VIII,* 1985, p. 195. For the dedication of the new Duke's Place see *AR 1766,* Chronicle, p. 131. For the brothel see Harris, *Harris's List* . . ., 1779, pp. 57–8; Harris also notes a couple of Jewish prostitutes in Covent Garden in this issue. • **49.** For Jewish street trading see Endelman, *The Jews of Georgian England,* pp. 180–81. For the arrest in the City of a Jewish hawker see *AR 1767,* Chronicle, p. 102. • **50.** Place, 'Papers', BL Add. MS 27,827, ff. 144–5. For Rag Fair see Thornton, *The New, Complete, and Universal History* . . ., 1784, p. 472. • **51.** City of London Coroner's Court: Inquests, 1794, CLA/041/IQ/02/007, Inquest 003, 7 January 1794. • **52.** For the Jewish fence generally see Endelman, *The Jews of Georgian England,* pp. 194–8. For the reward see *AR 1770,* Chronicle, p. 90. • **53.** OBP t17640113-42; t17720121-31; t17810425-67; t17810530-55; t17870221-19. • **54.** The swindlers are in Parker, *A View of Society and Manners* . . ., 1781, II, pp. 28–30; Archenholtz, *A Picture of England,* 1797, pp. 177–8. • **55.** On the Chelsea crime see Endelman, *The Jews of Georgian England,* pp. 198–200, and *AR 1771,* Chronicle, pp. 114, 153–4, 160–61 and Appendix to the Chronicle, pp. 210–15. The Moorfields events are in *AR 1775,* Chronicle, pp. 89, 111. The housebreakers are in Blizard, *Desultory Reflections on Police,* pp. 43–5. The New Prison is in *AR 1795,* Chronicle, pp. 13, 25. • **56.** The City Recorder is in Welch, *Modern History of the City of London,* p. 39; the child-killing is in *GM,* 1732, p. 773; for the events of 1753 see Endelman, *The Jews of Georgian England,* Ch. 3. • **57.** *AR 1763,* Chronicle, p. 80. See also Endelman, *The Jews of Georgian England,* p. 115. • **58.** Place, 'Papers', BL Add. MS 27,827, f. 145. • **59.** Mendoza, *Memoirs* . . ., 1816. See also Endelman, *The Jews of Georgian England,* pp. 219–22. • **60.** Elias (ed.), *Memoirs of Laetitia Pilkington,* 1997, I, p. 63. The people of energy etc. are in Lecky, *A History of England* . . ., 1877, II, pp. 257–60; Lecky himself was a Dubliner. • **61.** On Barker see *ODNB*; Altick, *The Shows of London,* 1978, Ch. 10; for Nelson see Whitley, *Artists and Their Friends* . . ., II, pp. 106–8. On Barry see *ODNB* and Whitley, *Artists and Their Friends* . . ., I, p. 284ff. • **62.** Copeland and others (eds.), *The Correspondence of Edmund Burke,* I, p. 335, 12 November 1767, and pp. 352–3, 9 June 1768. • **63.** Anon. [An Irish Clergyman], 'Journals of Visits to London in 1761 and 1772', ff. 24–5. • **64.** For the mythical society see, for instance, Anon. [A German Gentleman], *A View of London and Westminster,* 1725, pp. 15–20. • **65.** Nugent is in Wheatley (ed.), *The Historical and Posthumous Memoirs* . . ., I, p. 88ff.; for Concannen see Greig (ed.), *The Farington Diary,* p. 135, 21 January 1796; for Dowdale see Guthrie, *The Ordinary of Newgate* . . ., 1730, n.p. [p. 2]. • **66.** For the 'Irish literati' as legend see Smollett, *The Adventures of Roderick Random,* 1748, I, Ch. XLIX, where two have 'but one shirt, and half a pair of breeches' between them. Elias (ed.), *Memoirs of Laetitia Pilkington,* I, pp. 198–202. See also the excellent Clarke, *Queen of the Wits,* 2008. • **67.** Forster, *The Life and Times of Oliver Goldsmith,* 1854, I, pp. 181–2, 205–6. • **68.** Landers, *Death and the Metropolis,* 1993, pp. 48–9; for the Westminster Dispensary see *AR 1782,* Chronicle, pp. 229–30; and for the beggars, *Reports from the Committees on the State of Mendicity* . . ., First Report, p. 94. • **69.** Rossell, *The Ordinary of Newgate's Account* . . ., 1746, p. 49. • **70.** Welch, *A Proposal to Render* . . ., 1758, pp. 50–51. For the haymakers see Middleton, *View of the Agriculture of Middlesex,* 1798, pp. 237-8; for the milkmaids see Nelson, *The History, Topography, and Antiquities* . . ., 1811, p. 110; and the potato-pickers see VCH, *Essex*, VI, 1973, p. 15 (East Ham). • **71.** The mass-house is in *GM*, 1735, p. 106. For the Irish officers see Hunter, *The History of London* . . ., 1811, II, pp. 598-600; the spy was Bradstreet, *The Life and Uncommon Adventures* . . ., 1755, pp. 126-7; the chairmen's plot was according to Philip Thicknesse and reported in Nichols, *Literary Anecdotes* . . ., IX, pp. 272-3. • **72.** Ellis, *The History and Antiquities* . . ., 1798, pp. 362-3, citing correspondence of Sir Robert Walpole and the Duke of Newcastle. According to Malcolm, *Anecdotes* . . ., 1810, II, pp. 51-2, the Irish building workers would work for 5-6s a week while the 'English' demanded 12s. • **73.** The Brick Lane pub is in *GM*, 1736, p. 422; the troops are in Ellis, *The History and Antiquities* . . ., pp. 362-3. • **74.** OBP t17361013-5. A bavin was a bound bundle of firewood for bakers' ovens. • **75.** *GM*, 1736, p. 485. • **76.** For the effects of the 1736 riots on employers see Hervey, *Some Materials Towards Memoirs* . . ., 1931, II, pp. 565-7. The butchers are in *GM*, 1740, p. 142. The calico printers are in VCH, *Essex*, VI, p. 77. For the St Giles events see *GM*, 1755, pp. 375-6. The chairmen are in *AR 1763*, Chronicle, p. 62. The Hendon haymakers are in *AR 1774*, Chronicle, pp. 134-5. • **77.** OBP t17400903-31, trial of Stephen Jones, guilty, manslaughter; t17650918-54, trial of Thomas Bradley, not guilty, the house surgeon at the Middlesex Hospital swearing that Barry died of a fever contracted in hospital. The street is given as Banbury Street, and though there was a Banbury Court it is likely that Bainbridge Street was intended. • **78.** *AR 1793*, Chronicle, p. 29; *New AR 1796*, Principal Occurrences, p. 63; *AR 1798*, Chronicle, p. 18. For the extraordinary St Stephen's Night fracas see OBP t17990508-21, trial of Timothy Brian and several others, guilty, death for three.

5 *William Beckford's London – Commerce*

1. Beckford, *An Arabian Tale* . . ., 1786, p. 1. • **2.** William Beckford, 'Letters from Spanish Town, Jamaica, to James Knight, London', BL Add. MS 12,431, ff. 116-17, 11 October 1740. • **3.** Ireland, *Hogarth Illustrated*, 1884, p. 303; Uglow, *Hogarth*, 1997, pp. 666-7. In 1745 Beckford bought the eight paintings of Hogarth's *Rake's Progress*; they were sadly lost in the fire at his country mansion Fonthill nine years later. • **4.** For Beckford see *ODNB*; Alexander, *England's Wealthiest Son*, 1962, Ch. 1; Anon., *City Biography* . . ., 1800, pp. 63-80; the natural children are in Walpole, *Memoirs of the Reign of George the Third*, 1894, IV, p. 104n.; and the diarrhoea in Lewis, Troide, Martz and Smith (eds.), *Correspondence of Horace Walpole*, 38, 1974, p. 499, HW to Lord Hertford, 27 January 1765, citing Charles Townshend. Parker, *The Sugar Barons*, 2011, pp. 250-51, 299-300, 339. • **5.** Strype, *A Survey* . . ., 1720, II, Book V, p. 256. • **6.** Pennant, *Some Account of London*, 1805, pp. 47-8. • **7.** See Broodbank, *History of the Port of London*, 1921, I, Chs. VI-VIII. For the East India Company at Blackwall see SOL, *XLIV*, 1994, Ch. XIX. • **8.** The figures are in Bird, *The Geography of the Port of London*, 1957, pp. 38-9. See also Davis, *The Rise of the English Shipping Industry*, 1962, pp. 34-5, 40-43; Hancock, *Citizens of the World*, 1995, pp. 25-31. • **9.** For imports and exports see the useful table facing p. 22 in Colquhoun, *A Treatise on the Commerce and Police* . . ., 1800; for Beale's Wharf and others see Barfoot and Wilkes, *The Universal British Directory* . . ., 1793, pp. 621-32. • **10.** For the largely unsung Vaughan see *ODNB* and Broodbank, *History of the Port of London*, I, p.78ff. The proposals

are primarily in Vaughan, *On Wet Docks . . .*, 1793, but see his other works listed in the bibliography. • 11. *London Chronicle*, 20–22 January 1780, for the tragic accident. The Trinity House pilots are evidenced in *Report from the Committee . . . Port of London*, 1796, pp. vii–xi. For the fishing see Pennant, *Some Account of London*, pp. 403–5; Middleton, *View of the Agriculture of Middlesex*, 1798, p. 29; and for the whitebait see Pennant, *A Journey from London to the Isle of Wight*, 1801, I, p. 23. • 12. See Hoppit, *A Land of Liberty?*, 2000, pp. 318–23. • 13. For the numbers of East India Company ships see Keay, *The Honourable Company*, 1991, p. 220, and Colquhoun, *A Treatise on the Commerce and Police . . .*, table facing p. 22. Hickey, *Memoirs*, 1913–25, II, p. 186. For some great East India fortunes see Edwardes, *The Nabobs at Home*, 1991. • 14. Godwin, *Hansons of Eastcheap*, 1947, pp. 1–12, 45. • 15. On Newman see *AR 1799*, Chronicle, pp. 57–8. • 16. See Hancock, *Citizens of the World*. • 17. For the Exchange and its walks see Hatton, *A New View of London*, 1708, II, pp. 614–18; *The Spectator*, No. 69, 19 May 1711. • 18. Anon. [An Irish Clergyman], 'Journals of Visits to London in 1761 and 1772', f. 25, August 1761. • 19. For the numbers of coffee houses see Maitland, *The History and Survey . . .*, 1756, II, p. 719. The Russian is Karamzin, *Letters of a Russian Traveller . . .*, 1957, p. 289. For the list of premises destroyed in the Cornhill fire see *GM*, 1748, pp.148–9, April 1748. For a comprehensive directory of City and other coffee houses see Lillywhite, *London Coffee Houses*, 1963. • 20. For arrangements early in the century see Hatton, *A New View of London*, II, pp. 710–12; and for later see Barfoot and Wilkes, *The Universal British Directory . . .*, p. 711ff. Wendeborn, *A View of England . . .*, 1791, I, p. 340. • 21. Price (ed.), *Joshua Johnson's Letterbook*, 1979, p. 17; more generally see Hancock, *Citizens of the World*, Ch. 3. • 22. Chandler, *Four Centuries of Banking . . .*, 1964, pp. 21–3. See also Michie (ed.), *The Development of London . . .*, 2000, I, pp. 53–7. • 23. Carruthers, *City of Capita*, 1996, pp. 139–40. • 24. Macky, *A Journey Through England*, 1722, p. 309. • 25. Michie (ed.), *The Development of London . . .*, I, pp. 60–63. • 26. The figures for 1792 come from Barfoot and Wilkes, *The Universal British Directory . . .*, pp. 47–8; the earlier numbers are in Michie (ed.), *The Development of London . . .*, I, p. 58. • 27. For bankers living over the shop see Bradley and Pevsner, *The Buildings of England: London 1*, 1997, p. 94. For Coutts see Coleridge, *The Life of Thomas Coutts Banker*, 1920, I, pp. 43–6. • 28. For the tendency of merchants to diversify into finance by mid-century see Sutherland, *A London Merchant*, 1933, pp. 15–16. For Williams Deacon see Anon., *Williams Deacon's*, 1971, pp. 1–37. • 29. Davies, *An Account of the Formation . . .*, 1952, Ch. 3. • 30. On the Fire Watch see Drew, *The London Assurance*, 1949, p. 58. See also, for an overview of these years, Dickson, *The Sun Insurance Office*, 1960, Chs. 1–5; Supple, *The Royal Exchange Assurance*, 1970, Chs. 1–4; Michie (ed.), *The Development of London . . .*, I, Ch. 10. • 31. The quote from 1735 is cited ibid., p. 143; more generally see Gibb, *Lloyd's of London*, 1957, Chs. 1–3. • 32. *Daily Courant*, 10 January 1709. • 33. The Amicable's arrangements are set out in Dodsley, *London and Its Environs Described . . .*, 1761, I, pp. 164–70; Drew, *The London Assurance*, p. 62; Supple, *The Royal Exchange Assurance*, p. 54. • 34. Anderson, *The Birthplace and Genesis . . .*, 1937, pp. 9–21, 68. • 35. Anon. [An Irish Clergyman], 'Visits to London', f. 104, 13 August 1772. For the Alley see Morgan and Thomas, *The Stock Exchange*, 1962, pp. 35–7. • 36. Defoe, *A Tour . . .*, 1724–6, I, pp. 338–9. On the South Sea Company see Carswell, *South Sea Bubble*, 1993, pp. 45–9. • 37. Morgan and Thomas, *The Stock Exchange*, p. 68. • 38. Maitland, *The History and Survey*, I, p. 526. • 39. For a list of 156 bubbles see ibid., pp. 527–9. For the ruin see Noorthouck, *A New History of London . . .*, 1773, p. 317. • **40**. See *GM*, 1732, pp. 578–9, 766–8; 1733, pp. 265, 268; 1734, pp. 235–7; Hunter, *The History of London . . .*, 1811, II, pp. 639–40. • **41**. Price (ed.), *Joshua Johnson's Letterbook*, p. 40, 22 June 1772; p. 41, 4 July 1772. • **42**. On the panic of 1797 see *New AR 1797*, British and Foreign History, pp. 124–6, Principal Occurrences, pp. 38–40. For the vicissitudes of the London economy see Schwarz, *London in the Age of Industrialization*, 1992, Chs. 3–4. For business failures in London see Hoppit, *Risk and Failure . . .*, 1987, pp. 63–74. • **43**. Miège, *The New State of England . . .*, 1703, I, p. 182. Grosley, *A Tour to London*, 1772, I, p. 38. Archenholtz, *A Picture of England*, 1797, pp. 145–6. • **44**. Van Muyden (ed.), *A Foreign View of England . . .*, 1902, pp. 80–81, December 1725. For the importance of this artery in the 1690s see Spence, *London in the 1690s*, 2000, p. 124; and for its importance in the early years of the nineteenth century see McKendrick, Brewer and Plumb, *The Birth of a Consumer Society*, 1982, p. 82. • **45**. Anon. [A German Gentleman], *A View of London and Westminster*, 1725, pp. 33–4. • **46**. Burney, *Evelina*, 1778, I, Letter X. Roche, *Sophie in London . . .*, 1933, p. 87, and for window-shopping more generally see Styles, *The Dress of the People*, p. 167. Nourse's trade card is in Heal, *London Tradesmen's Cards . . .*, 1925, p. 82 and pl. LVIII, n.d., but before 1744. • **47**. Something of Cheapside before the mid-1760s can be gleaned from F. G. Hilton Price, 'Signs of Old London', *LTR*, 1907, pp. 27–111. Roche, *Sophie in London . . .*, pp. 141–3, 262. • **48**. Williams, *Memoirs of the Life and Correspondence of Mrs Hannah More*, 1835, I, p. 21, 12 February 1775; Ward, *The Man Who Buried Nelson*, 2007, p. 27, *c*. 1755. • **49**. Phillips, *Mid-Georgian London*, 1964, pp. 126–35, an indispensable overview of shopping at the west end of the town. • **50**. Frank Kelsall, 'Nos. 54–64 Strand: An Account of the Post-1737 Development of the Site', *LTR*, 1980, pp. 93–112; it was praised as late as 1729 for stocking 'the newest Fashion' for the Ladies': Anon., *The Foreigner's Guide*, 1729, p. 52. • **51**. Burney, *Evelina*, I, Letter X. • **52**. Pottle (ed.), *Boswell's London Journal*, 1950, pp. 59–60, 30 November 1762. • **53**. The Beaus are in Ward, *The London-Spy*, 1703, pp. 214–17. The distracted customer is Young Bookwit in Steele, *The Lying Lover*, 1703, Act II, Scene i. • **54**. Matthews (ed.), *The Diary of Dudley Ryder*, 1939, pp. 130–31, 3 November 1715. • **55**. See Jesse, *George Selwyn . . .*, 1843, IV, pp. 151–2, for a house-contents sale in Chesterfield Street in May 1779. On the streets selling second-hand goods see Strype, *A Survey . . .*, II, Book IV, pp. 112, 118, Book VI, pp. 63, 74. Colquhoun, *A Treatise on the Police of the Metropolis*, 1806, p. 115n., gives 213 licensed pawnbrokers in the Bills of Mortality at the end of the century. For Moorfields see Gay, *Trivia*, 1716, Book II, line 548; Burney, *Cecilia*, 1782, III, Ch. I. • **56**. Dawson is in Heal, *London Tradesmen's Cards*, pl. XVII; see also Styles, *The Dress of the People*, pp. 173–6. Smollett, *The Adventures of Roderick Random*, 1748, II, Ch. LIII. Yearsley (ed.), *The Diary of the Visits of John Yeoman*, 1934, p. 30, 9 April 1774. • **57**. Lackington, *Memoirs . . .*, 1795, pp. 204–6. • **58**. The later attempts to suppress the Fair are in City of London Police MSS, *Proclamation, Barnard Mayor, 31 January 1737* (CLA/048/PS/01/064) and *Proclamation, Lambert Mayor, 2 June 1741* (CLA/048/PS/01/065). Ward, *The London-Spy*, pp. 338–40; Pennant, *Some Account of London*, pp. 273–4. • **59**. Mazzinghy, *The New and Universal Guide . . .*, 1785, pp. 158–60. The marketing of the poor is in Legg, *Low-Life*, 1764, pp. 3, 54. The fruit cellar is in OBP t17341204-39. The turnips are in George, *London Life . . .*, 1925, p. 158, source uncited; see also pp. 89–90. • **60**. For Leadenhall see Maitland, *The History and Survey*, II, pp. 1002–1003. Lustig and

Pottle (eds.), *Boswell*, 1986, p. 83, 14 July 1786. On Southwark Market see Anon., *Reasons against Building a Bridge*, 1722, p. 7; *HCJ*, 27, p. 91, 16 January 1755, and pp. 158–60, 14 February 1755. • **61.** Copeland and others (eds.), *The Correspondence of Edmund Burke*, 1958–78, II, Burke to Arthur Young, 21 October 1770. • **62.** For the sums needed to set up business see Schwarz, *London in the Age of Industrialization*, pp. 61–2; see also Earle, *The Making of the English Middle Class*, 1989, p. 44ff. • **63.** Anon., *The London and Westminster Guide*, 1768, p. xv. • **64.** Defoe, *The Complete English Tradesman*, 1726, Ch. XIX. • **65.** For Perrott see *AR 1761*, Characters, pp. 63–73. • **66.** The ordinary tradesmen are in Defoe, *The Complete English Tradesman*, Ch. XXII; John Walker is in Brasbridge, *The Fruits of Experience*, 1824, p. 111, and Charcoal Dick, pp. 142–3. Sir William Plomer, perhaps scurrilously, is in Anon., *City Biography . . .*, 1880, pp. 23–5; Gibbs is in Pinks, *The History of Clerkenwell*, 1880, p. 293; Brasbridge, *The Fruits of Experience*, p. 111. • **67.** *The Spectator*, No. 251, 18 December 1711. Potter, *Life and Adventures . . .*, 1824, pp. 68–9. • **68.** For Handel see Keates, *Handel*, 2008, pp. 248–9; for the actors and artisans see Smith, *Nollekens and His Times*, 1829, I, pp. 196–201. For Sandby and a background to the 'Cries' see Bonehill and Daniels (eds.), *Paul Sandby*, 2009, pp. 130–39. Wheatley, *Cries of London*, 1929, pp. 8–9. Smith, *Ancient Topography of London*, 1815, has a number of plates drawn from 1789–99. There is a key to some of the street characters portrayed there in Smith, *Cries of London*, 1839, pp. 96–9. • **69.** *GM*, 1738, p. 660. • **70.** *HCJ*, 25, pp. 45–8, 31 January 1746, evidence of Richard Grainger. For half-profits see White, *London in the Nineteenth Century*, 2007, p. 207. The Stepney man, whose name isn't given in this source, is in *New Annual Register for the Year 1785*, Principal Occurrences, p. 20; *Annual Register for the Year 1767*, Chronicle, pp. 114–15. • **71.** Middleton, *View of the Agriculture of Middlesex*, p. 268. The posteriors are in Grose, *The Olio*, 1792, pp. 210–11; the rice-milk seller is in OBP t17400903-31; the modern mob is in Anon., *A Trip from St. James's . . .*, 1744, p. 48; the saloop sellers are in Anon., *A Sunday Ramble*, 1774, pp. 3–4; hot pies are in Smith, *A Book for a Rainy Day*, 1845, p. 11, and the muffin man, p. 128; John Bryson is in Smith, *Cries of London*, p. 96; Holloway cheesecakes are in Nelson, *The History, Topography, and Antiquities . . .*, 1811, p. 104; the other cries listed are from Bonehill and Daniels (eds.), *Paul Sandby*, pp. 134–9, and Wheatley, *Cries of London*, passim. Neats are oxen or cattle; hastings are 'Peas that come early' (Johnson). • **72.** The sticks are in Bonehill and Daniels (eds.), *Paul Sandby*, p. 134; Holcroft, *Memoirs . . .*, 1816, I, pp. 23–3; the horse quacks are in Ripley, *Select Original Letters . . .*, 1781, p. 26; the link boys are in Hitchcock, *Down and Out . . .*, 2004, pp. 59–61; the shoe-blacks are in Place, 'Papers', BL Add. MS 27,827, f. 100; the cry in Gay, *Trivia*, Book I, lines 71–3. The Meuse was the King's or Royal Mews, north of Charing Cross; Place says the cry was 'Black your Shoes, your Honour'. • **73.** Potter, *Life and Adventures . . .*, pp. 69–70. • **74.** Ibid., p. 78; Legg, *Low-Life*, pp. 9, 16 ('bunter' has many meanings but here refers to a rag and bone finder); Boswell, *The Life of Samuel Johnson*, 1799, IV, pp. 204–5. • **75.** Place, 'Papers', BL Add. MS 27,825, f. 148. • **76.** The drunken fools are in Legg, *Low-Life*, p. 4. Black, *The Cumberland Letters*, 1912, pp. 104–5. Todd (ed.), *The Collected Letters of Mary Wollstonecraft*, 2003, p. 140. The vipers are in Kalm, *Kalm's Account of his Visit to England . . .*, 1892, pp. 38–40. • **77.** Strutt, *The Sports and Pastimes . . .*, 1801, p. 189. • **78.** Lewis and Brown (eds.), *Horace Walpole's Correspondence . . .*, 9, 1941, p. 46, HW to George Montagu, 16 August 1746. • **79.** For link boys begging money to buy a torch see Legg, *Low-Life*, pp. 97–8. Mary Cox is in OBP t17650417-36. • **80.** Anon., *The Vices of the Cities of London and Westminster*, 1751, p. 17. The warnings to constables are in City of London Police MSS, *Proclamation, Blakiston Mayor, 25 November 1760* (CLA/048/PS/01/048) and *Proclamation, Glyn Mayor, 11 December 1798* (CLA/048/PS/01/049). Fielding, *A Brief Description . . .*, 1776, p. xxii (a later printing of the same text from Anon., *The London and Westminster Guide*, 1768, also p. xxii). • **81.** The parishioners are in Legg, *Low-Life*, p. 42; the field beggars are in Anon., *A Sunday Ramble*, pp. 47–8. Hutton, *A Journey to London*, 1818, pp. 18–19. For the generosity of Londoners to beggars see Hitchcock, *Down and Out . . .*, pp. xvi, 3. • **82.** For the stump see Malcolm, *Anecdotes . . .*, 1810, I, pp. 98–9, citing a case from 1702; the hanging women are ibid., pp. 146–7, citing a case from 1731, and *GM*, 1752, p. 88. The old soldier is in Parker, *A View of Society and Manners . . .*, 1781, II, p. 154ff. The clegms are in Davies, *Dramatic Miscellanies*, 1783–4, II, pp. 291–2. The Faquirs are in Grose, *Olio*, pp. 32–3. • **83.** The maimed coming to London are in Malcolm, *Anecdotes . . .*, I, pp. 286–7, citing 'an author'; Petticoat Lane is in *AR 1772*, Chronicle, p. 138. Archenholtz, *A Picture of England*, pp. 113–14. Anne Martin is in *AR 1761*, Chronicle, p. 96 (I can find no reference to her in the OBP); Elizabeth Parker is in *AR 1767*, Chronicle, pp. 135–6. • **84.** Rat's Castle is recalled in Smith, *Book for a Rainy Day*, p. 87; the Southwark places are in Strype, *A Survey . . .*, II, Book IV, pp. 28, 30, 31 (a mumper is a beggar); the pubs and slang are in *Attic*, I, pp. 401–5, August 1790. • **85.** For John Cornwall see *AR 1765*, Chronicle, p. 127; for Mary Simes see *AR 1772*, Chronicle, p. 154; for Mary Jones see *London Chronicle*, 20–22 June 1780. • **86.** For the large study see Hitchcock, *Down and Out . . .*, pp. 3–4; for the smaller see Bernard (ed.), *Reports of the Society for Bettering . . .*, 1800–1802, I, p. 122ff. • **87.** For the discharged prisoners see Lettsom, *Medical Memoirs . . .*, 1774, pp. 27–8. For the wooden legs see Meister, *Letters . . .*, 1799, pp. 184–6 and n. For the cripples etc. see Grose, *Olio*, pp. 213–14.

6 *Francis Place's London – Industry and Labour*

1. For the life of Place see *ODNB* (William Thomas); Wallas, *The Life of Francis Place*, 1918; Thale (ed.), *The Autobiography of Francis Place*, 1972. • **2.** Ibid., pp. 17–18, 44, 47–9. • **3.** Ibid., p. 71. • **4.** Ibid., p. 74. • **5.** Ibid., p. 104. • **6.** Ibid., p. 110. • **7.** Ibid., pp. 115–17, 128–9. • **8.** See Wallas, *The Life of Francis Place*, pp. 33–4. • **9.** See Barnett, *London, Hub of the Industrial Revolution*, 1998, pp. 3–4, 28–32, 219–20; Schwarz, *London in the Age of Industrialization*, 1992, p. 23; Ashton, *An Economic History of England*, 1955, pp. 91–2. • **10.** See Barnett, *London, Hub of the Industrial Revolution*, pp. 37–40. The schematic maps occasionally still in use that show Southwark as 'leather' or the City as 'commerce and finance' are far too crude to represent the diverse reality of London's economic life in these years. • **11.** For the leather trades of Southwark see VCH, *The Victoria County History of the County of Surrey, II*, 1905, pp. 336–7. Anon., *The London Directory . . .*, 1781. • **12.** A map of the 1748 fire is in *GM*, 1748, pp. 148–9. The airgun plot is in *NAR 1796*, Principal Occurrences, pp. 26–30; they were found not guilty. Unlucky Mrs Clitherow is in *AR 1791*, Chronicle, pp. 46–7. The special locations are to be found in Strype, *A Survey . . .*, 1720, I, Book II, pp. 24, 28, 107–8, 131–2; Book III, pp. 90–91, 94, 121, 196. The go-carts are in Smith,

Nollekens and His Times, 1829, I, p. 221; the women hair-pickers in Anon., *A Genuine Narrative of all the Street Robberies . . .*, 1728. • **13**. Anon., *The Case of the Parish of St Giles Criplegate*, 1712; *HCJ*, 24, p. 398, 1 February 1743. For an excellent oversight of City manufacturing at the end of the seventeenth century see Spence, *London in the 1690s*, 2000, p. 128ff. • **14**. These estimates are based on an analysis of some 750 addresses where goldsmiths and silversmiths were active over the century, taken from Heal, *The London Goldsmiths*, 1935. See also Jowett, *The Warning-Carriers*, 2005. • **15**. The numbers of tailors and shoemakers are in Corfield and Keene (eds.), *Work in Towns*, 1990, pp. 165–9. Poole and Dobson are in 'Album of Tradecards', pp. 33, 43. For Williams see Bondeson, *The London Monster*, 2003, pp. 117–21. For an overview of the West End shopping streets see the invaluable Phillips, *Mid-Georgian London*, 1964. • **16**. For Hatchett see Roche, *Sophie in London . . .*, 1933, pp. 158–9; for coachmaking in general see Corfield and Keene (eds.), *Work in Towns*, pp. 169–70; see also Campbell, *The London Tradesman*, 1747, pp. 229–33. • **17**. Ibid., pp. 250–52; see also Weiss, *Watch-Making in England*, 1982, pp. 30–50. • **18**. For Arnold's watch see *AR 1764*, Chronicle, pp. 78–9; Arnold moved to St James's Street in 1769 and to Adam Street in the Adelphi in 1771 (see *ODNB*). Lewis, Smith and Lam (eds.), *Horace Walpole's Correspondence . . .*, 21, 1960, pp. 295–6, HW to Sir Horace Mann, 8 June 1759. • **19**. Of a sample of eighty-three watchmakers etc. in Barfoot and Wilkes, *The Universal British Directory . . .*, 1793, thirty-two were in the City and twelve in Clerkenwell. For Clerkenwell watchmaking see SOL, *XLVI*, 2008, p. 9; George, *London Life . . .*, 1925, pp. 173–6. For Somers Town see Palmer, *St Pancras*, 1870, p. 59. For the shark see *NAR 1791*, Principal Occurrences, p. 47. • **20**. Brackett, *Thomas Chippendale*, 1924, pp. 15–25, and Ch. VI for his relations with Adam; Gilbert, *The Life and Work of Chippendale*, 1978, I, pp. 1–34. • **21**. For the fascinating Linnells see Hayward and Kirkham, *William and John Linnell*, 1980. • **22**. For Seddon see Edwards and Jourdain, *Georgian Cabinet-Makers*, 1955, pp. 79–80; Roche, *Sophie in London . . .*, pp. 173–5. Heal, *The London Furniture Makers*, 1953, identified some 2,500 furniture makers in London in the eighteenth century. An analysis of about 1,000 over the century divided into twenty-year periods (some makers appearing in more than one period) reveals around ninety-eight in the City and 103 in Westminster out of 282 listed in the period 1780–99. There is no evidence for the common assertion that furniture making moved from the City to Long Acre and St Martin's Lane by the 1730s. • **23**. For shipbuilding see Davis, *The Rise of the English Shipping Industry . . .*, 1962, pp. 70, 78–9; for stocking-frame knitters see Marshall, *The English Poor in the Eighteenth Century*, 1926, p. 197; for shoes and hats see Schwarz, *London in the Age of Industrialization*, pp. 34–7; for silk see Smith, *The History of East London . . .*, 1939, pp. 248–9. • **24**. Anon., *The State of the Silk . . .*, 1713, pp. 5, 7; lustring or lutestring was a fine lightweight shiny silk. • **25**. The detailed account of London silk weaving in George, *London Life . . .*, pp. 176–95, remains unsurpassed. See also VCH, *A History of the County of Middlesex*, II, 1911, pp. 132–8; VCH, *A History of the County of Middlesex*, XI, 1998, pp. 177–9; for Garthwaite and the other designers, with much else on the finer points of the trade, see Rothstein, *Silk Designs . . .*, 1990, pp. 20–21, 33–6. • **26**. Wyndham (ed.), *The Diary of the Late George Bubb Dodington*, 1784, p. 80. Rothstein, *Silk Designs . . .*, pp. 306–8. • **27**. Barnett, *London, Hub of the Industrial Revolution*, pp. 35–6. • **28**. Morris and Cozens, *Wapping*, 2009, pp. 34–7, 135–7, 169. For Bow see VCH, *A History of the County of Middlesex*, II, pp. 146–50; for Hackney see VCH, *Middlesex*, X, 1995, p. 97;

Berger, *A Century and a Half of the House of Berger*, 1910, pp. 12–17; for the
Limehouse Cut see Pennant, *Some Account of London*, 1805, p. 271, and Cherry,
O'Brien and Pevsner, *The Buildings of England: London 5*, 2005, p. 34. • **29.** On
Woolwich see Lysons, *The Environs of London*, 1792–6, IV, pp. 568–9; on the
Hounslow mills see *AR 1758*, Chronicle, pp. 85, 104, 118. • **30.** For Deptford see
Lysons, *The Environs of London*, IV, pp. 383–5. For Eleanor Coade see *ODNB*;
Messrs Doulton seem to have come to Lambeth only around 1815. For Battersea
enamels see VCH, *The Victoria History of the County of Surrey, II*, pp. 305–6.
Adams, *Chelsea Porcelain*, 2001; for the potteries and other Chelsea trades see
VCH, *Middlesex, XII*, 2004, pp. 158–9; for the charity children see Hitchcock and
Black (eds.), *Chelsea Settlement and Bastardy Examinations*, 1999, p. xv. For
Fulham see Lysons, *The Environs of London*, II, pp. 399–400; VCH, *A History of
the County of Middlesex, II*, pp. 142–6. • **31.** For Merton Abbey see Anon.,
Ambulator, 1800, pp. 154–5. • **32.** Colquhoun, *A Treatise on the Commerce and
Police . . .*, 1800, pp. 75, 179–88; the footpads are in Jackson, *The New and
Complete Newgate Calendar*, 1795, V, pp. 135–8. • **33.** For the physical strength
of the coalheavers see *AR 1768*, Chronicle, pp. 129–30, 139–40; see also Smith,
Sea-Coal for London, 1961, pp. 57–8. • **34.** Van Muyden (ed.), *A Foreign View of
England . . .*, 1902, pp. 169–71. For the watermen's regulations see Maitland, *The
History and Survey . . .*, 1756, II, pp. 1254–5. • **35.** Schwarz, *London in the Age
of Industrialization*, pp. 23–5. • **36.** Liability to arrest is in Dodsley, *London and
Its Environs Described . . .*, 1761, V, pp. 203–6. For the porters generally see the
invaluable Stern, *The Porters of London*, 1960; for the Fellowship of Billingsgate
Porters see Smith, *Sea-Coal for London*, pp. 56–7, 84–6. Moritz, *Travels of Carl
Philipp Moritz . . .*, 1795, p. 28. The good livelihood is in Macky, *A Journey
Through England*, 1722, p. 234. The women of Billingsgate are in Ward, *The
London-Spy*, 1703, pp. 40–2. • **37.** Swift, *Journal to Stella*, 1948, I, p. 198. • **38.** For
the census of horses see Maitland, *The History and Survey . . .*, I, pp. 532–4.
For the satire see Colman and Thornton, *The Connoisseur*, 1757, I, pp. 202, 204.
• **39.** Anon., *A Guide to Stage Coaches . . .*, 1783, pp. 109–65. Place, 'Papers', BL
Add. MS 27,827, f. 167. For the flash coachmen see Colquhoun, *A Treatise on the
Police of the Metropolis*, 1806, pp. 150, 547–8. For Scurrier see Guthrie, *The
Ordinary of Newgate . . .*, 1725, n.p. [p. 4]. • **40.** For the regulations see Anon.,
A Guide to Stage Coaches . . ., pp. 95–107; for the other carts see Maitland, *The
History and Survey . . .*, II, p. 1263. • **41.** There is a map of the coaching and
carrying inns around 1730 in Spence, *London in the 1690s*, pp. 34–5. The Wareham
wagons are in Anon., *A Guide to Stage Coaches . . .*, p. 85. The Friday Street inns
are in Strype, *A Survey . . .*, I, Book II, p. 207. The warehousing is in Earle, *The
Making of the English Middle Class*, p. 52. • **42.** For the White Hart and the
George see Rendle and Norman, *The Inns of Old Southwark . . .*, 1888, pp. 128–50,
159–60. • **43.** Matz, *The Inns & Taverns of 'Pickwick' . . .*, 1921, Ch. II; Phillips,
Mid-Georgian London, pp. 99–100. • **44.** For the growing demand for servants
see Earle, *The Making of the English Middle Class*, pp. 218–19; Hill, *Servants*,
1996, pp. 1–7; Horn, *Flunkeys and Scullions*, 2004, pp. 1–8. • **45.** The estimates
are in Hecht, *The Domestic Servant Class . . .*, 1956, pp. 33–4; Horn, *Flunkeys
and Scullions*, p. 5. Thale (ed.), *The Autobiography of Francis Place*, p. 124. • **46.** For
the importance of domestic service in women's employment see Schwarz, *London
in the Age of Industrialization*, pp. 17–19. • **47.** Thomson, *The Russells of
Bloomsbury*, 1940, Ch. XIII. • **48.** For Streatham see Hecht, *The Domestic Servant
Class . . .*, p. 8; Yorke (ed.), *The Diary of John Baker*, 1931, pp. 98–9. Richardson,

Pamela, 1740–41, III, Letter XLIII. The Westminster survey is in Horn, *Flunkeys and Scullions*, p. 17. • **49.** For Berry see Hecht, *The Domestic Servant Class . . .*, p. 7; the survey is in Earle, *The Making of the English Middle Class*, pp. 218–19. • **50.** Hecht, *The Domestic Servant Class . . .*, pp. 11, 23, 29. Devonshire, *The Sylph*, 1779, p. 31 [Letter 8]. • **51.** On these comparative privileges see Hecht, *The Domestic Servant Class . . .*, pp. 22–3. • **52.** Grosley, *A Tour to London*, 1772, I, pp. 81–2. See also Hecht, *The Domestic Servant Class . . .*, p. 119. • **53.** The porter is in West, *Fifty Years' Recollections . . .*, 1837, p. 49; see also Hecht, *The Domestic Servant Class . . .*, p. 120. • **54.** Climenson (ed.), *Elizabeth Montagu . . .*, 1906, I, p. 139. Balderston (ed.), *Thraliana*, 1951, I, p. 347. • **55.** Thomson, *The Russells of Bloomsbury*, p. 238; on the literacy of servants see Hill, *Servants*, pp. 226–9. • **56.** Balderston, *Thraliana*, I, p. 117. • **57.** Ibid., II, p. 682. • **58.** For the servant's settlement but not the lodger's see Shaw, *Parish Law*, 1753, pp. 259–60. St Clement Danes Poor Law Examinations as to Settlement (Plebeian Londoners Project), WCCDEP 358110031-84; on the vulnerability of maidservants to sexual advances by masters, lodgers etc., see Hill, *Servants*, p. 44ff. • **59.** Macdonald, *Memoirs . . .*, 1790, pp. 93–4. • **60.** Townley, *High Life Below Stairs*, 1759, Act I, Scene i. For the servant maids see, for example, Anon., *A Trip through the Town*, 1735, p. 15ff. • **61.** Angelo Family Papers, MSS 1, letter, Domenico Angelo to Mrs Angelo, London the 5th Aug. 1763. 'Home' is probably Carlisle House, Carlisle Street, Soho Square – not the more famous Carlisle House in Soho Square itself – where Angelo set up his school in 1763 or 1764. Paris and Mr Vernon are perhaps apprentices; 'harry' is his son, Henry Angelo, the memoirist, away at school in Chiswick. For Angelo see *ODNB*. • **62.** The useless set are in *GM*, 1732, p. 661. • **63.** For the taxation on dinner guests see Kielmansegge, *Diary of a Journey to England*, 1902, pp. 53–4. Elias (ed.), *Memoirs of Laetitia Pilkington*, 1997, I, p. 286. Plumb, *Sir Robert Walpole*, II, 1960, p. 78. • **64.** Boswell, *The Life of Samuel Johnson*, 1799, II, p. 78. Cited in Hecht, *The Domestic Servant Class . . .*, pp. 164–5; see also Horn, *Flunkeys and Scullions*, pp. 203–10. • **65.** *AR 1764*, Chronicle, pp. 74–5. • **66.** The half a crown a day is in Society for the Discharge and Relief of Persons Imprisoned for Small Debts, *An Account of the Rise . . .*, 1783, p. 59. See also Gilboy, *Wages in Eighteenth Century England*, 1934, pp. 2–38; Schwarz, *London in the Age of Industrialization*, pp. 168–70. For servants' wages see Hecht, *The Domestic Servant Class . . .*, pp. 145–8. • **67.** Mitchell and Deane, *Abstract of British Historical Statistics*, 1962, pp. 346–7; Schwarz, *London in the Age of Industrialization*, pp. 170–78. • **68.** For the season see ibid., pp. 105–6, and for the cold winters see p. 115. The two tragedies are in *Annual Register for 1763*, Chronicle p. 51; *Annual Register for 1768*, Chronicle p. 58. • **69.** OBP t17861025-38. • **70.** For an overview of the City companies in the eighteenth century see Kellett, 'The Breakdown of Gild and Corporation Control over the Handicraft and Retail Trade in London', *Economic History Review*, New Series, Vol. 10, No. 3, 1958, pp. 381–94. • **71.** For the tailors of 1708 see Malcolm, *Anecdotes . . .*, 1810, II, p. 5; for the weavers see *GM* 1736, p. 353; for the miniature coffin lids see Pyne, *Wine and Walnuts*, 1824, I, p. 9n.; for lamplighters' funerals see Ryskamp and Pottle (eds.), *Boswell*, 1963, pp. 344–5, 14 May 1776; for workers' friendly societies in this period more generally see Clark, *British Clubs and Societies*, 2000, pp. 83–8, 350ff. • **72.** *HCJ*, 20, esp. pp. 161 (5 March) and 180 (26 March 1723); pp. 744 (17 February 1727) and 776 (27 February 1727); 24, p. 583 (22 February 1744). The Frauds by Workmen Act, 1749, 22 Geo. 2 c.27. • **73.** For Dingley's sawmill see *AR 1767*, Chronicle, p. 85; *1768*, Chronicle, p. 108; OBP t17680706-47; John H. Appleby, 'Charles Dingley, Projector, and His Limehouse Sawmill', *LTR*, 1995, pp. 179–82. For the Albion see *AR 1791*, Chronicle, pp. 14–15; see also *Attic*, II, 1799, p. 233. • **74.** There is a good discussion of the lawfulness of combinations in Webb, *The History of Trade Unionism*, 1898, pp. 57–63. • **75.** *HCJ*, 13, p. 146, 27 January 1700. Bernard (ed.), *Reports of the Society for Bettering . . .*, 1800–1802, I, pp. 216–22. • **76.** For the events of 1721 see Maitland, *The History and Survey . . .*, I, p. 530. For 1739 see *GM 1739*, p. 602; Maitland, *The History and Survey . . .*, I, p. 605. For 1745 see *GM 1745*, p. 387. • **77.** *AR 1762*, Chronicle, pp. 119–20, for the severe winter. *AR 1763*, Chronicle, p. 105; *St James's Chronicle or the British Evening Post*, 11–13 October 1763. • **78.** For the tailors see *AR 1764*, Chronicle, p. 66. There are other interpretations of the Flint–Dung dichotomy, but this in the *Annual Register* for 1764 seems to be the origin of the term and an early mention in print: see, by contrast, Schwarz, *London in the Age of Industrialization*, p. 189. For the weavers see *AR 1764*, Chronicle, pp. 63–4; *AR 1765*, Chronicle, p. 57. • **79.** *AR 1765*, History of Europe, pp. 41–2; Entick, *A New and Accurate History . . .*, 1766, III, pp. 254–8; Noorthouck, *A New History of London*, pp. 431–3; Toynbee and Whibley (eds.), *Correspondence of Thomas Gray*, 1935, II, p. 875; Lewis, Smith and Lam (eds.), *Horace Walpole's Correspondence . . .*, 22, 1960, p. 301, HW to Sir Horace Mann, 25 May 1765. See also Walpole, *Memoirs of the Reign of King George III*, 2000, II, pp. 142–5, 149–50. For the events of May 1766 see *AR 1766*, Chronicle, p. 95. • **80.** *AR 1767*, Chronicle, pp. 139–40, 152, 158; 1768, Chronicle, pp. 57–8, 68; Hunter, *The History of London . . .*, 1811, II, p. 732. • **81.** *AR 1768*, Chronicle, p. 58. • **82.** For the coalheavers' grievances see George, *London Life . . .*, pp. 294–5; *HCJ*, 13, p. 168, 3 February 1700. Walpole, *Memoirs of the Reign of King George III*, IV, pp. 21–2. • **83.** *AR 1768*, Chronicle, p. 93, Appendix to Chronicle, pp. 222–7. OBP t17680706-46. See also Rudé, *Hanoverian London*, 1871, pp. 196–7; Shoemaker, *The London Mob*, 2004, pp. 140–45. • **84.** *AR 1768*, Chronicle, pp. 99, 105–8, 111, 113. • **85.** *AR 1768*, Chronicle, pp. 101–2, 108–9, 111. OBP t17680706-57. For the Tyburn and Sun Tavern Fields executions see *AR 1768*, Chronicle, pp. 129–30, 139–40. Lewis, Smith and Lam (eds.), *Horace Walpole's Correspondence*, 23, 1967, p. 39, HW to Sir Horace Mann, 4 August 1768. • **86.** *AR 1768*, Chronicle, p. 157; *AR 1769*, Chronicle, pp. 81, 124, 132–3, 138. • **87.** *AR 1769*, Chronicle, pp. 159–60, 162; Appendix to Chronicle, pp. 181–8; Noorthouck, *A New History of London*, pp. 471–4. See also Shoemaker, *The London Mob*, pp. 142–3, 146–7. • **88.** *AR 1771*, Chronicle, pp. 96, 122. OBP t17710703-59. • **89.** Smith, *The History of East London . . .*, pp. 248–50.

7 Eliza Haywood's London – Print, Pictures and the Professions

1. Lennox, *Henrietta*, 1758, I, Book I, Ch. VI. • **2.** Savage, *An Author to be Let*, 1729, n.p. [p. i]. Juno and the babes are in Pope, *The Dunciad*, 1729, Book II, lines 158, 163–4. For Haywood see *ODNB*, which states that she was 'probably born in Shropshire', a claim resting in part on her 'use of west country slang', and so on a muddled concept of English geography. Her first biographer says 'she was born at London': Baker, *Companion to the Play House*, 1764, reprinted in Haywood, *The History of Miss Betsy Thoughtless*, 1751 (1998 edn, Toronto, edited by Christine Blouch). • **3.** Steele, *The Tender Husband*, 1705, Act I, Scene i. For the importance of women readers in cultural production see Brewer, *The Pleasures of the Imagination*, 1997, pp. 77–8. On women writers see, for instance, Clarke, *Dr Johnson's Women*, 2000; Schellenberg, *The Professionalization of Women Writers . . .*, 2005. • **4.** The artifices are in Haywood, *The City Jilt*, 1726, p. 10; her education is in *The Female Spectator*, I, Book I, p. 9; for the poems see Brewster, *Aaron Hill*, 1913, pp. 185–8; for the servants see Hecht, *The Domestic Servant Class . . .*, 1956, pp. 73–4, 87. The publishing career is mentioned in Blouch's introduction to Haywood, *The History of Betsy Thoughtless*, Introduction, pp. 12–13; for women publishers and printers see McDowell, *The Women of Grub Street*, 1998. • **5.** The *Female Spectator*, I, Book I, p. 8. Oddly, she addresses the reader as 'him'. • **6.** Johnson, *Life of Savage*, 1744 (in *The Works . . .*, 1823), pp. 322–3. On the insult to Pope see Mack, *Alexander Pope*, 1985, p. 411. • **7.** Haywood, *The History of Betsy Thoughtless*, I, Ch. VIII. • **8.** Haywood, *The History of Jemmy and Jenny Jessamy*, 1753, III, Ch. XXI. • **9.** On literacy see J. Paul Hunter, 'The Novel and Social/ Cultural History', in Richetti (ed.), *The Cambridge Companion to the Eighteenth-Century Novel*, 1996, p. 20; Brewer, *The Pleasures of the Imagination*, pp. 167–8. St Clements Examinations as to Settlement, WCCDEP358110031-358120163; 358020191ff. • **10.** For the *Daily Courant* see Handover, *Printing in London*, 1960, p. 127; for 1709 see Nichols, *Literary Anecdotes . . .*, 1812–16, I, pp. 3–4n.; the business of reading newspapers is in *GM*, 1731, n.p., 'Introduction'; the mid-century figures are in Barker, *Newspapers . . .*, 2000, pp. 29–30; Pendred, *The London and Country Printers*, 1785, pp. 85–9; Barfoot and Wilkes, *The Universal British Directory . . .*, 1793, pp. 427–30. • **11.** Circulation figures are summarised in Andrew and McGowen, *The Perreaus and Mrs Rudd*, 2001, p. 56; Wilson, *First with the News*, 1985, pp. 9–10. • **12.** Archenholtz, *A Picture of England*, 1797, pp. 63–4, 314. • **13.** *London Chronicle*, 1 January 1757, 'Preliminary Discourse'. Piozzi, *Anecdotes . . .*, 1786, p. 128. The *Lying-Post* and *Grubstreet* are in *GM*, 1731, p. 12. • **14.** Garrick, *The Irish Widow*, 1772, Act II, Scene i. • **15.** Devonshire, *The Sylph*, 1779, Letter 40. • **16.** Raven, *The Business of Books*, 2007, pp. 7–8, 149–51. • **17.** Matthews (ed.), *The Diary of Dudley Ryder*, 1939, pp. 208–10, 31 March and 2 April 1716. Anon., *The Adventures of Lindamira*, 1702. Fielding, *Love in Several Masques*, 1727, Act I, Scene v. Johnson is in *London Chronicle*, 1 January 1757, 'Preliminary Discourse'. The three magazines of the 1750s were the *Literary Review*, *Critical Review* and *Monthly Review*; reviews were also carried in all the major magazines. • **18.** The number of London libraries in 1760 is in Raven, Small and Tadmor (eds.), *The Practice and Representation of Reading in England*, 1996, p. 175. Elias, *Memoirs of Laetitia Pilkington*, 1997, I, p. 168. Cross, *The Life and Times of Laurence Sterne*, 1925, I, pp. 132–3n. For Warburton see Jesse, *George Selwyn . . .*, 1843, III, pp. 61–2. The British Library is in Raven, Small and Tadmor (eds.), *The Practice and Representation of Reading in England*, p. 181. For other details and the London Library see Trusler, *The London Adviser and Guide*, 1786, pp. 121–2. • **19.** Lackington, *Memoirs . . .*, 1795, pp. 420–22, 450–51. • **20.** Cited in Clarke, *Dr Johnson's Women*, p. 3. • **21.** Goldsmith, *An Enquiry into the Present State of Polite Learning*, 1759, Ch. X. • **22.** For the sixpenny paragraph writers see Anon., *A Sunday Ramble*, 1774, p. 35. Johnson is in D'Arblay, *Diary and Letters . . .*, 1854, I, p. 356, Fanny Burney to Mrs Thrale, n.d. [prob. July 1780]. The foreigners are in Wendeborn, *View of England . . .*, 1791, I, p. 343. • **23.** For Sanders see *ODNB*; for Lennox see Small, *Charlotte Lennox*, 1935. For the background of some of Pope's dunces see Rogers, *Grub Street*, 1972, pp. 207–14. • **24.** Johnson, *Life of Pope*, 1781 (in *The Works . . .*,

1823), p. 155. • **25.** See Mack, *Alexander Pope*, esp. Ch. 19. The excrement is in Savage, *An Author to be Let*, n.p. [pp. ii–iv]. • **26.** Beloe, *The Sexagenarian . . .*, 1817, I, p. 196. • **27.** On the Chapter and Tom's see Lillywhite, *London Coffee Houses*, 1963, pp. 151–4, 590–93. For the King's Head see Hawkins, *The Life of Samuel Johnson*, 1787, pp. 219–20. • **28.** For Cochran see Lustig and Pottle (eds.), *Boswell*, 1986, pp. 127–8, 9 April 1787. For supportive authors more generally see Brewer, *The Pleasures of the Imagination*, pp. 158–9, 165. • **29.** For the geography of print see Rees and Britton, *Reminiscences of Literary London*, 1896; Myers, Harris and Mandelbrote (eds.), *The London Book Trade*, 2003, especially the chapters by Michael Harris and James Raven; Raven, *The Business of Books*, pp. 154–92. • **30.** See Pendred, *The London and Country Printers*, pp. 3–12; Howe and Waite, *The London Society of Compositors*, 1948, pp. 17, 23–4; Raven, *The Business of Books*, pp. 136–7. • **31.** Boswell, *The Life of Samuel Johnson*, 1799, II, p. 323. Franklin, *Autobiography of Benjamin Franklin*, 1868, pp. 146–8. • **32.** For Barber see *ODNB*; Anon., *The Life and Character of John Barber*, 1741; Nichols, *Literary Anecdotes . . .*, I, pp. 72–4n.; Trewin and King, *Printer to the House*, 1952; Hansard, *The Auto-Biography of Luke Hansard*, 1991. For Richardson the Cockney see Eaves and Kimpel, *Samuel Richardson*, 1971, pp. 527, 539–41. • **33.** Boswell, *The Life of Samuel Johnson*, I, pp. 303–4n. • **34.** Ralph, *The Case of Authors . . .*, 1758, pp. 20–21. • **35.** For the numbers of booksellers see Raven, *The Business of Books*, p. 136. The cost of a novel is in Schellenberg, *The Professionalization of Women Writers . . .*, p. 99. The auctions are in Cox and Chandler, *The House of Longman*, 1925, p. 7. For the *Dictionary*, see Boswell, *The Life of Samuel Johnson*, I, p. 183. • **36.** For Dodsley see Solomon, *The Rise of Robert Dodsley*, 1996, pp. 50–53, 111, 178–9, 189–91. For Millar see *ODNB*. Boswell, *The Life of Samuel Johnson*, I, pp. 287–8. • **37.** Eaves and Kimpel, *Samuel Richardson*, pp. 378–81. • **38.** Mack, *Alexander Pope*, pp. 266–9. For Churchill see Hamilton, *Doctor Syntax*, 1969, p. 90. Monger is in Campbell, *The London Tradesman*, 1747, p. 129. • **39.** Hawkins, *The Life of Samuel Johnson*, pp. 158–60n.; the letter to Cave is dated 21 July, a Wednesday, but says he has been in the house two nights since coming in on Tuesday evening; see also Boswell, *The Life of Samuel Johnson*, IV, pp. 446–7; Nichols, *Literary Anecdotes . . .*, IX, p. 477; Piozzi, *Anecdotes . . .*, p. 120. • **40.** Whyte, *Poems on Various Subjects . . .*, 1795, pp. 282–4. See also *ODNB*; Charke, *A Narrative of the Life . . .*, 1755. • **41.** Wheatley (ed.), *The Historical and Posthumous Memoirs . . .*, 1884, I, pp. 113–14; see also Foreman, *Georgiana Duchess of Devonshire*, 1998, p. 28n. • **42.** Northcote, *Memoirs of Sir Joshua Reynolds*, 1813, pp. 13–14. See also McIntyre, *Joshua Reynolds*, 2003, pp. 27–8. • **43.** *The Spectator*, No. 21, 24 March 1711. For an overview of the professions in Britain in these years see Corfield, *Power and the Professions . . .*, 1995, esp. Chs. 4 (lawyers) and 6 (doctors). • **44.** Fielding is cited in Battestin, *Henry Fielding*, 1993, pp. 116–17. The critics are in Fielding, *The History of Tom Jones*, 1749, Book XI, Ch. I. Danziger and Brady (eds.), *Boswell*, 1989, p. 123, 14 February 1791. For lawyers and Grub Street more generally see Rogers, *Grub Street*, pp. 287–90. • **45.** The 4,000 are in *GM*, 1731, p. 79. Pettifoggers are in Parker, *A View of Society and Manners . . .*, 1781, II, p. 89ff. The attorneys' law directory is in Barfoot and Wilkes, *The Universal British Directory . . .*, pp. 366–7, 370–92. • **46.** See Christian, *A Short History of Solicitors*, 1896, pp. 111–17; Kirk, *Portrait of a Profession*, 1976, pp. 16–23. For the scriveners see Brooks and Humphery-Smith, *A History of the Worshipful Company of Scriveners of London*, 2001, pp. 24–30. • **47.** Campbell, *The London Tradesman*, pp. 71–2. Hatton, *A*

New View of London, 1708, II, pp. 639–730. • **48.** For the numbers called see Lemmings, *Professors of the Law,* 2000, p. 63; the law directory is in Barfoot and Wilkes, *The Universal British Directory . . .,* pp. 359–65, 368–9. The common saying about the Inns is in Campbell, *The London Tradesman,* p. 74, who gives 'whores'. Ryder is in *ODNB* (David Lemmings). Prest, *William Blackstone,* 2008. • **49.** For the *Grub-Street Journal* see Hawkins, *The Life of Samuel Johnson,* pp. 31–2; Rogers, *Grub Street,* pp. 352–63. • **50.** Hamilton, *Doctor Syntax,* p. 2. • **51.** See Langford, *A Polite and Commercial People,* 1989, pp. 72–3, for the rise of fashionable medical men in this period. For an overview of the profession see Hamilton, 'The Medical Professions in the Eighteenth Century', *Economic History Review,* 2nd Series, IV, No. 2, 1951, pp. 141–69. • **52.** For the physicians see Hunt, *The Medical Society of London,* 1972, pp. ix–x; the coxcomb is in Campbell, *The London Tradesman,* p. 41. Anon., *The London and Westminster Guide,* 1768, p. xiv; for the canes see Hawkins, *The Life of Samuel Johnson,* p. 238n., and MacMichael, *The Gold-Headed Cane,* 1827. • **53.** Richardson, *Clarissa,* V, Letter XLV. Moore, *The History of St Bartholomew's Hospital,* 1918, II, p. 523ff. • **54.** Richardson, *Clarissa,* V, Letter XLV. Abernethy and Cheselden are in Turberville, *Johnson's England,* 1933, II, pp. 267–9. Campbell, *The London Tradesman,* Ch. IV. • **55.** Copeman, *The Worshipful Society of Apothecaries of London,* 1967; Hunt, *The Medical Society of London.* • **56.** Generally, see Thompson, *Quacks of Old London,* 1928, Chs. XVIII–XXIV. • **57.** Lewis (ed.), *Notes by Lady Louisa Stuart . . .,* 1928, pp. 34–5. • **58.** See Wheatley, *Hogarth's London,* 1909, p. 114ff. • **59.** *The Penny London Post,* 1–3 March 1749. • **60.** Boswell, *The Life of Samuel Johnson,* I, pp. 477–9. • **61.** Chesterfield, *Letters to His Son,* 1774, Letters LXXIII, LXXXVI. The comparison between art and print, in art's favour, is in Ralph, *The Case of Authors . . .,* p. 17. • **62.** Whitley, *Artists and Their Friends . . .,* 1928, I, p. 3. • **63.** For Northcote see McIntyre, *Joshua Reynolds,* pp. 223–4. • **64.** For the first academy and its rebirth in St Martin's Lane see Whitley, *Artists and Their Friends . . .,* I, Chs. 1–2. • **65.** For Hogarth see *ODNB* (David Bindman) and Uglow, *Hogarth,* 1997. • **66.** Whitley, *Artists and Their Friends . . .,* I, pp. 26–7. • **67.** Engraving Copyright Act 1734, 8 Geo. 2 c.13. • **68.** For Moser see Edgcumbe, *The Art of the Gold Chaser . . .,* 2000, p. 1ff. • **69.** Whitley, *Artists and Their Friends . . .,* I, pp. 4–5. • **70.** Northcote, *Memoirs of Sir Joshua Reynolds,* p. 12. For van Aken, variously spelt, see *ODNB*; Whitley, *Artists and Their Friends . . .,* I, pp. 53–9; for the location of his studio see Wedd, *Artists' London,* 2001, p. 32. • **71.** For Highmore see Whitley, *Artists and Their Friends . . .,* I, pp. 46–7; Uglow, *Hogarth,* p. 406. • **72.** Angelo, *Reminiscences . . .,* I, pp. 27 (equestrian portraits), 97 (the Pantheon painted by William Hodges with figures by Zoffany), 381 (Valenciennes). • **73.** For these clusters see the useful maps in Wedd, *Artists' London,* pp. 32, 66. The ten artists around the Piazza are in Angelo, *Reminiscences . . .,* I, p. 176. No. 104 St Martin's Lane is in Smith, *Nollekens and His Times,* 1829, II, pp. 230–31. • **74.** Ingamells and Edgcumbe (eds.), *The Letters of Sir Joshua Reynolds,* 2000, pp. 14–15, Reynolds to Joseph Wilton, 5 June 1753. For Reynolds's revolutionary way with portraits see Whitley, *Artists and Their Friends . . .,* I, p. 140. Marchi is in Northcote, *Memoirs of Sir Joshua Reynolds,* pp. 32–3; see also McIntyre, *Joshua Reynolds,* pp. 90–91 for another drapery painter used by Reynolds, Peter Toms. The fees for both Reynolds and Gainsborough are in McIntyre, *Joshua Reynolds,* pp. 95, 361. • **75.** Cited in Whitley, *Artists and Their Friends . . .,* I, pp. 23–4. • **76.** See ibid., pp. 162, 229–31; II, pp. 55–6, 245–6, 349. Joliffe is in Toynbee and Whibley (eds.), *Correspondence of*

Thomas Gray, 1935, II, pp. 546–7. Soros (ed.), *James 'Athenian' Stuart*, 2006, pp. 62–3. • 77. Thale (ed.), *Autobiography of Francis Place*, 1972, p. 54. The journeyman's wages are in Campbell, *The London Tradesman*, p. 140. • 78. Cited in Allan, *William Shipley*, 1968, p. 80. • 79. Kauffman's earnings are given in Greig (ed.), *The Farington Diary*, 1922, p. 13, 6 November 1793. For Grace see Turberville (ed.), *Johnson's England*, II, pp. 64–5. Mary Black is in Whitley, *Artists and Their Friends . . .*, I, p. 238 and *ODNB*. Mary Moser is described in Smith, *Nollekens and His Times*, I, p. 57. • 80. Heal, *London Tradesmen's Cards*, 1925, pl. LXXVIII. For the colourmen generally see Whitley, *Artists and Their Friends . . .*, I, pp. 330–35, and II, pp. 360–62. • 81. For Dyer see ibid., p. 281, and for White, II, pp. 265–6; Reynolds is in McIntyre, *Joshua Reynolds*, pp. 311–13, 354–5, 435. Frances is in Whitley, *Artists and Their Friends . . .*, II, p. 287. Nollekens is in Smith, *Nollekens and His Times*, I, pp. 49–50, 102–3, and Hercules in II, pp. 85–6. • 82. For Copley see Turberville (ed.), *Johnson's England*, II, pp. 58–9; the exhibitions are in Whitley, *Artists and Their Friends . . .*, I, Ch. 10. • 83. For Hogarth's French engravers see Uglow, *Hogarth*, pp. 386–90; for the City print sellers see Myers, Harris and Mandelbrote (eds.), *The London Book Trade*, pp. 72–5. • 84. For Boydell see *ODNB* (Timothy Clayton). Roche, *Sophie in London . . .*, 1933, pp. 237–9. • 85. Generally see Paston, *Social Caricature . . .*, 1905; Klingender (ed.), *Hogarth and English Caricature*, 1944; George, *English Political Caricature*, 1959; and for a vivid overview of all aspects of this age of caricature see Gatrell, *City of Laughter*, 2006. For the illustrated magazines see Handover, *Printing in London*, p. 145. For book illustration see Raven, *The Business of Books*, pp. 250–56. • 86. Lewis and Wallace (eds.), *Horace Walpole*, 1937, I, p. 286, Walpole to Rev. William Cole, 7 November 1772. For the journeymen see Campbell, *The London Tradesman*, Ch. XXII. Bentley, *The Stranger from Paradise*, 2001, pp. 30–31. Mrs Ryland is in Angelo, *Reminiscences . . .*, I, p. 482.

8 Teresa Cornelys's London – Public Pleasures

1. *Westminster Magazine*, January 1773, cited in McKinlay, *Mrs Cornely's Entertainments . . .*, 1840, pp. 12–13; *Middlesex Journal*, 21 January 1773; *Middlesex Journal*, 20 December 1774. For contemporary praise see, for example, Smollett, *The Expedition of Humphry Clinker* 1771, I, 31 May, Lydia Melford to Laetitia Willis. For posterity see *General Evening Post*, 4 June 1791: 'Since the days of Mrs. CORNELYS we have not attended a Masquerade so deserving our warmest praise, as that on Friday at Vauxhall . . .' See also generally Summers, *The Empress of Pleasure*, 2003. • 2. Her birthplace is sometimes given as Vienna and her nationality German but I have followed the *ODNB* (Judith Milhous). For Casanova's connection see Casanova, *His Life and Memoirs*, 1933, II, Ch. VIII; Bleackley (ed.), *Casanova in England*, 1925, pp. 2–3, 15–16. • 3. SOL, *XXXIII*, 1966, pp. 73–9. • 4. See Brackett, *Thomas Chippendale*, 1924, pp. 83–7, 138–41. The rooms are described in *Lloyd's Evening Post*, February 1776, cited in McKinlay, *Mrs Cornely's Entertainments . . .*, pp. 13–14. The puffer is in *Daily Universal Register*, 4 December 1786. Bleackley (ed.), *Casanova in England*, pp. 20–21. • 5. For an admirable history of the masquerade in Britain see Castle, *Masquerade and Civilization*, 1986. • 6. Fielding, *Amelia*, 1751, Book VI, Ch. V. • 7. Combe, *The First of April*, 1777, p16. • 8. Augusta's ball is in Lewis, Troide, Martz and Smith (eds.), *Horace Walpole's Correspondence . . .*, 38, 1974, pp. 291–2, HW to Lord Hertford, 22 January 1764.

McKinlay, *Mrs Cornely's Entertainments* . . ., pp. 6–7; *Morning Chronicle*, 18 July 1776. • **9**. *General Evening Post*, 27 February 1770. • **10**. *St James's Chronicle*, 29 December 1774; *Morning Chronicle*, 18 July 1776. • **11**. See the list of London musicians complied by Haydn in Landon, *The Collected Correspondence* . . ., 1959, pp. 262–7. • **12**. See Burrows (ed.), *The Cambridge Companion to Handel*, 1997, pp. 68–70; Foreman, *London*, 2005, pp. 5–7, 33–4; *Daily Courant*, 17 March 1719. For Britton see *ODNB*; *AR 1777*, Characters, pp. 41–5. • **13**. McKinlay, *Mrs Cornely's Entertainments* . . ., p. 6. • **14**. See Wheatley and Cunningham, *London Past and Present*, 1891, III, pp. 24–5; for its establishment as a rival to Carlisle House see *Town and Country Magazine*, December 1779, pp. 644–5. • **15**. Lewis, Smith and Lam (eds.), *Horace Walpole's Correspondence* . . ., 23, 1967, pp. 271–2, HW to Horace Mann, 22 February 1771. *SOL*, *XXXIII*, pp. 77–8. For Sophie see Taylor, *Records of My Life*, 1832, I, Ch. XXII. • **16**. *Morning Post*, 29 January 1777, for the French singers, and 25 April and 1 May for the court proceedings. Spring and summer masquerades continued at Carlisle House, but not under Mrs Cornelys's management, until the summer of 1780 at least: *London Chronicle*, 18–20 April, 16–18 May, 27–9 June 1780. Hickey, *Memoirs*, 1913–25, II, p. 294, is one who connects her name with the Promenades. • **17**. *Public Advertiser*, 27 June 1781; Hawkins, *The Life of Samuel Johnson*, 1787, pp. 262–3n. • **18**. SOL, *XXXIII*, p. 79; McKinlay, *Mrs Cornely's Entertainments* . . ., p. 18. The date of demolition of the front portion of Carlisle House is often given as 1788 but I have followed the authoritative Survey. • **19**. For the asses' milk see Taylor, *Records of My Life*, I, pp. 272–3; Davis, *The Memorials of the Hamlet of Knightsbridge*, 1859, pp. 156–8; SOL, *XLV*, 2000, pp. 30–31. The agonies and the possibility of breast cancer are cited in Bleackley (ed.), *Casanova in England*, p. 261. The notice of her death is in the *London Chronicle*, Saturday 19 August 1797, and begins, 'On Saturday last died in the Fleet Prison etc'. The wrong date for her death as 19 August was first given in the *GM*, 1797, pp. 890–91, an error carried into the *ODNB* and Summers. The final quote has 'goal' for gaol, which I've silently corrected. • **20**. For *The Spectator* see Blanchard (ed.), *The Correspondence of Richard Steele*, 1941, p. 47n. • **21**. Hogwood, *Handel*, 1984, pp. 86–7; Anon., *Devil to Pay at St. James's*, 1727, pp. 3–4. • **22**. Pearce, '*Polly Peachum*', 1913, has the full story. The veiled reference to Cuzzoni and Faustina is in the Beggar's introduction. • **23**. Hervey, *Some Materials Towards Memoirs* . . ., 1931, II, pp. 273–4; see also Flower, *George Friederic Handel*, 1923, pp. 213–15. • **24**. Ralph, *The Touchstone*, 1728, pp. 138–9; *Town and Country Magazine*, December 1772, p. 642. • **25**. Landon, *The Collected Correspondence* . . ., pp. 273–4. The tittering is in Burney, *Cecilia*, 1782, I, Book II, Ch. IV. • **26**. Wheatley and Cunningham, *London Past and Present*, II, pp. 126–9. • **27**. Boaden, *Memoirs of the Life* . . ., 1825, II, pp. 68–71. Wyndham, *The Annals of Covent Garden Theatre* . . ., 1906, I, pp. 255–6. • **28**. Anon., *The Tricks of the Town Laid Open*, 1747, pp. 37–8; see also Ralph, *The Touchstone*, Essay V. • **29**. The exhibition is in Boaden, *Memoirs of the Life*, I, pp. 140–41; the spectacles are in Goldsmith, *The Citizen of the World*, 1762, Letter XXI. Roche, *Sophie in London* . . ., 1933, p. 95. • **30**. *GM*, 1751, p. 425. Lewis and Wallace (eds.), *Horace Walpole's Correspondence* . . ., 11, 1944, p. 9, HW to Mary Berry, 14 April 1789. • **31**. Moritz, *Travels of Carl Philipp Moritz* . . ., 1795, pp. 70–71. • **32**. The crush for the King of Denmark was recalled in Harriott, *Struggles Through Life*, 1815, I, pp. 175–83. *NAR 1794*, Principal Occurrences, p. 7; City of London Coroner's Court: Inquests, 1794, CLA/041/IQ/02/007/017-19; Boaden, *Memoirs of the Life* . . ., II, pp. 112–14.

• 33. Cumberland's prologue opening the Covent Garden season of 1799–1800 cited in Boaden, *Memoirs of the Life . . .*, II, pp. 247–80. • 34. See Goldsmith, *The Citizen of the World*, Letter XXI. • 35. Malcolm, *Anecdotes . . .*, 1810, II, pp. 195–7. • 36. For the Chinese Festival see Davies, *Memoirs of the Life of David Garrick*, 1781, Ch. XVI. • 37. Collins (ed.), *Travels in Britain . . .*, 1994, p. 83. The audience of 1745 and the drama is in Colman and Thornton, *The Connoisseur*, 1757, II, No. XLIII, 21 November 1754, p. 55. • 38. *London Daily Post*, 19 March 1740; Climenson (ed.), *Elizabeth Montagu . . .*, 1906, I, pp. 44–5. *Public Advertiser*, 7 February 1760. *Star*, 11 February 1797. • 39. See 'The Drama and the Theatre' by W. J. Lawrence in Turberville (ed.), *Johnson's England*, 1933, II. • 40. Williams, Charles Hanbury MSS, Vol. 68, ff. 60–63, Richard Rigby to CHW, 23 January 1750; Rigby would be a pall bearer at Garrick's funeral nearly thirty years later. • 41. Anon., *Three Original Letters . . .*, 1763; Anon., *An Historical and Succinct Account of the Late Riots . . .*, 1763; Davies, *Memoirs of the Life of David Garrick*, II, Ch. I; Malcolm, *Anecdotes . . .*, II, p. 235ff. • 42. Percival MS, p. 22. • 43. Quarrell and Mare (eds.), *London in 1710 . . .*, 1934, pp. 38–9; for Exeter Change see Altick, *The Shows of London*, 1978, p. 38. The crown jewels are in Wendeborn, *A View of England . . .*, 1791, I, p. 332. • 44. The palace is in Anon., *The Foreigner's Guide*, 1729, pp. 96–8. Boswell, *The Life of Samuel Johnson*, 1799, II, pp. 374–5. For visiting days see O'Donoghue, *The Story of Bethlehem Hospital . . .*, 1914, Ch. XXVII. • 45. For the 1753 events see Boswell, *The Life of Samuel Johnson*, II, pp. 374–5n. Karamzin, *Letters of a Russian Traveller . . .*, 1957, pp. 284–7; see also Roche, *Sophie in London . . .*, pp. 166–71. • 46. Wood, *Giants and Dwarfs*, 1868, pp. 129–38, 289–90, 307, 350–51. • 47. For the crocodile see *Daily Advertiser*, 23 January 1752. For the pig see Strutt, *The Sports and Pastimes . . .*, 1801, p. 200. For the sea monster Yorke (ed.), *Diary of John Baker*, 1931, p. 110; for the siren see *AR 1775*, Chronicle, p. 127. • 48. Trusler, MS: 'Trusler's Memoirs Part 2', pp. 13–14. See Flavell, *When London was Capital of America*, 2010, pp. 181–4; for the 1782 visit see O'Keeffe, *Recollections . . .*, 1826, II, pp. 45–6. • 49. Wimsatt and Pottle (eds.), *Boswell for the Defence*, 1960, p. 54, 21 March 1772. Collins, *Travels in Britain . . .*, p. 76. For the Chinese shadows see Dobson, *Side-Walk Studies*, 1902, p. 95ff.; Altick, *The Shows of London*, pp. 117–19. For the Fantoccini and other shows see Speaight, *The History of the English Puppet Theatre*, 1955, p. 129ff. For the Eidophusikon see Altick, *The Shows of London*, Ch. 9. • 50. Morley, *Memoirs of Bartholomew Fair*, 1859; Frost, *The Old Showmen . . .*, 1874; Rosenfeld, *The Theatre of the London Fairs . . .*, 1960, Chs. I–III; the liveliest description of the fair is Ward, *The London-Spy*, 1703, pp. 239–75. • 51. Rosenfeld, *The Theatre of the London Fairs . . .*, Chs. V–VI. • 52. For the British Museum access arrangements see Carey, *The Stranger's Guide . . .*, 1808, pp. 274–5. *ODNB* (Sir Ashton Lever); the contents are fully described in Anon., *A Companion . . .*, 1799, pp. 89–94; it closed in 1806 and the collection sold at an auction lasting sixty-five days. • 53. Several dates are given for the beginning of Astley's, most commonly 1774; but it was open at least two years before that, as we know from the diary of the Irish clergyman, and I have followed the date given in Weinreb et al., *The London Encyclopaedia*, 2008. *The Times*, 1 April 1799. • 54. The West End attractions are all from the London daily press of 1 April to 5 May 1799; Morley, *Memoirs of Bartholomew Fair*, pp. 462–9. • 55. Pottle (ed.), *Boswell's London Journal*, 1950, p. 148, 18 January 1763. • 56. Balderston (ed.), *Thraliana*, II, pp. 732, 775. O'Rourke is in Angelo, *Reminiscences . . .*, 1828–30, II, pp. 88–9. • 57. For the King's ride see Anon. [An Irish Clergyman], 'Journals of Visits to

London in 1761 and 1772', f. 37. The liberty of the parks is in Prévost, *Memoirs*
. . ., 1770, II, pp. 109–10. Walpole, *Memoirs of King George II*, 1985, II, p. 160;
the story is sometimes given as 'three crowns' but I've relied on the memory of the
Great Man's son. For Queen Caroline and the parks see Tweedy, *Hyde Park*, 1908,
Ch. VII. • **58.** For the milk see Dobson, *Side-Walk Studies*, pp. 41–2, and the
syllabub Bielfeld, *Letters of Baron Bielfeld*, 1768–70, IV, pp. 158–9. The crowded
park is in Van Muyden (ed.), *A Foreign View of England* . . ., p. 48, September
1725; see Anon., *The Foreigner's Guide* . . ., p. 22. For Gray's Inn Walk see Bullock,
Woman is a Riddle, 1716, Act IV, Scene i. • **59.** GM, 1749, pp. 186–7; Lewis,
Smith and Lam (eds.), *Horace Walpole's Correspondence*, 20, 1960, pp. 46–9, HW
to Horace Mann, 3 May 1749; Flower, *George Friederic Handel*, pp. 305–9; Brewer,
The Pleasures of the Imagination, 1997, pp. 25–8. • **60.** Flower, *George Friederic
Handel*, pp. 105–6; *AR 1763*, Chronicle, pp. 69–70; *AR 1768*, Chronicle, pp. 167–8.
AR 1775, Appendix to Chronicle, pp. 216–18; Hoare, *Memoirs of Granville Sharp*,
1828, I, pp. 214–18 and n. • **61.** *Town and Country Magazine*, 1775, pp. 321–2;
Malcolm, *Anecdotes* . . ., II, pp. 293–300. • **62.** Boswell, *The Life of Samuel
Johnson*, II, pp. 168–9. Wroth, *The London Pleasure Gardens* . . ., 1896, pp.
199–218 – Wroth remains the indispensable source for this subject. Norton (ed.),
The Letters of Edward Gibbon, 1956, I, p. 226, EG to his mother, 18? April 1768.
Landon, *The Collected Correspondence* . . ., pp. 257–8. • **63.** GM, 1732, p. 823.
For the food see Colman and Thornton, *The Connoisseur*, II, No. LXVIII, p. 253ff.,
15 May 1755. • **64.** Lewis and Brown (eds.), *Horace Walpole's Correspondence*
. . ., 9, 1941, pp. 106–10, HW to George Montagu, 23 June 1750. • **65.** Walpole,
'Additional Notes' MS, pp. 3–4. • **66.** *The Female Spectator*, I, Book I, p. 51ff.
• **67.** Pottle (ed.), *Boswell's London Journal*, p. 278, 13 June 1763. Angelo,
Reminiscences . . ., II, pp. 1–3. For the end of season rioting see *AR 1776*, Chronicle,
p. 116; Wroth, *The London Pleasure Gardens* . . ., p. 306ff. • **68.** The wretched-
ness of Marybone Gardens is in Anon., *A Sunday Ramble*, 1774, p. 57ff.; see
Wroth, *The London Pleasure Gardens* . . ., pp. 93–110. • **69.** The milliners etc.
are in Anon., *A Sunday Ramble*, pp. 54–6; see generally Wroth, *The London Pleasure
Gardens* . . ., pp. 15–87; Cosh, *A History of Islington*, 2005, Ch. 7. • **70.** See Wroth,
The London Pleasure Gardens . . ., pp. 43–53; Pinks, *The History of Clerkenwell*,
1880, pp. 409–24; Williams, *Some London Theatres*, 1883, pp. 1–32. For the young
people dancing see Roche, *Sophie in London* . . ., pp. 132–3; for the programme
towards the end of the century see, for instance, *Diary, or Woodfall's Register*, 7
April 1790. For the younger Grimaldi see Stott, *The Pantomime Life of Joseph
Grimaldi*, 2009. • **71.** Woty, *The Shrubs of Parnassus*, 1760, pp. 107–11, 'Bagnigge-
Wells'. • **72.** Anon., *A Sunday Ramble*, pp. 20–23; Wroth, *The London Pleasure
Gardens* . . ., pp. 56–67; Palmer, *St Pancras*, 1870, pp. 77–90. • **73.** Danziger and
Brady (eds.), *Boswell*, 1989, pp. 265 (16 December 1793), 282–3 (4 February
1794), 58–9 (6–8 June 1790, for Jamie). Yearsley (ed.), *The Diary of the Visits of
John Yeoman*, 1934, pp. 22–3, 2 April 1774. Franklin, *Autobiography of Benjamin
Franklin*, 1868, pp. 146–7. *Report from Select Committee on Drunkenness*, 1834,
qq. 2033, 2065. • **74.** Maitland, *The History and Survey* . . ., 1756, II, p. 719ff.;
Mazzinghy, *The New and Universal Guide* . . ., 1785, p. 168. Colquhoun,
Observations and Facts Relevant to Licensed Ale-Houses . . ., 1794, p. 3. • **75.** GM,
1736, p10. • **76.** See, for example, Lecky, *A History of England* . . ., I, p. 476ff.;
Webb, *The History of Liquor Licensing* . . ., 1903, Ch. II; George, *London Life*
. . ., 1925, p. 36ff. • **77.** For the deaths see GM, 1736, p. 136. OBP t17270222-50.
• **78.** Hervey, *Some Materials Towards Memoirs* . . ., II, p. 569. Defoe, *Augusta*

Triumphans, 1728, p. 45. *GM*, 1735, p. 331; *GM*, 1751, p. 101. *HCJ*, 26, p. 85, 4 March 1751. Maitland, *The History and Survey . . .*, I, p. 544. • **79.** Ibid., II, p. 719ff.; *GM*, 1751, p. 136. • **80.** For the chemists see *GM*, 1736, p. 682. And see Warner, *Craze*, 2003, pp. 50–53, 221–4. • **81.** For the Gin Riots see Malcolm, *Anecdotes . . .*, II, pp. 49–53. For the informers' problems see *GM*, 1737, p. 701, and prosecutions generally see *GM*, 1738, p. 379 and esp. *HR 1738*, pp. 195–217 (pagination corrected). For production figures see Mitchell and Deane, *Abstract of British Historical Statistics*, 1962, p. 254ff. For a measured appraisal of the gin phenomenon see Clark, *The English Alehouse*, 1983, pp. 238–42. • **82.** Colquhoun, *Observations and Facts Relevant to Licensed Ale-Houses . . .*, pp. 15–17. • **83.** For Freemasons and the pub see Clark, *British Clubs and Societies*, 2000, pp. 309–13, 320–25; there is a useful list of pubs used by Freemasons' lodges in the index of Ginger (ed.), *John Grano*, 1998; see also pp. 340–52. Anon., *The Articles of the Mathematical Society . . .*, 1784. • **84.** Gladstone, *The Story of the Noblemen and Gentlemen's Catch Club*, 1930. On the social world of the public house in this period see Clark, *The English Alehouse*, pp. 225–42. • **85.** Fielding, *Extracts from such of the Penal Laws . . .*, 1769, pp. 186–7. For Barbican see *Attic*, II, 1790, pp. 33–4; the Tyburn pub is in King, *The Complete Modern London Spy . . .*, 1781, p. 112ff.; Whitechapel in *Town and Country Magazine*, 1769, pp. 18–19. • **86.** Brasbridge, *The Fruits of Experience*, 1824, passim. • **87.** The European comparison is in Anon., *The Vices of the Cities of London and Westminster*, 1751, pp. 23–4. Mrs Cornelys and the Lottery Office lamps are in *Gazetteer and New Daily Advertiser*, 25 December 1780. Foote, *The Cozeners*, 1774, Act I, Scene i. The offices are in *GM*, 1731, p. 25. • **88.** In general, see Langford, *A Polite and Commercial People*, 1989, p. 505. Jesse, *George Selwyn . . .*, 1843, I, pp. 67–72, 12 March 1745. The Duke of Ancaster is in Kielmansegge, *Diary of a Journey to England*, 1902, pp. 241–2, February 1762. *Morning Herald*, 29 March 1799. • **89.** For Hockley-in-the-Hole see SOL, *XLVI*, 2008, p. 67. Quarrell and Mare (eds.), *London in 1710 . . .*, pp. 58–9. *AR 1789*, Chronicle, p. 196; for Black Boy Alley see Malcolm, *Anecdotes . . .*, I, p. 216, and pp. 334–5 for cock-throwing; for the owl see Strutt, *The Sports and Pastimes . . .*, pp. 227–8. • **90.** Van Muyden (ed.), *A Foreign View of England . . .*, pp. 276–80. • **91.** The tailors and the women are cited in Pinks, *The History of Clerkenwell*, p. 151. *Bon Ton*, 1791, p. 40. • **92.** *AR 1788*, Chronicle, pp. 198–9. • **93.** For Barnet see Ripley, *Select Original Letters . . .*, 1781, pp. 9–10. *AR 1761*, Chronicle, p. 99. *GM*, 1738, p. 164. Lewis, Smith and Lam (eds), *Horace Walpole's Correspondence . . .*, 21, 1960, p. 7, HW to Horace Mann, 17 October 1756. • **94.** *AR 1775*, Chronicle, p. 143. For the sham matches see Anon., *The Tricks of the Town Laid Open*, p. 74. *AR 1763*, Chronicle, p. 58. • **95.** Pollnitz, *The Memoirs . . .*, 1737, II, p. 470. • **96.** For sharpers see Dobrée and Webb (eds.), *The Complete Works of Sir John Vanbrugh*, 1927, IV, JV to the Earl of Manchester, 18 July 1707. Seymour, *Court Gamester*, 1719, p. iii. • **97.** The royal family are in *GM*, 1731, pp. 24–5. *The Female Spectator*, I, Book III, p. 121, which also gives us the extravagant itch of gaming. For a recent survey of the Bluestockings see Eger, *Bluestockings*, 2010. • **98.** The City assembly is in Smyth (ed.), *Memoirs and Correspondence . . .*, 1849, II, pp. 6–7, General Conway to RMK, 12 April 1773. For the faro tables see Hanger, *The Life, Adventures, and Opinions . . .*, 1801, II, pp. 6–7. For the 3,000 guineas see *AR 1766*, Chronicle, p. 61. Foreman, *Georgiana Duchess of Devonshire*, 1998, pp. 134–5, 168, 183, 229–30, 281 and passim. • **99.** For an early raid see *GM*, 1731, p. 25. *The Female Spectator*, I, Book III, p. 124. The grand jury presentment is in

GM, 1744, p. 278. *Bon Ton*, 1791, p. 357. *AR 1798*, Chronicle, pp. 30–31. • 100. Walpole, 'Additional Notes' MS, p. 17. • 101. Lewis, Smith and Lam (eds.), *Horace Walpole's Correspondence . . .*, 23, p. 530, HW to Horace Mann, 28 November 1773. Roscoe and Clergue (eds.), *George Selwyn*, 1899, pp. 137–40, correspondence, May 1781. • 102. Ryskamp and Pottle (eds.), *Boswell*, 1963, pp. 318–19, 5 April 1776. • 103. Boulton, *The History of White's*, Vol. II, p. 13; Brooks's is cited in Mitchell, *Charles James Fox*, 1992, p. 96.

9 *Martha Stracey's London – Prostitution*

1. *General Evening Post*, 14–16 March 1745. • 2. OBP oA17440315, Ordinary's Account of the Malefactors who were Executed at Tyburn, on Friday 15 March 1744[/5]. • 3. OBP t17450116-6. • 4. Quarrell and Mare (eds.), *London in 1710 . . .*, 1934, p. 12; Defoe (attrib.), *Some Considerations Upon Street-Walkers*, 1726, p. 3; Van Muyden (ed.), *A Foreign View of England . . .*, 1902, p. 193, February 1727. See also Macky, *A Journey Through England*, 1722, p. 296; Defoe, *Augusta Triumphans*, 1728, p. 28. • 5. Welch, *A Proposal to Render . . .*, 1758, p. 7; Grosley, *A Tour to London*, 1772, I, pp. 59–60; Andrew, *London Debating Societies*, 1994, nos. 1270 (1 November 1787) and 1389 (15 October 1788). • 6. Colquhoun, *A Treatise on the Police of the Metropolis*, 1806, p. 340. • 7. See Henderson, *Disorderly Women . . .*, 1999, pp. 197–9, and Trumbach, *Sex and the Gender Revolution*, 1998, pp. 113–20, who take a similar view of the likely figures. • 8. Cited in Straus, *Robert Dodsley*, 1910, pp. 144–6. • 9. See the invaluable Henderson, *Disorderly Women . . .*, pp. 22–3, 26. • 10. The Southwark sample is ibid., p. 19; Hutton, *A Journey to London*, 1818, pp. 43–8. • 11. Ilive, *Reasons Offered . . .*, 1757, pp. 19–21. • 12. For Mary Brown see St Clement Danes Poor Law Examinations as to Settlement (Plebeian Londoners Project), WCCDEP358000216, 26 January 1786; Ambross, *The Life and Memoirs of the Late Miss Ann Catley . . .*, 1789, pp. 6–12; *AR 1759*, Chronicle, p. 86; Williams, *Memoirs of the Life and Correspondence of Mrs Hannah More*, 1835, II, pp. 333–5; GM, 1752, p. 141. • 13. *AR 1766*, Chronicle, pp. 51–2; Pottle (ed.), *Boswell's London Journal*, 1950, p. 227, 25 March 1763. • 14. Hutton, *A Journey to London*, pp. 44–5. The poor servant maid is in *AR 1758*, Chronicle, p. 107. Slaughter and Murray are among many others in St Clement's Examinations WCCDEP358020191-331, 6 September 1791, 31 October 1791; and Parker 358020224, 22 September 1790. Lustig and Pottle (eds.), *Boswell*, 1982, p. 320, 6 July 1785. • 15. Campbell, *The London Tradesman*, 1747, pp. 208–9. • 16. See Heartfree, *A Most Circumstantial Account . . .*, 1760; Holland, *A Circumstantial Account . . .*, 1760; OBP t17610225-18; Trusler, *Memoirs . . .*, 1806, p. 170. There is a full account in Cruickshank, *The Secret History . . .*, 2009, pp. 413–35, though Trusler's evidence for Moody's presence at Haddock's and Fowler's suicide has been missed. • 17. OBP t17431012-34, spelling silently corrected. • 18. OBP t17430629-30. • 19. OBP t17411204-55. • 20. Ilive, *Reasons Offered . . .*, p. 23. • 21. Cleland, *Fanny Hill*, 1749, p. 104. Miss Oliver is in Harris, *Harris's List . . .*, 1779, pp. 5–6; the Chinese ornaments in King, *The Complete Modern London Spy . . .*, 1781, pp. 73–4. Mackenzie, *The Man of Feeling*, 1771, p. 109. Brady and Pottle (eds.), *Boswell in Search of a Wife*, 1957, p. 169, 29–30 March 1768. • 22. OBP t17660702-12. • 23. Harris, *The Remonstrance of Harris . . .*, 1769, p. 3ff. For a full account of the *List* see

Rubenhold, *The Covent Garden Ladies* and *Harris's List . . .*, both 2005. • **24.** Ryskamp and Pottle (eds.), *Boswell*, 1963, p. 306, 31 March 1776. There is an excellent description of Haddock's Bagnio culled from inventories in Cruickshank, *The Secret History*, pp. 232–7, and a very useful map at pp. xvi–vii. The waiters are in King, *The Complete Modern London Spy . . .*, pp. 83–4. • **25.** For Elizabeth Needham see *ODNB*; Henderson, *Disorderly Women . . .*, pp. 28–9, is appropriately cautious on the role of the procurer in forcing women to a life of prostitution. For Wetherby's see Hickey, *Memoirs*, 1913–25, I, pp. 82–4, *c.* 1768. • **26.** Pottle (ed.), *Boswell's London Journal*, pp. 230–31, 31 March 1763. For the Mall see Anon., *A Sunday Ramble*, 1774, p. 20. Prévost, *Memoirs . . .*, 1770, II, pp. 110–11. • **27.** Percival MS, pp. 18–19; Casanova, *His Life and Memoirs*, 1933, II, p. 208; Moritz, *Travels of Carl Philipp Moritz . . .*, 1795, p. 41. For Cromwell's Tea Gardens see Anon., *A Sunday Ramble*, pp. 64–6. Burney, *Evelina*, 1778, II, Letter LIII. For Ranelagh see Cozens-Hardy (ed.), *The Diary of Sylas Neville*, 1950, p. 9, 1 June 1767. Harris, *Harris's List . . .*, pp. 6–7. • **28.** Pottle (ed.), *Boswell's London Journal*, pp. 83–4, 14 December 1762. • **29.** Gay, *Trivia*, 1716, Book III, lines 259–62. • **30.** Green, *The Art of Living in London*, 1768, p. 8; Thale (ed.), *The Autobiography of Francis Place*, 1972, pp. 77–8. • **31.** The Opera House attraction is cited in Pearce, *'Polly Peachum'*, 1913, pp. 73–4; Goodman's Fields theatre is in *GM*, 1735, p. 192. Matthews (ed.), *The Diary of Dudley Ryder*, 1939, p. 49, 8 July 1715. The flesh market is in Colman and Thornton, *The Connoisseur*, 1757, II, No. XLIII, pp. 58–9, 21 November 1754. The Little Theatre is in Holcroft, *Memoirs . . .*, 1816, II, p. 245, 24 June 1798. Collins (ed.), *Travels in Britain . . .*, 1994, p. 74, 24 February 1795. • **32.** Wheatley, *Hogarth's London*, 1909, pp. 285–7. • **33.** The only Earl's Court I can find on the maps was in Seven Dials, north of Long Acre and to the west of Drury Lane; on the other hand, many places at this time were too small for the map maker's art. • **34.** OBP t17351210-16. A moidore was a Portuguese gold coin current in England because of the lack of domestic coinage in the first half of the century. • **35.** The approximate numbers of brothels in various locations are given by Fielding in *HCJ*, 32, p. 881, 10 April 1770, Report of the Committee on Robberies and Burglaries in London and Westminster. The barmaids are in Van Muyden (ed.), *A Foreign View of England . . .*, pp. 164–5, October 1726. Fielding, *A Brief Description . . .*, 1776, pp. xxviii–ix; Fielding put his name to this but I doubt that he wrote it, for the text is identical to that in Anon., *The London and Westminster Guide*, 1768. The critic is Miles, *A Letter to Sir John Fielding . . .*, 1773, p. 13. • **36.** For an overview of the geography of prostitution in London see Henderson, *Disorderly Women . . .*, Ch. 3. The comments on masquerades are from *Morning Post*, 27 November and 21 June 1777 respectively; see also *Morning Chronicle and London Advertiser*, 21 February 1776. For the cloisters of Bart's and the Fair see Ward, *The London-Spy*, 1703, pp. 122, 267. • **37.** For Reynolds see Asleson (ed.), *Notorious Muse*, 2003, pp. 39–42. Smith, *Nollekens and His Times*, 1829, I, pp. 356–7; see also pp. 102–3. • **38.** *AR 1764*, Chronicle, p. 59. • **39.** Pottle (ed.), *Boswell's London Journal*, p. 47, 21 November 1762, p. 277, 10 June 1763. Williams, *Memoirs of the Life and Correspondence of Mrs Hannah More*, II, pp. 339–40. Hickey, *Memoirs*, II, p. 261. • **40.** Ambross, *The Life and Memoirs of the Late Miss Ann Catley . . .*, esp. pp. 44–56. Cozens-Hardy (ed.), *The Diary of Sylas Neville*, p. 254, 4 October 1776. • **41.** Murphy, *Genuine Memoirs . . .*, 1769. • **42.** Williams, Charles Hanbury MSS, 68, ff. 57–9, Richard Rigby to CHW, n.d., *c.* 1744. The fraenum is the ligament attaching the foreskin to the penis; his treatment presumably required cutting. For Rigby see

ODNB. • **43**. Williams, *The Works . . .*, 1822, I, p. viii. For Williams see *ODNB*.
• **44**. Williams, Charles Hanbury MSS, 68, ff. 43–4, Charles Wyndham to CHW,
Argyle Street, 9 July 1745; ff. 48–51, Charles Wyndham to CHW, Whitham,
Somerset, 5 April 1746. • **45**. Williams, Charles Hanbury MSS, 68, ff. 64–5, Richard
Rigby to CHW, 21 July [1744]. A cordee is 'a painful inflammatory downward
curving of the penis' (*OED*). • **46**. Williams, Charles Hanbury MSS, 68, ff. 66–7,
RR to CHW, 17 August 1745. • **47**. Williams, Charles Hanbury MSS, 70, ff. 29–30,
39–43. • **48**. For Mother Douglas see Cruickshank, *The Secret History*, pp. 47–8;
Rubenhold, *The Covent Garden Ladies*, pp. 64, 181–2. For the mob cap see
Bleackley, *Ladies Fair and Frail*, 1909, p. 11. • **49**. Williams, Charles Hanbury
MSS, 70, ff. 39–43. • **50**. Eaves and Kimpel, *Samuel Richardson*, 1971, p. 520.
• **51**. Matthews (ed.), *The Diary of Dudley Ryder*, pp. 67, 71–2, 85, 138, 218,
292, 331, 369. • **52**. Ryskamp and Pottle (eds.), *Boswell*, p. 306, 31 March 1776.
• **53**. 'John Wilkes. Lists of Addresses', BL Add. MS 30,892, throughout but esp.
ff. 44–6. • **54**. For Worsdale see Balderston (ed.), *Thraliana*, 1951, I, p. 237; for
the ailment see McIntyre, *Hester*, 2008, p. 121. • **55**. *Morning Herald*, 22 January
1782. • **56**. Morris, *Observations on the Past Growth . . .*, 1751, p. 2. Williams,
Charles Hanbury MSS 69, f. 72, 'Parody of His own Song in Comus'. • **57**. For
an overview of venereal disease in this period see Trumbach, *Sex and the Gender
Revolution*, Ch. 7. • **58**. Williams, Charles Hanbury MSS MISC. #26018, ff. 21–2,
Lady Frances to CHW, 1 November 1742. • **59**. The opinion of the Bath surgeon
is in *ODNB*. Williams, Charles Hanbury MSS, 48, ff. 26–7, Henry Fox to CHW,
Scotland Yard, 15? August 1741. I cannot explain the discrepancy in the date of
year. The context seems to fit precisely with August 1742 but the letter is not a
one-off and one from June 1741 deals with the same matter. It is just possible that
CHW was in Bath both years with similar 'Cholick' problems. The accusation of
indiscretion is referred to in Williams, Charles Hanbury MSS MISC. #26018, ff.
2–3, Dr J. Oldfield to CHW, 15 September 1742 (no letters from CHW about this
affair seem to have survived). Williams, Charles Hanbury MSS MISC. #26018, ff.
4–9, Lady Kildare to CHW, 10 September [1742]. Williams, Charles Hanbury MSS
MISC. #26018, ff. 6–7, Lady Frances to CHW, 13 September 1742. • **60**. Lady
Frances lived on till 1781. Sir Charles's wayward past was well known. There was
a rumour, which some believed, that he and not John Cleland was the real author
of *Fanny Hill*, but this seems to have been untrue: Danziger and Brady (eds.),
Boswell, 1989, p. 211, 1 January 1793. • **61**. Norton, *Mother Clap's Molly House*,
2006, pp. 17, 106–9. Ward, *The History of the London Clubs*, 1709, Part II; Ward,
The London Terrae-Filius, 1707–8, No. IV, p. 39; Anon., *Hell upon Earth*, 1729,
p. 42. • **62**. See generally Norton, *Mother Clap's Molly House*, Ch. 3; for Marygold
Court see Anon., *A Genuine Narrative of all the Street Robberies . . .*, 1728, pp.
35–6; for Seven Dials see *Daily Journal*, 26 March 1730. • **63**. For the link boys
and shoeblacks see Hitchcock, *Down and Out . . .*, 2004, p. 60; for Moorfields
see Norton, *Mother Clap's Molly House*, pp. 125–7; Anon., *Hell upon Earth*, pp.
42–3. • **64**. Parker, *A View of Society and Manners . . .*, 1781, II, pp. 85–6. • **65**. *NAR
1785*, Principal Occurrences, p. 24. • **66**. Balderston (ed.), *Thraliana*, I, pp. 517–18
(October 1781). For Bickerstaff see *ODNB* and Norton, *Mother Clap's Molly
House*, pp. 317–21. Alexander, *England's Wealthiest Son*, 1962, Chs. VIII–IX.
• **67**. Norton, *Mother Clap's Molly House*, Ch. 11 – he wrongly gives the boy's
age as thirteen. OBP t17720715-22. • **68**. Trusler, *Memoirs . . .*, pp. 57–8; Balderston
(ed.), *Thraliana*, II, p. 739, April 1789. • **69**. For the Duke of Norfolk see Angelo,
Reminiscences . . ., 1828–30, I, pp. 378–9; for Lord Baltimore see Flavell, *When*

London was Capital of America, 2010, pp. 152–3; for Gordon see Hibbert, *King Mob*, 1958, p. 12; for Old Q see Melville, *The Star of Piccadilly*, 1927, p. 143. • 70. *ODNB*; for the £20 note see Lewis and Brown (eds.), *Horace Walpole's Correspondence*, 9, 1941, p. 80, HW to George Montagu, 20 October 1748. Similar tales were told of Kitty Fisher and no doubt others but this seems to be the original. • 71. *ODNB*; Bleackley, *Ladies Fair and Frail*, Ch. II; Balderston (ed.), *Thraliana*, I, pp. 271–2. • 72. *ODNB*; Brewer, *Sentimental Murder*, 2004; Levy, *Love and Madness*, 2004. • 73. *ODNB*, Lavinia Fenton, Duchess of Bolton; Pearce, *'Polly Peachum'*. For Hogarth's many versions of *Beggar's Opera* see Uglow, *Hogarth*, 1997, pp. 137–40. • 74. For Nancy Parsons see *ODNB*; Bleackley, *Ladies Fair and Frail*, Ch. III. • 75. See Martin Postle, '"Painted Women": Reynolds and the Cult of the Courtesan', in Asleson (ed.), *Notorious Muse*, pp. 22–55. • 76. Byrne, *Perdita*, 2004. • 77. Hawkins, *Memoirs . . .*, 1824, II, p. 24. • 78. Brewer, *Sentimental Murder*, pp. 138–42. • 79. *The Trial of Elizabeth Duchess Dowager of Kingston . . .*, 1776, pp. 103–4. • 80. Ibid., p. 108.

10 *Mary Young's London – Crime and Violence*

1. OBP t17410116-15. • 2. Anon., *Drury-Lane in Tears*, c. 1738; London Lives 1690 to 1800 Online, Bridewell Royal Hospital, *Minutes of the Court of Governors*, 11 November 1737, 12 January 1738. • 3. OBP t17380412-40. • 4. See *ODNB* (Philip Rawlings); OBP OA17410318, No. 1 and No. 1 Part 2; the fatal trial and the Ordinary's Account are reprinted in Anon., *Select Trials . . .*, 1742, IV, pp. 335–60. • 5. *London and Country Journal*, 19 March 1741. • 6. Statistics calculated from OBP. • 7. For this type of crime see John Styles, 'Lodgings at the Old Bailey: Lodgings and Their Furnishings in 18th-Century London', in Styles and Vickery (eds.), *Gender, Taste, and Material Culture . . .*, 2006, pp. 61–80. • 8. These statistics come from an analysis of Hodgson, *The Whole Proceedings . . .*, Nos. I–VIII, 4 December 1782–29 October 1783. I have selected cases only where there is some evidence as to the methodology of the crime. • 9. *AR 1780*, Chronicle, p. 214. • 10. Colquhoun, *A Treatise on the Police of the Metropolis*, 1797, pp. vii–ix; see also Colquhoun, *A Treatise on the Commerce and Police . . .*, 1800, esp. Ch. II. • 11. See, for instance, Schwarz, *London in the Age of Industrialization*, 1992, p. 95; Beattie, *Policing and Punishment in London*, 2001, pp. 45–8. For six soldiers hanged as footpads see *GM*, 1746, p. 381. • 12. Hitchin, *A True Discovery . . .*, 1718, p. 8. The petition of 1744 is in Hughson, *London*, 1805–9, I, pp. 393–5. Lewis, Smith and Lam (eds.), *Horace Walpole's Correspondence*, 20, 1960, p. 312, 23 March 1752. *AR 1761*, Chronicle, p. 189. *AR 1772*, Chronicle, p. 80. *AR 1781*, Chronicle, p. 191; *AR 1782*, Chronicle, p. 220. • 13. Ginger (ed.), *John Grano*, 1998, pp. 252–3. Hardy, *Memoir of Thomas Hardy*, 1832, p. 75. Balderston (ed.), *Thraliana*, 1951, I, p. 483. • 14. *AR 1776*, Chronicle, p. 177; *NAR 1785*, Principal Occurrences, p. 11; *AR 1792*, Part II, Chronicle, p. 5. • 15. Danziger and Brady (eds.), *Boswell*, 1989, p. 221. • 16. Anon., *A Genuine Narrative of all the Street Robberies . . .*, 1728, pp. 16–18; OBP t17280501-30. Anon *Select Trials*, III, pp. 243–54. • 17. See Johnson, *Berkeley Square to Bond Street*, 1952, pp. 185–7; *GM*, 1756, p. 495. *AR 1770*, Chronicle, pp. 110, 129. • 18. The gentleman's cry is cited in Pinks, *The History of Clerkenwell*, 1880, p. 514. For Fryer see *NAR 1797*, Principal Occurrences, pp. 87–8, 97; OBP t17970531-1. *AR 1798*, Chronicle,

pp. 27–9. • **19.** For an affectionate remembrance of a gallant highwayman see Hanger, *The Life, Adventures, and Opinions* . . ., 1801, II, pp. 13–24. Anon., *A Genuine Account of the Life and Actions of James Maclean* . . ., 1750; see also *GM*, 1750, pp. 391–2. • **20.** For Turpin see Barlow, *Dick Turpin* . . ., 1973, p. 280. For Blackheath and around see Landmann, *Adventures and Recollections* . . ., 1852, I, pp. 46–54. • **21.** Barlow, *Dick Turpin* . . ., Book II. *AR 1775*, Chronicle, p. 104. • **22.** *AR 1784–85*, Chronicle 1785, p. 225. For householders tied and robbed see, for example, *AR 1798*, Chronicle, p. 1, for a robbery in Norton Street, Marylebone. • **23.** Guthrie, *The Ordinary of Newgate* . . ., 1726, [n.p.]; Guthrie, *The Ordinary of Newgate* . . ., 1727, [n.p.]; Taylor, *The Ordinary of Newgate's Account* . . ., 1747. • **24.** Hodgson, *The Whole Proceedings* . . ., p. 916, seventh session beginning 10 September 1783. *AR 1765*, Chronicle, p. 72. OBP t17870221-43, trial of William Welch (twelve) and Henry Conway (nine) for highway robbery, Welch transported, Conway acquitted. • **25.** *AR 1763*, Chronicle, p. 51. • **26.** Calculated from Old Bailey Proceedings Online. The figures are 48,756 between 1700 and 1799, 29,837 between 1750 and 1799. • **27.** *AR 1775*, Chronicle, pp. 140–41; *AR 1774*, Chronicle, p. 169. • **28.** OBP 0A17410318. • **29.** Anon., *Select Trials* . . ., II, pp. 345–62. • **30.** OBP t17280501-30. For Morris see Anon., *Select Trials* . . ., III, pp. 243–54. • **31.** Beattie, *Policing and Punishment in London*, pp. 406–11; OBP t17441205-48; OA17441224. For Jack Ketch's Common, Jack Ketch a generic name for the hangman, see Smith, *A Book for a Rainy Day*, 1845, p. 180n. • **32.** OBP t17400116-4; for the alias see *London and Country Journal*, 29 January 1740; for the transportation see *Daily Gazetteer*, 8 February 1740. • **33.** Hanway, *The Citizen's Monitor*, 1780, pp. xvi–vii. • **34.** Pinks, *The History of Clerkenwell*, pp. 355–6. • **35.** Coxe, *Memoirs of Sir Robert Walpole*, 1800, I, p. 233n. • **36.** I have excluded perjury from the deception charges (378 in the century, of which 141 were brought before 1750). • **37.** *Act for the Relief of the Creditors of Thomas Pitkin* . . ., 1704, pp. i–vi. *AR 1758*, Chronicle, p. 107. • **38.** Anon., *English Rogue Reviv'd*, 1718; OBP t17170911-51, fined £50 and two years' imprisonment. For Dignam see *AR 1777*, Chronicle, p. 187. • **39.** *AR 1769*, Chronicle, p. 87. *AR 1790*, Chronicle, p. 214; OBP t17900707-11. *AR 1798*, Chronicle, pp. 47–8. • **40.** *AR 1775*, Appendix to the Chronicle, pp. 222–33. The full story is brilliantly told in Andrew and McGowen, *The Perreaus and Mrs Rudd*, 2001. • **41.** Anon., *Authentic Memoirs of William Wynne Ryland* . . ., 1784. For offences in relation to the Bank see Radzinowicz, *A History of English Criminal Law* . . ., I, 1948, pp. 647–8. For some Bank forgery cases at the end of the century see Palk (ed.), *Prisoners' Letters* . . ., 2007, pp. 1–4. • **42.** *Daily Courant*, 26 January 1709. I can find no prosecutor called Samuel Robinson in the OBP for this period. • **43.** *GM*, 1751, p. 31. • **44.** *AR 1767*, Chronicle, pp. 107, 112, 129–30. *AR 1790*, Chronicle, p. 214; OBP t17900915-37. • **45.** *GM*, 1741, p. 277; OBP t17430223-26; *General Evening Post*, 7–9 July 1743. • **46.** *London Evening Post*, 27–29 June 1745. • **47.** *GM*, 1745, pp. 275, 385. Nothing more seems to have been heard of Mr Shuttleworth after July 1745. • **48.** *AR 1793*, Chronicle, pp. 43, 48, 58; OBP t17931030-69. • **49.** See Shoemaker, *The London Mob*, 2004, pp. 171–4, for the decline. • **50.** See, for instance, Grosley, *A Tour to London*, 1772, I, pp. 254–62. • **51.** HMC, *Manuscripts of the Duke of Portland*, V, 1899, p. 336, 17 September 1713, from a private newsletter. • **52.** OBP t17211206-18, tried for murder but guilty of manslaughter, burned in the hand. For Strafford see *GM*, 1731, pp. 268, 307. For the Shakespeare's Head see *GM*, 1756, p. 202. • **53.** See Angelo, *Reminiscences* . . ., 1828–30, II, pp. 298–9 for the fencing masters. • **54.** *AR 1779*,

Chronicle, p. 213; Sir John Hawkins was chairman of the bench and argued vociferously to retain the prison sentences but was outvoted. • 55. Lewis, Troide, Martz and Smith (eds), *Correspondence of Horace Walpole, 38*, 1974, p. 503, HW to Lord Hertford, 27 January 1765; see also *AR 1765*, Appendix to the Chronicle, pp. 208–12. • 56. *London Chronicle*, 1–4 January, 21–3 March, 28–30 March, 1–4 April, 24–27 June 1780. • 57. Paley (ed.), *Justice in Eighteenth-Century Hackney*, 1991, pp. xvii–viii. • 58. OBP t17330912-56, Lamb was sentenced to death. • 59. *AR 1791*, Chronicle, pp. 19–20. *NAR 1796*, Principal Occurrences, pp. 49–50, 61–2. • 60. *AR 1762*, Chronicle, pp. 132–8; OBP t17620714-30 and OA17620719; for the execution see *Gazetteer and London Daily Advertiser*, 20 July 1762. For poor Rooker see *AR 1763*, Chronicle, p. 55. • 61. *AR 1767*, Chronicle, pp. 115, 117–21, 129, 140–41; OBP t17670909-1 and OA17670914. • 62. *London Evening Post*, 12–15 and 15–17 September 1767. • 63. Henderson, *Disorderly Women . . .*, 1999, Ch. 6. • 64. *GM*, 1753, p441; for the 1757 event see Leslie-Melville, *The Life and Work of Sir John Fielding*, 1934, p. 91. • 65. Fielding, *A True State of the Case of Bosavern Penlez . . .*, 1749, p. 34. • 66. *GM*, 1749, p329; OBP t17490906-4. • 67. *GM*, 1749, p. 474. • 68. Fielding, *A True State of the Case of Bosavern Penlez . . .*, pp. 52–3; see also Battestin, *Henry Fielding*, 1993, pp. 482–4.

11 *The Fieldings' London – Police, Prison and Punishment*

1. For the respectful treatments of the Fieldings by historians of police there are numerous instances, but see Radzinowicz, *A History of English Criminal Law . . .*, I, 1948, Ch. 12, and *III*, 1956, Ch. 1; Emsley, *The English Police*, 1996, p. 15ff. • 2. See Battestin, *Henry Fielding*, 1993. • 3. Fielding, *An Enquiry into the Causes . . .*, 1751, pp. 6ff., 20ff. • 4. George, *London Life . . .*, 1925, pp. 5–6. • 5. Battestin, *Henry Fielding*, pp. 542–50. • 6. Gascoyne, *An Address . . .*, 1754, p. 15; see also Hill, *The Story of Elizabeth Canning . . .*, 1753. • 7. Anon., *Genuine and Impartial Memoirs . . .*, 1754, pp. 74, 146. • 8. Fielding, *A Clear State . . .*, 1753, pp. 6, 22. The mystery continues to fascinate: see, for instance, Treherne, *The Canning Enigma*, 1989, and Moore, *The Appearance of Truth*, 1994. I find the evidence compiled by Gascoyne entirely compelling, but others disagree. The trial of Squires and Wells is at OBP t17530221-47 and of Canning for perjury at OBP t17540424-60. • 9. Leslie-Melville, *The Life and Work of Sir John Fielding*, 1934. • 10. *Daily Courant*, 8 January 1709. • 11. Van Muyden (ed.), *A Foreign View of England . . .*, 1902, p. 132, February 1726. For Wild the most detailed and generally accurate account remains Howson, *It Takes a Thief*, 1987, first published in 1970. For thief-takers more generally see Beattie, *Policing and Punishment in London*, 2001, pp. 247–56, 376–83, 401–17. • 12. For de Veil see *ODNB* and Anon., *Memoirs of the Life and Times of Sir Thomas Deveil . . .*, 1748. For 4 Bow Street see SOL, *XXXIV*, 1966, pp. 188–9. For Black Boy Alley and de Veil see *GM*, 1744, p. 505. • 13. Fielding, *Journal of a Voyage to Lisbon*, 1755 (in *Works*, 1766, XII, pp. 227–9). • 14. Radzinowicz, *A History of English Criminal Law . . .*, III, pp. 54–8. • 15. For McDaniel see *ODNB*; Cox, *A Faithful Narrative . . .*, 1756; Fielding, *A Plan for Preventing Robberies*, 1755, p. 4ff. Pentlow, one of Henry Fielding's men, was recommended by Fielding as keeper of the New Prison at Clerkenwell and duly appointed; he is mentioned as possibly accompanying McDaniel at one of his

arranged arrests (Cox, *A Faithful Narrative* . . ., p. 92). • **16.** Radzinowicz, *History of English Criminal Law* . . ., III, pp. 41–54, 58–62. • **17.** Leslie-Melville, *The Life and Work of Sir John Fielding*, pp. 214–22, 280–86. Johnson, *Life of Gay* (in *The Works* . . ., 1823), pp. 248–9. • **18.** For the trading justice in Middlesex see Webb, *English Local Government* . . ., 1906, pp. 326–37; for less critical views see Dowdell, *A Hundred Years of Quarter Sessions*, 1932, Ch. II; Landau, *The Justices of the Peace*, 1984; Paley (ed.), *Justice in Eighteenth-Century Hackney*, 1991, Introduction; Hitchcock and Black (eds.), *Chelsea Settlement and Bastardy Examinations*, 1999, pp. xiii–iv. • **19.** The arrangements for the eight offices are detailed in *Twenty-Eighth Report* . . ., 1798; for the Thames police establishment see Colquhoun, *A Treatise on the Commerce and Police* . . ., 1800, pp. 199–200. For the riot see Harriott, *Struggles Through Life* . . ., 1815, III, pp. 116–24. • **20.** *London Chronicle*, 2–4 September 1783. For their hanging see the issue of 20–23 September. Their trial was not reported in the OBP. • **21.** For the City in the first half of the century see Beattie, *Policing and Punishment in London.* • **22.** For the king's arms to be displayed by constables see Trusler, *The London Adviser and Guide*, 1786, p. 58. Figures for watchmen in each ward around 1755 are in Maitland, *The History and Survey* . . ., 1756, II, summarised (with some contradictions in the figures) at pp. 1187–8. For Deputies in 1778 see Gray, *Crime, Prosecution and Social Relations*, 2009, p. 60. • **23.** Maitland, *The History and Survey* . . ., II, pp. 1351–80. • **24.** For Westminster see Webb, *English Local Government* . . ., 1908, Part I, Ch. IV; Reynolds, *Before the Bobbies*, 1998, Chs. 2 and 3. The *c.* 1755 Westminster figures are in Maitland, *The History and Survey* . . ., II, p. 1347 (two of the 'constables' were in fact headboroughs, but their duties appear very similar, the constable taking precedence); figures for the metropolis are at p. 1392. • **25.** *HCJ*, 32, pp. 878–82, 10 April 1770, Report of the Committee on Burglaries and Robberies in and around London and Westminster. *AR 1795*, Chronicle, p. 4. Massie, *An Essay* . . ., 1754, p. 23. • **26.** OBP t17500228-20. • **27.** OBP t17501205-22. • **28.** OBP t17500228-20; t17830910-84. • **29.** OBP t17531024-40. • **30.** OBP t17410514-21. • **31.** OBP t17700221-44; almost two centuries later a poker in London thieves' slang was known as a 'kennedy', though whether from this case or another I can't be sure; it was current too in the 1850s. • **32.** Jesse, *George Selwyn* . . ., 1843, II, pp. 381–8; Bleackley, *Ladies Fair and Frail*, 1909, Ch. IV. • **33.** *AR 1779*, Chronicle, p. 227. • **34.** Ward, *The London Terrae-Filius*, 1707–8, No. 2, pp. 22–4. • **35.** *NAR 1785*, Principal Occurrences, p. 72. • **36.** *The Times*, 13 January 1790. • **37.** OBP t17421013-19; see also t17420909-37. • **38.** Lewis and Smith (eds.), *Horace Walpole's Correspondence* . . ., 17, 1955, pp. 503–5, 21 July 1742. There are excellent recent accounts in Hitchcock and Shore (eds.), *The Streets of London*, 2003, pp. 69–81; and Hitchcock and Shoemaker, *Tales from Hanging Court*, 2006, p. 23ff. • **39.** Shenstone, *The Works* . . ., 1777, III, pp. 49–50; the letter 'From Town' to a friend is wrongly dated 1741. *AR 1774*, Chronicle, p. 123; *AR 1792 Part II*, Chronicle, pp. 23–4. • **40.** See, generally, Hayter, *The Army and the Crowd* . . ., 1978. • **41.** *AR 1775*, Chronicle, pp. 162–3; *AR 1778*, Chronicle, pp. 195–6 (the Fleet, in August); p. 180 (Blackfriars Bridge). • **42.** For militias generally see Western, *The English Militia* . . ., 1965; Angelo, *Reminiscences* . . ., 1828–30, I, pp. 267–8. • **43.** VCH, *A History of the County of Middlesex*, VIII, 1985, p. 201. Palmer, *St Pancras*, 1870. Bondeson, *The London Monster*, 2003, pp. 60–61. • **44.** Reddaway, *The Rebuilding of London*, 1940 pp. 89n., 122–3, 182. • **45.** Defoe, *A Tour* . . ., 1724–6, I, pp. 355–6. • **46.** For small debts in the Marshalsea Court see Anon., *An Account of the Rise* . . ., 1783, pp. 8–9n.,

15. For the 1779 figure see Howard, *The State of the Prisons . . .*, 1784, p. 489. For an excellent modern overview of debt in this period see Finn, *The Character of Credit*, 2003. • 47. For a full discussion of prison and the eighteenth-century novel see Bender, *Imagining the Penitentiary*, 1987. • 48. For a more detailed view of the Marshalsea see White, 'Pain and Degradation in Georgian London', 2009, pp. 69–98. • 49. We are fortunate in having a detailed diary from the Master's Side of the Marshalsea: see Grano, 'A Journal of My Life Inside the Marshalsea' (May 1728–Sept. 1729), Bodleian Library, MS Rawlinson d.34; Ginger (ed.), *John Grano*, 1998. • 50. *AR 1779*, Chronicle, pp. 216–17. • 51. See Brown, *A History of the Fleet Prison*, 1996; White, 'Pain and Degradation in Georgian London'. • 52. Smith, *The Comical and Tragical History . . .*, 1723, pp. 64–6. • 53. *HCJ*, 15, p. 147, 12 February 1706; pp. 169–70, 23 February 1706, Report from the Committee on Riotous Proceedings in the Mint; pp. 291–2, 12 February 1707. • 54. *HCJ*, 20, p. 32, 11 February 1723, and pp. 155–7, 27 February 1723. For a modern appraisal see Stirk, 'Arresting Ambiguity', 2000, pp. 316–29. For the New Mint see OBP t17241204-69. • 55. Ilive, *Reasons Offered . . .*, 1757, pp. 4–13. For Ilive see *ODNB*; Hitchcock, *Down and Out . . .*, 2004, pp. 164–76. • 56. Creighton, *A History of Epidemics in Britain*, II, 1894, pp. 93–5. • 57. Trewin and King, *Printer to the House*, 1952, p. 33. • 58. *GM*, 1736, pp. 230, 354. • 59. Bleackley, *Jack Sheppard*, 1933, pp. 1–46; Linebaugh, *The London Hanged*, 1991, Ch. 1. • 60. At the time of the riot in 1777 the gaol was still unfinished. *NAR 1785*, Principal Occurrences, p. 23. • 61. On Howard see *ODNB*; Aikin, *A View of the Character . . .*, 1792. • 62. Smith, *State of the Gaols . . .*, 1776, pp. 9–10. • 63. Patterson, *Sir Francis Burdett . . .*, 1931, I, p. 38. • 64. Neild, *An Account of the Rise . . .*, 1808, pp. 96, 287, 397. For a scholarly overview see McConville, *A History of English Prison Administration*, 1981. • 65. Ward (ed.), *Journal and Letters of the Late Samuel Curwen . . .*, 1842, p. 277. For an excellent recent overview of public punishments in this period see Robert Shoemaker, 'Streets of Shame? The Crowd and Public Punishments in London, 1700–1820', in Devereaux and Griffiths (eds.), *Penal Practice and Culture*, 2004, pp. 232–57. • 66. For Defoe see Novak, *Daniel Defoe . . .*, 2001, pp. 189–94. *AR 1765*, Chronicle, p. 65; *AR 1763*, Chronicle, pp. 79–80. • 67. *AR 1763*, Chronicle, p. 67. • 68. *AR 1780*, Chronicle, pp. 207–9; *London Chronicle*, 8–11, 11–13, 13–15, 20–22 and 27–29 April 1780; Copeland and others (eds.), *The Correspondence of Edmund Burke*, 1958–78, IV, pp. 230–32, 350–51. • 69. *British Spy*, 13 March 1756. • 70. *Gazetteer and London Daily Advertiser*, 9 March 1756; *British Spy*, 13 March 1756; *GM*, 1756, pp. 146 and 166, the latter from April seeming to suggest that Salmon was still alive, though the *ODNB* (Stephen McDaniel) reports them both dying, while giving the year wrongly as 1755. See also Shoemaker, 'Streets of Shame?' • 71. See Radzinowicz, *A History of English Criminal Law . . .*, I, pp. 31–3. • 72. Pottle (ed.), *Boswell's London Journal*, 1950, p. 252, 4 May 1763; Danziger and Brady (eds.), *Boswell*, 1989, p. 51. • 73. For the numbers of hangings see Radzinowicz, *A History of English Criminal Law . . .*, I, pp. 147–64. *Public Advertiser*, 10 December 1783. For excellent modern accounts of hanging in eighteenth-century London see Linebaugh, *The London Hanged*; Gatrell, *The Hanging Tree*, 1994. • 74. Jesse, *George Selwyn . . .*, I, p. 126, T. Phillips to GS, 14 July (1746). • 75. Place, 'Papers', BL Add. MS 27,826, ff. 97, 100–101. For a modern study of the gallows crowd see Gatrell, *The Hanging Tree*, Ch. 2. • 76. *AR 1767*, Chronicle, p. 49. • 77. Radzinowicz, *A History of English Criminal Law . . .*, I, pp. 209–13; for a coiner's disembowelling after death see *AR 1767*, Chronicle, p. 112.

• **78.** *AR 1763*, Chronicle, p. 67. • **79.** For the curative power of a hanged man see for instance *AR 1758*, Chronicle, pp. 90–91. *AR 1793*, Chronicle, p. 58. *AR 1763*, Chronicle, pp. 95–6. • **80.** Bleackley, *Jack Sheppard*, pp. 53–5; see also Hay et al., *Albion's Fatal Tree*, 1975, Ch. 2. • **81.** *AR 1763*, Chronicle, p. 96; *AR 1764*, Chronicle, p. 74; *AR 1774*, Chronicle, p. 165. • **82.** Place, BL Add. MS 27,826, f. 107. For Fielding see Radzinowicz, *A History of English Criminal Law . . .*, I, p. 410ff. and *Covent Garden Journal*, No. 49, 20 June 1752. Boswell, *The Life of Samuel Johnson*, 1799, IV, pp. 188–9; Johnson's position on capital punishment was in fact more nuanced, as the editors' notes reveal. • **83.** Cited in Radzinowicz, *A History of English Criminal Law . . .*, I, p. 410ff. • **84.** Trusler, MS: 'Trusler's Memoirs Part 2', pp. 41–3. 'Twig' here presumably means observe or mark.

12 *Jonas Hanway's London – Religion and Charity*

1. Hanway, *The Defects of Police . . .*, 1775, p. 175. • **2.** Hanway, *Observations on the Causes of the Dissoluteness . . .*, 1772, p. 7. On the relationship between charity and discipline, and Hanway's place within it, see Andrew, *Philanthropy and Police*, 1989, esp. Ch.3. • **3.** Pugh, *Remarkable Occurrences . . .*, 1787, pp. 218–19. • **4.** Ibid., pp. 224–5. Pugh was Hanway's long-suffering amanuensis as well as his biographer. • **5.** City of London Commissioners of Sewers and Pavements: Proceedings 1766–7, p. 23ff., 9 June 1766. • **6.** Hanway, *A Review of the Proposed Naturalization of the Jews . . .*, 1753, Ch. III. • **7.** Pugh, *Remarkable Occurrences . . .*, pp. 220–22. See also *ODNB* and Taylor, *Jonas Hanway . . .*, 1985, which includes a full Hanway bibliography. • **8.** Gray, *A Sermon . . .*, 1803, [pp. 103–10]; Jones, *The Charity School Movement*, 1938, esp. Chs. I–II. • **9.** Hanway, *Observations on the Causes of the Dissoluteness . . .*, p. 57, and *A Comprehensive View of Sunday Schools*, 1786, p. xiii; Gibson, *Directions given by Edmund Lord Bishop of London . . .*, 1724, pp. 4–5. • **10.** *The Church Catechism . . .*, 1709, p. 14; Gibson, *Directions given by Edmund Lord Bishop of London . . .*, p. 6. • **11.** Ireland, *Hogarth Illustrated*, 1884, pp. 214–15; Gray, *A Sermon . . .*, [p. 110]. • **12.** Brownlow, *Memoranda*, 1847, pp. 114–15, citing Dr Richard Brocklesby, Coram's friend. For Coram generally see Wagner, *Thomas Coram . . .*, 2004. • **13.** See Nichols and Wray, *The History of the Foundling Hospital*, 1935; McClure, *Coram's Children*, 1981. • **14.** Ibid., pp. 47–8, 226–8. • **15.** For Hanway and the Foundling see Taylor, *Jonas Hanway . . .*, pp. 61–2, 158–9. • **16.** For the Cockney Feasts see Lysons, *The Environs of London*, 1792–6, III, p. 488. Leslie-Melville, *The Life and Work of Sir John Fielding*, 1934, p. 114. • **17.** Taylor, *Jonas Hanway . . .*, Ch. VI; Owen, *English Philanthropy*, 1960, pp. 59–60. • **18.** Taylor, *Jonas Hanway . . .*, Ch. IX; see also Hanway, *A Sentimental History of Chimney Sweepers*, 1785. • **19.** Highmore, *Pietas Londinensis*, 1810, pp. 600–608. • **20.** Ibid., pp. 215–23. See also Compston, *The Magdalen Hospital*, 1917; Taylor, *Jonas Hanway . . .*, pp. 76–9; Ogborn, *Spaces of Modernity*, 1998, Ch. 2. • **21.** Langdon-Davies, *Westminster Hospital*, 1952, pp. 23–6. • **22.** Cameron, *Mr Guy's Hospital*, 1954, Ch. 1. • **23.** See Lettsom, *Of the Improvement of Medicine in London . . .*, 1775. • **24.** For an excellent overview see Owen, *English Philanthropy*, pp. 41–61. • **25.** Hawkins, *The Life of Samuel Johnson*, 1787, p. 236ff. • **26.** For the Westminster see Highmore, *Pietas Londinensis*, pp. 311–12, and Langdon-Davies, *Westminster Hospital*, p. 28. Clark-Kennedy, *The London*, 1962, p. 34. For Guy's see Cameron, *Mr Guy's Hospital*, pp. 74–8. For the Middlesex see Highmore, *Pietas Londinensis*, p. 224. • **27**. Pugh, *Remarkable Occurrences* . . ., pp. 248-9. • **28**. For Sunday schools see *NAR 1785*, Principal Occurrences, p. 109. For the Philanthropic Society see Highmore, *Pietas Londinensis*, pp. 859-71. • **29**. Bernard (ed.), *Reports of the Society for Bettering* . . ., 1800-1802, I, pp. xi-xiv. For Bernard see *ODNB*. • **30**. Bernard, *Reports of the Society for Bettering* . . ., I, pp. 153-61; III, p. 143ff. • **31**. Ibid., II, p. 237ff. • **32**. Hanway, *The Defects of Police* . . ., p. 7. • **33**. Ibid., p. 9. • **34**. *Daily Courant*, 19 February 1709. • **35**. Taylor, *Jonas Hanway* . . ., pp. 105-9; Hanway, *An Earnest Appeal for Mercy* . . ., 1766, p. 8. • **36**. Ibid., pp. iii-iv; this is usually said of Hanway's Act of 1767, many authorities citing Pugh, *Remarkable Occurrences* . . ., pp. 185-92, who seems to have misremembered here. See George, *London Life* . . ., 1925, pp. 46-7. • **37**. Hanway, *An Earnest Appeal for Mercy* . . ., p. 77; Foundling Hospital data courtesy of David Allin. • **38**. Ibid., p. 135, for the Brownrigg apprentice. • **39**. Pennant, *Some Account of London*, 1805, p. 190. • **40**. Highmore, *Pietas Londinensis*, pp. 780-86. • **41**. Anon., *An Account of Several Work-Houses* . . ., 1725; Anon., *An Account of the Work-Houses in Great Britain* . . ., 1786. Green, *Pauper Capital*, 2010, pp. 57-69. • **42**. Webb, *English Poor Law History*, 1927, Ch. IV, still indispensable. • **43**. For St Martin-in-the-Fields see Eden, *The State of the Poor*, 1797, II, p. 440ff. Brown, *A Memoir of Robert Blincoe*, 1832, pp. 7-13. • **44**. For Aldgate see Hitchcock, *Down and Out* . . ., 2004, pp. 136-8; OBP t17550910-41. *AR 1768*, Chronicle, p. 98; *Gazetteer and New Daily Advertiser*, 25 April 1768. *NAR 1785*, Principal Occurrences, pp. 16, 33. • **45**. Mazzinghy, *The New and Universal Guide* . . ., 1785, p. 186. • **46**. Anon., *An Account of the Work-Houses in Great Britain* . . ., pp. vii, 22. • **47**. See Hervey, *Some Materials Towards Memoirs* . . ., 1931, III, pp. 906-8 for the extraordinary manoeuvres attending the death of Queen Caroline. • **48**. *GM*, 1733, p. 641, citing the *Grubstreet Journal* of 13 December 1733. • **49**. Hutton, *A Journey to London*, 1818, pp. 21-2. R. Michael Robbins, 'Some Designs for St Marylebone Church with Notes on the Chapels of the District', *LTR*, 1972, pp. 105-6. • **50**. For complaints of empty City churches at the end of the century see Abbey and Overton, *The English Church in the Eighteenth Century*, 1878, II, pp. 457-8. Anon. [An Irish Clergyman], 'Journals of Visits to London in 1761 and 1772', f. 116. For City churchgoing early in the century see Earle, *The Making of the English Middle Class*, 1989, pp. 245-7. • **51**. Voltaire, *Letters* . . ., 1733, Letter V. Maitland, *The History and Survey* . . ., 1756, II, pp. 1189-90; I'm very grateful for information from John Seed that charts some small decline in meeting-house numbers across the century. See also Hollaender and Kellaway (eds.), *Studies in London History* . . ., 1969, pp. 392-7. • **52**. Kevan, 'Autobiographical Memoir and Diary', f. 16. • **53**. Ibid., f. 36. • **54**. Ibid., f. 44. • **55**. Woodman, 'Diary, September 1706-March 1707' and 'Diary, September 1707-March 1709', d.1334, f. 7, 3 November 1706. These diaries are catalogued as Anon., and as if they were written by different hands, but they are both plainly Woodman's. • **56**. Ibid., f. 8, 8 November 1706. • **57**. Ilive, *Reasons Offered* . . ., 1757, pp. 22-3. • **58**. Sherwood, *A Letter from the Bishop of London* . . ., 1750. Lewis, Troide, Martz and Smith (eds.), *Horace Walpole's Correspondence*, 37, 1974, pp. 430, 437-8, HW to Henry Conway, 22 January and 12 February 1756. On Brothers see esp. Binns, *Recollections* . . ., 1854, pp. 48-50. • **59**. Whitefield, *Journals*, 1965, p. 260ff. For the attacks on Wesley's meetings see Curnock (ed.), *The Journal* . . ., 1909, II, pp. 221-2, 475, 522-4. *AR 1760*, Chronicle, p. 86. For the influence of Methodism among the poor see Christie, *Stress and Stability* . . ., 1984, pp. 206-14. • **60**. Curnock (ed.), *The Journal* . . ., IV, p. 52. • **61**. Ibid., VII, pp. 235-6, January

1787. • **62.** For the Quaker workhouse see Hitchcock (ed.), *Richard Hutton's Complaints Book*, 1987, Introduction; for Lettsom see Abraham, *Lettsom*, 1933, pp. 16–34; Lackington, *Memoirs . . .*, 1795, pp. 200, 215. • **63.** Ibid., pp. 202–3. • **64.** SPRM, *An Account . . .*, 1701; SPRM, *The Eight and Twentieth Account . . .*, 1722, p. 1; Simpson, *A Sermon Preached . . .*, 1738, pp. 28–9. For Cooper see OBP t17030707-2; for Dent see Bristow, *Vice and Vigilance*, 1977, p. 24. • **65.** Paley (ed.), *Justice in Eighteenth-Century Hackney*, 1991, pp. xxvi–vii, 185ff. The proclamation is in *NAR 1787*, Public Papers, pp. 62–4. • **66.** *AR 1799*, Chronicle, p. 20. For modern appraisals see Corfield, *Power and the Professions . . .*, 1995, pp. 102–36; Jacob, *The Clerical Profession . . .*, 2007. • **67.** Boswell, *The Life of Samuel Johnson*, 1799, II, p. 222n. Hiccup is in Jesse, *George Selwyn . . .*, 1843, I, p. 339, Gilly Williams to George Selwyn, Christmas Day 1764. For Lloyd see OBP t17830723-25 and *London Chronicle*, 12–15 July and 28–30 August 1783. For Russen see *AR 1777*, Chronicle, pp. 205, 207–8, 215. • **68.** The St Clements Danes examinations as to settlement of 1752–3 are eloquent testimony to the popularity of Fleet marriages, in a sample of 100 cases far outnumbering all regular marriages put together, at least among these very poorest of Londoners: WCC DEP 35811031-84, 35811032-157. Pennant, *Some Account of London*, p. 194; see also Ashton, *The Fleet*, 1889, Chs. XXVI–XXX. • **69.** *GM*, 1735, p. 93. For the Savoy marriages see *GM*, 1755, pp. 328, 569; Wilkinson, *Memoirs . . .*, 1790, I, pp. 74–97. • **70.** *ODNB*; Wheatley, *Hogarth's London*, 1909, pp. 211–14. • **71.** Brasbridge, *The Fruits of Experience*, 1824, p. 51; for Sandwich's chaplain see Brewer, *Sentimental Murder*, 2004, pp. 44–5. Trusler MS: 'Trusler's Memoirs Part 2', p. 273ff. • **72.** Taylor, *Records of My Life*, 1832, I, pp. 102–6; see *ODNB*. • **73.** For the mistress see Hawkins, *The Life of Samuel Johnson*, p. 435. The verse is from Thompson, *The Courtesan*, 1765, p. 32; I've not been able to identify the penitent Talbot. For Dodd and the Magdalen generally see Compston, *The Magdalen Hospital*, Ch. IX. • **74.** Carlyle, *The Autobiography . . .*,1910, pp. 528–9. • **75.** Brasbridge, *The Fruits of Experience*, pp. 98–100. • **76.** Boswell, *The Life of Samuel Johnson*, III, p. 143. • **77.** See *ODNB*; the trial is at OBP t17770219-1. • **78.** Wheatley (ed.), *The Historical and Posthumous Memoirs . . .*, 1884, IV, pp. 248–9. • **79.** Calamy, *An Historical Account . . .*, 1829, II, pp. 227–9; see also Lecky, *A History of England . . .*, I, pp. 51–7. • **80.** Maitland, *The History and Survey . . .*, I, p. 508. • **81.** HMC, *Manuscripts of the Duke of Portland, IV*, 1897, pp. 532–3, Abigail Harley to her nephew Edward Harley, 2 March 1710. Dolben died three months later. • **82.** OBP t17150713-14; see also t17150907-7; t17150907-13. • **83.** Maitland, *The History and Survey . . .*, I, p. 521. OBP t17160906-2; t17161010-1; see also t17161010-2 for trouble after the first executions of the Salisbury Court rioters. For the Salisbury Court mug-house see Matthews (ed.), *The Diary of Dudley Ryder*, 1939, pp. 279–83. • **84.** *HR 1719*, Chronological Diary, pp. 14, 17–19. For Atterbury see Henderson, *London and the National Government*, 1945, p. 72n. Anon., *Hell upon Earth*, 1729, p. 8. • **85.** *GM*, 1744, pp. 102–7; 1745 pp. 441, 501, 557, 641–2, 665–7. • **86.** Hoppit, *A Land of Liberty?*, 2000, pp. 221–2. • **87.** See Dodsley, *London and Its Environs Described . . .*, 1761, V, pp. 201–2. • **88.** For the Monument see Strype, *A Survey . . .*, 1720, I, Book II, pp. 180–81. For Guy Fawkes and other celebrations see Swift, *Journal to Stella*, 1948, II, pp. 404, 415–16 (1711); *GM*, 1735, p. 105. • **89.** *GM*, 1734, pp. 450–51, 702; 1738, p. 378; 1736, p. 290; see also Langford, *A Polite and Commercial People*, 1989, pp. 39–40. Langdon-Davies, *Westminster Hospital*, pp. 50–52. • **90.** *GM*, 1756, p. 89; *AR 1759*, Chronicle, p. 98. • **91.** *GM*, 1744, p. 275; *AR 1762*, Chronicle, p. 92.

13 *John Wilkes's London – Politics and Government*

1. John Wilkes has understandably been the subject of many biographies and much historical enquiry. For a useful introduction to the main outline of his life and character see the article in *ODNB* (Peter D. G. Thomas). In the narrative of Wilkes's life that follows I have drawn mainly on Bleackley, *Life of Wilkes*, 1917; Treloar, *Wilkes and the City*, 1917; Postgate, 'That Devil Wilkes', 1956; Rudé, *Wilkes and Liberty*, 1983; Thomas, *John Wilkes*, 1996; and Cash, *John Wilkes*, 2006. • 2. SOL, XLVI, 2008, pp. 120–22. • 3. Bleackley, *Life of Wilkes*, p. 17. • 4. Cash, *John Wilkes*, pp. 27–9, 126. • 5. Cited ibid., p. 101. • 6. Ibid., pp. 101–8. • 7. Bleackley, *Life of Wilkes*, pp. 105–6. • 8. Thomas, *John Wilkes*, pp. 54–5; Cash, *John Wilkes*, p. 262. • 9. Bleackley, *Life of Wilkes*, pp. 130–31. • 10. Cited in Cash, *John Wilkes*, p. 151. • 11. Ibid., p. 153. • 12. Webb, *English Local Government . . .*, 1908, II, Ch. X, remains an indispensable guide to the City's government. See also Oldfield, *An Entire and Complete History . . .*, 1792, III, pp. 243–7. • 13. For excise see Hervey, *Some Materials Towards Memoirs . . .*, 1931, I, pp. 133–51. For the full story of these years see Henderson, *London and the National Government*, 1945. • 14. Sharpe, *London and the Kingdom*, 1894–5, III, p. 57ff. • 15. AR 1763, Chronicle, p. 67. • 16. Entick, *A New and Accurate History . . .*, 1766, III, p. 225ff.; Noorthouck, *A New History of London*, 1773, pp. 418–19. • 17. Sutherland, *The City of London . . .*, 1959, pp. 9–10; see also Parker, *The Sugar Barons*, 2011, Ch. 25. • 18. Treloar, *Wilkes and the City*, pp. 62–3. • 19. Thomas, *John Wilkes*, pp. 70–72. • 20. On the disconnectedness between Wilkes and the industrial strife of 1768–70 see Rudé, *Wilkes and Liberty*, Ch. VI. • 21. Bleackley, *Life of Wilkes*, pp. 192–3. • 22. Rudé, *Wilkes and Liberty*, pp. 62–6. • 23. Bleackley, *Life of Wilkes*, pp. 220–21. • 24. Sharpe, *London and the Kingdom*, III, pp. 84–5. • 25. Ibid., pp. 90–91. • 26. Lewis, Smith and Lam (eds.), *Horace Walpole's Correspondence*, 23, 1967, pp. 195–6, HW to Mann, 15 March 1770. • 27. Junius, *The Letters of Junius*, 1775, I, pp. 285–6, Letter XLIII, 19 March 1770. Many scholars now consider that Junius was Sir Philip Francis. • 28. Cited in Sutherland, *The City of London . . .*, p. 2. • 29. Sharpe, *London and the Kingdom*, III, pp. 102–5; Ward-Jackson, *Public Sculpture of the City of London*, 2003, pp. 163–5. • 30. Bleackley, *Life of Wilkes*, p. 256. For the later period see Pickett, 'Manuscripts and Publications', 1782–96, ff. 65, 166–72. • 31. For Wilkes's part see Almon, *The Correspondence of the Late John Wilkes . . .*, 1805, V, pp. 52–64. • 32. Bleackley, *Life of Wilkes*, pp. 262–3. • 33. Cash, *John Wilkes*, pp. 284–5. • 34. The obelisk was designed by Robert Mylne, architect of Blackfriars Bridge, and had been ordered in 1770, before the affair of the printers. See Bowers, *Sketches of Southwark . . .*, 1905, p. 606ff. • 35. Almon, *The Correspondence of the Late John Wilkes . . .*, V, p. 63. • 36. Cash, *John Wilkes*, pp. 348–9. • 37. *London Chronicle*, 8–11 April, 6–9 May 1780. • 38. Mitchell, *Charles James Fox*, 1992, pp. 28–9. • 39. For Terrick see Walpole, *Memoirs of the Reign of King George III*, 2000, II, pp. 186–7, and for Payne see *ODNB*. For Catholic intrigue see Blom et al. (eds.), *The Correspondence of James Peter Coghlan*, 2007, pp. 51–2, 55. Andrew, *London Debating Societies*, 1994, for instance nos. 10, 76, 79, 337. • 40. *London Chronicle*, 4–8 January; 5–8 February (Wesley); 7–9 March; 30 May–1 June 1780. See also De Castro, *The Gordon Riots*, 1926, Ch. 1; Hibbert, *King Mob*, 1958, Chs. 2–3. • 41. *London Chronicle*, 1–3 June 1780. Unless where cited, I have followed the narratives of De Castro, *Gordon Riots*, and Hibbert, *King Mob*; the best

contemporary account is Holcroft, *A Plain and Succinct Narrative . . .*, 1780.
• **42**. *London Chronicle*, 6–8 June 1780. • **43**. Crabbe, *The Life of George Crabbe*,
1834, p. 72: Crabbe put this on 7 June but seems to have been in error. • **44**. Nelson,
The History, Topography, and Antiquities . . ., 1811, p. 260. • **45**. Cited in De
Castro, *Gordon Riots*, p. 92. • **46**. OBP t17800628-34. • **47**. Boswell, *The Life of
Samuel Johnson*, 1799, III, p. 429. • **48**. See Rudé, *Paris and London . . .*, 1974,
p. 289; OBP t17800628-23; t17800628-89. • **49**. Hunter, *The History of London
. . .*, 1811, II, p. 777ff. • **50**. OBP t17800628-113. See also Rudé, *Paris and London*,
pp. 268–92. • **51**. For the total losses see *AR 1780*, Chronicle, p. 233. The Paris
comparison is in Blanning, *The Pursuit of Glory*, 2007, p. 326. For Langdale's see
AR 1784–5, Chronicle 1785, pp. 225–6: the insurers lost their claim. • **52**. *AR
1781*, History of Europe, pp. 137–8 for the judgement on Kennett; De Castro,
Gordon Riots, p. 216ff. for the conspiracy theories. For the end of Kennett see
ODNB. • **53**. De Castro, *Gordon Riots*, p. 208, says twenty-one were hanged;
Thornton, *The New, Complete, and Universal History . . .*, 1784, pp. 520–21, says
nineteen were executed in London and Middlesex and six in Southwark. • **54**. *AR
1783*, Chronicle, pp. 198, 204. • **55**. Russell, *Memorials and Correspondence . . .*,
1853–7, I, p. 258. • **56**. Oldfield, *An Entire and Complete History . . .*, II, p. 255.
• **57**. Hartley and another (eds.), *History of the Westminster Election . . .*, 1784,
p. 54. • **58**. Ibid., pp. 61, 99–100, 112–13, 163–5. • **59**. Ibid., pp. 379–410.
• **60**. Mitchell, *Charles James Fox*, p. 252 ff. • **61**. See Cartwright (ed.), *The Life
and Correspondence of Major Cartwright*, 1826, II, pp. 343–7, for a list of the
founder members. • **62**. Hardy, *Memoir of Thomas Hardy*, 1832, pp. 8–14; Thale
(ed.), *Selections from the Papers . . .*, 1983, p. 10. • **63**. The proclamation is in *AR
1792*, Part II, State Papers, pp. 192*–4*. Keane, *Tom Paine*, 1995, pp. 334–48.
• **64**. For the panic see *AR 1792*, Part II, Chronicle, p. 46; Lambert, *The History
and Survey of London . . .*, 1806, II, pp. 319–22; Hunter, *The History of London
. . .*, II, pp. 814–15. For the City and the Bank guard, which inspired one of James
Gillray's happiest cartoons in 1787, see Pickett, 'Manuscripts and Publications', ff.
12, 138–46. • **65**. For the numbers of divisions and members see Thale (ed.),
Selections from the Papers . . ., pp. xxiii–xxiv, 42. Thale (ed.), *The Autobiography
of Francis Place*, 1972, pp. 131–2 and n. • **66**. *AR 1793*, Chronicle, pp. 25, 28,
59; Barrell, *The Spirit of Despotism*, 2006, Ch. 2. • **67**. *Lloyd's Evening Post*, 5–7
November 1794. • **68**. *NAR 1794*, Principal Occurrences, p. 55; *AR 1795*, Chronicle,
pp. 2–3, 29, 37, 43. • **69**. *AR 1795*, Chronicle, pp. 37–9; Thale (ed.), *The
Autobiography of Francis Place*, pp. 148–9; Thale, (ed.), *Selections from the Papers
. . .*, p. 429. • **70**. See Reid, *The Rise and Dissolution . . .*, 1800. • **71**. Cash, *John
Wilkes*, p. 329. • **72**. Angelo, *Reminiscence . . .*, 1828–30, I, pp. 55–6. • **73**. Wheatley
(ed.), Wheatley (ed.), *The Historical and Posthumous Memoirs . . .*, 1884, II,
pp. 48–9.

BIBLIOGRAPHY

The place of publication is London unless indicated otherwise.

Abbreviations

AR	*Annual Register for the Year . . .*
BL Add. MS	British Library Additional Manuscript
Bodleian	Bodleian Library
DNB	*Dictionary of National Biography*
GM	*Gentleman's Magazine*
HCJ	*House of Commons Journal*
HMC	Historical Manuscripts Commission
HR	*The Historical Register for the Year . . .*
LMA	London Metropolitan Archive
LTR	*London Topographical Record*
LWL	Lewis Walpole Library, Farmington, Connecticut
NAR	*New Annual Register for the Year . . .*
OBP	Old Bailey Proceedings Online
ODNB	*Oxford Dictionary of National Biography*
OED	*Oxford English Dictionary*
SOL	Survey of London
SPRM	Societies for Promoting a Reformation of Manners
VCH	Victoria County History

Manuscript Sources

'Album of Tradecards' (LWL)

Angelo Family Papers (LWL)

Anon. [An Irish Clergyman], 'Journals of Visits to London in 1761 and 1772', BL Add. MS 27,951

Beckford, William, 'Letters from Spanish Town, Jamaica, to James Knight, London', BL Add. MS 12,431

City of London Commissioners of Sewers and Pavements: Proceedings 1765–9 [Minutes of Courts of Sewers and Pavements], CLA/oo6/AD/o4/oo1 (LMA)

City of London Commissioners of Sewers and Pavements: Proceedings 1766–7 [Minutes of Public Meetings for Implementing the New Act for Improving the Streets of London etc.], CLA/oo6/AD/o4/oo4 (LMA)

City of London Coroner's Court: Inquests, 1794, CLA/o41/IQ/o2/oo7 (LMA)

City of London Police MSS (LMA)

Cumberland, George, 'Cumberland Papers Vol. I: Correspondence 1748–1777', BL Add. MS 36,491

Grano, John Baptist (Giovanni Battista), 'A Journal of My Life Inside the Marshalsea' [May 1728–September 1729], Bodleian, MS Rawlinson d.34

Gulston, Joseph, 'The Effusions of Fancy and Fun Compiled by Joseph Gulston 1784' (LWL)

Kevan, Samuel, 'Autobiographical Memoir and Diary', memoir 1826, diary 7 June 1798–19 May 1827, BL Add. MS 42,556

Percival MS, 'Observations made by Mrs Percivall when in London Anno 1713 or 1714 in Letters to a Friend', 1713–14 (LWL)

Pickett, William, 'Manuscripts and Publications', 1782–96 (LWL)

Place, Francis, 'Papers' (BL)

St Clement Danes Poor Law Examinations as to Settlement (Plebeian Londoners Project)

Trusler, John MS: 'Trusler's Memoirs Part 2' (LWL)

Walpole, Horace, 'Additional Notes' (MS) at the end of his copy of Thomas Pennant, *Some Account of London*, 1790 (LWL)

Warwick Wroth Collection, Museum of London

Williams, Charles Hanbury MSS (LWL)

Woodman, William, 'Diary, September 1706–March 1707' and 'Diary, September 1707–March 1709', MS Rawlinson d.1334 and c.861 (Bodleian)

Newspapers and Journals

Attic
Bon Ton
British Spy or New Universal London Weekly Journal
Covent Garden Journal
Daily Advertiser
Daily Courant
Daily Gazetteer
Daily Journal
Daily Post
Daily Universal Register
Diary, or Woodfall's Register
Gazetteer and London Daily Advertiser
Gazetteer and New Daily Advertiser
General Evening Post
Gentleman's Magazine (GM)
Lloyd's Evening Post
London and Country Journal
London Chronicle
London Daily Post and General Advertiser
London Evening Post
London Morning Penny Post
Middlesex Journal or Universal Evening Post
Morning Chronicle and London Advertiser
Morning Herald and Daily Advertiser
Morning Post and Daily Advertiser
Public Advertiser
St James's Chronicle or the British Evening Post
Star
The Female Spectator
The Museum
The Penny London Post or the Morning Advertiser
The Post-Man
The Spectator
The Times
The World
Town and Country Magazine

Primary Sources: Printed Books and Pamphlets

Act for the Relief of the Creditors of Thomas Pitkin, a Bankrupt, and for the Apprehending of him, and the Discovery of the Effects of the said Thomas Pitkin, and his Accomplices, 1704

Address from the Committee for the Relief of the French Refugee Clergy and Laity, 1796

Aikin, John, *A View of the Character and Public Services of the late John Howard, Esq. LL.D., F.R.S.*, 1792

Alcock, Thomas, *Some Memoirs of the Life of Dr. Nathan Alcock, Lately Deceased*, 1780

Almon, John, *The Correspondence of the Late John Wilkes, with his friends, printed from the original manuscripts, in which are introduced memoirs of his Life*, 5 vols., 1805

Ambross, Miss, *The Life and Memoirs of the Late Miss Ann Catley, the Celebrated Actress . . .*, 1789

Andrew, Donna T., *London Debating Societies 1776–1799*, 1994

Angelo, Henry, *Reminiscences of Henry Angelo, with Memoirs of His Late Father and Friends . . .*, 2 vols., 1828–30

Anon., *A Companion to all the principal Places of Curiosity and Entertainment in and about London and Westminster*, 1799

Anon. [P. Cox?], *A Compleat History of Middlesex . . . to which is Added a . . . Description of the Cities of London and Westminster*, 1730

Anon., *A Genuine Account of the Life and Actions of James Maclean, Highwayman, to the Time of his Trial and receiving Sentence at the Old Bailey . . .*, 1750

Anon., *A Genuine Narrative of all the Street Robberies Committed since October Last by James Dalton and His Accomplices . . .*, 1728

Anon., *A Guide to Stage Coaches, Diligences, Waggons, Carts, Coasting Vessels, Barges, and Boats, which Carry Passengers and Merchandise from London to the Different Towns in Great Britain . . .*, 1783

Anon., *A State of the Case of the New Parish Church of St John Clerkenwell in the County of Middlesex, with Respect to the Endowment of the Said Church*, n.d. [1725?]

Anon., *A Sunday Ramble; or Modern Sabbath-Day Journey; In and about the Cities of London and Westminster*, 1774

Anon., *A Trip from St. James's to the Royal Exchange. With Remarks Serious and Diverting, on the Manners, Customs, and Amusements of the Inhabitants of London and Westminster*, 1744

Anon., *A Trip through the Town. Containing Observations on the Customs and Manners of the Age*, 1735

Anon. [A German Gentleman], *A View of London and Westminster: or, the Town Spy*, 1725

Anon., *Ambulator: or, A Pocket Companion in a Tour Round London, within the Circuit of Twenty-Five Miles . . .*, 1800

Anon., *An Account of Several Work-Houses for Employing and Maintaining the Poor . . .*, 1725

Anon., *An Account of the Rise, Progress, and Present State of the Society for the Discharge and Relief of Persons Imprisoned for Small Debts*, 6th edition, 1783

Anon., *An Account of the Work-Houses in Great Britain, in the Year M,DCC,XXXII . . .*, 1786

Anon., *An Historical and Succinct Account of the Late Riots at the Theatres of Drury-Lane and Covent-Garden*, 1763

Anon., *An Impartial State of the Case of the French Comedians, Actors, Players, or Strollers, who lately opened a Theatre at the Hay-Market . . .*, 1750

Anon., *Authentic Memoirs of William Wynne Ryland, containing a Succinct Account of the Life and Transactions of that great but unfortunate Artist . . .*, 1784

Anon., *City Biography, containing Anecdotes and Memoirs of the Rise, Progress, Situation, & Character of the Aldermen and other Conspicuous Personages of the Corporation and City of London*, 1800

Anon., *Drury-Lane in Tears: or, the Ladies of Pleasure in Mourning. Being a Full and Genuine Account of the Life intrigues, and merry transactions, of that famous and well-known Pickpocket Jane Webb, otherwise Jenny Diver . . .*, n.d. [*c.* 1738]

Anon., *Genuine and Impartial Memoirs of Elizabeth Canning, containing a complete History of that Unfortunate Girl, from Her Birth to the present Time . . .*, 1754

Anon., *Hell upon Earth: or the Most Pleasant and Delectable History of Whittington's Colledge, Otherwise (vulgarly) called Newgate*, 1703

Anon., *Hell upon Earth: or the Town in an Uproar*, 1729

Anon., *Memoirs of the Life and Times of Sir Thomas Deveil . . .*, 1748

Anon., *Reasons against Building a Bridge from Lambeth to Westminster. Shewing the Inconveniencies of the same to the City of London, and Borough of Southwark*, 1722

Anon., *Reasons for a Pound-Rate in the Intended New Parishes in Stepney Answered and Confuted*, 1727

Anon., *Reasons for erecting a Bridge Cross the River Thames, from Westminster to the opposite Shore in the County of Surrey*, n.d. [1736]

Anon., *Select Trials at the Sessions-House in the Old-Bailey . . .*, 4 vols., 1742

Anon., *Some Considerations on the Establishment of the French Strolers; The Behaviour of their Bully-Champions. And other Seasonable Matters*, 1750

Anon., *The Adventures of Lindamira, A Lady of Quality*, 1702, edited by Benjamin Boyce, Minnesota, 1949

Anon., *The Articles of the Mathematical Society, meeting at the Sign of the Black Swan in Brown's-Lane, Spitalfields, London*, 1784

Anon., *The Case of the Parish of St Giles Criplegate*, 1712

Anon., *The Devil to Pay at St. James's; or, a full and true Account of a most horrid and bloody Battle between Madam Faustina and Madam Cuzzoni*, 1727

Anon., *The English Rogue Reviv'd. Or, the Life of William Fuller, Cheat-Master-General of Great-Britain*, 1718

Anon., *The Foreigner's Guide: Or, a necessary and instructive Companion Both for the Foreigner and Native, in their Tour through the Cities of London and Westminster*, 1729

Anon., *The Life and Character of John Barber, Esq.; Late Lord-Mayor of London, Deceased*, 1741

Anon., *The London and Westminster Guide, through the Cities and Suburbs*, 1768

Anon., *The London Directory for the Year 1781*, 1781

Anon., *The London Guide, Describing the Private and Public Buildings of London, Westminster & Southwark . . .*, c. 1782

Anon., *The Midnight Spy or, A View of the Transactions of London and Westminster from the Hours of Ten in the Evening, till Five in the Morning*, 1766

Anon., *The State of the Silk and Woollen Manufacture Considered . . .*, 1713

Anon., *The Tricks of the Town Laid Open: or, a Companion for Country Gentlemen*, 1747

Anon., *The Vices of the Cities of London and Westminster. Trac'd from their Original*, Dublin, 1751

Anon. [An Old Man of the Town], *Three Original Letters to a Friend in the Country, on the Cause and Manner of the Late Riot at the Theatre-Royal in Drury-Lane*, 1763

Archenholtz, W. de, *A Picture of England: containing a Description of the Laws, Customs, and Manners of England*, 1797

Argent, Mark (ed.), *Recollections of R. J. S. Stevens. An Organist in Georgian London*, Carbondale and Edwardsville, 1992

Baker, David, *Companion to the Play House*, 2 vols., 1764

Balderston, Katharine C. (ed.), *Thraliana. The Diary of Mrs. Hester Lynch Thrale (later Mrs Piozzi) 1779–1809*, 2 vols., Oxford, 2nd edition, 1951

Barfoot, Peter, and Wilkes, John, *The Universal British Directory of Trade,*

Commerce, and Manufacture, Comprehending Lists of the Inhabitants of London, Westminster, and Borough of Southwark . . ., 2nd edition, 1793

Beckford, William, *An Arabian Tale, from an Unpublished Manuscript: with Notes Critical and Explanatory. The History of the Caliph Vathek, with Notes*, 1786

Beloe, William, *The Sexagenarian, or, the Recollections of a Literary Life*, 2 vols., 1817

Bernard, Sir Thomas (ed.), *Reports of the Society for Bettering the Condition and Increasing the Comforts of the Poor*, 3 vols., 1800–1802

Bickerstaffe, Isaac, *The Hypocrite*, 1769

Bielfeld, Jacob Friedrich von, *Letters of Baron Bielfeld, Secretary of Legation to the King of Prussia*, 4 vols., 1768–70

Binns, John, *Recollections of the Life of John Binns: Twenty-Nine Years in Europe and Fifty-Three in the United States*, Philadelphia, 1854

Birch, Busby, *City Latin, or Critical and Political Remarks on the Latin Inscription on Laying the First Stone on the intended New Bridge at Black-Fryars*, 2nd edition, 1761

Black, Clementina (ed.), *The Cumberland Letters. Being the Correspondence of Richard Dennison Cumberland & George Cumberland between the Years 1771 & 1784*, 1912

Blanchard, Rae (ed.), *The Correspondence of Richard Steele*, 1941

Blizard, William, *Desultory Reflections on Police: with an Essay on the Means of Preventing Crimes and Amending Criminals*, 1785

Blom, Frans et al. (eds.), *The Correspondence of James Peter Coghlan (1731–1800)*, Woodbridge, 2007

Boaden, James, *Memoirs of the Life of John Philip Kemble Esq. including A History of the Stage from the time of Garrick to the Present Period*, 2 vols., 1825

Boswell, James, *The Life of Samuel Johnson, LL.D.*, 3rd edition, 1799, edited by George Birkbeck Hill and L. F. Powell, 6 vols., 1934–50

Bradstreet, Dudley, *The Life and Uncommon Adventures of Capt. Dudley Bradstreet, being the most Genuine and Extraordinary, perhaps, ever Published*, Dublin, 1755

Brady, Frank, and Pottle, Frederick A. (eds.), *Boswell in Search of a Wife 1766–1769*, 1957

Brasbridge, Joseph, *The Fruits of Experience; or, Memoir of Joseph Brasbridge, written in his 80th and 81st Years*, 2nd edition, 1824

Brayley, Edward Wedlake, and others, *London and Middlesex; or, an Historical, Commercial, and Descriptive Survey of the Metropolis of Great Britain* . . ., 4 vols., 1810–16

Brown, John, *A Memoir of Robert Blincoe, An Orphan Boy . . .*, Manchester, 1832

Bullock, Christopher, *Woman is a Riddle. A Comedy*, 1716

Burney, Fanny, *Camilla: or A Picture of Youth*, 3 vols., Dublin, 1796

Burney, Fanny, *Cecilia. Or, Memoirs of an Heiress*, 3 vols., 1782

Burney, Fanny, *Evelina. Or, The History of a Young Lady's Entrance into the World*, 2 vols., 1778

Calamy, Edmund, *An Historical Account of My Own Life, with some Reflections on the Times I have Lived in (1671–1731)*, 2 vols., 1829

Campbell, R., *The London Tradesman. Being a Compendious View of All the Trades, Professions, Arts, both Liberal and Mechanic, now practised in the Cities of London and Westminster*, 1747

Carey, William, *The Stranger's Guide through London; Or, a View of the British Metropolis*, 1808

Carlyle, Alexander, *The Autobiography of Dr Alexander Carlyle of Inveresk 1722–1805*, edited by John Hill Burton, new edition, 1910

Cartwright, F. D. (ed.), *The Life and Correspondence of Major Cartwright*, 2 vols., 1826

Casanova, Giacomo, *His Life and Memoirs*, 2 vols., edited by Arthur Machen, 1933

Census of Great Britain, 1851: Population Tables Vols. I and II. Numbers of Inhabitants in the Years 1801, 1811, 1821, 1831, 1841, & 1851, 2 vols., 1852

Chamberlayne, John, *Magna Britannia Notitia: or, the Present State of Great-Britain, with divers Remarks upon the Antient State thereof*, 1710

Charke, Charlotte, *A Narrative of the Life of Mrs Charlotte Charke*, 1755, edited and with an introduction by Robert Rehder, 1999

Chesterfield, Earl of, *Letters to His Son. On the Fine Art of Becoming a Man of the World and a Gentleman*, 1774, 2 vols., Navarre Society edition, 1926

The Church Catechism Broke into Short Questions, With . . . Prayers for the Charity-Schools, 1709

Cleland, John, *Fanny Hill. Memoirs of a Woman of Pleasure*, 1749, Guild Publishing edition, 1979

Climenson, Emily J. (ed.), *Elizabeth Montagu, the Queen of the Blue-Stockings. Her Correspondence from 1720 to 1761*, 2 vols., 1906

Collins, Aileen Sutherland (ed.), *Travels in Britain 1794–1795. The Diary of John Aspinwall Great-grandfather of Franklin Delano Roosevelt with a Brief History of his Aspinwall Forebears*, Virginia Beach, 1994

Colman, George, *The Man of Business*, 1774

Colman, George, and Garrick, David, *The Clandestine Marriage*, 1766

BIBLIOGRAPHY 615

Colman, George, and Thornton, Bonnell, *The Connoisseur. By Mr Town, Critic and Censor-General*, 4 vols., 1757

Colquhoun, Patrick, *An Account of a Meat and Soup Charity. Established in the Metropolis in the Year 1797 . . .*, 1797

Colquhoun, Patrick, *A Treatise on the Commerce and Police of the River Thames . . .*, 1800

Colquhoun, Patrick, *A Treatise on the Police of the Metropolis . . .*, 5th edition, 1797

Colquhoun, Patrick, *A Treatise on the Police of the Metropolis . . .*, 7th edition, 1806

Colquhoun, Patrick, *Observations and Facts Relative to Licensed Ale-Houses, in the City of London and its Environs*, 1794

Colquhoun, Patrick, *The State of Indigence, and the Situation of the Casual Poor in the Metropolis, Explained . . .*, 1799

Combe, William, *The First of April: or, The Triumphs of Folly: A Poem*, 1777

Committé, François, *Le Estat de la Distribution de la Somme de Douze Mille Livres Sterling, Accordée par la Reine aux Pauvres Protestants François Refugiez en Angleterre, pour l'An 1705*, 1707

Concanen, M., Jr, and Morgan, A., *The History and Antiquities of the Parish of St. Saviour's, Southwark*, 1795

Copeland, Thomas W., and others (eds.), *The Correspondence of Edmund Burke*, 9 vols., Cambridge, 1958–78

Cox, Joseph, *A Faithful Narrative of the Most Wicked Gang of Thief-Takers, alias Thief-Makers, Macdaniel, Berry, Salmon, Eagan alias Gahagan . . .*, 1756

Coxe, William, *Memoirs of the Life and Administration of Sir Robert Walpole, Earl of Orford*, 3 vols., 1800

Cozens-Hardy, Basil (ed.), *The Diary of Sylas Neville 1767–1788*, 1950

Crabbe, George the Younger, *The Life of George Crabbe. By His Son*, 1834

Cumberland, Richard, *Memoirs of Richard Cumberland. Written by Himself*, 2 vols., 1807

Cumberland, Richard, *The West Indian*, 1771

Curnock, Nehemiah (ed.), *The Journal of the Rev. John Wesley, AM*, 8 vols., 1909

Danziger, Marlies K., and Brady, Frank (eds.), *Boswell: The Great Biographer 1789–1795*, 1989

D'Arblay, Madame, *Diary and Letters of Madame D'Arblay, author of 'Evelina', 'Cecilia', &c. Edited by her Niece*, 7 vols., new edition, 1854

Davies, Thomas, *Dramatic Miscellanies: consisting of Critical Observations on several Plays of Shakespeare*, 3 vols., 1783–4

Davies, Thomas, *Memoirs of the Life of David Garrick, Esq . . .*, 2 vols., 1781

De Castro, J., *The Memoirs of J. Decastro, Comedian* . . . , 1824

Defoe, Daniel *A Tour Through the Whole Island of Great Britain*, 2 vols., 1724–6

Defoe, Daniel, *An Historical Narrative of the Great and Tremendous Storm which happened on Nov. 26th, 1703*, 1769

Defoe, Daniel, *Augusta Triumphans: or, the Way to Make London the most Flourishing City in the Universe*, 1728

Defoe, Daniel, *Due Preparations for the Plague, As Well for Soul as Body*, 1722

Defoe, Daniel [attrib.], *Some Considerations Upon Street-Walkers* . . ., 1726

Defoe, Daniel, *The Complete English Tradesman*, 1726

Defoe, Daniel, *The Fortunes and Misfortunes of the Famous Moll Flanders* . . ., 1722, Folio Society edition, 1965

Defoe Daniel, *The Great Law of Subordination Consider'd; or, the Insolence and Insufferable Behaviour of Servants in England duly enquir'd into*, 1724

Defoe, Daniel, Richardson, Samuel, and another, *A Tour Through the Whole Island of Great Britain. Divided into Circuits or Journeys*, 4 vols., 1769

Devonshire, Georgiana Duchess of, *The Sylph*, 1779, York, 2001 edition

Dobrée, Bonamy, and Webb, Geoffrey (eds.), *The Complete Works of Sir John Vanbrugh*, 4 vols., 1927

Dodsley, Robert [publisher], *London and Its Environs Described* . . ., 6 vols., 1761

Eden, Sir Frederic Morton, *The State of the Poor. A History of the Labouring Classes in England, with Parochial Reports*, 3 vols., 1797

Edgeworth, Richard Lovell, *Memoirs of Richard Lovell Edgeworth, Esq., Begun by Himself, and Concluded by His Daughter, Maria Edgeworth*, 2 vols., 1821, 2nd edition corrected

Edwards, Paul, and Rewt, Polly (eds.), *The Letters of Ignatius Sancho*, 1994, Edinburgh, p. 168, to John Rush, May 1779

Elias, A. C., Jr (ed.), *Memoirs of Laetitia Pilkington*, 2 vols., Athens, Georgia, 1997

Ellis, Sir Henry, *The History and Antiquities of the Parish of Saint Leonard Shoreditch, and Liberty of Norton Folgate, in the Suburbs of London*, 1798

Entick, John, *A New and Accurate History and Survey of London, Westminster, Southwark, and Places Adjacent* . . ., 4 vols., 1766

Equiano, Olaudah, *The Interesting Narrative of the Life of Olaudah Equiano, or Gustavas Vassa, Written by Himself*, 1789

Faujas de Saint Fond, B., *A Journey Through England and Scotland to the Hebrides in 1784*, 2 vols., Glasgow, 1907

Fielding, Henry, *A Clear State of the Case of Elizabeth Canning . . .*, 1753

Fielding, Henry, *A Proposal for Making an Effectual Provision for the Poor, for Amending their Morals, and for Rendering them useful Members of the Society*, 1753

Fielding, Henry, *A True State of the Case of Bosavern Penlez, who suffered on Account of the Late Riot in the Strand . . .*, 1749

Fielding, Henry, *Amelia*, 1751

Fielding, Henry, *An Enquiry into the Causes of the Late Increase of Robbers, &c. with some Proposals for Remedying this Growing Evil*, 2nd edition, 1751

Fielding, Henry, *History of Joseph Andrews*, 1742

Fielding, Henry, *Journal of a Voyage to Lisbon*, 1755

Fielding, Henry, *Love in Several Masques. A Comedy*, 1727

Fielding, Henry, *The History of Tom Jones, A Foundling*, 6 vols., 1749

Fielding, Sir John, *A Brief Description of the Cities of London and Westminster . . .*, 1776

Fielding, [Sir] John, *A Plan for Preventing Robberies within Twenty Miles of London. With an Account of the Rise and Establishment of the Real Thieftakers. To which is added, Advice to Pawnbrokers, Stable-Keepers, and Publicans*, 1755

Fielding, Sir John, *Extracts from such of the Penal Laws as Particularly relate to the Peace and Good Order of the Metropolis . . .*, new edition, 1769

Fielding, Sarah, *The Adventures of David Simple; Containing an Account of His Travels Through the Cities of London and Westminster in Search of a Real Friend*, 1744

Foote, Samuel, *A Trip to Calais*, 1776

Foote, Samuel, *The Commissary*, 1765

Foote, Samuel, *The Cozeners*, 1774

Foote, Samuel, *The Liar*, 1762

Foote, Samuel, *The Nabob*, 1772

Franklin, Benjamin, *Autobiography of Benjamin Franklin. Edited from his Manuscript, with Notes and an Introduction, by John Bigelow*, Philadelphia, 1868

Garrick, David, *A Peep Behind the Curtain*, 1767

Garrick, David, *The Irish Widow*, 1772

Garrick, David, *The Male-Coquette*, 1757

Gascoyne, Sir Crisp, *An Address to the liverymen of the City of London, from Sir Crisp Gascoyne, Knt. late Lord-Mayor, relative to his conduct in the cases of Elizabeth Canning and Mary Squires*, 1754

Gay, John, *Trivia; or, The Art of Walking the Streets of London*, 1716

Gibbon, Edward, *The Memoirs of the Life of Edward Gibbon. With Various Observations and Excursions. By Himself*, 1795, 1900 edition

Gibson, Edmund, *Directions given by Edmund Lord Bishop of London to the Masters and Mistresses of the Charity-Schools within the Bills of Mortality, and the Diocese of London . . .*, 1724

Ginger, John (ed.), *John Grano: Handel's Trumpeter. The Diary of John Grano*, New York, 1998

Goldsmith, Oliver, *An Enquiry into the Present State of Polite Learning*, 1759

Goldsmith, Oliver, *The Citizen of the World, or Letters from a Chinese Philosopher residing in London to His Friends in the East*, 1762

Gomme, George Laurence (ed.), *The Gentleman's Magazine Library . . . London Vols. I–III*, 3 vols., 1904–5

Gray, Robert, *A Sermon Preached in the Cathedral Church of St Paul, London: On Thursday, May 26, 1803. Being the Time of the Yearly Meeting of the Children Educated in the Charity-Schools, in and about the Cities of London and Westminster . . .*, 1803

Green, William, *The Art of Living in London*, 1768

Greig, James (ed.), *The Farington Diary by James Farington R.A. Vol. I (July 13, 1793, to August 24, 1802)*, 1922

Grose, Francis, *The Olio: being a Collection of Essays, Dialogues . . . by the late Francis Grose, Esq. F.A.S.*, 1792

Grosley, Pierre Jean, *A Tour to London: or, New Observations on England, and its Inhabitants*, 3 vols., Dublin, 1772

Guthrie, James, *The Ordinary of Newgate His Account of the Behaviour, Confession, and dying Words of the Malefactors who were Executed on Wednesday the 22d of this Instant December at Tyburn*, 1725

Guthrie, James, *The Ordinary of Newgate His Account of the Behaviour, Confession, and dying Words of the Malefactors who were Executed on Monday the 9th of this Instant May, 1726, at Tyburn*, 1726

Guthrie, James, *The Ordinary of Newgate His Account of the Behaviour, Confession, and dying Words of the Malefactors who were Executed at Tyburn, on Monday the 20th of Novem. 1727*, 1727

Guthrie, James, *The Ordinary of Newgate His Account of the Behaviour, Confession, and dying Words of the Malefactors who were Executed at Tyburn, on Monday the 12th of this Instant February, 1728*, 1728

Guthrie, James, *The Ordinary of Newgate His Account of the Behaviour, Confession, and dying Words of the Malefactors who were Executed at Tyburn on Friday the 17th, of this Instant April, 1730*, 1730

Gwynn, John, *London and Westminster Improved, Illustrated by Plans*, 1766

Hanger, George, *The Life, Adventures, and Opinions of Col. George Hanger, Written by Himself*, 2 vols., 1801

Hansard, Luke, *The Auto-Biography of Luke Hansard. Printer to the House, 1752–1828*, 1991

Hanway, Jonas, *A Comprehensive View of Sunday Schools . . .*, 1786

Hanway, Jonas, *A Letter to Mr. John Spranger, on his Excellent Proposal for Paving, Cleansing and Lighting the Streets of Westminster, and the Parishes in Middlesex*, 1754

Hanway, Jonas, *A Review of the Proposed Naturalization of the Jews . . .*, 1753

Hanway, Jonas, *A Sentimental History of Chimney Sweepers, in London and Westminster . . .*, 1785

Hanway, Jonas, *An Earnest Appeal for Mercy to the Children of the Poor, particularly those belonging to the Parishes within the Bills of Mortality . . .*, 1766

Hanway, Jonas, *Observations on the Causes of the Dissoluteness which reigns among the Lower Classes of the People . . .*, 1772

Hanway, Jonas, *The Citizen's Monitor: Shewing the Necessity of a Salutary Police . . .*, 1780

Hanway, Jonas, *The Defects of Police the Cause of Immorality, and the Continued Robberies Committed, particularly in and about the Metropolis . . .*, 1775

Hardy, Thomas, *Memoir of Thomas Hardy, Founder of, and Secretary to, the London Corresponding Society . . .*, 1832

Harriott, John, *Struggles Through Life, exemplified in the Various Travels and Adventures in Europe, Asia, Africa, and America, of John Harriott, Esq.*, 3 vols., 1815

Harris, Jack, *Harris's List of Covent-Garden Ladies: or Man of Pleasure's Kalendar For the Year 1779*, 1779

Harris, Jack, *The Remonstrance of Harris, Pimp-General to the People of England. Setting Forth His many Schemes in Town and Country, for the Service of the Public, and The ungrateful Treatment he has met With*, 1769

Harrison, Walter, *The Universal History, Description and Survey of London, Westminster and Southwark*, 1777

Hartley, James, and another (eds.), *History of the Westminster Election . . . By Lovers of Truth and Justice*, 1784

Hatton, Edward, *A New View of London; or, An Ample Account of that City*, 2 vols., 1708

Hawkins, Sir John, *The Life of Samuel Johnson, LL.D.*, 2nd edition revised and corrected, 1787

Hawkins, Laetitia-Matilda, *Memoirs, Anecdotes, Facts, and Opinions*, 2 vols., 1824

Haywood, Eliza, *The City Jilt*, 1726

Haywood, Eliza, *The History of Jemmy and Jenny Jessamy*, 3 vols., 1753

Haywood, Eliza, *The History of Miss Betsy Thoughtless*, 4 vols., 1751

Heartfree, *A Most Circumstantial Account of the Unfortunate Young Lady Miss Bell, otherwise Sharpe, who Died at Marybone on Saturday October 4 . . .*, 1760

Heberden, William, *Observations on the Increase and Decrease of Different Diseases, and Particularly of the Plague*, 1801

Hervey, Lord John, *Some Materials Towards Memoirs of the Reign of King George II*, 3 vols., 1931

Hickey, William, *Memoirs*, 4 vols., 1913–25

Highmore, Anthony, *Pietas Londinensis: The History, Design, and Present State of the Various Public Charities in London*, 1810

Hill, John, *The Story of Elizabeth Canning considered by Dr Hill . . .*, 1753

Hitchcock, Tim (ed.), *Richard Hutton's Complaints Book. The Notebook of the Steward of the Quaker Workhouse at Clerkenwell, 1711–1737*, 1987

Hitchcock, Tim, and Black, John (eds.), *Chelsea Settlement and Bastardy Examinations, 1733–1766*, 1999

Hitchin, Charles, *A True Discovery of the Conduct of Receivers and Thief-Takers in and about the City of London . . .*, 1718

HMC, *Report on the Manuscripts of His Grace the Duke of Portland, Preserved at Welbeck Abbey, Vol. IV*, 1897

HMC, *Report on the Manuscripts of His Grace the Duke of Portland, Preserved at Welbeck Abbey, Vol. V*, 1899

Hoare, Prince, *Memoirs of Granville Sharp, Esq. Composed from his own Manuscripts, and other Authentic Documents in the Possession of his Family and of the African Institution*, 2 vols., 2nd edition, 1828

Hodgson, E., *The Whole Proceedings on the King's Commission of the Peace, Oyer and Terminer, and Gaol Delivery for the City of London; and also for the County of Middlesex; held at Justice Hall in the Old Bailey . . .*, Nos. I–VIII, 4 December 1782–29 October 1783

Holcroft, Thomas [pseudonym William Vincent], *A Plain and Succinct Narrative of the Late Riots and Disturbances in the Cities of London and Westminster, and Borough of Southwark . . .*, 1780

Holcroft, Thomas, *Memoirs of the Late Thomas Holcroft, written by Himself, and continued to the Time of His Death, from His Diary, Notes, and other Papers*, 3 vols., 1816

Holland, Thomas, *A Circumstantial Account, Relating to the Unfortunate Young Woman Miss Anne Bell, Alias Sharpe, (Who died at St Mary le Bone.) . . .*, 1760

Howard, John, *The State of the Prisons in England and Wales, with Preliminary Observations, and an Account of Some Foreign Prisons and Hospitals*, Warrington, 1784

Hughson, David, *London; being an Accurate History and Description of the British Metropolis and its Neighbourhood to Thirty Miles Extent, from an Actual Perambulation*, 6 vols., 1805–9

Hunter, Henry, *The History of London, and Its Environs . . .*, 2 vols., 1811

Hutton, William, *A Journey to London; comprising a description of the most interesting objects of curiosity to a visitor of the Metropolis, 1785*, 2nd edition, 1818

Ilive, Jacob, *Reasons Offered for the Reformation of the House of Correction in Clerkenwell . . .*, 1757

Ingamells, John, and Edgcumbe, John (eds.), *The Letters of Sir Joshua Reynolds*, 2000

Jackson, William, *The New and Complete Newgate Calendar . . .*, 6 vols., 1795

Jesse, John Heneage, *George Selwyn and His Contemporaries. With Memoirs and Notes*, 4 vols., 1843, 1901 edition

Johnson, Samuel, *Life of Gay*, 1779–81 (in *The Works of Samuel Johnson*, 12 vols., 1823, Vol. VII)

Johnson, Samuel, *Life of Pope*, 1781 (in *The Works of Samuel Johnson*, 12 vols., 1823, Vol. VIII)

Johnson, Samuel, *Life of Savage*, 1744 (in *The Works of Samuel Johnson*, 12 vols., 1823, Vol. VII)

Johnson, Samuel, *London: A Poem, in Imitation of the Third Satire of Juvenal*, 1738

Junius, *The Letters of Junius*, 2 vols., 1775

Kalm, Pehr, *Kalm's Account of his Visit to England on his Way to America in 1748*, 1892

Karamzin, N. M., *Letters of a Russian Traveller 1789–90. An Account of a Young Russian Gentleman's Tour Through Germany, Switzerland, France, and England*, New York, 1957

Kielmansegge, Count Frederick, *Diary of a Journey to England in the Years 1761–1762*, 1902

King, Richard, *The Complete Modern London Spy . . .*, 1781

King, Richard, *The New Cheats of London Exposed; or, The Frauds and Tricks of the Town Laid Open to Both Sexes*, n.d. [1790?]

Knox, Vicesimus, *Winter Evenings: or, Lucubrations on Life and Letters*, 2 vols., 2nd edition corrected and enlarged, 1790

Lackington, James, *Memoirs of the Forty-Five First Years of the Life of James Lackington, the present Bookseller in Finsbury Square, London. Written by Himself*, 1795

Lambert, B., *The History and Survey of London and Its Environs. From the Earliest Period to the Present Time*, 4 vols., 1806

Landmann, George T., *Adventures and Recollections of Colonel Landmann*, 2 vols., 1852

Landon, H. C. Robbins, *The Collected Correspondence and London Notebooks of Joseph Haydn*, 1959

Le Blanc, Jean Bernard, *Letters on the English and French Nations . . .*, 2 vols., 1747

Legg, Thomas, *Low-Life: or One Half of the World, Knows not how The Other Half Live . . .*, 1764

Lennox, Charlotte, *Henrietta*, 2 vols., 1758

Lettsom, John Coakley, *Hints Respecting the Distresses of the Poor*, 1795

Lettsom, John Coakley, *Medical Memoirs of the General Dispensary in London, for part of the Years 1773 & 1774*, 1774

Lettsom, John Coakley, *Of the Improvement of Medicine in London, on the Basis of Public Good*, 2nd edition, 1775

Lewis, W. S. (ed.), *Notes by Lady Louisa Stuart on George Selwyn and His Contemporaries by John Heneage Jesse*, 1928

Lewis, W. S., and Brown, Ralph S. (eds.), *Horace Walpole's Correspondence with George Montagu*, 2 vols., 1941 (*Complete Correspondence of Horace Walpole, Vols. 9–10*)

Lewis, W.S., and Smith, Robert A. (eds.), *Horace Walpole's Correspondence with George Selwyn, Lord Lincoln, Sir Charles Hanbury Williams, Henry Fox, Richard Edgcumbe*, 1961 (*Complete Correspondence of Horace Walpole, Vol. 30*)

Lewis, W. S., and Smith, Warren Hunting (eds.), *Horace Walpole's Correspondence with Sir Horace Mann*, 3 vols., 1955 (*Complete Correspondence of Horace Walpole, Vols. 17–19*)

Lewis, W. S., and Wallace, A. Dayle (eds.), *Horace Walpole's Correspondence with Mary and Agnes Berry and Barbara Cecilia Seton*, 2 vols., 1944 (*Complete Correspondence of Horace Walpole, Vols. 11 and 12*)

Lewis, W. S., and Wallace, A. Dayle (eds.), *Horace Walpole's Correspondence with the Countess of Upper Ossory*, 3 vols., 1965 (*Complete Correspondence of Horace Walpole, Vols. 32–34*)

Lewis, W. S., and Wallace, A. Dayle (eds.), *Horace Walpole: Correspondence Vols. I and II With the Rev. William Cole*, 2 vols., 1937

Lewis, W. S., Smith, Robert A., and Bennett, Charles H. (eds.), *Horace Walpole's Correspondence with Hannah More, Lady Browne, Lady George Lennox, Lady Mary Cole, Anne Pitt, Lady Hervey, Lady Suffolk, Mary Hamilton (Mrs John Dickenson)*, 1961 (*Complete Correspondence of Horace Walpole, Vol. 31*)

Lewis, W. S., Smith, Warren Hunting, and Lam, George L. (eds.), *Horace Walpole's Correspondence with Sir Horace Mann*, 3 vols., 1960 (*Complete Correspondence of Horace Walpole, Vols. 20–22*)

Lewis, W. S., Smith, Warren Hunting, and Lam, George L. (eds.), *Horace

Walpole's Correspondence with Sir Horace Mann, 2 vols., 1967 (Complete Correspondence of Horace Walpole, Vols. 23 and 24)

Lewis, W. S., Smith, Warren Hunting, and Lam, George L. (eds.), Horace Walpole's Correspondence with Sir Horace Mann and Sir Horace Mann the Younger, 1971 (Complete Correspondence of Horace Walpole, Vol. 25)

Lewis, W. S., Troide, Lars E., Martz, Edwine M., and Smith, Robert A. (eds.), Horace Walpole's Correspondence with Henry Seymour Conway, Lady Ailesbury, Lord and Lady Hertford, Mrs Harris [and others], 3 vols., 1974 (Complete Correspondence of Horace Walpole, Vols. 37–9)

Lewis, W. S., Wallace, A. Dayle, and Smith, Robert A. (eds.), Horace Walpole's Correspondence with John Chute, Richard Bentley, The Earl of Strafford, Sir William Hamilton, The Earl and Countess Harcourt, George Hardinge, 1973 (Complete Correspondence of Horace Walpole, Vol. 35)

Little, David M., and Kahrl, George M. (eds.), The Letters of David Garrick, 3 vols., 1963

Lustig, Irma S., and Pottle, Frederick A. (eds.), Boswell: The Applause of the Jury 1782–1785, 1982

Lustig, Irma S., and Pottle, Frederick A. (eds.), Boswell: The English Experiment 1785–1789, 1986

Lysons, Daniel, The Environs of London, being an historical account of the towns, villages, and hamlets, within twelve miles of that capital . . ., 4 vols., 1792–6

Macdonald, John, Memoirs of an Eighteenth-Century Footman. Travels (1745–1779), 1790, 1927 edition

Mackenzie, Henry, The Man of Feeling, 1771, new edition 1799

Macky, John, A Journey Through England. In Familiar Letters from a Gentleman Here, to His Friend Abroad, 2nd edition, 1722

Maitland, William, The History and Survey of London from its Foundation to the Present Time, 2 vols., 1756

Maitland, William, The History of London, from its Foundation by the Romans, to the Present Time, 1739

Malcolm, James Peller, Anecdotes of the Manners and Customs of London during the Eighteenth Century, 2 vols., 1810

Mandeville, Bernard, The Fable of the Bees: or, Private Vices Publick Benefits, 1714

Manning, Owen, and Bray, William, The History and Antiquities of the County of Surrey, 3 vols., 1804–14

Marchand, Jean (ed.), A Frenchman in England 1784. Being the Mélanges sur l'Angleterre of François de la Rochefoucauld, Cambridge, 1933

Massie, Joseph, An Essay on the Many Advantages Accruing to the

Community, from the Superior Neatness, Conveniencies, Decorations and Embellishments of Great and Capital Cities. Particularly Apply'd to the City and Suburbs of London . . ., 1754

Matthews, William (ed.), The Diary of Dudley Ryder 1715–1716, 1939

Mazzinghy, John, The New and Universal Guide through the Cities of London and Westminster, the Borough of Southwark, and Parts Adjacent, 1785

Meister, Henry, Letters Written during a Residence in England. Translated from the French, 1799

Mendoza, Daniel, Memoirs of the Life of Daniel Mendoza, 1816

Middleton, John, View of the Agriculture of Middlesex; with Observations on the Means of Its Improvement, and Several Essays on Agriculture in General, 1798

Miège, Guy, The New State of England, under our Present Sovereign Queen Anne, 1703

Miles, William Augustus, A Letter to Sir John Fielding, Knt. Occasioned by His extraordinary Request to Mr Garrick for the Suppression of the Beggars Opera. To which is added a Postscript to D. Garrick, Esq., 1773

Misson, Henri, M. Misson's Memoirs and Observations in his Travels over England. With some Account of Scotland and Ireland. Dispos'd in Alphabetical Order, 1719

Moritz, Carl Philipp, Travels of Carl Philipp Moritz in England in 1782, 1795, 1924 edition, edited by P. E. Matheson

Morris, Corbyn, Observations on the Past Growth and Present State of the City of London, 1751

Murphy, Arthur, An Essay on the Life and Genius of Samuel Johnson, LL.D., 1792

Murphy, Arthur, Genuine Memoirs of the Life and Adventures of the Celebrated Miss Ann Elliot. Written by a Gentleman . . ., 1769

Murphy, Arthur, The Citizen, 1763

Murray, T. A., Remarks on the Situation of the Poor in the Metropolis, as Contributing to the Progress of Contagious Diseases; with a Plan for the Institution of Houses of Recovery, for Persons Infected by Fever, 1801

Napier, Robina (ed.), Johnsoniana. Anecdotes of the Late Samuel Johnson, LL.D., 1892

Neild, James, An Account of the Rise, Progress, and Present State of the Society for the Discharge and Relief of Persons Imprisoned for Small Debts throughout England and Wales, 1808

Nelson, John, The History, Topography, and Antiquities of the Parish of St. Mary Islington, in the County of Middlesex . . ., 1811

Nelson, Robert, An Address to Persons of Quality and Estate . . ., 1715

Nichols, John, *Illustrations of the Literary History of the Eighteenth Century* . . ., 8 vols., 1817–58

Nichols, John, *Literary Anecdotes of the Eighteenth Century* . . ., 9 vols., 1812–16

Nokes, David, *Samuel Johnson. A Life*, 2009

Noorthouck, John, *A New History of London, including Westminster and Southwark*, 1773

Northcote, James, *Memoirs of Sir Joshua Reynolds* . . ., 1813

Norton, J. E. (ed.), *The Letters of Edward Gibbon*, 3 vols., 1956

O'Keeffe, John, *Recollections of the Life of John O'Keeffe, Written by Himself*, 2 vols., 1826

Oldfield, Thomas Hinton Burley, *An Entire and Complete History, Political and Personal, of the Boroughs of Great Britain* . . ., 3 vols., 1792

Paley, Ruth (ed.), *Justice in Eighteenth-Century Hackney: The Justicing Notebook of Henry Norris and the Hackney Petty Sessions Book*, 1991

Palk, Deirdre (ed.), *Prisoners' Letters to the Bank of England 1781–1827*, 2007

Parker, George, *A View of Society and Manners in High and Low Life*, 2 vols., 1781

Pendred, J., *The London and Country Printers, Booksellers and Stationers Vade Mecum* . . ., 1785

Pennant, Thomas, *A Journey from London to the Isle of Wight*, 2 vols., 1801

Pennant, Thomas, *Some Account of London*, 4th edition, 1805

Pickett, William, *Public Improvement; or, A Plan for Making a Convenient and Handsome Communication between the Cities of London and Westminster*, n.d. [1789]

Piozzi, Hester Lynch, *Anecdotes of the Late Samuel Johnson, LL.D., during the last Twenty Years of his Life*, 2nd edition, 1786

Pollnitz, Charles-Lewis, Baron de, *The Memoirs of Charles-Lewis, Baron de Pollnitz, being the Observations he made in his late Travels* . . ., 2 vols., 1737

Pope, Alexander, *The Dunciad*, 1729, in *The Works of Alexander Pope, Esq. In Six Volumes Complete. With His Last Corrections, Additions, and Improvements; together with all His Notes*, 6 vols., Edinburgh, 1767

Port, M. H. (ed.), *The Commissions for Building Fifty New Churches. The Minute Books, 1711–27, A Calendar*, 1986

Potter, Israel R., *Life and Adventures of Israel R. Potter, (A Native of Cranston, Rhode-Island,) Who Was a Soldier in the American Revolution* . . ., Providence, RI, 1824

Pottle, Frederick A. (ed.), *Boswell's London Journal 1762–1763*, 1950

Prévost, Antoine François, l'Abbé, *Memoirs of a Man of Quality. Written Originally in the French Tongue, by Himself, after His retirement from the World*, 2 vols., 1770

Price, Jacob M. (ed.), *Joshua Johnson's Letterbook, 1771–1774. Letters from a Merchant in London to His Partners in Maryland*, 1979

Pryor, F. R. (ed.), *Memoirs of Samuel Hoare by his Daughter Sarah and his Widow Hannah. Also some Letters from London during the Gordon Riots*, 1911

Pugh, John, *Remarkable Occurrences in the Life of Jonas Hanway, Esq*, 1787

Pyne, W. H., *Wine and Walnuts; or, After Dinner Chit-Chat*, 2 vols., 2nd edition, 1824

Quarrell, W. H., and Mare, Margaret (eds.), *London in 1710 from the Travels of Zacharias Conrad von Uffenbach*, 1934

Ralph, James, *A New Critical Review of the Public Buildings, Statues and Ornaments, in and about the Cities of London and Westminster*, 2nd edition corrected, 1736

Ralph, James, *The Case of Authors by Profession or Trade, Stated*, 1758

Ralph, James, *The Touchstone: or, Historical, Critical, Political, Philosophical, and Theological Essays on the Reigning Diversions of the Town . . .*, 1728

Reed, Joseph W., and Pottle, Frederick A. (eds.), *Boswell Laird of Auchinleck 1778–1782*, Edinburgh, 1993

Rees, Thomas, and Britton, John, *Reminiscences of Literary London, from 1779 to 1853*, New York, 1896

Reid, William Hamilton, *The Rise and Dissolution of the Infidel Societies in this Metropolis*, 1800

Report from the Committee appointed to Enquire into the best Mode of providing sufficient Accommodation for the increased Trade and Shipping of the Port of London; &c. &c. &c., 1796

Report from the Committee Appointed to Enquire into the State of the Goals [sic] of this Kingdom: Relating to the Fleet Prison, 1729

Report from the Committee Appointed to Enquire into the State of the Goals [sic] of this Kingdom: Relating to the Marshalsea Prison; and farther Relating to the Fleet Prison, 1729

Reports from the Committees on the State of Mendicity in the Metropolis, 1815–16

Report from the Select Committee on Inquiry into Drunkenness, with Minutes of Evidence, and Appendix, 1834

Richardson, Samuel, *Clarissa; or, The History of a Young Lady*, 5 vols., 1747–8, 1883 edition

Richardson, Samuel, *Pamela; or, Virtue Rewarded*, 3 vols., 1740–41, 1883 edition

Ripley, James, *Select Original Letters on Various Subjects*, 1781

Roche, Sophie von la, *Sophie in London 1786 being the Diary of Sophie v. La Roche*, 1933

Romilly, Samuel, *Memoirs of the Life of Sir Samuel Romilly, written by Himself; with a Selection from His Correspondence. Edited by His Sons*, 3 vols., 1840

Rossell, Samuel, *The Ordinary of Newgate's Account of the Behaviour, Confession, & Dying Words of the Seven Malefactors who were executed at Tyburn on Friday the 1st of August 1746 . . .*, 1746

Russell, Lord John, *Memorials and Correspondence of Charles James Fox*, 4 vols., 1853–7

Ryskamp, Charles, and Pottle, Frederick A. (eds.), *Boswell: The Ominous Years 1774–1776*, 1963

St. Giles in the Fields and St George, Bloomsbury: Plane of Association for Preserving Tranquillity in the Metropolis, and Protecting and Defending the Lives and Properties of Its Inhabitants, 1797

Savage, Richard, *An Author to be Let*, 1729

Saxby, Mary, *Memoirs of a Female Vagrant, Written by Herself*, 1806

Seymour, Richard, *The Court Gamester: or, Full and Easy Instructions for Playing the Games now in Vogue . . .*, 1719

Shaw, Joseph, *Parish Law: or, A Guide to Justices of the Peace, Ministers, Churchwardens, Overseers of the Poor, Constables, Surveyors of the Highways, Vestry-Clerks, and all Others concern'd in Parish Business . . .*, 8th edition, 1753

Shenstone, William, *The Works, in Verse and Prose, of William Shenstone, Esq*, 3 vols., 1777

Sheridan, Richard Brinsley, *The School for Scandal*, 1777

Sherwood, Thomas, *A Letter from the Bishop of London, to the Clergy and People of London and Westminster, on Occasion of the Late Earthquake*, 1750

Simpson, William, *A Sermon Preached to the Societies for Reformation of Manners, at St Mary-le-Bow, on Monday, March 20th, 1737 [containing] The Forty-Third Account of the Progress made in the Cities of London and Westminster, and Places adjacent, by the Societies for Promoting a Reformation of Manners*, 1738

Smith, Alexander, *The Comical and Tragical History of the Lives and Adventures of the Most Noted Bayliffs in and about London and Westminster . . .*, 1723

Smith, John Thomas, *A Book for a Rainy Day, or Recollections of the Events of the Years 1766–1833*, 1845, 1905 edition

Smith, John Thomas, *Ancient Topography of London*, 1815

Smith, John Thomas, *Nollekens and His Times: comprehending a Life of*

*that Celebrated Sculptor; and Memoirs of Several Contemporary Artists
. . .*, 2 vols., 1829

Smith, John Thomas, *The Cries of London: Exhibiting Several of the
Itinerant Traders of Antient and Modern Times*, 1839

Smith, John Thomas, *Vagabondiana or, Anecdotes of Mendicant Wanderers
through the Streets of London; with portraits of the most remarkable,
drawn from the life*, 1817

Smith, Thomas, *A Topographical and Historical Account of the Parish of
St Mary-Le-Bone*, 1833

Smith, William, *State of the Gaols in London and Westminster, and Borough
of Southwark . . .*, 1776

Smollett, Tobias, *The Adventures of Roderick Random*, 2 vols., 1748

Smollett, Tobias, *The Expedition of Humphry Clinker*, 2 vols., 1771

Smyth, Mrs Gillespie (ed.), *Memoirs and Correspondence (official and
familiar) of Sir Robert Keith, K.B.*, 2 vols., 1849

Society for the Discharge and Relief of Persons Imprisoned for Small Debts,
*An Account of the Rise, Progress, and Present State of the Society for
the Discharge and Relief of Persons Imprisoned for Small Debts. The
sixth edition*, 1783

Somerville, Thomas, *My Own Life and Times 1741–1814*, Edinburgh, 1861

Southey, Robert, *Letters from England: by Don Manuel Alvarez Espriella.
Translated from the Spanish*, 1807, Cresset Press edition, 1951

Spranger, John, *A Proposal or Plan for an Act of Parliament for the Better
Paving, Lighting, Cleansing . . . of the City and Liberty of Westminster
. . .*, 1754

SPRM, *An Account of the Societies for Reformation of Manners, in England
and Ireland . . .*, 1701

SPRM, *The Eight and Twentieth Account of the Progress Made in the
Cities of London and Westminster, and Places adjacent, by the Societies
for Promoting a Reformation of Manners . . .*, 1722

Steele, Richard, *The Funeral*, 1702

Steele, Richard, *The Lying Lover*, 1703

Steele, Richard, *The Tender Husband*, 1705

Sterne, Laurence, *The Life and Opinions of Tristram Shandy, Gentleman*,
9 vols., 1759–67

Stevens, George Alexander, *A Lecture on Heads . . .*, 1799

Stow, William, *Remarks on London; Being an Exact Survey of the Cities
of London and Westminster, Borough of Southwark, and the Suburbs
and Liberties contiguous to them . . .*, 1722

Strutt, Joseph, *The Sports and Pastimes of the People of England*, 1801,
1903 edition, enlarged and corrected by J. Charles Cox

Strype, John, *A Survey of the Cities of London and Westminster*, 2 vols., 1720

Stuart, James, *Critical Observations on the Buildings and Improvements of London*, 1771

Swift, Jonathan, *Gulliver's Travels*, 1726

Swift, Jonathan, *Journal to Stella*, edited by Harold Williams, 2 vols., Oxford, 1948

Taylor, John, *Records of My Life*, 2 vols., 1832

Taylor, John, *The Ordinary of Newgate's Account of the Behaviour, Confession, & Dying Words of the . . . Malefactors who were executed at Tyburn . . . [June and July] 1747. . .*, 1747

Thale, Mary (ed.), *Selections from the Papers of the London Corresponding Society 1792–1799*, Cambridge, 1983

Thale, Mary (ed.), *The Autobiography of Francis Place (1771–1854)*, Cambridge, 1972

Thompson, Edward, *The Courtesan*, 1765

Thornton, William, *The New, Complete, and Universal History, Description, and Survey of the Cities of London and Westminster, the Borough of Southwark, and the Parts Adjacent . . .*, 1784

Todd, Janet (ed.), *The Collected Letters of Mary Wollstonecraft*, New York, 2003

Townley, James, *High Life Below Stairs*, 1759

Toynbee, Paget, and Whibley, Leonard (eds.), *Correspondence of Thomas Gray*, 3 vols., Oxford, 1935

The Trial of Elizabeth Duchess Dowager of Kingston for Bigamy, before the Right Honourable the House of Peers, in Westminster-Hall, in full Parliament . . ., 1776

True-Born Englishman, A, *A Ramble through London: Containing Observations on Men and Things . . .*, 1738

Trusler, John, *Memoirs of the Life of the Rev. Dr. Trusler, with, His Opinions on a Variety of Interesting Subjects, and His Remarks Through a Long Life, on Men and Manners*, Bath, 1806

Trusler, John, *The London Adviser and Guide: Containing Every Instruction and Information Useful and Necessary to Persons Living in London, and Coming to Reside there . . .*, 1786

Trusler, John, *The Works of William Hogarth*, 2 vols., 1821

Tucker, Josiah, *Four Letters on Important National Subjects, Addressed to the Right Honourable the Earl of Shelburne, His Majesty's First Lord Commissioner of the Treasury*, 2nd edition, 1783

Twenty-Eighth Report of the Select Committee of the House of Commons on Finance: Police, including Convict Establishments, 1798

Van Muyden, Madame (ed.), *A Foreign View of England in the Reigns of George I & George II. The Letters of Monsieur César de Saussure to his Family*, 1902

Vaughan, William, *A Comparative Statement of the Advantages and Disadvantages of the Docks in Wapping and the Docks in the Isle of Dogs . . .*, 1799

Vaughan, William, *Examination of William Vaughan, Esq. In a Committee of the Honourable House of Commons, April 22, 1796 . . .*, 1796

Vaughan, William, *On Wet Docks, Quays, and Warehouses for the Port of London; with Hints Respecting Trade*, 1793

Vaux, James Hardy, *Memoirs of James Hardy Vaux. Written by Himself*, 2 vols., 1819

Voltaire, *Letters Concerning the English Nation*, 1733

Wales, William, *An Inquiry into the Present State of Population in England and Wales . . .*, 1781

Walpole, Horace, *Anecdotes of Painting in England; with some Account of the principal Artists; And incidental Notes on the other Arts . . .*, 2nd edition with additions, 4 vols., 1782

Walpole, Horace, *Memoirs of King George II*, 3 vols., 1985

Walpole, Horace, *Memoirs of the Reign of King George the Third*, 4 vols., 1894

Walpole, Horace, *Memoirs of the Reign of King George III*, 4 vols., 2000

Warburton, John, *London and Middlesex Illustrated*, 1749

Ward, Edward, *The History of the London Clubs, or, The Citizens' Pastime*, 1709

Ward, Edward, *The London-Spy, Compleat, In Eighteen Parts*, 1703, 1924 edition

Ward, Edward, *The London Terrae-Filius: or the Satyrical Reformer. Being Drolling Reflections on the Vices and Vanities of Both Sexes*, 1707–8

Ward, Edward, *Vulgus Britannicus: or the British Hudibras. In Fifteen Cantos*, 1710

Ward, Edward, *Miscellaneous Writings, in Verse and Prose, both Serious and Comical*, 4 vols., 1718

Ward, George Atkinson (ed.), *Journal and Letters of the Late Samuel Curwen, Judge of Admiralty, etc., an American Refugee in England, from 1775 to 1784 . . .*, 1842

Welch, Saunders, *A Proposal to Render Effectual a Plan, to Remove the Nuisance of Common Prostitutes from the Streets of this Metropolis . . .*, 1758

Wendeborn, Frederick Augustus, *A View of England Towards the Close of the Eighteenth Century*, 2 vols., 1791

West, William, *Fifty Years' Recollections of an Old Bookseller*, 1837

Wheatley, Francis, *Cries of London*, 1929

Wheatley, Henry B. (ed.), *The Historical and the Posthumous Memoirs of Sir Nathaniel William Wraxall 1772–1784*, 5 vols., 1884

Whitefield, George, *Journals*, 1965

Whyte, Samuel, *Poems on Various Subjects . . . Illustrated with Notes, Original Letters and Curious Incidental Anecdotes*, 3rd edition, Dublin, 1795

Wilkinson, Tate, *Memoirs of His Own Life, by Tate Wilkinson*, 4 vols., 1790

Willan, Robert, *Reports on the Diseases in London, particularly During the Years 1796, 97, 98, 99, and 1800*, 1801

Williams, Sir Charles Hanbury, *The Works of the Right Honourable Sir Charles Hanbury Williams, K.B . . . With Notes by Horace Walpole, Earl of Orford*, 3 vols., 1822

Williams, Robert, *Memoirs of the Life and Correspondence of Mrs Hannah More*, 4 vols., 2nd edition, 1835

Wimsatt, William K., Jr, and Pottle, Frederick A. (eds.), *Boswell for the Defence 1769–1774*, 1960

Woty, William, *The Shrubs of Parnassus. Consisting of a Variety of Poetical Essays, Moral and Comic*, 1760

Wyndham, Henry Penruddocke (ed.), *The Diary of the Late George Bubb Dodington, Baron of Melcombe Regis: From March 8, 1748–9, to February 6, 1761*, Salisbury, 1784

Yearsley, Macleod (ed.), *The Diary of the Visits of John Yeoman to London in the Years 1774 and 1777*, 1934

Yorke, Philip C. (ed.), *The Diary of John Baker, Barrister of the Middle Temple, Solicitor-General of the Leeward Islands*, 1931

Young, Arthur, *The Farmer's Letter to the People of England*, 1768

Secondary Sources

Abbey, Charles J., and Overton, John H., *The English Church in the Eighteenth Century*, 2 vols., 1878

Abraham, James Johnston, *Lettsom: His Life, Times, Friends and Descendants*, 1933

Adams, Elizabeth, *Chelsea Porcelain*, 2001

Aitken, George A., *The Life of Richard Steele*, 2 vols., 1889

Alexander, Boyd, *England's Wealthiest Son: A Study of William Beckford*, 1962

Allan, D. G. C., *William Shipley: Founder of the Royal Society of Arts*, 1968

Altick, Richard D., *The Shows of London*, Cambridge, MA, 1978

Anderson, J. G., *The Birthplace and Genesis of Life Assurance*, 1937

Andrew, Donna T., *Philanthropy and Police: London Charity in the Eighteenth Century*, Princeton, NJ, 1989

Andrew, Donna T., and McGowen, Randall, *The Perreaus and Mrs Rudd: Forgery and Betrayal in Eighteenth-Century London*, Berkeley, 2001

Andrews, Alexander, *The Eighteenth Century or Illustrations of the Manners and Customs of our Grandfathers*, 1856

Anon., *Williams Deacon's 1771–1970*, Manchester, 1971

Ashton, John, *The Fleet: Its River, Prison, and Marriages*, popular edition, 1889

Ashton, T. S., *An Economic History of England: The Eighteenth Century*, 1955, 1966 edition

Asleson, Robyn (ed.), *Notorious Muse: The Actress in British Art and Culture 1776–1812*, 2003

Baines, Paul, and Rogers, Pat, *Edmund Curll, Bookseller*, Oxford, 2007

Baker, T. M. M., *London: Rebuilding the City after the Great Fire*, 2000

Barker, Hannah, *Newspapers, Politics and English Society, 1695–1855*, 2000

Barlow, Derek, *Dick Turpin and the Gregory Gang*, Chichester, 1973

Barnard, Toby, and Clark, Jane (eds.), *Lord Burlington: Architecture, Art and Life*, 1995

Barnett, David, *London, Hub of the Industrial Revolution: A Revisionary History 1775–1825*, 1998

Barrell, John, *The Spirit of Despotism: Invasions of Privacy in the 1790s*, Oxford, 2006

Battestin, Martin C., with Ruthe R. Battestin, *Henry Fielding: A Life*, 1993

Beattie, J. M., *Policing and Punishment in London, 1660–1750: Urban Crime and the Limits of Terror*, Oxford, 2001

Beaven, Alfred B., *The Aldermen of the City of London*, 2 vols., 1908–13

Beier, A. L., and Finlay, Roger (eds.), *London 1500–1700: The Making of the Metropolis*, 1986

Bell, Walter G., *The Great Fire of London in 1666*, 1920

Bender, John, *Imagining the Penitentiary: Fiction and Architecture of Mind in Eighteenth-Century England*, Chicago, 1987

Bentley, G. E., Jr, *The Stranger from Paradise: A Biography of William Blake*, New Haven, 2001

Berger, Thomas B., *A Century and a Half of the House of Berger: Being a Brief History of the 150 Years of Trading of Lewis Berger and Sons, Ltd., Manufacturers of Fine Dry Colours, Paints and Varnished*, Homerton, London, N.E., 1910

Birch, George H., *London Churches of the XVIIth and XVIIIth Centuries*, 1896

Bird, James, *The Geography of the Port of London*, 1957

Blanning, Tim, *The Pursuit of Glory: Europe 1648–1815*, 2007

Bleackley, Horace, *Jack Sheppard: With an Epilogue on Jack Sheppard in Literature and Drama etc. by S. M. Ellis*, 1933

Bleackley, Horace, *Ladies Fair and Frail: Sketches of the Demi-Monde During the Eighteenth Century*, 1909, 1925 edition

Bleackley, Horace, *Life of John Wilkes*, 1917

Bleackley, Horace (ed.), *Casanova in England*, 1925

Bolton, Arthur T., *The Architecture of Robert and James Adam (1758–1794)*, 2 vols., 1922

Bondeson, Jan, *The London Monster: Terror on the Streets in 1790*, 2003

Bonehill, John, and Daniels, Stephen (eds.), *Paul Sandby: Picturing Britain*, 2009

Boulton, W. B., *The History of White's*, 2 vols., 1892

Bowers, Robert Woodger, *Sketches of Southwark Old and New*, 1905

Brackett, Oliver, *Thomas Chippendale: A Study of His Life, Work and Influence*, 1924

Bradley, Simon, and Pevsner, Nikolaus, *The Buildings of England: London 6. Westminster*, 2003

Bradley, Simon, and Pevsner, Nikolaus, *The Buildings of England: London 1. The City of London*, 1997

Braidwood, Stephen J., *Black Poor and White Philanthropists: London's Blacks and the Foundation of the Sierra Leone Settlement 1786–1791*, Liverpool, 1994

Brett-James, Norman G., *The Growth of Stuart London*, 1935

Brewer, John, *Sentimental Murder: Love and Madness in the Eighteenth Century*, 2004

Brewer, John, *The Pleasures of the Imagination: English Culture in the Eighteenth Century*, 1997

Brewster, Dorothy, *Aaron Hill: Poet, Dramatist, Projector*, New York, 1913

Bristow, Edward J., *Vice and Vigilance: Purity Movements in Britain since 1700*, Dublin, 1977

Broodbank, Joseph G., *History of the Port of London*, 2 vols., 1921

Brooks, Brian, and Humphery-Smith, Cecil, *A History of the Worshipful Company of Scriveners of London. Volume II*, Chichester, 2001

Brown, Roger Lee, *A History of the Fleet Prison, London: The Anatomy of the Fleet*, Lampeter, 1996

Brownlow, John, *Memoranda; or, Chronicles of The Foundling Hospital, including Memoirs of Captain Coram, &c. &c.*, 1847

Burrows, Donald (ed.), *The Cambridge Companion to Handel*, Cambridge, 1997

Byrd, Max, *London Transformed: Images of the City in the Eighteenth Century*, 1978

Byrne, Paula, *Perdita: The Life of Mary Robinson*, 2004

Cameron, H. C., *Mr Guy's Hospital 1726–1948*, 1954

Campbell, Peter (ed.), *A House in Town: 22 Arlington Street, Its Owners and Builders*, 1984

Capper, Charles, *The Port and Trade of London, Historical, Statistical, Local and General*, 1862

Carretta, Vincent, *Equiano the African: Biography of a Self-Made Man*, 2006

Carruthers, Bruce G., *City of Capital: Politics and Markets in the English Financial Revolution*, Princeton, NJ, 1996

Carswell, John, *The South Sea Bubble*, Stroud, 1993

Cash, Arthur H., *John Wilkes: The Scandalous Father of Civil Liberty*, 2006

Castle, Terry, *Masquerade and Civilization: The Carnivalesque in Eighteenth-Century English Culture and Fiction*, 1986

Chancellor, E. Beresford, *Memorials of St. James's Street together with the Annals of Almack's*, 1922

Chancellor, E. Beresford, *The Eighteenth Century in London: An Account of its Social Life and Arts*, 1920

Chancellor, E. Beresford, *The Private Palaces of London Past and Present*, 1908

Chandler, George, *Four Centuries of Banking as illustrated by the Bankers, Customers and Staff associated with the constituent banks of Martins Bank Limited. Vol. I The Grasshopper and the Liver Bird: Liverpool and London*, 1964

Cherry, Bridget, and Pevsner, Nikolaus, *The Buildings of England: London 2. South*, 1983

Cherry, Bridget, and Pevsner, Nikolaus, *The Buildings of England: London 3. North West*, 1999

Cherry, Bridget, and Pevsner, Nikolaus, *The Buildings of England: London 4. North*, 1999

Cherry, Bridget, O'Brien, Charles, and Pevsner, Nikolaus, *The Buildings of England: London 5. East*, 2005

Christian, Edmund B. V., *A Short History of Solicitors*, 1896

Christie, Ian R., *Stress and Stability in Late Eighteenth-Century Britain: Reflections on the British Avoidance of Revolution*, Oxford, 1984

Clark, Peter, *British Clubs and Societies 1580–1800: The Origins of an Associational World*, Oxford, 2000

Clark, Peter, *The English Alehouse: A Social History 1200–1830*, 1983

Clark-Kennedy, A. E., *The London: A Study in the Voluntary Hospital System. Vol. I The First Hundred Years 1740–1840*, 1962

Clarke, Norma, *Dr Johnson's Women*, 2000

Clarke, Norma, *Queen of the Wits: A Life of Laetitia Pilkington*, 2008

Clinch, George, *Marylebone and St Pancras: Their History, Celebrities, Buildings, and Institutions*, 1890

Cochrane, J. A., *Dr Johnson's Printer: The Life of William Strahan*, 1964

Coleridge, Ernest Hartley, *The Life of Thomas Coutts Banker*, 2 vols., 1920

Colson, Percy, *White's 1693–1950*, 1951

Compston, H. F. B., *The Magdalen Hospital: The Story of a Great Charity*, 1917

Copeman, W. S. C., *The Worshipful Society of Apothecaries of London: A History 1617–1967*, 1967

Corfield, Penelope J., *Power and the Professions in Britain 1700–1850*, 1995

Corfield, Penelope J., and Keene, Derek (eds.), *Work in Towns 850–1850*, Leicester, 1990

Cosh, Mary, *A History of Islington*, 2005

Cox, Harold, and Chandler, John E., *The House of Longman: With a Record of Their Bicentenary Celebrations 1724–1924*, 1925

Cragoe, Matthew, and Taylor, Antony (eds.), *London Politics, 1760–1914*, Basingstoke, 2005

Creighton, Charles, *A History of Epidemics in Britain Vol. II: From the Extinction of Plague to the Present Time*, Cambridge, 1894

Cross, Wilbur L., *The Life and Times of Laurence Sterne*, 2 vols., New Haven, 1925

Cruickshank, Dan, *The Secret History of Georgian London: How the Wages of Sin Shaped the Capital*, 2009

Dabydeen, David, *Hogarth's Blacks: Images of Blacks in Eighteenth Century English Art*, Kingston-upon-Thames, 1985

Dabydeen, David, Gilmore, John, and Jones, Cecily, *The Oxford Companion to Black British History*, Oxford, 2007

Darby, H. C. (ed.), *An Historical Geography of England Before A.D. 1800*, Cambridge, 1951

Dasent, Arthur Irwin, *A History of Grosvenor Square*, 1935

Dasent, Arthur Irwin, *The History of St. James's Square and the Foundation of the West End of London. With a Glimpse of Whitehall in the Reign of Charles the Second*, 1895

Davies, E. A., *An Account of the Formation and Early Years of the Westminster Fire Office*, 1952

Davis, Cecil T., *Industries of Wandsworth: Past and Present*, 1898, 1983 edition

Davis, Henry George, *The Memorials of the Hamlet of Knightsbridge. With Notices of Its Immediate Neighbourhood*, 1859

Davis, Ralph, *The Rise of the English Shipping Industry in the Seventeenth and Eighteenth Centuries*, 1962

Dawe, Donovan, and Oswald, Adrian, *11 Ironmonger Lane: The Story of a Site in the City of London*, 1952

De Castro, J. Paul, *The Gordon Riots*, 1926

Devereaux, Simon, and Griffiths, Paul (eds.), *Penal Practice and Culture, 1500–1900: Punishing the English*, 2004

Dickson, P. G. M., *The Sun Insurance Office 1710–1960*, 1960

Dobson, Austin, *Side-Walk Studies*, 1902

Dowdell, E. G., *A Hundred Years of Quarter Sessions: The Government of Middlesex from 1660 to 1760*, Cambridge, 1932

Downes, Kerry, *Hawksmoor*, 1959

Drew, Bernard, *The London Assurance: A Second Chronicle*, 1949

Dudden, F. Homes, *Henry Fielding: His Life, Works, and Times*, 2 vols., Oxford, 1952

Dyos, H. J., *Victorian Suburb: A Study of the Growth of Camberwell*, Leicester, 1973

Earle, Peter, *The Making of the English Middle Class: Business, Society and Family Life in London, 1660–1730*, 1989

Eaves, T. C. Duncan, and Kimpel, Ben D., *Samuel Richardson: A Biography*, 1971

Edgcumbe, Richard, *The Art of the Gold Chaser in Eighteenth-Century London*, Oxford, 2000

Edwardes, Michael, *The Nabobs at Home*, 1991

Edwards, Ralph, and Jourdain, Margaret, *Georgian Cabinet-Makers c. 1700–1800*, 1955

Eeles, Henry S., and Spencer, Earl, *Brooks's 1764–1964*, 1964

Eger, Elizabeth, *Bluestockings: Women of Reason from Enlightenment to Romanticism*, 2010

Ellis, Aytoun, *The Penny Universities: A History of the Coffee-Houses*, 1956

Emsley, Clive, *The English Police: A Political and Social History*, 2nd edition, 1996

Endelman, Todd M., *The Jews of Georgian England 1714–1830: Tradition and Change in a Liberal Society*, Philadelphia, 1979

Farmer, John S., and Henley, W. E., *Slang and its Analogues, Past and Present*, 7 vols., 1890–1904

Finn, Margot C., *The Character of Credit: Personal Debt in English Culture, 1740–1914*, Cambridge, 2003

Fitzgerald, Percy, *A Famous Forgery being the Story of 'The Unfortunate' Doctor Dodd*, 1865

Flavell, Julie, *When London was Capital of America*, 2010

Fleming, John, *Robert Adam and His Circle*, 1962

Flower, Newman, *George Frideric Handel: His Personality and His Times*, 1923

Foreman, Amanda, *Georgiana Duchess of Devonshire*, 1998

Foreman, Lewis, and Foreman, Susan, *London: A Musical Gazetteer*, 2005

Forster, John, *The Life and Times of Oliver Goldsmith*, 2 vols., 1854

Friedman, Terry, *James Gibbs*, 1984

Frost, Thomas, *The Old Showmen, and the Old London Fairs*, 1874

Fryer, Peter, *Staying Power: The History of Black People in Britain*, 1984

Fulford, Roger, *Boodle's 1762–1962*, 1962

Garrard's 1721–1911: Crown Jewellers and Goldsmiths during Six Reigns and in Three Centuries, 1912

Gatrell, Vic, *City of Laughter: Sex and Satire in Eighteenth-Century London*, 2006

Gatrell, Vic, *The Hanging Tree: Execution and the English People 1770–1868*, Oxford, 1994

George, M. Dorothy, *English Political Caricature to 1792: A Study of Opinion and Propaganda*, Oxford, 1959

George, M. Dorothy, *London Life in the XVIIIth Century*, 1925

Gerzina, Gretchen, *Black London: Life before Emancipation*, New Brunswick, 1995

Gibb, D. E. W., *Lloyd's of London: A Study in Individualism*, 1957

Gilbert, Christopher, *The Life and Work of Thomas Chippendale*, 2 vols., 1978

Gilboy, Elizabeth W., *Wages in Eighteenth Century England*, Cambridge, MA, 1934

Gladstone, Herbert G., *The Story of the Noblemen and Gentlemen's Catch Club*, 1930

Glass, D. V., *Numbering the People: The Eighteenth-century Population Controversy and the Development of Census and Vital Statistics in Britain*, Farnborough, 1973

Godwin, George, *Hansons of Eastcheap: The Story of the House of Samuel Hanson and Son Ltd*, 1947

Gray, Drew D., *Crime, Prosecution and Social Relations: The Summary Courts of the City of London in the Late Eighteenth Century*, Basingstoke, 2009

Green, David R., *Pauper Capital: London and the Poor Law, 1790–1870*, 2010

Griffiths, Paul, *Lost Londons: Change, Crime, and Control in the Capital City, 1550–1660*, Cambridge, 2008

Guillery, Peter, *The Small House in Eighteenth-Century London: A Social and Architectural History*, 2004

Gwynn, Robin D., *Huguenot Heritage: The History and Contribution of the Huguenots in Britain*, 1985

Hamilton, Bernice, 'The Medical Professions in the Eighteenth Century', *Economic History Review*, 2nd Series, Vol. IV, No. 2, 1951, pp. 141–69

Hamilton, Harlan W., *Doctor Syntax: A Silhouette of William Combe, Esq. (1742–1823)*, 1969

Hancock, David, *Citizens of the World: London Merchants and the Integration of the British Atlantic Community, 1735–1785*, Cambridge, 1995

Handover, P. M., *Printing in London: From 1476 to Modern Times*, 1960

Harding, Vanessa, 'The Population of London, 1550–1700: A Review of the Published Evidence', *London Journal*, 15 (2), 1990, pp. 111–28

Harris, Eileen, *The Genius of Robert Adam: His Interiors*, 2001

Harris, John, *Sir William Chambers: Knight of the Polar Star*, 1970

Hay, Douglas, et al., *Albion's Fatal Tree: Crime and Society in Eighteenth-Century England*, 1975

Hayter, Tony, *The Army and the Crowd in Mid-Georgian England*, 1978

Hayward, Helena, and Kirkham, Pat, *William and John Linnell: Eighteenth Century London Furniture Makers*, 2 vols., 1980

Heal, Ambrose, *London Tradesmen's Cards of the XVIII Century: An Account of Their Origin and Use*, 1925

Heal, Ambrose, *The London Furniture Makers: From the Restoration to the Victorian Era 1660–1840*, 1953

Heal, Ambrose, *The London Goldsmiths 1200–1800: A Record of the Names and Addresses of the Craftsmen, their Shop-Signs and Trade-Cards*, Cambridge, 1935

Hecht, J. Jean, *The Domestic Servant Class in Eighteenth-Century England*, 1956

Henderson, Alfred James, *London and the National Government, 1721–1742: A Study of City Politics and the Walpole Administration*, Durham, NC, 1945

Henderson, Tony, *Disorderly Women in Eighteenth-Century London: Prostitution and Control in the Metropolis, 1730–1830*, 1999

Hibbert, Christopher, *King Mob: The Story of Lord George Gordon and the Riots of 1780*, 1958

Hill, Bridget, *Servants: English Domestics in the Eighteenth Century*, Oxford, 1996

Hitchcock, Tim, *Down and Out in Eighteenth-Century London*, 2004

Hitchcock, Tim, and Shoemaker, Robert, *Tales from Hanging Court*, 2006

Hitchcock, Tim, and Shore, Heather (eds.), *The Streets of London: From the Great Fire to the Great Stink*, 2003

Hogwood, Christopher, *Handel*, 1984

Hollaender, A. E. J., and Kellaway, William (eds.), *Studies in London History Presented to Philip Edmund Jones*, 1969

Home, Gordon, *Old London Bridge*, 1931

Hoppit, Julian, *A Land of Liberty? England 1689–1727*, Oxford, 2000

Hoppit, Julian, *Risk and Failure in English Business 1700–1800*, Cambridge, 1987

Horn, Pamela, *Flunkeys and Scullions: Life Below Stairs in Georgian England*, Stroud, 2004

Howe, Ellic, and Waite, Harold E., *The London Society of Compositors: A Centenary History*, 1948

Howson, Gerald, *It Takes A Thief: The Life and Times of Jonathan Wild*, 1987

Hunt, Thomas (ed.), *The Medical Society of London 1773–1973*, 1972

Inwood, Stephen, *A History of London*, 1998

Ireland, John, *Hogarth Illustrated*, 2nd edition, 1884

Jacob, W. M., *The Clerical Profession in the Long Eighteenth Century 1680–1840*, Oxford, 2007

Jeffery, Sally, *The Mansion House*, 1993

Johnson, B. H., *Berkeley Square to Bond Street: The Early History of the Neighbourhood*, 1952

Jones, M. G., *The Charity School Movement: A Study of Eighteenth Century Puritanism in Action*, Cambridge, 1938

Jowett, Judy, *The Warning-Carriers: How Messengers of The Goldsmiths' Company Warned the Luxury Trades of Criminal Activities in Eighteenth-century London*, 2005

Keane, John, *Tom Paine: A Political Life*, 1995

Keates, Jonathan, *Handel: The Man and His Music*, 2008

Keay, John, *The Honourable Company: A History of the English East India Company*, 1991

Keene, Derek, Burns, Arthur, and Saint, Andrew (eds.), *St Paul's, The Cathedral Church of London 604–2004*, 2004

Kellett, J. R., 'The Breakdown of Gild and Corporation Control over the Handicraft and Retail Trade in London', *Economic History Review*, New Series, Vol. 10, No. 3, 1958, pp. 381–94

King, Reyahn, Sandhu, Sukhdev, Walvin, James, and Girdham, Jane, *Ignatius Sancho: An African Man of Letters*, 1997

King-Dorset, Rodreguez, *Black Dance in London, 1730–1850: Innovation, Tradition and Resistance*, Jefferson, NC, 2008

Kirk, Harry, *Portrait of a Profession: A History of the Solicitor's Profession, 1100 to the Present Day*, 1976

Klingender, F. D. (ed.), *Hogarth and English Caricature*, 1944

Knowles, C. C., and Pitt, P. H., *The History of Building Regulation in London 1189–1972 with an Account of the District Surveyors' Association*, 1972

Landau, Norma, *The Justices of the Peace, 1679–1760*, Berkeley, CA, 1984

Landers, John, *Death and the Metropolis: Studies in the Demographic History of London 1670–1830*, Cambridge, 1993

Langdon-Davies, John, *Westminster Hospital: Two Centuries of Voluntary Service 1719–1948*, 1952

Langford, Paul, *A Polite and Commercial People: England 1727–1783*, Oxford, 1989

Lecky, William Edward Hartpole, *A History of England in the Eighteenth Century*, 8 vols., 1877

Lemmings, David, *Professors of the Law: Barristers and Legal Culture in the Eighteenth Century*, Oxford, 2000

Leslie-Melville, R., *The Life and Work of Sir John Fielding*, 1934

Levy, Martin, *Love and Madness: The Murder of Martha Ray, Mistress of the Fourth Earl of Sandwich*, New York, 2004

Lillywhite, Bryant, *London Coffee Houses: A Reference Book of Coffee Houses of the Seventeenth, Eighteenth and Nineteenth Centuries*, 1963

Linebaugh, Peter, *The London Hanged: Crime and Civil Society in the Eighteenth Century*, 1991

Lipman, V. D., *Social History of the Jews in England 1850–1950*, 1954

Little, Bryan, *The Life and Work of James Gibbs 1682–1754*, 1955

London County Council, *Bridges*, 1914

McClure, Ruth, *Coram's Children: The London Foundling Hospital in the Eighteenth Century*, 1981

McConville, Seán, *A History of English Prison Administration: Volume I 1750–1877*, 1981

McDowell, Paula, *The Women of Grub Street: Press, Politics, and Gender in the London Literary Marketplace 1678–1730*, Oxford, 1998

McIntyre, Ian, *Hester: The Remarkable Life of Dr Johnson's 'Dear Mistress'*, 2008

McIntyre, Ian, *Joshua Reynolds: The Life and Times of the First President of the Royal Academy*, 2003

Mack, Maynard, *Alexander Pope: A Life*, 1985

McKellar, Elizabeth, *The Birth of Modern London: The Development and Design of the City 1660–1720*, Manchester, 1999

McKendrick, Neil, Brewer, John, and Plumb, J. H., *The Birth of a Consumer Society: The Commercialization of Eighteenth-century England*, 1982, 1983 paperback edition

McKinlay, Thomas, *Mrs Cornely's Entertainments at Carlisle House, Soho Square*, 1840

McMaster, John, *A Short History of the Royal Parish of St. Martin-in-the-Fields, London, W.C.*, 1916

Macmichael, J. Holden, *The Story of Charing Cross and Its Immediate Neighbourhood*, 1906

MacMichael, William, *The Gold-Headed Cane*, 1827

Malcolm, Joyce Lee, *To Keep and Bear Arms: The Origins of an Anglo-American Right*, Cambridge, MA, 1994

Marshall, Dorothy, *The English Poor in the Eighteenth Century: A Study in Social and Administrative History*, 1926

Mathias, Peter, *The Brewing Industry in England 1700–1830*, Cambridge, 1959

Matz, B. W., *The Inns & Taverns of 'Pickwick' with Some Observations on Their Other Associations*, 1921

Mayer, Edward, *The Curriers and the City of London: A History of the Worshipful Company of Curriers*, 1968

Mayhew, Henry, *London Labour and the London Poor*, 4 vols., 1861–2, 1864 edition

Melville, Lewis, *The Life and Letters of Tobias Smollett (1721–1771)*, 1926

Melville, Lewis, *The Star of Piccadilly: A Memoir of William Douglas Fourth Duke of Queensberry, K.T. (1725–1810)*, 1927

Michie, R. C. (ed.), *The Development of London as a Financial Centre*, 4 vols., 2000

Mitchell, B. R., and Deane, Phyllis, *Abstract of British Historical Statistics*, Cambridge, 1962

Mitchell, L. G., *Charles James Fox*, Oxford, 1992

Moore, Judith, *The Appearance of Truth: The Story of Elizabeth Canning and Eighteenth-Century Narrative*, Newark, NJ, 1994

Moore, Lucy, *The Thieves' Opera: The Remarkable Lives of Jonathan Wild, Thief-Taker, and Jack Sheppard, House-Breaker*, 1997

Moore, Norman, *The History of St. Bartholomew's Hospital*, 2 vols., 1918

Morgan, E. Victor, and Thomas, W. A., *The Stock Exchange: Its History and Functions*, 1962

Morley, Henry, *Memoirs of Bartholomew Fair*, 1859

Morris, Derek, *Mile End Old Town 1740–1780: A Social History of an Early Modern London Suburb*, 2nd edition, 2007

Morris, Derek, and Cozens, Ken, *Wapping 1600–1800: A Social History of an Early Modern London Maritime Suburb*, 2009

Myers, Norma, *Reconstructing the Black Past: Blacks in Britain 1780–1830*, 1996

Myers, Robin, Harris, Michael, and Mandelbrote, Giles (eds.), *The London Book Trade: Topographies of Print in the Metropolis from the Sixteenth Century*, 2003

Nichols, R. H., and Wray, F. A., *The History of the Foundling Hospital*, 1935

Norman, Philip, *London Signs and Inscriptions*, 1893

Norton, Rictor, *Mother Clap's Molly House: The Gay Subculture in England 1700–1830*, Stroud, 2006

Novak, Maximillian E., *Daniel Defoe, Master of Fictions: His Life and Ideas*, Oxford, 2001

O'Donoghue, Edward George, *The Story of Bethlehem Hospital from its Foundation in 1247*, 1914

Ogborn, Miles, *Spaces of Modernity: London's Geographies, 1680–1780*, 1998

Olsen, Donald, *Town Planning in London, the Eighteenth and Nineteenth Centuries*, 1964

Owen, David, *English Philanthropy 1660–1960*, Cambridge, MA, 1960

Palmer, Samuel, *St Pancras: Being Antiquarian, Topographical, and Biographical Memoranda . . .*, 1870

Panayi, Panikos (ed.), *Germans in Britain since 1500*, 1996

Parker, Matthew, *The Sugar Barons: Family, Corruption, Empire and War*, 2011

Paston, George, *Social Caricature in the Eighteenth Century*, 1905

Patterson, M. W., *Sir Francis Burdett and His Times (1770–1844)*, 2 vols., 1931

Pearce, Charles E., *'Polly Peachum': Being the Story of Lavinia Fenton (Duchess of Bolton) and 'The Beggar's Opera'*, 1913

Perks, Sydney, *The History of the Mansion House*, Cambridge, 1922

Phillips, Hugh, *Mid-Georgian London: A Topographical and Social Survey of Central and Western London About 1750*, 1964

Phillips, Hugh, *The Thames about 1750*, 1951

Pinks, William J., *The History of Clerkenwell*, 2nd edition, 1880

Plumb, J. H., *Sir Robert Walpole: Vol. II The King's Minister*, 1960, 1972 edition

Porter, Roy, *London: A Social History*, 1994

Postgate, Raymond, *'That Devil Wilkes'*, 1956

Postle, Martin (ed.), *Joshua Reynolds: The Creation of Celebrity*, 2005

Prest, Wilfrid, *William Blackstone: Law and Letters in the Eighteenth Century*, Oxford, 2008

Radzinowicz, Leon, *A History of English Criminal Law and its Administration from 1750, Vol. I The Movement for Reform*, 1948

Radzinowicz, Leon, *A History of English Criminal Law and its Administration from 1750, Vol. III The Reform of the Police*, 1956

Radzinowicz, Leon, *A History of English Criminal Law and its Administration from 1750, Vol. IV Grappling for Control*, 1968

Raven, James, *The Business of Books: Booksellers and the English Book Trade 1450–1850*, 2007

Raven, James, Small, Helen, and Tadmor, Naomi (eds.), *The Practice and Representation of Reading in England*, Cambridge, 1996

Reddaway, T. R., *The Rebuilding of London*, 1940

Rendle, William, and Norman, Philip, *The Inns of Old Southwark and Their Association*, 1888

Reynolds, Elaine A., *Before the Bobbies: The Night Watch and Police Reform in Metropolitan London, 1720–1830*, 1998

Richetti, John (ed.), *The Cambridge Companion to the Eighteenth-Century Novel*, Cambridge, 1996

Robins, William, *Paddington: Past and Present*, 1853

Rogers, Nicholas, *The Press Gang: Naval Impressments and Its Opponents in Georgian Britain*, 2007

Rogers, Pat, *Grub Street: Studies in a Subculture*, 1972

Rogers, Pat, *Literature and Popular Culture in Eighteenth Century England*, Brighton, 1985

Roscoe, E. S., and Clergue, Helen (eds.), *George Selwyn: His Letters and His Life*, 1899

Rosenfeld, Sybil, *The Theatre of the London Fairs in the Eighteenth Century*, Cambridge, 1960

Rothstein, Andrew, *A House on Clerkenwell Green*, 1972

Rothstein, Natalie, *Silk Designs of the Eighteenth Century in the Collection of the Victorian and Albert Museum, London. With a Complete Catalogue*, 1990

Rubenhold, Hallie, *Harris's List of Covent-Garden Ladies: Sex in the City in Georgian Britain*, 2005

Rubenhold, Hallie, *The Covent Garden Ladies: Pimp General Jack & The Extraordinary Story of Harris's List*, 2005

Rudé, George, *Hanoverian London 1714–1808*, 1971

Rudé, George, *Paris and London in the Eighteenth Century: Studies in Popular Protest*, 1974

Rudé, George, *Wilkes and Liberty: A Social Study*, 1983

Rutter, Owen, *At the Three Sugar Loaves and Crown: A Brief History of the Firm of Messrs. Davison, Newman and Company Now Incorporated with the West Indian Produce Association Ltd*, 1938

St Aubyn-Brisbane, F., *If Stones Could Speak: The Old City of London Churches: Their Ancient and Romantic Traditions, Customs and Legends from Earliest Days*, 1929

Sale, William M., *Samuel Richardson: Master Printer*, Ithaca, NY, 1950

Schellenberg, Betty A., *The Professionalization of Women Writers in Eighteenth-Century Britain*, Cambridge, 2005

Schlarman, Julie, 'The Social Geography of Grosvenor Square: Mapping Gender and Politics, 1720–1760', *London Journal*, No. 28, 2003, pp. 8–28

Schwarz, L. D., *London in the Age of Industrialization: Entrepreneurs, Labour Force and Living Conditions, 1700–1850*, Cambridge, 1992

Sharpe, Reginald R., *London and the Kingdom*, 3 vols., 1894–5

Sheppard, Francis, *London: A History*, Oxford, 1998

Shoemaker, Robert, *The London Mob: Violence and Disorder in Eighteenth-Century England*, 2004

Small, Miriam Rossiter, *Charlotte Lennox: An Eighteenth Century Lady of Letters*, New Haven, 1935

Smith, Sir Hubert Llewellyn, *The History of East London from the Earliest Times to the End of the 18th Century*, 1939

Smith, Raymond, *Sea-Coal for London: History of the Coal Factors in the London Market*, 1961

Solomon, Harry M., *The Rise of Robert Dodsley: Creating the New Age of Print*, Carbondale and Edwardsville, IL, 1996

Soros, Susan Weber (ed.), *James 'Athenian' Stuart 1713–1788: The Rediscovery of Antiquity*, 2006

Speaight, George, *The History of the English Puppet Theatre*, 1955

Spence, Craig, *London in the 1690s: A Social Atlas*, 2000

Stern, Walter M., *The Porters of London*, 1960

Stewart, Rachel, *The Town House in Georgian London*, 2009

Stirk, Nigel, 'Arresting Ambiguity: The Shifting Geographies of a London Debtors' Sanctuary in the Eighteenth Century', *Social History*, Vol. 25, No. 3, 2000

Stott, Andrew McConnell, *The Pantomime Life of Joseph Grimaldi: Laughter, Madness and the Story of Britain's Greatest Comedian*, 2009

Straus, Ralph, *Robert Dodsley: Poet, Publisher & Playwright*, 1910

Styles, John, *The Dress of the People: Everyday Fashion in Eighteenth-Century England*, 2007

Styles, John, and Vickery, Amanda (eds.), *Gender, Taste, and Material Culture in Britain and North America 1700–1800*, 2006

Summers, Judith, *The Empress of Pleasure: The Life and Adventures of Teresa Cornelys – Queen of Masquerades and Casanova's Lover*, 2003

Summerson, John, *Architecture in Britain 1530 to 1830*, 1953

Summerson, John, *Georgian London*, 1945

Supple, Barry, *The Royal Exchange Assurance: A History of British Insurance 1720–1970*, Cambridge, 1970

Survey of London, *Vol. X. The Parish of St Margaret, Westminster (Pt. I)*, 1926

Survey of London, *Vol. XVI. Charing Cross (The Parish of St Martin-in-the-Fields, Part I)*, 1935

Survey of London, *Vol. XX. Trafalgar Square and Neighbourhood (The Parish of St Martin-in-the-Fields, Part III)*, 1940

Survey of London, *Vol. XXII. Bankside (The Parishes of St Saviour and Christchurch, Southwark)*, 1950

Survey of London, *Vol. XXIII. South Bank and Vauxhall. The Parish of St. Mary Lambeth Pt. I,* 1951

Survey of London, *Vol. XXIV. The Parish of St Pancras Pt. IV: King's Cross Neighbourhood,* 1952

Survey of London, *Vol. XXVII. The Parish of Christ Church and All Saints (Spitalfields and Mile End New Town),* 1957

Survey of London, *Vols. XXXIII–IV. The Parish of St Anne Soho,* 1966

Survey of London, *Vol. XXXIX. The Grosvenor Estate in Mayfair. Part I General History,* 1977, and *Vol. XL. The Grosvenor Estate in Mayfair. Part II The Buildings,* 1980

Survey of London, *Vols. XLIII–IV. Poplar, Blackwall and the Isle of Dogs. The Parish of All Saints,* 1994

Survey of London, *Vol. XLV, Knightsbridge,* 2000

Survey of London, *Vol. XLVI. South and East Clerkenwell,* 2008

Sutherland, Lucy S., *A London Merchant 1695–1774,* 1933

Sutherland, Lucy S., *The City of London and the Opposition Government 1768–1774: A Study in the Rise of Metropolitan Radicalism,* 1959

Swarbrick, John, *Robert Adam and His Brothers: Their Lives, Work and Influence on English Architecture, Decoration and Furniture,* 1915

Taylor, James Stephen, *Jonas Hanway, Founder of the Marine Society: Charity and Policy in Eighteenth-Century Britain,* 1985

Taylor, Justine, *A Cup of Kindness: The History of the Royal Scottish Corporation, a London Charity, 1603–2003,* East Linton, 2003

Thomas, Keith, *The Ends of Life: Roads to Fulfilment in Early Modern England,* Oxford, 2009

Thomas, Peter D. G., *John Wilkes: A Friend to Liberty,* Oxford, 1996

Thompson, C. J. S., *Quacks of Old London,* 1928

Thomson, Gladys Scott, *The Russells of Bloomsbury 1669–1771,* 1940

Thorold, Peter, *The London Rich: The Creation of a Great City, from 1666 to the Present,* 1999

Treherne, John, *The Canning Enigma,* 1989

Treloar, William Purdie, *Wilkes and the City,* 1917

Trewin, J. C., and King, E. M., *Printer to the House: The Story of Hansard,* 1952

Troyer, Howard William, *Ned Ward of Grubstreet: A Study of Sub-Literary London in the Eighteenth Century,* Cambridge, MA, 1946

Trumbach, Randolph, *Sex and the Gender Revolution. Volume One: Heterosexuality and the Third Gender in Enlightenment London,* 1998

Turberville, A. S. (ed.), *Johnson's England: An Account of the Life and Manners of his Age,* 2 vols., Oxford, 1933

Tweedy, Mrs Alec, *Hyde Park: Its History and Romance,* 1908

Uglow, Jenny, *Hogarth: A Life and a World,* 1997

Unwin, George, *The Gilds and Companies of London*, 1908
Vickery, Amanda, *Behind Closed Doors: At Home in Georgian England*, 2009
Victoria County History, *Essex. Vol. VI*, Oxford, 1973
Victoria County History, *A History of the County of Middlesex Vol. II*, 1911
Victoria County History, *A History of the County of Middlesex Vol. VIII Islington and Stoke Newington Parishes*, Oxford, 1985
Victoria County History, *Middlesex. Vol. IX, Hampstead and Paddington Parishes*, Oxford, 1989
Victoria County History, *Middlesex. Vol. X, Hackney Parish*, Oxford, 1995
Victoria County History, *A History of the County of Middlesex Vol. XI Early Stepney with Bethnal Green*, Oxford, 1998
Victoria County History, *Middlesex. Vol. XII Chelsea*, Woodbridge, 2004
Victoria County History, *The Victoria History of the County of Surrey. Vol. II*, 1905
Victoria County History, *The Victoria History of the County of Surrey. Vol. IV*, 1912
Visram, Rozina, *Asians in Britain: 400 Years of History*, 2002
Wagner, Gillian, *Thomas Coram, Gent. 1668–1751*, Woodbridge, 2004
Wain, John, *Samuel Johnson: A Biography*, 1974
Walcott, Mackenzie E. C., *Westminster: Memorials of the City, Saint Peter's College, The Parish Churches, Palaces, Streets, and Worthies*, 1849
Wallas, Graham, *The Life of Francis Place 1771–1854*, 1918
Ward, Robert, *The Man Who Buried Nelson: The Surprising Life of Robert Mylne*, Stroud, 2007
Ward-Jackson, Philip, *Public Sculpture of the City of London*, Liverpool, 2003
Warner, Jessica, *Craze: Gin and Debauchery in an Age of Reason*, 2003
Webb, Sidney and Beatrice, *English Local Government: Statutory Authorities for Special Purposes*, 1922
Webb, Sidney and Beatrice, *English Local Government from the Revolution to the Municipal Corporations Act: The Manor and the Borough*, 2 vols., 1908
Webb, Sidney and Beatrice, *English Local Government from the Revolution to the Municipal Corporations Act: The Parish and the County*, 1906
Webb, Sidney and Beatrice, *English Poor Law History. Part I: The Old Poor Law*, 1927
Webb, Sidney and Beatrice, *The History of Liquor Licensing in England Principally from 1700 to 1830*, 1903
Webb, Sidney and Beatrice, *The History of Trade Unionism*, 1898
Wedd, Kit, with Lucy Peltz and Cathy Ross, *Artists' London: Holbein to Hirst*, 2001

Weinreb, Ben, Hibbert, Christopher, Keay, Julia, and Keay, John, *The London Encyclopaedia*, 3rd edition, 2008

Weiss, Leonard, *Watch-Making in England 1760–1820*, 1982

Welch, Charles, *Modern History of the City of London: A Record of Municipal and Social Progress from 1760 to the Present Day*, 1896

Western, J. R., *The English Militia in the Eighteenth Century: The Story of a Political Issue 1660–1802*, 1965

Wheatley, Henry B., *Hogarth's London: Pictures of the Manners of the Eighteenth Century*, 1909

Wheatley, Henry B., *The Adelphi and Its Site*, 1885

Wheatley, Henry B., and Cunningham, Peter, *London Past and Present: Its History, Associations and Traditions*, 3 vols., 1891

Whistler, Laurence, *Sir John Vanbrugh: Architect and Dramatist 1664–1726*, 1938

White, Jerry, *London in the Nineteenth Century: A Human Awful Wonder of God*, 2007

White, Jerry, 'Pain and Degradation in Georgian London: Life in the Marshalsea Prison', *History Workshop Journal*, Issue 68, Autumn 2009, pp. 69–98

Whitley, William T., *Artists and Their Friends in England 1700–1799*, 2 vols., 1928

Williams, Michael, *Some London Theatres: Past and Present*, 1883

Wilson, Charles, *First with the News: The History of W. H. Smith 1792–1972*, 1985

Wood, E. J., *Giants and Dwarfs*, 1868

Wrigley, E. A., 'A Simple Model of London's Importance in Changing English Society and Economy 1650–1750', *Past and Present*, Vol. 37, 1967, pp. 44–70

Wrigley, E. A., and Schofield, R. S., *The Population History of England 1541–1871*, 1981

Wroth, Warwick, *The London Pleasure Gardens of the Eighteenth Century*, 1896

Wyndham, Henry Saxe, *The Annals of Covent Garden Theatre from 1732 to 1897*, 2 vols., 1906

INDEX

Macklin, Charles (*c*.1699–1797, actor and playwright) 153, 260, 311, 363

Maclean, James (1724–50, highwayman) 392, 395, 397

Magdalen Hospital 362–3, 476, 478, 480, 499–500

Mahon, Gertrude (1752–*c*.1808, actress) 154

Maitland, William (*c*.1693–1757, antiquary) 97, 328, 330, 489–90

Mall, The (St James's) 11, 320, 357, 391, 550

Mallet, David (*c*.1702–65, poet) 97

Mallors, James (builder) 46

Malone, Edmond (1741–1812, writer) 154

Manchester 217, 484

Manchester Square (Marylebone) 70–1

Mandeville, Bernard (*c*.1670–1733, writer) 9

Manley, Delarivière (*c*.1670–1724, writer) 263

Mansfield Street (Marylebone) 55–6

Mansfield, William Murray Earl of (1705–93, lawyer and politician) 51, 54, 96, 130, 165, 301, 501, 513, 517–20, 524, 526, 536, 538, 543

Mansion House (City) 44, 130, 217, 319, 383, 426, 524, 530, 532, 537

manufacturing 2–3, 74–5, 100, 142, 207–10, 212–20, 234–6, 553; *see also individual trades*

maps and guides 9, 117–8

Mar, John Erskine Earl of (*c*.1675–1732, politician) 18, 21, 22, 47

Margate 105

Marine Society 474–5

Mark Lane (City) 63

markets 192–4

Marlborough, John Churchill 1st Duke of (1650–1722, politician and soldier) 25, 319

Marseille 116

Marshalsea Prison (Southwark) 156, 207, 301, 391, 446–51, 454, 541

Martin, Samuel (1695–1776, politician) 519

Martin's Bank (Lombard Street) 65, 177

Marylebone 26–7, 29, 31, 55–7, 62, 68–72, 78, 119, 224, 282, 336–7, 362, 378, 439, 478, 489, 553

Marylebone Gardens 70–1, 316, 324, 358, 375

Marylebone High Street 71, 324

Marylebone Lane 55, 69, 71

Masquerades 294–5, 297–8, 301–2, 322, 335, 361, 492

Massie, Joseph (d.1784, merchant and writer) 58–61

Mathematical Society of Spitalfields 333

Matthew Martin (1748–1838, philanthropist) 204

May Day 107

Mayfair (Westminster) 29–31, 38, 57, 69, 95, 107, 216, 300, 317, 358, 444, 506

McDaniel, Stephen (*fl.* 1741–55, thief-taker) 434, 443, 458–9

Mead, Richard (1672–1754, physician and collector) 24, 274

Mecklenburgh Square 73